PSYCHOLOGY LIBRARY EDITIONS:
COGNITIVE SCIENCE

Volume 22

CONNECTIONIST APPROACHES TO NATURAL LANGUAGE PROCESSING

CONNECTIONIST APPROACHES TO NATURAL LANGUAGE PROCESSING

Edited by
RONAN G. REILLY AND NOEL E. SHARKEY

Routledge
Taylor & Francis Group

LONDON AND NEW YORK

First published in 1992 by Lawrence Erlbaum Associates Ltd.

This edition first published in 2017
by Routledge
2 Park Square, Milton Park, Abingdon, Oxon OX14 4RN

and by Routledge
711 Third Avenue, New York, NY 10017

Routledge is an imprint of the Taylor & Francis Group, an informa business

© 1992 by Lawrence Erlbaum Associates Ltd.

British Library Cataloguing in Publication Data
A catalogue record for this book is available from the British Library

ISBN: 978-1-138-19163-1 (Set)
ISBN: 978-1-315-54401-4 (Set) (ebk)
ISBN: 978-1-138-64006-1 (Volume 22) (hbk)
ISBN: 978-1-315-63686-3 (Volume 22) (ebk)

Publisher's Note
The publisher has gone to great lengths to ensure the quality of this reprint but points out that some imperfections in the original copies may be apparent.

Disclaimer
The publisher has made every effort to trace copyright holders and would welcome correspondence from those they have been unable to trace.

Connectionist Approaches
to Natural Language Processing

edited by

Ronan G. Reilly

Department of Computer Science, University College Dublin, Ireland

Noel E. Sharkey

Department of Computer Science, University of Exeter, U.K.

LAWRENCE ERLBAUM ASSOCIATES, PUBLISHERS
Hove (UK)   Hillsdale (USA)

Lawrence Erlbaum Associates Ltd., Publishers
27 Palmeira Mansions
Church Road
Hove
East Sussex, BN3 2FA
U.K.

British Library cataloguing in Publication Data

Connectionist approaches to natural language processing
  I. Reilly, Ronan G., *1955*– II. Sharkey, N.E. (Noel E)
  006.35

  ISBN 0-86377-179-3

Typeset by DP Photosetting, Aylesbury, Bucks.
Printed and bound by BPCC Wheatons, Exeter.

We dedicate this book to our daughters Aifric Reilly and Autumn Sharkey who were born while we were preparing it.

Contents

List of Contributors[1]

Marlene Behrmann, Sunnybrook Medical Centre, University of Toronto, Toronto, Ontario M5S 1A1, Canada.

George Berg, Department of Computer Science, Department of Linguistics and Cognitive Science, State University of New York at Albany, LI67A, Albany, NY 12222, U.S.A.

Thomas G. Bever, Department of Psychology, University of Rochester, Wilson Blvd., Rochester, NY 14627, U.S.A.

Gary S. Dell, Beckman Institute, University of Illinois, Urbana, Illinois, U.S.A.

Georg Dorffner, Austrian Research Institute for Artificial Intelligence, Schottengasse 3, 1010 Vienna, Austria, and Indiana University, Computer Science Dept., Lindley Hall, Bloomington, Indiana 47405, U.S.A.

R. Doust, Sprachwissenschaftliches Institut, Ruhr-Universitat, Universitätsstr. 150, 4630 Bochum, Germany.

Michael G. Dyer, 3532 Boelter Hall, Computer Science Department, University of California, Los Angeles, CA 90024, U.S.A.

Margot Flowers, 3532 Boelter Hall, Computer Science Department, University of California, Los Angeles, CA 90024, U.S.A.

Cornell Juliano, University of Rochester, Wilson Blvd, Rochester, NY 14627, U.S.A.

Wendy G. Lehnert, Department of Computer and Information Science, University of Massachusetts, Amherst, MA 01003, U.S.A.

Dominic W. Massaro, Program in Experimental Psychology, University of California, Santa Cruz, CA 95064, U.S.A.

---

[1] This is the list of current (at time of publication) addresses for correspondence with the authors who have contributed to this volume.

James L. McClelland, Department of Psychology, Carnegie-Mellon University, Pittsburgh, Pennsylvania, PA 15213, U.S.A.

Michael C. Mozer, Department of Computer Science and Institute of Cognitive Science, University of Colorado, Boulder, CO 80309-0430, U.S.A.

Dennis Norris, Medical Research Council Applied Psychology Unit, 15 Chaucer Road, Cambridge CB2 2EF, U.K.

Padraig G. O'Seaghdha, Lehigh University, Bethlehem, Pennsylvania, PA 18015, U.S.A.

Robert R. Peterson, Indiana University, Bloomington, Indiana, U.S.A.

John E. Rager, Department of Mathematics and Computer Science, Amherst College, Amherst, MA 01002, U.S.A.

Ronan G. Reilly, Department of Computer Science, University College Dublin, Belfield, Dublin 4, Ireland.

H. Schnelle, Sprachwissenschaftliches Institut, Ruhr-Universität, Universitätsstr. 150, 4630 Bochum, Germany.

Noel E. Sharkey, Department of Computer Science, University of Exeter, Exeter EX4 4PT, U.K.

Mark F. St. John, Department of Cognitive Science, University of California at San Diego, La Jolla, CA 92093, U.S.A.

Richard F.E. Sutcliffe, Department of Computer Science and Information Systems, University of Limerick, Limerick, Ireland.

Yih-Jih Alan Wang, 3532 Boelter Hall, Computer Science Department, University of California, Los Angeles, CA 90024, U.S.A.

Stefan Wermter, Universität Hamburg, Fachbereich Informatik, D-2000 Hamburg 50, Germany.

Preface

It is always challenging to take a cross-section of research in a rapidly evolving field such as connectionist natural language processing (CNLP) and attempt to provide a representative account of the research enterprise. In solving this constraint satisfaction problem, we feel we have succeeded in producing a volume that presents a broad picture of current CNLP research. The structure of the volume reflects the traditional division of labour in linguistics. There are, for example, sections on semantics and syntax. Nevertheless, the content of each chapter is far from traditional in outlook, and overall the volume represents a radical perspective on natural language processing. Given the time taken to put together an edited book and get it into print, much of the work described here will inevitably have been superseded by the time it reaches the reader. This is especially the case for CNLP, because of the significant increase in research effort over the last few years. However, regardless of rapid developments, the chapters in this book will always represent some of the more important foundational research in the area.

1

Connectionist Natural Language Processing

Noel E. Sharkey
Department of Computer Science, University of Exeter, Exeter, U.K.

Ronan G. Reilly
Department of Computer Science, University College Dublin, Dublin, Ireland

INTRODUCTION

Computational research on natural language has been going on for decades in artificial intelligence and computational linguistics. These disciplines generated enormous excitement in the '60s and '70s, but they have not entirely realised their promise and have now reached what seems to be a plateau. Why should connectionist natural language processing (CNLP) be any different? There are a number of reasons. For many, the connectionist approach provides a new way of looking at old issues. For these researchers, connectionism provides an expanded toolkit with which to invigorate old research projects with new ideas. For instance, connectionist systems can learn from examples so that, in the context of a rule-based system, all of the rules need not be specified a priori. Connectionist systems have very powerful generalisation capabilities. Content addressable memory or pattern completion falls naturally out of distributed connectionist systems, making them ideal for filling in missing information.

However, for many new researchers, connectionism is a whole new way of looking at language. The big promise is that the integration of learning and representation (e.g. Hanson & Burr, 1990) will be a source of new theoretical ideas. Connectionist devices are very good at constructing representations from the statistical regularities of a domain. They do so in a form that is not directly interpretable. Nevertheless, it is the nature of these representations, uninfluenced by a priori theoretical considerations, that hold the most promise for the discipline. Currently, connectionists are seeking ways of analysing such

1

representations as a means of developing a new understanding of the problems facing automated language processing.

A Brief History

As far as we know, the first paper that discussed language in terms of parallel distributed processing was by Hinton (1981)[1]. Although that paper was really about implementing semantic nets in parallel hardware, many of the problem areas described by Hinton have been explored further in the natural language papers of the 1980s. The Hinton system took as input a distributed representation of word triples consisting of ROLE1 RELATION ROLE2. In other words, simple propositions such as ELEPHANT COLOUR GREY. When the system had finished learning the propositions, its task was to complete the third term of an input triple given only two of the terms. For example, given the terms ELEPHANT and COLOUR the system filled in the missing term GREY. This was very similar to the notion of default reasoning in AI. But Hinton went further, to discuss how his system could generalise its experience to novel examples. If the system knew that CLYDE was an elephant (i.e. the token CLYDE contained the type ELEPHANT microfeatures), then, given the two terms CLYDE and COLOUR, the third term GREY would be filled in.

What was interesting about Hinton's work was that he described two types of representation that have become commonplace in CNLP. The first concerns the input to a language system. In any sort of natural language system it is important to preserve the ordering of the input elements. Hinton did this by partitioning the input vector so that the first n bits represented the ROLE1 words, the second n bits represented the RELATION words, and the final n bits represented the ROLE2 words. There are a number of problems with this representational approach, such as redundancy, fixed length, and absence of semantic similarity among identical elements in different roles. Nonetheless, it has been widely used in the literature, both for input and output, and has only been superseded in the last two years, as we shall see.

The second type of representation used by Hinton was a distributed coarse-coded or compact representation. That is, the vector of input activations was recoded into a compact representation by random weights connected to a second layer of units. The states of this second layer of units were then fed back to the input layer and the weights were adjusted until the states from the second layer accurately reproduced the input. This is how the system filled in the missing term. It was also from the distributed representation that this system gained its generalisation abilities. Although such content-addressable memory systems

---

[1] We are not discussing word recognition here, nor are we dealing with the bulk of research in speech processing.

were already well known, no one had used them in a language-related problem before.

The next four years from 1981 onwards saw only a few published papers, and most of these did not employ distributed representations. Distributed representations have a number of advantages over nondistributed or "localist" representations. For example, they have a greater psychological plausibility, they are more economical in the use of memory resources, and they are more resistant to disruption. However, prior to the development of sufficiently powerful learning algorithms, researchers found localist representations to be easier to work with, since they could readily be hand-coded. Small, Cottrell, and Shastri (1982) made a first brave stab at connectionist parsing. Though not greatly successful, this localist work opened the way for other linguistic-style work and provided a basis for Cottrell's (1985) thesis research, at Rochester, on word sense disambiguation. That year also saw a Technical Report from another Rochester student, Fanty (1985), that attempted to employ localist techniques to do context-free parsing. The same year, Selman (1985) presented a master's thesis that utilised the Boltzmann learning algorithm (Hinton, Sejnowski & Ackley, 1984) for syntactic parsing. There were many interesting ideas in Selman's thesis, but the use of simulated annealing proved to be too cumbersome for language (but see Sampson, 1989). Also in that year, a special issue of the *Cognitive Science* journal featured a language article by Waltz and Pollack (1985) who were not only concerned with parsing but also with contextual semantics. Prior to this paper, only Reilly (1984) had attempted a connectionist approach to the higher-level phenomena in his paper on anaphoric resolution.

Then, in 1986, there was a relative explosion of language-related papers. First, there were papers on the use of connectionist techniques for language work using AI style theory (e.g. Golden, 1986; Lehnert, 1986; Sharkey, Sutcliffe, & Wobcke, 1986). These papers were followed closely by the publication of the two volumes on parallel distributed processing (PDP) edited by David Rumelhart and Jay McClelland (Rumelhart & McClelland, 1986b; McClelland & Rumelhart, 1986). The two volumes contained a number of papers relating to aspects of natural language processing such as case-role assignment (McClelland & Kawamoto, 1986); learning the past tense of verbs (Rumelhart & McClelland, 1986a); and word recognition in reading (McClelland, 1986). Furthermore, the two volumes opened up the issue of representation in natural language which had started with Hinton (1981).

However, one paper (Rumelhart, Hinton, & Williams, 1986) in the PDP volumes significantly changed the style of much of connectionist research. This paper described a new learning algorithm employing a generalisation of a learning rule first proposed by Widrow and Hoff (1960). The new algorithm, usually referred to as the backpropagation algorithm, opened up the field of connectionist research, because now we could process input patterns that were not restricted by the constraint that they be in linearly separable classes (c.f.

Allen, 1987 for a number of language studies employing the new algorithm). In the same year, Sejnowski and Rosenberg (1986) successfully applied the backpropagation algorithm to the problem of text-to-speech translation. And Hinton (1986) applied it to the learning of family trees (inheritance relations). These papers began a line of research devoted to examining the type of internal representation learned by connectionist networks in order to compute the required input–output mapping (c.f. Hanson & Burr, 1990).

A significant extension to the representational capacity of connectionist networks was made by Jordan (1986). He proposed an architectural variant of the standard feed-forward backpropagation network. This variant involved feedback from the output layer to the input layer (thus, forming a recurrent network) which enabled the construction of powerful sequencing systems. By using the recurrent links to store a contextual history of any particular sequence, they overcame many of the difficulties that connectionist systems had in dealing with problems having a temporal structure. Later work by Elman (1988; 1989) utilised a similar architecture, but ran the recurrent links from the hidden units rather than from the output units. This variant enabled Elman to develop a CNLP model that appeared to have many of the properties of conventional symbol-processing models, such as sensitivity to compositional structure. This latter property had earlier been pinpointed by Fodor and Pylyshyn (1988) in their critique of connectionism as a significant and irredeemable deficit in CNLP systems. Another important advantage of Elman's approach was that words (from a sentence) could be presented to the system in sequence. This departure from Hinton's (1981) vector partitioning approach overcame problems of redundancy, lack of semantic similarity between identical items, and fixed input length.

Since 1986, many more papers on language issues have begun to appear which are too numerous to mention here. Among these was further work on the application of world knowledge to language understanding (e.g. Chun & Mimo, 1987; Dolan & Dyer, 1987; Miikkulainen, 1990; Sharkey, 1989a). Research on various aspects of syntax and parsing has increased sharply (e.g. Benello, Makie, & Anderson, 1989; Hanson & Kegl, 1987; Howells, 1988; Kwasny & Faisal, 1990; Rager & Berg, 1990). Moreover, there has been an increase in research on other aspects of natural language such as speech production (Dell, 1986; Seidenberg & McClelland, 1989), sentence and phrase generation (e.g. Gasser, 1988; Kukich, 1987), question answering (Allen, 1988), prepositional attachment (e.g. Cosic & Munro, 1988), anaphora (Allen & Riecken, 1988), cognitive linguistics (Harris, 1990), discourse topic (Karen, 1990), lexical processing (Sharkey, 1989b; Sharkey & Sharkey, 1989; Kawamoto, 1989), variable binding (Smolensky, 1987), and speech processing (e.g., Kohonen, 1989; Hare, 1990; Port, 1990).

OVERVIEW OF CHAPTERS

The book is divided into four sections. The first section (Semantics) contains four chapters that deal with connectionist issues in both lexical and structural semantics. The second section (Syntax) contains two chapters dealing with connectionist parsing. The third section (Representational Adequacy) contains three chapters dealing with the controversial issue of the representational adequacy of connectionist representations. The fourth and final section (Computational Psycholinguistics) contains four chapters which focus on the cognitive modelling role of connectionism and which address a variety of topics in the area of computational psycholinguistics.

In what follows we will give a brief introduction to each of the chapters. For a more detailed discussion of some of the relevant issues, we provide an introduction at the beginning of each section.

Semantics

The four chapters in this section can be divided into two. The first pair of chapters deal with what can be best characterised as lexical semantics and the second pair with sentential or structural semantics.

In the first chapter of this section, Dyer et al. discuss a method for modifying distributed representations dynamically, by maintaining a separate, distributed connectionist network as a symbol memory, where each symbol is composed of a pattern of activation. Symbol representations start out as random patterns of activation. Over time they are "recirculated" through the symbolic tasks being demanded of them, and as a result, gradually form distributed representations that aid in the performance of these tasks. These distributed symbols enter into structured relations with other symbols, while exhibiting features of distributed representations, e.g. tolerance to noise and similarity-based generalisation to novel cases. Dyer et al. discuss in detail a method of symbol recirculation based on using entire weight matrices, formed in one network, as patterns of activation in a larger network. In the case of natural language processing, the resulting symbol memory can serve as a store for lexical entries, symbols, and relations among symbols, and thus represent semantic information.

In his chapter, Sutcliffe focuses on how the meaning of concepts is represented using microfeatures. He shows how microfeatural representations can be constructed, how they can be compared using the dot product, and why normalisation of microfeature vectors is required. He then goes on to describe the use of such representations in the construction of a lexicon for a story-paraphrasing system. Finally, he discusses the properties of the chosen representation and describes possible further developments of the work.

Wermter and Lehnert describe an approach combining natural language processing and connectionist learning. Concentrating on the domain of scientific language and the task of structural noun phrase disambiguation they present NOCON, a system which shows how learning can supply a memory model as the basis for understanding noun phrases. NOCON consists of two levels: a learning level at the bottom for learning semantic relationships between nouns and an integration level at the top for integrating semantic and syntactic constraints needed for structural noun phrase disambiguation. Wermter and Lehnert argue that this architecture is potentially strong enough to provide a learning and integrating memory model for natural language systems.

In the final chapter of this section St. John and McClelland argue that the parallel constraint satisfaction mechanism of connectionist models is a useful language comprehension algorithm; it allows syntactic and semantic constraints to be combined easily so that an interpretation which satisfies the most constraints can be found. It also allows interpretations to be revised easily, knowledge from different contexts to be shared, and it makes inferences an inherent part of comprehension. They present a model of sentence comprehension that addresses a range of important language phenomena. They show that the model can be extended to story comprehension. Both the sentence and story models view their input as evidence that constrains a complete interpretation. This view facilitates difficult aspects of sentence comprehension such as assigning thematic roles. It also facilitates difficult aspects of story comprehension such as inferring missing propositions, resolving pronouns, and sharing knowledge between contexts.

Syntax

The section on syntax provides a number of differing perspectives on how to deal with syntax in a connectionist network. The chapters are similar in that the models described are predominantly localist in nature. Rager focuses on robustness in parsing and Schnelle and Doust examine the capacity of connectionist networks to deal with complex linguistic structure.

Rager discusses methods for syntactic connectionist parsing in the presence of input errors. Using localist connectionist networks and a linguistic theory based on two-level grammars, he describes methods for detecting and recovering from errors in agreement, errors in lengths of constituent strings, and errors of missing constituents. The same mechanisms can be used to alter a phrase to a different, syntactically related, phrase, in the sense often discussed in transformational grammars. In this context, the paper discusses a method of representing constituent motion in a connectionist network.

Schnelle and Doust argue that notation is secondary to the content of a linguistic system: Linguistic structure should be conceived as a fundamentally abstract entity that can, however, be notationally represented in different ways (e.g. as a connectionist network or as a symbolic rule system). Since symbolic rule systems are the standard descriptive means in theoretical linguistics, the challenge is to find out whether combinatorially and compositionally complex linguistic contents, such as those represented in phrase structure rules, can also be defined in connectionist architectures. The challenge has been put forward explicitly by Fodor and Pylyshyn (1988). This chapter tries to justify a positive answer to this challenge. In support of their case, Schnelle and Doust present a general translation algorithm which defines a localist connectionist system given an arbitrary context-free constituent structure grammar.

Representational Adequacy

The three chapters of this section present a number of different perspectives on the adequacy of connectionist representations.

In his chapter, Bever argues that an enduring insight of behavioural science is that most of what we do is a function of habit. This was the basis for the enduring popularity of S-R psychology, despite its empirical inadequacies, which ultimately led to its downfall. Connectionism, he suggests, appears to be rehabilitating the image of associationistic models of behaviour by increasing the adequacy of activation models to account for structural phenomena invoked by cognitive psychologists as the basis for rejecting S-R psychology. He argues that connectionist models can capture only habits and are therefore inadequate in principle to capture structural processes. Nevertheless, he proposes a positive interpretation of this inadequacy, which is that connectionist models represent an important new tool in the study of how habitual knowledge interacts with structural processes.

In his chapter Berg examines the representational adequacy of the knowledge representation mechanisms underlying connectionist natural language processing systems. He contends that in two key respects—static adequacy and dynamic adequacy—current connectionist systems are lacking. He introduces a hybrid model, Autonomous Semantic Networks, and shows how it possesses the required properties while retaining the massive parallelism of connectionist models.

The main hypothesis of Dorffner's chapter is that the knowledge used by a cognitive system cannot be described or implemented sufficiently using the symbol structures of classical AI and computational linguistics. The chapter also proposes that many cognitive processes work on an intuitive and associative level where sub-symbolic knowledge is of key importance. Dorffner examines the notion that cognitive behaviour is not based on representations (i.e. an internal mirror image of the external world) but on self-organisation through motivated interaction with the environment. Finally, a connectionist implementation of the ideas he develops in the chapter is described, and extensions to the model allowing it to deal with more complex aspects of language are proposed.

Computational Psycholinguists

The four chapters in this section represent a sample of applications of connectionism to the task of cognitive modelling in the domain of computational psycholinguistics. The first two chapters deal primarily with speech perception, and the latter two chapters with speech production and attentional dysfunction, respectively.

The goal of Massaro's chapter is to test various assumptions of connectionist models. A set of prototypical results and a successful process model are described to serve as "landmarks" for an accurate connectionist model. Two classes of connectionist models of speech perception are described, evaluated, and tested. The classes are interactive-activation connectionist models and feed-forward connectionist models. A distinguishing feature of interactive activation models is that separate sources of information are not maintained independently of one another at any level of processing. Feed-forward models assume activation feeds only forward. Two-layer and three-layer models are described. Two-layer models have only input and output layers, whereas three-layer models postulate a layer of hidden units between input and output layers. Several sources of evidence are used to distinguish among these classes of models. These empirical domains include the integration of top-down and bottom-up sources of information and the integration of auditory and visual speech in bimodal speech perception. Results from several experiments indicate that several sources of information simultaneously influence speech perception, but that their representations remain independent of one another. Massaro claims that this independence is strong evidence against interactive activation in speech perception.

In the second chapter of this section Norris considers one aspect of the relation between connectionism and the traditional information-processing approach to cognitive psychology. It is often claimed that connectionism gives us a new language for describing psychological theories. Norris asks whether the new language simply gives us a way of describing and implementing the processes represented by the boxes of traditional box-models, or whether connectionist models behave in ways which mean that there is no simple mapping between the connectionist models and the box-models. Norris examines these issues by concentrating on the problem of deciding whether two processes interact or not. In particular he considers the relation between lexical processes and the sub-lexical processes of letter and phoneme identification.

In the third chapter of this section, O'Seaghdha et al. evaluate two different connectionist models in the light of recent evidence on the effect of context on phonological activation in word recognition and production. The first model is a distributed sequential backpropagation learning model of word pronunciation. Priming effects simulated by means of the model's learning mechanism are determined by two factors, prime-target similarity and degree of learning, and they are always facilitatory. This model, therefore, cannot simulate empirically observed inhibitory outcomes in similar-prime contexts. The second model is an interactive activation model that is specifically designed to reproduce the empirical effects. This model incorporates a distinction drawn from language production theory between a level at which lexical items are activated and a level at which their sounds are specified, and implements their hypothesis that, whereas facilitation arises at a lexical level, inhibition is a product of phonological competition. O'Seaghdha et al. present data from a variety of receptive and productive priming tasks to support their view of form-related priming.

Finally, Mozer and Behrmann describe an application of Mozer's BLIRNET word recognition model to the problem of neglect dyslexia. Neglect dyslexia, a reading impairment acquired as a consequence of brain injury, is traditionally interpreted as a disturbance of selective attention. Patients with neglect dyslexia may ignore the left side of an open book, the beginning words of a line of text, or the beginning letters of a single word. These patients provide a rich but sometimes contradictory source of data regarding the locus of attentional selectivity. Mozer and Behrmann show that the effects of damage to the BLIRNET model resemble the reading impairments observed in neglect dyslexia. In simulation experiments, they account for a broad spectrum of behaviours including the following: (1) when two noncontiguous stimuli are presented simultaneously, the contralesional stimulus is neglected (extinction); (2) explicit instructions to the patient can reduce the severity of neglect; (3) stimulus position in the visual field affects reading performance; (4) words are read much better than pronounceable nonwords; (5) the nature of error responses depends on the morphemic composition of the stimulus; and (6) extinction interacts with lexical knowledge (if two words are presented that form a compound, e.g. COW and BOY, the patient is more likely to report both than in a control condition, e.g. SUN and FLY). The convergence of findings from the neuropsychological research and the computational modelling sheds light on the role of attention in normal visuo-spatial processing, supporting a hybrid view of attentional selection that has properties of both early and late selection.

ACKNOWLEDGEMENTS

This chapter was written while Ronan G. Reilly was a visiting associate professor at the University of Illinois at Urbana-Champaign.

REFERENCES

Allen, R.B. (1987). Several studies on natural language and back-propagation. *Proceedings of IEEE First International Conference on Neural Nets, San Diego, June 21–24, II*, 335–341.

Allen, R.B. (1988). Sequential connectionist networks for answering simple questions about a microworld. *Proceedings of the 10th Annual Conference of the Cognitive Science Society, Montreal.*

Allen, R.B. & Riecken, M.E. (1988). Anaphora and reference in connectionist language users. *International Computer Science Conference, Hong Kong.*

Benello, J., Makie, A.W., & Anderson, J.A. (1989). Syntactic category disambiguation with neural networks. *Computer Speech and Language, 3*, 203–217.

Chun, H.W. & Mimo, A. (1987). A model of schema selection using marker parsing and connectionist spreading activation. *Proceedings of the 9th Annual Conference of the Cognitive Science Society, Seattle, Washington,* 887–896.

Cosic, C. & Munro, P. (1988). *Learning to represent and understand locative prepositional phrases.* TR LIS002/IS88002. Pittsburgh, Penn.: School of Library and Information Science, University of Pittsburgh.

Cottrell, G.W. (1985). A connectionist approach to word sense disambiguation. *Phd. Thesis, TR154.* Rochester, New York: Department of Computer Science, University of Rochester.

Dell. G. (1986) A spreading activation model of retrieval in sentence production. *Psychological Review, 93,* 283–321.

Dolan, C.P. & Dyer, M.G. (1987). Symbolic schemata, role binding, and the evolution of structure in connectionist memories. *IEEE First International Conference on Neural Networks, San Diego, June 21–24, II,* 287–298.

Dolan, C.P. & Dyer, M.G. (1988). *Parallel retrieval and application of conceptual knowledge.* Technical Report UCLA-AI-88-3. Los Angeles: AI Lab, Computer Science department, University of California at Los Angeles.

Elman, J.L. (1988). *Finding structure in time.* CRL TR 8801. San Diego, Calif.: Center for Research in Language, University of California.

Elman, J.L. (1989). *Representation and structure in connectionist models.* CRL TR 8903. San Diego, Calif.: Center for Research in Language, University of California.

Fanty, M. (1985).*Context-free parsing in connectionist networks.* Technical Report TR-174. Rochester, New York: University of Rochester, Department of Computer Science.

Fodor, J.A. & Pylyshyn, Z.W. (1988). Connectionism and cognitive architecture: A critical analysis. *Cognition, 28,* 2–71.

Gasser, M.E. (1988). *A connectionist model of sentence generation in a first and second language.* TR UCLA-AI-88-13. Los Angeles, Calif.: AI Lab, Computer Science Department, U.C.L.A.

Golden, R.M. (1986). Representing causal schemata in connectionist systems. *Proceedings of the 8th Annual Conference of the Cognitive Science Society,* 13–21.

Hanson, S.J. & Burr, D.J. (1990). What connectionist models learn: Learning and representation in connectionist networks. *Behavioral and Brain Sciences, 13,* 471–518.

Hanson, S.J. & Kegl, J. (1987). PARSNIP: A connectionist network that learns natural language grammar from exposure to natural language sentences. *Proceedings of the 9th Annual Conference of the Cognitive Science Society, Washington,* 106–119.

Hare, M. (1990). The role of similarity in Hungarian vowel harmony: A connectionist account. *Connection Science, 2,* 123–150.

Harris, C.L. (1990). Connectionism and cognitive linguistics. *Connection Science, 2.*

Hinton, G.E. (1981) Implementing semantic networks in parallel hardware. In G.E. Hinton & J.A. Anderson (Eds.), *Parallel models of associative memory.* Hillsdale, N.J.: Lawrence Erlbaum Associates Inc. 161–187.

Hinton, G.E. (1986). Learning distributed representations of concepts. *Proceedings of the 8th Annual Conference of the Cognitive Science Society, 1986,* 1–12.

Hinton, G.E., McClelland, J.L., & Rumelhart, D. E. (1986). Distributed representations. In D. E. Rumelhart & J. L. McClelland (Eds.), *Parallel distributed processing: Explorations in the microstructure of cognition. Volume I: Foundations.* Cambridge, Mass.: M.I.T. Press, 77–109.

Hinton, G.E., Sejnowski, T.J., & Ackley, D.H. (1984). *Boltzmann machines: Constraint satisfaction networks that learn* (Technical Report No. CMU-CS-84-119).

Howells, T. (1988). VITAL, A connectionist parser. *Proceedings of the 10th Annual Conference of the Cognitive Science Society, Montreal.*

Jordan, M.I. (1986). Attractor dynamics and parallelism in a connectionist sequential machine. *Proceedings of the 8th Annual Conference of the Cognitive Science Society, Amherst Mass.*, 531–545.

Karen, L.F.P. (1990). Identification of topical entities in discourse: A connectionist approach to attention mechanisms in language. *Connection Science, 2* 103–118.

Kawamoto, A.H. (1989). Distributed representations of ambiguous words and their resolution in a connectionist network. In S.L. Small, G.W. Cottrell, & M.K. Tanenhaus (Eds.), *Lexical ambiguity resolution*. San Mateo, Calif.: Morgan Kaufmann Publishers Inc.

Kohonen, T. (1989). Speech recognition based on topology-preserving neural maps. In I. Aleksander (Ed.), *Neural computing architectures*. Cambridge, Mass.: MIT Press, 26–40.

Kukich, K. (1987). Where do phrases come from: Some preliminary experiments in connectionist phrase generation. In G. Kempen (Ed.), *Natural language generation: New results from artificial intelligence, psychology, and linguistics*. Dordrecht, Holland, & Boston, Mass.: Kluwer Academic Press, 405–421.

Kwasny, S.C. & Faisal, K.A. (1990). Connectionism and determinism in a syntactic parser. *Connection Science, 2*, 63–82.

LeCun, Y. (1985). A learning scheme for asymmetric threshold networks. In *Proceedings of Cognitivia '85, Paris, France*.

Lehnert, W.G. (1986). Possible implications of connectionism. *Theoretical issues in natural language processing*. University of New Mexico, New Mexico, U.S.A, 78–83.

McClelland, J.L. (1986). Parallel distributed processing and role assignment constraints. *Theoretical Issues in Natural Language Processing*. University of New Mexico, New Mexico, U.S.A., 73–77.

McClelland, J.L. & Kawamoto, A.H. (1986). Mechanisms of sentence processing: Assigning roles to constituents. In J.L. McClelland, D.E. Rumelhart, & PDP group, *Parallel distributed processing, Volume II*. Cambridge, Mass.: M.I.T. Press, 272–326.

McClelland, J.L. & Rumelhart, D.E. (Eds.). (1986). *Parallel distributed processing: Explorations in the microstructure of cognition, Volume 2: Psychological and biological models*. Cambridge, Mass.: M.I.T. Press.

Miikkulainen, R. (1990). Script recognition with hierarchical feature maps. *Connection Science, 2*, 83–102.

Parker, D.B. (1985). *Learning-logic*. TR-47. Massachusetts: Center for Computational Research in Economic and Management Science, M.I.T.

Port, R. (1990). Representation and recognition of temporal patterns. *Connection Science, 2*, 151–176.

Rager, J. & Berg, G. (1990). A connectionist model of motion and government in Chomsky's government-binding theory. *Connection Science, 2*, 35–52.

Reilly, R.G. (1984). A connectionist model of some aspects of anaphor resolution. *Proceedings of the Tenth International Conference on Computational Linguistics, Stanford, July*, 144–149.

Rumelhart, D.E., Hinton, G.E., & Williams, R. J. (1986). Learning internal representations by error propagation. In D.E. Rumelhart & J.L. McClelland (Eds.), *Parallel distributed processing, Volume 1*. Cambridge, Mass.: M.I.T.

Rumelhart, D.E. & McClelland, J.L. (1986a). On learning the past tenses of English verbs. In J.L. McClelland & D. E. Rumelhart (Eds.), *Parallel distributed processing: Explorations in the microstructure of cognition, Volume II: Psychological and biological models*. Cambridge, Mass.: M.I.T. Bradford, 216–271.

Rumelhart, D.E. & McClelland, J.L. (Eds.) (1986b). *Parallel distributed processing: Explorations in the microstructure of cognition. Volume I: Foundations*. Cambridge, Mass.: M.I.T. Press.

Sampson, G.E. (1989). Simulated annealing as a parsing technique. In N.E. Sharkey (Ed.), *Models of cognition*. New Jersey: Ablex.

Seidenberg, M.S. & McClelland, J.L. (1989). A distributed, developmental model of word recognition and naming. *Psychological Review, 96*, 523–568.

Sejnowski, T.J. & Rosenberg, C.R. (1986). NET TALK: *A parallel network that learns to read aloud* (Technical Report JHU/EECS-86/01). Baltimore, MD: Johns Hopkins University.

Selman, B. (1985). *Rule-based processing in a connectionist system for natural language understanding.* TR CSRI-168. Toronto: Computer Systems Research Institute, University of Toronto.

Sharkey, A.J.C. & Sharkey, N.E. (1989). Lexical processing and the mechanism of context effects in text comprehension. *Proceedings of the Cognitive Science Society, 11.*

Sharkey, N.E. (1988). A PDP system for goal-plan decisions. In R. Trappl (Ed.), *Cybernetics and systems.* Dordrecht: Kluwer Academic Publishers, 1031–1038.

Sharkey, N.E. (1989a). A PDP learning approach to natural language understanding. In I. Aleksander (Ed.), *Neural computing architectures.* London: Kogan Page.

Sharkey, N.E. (1989b). The lexical distance model and word priming. *Proceedings of the Cognitive Science Society, 11.*

Sharkey, N.E., Sutcliffe, R.F.E., & Wobcke, W.R. (1986). Mixing binary and continuous connection schemes for knowledge access. *Proceedings of the American Association for Artificial Intelligence.*

Small, S.L., Cottrell, G.W., & Shastri, L. (1982). Towards connectionist parsing. *Proceedings of the National Conference on Artificial Intelligence.* Pittsburgh, Penn.

Smolensky, P. (1987). *On variable binding and the representation of symbolic structures in connectionist systems.* TR CU-CS-355-87. Boulder, Colorado: Department of Computer Science, University of Colorado.

Waltz, D.L. & Pollack, B.B. (1985). Massively parallel parsing: A strongly interactive model of natural language interpretation. *Cognitive Science, 9,* 51–74.

Werbos, P.J. (1974). *Beyond regression: New tools for prediction and analysis in the behavioral sciences.* Unpublished thesis. Department of Applied Mathematics, Harvard University.

Widrow, G. & Hoff, M.E. (1960). Adaptive switching circuits. *Institute of Radio Engineers, Western Electronic Show and Convention, Convention Record, Part 4,* 96–104.

SEMANTICS

SEMANTICS

INTRODUCTION

All of the chapters in this section deal, in one way or another, with semantics. It is possible to make a loose distinction between lexical semantics and structural semantics, the former being concerned with the meaning of individual words and the latter with the meaning of larger units such as phrases and sentences. Such a distinction is often blurred in connectionist research, but is roughly paralleled in the arrangement of the chapters in this section; the first two chapters focus primarily on lexical semantics, and the latter two deal mainly with phrasal and sentential semantics.

Semantic Representation

In conventional semantics a distinction is made between semantic *representation* and semantic *interpretation*. Representation refers to the meaning constructs at the current level of analysis (e.g. lexical, sentential). Interpretation is the process whereby representations at one level are transformed to representations at another. In a connectionist context, representation can be thought of as a pattern of activation on a set of units, and interpretation can be viewed as the transmission of activation from one level of representation to the next over the weights of the network.

There are two main styles of representation found in connectionist models: one is localist and the other distributed. Localist representations are usually characterised as having one unit representing a given concept. A distributed representation, on the other hand, entails a concept being represented by a pattern of activation over a number of units. One can often find both forms used in the same model. However, the continuous distributed form of representation is typical of models in which some form of learning algorithm has been used in the construction of the representation, such as error backpropagation. Localist representations, on the other hand, are more commonly found either as the input to, or output from, networks that learn. Nevertheless, one can still find networks that are comprised entirely of localist units. As has been pointed out by Hinton (1989), the terms *localist* and *distributed* are not absolute definitions, and should be understood in the context of the relationship between some descriptive language and its connectionist implementation.

A common form of distributed representation involves the use of vectors of microfeatures. It is possible to distinguish between three classes of microfeatural representation: those in which the microfeatures are (1) symbolic, (2) nonsymbolic, or (3) learned (Sharkey, 1991). In the first case, a concept is represented as a pattern of activation over a set of units, where each of these units stands for a meaningful feature such as gender. In the second case, the features have no immediate interpretation, and merely serve to distinguish one input vector from another. Typically, in both these cases the presence of a feature is indicated by the relevant unit having a value of one, and zero otherwise. In the final case, where the microfeatures are learned, the network devises the best set of features to perform the mapping task. The main difference between learned and symbolic features is that the latter tend to have greater generality because they have the capacity to encode information beyond that contained in the training corpus of a network. Learned features, however, are devised solely within the context of a training task, and their generality is dependent on the representativeness of the training set.

The chapter by Sutcliffe (Chapter 3) explores the symbolic type of microfeatural representation. One of the interesting aspects of his work is the attempt made to develop a comprehensive set of microfeatures to cover a range of lexical items. He claims that as the lexicon is expanded, the number of additional microfeatures required significantly decreases. However, the size of the lexicon is still rather small (some 217 nouns and verbs). Another aspect of interest is the use made of *centralities* to weight individual microfeatures in terms of their importance in defining a particular concept (Robins, 1989). Though not described as such, this can be thought of as a compromise between conventional bivalent microfeatures and continuous-valued learned microfeatures. It gives additional representational capacity to the microfeatures, in particular when dealing with words that are almost synonymous.

Dyer, Flowers, and Wang (Chapter 2) tackle the problem of selecting appropriate microfeatures by allowing the network to learn them, rather than specifying them in advance. The nature of the resulting microfeatures reflects the context in which the concept is used in the training corpus. Concepts used in similar contexts acquire similar representations. A limitation on this approach, as mentioned earlier, is the possibility of poor generalisation outside the training corpus.

St. John and McClelland (Chapter 5) also make use of learned distributed representations, though in this case internally rather than at the input level. The backpropagation learning algorithm is used to create what they refer to as *gestalt* representations for representing sentence content. The input to the network is a surface representation of a sentence, and the output is a set of correctly assigned thematic role/filler pairs. The sentence gestalt contains a meaning representation for the entire sentence, details of which can be extracted by a process of probing for thematic role fillers.

In some respects it is one of the strengths of connectionist representations that a vector of activation values can be used to represent a single lexical item as in Sutcliffe's model, or a whole sentence as in St. John and McClelland's model. Connectionism provides a common currency of representation for all levels of analysis, from pixel to predicate. Nevertheless, as will be seen in the discussion of compositionality below, the failure on the part of connectionist representations directly to reflect the structural complexity of what they represent lies at the root of a major criticism of this type of representation.

Ambiguity and Similarity

An important task for any system of semantic representation is to deal with ambiguity. An adequate semantic representation must give a complete account of all potential interpretations of a sentence. Furthermore, sentences that have similar meanings (e.g. sentences that paraphrase each other) should also have similar semantic representations.

Wermter and Lehnert (Chapter 4) tackle the problem of ambiguity explicitly by using a set of real-valued numbers to represent the plausibility of various interpretations of inherently ambiguous complex noun phrases. They deal with the problem of prepositional-phrase (PP) attachment in complex noun phrases using a two-stage model. During the first stage, a backpropagation network is used to learn the semantic plausibility of a wide range of PP-attachments. The second stage involves the use of a localist constraint-satisfaction network to select the most plausible parse/interpretation of a specific sentence. In doing so, it makes use of the learned plausibility ratings from the first stage. An interesting aspect of this chapter is its use of a hybrid strategy in solving the problem. Another point of note is the attempt made to motivate the selection of microfeatures for the representation of nouns in the first stage by consulting a domain-related thesaurus. In general, the selection of suitable microfeatures is very much an ad hoc affair, and any attempt to formalise it must be welcomed.

One of several goals of St. John and McClelland (Chapter 5) is to give an account of lexical and sentential ambiguity. As a sentence is input word by word, the network is forced to anticipate the role/filler pairs for the whole event described in the sentence. The relative activation levels of the output units reflect the range of possible interpretations open at a given point in the sentence. As more of the sentence is input, the range of possibilities narrows, until one is left with, in the case of a sentence having a single interpretation, a unique set of role/filler pairs. However, in the case of an ambiguity, all relevant sets of role/filler pairs remain active.

The related requirement that the representations of similar concepts should themselves be similar is a problematic question when it comes to comparing learned internal representations (those created in hidden units). However, there are a number of techniques available for exploring the structural similarities of internal representations. One of these involves performing cluster analyses on the activation values of internal representation units, and finding what patterns get classified as similar in terms of distance measure (e.g. Euclidean distance; cf. Elman, 1988). If the network is performing its task satisfactorily, one finds that inputs treated in a similar way by the network have similar internal representations as indicated by the relative proximity of their hidden unit activation vectors.

In general, measures of ambiguity and similarity fall out very naturally from the nature of connectionist representations. Since the representations comprise vectors of unit activations, ambiguity can be conveyed by the ambiguous vector being more or less equidistant from vectors representing competing interpretations. Furthermore, similarity of two representations is simply a measure of the distance between vectors.

Compositionality

The compositionality requirement for a semantic representation entails that the meaning of a sentence as a whole should, with certain exceptions, be equivalent to the "sum" or composition of the meaning of its constituents. One obvious exception to this is the semantic representation of idiomatic phrases (e.g. "kick the bucket"). Nevertheless, in general the Fregean principle of semantic compositionality holds true (Frege, 1892).

It is in the domain of compositionality that much criticism has been aimed at the connectionist approach from the advocates of symbolic representation (Fodor & McLaughlin, 1990; Fodor & Pylyshyn, 1988). Microfeatures, in particular, have been the subject of some criticism. Fodor and Pylyshyn (1988) have argued that microfeatural representations are not compositional, and therefore they cannot provide a suitable medium for the operation of cognitive processes. The compositionality issue hinges on whether a system of conceptual representation reflects the fact that the elements of cognitive computation are composable into complex structures and that this constituent structure causally determines the steps of the cognitive algorithm. Fodor and Pylyshyn have argued that microfeatural representations are not compositional in the right sense. So, for example, if one wanted to represent the concept "a cup of coffee" using microfeatures, all you would end up with is a representation of "cup" with a representation of "coffee'. They argue that without creating ad hoc features, there is no way to represent the predicate relationship that exists between the two constituents of the concept.

There are two notable ways in which Fodor and Pylyshyn's arguments have been addressed by connectionists. Both differ in their consideration of microfeatures. In the first case, it is argued that microfeatural representations implement a weak form of compositionality, and the predication is implicitly represented by the context dependent nature of the constituent representations (Smolensky, 1988). Thus, given a vector of features representing a cup of coffee, the representation of coffee obtained by removing the representation of cup would have certain context-independent features such as +*brown-colour*, +*hot-liquid*, and +*burnt-odour*. However, in addition to these, an adequate representation would have certain context-dependent features such as +*curved-sides*, or +*3D-volume*. These latter features, Smolensky argues, capture the predicate relationship that exists between cup and coffee.

Van Gelder (1990) takes a more radical stance in pointing out that Fodor and Pylyshyn are implicitly discussing only one type of compositionality: spatially concatenative composition. In this mode of composition, the spatial layout of the symbols (reading from left to right) is important (indeed crucial) for symbol manipulation and inference. Van Gelder (1990, p. 360) states that for a mode of combination to be concatenative "it must preserve tokens of an expression's constituents (and the sequential relations among tokens) in the expression itself."

In contrast to the classical concatenative representations are connectionist representations that have been learned (e.g. hidden unit representations in backpropagation). In this type of representation it is only the pattern of activation across microfeatures as a whole that is semantically interpretable and not the individual microfeatures, since the same microfeatures are used in all of the representations. These uniquely connectionist representations should be considered to have a different mode of composition. That is, they are not concatenative, but are functionally compositional nonetheless. According to van Gelder (1990, p. 361), "we have functional compositionality when there are general, effective, and reliable processes for (a) producing an expression given its constituents, and (b) decomposing the expression back into its constituents." Connectionist models can certainly perform (a) and (b) as well as meet the criteria that the processes be general, effective, and reliable. By *general*, van Gelder means that the process can be applied to the construction and decomposition of arbitrarily complex representations. We have seen how a simple feedforward backpropagation network can learn to encode and decode representations. To be *effective* the process must be mechanistically implementible and to be *reliable* it must always generate the same answer for the same inputs. Clearly, these criteria have been satisfied by a number of recent connectionist systems (cf. Sharkey, 1991, for a review and discussion of these systems).

Wermter and Lehnert (Chapter 4) sidestep the issue by using a sentence representation network that is more akin to a conventional semantic network than a connectionist one, given the variety of different unit types employed. The sentence gestalt of St. John and McClelland (Chapter 5) does seem to demonstrate some of the properties that one would expect from a compositional representation. It appears to have internal structure that can be accessed, though not in a direct way.

The debate engendered by the Fodor and Pylyshyn critique still goes on, and the general strategy adopted by the connectionist research community has been twofold. The first has been to demonstrate a functionality in networks that is consistent with a sensitivity to compositional structure (e.g. Elman, 1989; Pollack, 1990; Servan-Schreiber, Cleeremans, & McClelland, 1989). The resulting solutions, however, tend not to map very readily onto conventional symbolic approaches. A second approach has been to try to merge symbolic and connectionist systems of representations into a hybrid system. Dyer, Flowers and Wang (Chapter 2) adopt this strategy. They attempt to marry the strengths of connectionist representation (graceful degradation, automatic learning, parallelism, etc.) with the power of conventional symbol-processing systems.

REFERENCES

Elman, J.L. (1988) *Finding structure in time*. C.R.L. Technical Report 8801. La Jolla, Calif.: U.C.S.D.

Elman, J.L. (1989). *Representation and structure in connectionist models*. C.R.L. Technical Report 8903. La Jolla, Calif.: Center for Research in Language, U.C.S.D.

Fodor, J. & McLaughlin, B.P. (1990). Connectionism and the problems of systematicity. *Cognition, 35*, 183–204.

Fodor, J. & Pylyshyn, Z. (1988). Connectionism and cognitive architecture. *Cognition, 28*, 3–71.

Frege, G. (1892). On sense and reference. Reprinted in D. Davidson & G. Harman (1972) (Eds.), *Semantics of natural language*. Dordrecht: Reidel, 116–128.

Hinton G.E. (1989). Connectionist learning procedures. *Artificial Intelligence, 40*, 185–234.

Jordan, M.I. (1986). Attractor dynamics and parallelism in a connectionist sequential machine, *Proceedings of the Cognitive Science Society*. Amherst, Mass., August, 531–546.

Pollack, J.B. (1990). Recursive distributed representations. *Artificial Intelligence, 46*, 77–105.

Robins, A. (1989). Distributed representations of type and category. *Connection Science, 1*, 345–364.

Servan-Schreiber, D., Cleeremans, A., & McClelland, J. (1989). Learning sequential structure in simple recurrent networks. In D. Touretzsky (Ed.), *Advances in neural information processing systems, 2*. San Mateo, Calif.: Morgan-Kaufmann.

Sharkey, N.E. (1991). Connectionist representation techniques. *AI Review, 5*, 143–167.

Smolensky, P. (1988). *The constituent structure of connectionist mental states*. Technical Report CU-CS-394-88. Boulder, Colorado: Department of Computer Science, University of Colorado.

Van Gelder, T. (1990). Compositionality: A connectionist variation on a classical theme. *Cognitive Science, 14*, 355–384.

2

Distributed Symbol Discovery through Symbol Recirculation: Toward Natural Language Processing in Distributed Connectionist Networks

Michael G. Dyer, Margot Flowers, and Yih-Jih Alan Wang
3532 Boelter Hall, Computer Science Department, University of California, Los Angeles, CA 90024, U.S.A.

INTRODUCTION

The standard position in both AI and linguistics, that natural language processing (NLP) is highly symbolic in nature, has recently come under critical review (e.g. Churchland & Sejnowski, 1989; Dreyfus & Dreyfus, 1988; Reeke & Edelman, 1988; Smolensky, 1988b). Researchers in the distributed connectionist systems (DCS) camp have built architectures in which language-related tasks are reformulated as mapping tasks that are fundamentally associative in nature. Examples are: mapping syntax to semantics (McClelland & Kawamoto, 1986); mapping present to past tense (Rumelhart & McClelland, 1986b); translating language L1 to L2 (Allen, 1986); and mapping orthography to morphemes (Sejnowski & Rosenberg, 1987). What motivates these researchers are the useful features displayed by distributed connectionist networks, namely: (1) graceful degradation to noise and damage; (2) automatic learning and generalisation to novel inputs; (3) massive parallelism; (4) self-organisation and reconstructive memory; and (5) increased neural plausibility, including lesionability (Rumelhart and McClelland, 1986c; Smolensky, 1988a).

The enthusiasms generated by initial successes in connectionism, (e.g. Rumelhart & McClelland, 1986c), have prompted a counterattack by symbolically oriented psychologists and linguists (e.g. Fodor & Pylyshyn, 1988; Pinker & Prince, 1988), who have pointed out a number of fundamental weaknesses in language-related DCS models. Other researchers have responded by attempting to construct distributed connectionist architectures and hybrid symbolic-connectionist systems capable of various degrees of symbol processing (e.g. Dolan, 1989; Dolan & Smolensky, 1989; Dyer, 1991; Gasser, 1988; Gasser & Dyer, 1988; Hendler, 1987; 1989; Lange & Dyer, 1989a; 1989b; Pollack, 1988; Shastri, 1988; Smolensky, 1990; Sumida & Dyer, 1989; Touretzky & Hinton, 1988).

In this chapter, we take the position that NLP requires symbol processing (Dyer, 1991; Touretzky, 1989). Thus, if distributed connectionist systems are to handle natural language input with full generality, they must be able to exhibit the capabilities of symbol processing systems, namely: (1) representation of abstract and recursive structure; (2) implementation of rules and schemas; (3) inference chaining through propagation of bindings; and (4) formation of new instances and episodes in long-term memory.

The rest of this chapter is organised as follows. First, we discuss requirements for NLP, pointing out the symbolic nature of natural language comprehension through the use of an example involving abstract knowledge. Second, we examine in detail one method for forming distributed symbol representations dynamically. This method uses the technique of manipulating entire weight matrices in one network as a pattern of activation in another network, storing these distributed representations in a symbol memory, and then recirculating them as the system is required to relate symbols to each other in specified ways. As a result of this *symbol recirculation*, symbol representations are dynamically altered and converge on representations that aid in those tasks demanded of them. Third, we review briefly related methods of symbol recirculation. Finally, we discuss open problems in distributed connectionist symbol processing for natural language tasks and conclude with a brief description of some current approaches toward resolving these problems.

NATURAL LANGUAGE PROCESSING: CONSTRAINTS FROM THE TASK DOMAIN

Natural language processing systems must manipulate very abstract forms of knowledge, e.g. the goals, plans, and beliefs of narrative agents. Consider just a fragment of the abstract knowledge needed to understand, and answer questions about, the following narrative segment:

Irresponsible Babysitter

John promised to watch the baby for Mary. John decided to talk to a friend on the phone. The baby crawled outside and fell into the swimming pool and nearly drowned.
Q: Why did Mary accuse John of being irresponsible?
A: John had agreed to protect the baby from harm, but the baby nearly drowned.

A portion of the necessary background knowledge needed to understand "Irresponsible Babysitter" includes abstract structures of the following sort (informally stated below):

<x "promise" y that z> =
    <x communicated to y that x has goal G, satisfied by z>
    <y communicated to x that y has goal G', to be agent for x>
    <after communications, y believes that G(x), x believes that G'(y)
        and y believes that x will execute action A to achieve G>

<x "watch" y "for" z> =
    <x attends eyes(x) to y and
        if possible act A of y can cause harm to y,
        then x performs act B to block A>

<x can know act A of y by attending eyes of x to y at the time of A>
<possibility of drowning(x) threatens preservation health goal G(x)>
<if x loves y, then x has goal to block failure of health goal G(y)>
<"irresponsible" x (wrt y)> = <promise by x to achieve G(y)
                             followed by goal failure for y>

In addition we need to know facts such as:

<babies cannot swim and may drown in water>
<mothers love their babies>

The traditional approach to the NLP comprehension problem is to handcode such abstract symbolic structures in a semantic network of labelled relationships, then instantiate instances of such structures and bind them into larger structures in episodic memory. Once episodic memory is built, questions can be mapped into conceptual representations that direct retrieval strategies.

The mapping from natural language to conceptual representations is usually accomplished via instantiation and binding operations over symbol structures, performed by a conceptual parser (e.g. Dyer, 1983). Basically, as the parser encounters each word and/or phrase in the input (e.g. a sentence of a story or question about the story), it accesses a corresponding entry in lexical memory. Each lexical entry refers to one or more fragments of associated symbol structures (schemas) in a general semantic memory. These fragments are either explicitly connected to other schemas, via labelled links, or implicitly connected via rules. Examples of (informal) rules are:

if x communicates message m to y
then y knows m

if x cannot perform an act z
then x may ask y to perform z for x

if x loves y and x believes that y might perform an act z to cause harm to y,
then x will do an act r to keep y from doing z

Such rules are needed in order to interpret phrases such as "watch the baby," which are actually ambiguous. For example, in "Irresponsible Babysitter," John could conceivably argue that he was not irresponsible:

> I am not irresponsible. I agreed to watch the baby and I did. I watched the baby crawl out of the crib. I watched him crawl to the pool, and I watched him fall in. You wanted me to watch the baby and that is exactly what I did.

To interpret "watch" correctly, we need many inferences. We need to infer from John's promise to Mary that Mary believes that John will do what he promises; otherwise, we could accuse Mary of being irresponsible. We need to know that unattended babies may perform actions that will cause them harm (e.g. "watching a television" does not involve keeping the television set from harming itself). We also need to know that guardians often observe incompetent individuals to prevent them from coming to harm, so we need rules such as:

if x is a baby
then x may do an act that causes harm to x

if x is attending eyes to y and y typically performs acts that can cause harm
then x is probably attending eyes in order to be aware of such acts,
in order to block them

Given such rules, a conceptual parser must link conceptual representations for "promise," "watch," and "baby" into a coherent set of interrelated instantiations. Before this task can be performed by a distributed connectionist system, we must solve the problems of: (1) representing these abstract schemas; (2) representing these rules, along with their variable portions; (3) propagating dynamic bindings along the variable portions; and (4) creating long-term episodes in memory.

Notice that these operations, although traditionally performed by symbol processing systems, need not necessarily be implemented as in von Neumann architectures. Symbols and symbol manipulations could conceivably be implemented via associative operations over distributed patterns of activation. However, no matter how they are implemented, capabilities of structure, inference, and instantiation must be realised (Feldman, 1989). Notice also that the existence of symbols in distributed connectionist systems does not imply the denial of nonsymbolic forms of knowledge. For instance, visual images (e.g. of John talking on the phone while the baby crawls off) could very well be nonsymbolic in nature. But without the capabilities to form and manipulate abstract structures (e.g. irresponsibility), it will be impossible to represent, infer, acquire, or interpret instances of such abstract situations.

Once we accept the necessity for entities that behave as symbols, major issues of research in designing distributed connectionist systems for high-level cognition become: How are distributed symbols automatically formed? How do such distributed symbols enter into structured relationships with other symbols?

DYNAMIC VS. STATIC SYMBOL REPRESENTATIONS

The purely symbolic approach to NLP can exhibit impressive performance on short segments of text within constrained domains of knowledge, e.g. narrative understanding and question answering (Dyer, 1983; 1989; Dyer, Cullingford, & Alvarado, 1987), argument comprehension in editorials (Alvarado, Dyer, & Flowers, 1990; in press), legal analyses (Goldman, Dyer, & Flowers, 1988), advice giving (Quilici, Dyer, & Flowers, 1988), and moral evaluation of text (Reeves, 1988). But the resulting complexity of knowledge interactions, the difficulty of engineering the knowledge by hand, and the fragility of the resulting systems is well known. Connectionists hope to overcome these problems through automatic learning of distributed structures. One positive consequence of the connectionist approach is the resulting re-examination of the nature of symbols and symbolic operations.

How should symbols be implemented? In von Neumann machines, symbols are implemented as bit patterns residing in separate memory registers. The bit patterns are specified by a predetermined coding scheme, such as ASCII. The encoding scheme is both arbitrary and static; e.g. the ASCII code for "CAT" remains the same throughout all system executions. In purely symbolic systems, the arbitrary and static nature of symbol representations are not viewed as any problem, since it is assumed that the semantics of a given symbol develops only in terms of the structured relationships it enters into with other symbols. Although it is the case that symbols enter into structured relationships with other symbols, the arbitrary and static nature of von Neumann symbol representations results in the inability of standard symbolic models to perform associative inference, handle noise and damage, complete partial patterns, or generalise to novel cases.

In contrast, distributed connectionist systems can represent symbols as patterns of activation over a set of processing units in the input/output layers of a given network. These patterns of activation are intimately involved in the success (or failure) of the associative operations that are demanded of them. The generalisation and noise handling capabilities of distributed connectionist networks depend on similar patterns in the input layer reconstructing related patterns (related by some similarity metric) in the output layer, based on the energy landscape established in "weight space."

In the prototypical case, a mapping task is established via a set of input/output pairs. During the training phase, a subset of these I/O pairs is presented to the network and the connection weights are adjusted incrementally, using some adaptive learning algorithm, such as back-error propagation (Rumelhart & McClelland, 1986a) or reinforcement learning (Sutton, 1984). Once the network has been trained, the reserved subset of I/O pairs is used to test the generalisation capabilities of the network. From an architectural point of view, the particular weight-update rule is not centrally important, just as long as the update rule is capable of finding a set of weights that realise the desired associations.

In most distributed connectionist systems, only the weights are altered during learning. The representations of the training set, encoded in the input/output layers, are not modified. In the cases where the input is language related, the input/output representations are usually encoded by hand, using some sort of microfeature scheme. For instance, McClelland and Kawamoto (1986) trained a network to associate a representation of syntactic input with semantic output. Both the input and output layers were divided up into segments (e.g. subject, object, prepositional phrase, etc. in the syntax layer; actor, action, instrument, etc. in the semantics layer), where a pattern of activation (PoA) over each segment represented a symbol. For instance, the symbol "John" might be represented by activating those units representing the microfeatures: animate, human, male, etc. The reason the network could generalise to novel mappings relied greatly on the similarity between symbols. Suppose the network learns the following mappings:

syntax layer		*semantics layer*
SUBJECT: John		ACTION: ingest
VERB: eats	$\longrightarrow$	ACTOR: John
OBJECT: hamburger		OBJECT: hamburger
PREP-PH: with a fork		INSTRUMENT: fork
		OBJ-MODIFIER: xx
SUBJECT: Fred		ACTION: ingest
VERB: eats	$\longrightarrow$	ACTOR: Fred
OBJECT: hamburger		OBJECT: hamburger
PREP-PH: with cheese		INSTRUMENT: xx
		OBJ-MODIFIER: cheese

If the network is given the novel input:

SUBJECT: Mary
VERB: eats
OBJECT: hotdog
PREP-PH: with ketchup

then the extent to which it arrives at the correct interpretation of "with ketchup" (i.e. as either the modifier of the OBJECT or the INSTRUMENT of the ACT) will depend on how closely "Mary," "hotdog," and "ketchup" share microfeatures with previous inputs. Clearly, if their patterns of activation do not share microfeatures, then the network will fail to generalise properly.

Unfortunately, microfeature encodings suffer from four major problems:

1. *Knowledge engineering bottleneck*—the initial set of microfeatures must be determined. As is well known by AI researchers, the selection of a primitive set of features is itself a difficult knowledge engineering problem.

2. *Flatness*—microfeature vectors are impoverished as a representation scheme since they are flat; i.e. they lack the ability to represent recursive and constituent structure. Such structures are necessary to capture embedded grammatical and conceptual regularities, as in "John told Mary that Bill thought Mary wanted to be kissed."

3. *Inapplicability*—Many microfeatures will be inapplicable when representing various entities. For example, the microfeature say, METAL = {aluminium, copper, etc.} will not be applicable for representing people. This results in requiring a huge number of microfeatures specified ahead of time, with most of them specified as negative or not applicable. It seems counterintuitive to represent a person or a building, for example, in terms of the very large number of features that they lack.

4. *Tokens vs. Types*—It is awkward to distinguish a specific instance from a general concept using the microfeature approach. For example, the representations for a car, John's car, a convertible, a broken car, and an antique car must all be differentiated in terms of microfeatures. In the case of "John's car," it might seem sufficient to have some "ownership" microfeatures, but what do such microfeatures look like? Must we establish an ownership microfeature for each of the possible owners, so that "my car" and "John's car" can be distinguished?

SYMBOL RECIRCULATION

What we want is a method by which symbols can enter into structured, recursive relationships with one another, but without microfeatures, while at the same time forming distributed patterns of activation. The general technique for accomplishing this goal we refer to as *symbol recirculation*. Symbols are maintained in a separate connectionist network that acts as a global symbol memory, where each symbol is composed of a pattern of activation. Symbol representations start out as random patterns of activation. Over time they are "recirculated" through the symbolic tasks being demanded of them, and as a result, gradually form distributed representations that aid in the performance of these tasks. Symbol representations arise as a result of teaching the system to form associative mappings among symbols, where these mappings capture structured relationships.

For instance, in NLP tasks, structured relationships among symbols can be represented as triples of the form (PREDICATE SLOT FILLER). For instance, "John told Mary that he drank the milk at home on Tuesday" can be represented as:

```
(MTRANS1 ACTOR HUMAN1)
(MTRANS1 TO HUMAN2)
(MTRANS1 OBJECT INGEST1)
(MTRANS1 ISA MTRANS)
(INGEST1 ACTOR HUMAN1)
(INGEST1 OBJECT MILK)
(INGEST1 TIME TUESDAY)
(INGEST1 LOCATION HOME)
(INGEST1 ISA INGEST)
(HUMAN1 ISA HUMAN)
(HUMAN1 NAME "JOHN")
(HUMAN1 GENDER MALE)
(HUMAN2 ISA HUMAN)
(HUMAN2 NAME "MARY")
(HUMAN2 GENDER FEMALE)
(INGEST ISA ACT)
    . . .
```

Structured relationships among symbols can also be interpreted as a semantic network (Fig. 2.1), where each SLOT is the name of a relation that links together

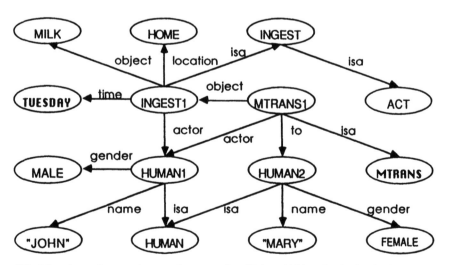

FIG. 2.1.   A sample semantic network representing: "John told Mary that he drank milk at home on Tuesday."

two nodes (i.e. PREDICATE and FILLER). In a distributed connectionist architecture, each symbol is represented as a pattern of activation over a set of processing units in the input layer of a distributed connectionist network.

The basic technique of symbol recirculation involves: (1) starting with an arbitrary representation for each symbol; (2) loading these symbols into the input/output layers of a network performing a mapping task; (3) forming a distributed symbol representation that aids in the mapping task; (4) storing the modified symbol representations back in the global symbol memory; and (5) iterating over all symbols for all mapping tasks, until all symbol representations converge. As the same I/O pairs are presented to the mapping network, the representations of the symbols making up these pairs undergo modification. As a result, the system is "shooting at a moving target," since the representations (of the mappings that the network must learn) are being altered while the network is attempting to learn the mapping. So not only are weights being modified, but also the encodings of the representations that are being associated. Thus, the training environment is reactive.

The approach we will describe in detail in this chapter is based on the following observation:

> Any distributed connectionist network whose long-term memory is representable as a weight matrix (WMx), can be transformed into a pattern of activation (PoA) in the input layer of a larger network. Likewise, the PoA output by one network can be used to dynamically construct another network (WMx).

This fundamental relationship can be exploited in many ways. We describe one such method next.

ENCODING SEMANTIC NETWORKS IN DUAL: A DISTRIBUTED CONNECTIONIST ARCHITECTURE

DUAL is an architecture designed to form distributed representations of symbols that are related in the form of a semantic network. For our purposes here, a semantic network is a directed graph of nodes {...A_i...} and named

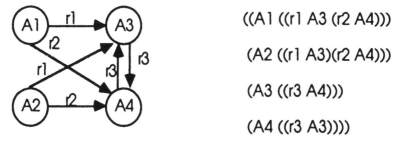

$$((A1 ((r1 A3 (r2 A4)))$$

$$(A2 ((r1 A3)(r2 A4)))$$

$$(A3 ((r3 A4)))$$

$$(A4 ((r3 A3))))$$

FIG. 2.2.   A sample semantic network (SSN) with four nodes and three relations.

links {...r_i...}. It can be represented pictorially (Fig. 2.2a) or as a case frame (Fig. 2.2b). This sample semantic network (SSN) has four nodes: A_1, A_2, A_3, A_4; and three distinct links: r_1, r_2, r_3.

The essence of our approach (Dyer, Flowers, & Wang, 1988) is to maintain two distributed connectionist networks, STM and LTM (each with its own input, output, and hidden layers). STM acts as a short-term memory and encodes link-node pairs associated with a given node (symbol) in the semantic network (SN). LTM acts as a long-term memory and encodes an entire semantic network. STM and LTM are illustrated in Fig. 2.3.

STM contains m input and n output units, connected by N1 weights to the hidden units and N2 weights to the output units. An entire matrix S of the STM

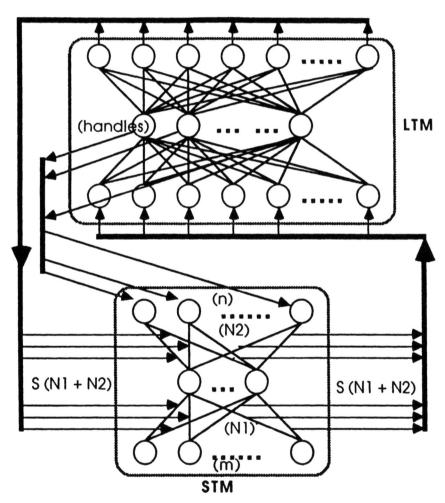

FIG. 2.3.   DUAL architecture: STM and LTM.

contains N = N1 + N2 weights. LTM consists of N input units Thus, the complete weight matrix (WMx) of STM is the input to LTM, as a pattern of activation (PoA). LTM acts as an autoassociator, with n hidden units. A pattern of activation over the hidden units in LTM, which we term a *handle*, can be used to retrieve a weight matrix S from LTM. Thus, LTM functions to compress an S into a handle and to store a number of S's into a single, long-term memory weight matrix.

In addition to STM and LTM, DUAL contains a Distributed Symbol Memory (DSM), where handles are stored. Each handle actually represents a symbol in the semantic memory, which indirectly encodes all of the link-node relationships associated with it. Over time, the representation of each handle changes, converging on a final representation for each symbol. At any given point in time, STM holds all (r_j A_j) link-node pairs associated with a given semantic network node A_i; DSM holds handles (symbols) that retrieve, from LTM, nodes $A_1 \ldots A_p$ (assuming p nodes in the semantic network); LTM holds the entire semantic network as a set of autoassociated, STM weight matrices.

Each link r_j in DUAL is represented as an arbitrary, handcoded PoA over the input units in STM. In the current version of DUAL, the activity patterns for the links remain unchanged during encoding; only node representations are dynamically formed. A set of orthogonal representations is used for the links, in order to minimise interferences, since we want to keep links discriminated. For example, the three links r_1, r_2, r_3 of SNN may be represented by the PoAs illustrated in Fig. 2.4a. Each node A_i is represented by its handle and the PoA of its handle is randomly set up initially and varies dynamically as the semantic network is encoded. The encoding process involves iterating over all nodes until a consistent set of handles have emerged. In the process of encoding, *DUAL discovers distributed representations for the nodes of the semantic network*, representations consistent with the desired operations over the semantic network. Figure 2.4b illustrates a possible set of initial PoAs of the handles for the nodes of SSN.

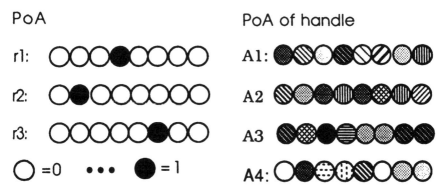

PoA   PoA of handle

FIG. 2.4.   Initial PoAs of SSN from Fig. 2.2.

Encoding Semantic Memory Nodes in STM

A given node A_i in a semantic network is defined by the link-node pairs $(r_j A_k)$ that are associated with it. To encode A_i we perform the operation ENCODE-NODE(A_i):

> ENCODE-NODE(A_i)—Let all the $(r_j A_k)$ relationships associated with A_i be encoded into STM by using standard back-error propagation techniques (Rumelhart & McClelland, 1986), where the input pattern is PoA(r_j) and the desired output pattern is the current PoA(handle [A_k]). Initially, the representation of each A_k is represented by an arbitrary PoA. The resulting weight matrix of STM is S_i.

For example, in SNN (Fig. 2.2), the node A_1 has two relationships $(r_1 A_3)$ and $(r_2 A_4)$. Therefore, ENCODE-NODE (A_1) involves training the STM with two sets of input-output patterns: $[PoA(r_1) \rightarrow PoA(handle[A_3])]$ and $[PoA(r_2) \rightarrow PoA(handle[A_4])]$. After training STM on these two patterns, the weight matrix in STM is designated as S_1 (Fig. 2.5).

Encoding STM Weight Matrices in LTM

To encode a set of STM weight matrices $\{S_1 \ldots S_p\}$ in LTM, we perform the operation LOAD-LTM:

> LOAD-LTM—Train LTM with the set of $\{\ldots S_i \ldots\}$ from the STM phase, using the LTM as an autoassociator. At the end of the training, the PoA over the hidden units in LTM for each autoassociated S_i replaces the corresponding handle H_i (for A_i) in DSM. That is, each pattern of activation over the hidden layer in LTM constitutes a compression of an entire STM weight matrix.

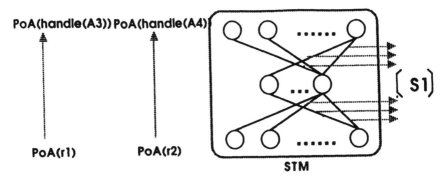

FIG. 2.5.   ENCODE-NODE(A1) for SSN from Fig. 2.4.

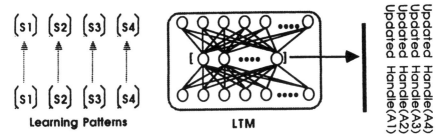

FIG. 2.6.   LOAD-LTM for the sample semantic network (SSN) in Fig. 2.2.

Figure 2.6 illustrates the encoding of each S_i through autoassociation and the updating of handles in the distributed symbol memory for each symbol/node/handle.

Recirculation to Convergence

At this point, each handle H_i, if placed in the hidden layer of LTM, will cause the corresponding S_i to be reconstructed to the output layer of LTM. The resulting S_i is then loaded into STM, through modification of the weights of STM. Figure 2.7 illustrates the operation of LS-TRANSF(H_1), which consists of both loading

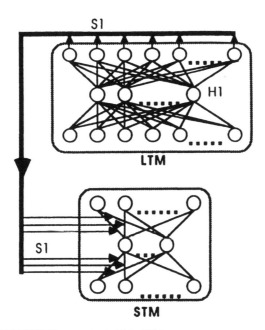

FIG. 2.7.   LS-TRANSFS(H1) reconstructs S1 in STM.

handle H_1 (of semantic node A_1) into LTM and loading the resulting S_1 into STM. Now, suppose STM has S_i as its weight matrix. If we want to retrieve any relationship, say $(r_j \ A_k)$ associated with A_i, we simply place link r_j on the STM input layer and a handle for A_k will appear on the output layer. Notice, however, that *this handle is obsolete*! That is, DSM contains a more current version H_k of A_k. Since we do not want A_i's link, r_j, pointing to an obsolete version of A_k, we need to retrain STM with the new pair $(r_j \ A_k)$, where $A_k = H_k$.

Consider a concrete example, where we focus on just two nodes in a hypothetical semantic network:

node	associated link-node pairs
JOHN	(LIKES MARY), (GENDER HUMAN), (OWNS FIDO)...
MARY	(LIKES JOHN), (GENDER FEMALE), (OCCUPATION STUDENT)...

To encode JOHN in STM we must encode the associations [LIKES → MARY, ...]; but what is the teaching pattern we are going to use for the output layer of STM? Since we have not yet encoded MARY, we must select a random pattern, say P1. So we have really encoded JOHN LIKES P1, where P1 is a poor initial representation for the MARY symbol. Likewise, the pattern for JOHN (when encoding that MARY LIKES JOHN) must also be a random pattern, say P2. But once both JOHN and MARY have been encoded in LTM (via LOAD-LTM) and updated in DSM, then both JOHN and MARY now have patterns that are no longer as random, but which aid in reconstructing the respective weight matrices in STM that will allow their associated link-node pairs to be retrieved. So now we must again execute LS-TRANSF and ENCODE-NODE for both JOHN and MARY, followed again by LOAD-LTM. But this encoding operation will cause yet a new set of handles to be created for JOHN and MARY.

Each time JOHN LIKES MARY, JOHN is learning to LIKE a new representation of MARY. This associative learning operation is changing the weight matrix in STM that represents JOHN. As a result, the representation of JOHN is now different, which means that MARY must learn to LIKE this new representation of JOHN, which causes the representation for MARY again to be altered. So the process of ENCODE-NODE and LOAD-LTM (along with updating DSM) must recirculate, until the representations in DSM cease changing. At this point, convergence is achieved. After convergence, each semantic node A_i has a distributed representation H_i that encodes all of its structural information where the distributed representation is central in retrieving the weight matrix that makes this structural information available.

To summarise: In the encoding cycle we start the training of STM with one set of handles (node representations) and end up with a new set of handles in LTM. Therefore, the information we have encoded in the STM matrices (about the old handles) no longer holds for the new handles. However, updating old handles with new ones will require yet another encoding cycle to be performed. Thus, to encode the entire semantic network, DUAL must successively perform this encoding cycle repeatedly, until convergence of handles is achieved. This approach is analogous to "shooting at a moving target," where the act of shooting causes the target to move. As one "shoots," the target location has moved, so the aim has to be adjusted repeatedly. After convergence, we end up with only one set of consistent handles representing the semantic network nodes. Figure 2.8 illustrates a sample set of handles for SSN after convergence.

Retrieval and Accuracy/Capacity in DUAL

To retrieve the value of r_i for node A_i (with handle H_i), we do the operation GET(A_i, r_i):

GET(A_i, r_i)—Place H_i in the hidden layer of LTM to get S_i. Then perform LS-TRANSF(S_i), followed by placing r_i on the input layer of STM to obtain the associated node.

By repeatedly using GET(node, link), we can traverse the entire semantic network. However, due to the nature of distributed connectionist networks, a certain degree of inaccuracy is likely to be introduced as each S_i is encoded into LTM.

To test both for change in accuracy of retrieval during recirculation, and to gain a rough estimate of time to convergence, a semantic network SNET was created, with 10 nodes and an average number of relations per node being 5. Each node of SNET was represented in the distributed symbol memory (DSM) as a handle 8 bits long. Execution time was measured in terms of CPU seconds as epochs of symbol recirculation were run (Table 2.1). Here, a single epoch consists of: (1) setting the weights in STM (via back-error propagation) for a

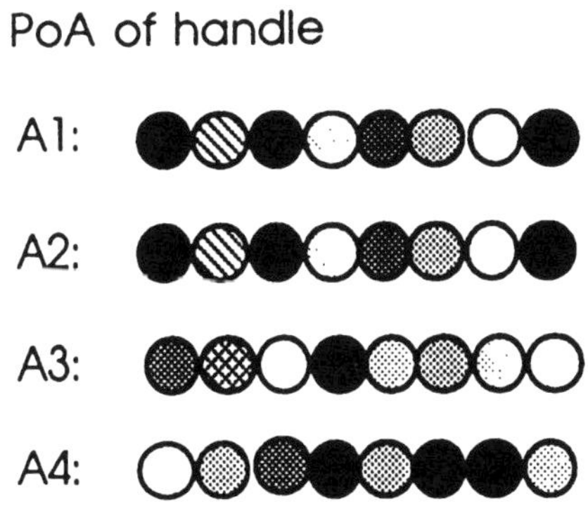

PoA of handle

FIG. 2.8. Handlers of the nodes (from Fig. 2.4) after convergence.

TABLE 2.1
Sample DUAL Experiment on Semantic Network
SNET; C.P.U. Time Calculated on a Hewlett-Packard
Workstation (Model HP 9000/320, ~ 1.7 M.I.P.s).

Epochs	Avg. Error	C.P.U. Time (Sec.)
0	84.2%	1.2
2	28.5%	943
4	21.3%	1886
6	13.7%	2830
8	12.6%	3773
10	11.6%	4717

given node; (2) iterating over all nodes in SNET; and (3) storing/compressing all S_i in LTM. The representations of the handles $\{\ldots H_i \ldots\}$, and thus also the weight matrices $\{\ldots S_i \ldots\}$, will get updated from one epoch to the next.

The retrieval error was calculated at the end of each epoch by collecting the VALUEs from the DUAL network for all the (PREDICATE REL VALUE) triples in SNET and comparing them with the current handle representation for that VALUE in DSM. For example, to calculate the accuracy of retrieving the triple (A → r → C) during symbol recirculation, we first load the STM with the current weight matrix of A (i.e. S_A). Then we input pattern r to STM and collect the output as C'. We then compute the difference between C' and the current handle of C (i.e. H[C] in DSM) and divide by H(C). This is the measure of error. We do this operation for all triples and calculate the average to get the average error over all triples for that epoch.

The average error roughly indicates the degree of convergence. The lower the error, the more consistency exists in the representation set in DSM and thus the closer to convergence is the set of handles (distributed representations of nodes in SNET). In Table 2.1, the error drops as the set of handles converges.

Nature of Discovered Representations

In a von Neumann architecture, a unique address can be assigned initially to each node, whereupon the pointer fields for each link can be trivially specified. In DUAL, however, the representations for each node A_i are constantly changing as the representations of the nodes in each link-node pair (associated with A_i) undergo changes. This process occurs because each link must supply a handle for retrieving an entire weight matrix. In DUAL, *each handle reconstructs its own, virtual distributed connectionist network*, encoded within another, larger network.

DUAL is able to encode the structural relations of a semantic network while at the same time dynamically forming distributed representations for each node, from an initially random set of patterns; as a result, microfeature-based representations are not needed. DUAL solves the microfeature representation problems of flatness, inapplicability, and tokens vs. types by using patterns of activation to represent links that function as normal property names in AI systems. In a semantic network, the node pointed to by a link is interpreted as the value of that property. Only relevant properties (and their values) are associated with a given node. Although only a small number of the relevant properties need be used per node, the potential number of different properties representable in a pattern of activation (PoA) can be very large. By using PoAs also to represent nodes, we solve the type-token problem, since a given PoA can represent a unique person, event, plan instance, object, etc. We also solve the problems of constituent and recursive structures since a semantic network with labelled links can represent such structures directly.

Experiments show that *DUAL discovers distributed representations of the semantic nodes* input to the system and that these representations are formed to facilitate the demanded retrieval tasks. Furthermore, DUAL automatically forms representations that reflect the similarity of nodes, with respect to the similarity of their structural relationships.

Similar semantic nodes are those with similar link-node associations. Before convergence, similar nodes may be represented by very different handles, although they are computing similar link-node associations. *After convergence, however, similar nodes contain similar representations.* For example, nodes A_1 and A_2 in SNN are similar nodes (Fig. 2.2). Their initial handles are distinct (Fig. 2.4b). After convergence, their representations are identical (Fig. 2.8). In general, representations become similar to the extent that they share similar link-node pairs.

In addition, similar distributed representations among similar semantic nodes results in some statistical generalisation to novel cases. That is, if A_i and A_j are nearly identical, except that A_i has link r_k and A_j does not, then one can perform GET(A_j, r_k) for a node A_j *without* relation r_k, and have a likelihood of retrieving the value of GET(A_i, r_k).

Consider two similar nodes A and B that share all identical relations, except that A has *one more* relation, say, $(A \rightarrow r \rightarrow C)$. How will DUAL behave if we attempt to traverse link r from node B? This experiment was performed, for nodes having from 2 to 8 nodes in common (see Table 2.2). Here, the normal case retrieval error is calculated by the relative difference between H(C) and the output C' we get by actually loading the STM with S_A and setting the input in STM to r. The generalisation error is calculated in the same way for S_B. The actual formula for measuring these two columns of error is similar to the one used for Table 2.1. As demonstrated in Table 2.2, the more two similar nodes have relations in common, the less the retrieval error will be when the network is asked to generalise.

Whether this form of statistical generalisation is a feature or a bug remains to be seen. In the case of instance nodes, generalisation is an advantage, since many

TABLE 2.2
Generalisation Experiment

No. of Relations in Common for A and B	Normal Case: Error in Traversing r from A	Generalisation: Error in Traversing r from B
2	0.20%	13.5%
4	0.87%	5.50%
6	0.99%	4.85%
8	0.68	3.37%

similar instances (e.g. of eating the same food regularly at the same restaurant—normally represented as distinct symbols INGEST1, INGEST2. . . in symbolic systems) will be merged into a single prototype.

OTHER SYMBOL RECIRCULATION METHODS

Symbol recirculation is a relatively recent technique and thus the relative advantages and disadvantages of various recirculation methods are not yet well understood. The earliest symbol recirculation method that we are aware of was first described by Miikkulainen and Dyer (1987). The method, subsequently called FGREP (Miikkulainen & Dyer, 1988; 1989a), involves maintaining a global symbol memory, where each symbol is represented as a set of weights and where backpropagation is extended into this global memory. FGREP was first used to learn distributed representations of lexical items, where a three-layer feed-forward PDP network is used to map a syntactic representation to a semantic representation. To learn the mapping task, back-error propagation is used, with the additional step of extending the back-error propagation weight update rule through the weights that connect a subset of the symbols (in the global symbol memory) to the input layer. For example, suppose the current

TABLE 2.3
Sample Syntax-semantic Mapping Task

I/O Pair 1					
Input banks	subject	verb	object	prep-phrase	
Symbols	JOHN	EATS	CHICKEN	WITH FORK	
Output	action	actor	instrument	object	obj-modifier
Symbols	EATS	JOHN	FORK	CHICKEN	XX
I/O Pair 2					
Input banks	subject	verb	object	prep-phrase	
Symbols	JOHN	EATS	HAM	WITH CHEESE	
Output	action	actor	instrument	object	obj-modifier
Symbols	EATS	JOHN	XX	HAM	CHEESE

mapping task contains the two I/O pairs shown in Table 2.3, where different syntactic roles must be mapped to different semantic case roles, depending upon the semantics of the words that are bound to the different syntactic roles.

For I/O PAIR 1, backpropagation via FGREP results in modifying the weights that connect the symbols in the input layer to the corresponding symbols in the global symbol memory. When the PDP network is called upon to learn I/O PAIR 2, the representations of JOHN, EATS, HAM, and CHEESE are taken from the global symbol memory and their weights (from the global symbol memory to the input layer) are modified. As a result, each subsequent time the same I/O pair is presented to the mapping network, the representations of the symbols will be different. Over time, these representations will converge for a given training corpus. After training, the network shows better generalisation to novel cases than with handcoded microfeature representations. In addition, the symbol memory forms representations in which symbols with similar uses (e.g. eating utensils, such as KNIFE, FORK, SPOON versus foods, such as HAM, CHICKEN) form similar representations. Ambiguous words share representations across semantic categories (e.g. CHICKEN is animate in "FOX EATS CHICKEN", while CHICKEN is a prepared food in "JOHN EATS CHICKEN WITH FORK"). The FGREP method of symbol recirculation has since been generalised to recurrent PDP networks and FGREP modules have been formed into an architecture to acquire scripts dynamically and generate paraphrases of script-based stories (Miikkulainen & Dyer, 1989b).

The method of extending backpropagation over PDP networks with more than three layers had been used prior to the work of Miikulainen and Dyer. For example, Hinton (1986) used additional layers to form representations of family trees. However, Hinton did not save these representations in a global memory and then reuse and remodify them. Thus, the representations formed were not global (i.e. the input and output layers formed different representations) and also symbol recirculation did not occur.

Recently, Pollack (1988) has shown that a three-layer PDP network can learn stack and tree structures. In his method, called "recursive auto-association memory (RAAM)," a three-layer PDP network is given an auto-associative mapping task, in which the input/output layers have encoded in them the same pair of symbols. Once a symbol pair has been learned, say [A B], the pattern of activation on the hidden layer (call it C) is then used to represent the pair [A B]. To build up a tree structure, the network is now trained to auto-associate the pair [C D], where the pattern over its hidden layer now represents E = [C D]. Consequently, we have encoded the structure illustrated in Fig. 2.9.

More recently, we have extended Pollack's RAAM technique. In our model (Lee, Flowers, & Dyer, 1989), a number of RAAMs are augmented with a global lexicon. The distributed representation of a symbol, e.g. MILK, is gradually built up by training a recursive auto-associative network to learn a set of propositions concerning MILK, such as:

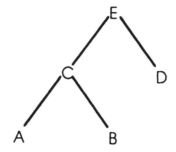

FIG. 2.9.   Tree encoded via recursive auto-association.

(COWS PRODUCE MILK)
(CHILDREN DRINK MILK)
(MILK HAS-COLOUR WHITE)
. . .

As each triple is learned, the pattern of activation over the hidden layer is fed back into the position (a bank in the input layer) in the next triple in which MILK occurs. Once a stable pattern of activation for MILK has been formed, it is used in forming the distributed representation for all other symbols involving MILK, e.g. COWS, CHILDREN, WHITE, etc. This recirculation causes the representation for COWS to be modified, resulting in the need to recirculate MILK. After convergence has occurred for all symbols, each has encoded, within its pattern of activation, the structural information associated with it.

The related technique to the one presented in DUAL is that described in Pollack (1988). Here, Pollack uses what he calls "cascaded" networks. Essentially, he links the output layer of one network to the conection weights of another network, thus forming higher-order connections. Pollack also shows how cascaded networks can receive feedback and thus form sequential cascaded networks. The resulting networks can learn finite state languages. Although many of the details are different, DUAL also uses this general technique of having one network manipulate the connection weights of another network.

OPEN PROBLEMS

There are many open problems, both in symbol recirculation and in representing semantic information in distributed connectionist networks. Two such problems are described here.

Convergence

The issue of convergence is central in DUAL networks. The nice features of symbol representations in DUAL will not be maintained if the symbol representation set in DSM does not converge. Unfortunately, there is no theoretic proof at this point for convergence in DUAL (or in other recirculation methods). Currently, there are three potential problems that can arise in DUAL:

1. Oscillation—The representation set for the handles oscillates and thus does not settle down to one consistent pattern.

2. Degenerate cases—This problem occurs when all representations converge to identical patterns, e.g. 1101111. (*Note.* This degenerate representation set *also* satisfies our constraints.) Degeneration can occur when the initial handle set already carries some similarity in it and may be caused and/or aggravated by the way in which we normalise a weight matrix S_i when encoding it in the input layer of LTM.

3. Time problems—For a small DUAL network (i.e. 8-bit long representations, 10 semantic nodes, 5 relationships per node on average, and running 50 epochs) symbol recirculation usually takes around 8 hours CPU-time on an HP 9000/320 workstation.

When (1) and (2) occasionally arise, we have to start with a new set of initial handles to get around the oscillation or degenerate case. Since DUAL makes use of back-error propagation during symbol recirculation, any problems in back-error propagation (e.g. local minima) will affect DUAL's performance.

For (3), we are currently working on a project to speed up the convergence procedure (when convergence occurs).

One might ask why the handles *do* converge in any case. Recall that the operation of auto-associating and compressing all S_i in LTM causes the hidden units to find an efficient encoding (Rumelhart & McClelland, 1986c) of the shared structure in each weight matrix S_i. Although each weight matrix that performs a similar function may appear very different, what they share in common are the structural relations they encode at the semantic network level. It is this shared structure that is apparently being encoded in the hidden units of LTM. This shared structure then directs subsequent learning as the node representations are recirculated.

Rules with Variables vs. Statistical Associations

The preceding sections have discussed at length the dynamic formation of symbol representations. One very special type of symbol is one that plays the role of a *variable*. In order to implement rules, one needs both structure and variables. One major problem facing connectionist researchers is resolving the nature of statistical versus logical (rule-based) inferences. High-level cognitive tasks, such as NLP, require both the ability to make logical (rule-based) and statistically based inferences. Rumelhart and McClelland have pointed out the usefulness of statistically based inferences. For example, they suppose a PDP system has encountered many cases of babies interacting with objects in the world and then receives input "the baby kicked the ball." The network will automatically infer that the ball is large, light, and soft. It would be painful to have to anticipate and build in such inferences by hand, as rules of the sort:

if a baby kicks a ball
then the ball will be soft

Instead, we want such inferences to arise from the fact that most of the objects parents will allow a baby to encounter tend to be light, soft, and harmless. A nice feature of distributed connectionist systems is the ability to apply such experiences to a novel case, in the form of a statistically based associative generalisation or conclusion.

On the other hand, actual rule-based inferences are also required. For example, we know the rule:

if x tells y message z
then y knows z

Though such a rule may have arisen from experiences with telling, the application of the rule is not biased by previous experiences. Furthermore, this rule will work for an infinite number of cases.

Standard PDP models are not capable of implementing a simple rule. Why is this the case? For example, consider the following rule, with 3 variables, that is represented as a relationship between two knowledge structures (schemas):

(TELL ACTOR X $\longrightarrow$ (KNOWS ACTOR Y
    TO Y   OBJECT Z)
    OBJECT Z)

Imagine that a 3-layer PDP network is trained to associate instances of TELL frames (on the input layer) with KNOWS instances on the output layer. Here is a sample training set:

input layer	*output layer*
John told Mary that Bill is sick.	Mary knows that Bill is sick.
John told Fred that Bill is well.	Fred knows that Bill is well.
John told Betty that Bill is sick.	Betty knows that Bill is sick.
Frank told George that Fred is well.	George knows that Fred is well.
. . .	. . .

Upon learning such a training set, the network might be able to complete known patterns and, depending on the input representations, the network might even be able to generalise to some new cases. For instance, in the sample set above, males tell females that males are sick, but they tell males that males are well. So perhaps it will be able to generalise (even with some noise and/or incomplete patterns). For example:

input layer	*output layer*
John told Gxxrge that Bill is xx.	George knows that Bill is well.

However, there are many problems with this implementation of a rule as a statistically based association. Two problems are:

1. Inability to handle novel symbols—For instance, if we place a novel symbol (say "Glotz") in the TO slot of the TELL frame, then "Glotz" will fail to get propagated properly into the ACTOR slot of the KNOWS frame. Why is this the case? The network has never seen "Glotz" before; therefore, "Glotz" will be treated as a "noisy" version of a known pattern that is close to it in the input space. As a result, either mush (i.e. an intermediate pattern) will come out in the KNOWS:ACTOR slot, or, if the network is set up to complete mush to known patterns, then a known symbol (e.g. "Fred") will appear. In either case, the "Glotz" binding has failed to be propagated.

2. Inability to handle novel structures—This problem is just an extension of the "novel symbol" problem. That is, no matter how many instances of the rule we train the network on, it will not handle completely novel instances. Remember, in a real rule, variables can be bound to any recursive structure. For example, given the novel input:

John told Frank that, although he had worked for months trying to lose weight, he was heavier than ever.

we want the system to conclude:

Frank knows that, although John has worked for months trying to lose weight, John is heavier than ever.

The PDP network that was trained on the cases where the message was "Male/female is well/sick" will be unable to generalise to messages about dieting. Since PDP implementations of rules are statistical in nature, they do not really create or propagate bindings. Without rules and virtual (unlimited) memory, there is no infinite generative capacity. Other problems with association-based models are discussed in Dyer (1991) and Touretzky (1989).

VARIABLE BINDING RESEARCH AND SYMBOL FORMATION

Although the problem of variable bindings has not yet been adequately solved for distributed connectionist systems, there are a number of researchers working on it. Touretzky and Hinton (1988), for example, have addressed the problem of encoding semantic relations and implementing variables and bindings in a PDP architecture that operates as a production interpreter. In their case, instead of using a DUAL network approach, they encode the link r_j from A_i to A_j as a triple $(A_i\ r_j\ A_j)$ in the input layer. As a result, the entire semantic network can be encoded in a single PDP network.[1] However, since there is no global symbol memory or recirculation method, the representations for their symbols remain static throughout processing.

Dolan (1989) has constructed a PDP natural language processing architecture, based on tensors, which are a generalisation of conjunctive coding techniques (Dolan & Dyer, 1987; 1989). The use of tensors (Smolensky, in press) and tensor manipulation networks (Dolan & Smolensky, 1989) allows Dolan's system, CRAM, to bind and unbind symbols dynamically, through tensor outer products and dot products. The representations for each symbol, however, are static and prespecified as a set of microfeatures.

Sumida and Dyer (1989) have developed what they call "parallel distributed semantic" networks. Each semantic node consists of a layer of PDP units and specific instances of symbols can reside as a pattern of activation over a given PDP layer (semantic node). Although novel patterns are learned that represent instances of new episodes, the basic level symbols (e.g. from the lexicon) currently contain static representations.

Lange and Dyer (1989a; 1989b) have developed a method for using one type of activation (called "signature activation") to represent a binding. Basically, each symbol (e.g. JOHN) produces a constant activation value (e.g. JOHN = 4.3). To represent that the ACTOR of TELL is bound to JOHN, the activation value of 4.3 is propagated to that ACTOR node and causes that node also to produce a constant activation value of 4.3. Currently, the signatures are assigned initial values at random that remain the same throughout processing. A future research project is to form signature values dynamically through learning.

It is important to point out that the technique of symbol recirculation appears to be compatible with the symbol processing systems developed by researchers such as Dolan, Dyer , Hinton, Lange, Lee, Sumida, and Touretzky. That is, symbol recirculation could be used to form distributed symbol representations dynamically and then these symbols could be manipulated via PDP production

---

[1] Touretzky and Hinton also have various short-term (or working) memories in their system, but these modules are used for other purposes, e.g. to represent bindings or trigger production rules.

interpreters and other distributed connectionist symbol processing architectures. This is an area of future research.

SUMMARY AND CONCLUSIONS

Using the insight that WMx = PoA (i.e. that weight matrices and patterns of activation are two sides of the same coin), we have designed and implemented DUAL, a PDP memory management architecture, to encode and manipulate a symbolically specified semantic network as a virtual, distributed, directed graph in a PDP architecture. DUAL consists mainly of two PDP networks. The STM network functions as a working memory to hold temporarily all of a given node's associations, while the LTM network functions as a long-term memory for the entire semantic network. The process of encoding causes DUAL to find distributed representations for all nodes in the semantic network. As a result, nodes with similar associational links are merged and generalised. The DUAL architecture allows us to manipulate the virtual semantic network at a symbolic level, while at the same time retaining many of the robust features (of adaptive learning, generalisation to novel cases, graceful error degradation, etc.) associated with distributed connectionist networks.

The method of automatic distributed symbol discovery in DUAL is an instance of a more general method, dubbed *symbol recirculation*, in which symbols start out with random patterns of activation and, through the attempt of the system to form structural relations via associative mapping, new representations are formed. The resulting symbol representations are then actively involved in the operations that are demanded of them. Distributed representations of similar semantic nodes converge to similar representations, resulting in features exhibited by distributed connectionist networks, such as similarity-based generalisations to novel cases.

ACKNOWLEDGEMENTS

This work was supported in part by a contract with the J.T.F. program of the D.o.D., monitored by J.P.L., and by a grant from the I.T.A. Foundation. Simulations were carried out on equipment donated by Hewlett Packard.

REFERENCES

Allen, R.B. (1986). Several studies in natural language and backpropagation. *Proceedings of IEEE First International Conference on Neural Networks*, II-335–II-341.

Alvarado, S., Dyer, M.G., & Flowers, M. (1986). Editorial comprehension in OpEd through argument units. *Proceedings of American Association of Artificial Intelligence (AAAI-86)*, Philadelphia, Penn., 250–256.

Alvarado, S.J., Dyer, M.G., & Flowers, M. (1990). Natural language processing: Computer comprehension of editorial text. In H. Adeli (Ed.), *Knowledge engineering* (Vol. 1), 286–344. New York: McGraw-Hill.

Churchland, P.S. & Sejnowski, T.J. (1989). Neural representation and neural computation. In L. Nadel, L.A. Cooper, P. Culiver, & R.M. Harnish (Eds.), *Neural connections, mental computation*. Cambridge, Mass.: Bradford Books/MIT Press.

Dolan, C.P. (1989). *Tensor manipulation networks: Connectionist and symbolic approaches to comprehension, learning, and planning*. UCLA Ph.D. Dissertation.

Dolan, C. & Dyer, M.G. (1987). Symbolic schemata, role binding, and the evolution of structure in connectionist memories. *Proceedings of the IEEE First Annual International Conference on Neural Networks*. San Diego, California, June.

Dolan, C.P. & Dyer, M.G. (1989). Parallel retrieval and application of conceptual knowledge. In D.S. Touretzky, G. Hinton, & T. Sejnowsky (Eds.), *Proceedings of the 1988 Connectionist Models Summer School*. San Mateo, Calif.: Morgan Kaufmann, 273–280.

Dolan, C.P. & Smolensky, P. (1989). Tensor product production system: A modular architecture and representation. *Connection Science, 1* (1), 53–68.

Dreyfus, H.L. & Dreyfus, S.E. (1988). Making a mind versus modeling the brain: Artificial intelligence at a branchpoint. In S.R. Graubard (Ed.), *The artificial intelligence debate: False starts, real foundations*. Cambridge, Mass.: M.I.T. Press. 15–43.

Dyer, M.G. (1983). *In-depth understanding*. Cambridge, Mass.: MIT Press.

Dyer, M.G. (1989). Knowledge interactions and integrated parsing for narrative comprehension. In D. Waltz (Ed.), *Advances in natural language processing*. Hillsdale, N.J.: Lawrence Erlbaum Associates Inc., 1–56.

Dyer, M.G. (1991). Symbolic neuroengineering for natural language processing: A multilevel research approach. In J. Barnden & J. Pollack (Eds.), *Advances in connectionist and neural computation*. Norwood, N.J.: Ablex Publishers, 32–86.

Dyer, M.G., Cullingford, R. & Alvarado, S. (1987). SCRIPTS. In S.C. Shapiro (Ed.), *Encyclopedia of artificial intelligence*. New York, N.Y.: John Wiley & Sons, 980–994.

Dyer, M.G., Flowers, M., & Wang, Y.A. (1988). *Weight-matrix = Pattern of activation: Encoding semantic networks as distributed representations in DUAL, a PDP architecture*. Technical Report UCLA-AI-88-5. Los Angeles: CS Dept., U.C.L.A.

Feldman, J.A. (1989). Neural representation of conceptual knowledge. In L. Nadel, L.A. Cooper, P. Culiver & R.M. Harnish (Eds.), *Neural connections, mental computation*. Cambridge, Mass.: Bradford Books/M.I.T. Press.

Fodor, J.A. & Pylyshyn, Z.W. (1988). Connectionism and cognitive architecture: A critical analysis. In S. Pinker & I. Mehler (Eds.), *Connections and symbols*. Cambridge, Mass.: Bradford Books/M.I.T. Press, 3–71.

Gasser, M. (1988). *A connectionist model of sentence generation in a first and second language*. UCLA Ph.D. and Technical Report UCLA-AI-88-13, July.

Gasser, M. & Dyer, M.G. (1988). Sequencing in a connectionist model of language processing. *Proceedings of Twelfth Internal Conference on Computational Linguistics (COLING-88)*. Budapest, Hungary, 185–190.

Goldman, S., Dyer, M.G., & Flowers, M. (1988). Representing contractual situations. In C. Walter (Ed.), *Computer power and legal language*. N.Y.: Quorum Books, 99–118.

Hendler, J.A. (1987). *Integrated marker-passing and problem solving: A spreading activation approach to improved choice in planning*. Hillsdale, N.J.: Lawrence Erlbaum Associates Inc.

Hendler, J. (1989). Spreading activation over distributed microfeatures. In D.S. Touretzky (Ed.), *Advances in neural information processing systems 1*. San Mateo, Calif.: Morgan Kaufmann, 553–559.

Hinton, G.E. (1986). Learning distributed representations of concepts, *Proceedings of the Eighth Annual Conference of the Cognitive Science Society*. Hillsdale, N.J.: Lawrence Erlbaum Associates Inc.

Lange, T.E. & Dyer, M.G. (1989a). Dynamic, non-local role bindings and inferencing in a localist network for natural language understanding. In D.S. Touretzky (Ed.), *Advances in neural information processing systems 1*. San Mateo, Calif.: Morgan Kaufmann, 545–552.

Lange, T.E. & Dyer, M.G. (1989b). High-level inferencing in a connectionist network. *Connection Science, 1* (2), 181–217.

Lee, G., Flowers, M., & Dyer, M.G. (1989). A symbolic/connectionist script applier mechanism. *Proceedings of the Eleventh Annual Conference of the Cognitive Science Society (CogSci-89)*. Hillsdale, N.J.: Lawrence Erlbaum Associates Inc., 714–721.

McClelland, J.L. & Kawamoto, A.H. (1986). Mechanisms of sentence processing: Assigning roles to constituents of sentences. In J.L. McClelland & D.E. Rumelhart (Eds.), *Parallel distributed processing, Vol. 2*. Cambridge, Mass.: Bradford Books/M.I.T. Press.

Miikkulainen, R. & Dyer, M.G. (1987). *Building distributed representations without microfeatures*. Technical Report UCLA-AI-87-17. Los Angeles: Computer Science Dept., U.C.L.A., August.

Miikkulainen, R. & Dyer, M.G. (1988). Forming global representations with extended backprop-agation. *Proceedings of the IEEE Second Annual International Conference on Neural Networks (ICNN-88)*, San Diego, Calif., July, I-285–I-292.

Miikkulainen, R. & Dyer, M.G. (1989a). Encoding input/output representations in connectionist cognitive systems. In D.S. Touretzky, G. Hinton, & T. Sejnowski (Eds.), *Proceedings of the 1988 Connectionist Models Summer School*. San Mateo, Calif.: Morgan Kaufmann, 347–356.

Miikkulainen, R. & Dyer, M.G. (1989b). A modular neural network architecture for sequential paraphrasing of script-based stories. *Proceedings of the International Joint Conference on Neural Networks (IJCNN-89)*, Washington D.C., June, II-49–II-56.

Pinker, S. & Prince, A. (1988). On language and connectionism: Analysis of a parallel distributed processing model of language acquisition. In S. Pinker & J. Mehler (Eds.), *Connections and symbols*. Cambridge, Mass.: Bradford Books/M.I.T. Press, 73–193. (Special issue of *Cognition: An International Journal of Cognitive Science, 28*.)

Pollack, J. (1988). Recursive auto-associative memory: Devising compositional distributed representations. *Proceedings of the Tenth Annual Conference of the Cognitive Science Society*. Hillsdale, N.J.: Lawrence Erlbaum Associates Inc., 33–39.

Pollack, Jordan B. (1987). Cascaded back-propagation on dynamic connectionist networks. *Proceedings of Ninth Annual Conference of the Cognitive Science Society*, Hillsdale, N.J.: Lawrence Erlbaum Associates Inc., 391–404.

Quilici, A., Dyer, M.G., & Flowers, M. (1988). Recognizing and responding to plan-oriented misconceptions. *Computational Linguistics, 14* (3), 38–51.

Reeke Jr., G.N. & Edelman, G.M. (1988). Real brains and artificial intelligence. In S.R. Graubard (Ed.), *The artificial intelligence debate: False starts, real foundations*. Cambridge, Mass.: M.I.T. Press, 143–173.

Reeves, J.F. (1988). Ethical understanding: Recognizing and using belief conflict in narrative processing. *Proceedings of the Seventh National Conference on Artificial Intelligence (AAAI-88)*, San Mateo, Calif.: Morgan Kaufmann, 227–232.

Rumelhart, D.E. & McClelland, J.L. (1986a). Learning internal representations by error propaga-tion. In D.E. Rumelhart & J.L. McClelland, *Parallel distributed processing, Vol. 1*. Cambridge, Mass.: M.I.T. Press/Bradford Books, 318–362.

Rumelhart, D.E. & McClelland, J.L. (1986b). On learning the past tense of English verbs. In D.E. Rumelhart & J.L. McClelland, *Parallel distributed processing, Vol. 2*. Cambridge, Mass.: M.I.T. Press/Bradford Books, 216–271.

Rumelhart, D.E. & McClelland, J.L. (1986c). *Parallel distributed processing, Vols. 1 & 2*. Cambridge, Mass.: M.I.T. Press/Bradford Books.

Sejnowski, T.J. & Rosenberg, C.R. (1987). Parallel networks that learn to pronounce English text. *Complex Systems, 1*, 145–168.

Shastri, L. (1988). A connectionist approach to knowledge representation and limited inference. *Cognitive Science, 12*, 331–392.

Smolensky, P. (1988a). On the proper treatment of connectionism. *The Behavioral and Brain Sciences, 11* (1), 1–23.

Smolensky, P. (1988b). The constituent structure of connectionist mental states: A reply to Fodor and Pylyshyn. In T. Horgan & J. Tienson (Eds.), *Connectionism and the philosophy of mind*, Department of Philosophy, Memphis State University, 137–161. (*The Southern Journal of Philosophy*, 1987, Vol. XXVI, Supplement.)

Smolensky, P. (1990). Tensor product variable binding and the representation of symbolic structures in connectionist systems. *Artificial Intelligence 46*, (1–2), 159–216.

Sumida, R.A. & Dyer, M.G. (1989). Storing and generalizing multiple instances while maintaining knowledge-level parallelism. *Proceedings of Eleventh International Joint Conference on Artificial Intelligence (IJCAI-89)*, San Mateo, Calif.: Morgan Kaufmann.

Sutton, R.S. (1984). *Temporal credit assignment in reinforcement learning*. Ph.D. Dissertation, University of Massachusetts.

Touretzky, D.S. (1989). Connectionism and PP attachment. In D.S. Touretzky, G. Hinton & T. Sejnowski (Eds.), *Proceedings of the 1988 Connectionist Models Summer School*. San Mateo, Calif.: Morgan Kaufmann, 325–332.

Touretzky, D.S. & Hinton, G.E. (1988). A distributed connectionist production system. *Cognitive Science, 12* (3), 423–466.

3 Representing Meaning Using Microfeatures

Richard F.E. Sutcliffe[1]
Department of Computer Science, University of Exeter, EX4 4PT, U.K.

INTRODUCTION

Any program which is capable of processing natural language must incorporate some scheme for representing meaning. Yet, despite a great deal of intensive research in this area, workers within artificial intelligence (AI) have failed to come up with any general method for capturing the underlying content of even simple passages of English.

Two important aspects of linguistic meaning are as follows. Firstly, the meaning of a sentence has an underlying semantic structure (called a *proposition* in this work), which enables the constituent parts of the sentence to be kept separate. One conventional approach to the representation of this kind of structure is to use a case-based system involving slots for action, agent, instrument, patient, and so on. Although this idea originated in linguistics (Fillmore, 1968), perhaps the most successful implementation of it in an AI system is Schank's conceptual dependency (CD) (Schank, 1972). Schank postulated that all meanings could be captured using only a very few semantic primitives. The meaning of an arbitrarily complex sentence could be captured using only a very few semantic primitives. The meaning of an arbitrarily complex sentence could then be expressed by building up a structure based on these primitives.

---

[1]The author is now at the Department of Computer Science and Information Systems, University of Limerick, Ireland.

However, a second aspect of language is that it is possible to describe and refer to amorphous concepts which possess an infinity of subtle nuances, implications, and colours. One approach which attempts to address this is the idea of a semantic feature (Chomsky, 1965; Katz & Fodor, 1963; Rosch, 1973; 1977; Schaeffer & Wallace, 1969; Smith, Shoben, & Rips, 1974).

Both these approaches suffer from the shortcoming that neither can capture the power of the other. A case frame approach to meaning, based as it is on list structures, cannot readily be adapted to capture subtle differences in meaning. A representation based only on features cannot express the structured aspects of language.

I recently implemented a prototype AI system based on a mixture of conventional and connectionist principles (Sutcliffe, 1988). The system, called PARROT (PARallel Recall Of Text), could extract the gist from "stories" (really only sequences of actions) that were presented to it. The thinking behind the system was strongly influenced by Schank's concept of a script, together with the work of other schema theorists (Schank & Abelson, 1977; Rumelhart, 1975; Arbib, 1975; etc.)[2]. However, the implementation was completely different. One of the successes of the project was that it showed quite persuasively how distributed representations can capture at least the amorphous aspects of word meaning. It is this aspect of the system which I will report on here. The PARROT project also attempted to address the issue of representing compositional language structures. The details may be found in Sutcliffe (1988).

In PARROT, word meanings were represented using semantically interpretable microfeatures[3], which were structured and processed in a specific way. In the first section, I will introduce the notion of a microfeature and develop the essential ideas that formed the basis of PARROT's meaning representation. The second section goes on to describe how the microfeature sets were constructed and how the representation for each word in the lexicon was encoded. The section concludes with a discussion of the important characteristics that the chosen representational scheme embodies. The final section discusses further issues relating to the lexicon, as well as discussing future steps in the research.

---

[2]I am grateful to Noel Sharkey, who made a large contribution to the knowledge access parts of the system; these were derived from his BACAS (Sharkey, Sutcliffe, & Wobcke, 1986) and SKAM (Sharkey & Sutcliffe, 1987) systems. These aspects are not, however, discussed here—see Sutcliffe (1988) for the details.

[3]One of the earliest uses of the term *microfeature* is in Hinton (1981, p. 172, para. 3). Although Hinton's microfeatures were not strictly speaking semantically interpretable in the sense described here, the idea of such microfeatures is clearly hinted at in the text.

MICROFEATURE REPRESENTATIONS IN PARROT

What is a Microfeature?

Let me introduce the concept of a microfeature by means of an extended example. Consider the meaning of the word "book." A book is a smallish object made of sheets of paper on which text about something is written. We see books the whole time, in bookshops, offices, and people's homes. Books primarily serve the function of providing information although they may be aesthetically pleasing as well.

All of this description conceals an important underlying idea: The concept of "book" can be defined by relating it explicitly to other concepts or properties which people know about. We can see this more clearly if we arrange the information just conveyed in the form of a table:

Book

size	smallish
constructional material	paper
frequency of occurrence	high
place of occurrence	bookshops, offices, homes
purpose	functional, involving information
	may also be aesthetically pleasing

Now consider the meaning of "food." Food is something generally found in smallish amounts which is made of edible organic material. It is very common, being found in foodshops, kitchens, etc. The main purpose of food is that we can eat it. It may be aesthetically pleasing as well.

Transforming the definition of food into another table yields the following:

Food

size	generally smallish
constructional material	organic
frequency of occurrence	high
place of occurrence	foodshops, kitchens
purpose	functional, being edible
	also aesthetically pleasing

This procedure suggests that disparate concepts like book and food can be expressed in a similar way by saying what properties (like *made of paper* or *aesthetically pleasing*) apply to each. We can now go one stage further by simply expressing the meaning of each word as a list of predicates:

Book	Food
small_size	small_size
made_of_paper	made_of_organic_material
is_common	is_common
found_in_bookshops	found_in_foodshops
found_in_offices	found_in_kitchens
found_in_homes	found_in_homes
is_functional	is_functional
involves_information	is_edible
is_aesthetically_pleasing	is_aesthetically_pleasing

We have now introduced the main idea of microfeature representations: The meaning of a concept is expressed as a list of predicates called *microfeatures* which apply to that concept. A microfeature representation has two important properties:

1. The same set of microfeatures can be used to encode many different concepts by choosing a different subset of those microfeatures to represent each concept. We can thus increase the number of concepts which are currently represented without necessarily increasing the number of microfeatures.

2. Two concepts can be compared by examining their corresponding microfeature sets. In particular, it is possible to assess how *similar* two concepts are by seeing which microfeatures they have in common, and how *different* they are by determining which microfeatures the concepts do *not* have in common.

Let us consider these two points in the light of our examples. Firstly, we have represented 2 concepts so far using a set of 13 microfeatures. The claim of the first point is that we can represent other words using the same set. Here are some examples:

Light Bulb	Cooker	Compact Disc
small_size	is_common	small_size
is_common	found_in_kitchens	is_common
found_in_bookshops	found_in_homes	found_in_homes
found_in_offices	is_functional	is_functional
found_in_homes		involves_information
found_in_foodshops		is_aesthetically_pleasing
found_in_kitchens		
found_in_homes		
is_functional		

We can continue this process for a long time, although the microfeature set in question will obviously be more suitable for representing some concepts than others. This is because its coverage of the different kinds of property that can be true of concepts is very limited and uneven. We will discuss this in greater detail later.

Turning to the second point, that the meanings of concepts can be compared by examining the differences and similarities between the microfeature sets encoding these concepts, we can immediately undertake this kind of exercise. For example, how similar is "book" to "food." They have in common their size (*small_size*), frequency of occurrence (*is_common*), practicality (*is_functional*), and potential to satisfy (*is_aesthetically_pleasing*).

Examples of ways in which they differ are that a book is made of paper and involves information (*made_of_paper*, *involves_information*), whereas food is organic and edible (*made_of_organic_material*, *is_edible*). The ability to make comparisons of this kind between concepts, however different, may not seem that important in itself. However, it turns out to be extremely useful, because simple algorithms can be employed for the automatic comparison or matching of concepts. We will return to this topic later.

Weighting Individual Microfeatures

In a previous section we saw how it is possible to represent the meaning of concepts using a set of microfeatures. An obvious problem with the scheme presented so far is as follows: some microfeatures seem to apply more strongly to a given concept than other microfeatures. For example, the crucial thing about a book is that it involves *information*. By comparison, the size of a book is less important.

The approach adopted in this work is thus to associate an integer *centrality* with every microfeature in an encoding. A possible association of centralities to the microfeatures defining "book" might be:

Book

small_size	5
made_of_paper	5
is_common	5
found_in_bookshops	10
found_in_offices	5
found_in_homes	5
is_functional	10
involves_information	15
is_aesthetically_pleasing	5

In this encoding we have chosen to emphasise *involves_information*, *is_functional*, and *found_in_bookshops* to a greater extent than the other microfeatures. The idea behind this process is to reflect the relative importance of the first three microfeatures. The major feature of a book is that it involves information. After this, the important features are that it is functional and found in bookshops. Finally, a book has some less important features relating to its size, etc.

The use of centralities gives a considerable degree of subtlety to the microfeature approach. In this work we call a microfeature encoding with centralities for each microfeature a *microfeature profile*.

Now consider how the profile for the word "book" relates to its definition shown here. This profile consists of a vector of integers, with one element for each microfeature. The integer corresponding to the microfeature *small_size* will have value 5, as will those corresponding to *made_of_paper*, *is_common*, *found_in_offices*, *found_in_homes*, and *is_aesthetically_pleasing*. The integers in the profile corresponding to the microfeatures *found_in_bookshops* and *is_functional* will have value 10, while the number corresponding to the microfeature *involves_information* will be 15. All microfeatures which are not shown in a definition are assumed to have zero centrality. Thus all other elements in the profile for "book" will be 0.

We have seen how microfeatures can be emphasised strongly if they are crucial to the meaning of a concept. In addition, it is possible to express the subtle differences in meaning between closely related concepts. For example magazines, newspapers, textbooks, and pamphlets all involve microfeatures like *involves_information, involves_work* and *involves_leisure*, but to different extents. A magazine is likely to be more entertaining than a textbook. Conversely, a textbook is likely to be more closely associated with work than a newspaper. We can reflect these differences in the centralities chosen for the microfeatures *involves_information, involves_entertainment, involves_work*, and *involves_leisure*, when encoding these concepts as microfeature profiles. The resulting representations will bear an overall similarity to one another compared to, say, the profile for "bread." At the same time, however, the profiles for these concepts will exhibit small differences reflecting the more fine-grained shades of meaning which they encapsulate. The ability to represent both small and large differences in meaning among a set of concepts is a major strength of the microfeature approach.

Comparing Microfeature Profiles

So far, we have made references to the comparison of different microfeature profiles without saying what this means. At the beginning of the chapter, direct comparison between two sets of microfeatures (those encoding the concepts "book" and "food") was made by seeing which microfeatures the sets had in common, and conversely, which microfeatures they did not have in common. It was possible to perform such comparisons because there were no centralities associated with the microfeatures. However, for profiles a better similarity profile is required.

There are a number of standard functions used for this purpose within connectionism, and the dot product was chosen from these. For completeness we define this as follows:

$$P1 \cdot P2 = \sum_{k=1}^{k=n} P1_k * P2_k$$

where both P1 and P2 have n elements, $P1_k$ is the kth element of P1, and $P2_k$ is the kth element of P2. For the dot product to work it is necessary to normalise or scale down the profiles so that the dot product of each with itself is equal to a constant (normally one). To see this, consider what can happen if centralities are unrestricted. Here is the "bread" profile defined earlier, but this time including zero centralities, together with example profiles for "magazine" and "cornflakes":

	Book	*Magazine*	*Cornflakes*
small_size	5	4	5
made_of_paper	5	5	0
made_of_organic_matter	0	0	10
is_common	5	5	5
found_in_bookshops	10	5	0
found_in_offices	5	5	0
found_in_foodshops	0	0	10
found_in_kitchens	0	0	10
found_in_homes	5	5	5
is_functional	10	5	100
involves_information	15	15	0
is_aesthetically_pleasing	5	3	25
is_edible	0	0	10

Suppose we wish to see how similar the profiles for "magazine" and "cornflakes" are to the profile for "book." The dot product of "book" with "magazine" (which we shall write book . magazine) is 460. On the other hand, book . cornflakes is 1300. Thus the meaning of "book" is more like the meaning of "cornflakes" than it is like the meaning of "magazines." The reason is simple. Whereas the profiles for "book" and "magazine" have microfeatures in common with similar centralities in each case, the absolute value of these centralities is low. By contrast, "book" and "cornflakes" share only 5 microfeatures. However, *is_functional* has a centrality of 100 in "cornflakes", which causes this microfeature to contribute 1000 to the dot product book . cornflakes. The undesirable result is that book . cornflakes is very high, whereas book . magazine is much lower.

When the 3 profiles have been normalised the result (with centralities rounded to 3 decimal places) is as follows:

	Book	Magazine	Cornflakes
small_size	0.209	0.200	0.048
made_of_paper	0.209	0.250	0
made_of_organic_material	0	0	0.095
is_common	0.209	0.250	0.048
found_in_bookshops	0.417	0.250	0
found_in_offices	0.209	0.250	0
found_in_foodshops	0	0	0.095
found_in_kitchens	0	0	0.095
found_in_homes	0.209	0.250	0.048
is_functional	0.417	0.250	0.949
involves_information	0.626	0.750	0
is_aesthetically_pleasing	0.209	0.150	0.237
is_edible	0	0	0.095

Now book . cornflakes is 0.474. This time, book . magazine is much higher than book . cornflakes. The reason is that although the centrality for is_functional in the profile for "cornflakes" is still much higher than that for other microfeatures in the same profile, all centralities in the profile have had to be reduced to ensure that cornflakes . cornflakes = 1. For example, in the un-normalised profiles, the centrality for is_common had the same value for all 3 words, namely 5. Here, however, the centrality of this microfeature is different for all 3 words. Whereas "book" and "magazine" have the roughly similar values of 0.209 and 0.250 respectively associated with this microfeature, "cornflakes" has the value 0.048, that is about 5 times smaller than either 0.209 or 0.250. Thus although the is_functional microfeature still makes a bigger contribution to the dot product book . cornflakes than any other microfeature, as was the case in the un-normalised examples, normalisation ensures that this contribution is not sufficient to make book . cornflakes higher than book . magazine.

The discussion of normalisation can be summed up as follows. Normalisation ensures that it is the *relative* centralities assigned to different microfeatures within a profile which is important. Without normalisation, the absolute values which happen to have been chosen for centralities will affect the comparison process. Normalisation also ensures that the dot product of two profiles will always lie within a fixed range of values. As a result, two or more dot products can be compared, for example when trying to decide how similar the concepts "book," "magazine," and "cornflakes" are.

In this section we have presented three key ideas which are central to the operation of the PARROT system. Firstly, we can encode the meaning of a concept by assigning centralities to a set of microfeatures, thus producing a microfeature profile. Secondly, if two concepts are encoded as profiles, we can determine how similar in meaning those concepts are by computing the dot product of the two profiles. Thirdly, it is essential that profiles should be normalised before such comparisons are carried out.

The importance of these three ideas is as follows. Microfeature profiles can be used to encode the meanings underlying words, propositions, and knowledge structures. Moreover, networks can be constructed whose update rules compute large numbers of dot products simultaneously, and in so doing compare many meanings in parallel. The principle of normalisation is used extensively when constructing such networks. The next stage is to see how microfeature profiles are constructed, and where the microfeatures which are actually used come from. These topics are addressed in the next section.

IMPLEMENTATION OF THE MICROFEATURE CONCEPT WITHIN PARROT

We have now introduced the concept of a microfeature together with techniques for normalising and comparing representations using them. In this section we will go on to describe how microfeature profiles are used within the PARROT system.

The Lexicon

In PARROT there are three types of concept which can be encoded: *contexts*, *objects*, and *actions*. Each type of concept is encoded using a different set of microfeatures. Contexts are encoded using the *context microfeatures*, objects are encoded using the *object microfeatures*, and actions are encoded using the *action microfeatures*.

An *action* is any action or set of actions we choose to describe. Getting up and walking are both examples of actions. Any type of object or group of objects is encoded as a concept of type *object*. People, animals, household artefacts, and buildings all count as objects. Finally, we use microfeatures of type *context* to represent the spatial and temporal context in which some action occurs. For example, night and winter are contexts.

The system can deal with three kinds of words; *nouns*, *verbs*, and *context words*. A noun is any word which describes an object, for example "person" or "house." A verb is any word which describes an action, e.g. "get_up" or 'walk." Lastly, a context word describes a context in which some action might occur, for example "night" or "winter." Definitions of nouns, verbs, and context words are contained in a lexicon.

The lexicon specifies all words which may be used for input to, and output from, the system. Each entry for a noun defines it as a profile consisting of microfeatures drawn from the set of object microfeatures. Similarly an entry for a verb defines it as a profile consisting of microfeatures drawn from the set of action microfeatures. An entry for a context word defines it as a profile of microfeatures from the set of context microfeatures.

Choosing Microfeatures and Encoding Concepts

In the examples discussed earlier, a set of 13 microfeatures was used to present the idea of profiles as a technique for representing meaning. We now describe how the three microfeature sets were devised and how concepts were encoded using them. Devising a large set of microfeatures is not an easy task. However, it turned out that although generating a long list of microfeatures in the abstract is very difficult, it is usually quite easy to determine what, if anything, is wrong with the representation of a concept when it is encoded using such a set of microfeatures. For this reason, the microfeatures sets were developed in parallel with the construction of the lexicon.

The process of constructing a lexicon was started off by generating a small initial set of microfeatures. This first task was accomplished by assembling a set of *dimensions* (McClelland & Kawamoto, 1986) that seemed suitable for describing concepts of the given type (verb, noun, or context). For example, if an object was to be encoded, some possible dimensions are *size, weight, frequency of occurrence, colour, place of occurrence, time of usage,* and *animacy*.

Along each of these dimensions, a set of microfeatures was then proposed. It was found that various microfeatures came to mind quite naturally once a specific dimension was considered. For example, the *size* dimension suggests microfeatures like *tiny, small, large* and *very large*. Likewise for a *time of usage* dimension we might have *early morning, morning, lunchtime, afternoon, evening,* and *night*. Similar sets were generated for all dimensions. Having constructed a suitable initial set of microfeatures it was then possible to start expressing concepts as profiles over that microfeature set. Note that the dimensions of a profile are purely conceptual devices for suggesting new microfeatures. At present, dimensions themselves take no part in the processing.

In order to represent a concept we must assign centralities to all microfeatures which occur in the appropriate microfeature set for that concept. In practice, it has proved easiest to start with a version of the microfeatures in which the same default centrality, 5 say, is already associated with each microfeature. Microfeatures which definitely do not apply can then be deleted from this set. The main business of altering centralities on the remaining microfeatures can then be turned to.

At present the technique for setting centralities has been simply to go through the elements of the profile assigning high centralities to those which seem especially important to the concept being encoded. For example, when encoding "breakfast," it seems natural to emphasise the time of day during which this event is most likely to occur, namely *obj_time_early_morning*. Similarly, when coding "paper," *obj_white* should receive a high centrality as this is particularly important. In all cases, such judgements are completely subjective, being performed according to the intuitions of the person doing the implementation. See later in the chapter for a discussion of alternative techniques.

The "breakfast" example suggests a further aspect to the encoding process: Different microfeatures within a dimension may all apply to some concept but to different extents. Thus breakfast is most likely to occur in the early morning, but it could also occur in the morning or at lunchtime. This can be reflected directly in the part of the profile that covers the time dimension, as follows:

Breakfast

.
.
.

obj_time_early_morning	15
obj_time_morning	10
obj_time_lunchtime	4
obj_time_afternoon	3
obj_time_evening	1
obj_time_night	1

.
.
.

When the representation of a given concept is complete, it may become apparent that more microfeatures must be added to the microfeature set, either by adding them to an existing dimension or by adding a new dimension consisting of a whole set of new elements. A deficiency in the existing microfeature set may become apparent in two ways:

1. The resulting profile may not have encapsulated the meaning of the concept in question successfully, according to the encoder's intuitions.
2. The profile may be very similar to the profile of another concept which has already been encoded, despite the concepts in question being significantly different, again according to the encoder's intuitions.

For an example of the first problem, consider encoding *skyscraper* using our original set of 13 microfeatures:

Skyscraper

is_common	3
is_functional	10
involves_information	3
is_aesthetically_pleasing	3

Somehow this seems an incomplete description of a skyscraper. What about the size and shape? What are skyscrapers used for? Questions such as these suggest that we need more microfeatures under the *size* dimension and in addition that new dimensions like *shape* and *usage* may be needed.

For an example of the second problem, consider a profile for "rolling_pin" as compared with that for "cooker" (as before, but with centralities added):

Rolling pin		Cooker	
is_common	5	is_common	5
found_in_kitchens	5	found_in_kitchens	5
found_in_homes	10	found_in_homes	10
is_functional	10	is_functional	10

These profiles are identical and so it is necessary to tease the concepts apart by adding more dimensions. Use of a rolling pin involves horizontal movement and rotation which cookers do not involve to the same extent. This suggests having a dimension for type of movement. Likewise, cookers cook things using heat, suggesting a dimension for temperature.

These examples should give a flavour of the kinds of mishaps that can occur, and how they in turn suggest amendments and improvements to the microfeature sets.

The procedure adopted in this work may thus be summarised as follows: Nouns, verbs, and context words were treated separately. Consider nouns as an example. A set of dimensions was first generated by considering the obvious properties which an object denoted by a noun could have. Each noun was encoded by assigning a centrality to each microfeature. When dissimilar words ended up with similar representations, further microfeatures were added to the microfeature set, and the encodings of words already done were checked again. Verbs and context words were encoded similarly, but using disjoint sets of microfeatures. One person performed the entire encoding task.

Properties of the Representation

We will now outline the important properties of the PARROT system which depend on the way in which words are represented in the lexicon. First of all, we will look at how profiles are transformed into words and vice versa.

Each word in the lexicon is encoded as a profile in the manner which we have just described. The PARROT system incorporates a method for converting a word in the lexicon into its profile, and conversely for transforming a profile into the word to which it corresponds. The first of these processes is straightforward. All that is necessary is to search for the word in the lexicon and to retrieve its profile. This was effectively implemented as a symbolic program which simply searches for the appropriate word in a table and returns its profile.

The second process, choosing a word to express a profile, is slightly more complex. We saw earlier that the dot product of one normalised profile with another is never greater than 1. In addition, the dot product of a profile with itself is always 1. When it is required to transform a profile into a word, the system computes the dot product of the profile with each and every profile corresponding to a lexicon entry. The lexicon word whose dot product is greatest is then chosen. Intuitively, we are determining which word in the lexicon is closest in meaning to the profile we wish to decode.

Clearly, if the profile corresponding to a particular word is decoded, we will obtain the same word again. In this case the greatest dot product found will be 1 (the word with itself). However, it is also possible to decode a profile even if it does not exactly match the profile of any lexicon word. In this case the word in the lexicon whose profile matches the search profile most closely will be chosen. It is of course the hypothesis underlying this work that the word chosen will also be the one closest in meaning to the underlying meaning of the search profile. The decoding technique which we have just outlined has several useful properties to which we now turn.

Firstly, synonyms and words which are close in meaning can be handled. Synonyms are represented using identical profiles. Note that if a word for which synonyms exist in the lexicon is encoded and then decoded, we may end up with one of the synonyms rather than the original word itself. (In the original implementation, the first word with an optimal match was chosen, but this was an arbitrary design decision.) Words with similar meanings are represented using profiles which are similar but not identical. A whole spectrum of word similarity can therefore be captured by the microfeature/dot product approach. This is not the case with conventional symbolic approaches to the representation of meaning.

A second property is that the lexicon can be updated during the lifetime of the system. Consider an example concept which is not expressed closely by any word in the lexicon, for example "breakfast." If the profile corresponding to this concept is decoded into a word, then a reasonably suitable word will be chosen, such as "meal." Suppose that the lexicon is then updated to include the word "breakfast." This can be accomplished simply by adding the word and its corresponding profile to a table. If the same profile is decoded again, the word "breakfast" will probably be chosen. Thus at any time, the most suitable word in the lexicon will automatically be used when decoding a profile.

Finally, it is possible to combine the meanings of a set of concepts by adding up the profiles by which those concepts are represented. The result after normalisation is simply another profile, which can then be decoded into a word in the normal way. Consider a trivial example. Adding up the profiles for "green" and "bird" might yield the profile for "parrot". In fact the main use of this technique in the system was to combine the meanings of constituent actions in a knowledge structure. For example there was a knowledge structure for washing-up which consisted of the actions putting on an apron, filling a basin, squirting washing-up liquid, etc. However, on adding up the profiles corresponding to these actions a profile was obtained which decoded to "wash." In other words the systems could determine that the gist of the washing-up event was washing, solely by an analysis of the constituent actions.

EXAMPLES

In this section I shall show briefly how the ideas discussed earlier have actually worked when applied to the PARROT system. PARROT is primarily a system capable of paraphrasing its input. This is accomplished by the use of sequences of actions called knowledge structures. Both input to and output from the system is also by means of actions. Each action is a triple such as "person ride bicycle." The lexicon contains definitions of all words which can appear in the input or output of the system. Thus there are entries for "person," "ride," and "bicycle." These are shown in Appendix II.

Note first of all that "person" and "bicycle" are defined as profiles over the same set of microfeatures. This is because both count as *objects* in the terminology of the system. There are 166 object microfeatures in total and 106 nouns have so far been encoded in the system using these.

As can be seen from Appendix II, actions like "ride" are defined using the action microfeature set. There are 151 action microfeatures which have been used to encode the 111 verbs in the system. For all words in the lexicon, centralities are initially stated as integers ranging between 0 and about 40. Although it will be recalled that all the profiles are unit normalised before they are actually used, this gives an idea of how accurately the centralities were actually specified in the first place.

DISCUSSION AND NEXT STEPS

In previous sections we have discussed how words in the PARROT lexicon are represented using microfeature profiles. We have described how the microfeature sets and lexicon entries were generated, as well as showing how profiles can be compared using the dot product, and why profiles must be normalised for this to work properly. In addition, we showed how profiles could be converted back into words using these ideas. In this final section, we conclude by looking more critically at these aspects of the PARROT project. In addition, we isolate important areas for further work.

How Many Microfeatures?

We have described how the microfeature sets used to encode the lexicon were gradually expanded as the lexicon was encoded, by identifying gaps in their coverage. What was not addressed was the question of how many microfeatures are actually necessary in order to encode a large set of concepts. In other words, will the microfeature sets continue to grow indefinitely as more and more words are added to the lexicon? Clearly the answer here depends on the sets themselves and the concepts to be encoded. It was originally expected in the PARROT project that the size of the different microfeature sets would initially grow very rapidly, but that the rate of growth would tail off once a variety of different concepts had been encoded using the microfeatures in a given set. This expectation has been confirmed so far. As we have already seen, there are currently 106 nouns and 111 verbs in the lexicon, encoded using 166 object microfeatures and 151 action microfeatures respectively. Only a handful of microfeatures have been added to the sets in recent times. Thus initial results suggest that many concepts can be represented effectively using the same microfeature set.

Of course, the technique of adding microfeatures as the encoding of the lexicon proceeds suffers from a rather serious flaw: The representations of all existing words in the lexicon must be reconsidered in the light of the new additions. If the lexicon is small, this presents no difficulty. However, if the lexicon is already large, such a procedure may not be practicable. An alternative is to ignore the new microfeatures. This will tend to cause degradation of the lexicon, but may be acceptable under some circumstances. The best solution, if this general approach is to be adopted at all, would be to start with a large set of microfeatures (generated during the encoding of a previous lexicon), so that no serious deficiency in the set emerges during the encoding process.

Choice of Microfeatures

Another issue relates to the sets of microfeatures themselves. It might be argued that PARROT only worked because the microfeatures were chosen carefully in order to make it work. However, it is my conjecture that the precise choice of microfeatures is not crucial, provided that it is always possible to differentiate between two concepts if one's intuitions indicate that they are indeed different in meaning. I have yet to show this empirically, but I would predict that if the dimensions on which the microfeatures lay were elicited systematically from people, then certain key dimensions (such as weight and size for objects) would always appear, but that less important dimensions (such as definedness of limits or association) might not occur. It would still be possible to generate profiles for words even if the less important dimensions were excluded. This would fit well with one's intuitions about the meaning of words: Generally, people will agree about the essential meaning of a given word, but they are likely to disagree on the finer points of its meaning. In this account, the essential meaning would be captured by the key dimensions whereas the finer points would be handled by the less important dimensions.

Assigning Centralities to Microfeatures

One possible shortcoming of the work that has been described is as follows: Centralities were assigned to microfeatures by a single individual. I have presented no evidence to suggest tha the system would still work if someone else had done the encoding. The work is thus open to the criticism of being ad hoc. However, the use of distributed representations has a considerable advantage over list-based approaches to lexical encoding: Empirical methods can be used in the encoding process. For example, it is possible to perform a norming study in which subjects assign centralities to a set of microfeatures in order to encode a given concept. The representations so obtained can then be used in an NLU system. This approach uses people's linguistic knowledge in a systematic fashion and therefore starts to address the problem of AI being subjective and unreplicable. Sharkey & Brown (1986) have already argued that AI needs an empirical foundation based on psychology. Distributed representations of the kind discussed here are one means by which this can be achieved. There is already an established literature on norming procedures which is effectively relevant to the work being discussed here (e.g. Katz, 1983). All that is needed now is to find out to what extent existing techniques are applicable to AI.

Labelled Versus Unlabelled Microfeatures

In this work I have opted for named microfeatures that have a clearly defined meaning, captured by their labels. The work therefore follows in the tradition of Waltz and Pollack (1985) and McClelland and Kawamoto (1986), where labelled microfeatures are also used. However it is also possible to generate microfeature-type representations by learning; (Elman, 1988; Hinton & Sejnowski, 1984; Hinton 1986; Miikkulainen & Dyer, 1987). In this case the semantic significance of each microfeature is not determined in advance by the implementor. Rather, it is determined while learning to perform a specific task. The issue of whether to adopt one approach or the other is a somewhat contentious one. There is no question that the use of unlabelled microfeatures is experimentally sound and has already produced some very interesting results. For example, Miikkulainen and Dyer (1989) have produced a complete paraphraser for script-based stories which learns distributed representations. However, as an approach within AI, unlabelled microfeatures have severe limitations. The most notable of these is that a learning system will only learn in its hidden units to capture the uniformities underlying the data with which it is presented. This raises the question of how the data can be made to capture the right uniformities. Language is extremely complicated, and there seems no easy way of generating linguistic data which can cause a system to learn something specific about language except in very restricted cases. Another problem with learned microfeatures is that the learning process is extremely slow even if a data set with the required properties can be generated. By contrast, it should be tractable to construct a lexicon, using labelled microfeatures, which is not only quite large but also generally applicable. Therefore I consider that it will be most fruitful if both approaches continue to be developed in parallel.

Use of Multiple Microfeature Sets

In PARROT there are three disjoint sets of microfeatures, one set each for representing contexts of nouns, objects, and actions. Each word in the lexicon is therefore encoded as a profile over one of these three microfeature sets. However, a word suggests more than its simple literal meaning, considered in isolation. For example, the noun "food" might suggest the actions of eating, cooking, and perhaps shopping. Moreover, it suggests certain times of day when one might eat, a likely goal, namely hunger, and certain places like kitchens, dining rooms, and cafeterias. Thus the word food conjures up a great deal more than its "literal" meaning. Now consider the action "reading." This word suggests certain objects, for example books and newspapers, which people read. It also suggests certain stereotypical contexts, like sitting at a desk, where reading might take place. If all words were encoded as profiles over just one microfeature set, encompassing all existing sets, then we would be able to express some of the information implied by a word's meaning, and not just its "literal" meaning.

Thus, for example, verbs of state like is_asleep could be defined mainly in terms of the context they imply, using context microfeatures. As it is, it has effectively proved necessary to add context microfeatures to the action microfeature set (describing posture, for example) in order to handle verbs of state. This is undesirable because it does not provide a link between verbs of state and the context of other actions which might follow such a state description in a narrative text of some kind.

What I am arguing for, effectively, is that a word's meaning should be represented as a partial specification of all the complete propositions[4] in which that word might occur. A very similar idea, proposed by Rumelhart (1979) and discussed further in McClelland and Kawamoto (1986, p. 316) is the word meanings provide clues to the scenarios described by the propositions in which they take part. Outside connectionism, there have also been discussions on similar lines (e.g. Mitchell & Zagar, 1986, p. 277). However, a distributed representation based on microfeatures appears to be a good format within which to develop this idea further.

Next Steps

Before concluding, let us summarise some of the important areas for further research which have been identified by the work reported here. We have already isolated certain weaknesses in the present representation scheme. We outline

---

[4]The general issue of how to represent propositions within a connectionist NLU system is outside the scope of this chapter. However, this aspect of PARROT is discussed in Sutcliffe (1988). A review of other connectionist work on propositional representation can also be found in Chapter 3 of the same work. Note however that there has been a lot more work in this area since then.

here how some of these could be addressed. First of all, three sets of microfeatures were used in order to encode words in the lexicon. We have argued that a single microfeature set for all words would have certain advantages. The consequences of using a single set are currently being investigated.

Second, words were encoded by assigning centralities to microfeatures within a given set. This was done by a single person. We are currently engaged in showing that when a group of subjects encode lexical items by means of a norming study that consistent results are obtained. This will undermine the criticism that PARROT's implementor manipulated the profiles in order to make the system work.

Third, we have asserted that the choice of microfeatures is not crucial to the operation of the system, provided that they satisfy certain criteria. This needs to be demonstrated. Moreover, a general means of generating microfeature sets in a systematic and objective fashion needs to be devised. We are investigating these issues by working on predicate elicitation schemes within a limited domain.

Finally, we have pointed out that microfeature profiles cannot capture the propositional richness of language. There is already a large body of work in the area of propositional structures (see Sutcliffe, 1988, Chapter 3 for a review up to 1988). My own approach at present is to investigate the extent to which the proposition can be elided, rather than attempting to address it directly. This is possible in certain NLU applications. Such an approach may in any case suggest new candidate representation schemes.

Summary

In this chapter we have dealt with one aspect of PARROT, namely how words are represented in the lexicon using microfeature profiles. We have described in some detail how microfeature sets are created, and how word meanings are encoded using those microfeatures. We have also outlined some of the properties which might make these representations useful in an NLU system. Finally, we have shown some of the shortcomings of the present work and have identified some areas for further study.

Microfeatures are not a panacea for language understanding. However, they seem to offer something new when compared to traditional approaches to the representation of meaning. In particular, the meanings of many words can be captured using one set of microfeatures. Such words can range from the concrete to the abstract, and in addition both small and large differences between the definition of words can be encapsulated. Moreover, microfeatures offer the promise of both systematic encoding procedures using norming strategies, and representations which are entirely generated from data, via multiple layer network learning algorithms. Connectionist AI systems are still in their infancy. However, distributed representations for encoding word meanings, either learned or otherwise, are likely to play an important part in future AI research.

ACKNOWLEDGEMENTS

I am indebted to Noel Sharkey, Paul Day, Nick Reeves, and Lindsey Ford for making many helpful comments and suggestions relating to this work. I am also grateful to Khalid Sattar, Eby Zafari, Lyn Shackleton, Marlene Teague, Jane Stevens, and Joanne O'Donoghue. The author's email is sutcliffer @ ul.ie.

REFERENCES

Arbib, M.A. (1975). Artificial intelligence and brain theory: Unities and diversities. *Annals of Biomedical Engineering, 3,* 238–274.

Chomsky, N. (1965). *Aspects of the theory of syntax.* Cambridge, Mass.: M.I.T. Press.

Clark, H.H. & Clark, E.V. (1977). *Psychology and language. An introduction to psycholinguistics.* New York: Harcourt Brace Jovanovich Inc.

Elman, J.L. (1988). *Finding structure in time.* TR 8801. San Diego, Calif.: Center for Research in Language, University of California, April.

Fillmore, C. (1968). The case for case. In E. Bach and R.T. Harms (Eds.), *Universals of linguistic theory,* (1–88). New York, N.Y.: Holt, Rinehart & Winston.

Garnham, A. (1985). *Psycholinguistics: Central topics.* New York: Methuen.

Golden, R.M. (1986). Representing causal schemata in connectionist systems. *Proceedings of the 8th Annual Conference of the Cognitive Science Society,* 13–21.

Grossberg, S. (1980). How does a brain build a cognitive code? *Psychological Review, 87,* 1–51.

Hinton, G.E. (1981). Implementing semantic networks in parallel hardware. In G.E. Hinton & J.A. Anderson (Eds.), *Parallel models of associative memory. Hillsdale, N.J.:* Lawrence Erlbaum Associates Inc., 161–187.

Hinton, G.E. (1986). Learning distributed representations of concepts. *Proceedings of the 8th Annual Conference of the Cognitive Science Society,* 1–12.

Hinton, G.E. & Sejnowsi, T.J. (1984). Learning semantic features. *Proceedings of the 6th Annual Conference of the Cognitive Science Society,* 63–70.

Jordan, M.I. (1986a). An introduction to linear algebra in parallel distributed processing. In D.E. Rumelhart & J.L. McClelland (Eds.), *Parallel distributed processing: Explorations in the microstructure of cognition. Volume I: Foundations.* Cambridge, Mass.: M.I.T. Press, 365–422.

Jordan, M.I. (1986b). Attractor dynamics and parallelism in a connectionist sequential machine. *Proceedings of the 8th Annual Conference of the Cognitive Science Society, Amherst, Mass.,* 531–545.

Katz, A.N. (1983). Dominance and typicality norms for properties: Convergent and discriminant validity. *Behavior Research Methods and Instrumentation, 15,* (1), 28–38.

Katz, J.J. & Fodor, J.A. (1963). The structure of a semantic theory. *Language, 39* (2), 170–210. Also in J.A. Fodor & J.J. Katz (Eds.), *The structure of language.* Englewood Cliffs, N.J.: Prentice Hall, 1964.

Lehnert, W.G. & Burstein, M.H. (1979). The role of object primitives in natural language processing. *Proceedings of the 6th IJCAI.*

McClelland, J.L. & Kawamoto, A.H. (1986). Mechanisms of sentence processing: Assigning roles to constituents. In J.L. McClelland & D.E. Rumelhart, & PDP group, *Parallel distributed processing, Volume II.* Cambridge, Mass.: M.I.T. Press, 272–326.

Miikkulainen, R. & Dyer, M.G. (1987). *Building distributed representations without microfeatures.* Technical Report UCLA-AI-87-17. Los Angeles, Calif.: AI Laboratory, Computer Science Department, University of California at Los Angeles.

Miikkulainen, R. & Dyer, M.G. (1989). *A modular neural network architecture for sequential paraphrasing of script-based stories.* Technical Report UCLA-AI-89-02. Los Angeles, Calif.: AI Laboratory, Computer Science Department, University of California at Los Angeles.

Mitchell, C.C. & Zagar, D. (1986). Psycholinguistic work on parsing with lexical functional grammars. In N.E. Sharkey (Ed.), *Advances in cognitive science I*. Chichester: Ellis Horwood, 276–289.

Quillian, M.R. (1968). Semantic memory. In M. Minsky (Ed.), *Semantic information processing*. Cambridge, Mass.: M.I.T. Press, 216–270.

Rosch, E. (1973). Natural categories. *Cognitive Psychology, 4,* 328–350.

Rosch, E. (1977). Human categorization. In N. Warren (Ed.), *Advances in cross-cultural psychology, Vol. I*. London: Academic Press.

Rumelhart, D.E. (1975). Notes on a schema for stories. in D.G. Bobrow & A. Collins (Eds.), *Representation and understanding*, New York: Academic Press, 211–236.

Rumelhart, D.E. (1979). Some problems with the notion of literal meanings. In A. Ortony (Ed.), *Metaphor and thought*. Cambridge: Cambridge University Press.

Rumelhart, D.E., Hinton, G.E., & Williams, R.J. (1986). Learning internal representations by error propagation. In D.E. Rumelhart & J.L. McClelland (Eds.), *Parallel distributed processing: Explorations in the microstructure of cognition. Volume I: Foundations*. Cambridge, Mass.: M.I.T. Press, 318–362.

Schaeffer, B. & Wallace, R. (1969). Semantic similarity and the comprehension of meanings. *Journal of Experimental Psychology, 82,* 342-346.

Schank, R.C. (1972). Conceptual dependency: A theory of natural language understanding. *Cognitive Psychology, 3* (4), 552–630.

Schank, R.C. & Abelson, R.P. (1977). *Scripts, plans, goals, and understanding*. Hillsdale, N.J.: Lawrence Erlbaum Associates Inc.

Sharkey, N.E. & Brown, G.D.A. (1986). Why AI needs an empirical foundation. In M. Yazdani (Ed.), AI: *Principles and applications*. London: Chapman-Hall, 267–293.

Sharkey, N.E., Sutcliffe, R.F.E., & Wobcke, W.R. (1986). Mixing binary and continuous connection schemes for knowledge access. *Proceedings of the American Association for Artificial Intelligence*.

Sharkey, N.E. & Sutcliffe, R.F.E. (1987, June). *Memory attraction: Learning distributed schemata for language understanding*. Paper presented at Edinburgh Parallel Distributed Processing meeting.

Smith, E.E., Shoben, E.J., & Rips, L.J. (1974). Structure and process in semantic memory: A featural model of semantic decisions. *Psychological Review, 81,* 214–241.

Sutcliffe, R.F.E. (1988). *A parallel distributed processing approach to the representation of knowledge for natural language understanding*. Unpublished doctoral thesis, University of Essex, U.K.

Waltz, D.L. & Pollack, J.B. (1985). Massively parallel parsing: A strongly interactive model of natural language interpretation. *Cognitive Science, 9,* 51–74.

Wilks, Y. (1975). An intelligent analyser and understander of English. *Communications of the Association for Computing Machinery, 8* (18), 264–274.

APPENDIX I: OUTLINE OF THE PARROT SYSTEM

PARROT is a prototype natural language understanding system that uses connectionist rather than conventional artificial techniques. Knowledge about the world is stored in a set of knowledge structures, each of which describes a stereotypical event from some level of abstraction. Each knowledge structure contains a sequence of actions, represented as distributed patterns of activity over many different processing elements. Word meanings are also represented as distributed patterns.

When presented with a partial description of some event as input, the system can map the constituent actions of this description onto different parts of its knowledge structures. This process occurs in parallel, and as a result, various knowledge structures become active to different degrees, depending on how closely they describe the input event.

The system can perform three main functions. First, a *paraphrase* can be generated which uses the most active knowledge structure to fill in information missing from the input. At the same time, binding of character's names to roles in the knowledge structure occurs. Second, a one action *compaction* encapsulating an event can also be output. Third, a mechanism for *expanding* actions using system knowledge structure is also supported.

There are 151 action microfeatures, 166 object microfeatures, and 99 context microfeatures defining 106 nouns and 111 verbs in the lexicon. There are a total of 202 actions among the 20 knowledge structures of the system.

Here is an example paraphrase. Suppose the following actions are input to the system:

John hear alarm
John wake_up nonoun
John go_to bathroom

Notice that each action consists of a verb like "hear" and two nouns, like "John" and "alarm." As each action is entered, the system attempts to map it onto one of its knowledge structures (KSs)—sequences of actions representing a stereotypical event like getting up, washing, or going shopping. The system works under the assumption that the input is a partial description of some event characterised by one or more of its KSs. It therefore keeps track of how likely the input is to be about each such KS. Thus, as processing of this input continues, the system accumulates more and more evidence to support the hypothesis that it is about getting up, an event described by the KS called *getting_up*.

In order to generate a paraphrase at the end of the input, the system goes through the following steps. Firstly, it selects the KS that it deems most likely to describe the input. Secondly, the process of schema role binding takes place. The role binding enables the information that John (rather than Susan or Mary, say) is getting up to spread to all the constituent actions of the KS. Finally, all the KS's actions are output in order. The result is the following:

John is_asleep bed
alarm_clock go_off nonoun
John hears alarm_clock
John wake_up nonoun
John lie_in bed
John get_out bed
John go_to bathroom
John wash face
John clean teeth
John go_to bedroom
John shave face
John go_to kitchen

The paraphrase thus consists of all the actions in an appropriate KS being output with roles bound. The compaction process, on the other hand, generates a single action as output which "sums up" the input. For example, suppose the system is presented with exactly the same input as before. As the actions are input, exactly the same process of KS access occurs as did previously. When the command for generating a single action compaction is invoked, the following occurs. Firstly, the KS that has gathered most evidence is selected to form the basis of the compaction. Secondly, a process takes place that accomplishes role binding in that KS. Thirdly, a single action is output, which consists of the sum of the constituent actions of the KS. (See the main text for more discussion about summing up concepts represented as profiles.) The result is the following:

John wake_up bedroom

The final process is expansion. If a single action is input, the system can tell what the action is about, and as a result specify the constituent actions which might make up the input action. For example, suppose we wish to expand the action *go_to_bed* in the KS *day* (*day* represents the activities a person indulges in on a typical day). The system first determines which KS is the best expansion. Secondly, some processing associated with role binding is carried out. Finally, the expansion is output as follows:

person walk_to bathroom
person wash face
person clean teeth
person walk_to bedroom
person take_off clothes
person get_into bed
person lie_in bed
person is_asleep bed

The expansion process also involves the process of adding up the profiles corresponding to individual actions within a KS—the most appropriate KS for expanding the input is determined by comparing the input action directly with a set of special actions, each of which is the sum of all the actions in one KS.

The work shows that connectionist NLU systems can be given at least some of the representational power of their symbolic counterparts while at the same time allowing parallel access of event knowledge. In addition some of the subtle nuances of linguistic meaning can be captured using distributed representations. For more information about the whole system, see Sutcliffe (1988).

APPENDIX II: EXAMPLE ENTRIES FROM THE LEXICON

The Lexical Entry for "Person"

This is defined as a profile over the *object* microfeature set. The microfeatures are grouped together into dimensions by blank lines. Microfeatures which are not mentioned in the definition are assumed to have a centrality of zero. All lexical entries are unit normalised before being used in the system, as discussed in the text.

Person Noun
{

obj_one_to_three_letters	10	obj_solid	10
obj_four_to_six_letters	10		
obj_more_than_six_letters	10	obj_living_material	15
		obj_cloth	2
obj_starts_with_vowel	10		
obj_ends_with_vowel	10	obj_shiny	1
obj_starts_with_consonant	10	obj_smooth	5
obj_ends_with_consonant	10	obj_carpet_texture	10
		obj_road_texture	5
obj._one_syllable	10	obj_ploughed_field_texture	1
obj_two_syllables	10		
obj_three_syllables	10	obj_opaque	5
obj_first_vowel_a	10	obj_person_weight	10

obj_first_vowel_e	10			
obj_first_vowel_i	10	obj_person_size	10
obj_first_vowel_o	10		
obj_first_vowel_u	10	obj_specific_limits	5
obj_second_vowel_a	10	obj_vertical	8
obj_second_vowel_e	10	obj_horizontal	2
obj_second_vowel_i	10		
obj_second_vowel_o	10	obj_cubical	2
obj_second_vowel_u	10	obj_cuboidical	6
		obj_spherical	1
obj_time_early_morning	5	obj_rugby_ballical	8
obj_time_morning	5	obj_cylindrical	8
obj_time_lunchtime	5		
obj_time_afternoon	5	obj_room_temp	5
obj_time_evening	5	obj_person_temp	5
obj_time_night	5		
		obj_involves_one_object	10
obj_lasts_half_lifetime	5		
obj_lasts_lifetime	10	obj_red	1
		obj_blue	1
obj_found_kitchen	5	obj_green	1
obj_found_bathroom	5	obj_orange	1
obj_found_living_room	5	obj_yellow	1
obj_found_bedroom	5	obj_white	1
obj_found_garden	5	obj_black	1
obj_found_office	5	obj_brown	1
obj_found_inside	10		
obj_found_outside	5	obj_one_colour	5
obj_found_upstairs	5	obj_several_colours	5
obj_found_downstairs	5	obj_many_colours	5
obj_found_shopping_area	5		
obj_found_residential_area	5	obj_living	10
obj_found_urban_area	5	obj_conscious	25
obj_found_countryside	5		
		obj_one_person	15
obj_squashy	10		
obj_rubbery	10	obj_male	5
obj_pliable	5	obj_female	5
		}	

The Lexical Entry for "Ride"

This is defined as a profile over the *action* microfeature set.

Bicycle Noun
{

obj_one_to_three_letters	5	obj_solid	5
obj_four_to_six_letters	5		
obj_more_than_six_letters	5	obj_plastic	5
		obj_metal	15
obj_starts_with_vowel	5		

obj_ends_with_vowel	5	obj_shiny	5
obj_starts_with_consonant	5	obj_smooth	5
obj_ends_with_consonant	5		
		obj_opaque	5
obj._one_syllable	5		
obj_two_syllables	5	obj_dog_weight	5
obj_three_syllables	5		
		obj_person_size	8
obj_first_vowel_a	5	obj_dog_size	5
obj_first_vowel_e	5		
obj_first_vowel_i	5	obj_specific_limits	2
obj_first_vowel_o	5	obj_holey	12
obj_first_vowel_u	5	obj_hollow	8
		obj_sparse_filling	18
obj_second_vowel_a	5		
obj_second_vowel_e	5	obj_vertical	5
obj_second_vowel_i	5		
obj_second_vowel_o	5	obj_square_lamina	8
obj_second_vowel_u	5	obj_rect_lamina	15
		obj_round_lamina	5
obj_time_early_morning	15	obj_oval_lamina	5
obj_time_morning	12		
obj_time_lunchtime	10	obj_very_cold	5
obj_time_afternoon	5	obj_cold	5
obj_time_evening	12		
obj_time_night	2	obj_functional	5
obj_lasts_several_years	5	obj_concerns_tiredness	5
obj_lasts_decade	10		
obj_lasts_half_lifetime	10	obj_concerns_action	12
obj_lasts_lifetime	5		
		obj_involves_one_object	5
obj_found_garden	10		
obj_found_outside	10	obj_horiz_motion	25
obj_found_shopping_area	5		
obj_found_residential_area	12	obj_red	1
obj_found_urban_area	12	obj_blue	1
obj_found_countryside	3	obj_green	1
		obj_orange	1
obj_rubbery	1	obj_yellow	1
obj_rigid_pliable	15	obj_white	1
		obj_black	1
		obj_brown	1
		obj_one_colour	10
		obj_several_colours	5
		obj_many_colours	1
		obj_inanimate	5
		obj_one_person	5
			}

The Lexical Entry for "Bicycle"

Ride Verb
{

act_by_subj	5	act_mundane_action	5
act_with_others	5	act_usual_action	5
		act_unusual_action	5
act_sound	5		
act_sight	5		
act_sensation	5	act_typically_normal_health	5
act_move_in_locality	5	act_typically_confident	5
act_move_in_region	5		
act_move_in_country	5	act_typically_awake	5
act_move_plane_speed	3	act_typically_neutral	5
act_move_car_speed	5		
act_move_bicycle_speed	5	act_takes_second	2
		act_takes_minute	5
act_typically_standing	5	act_takes_few_minutes	10
act_typically_sitting	15	act_takes_hour	10
		act_takes_half_day	2
act_typically_easy_thinking	5	act_takes_day	2
		act_done_in_early_morning	8
act_very_complex_action	5	act_done_in_morning	5
act_fairly_complex_action	5	act_done_in_lunchtime	5
act_simple_action	5	act_done_in_afternoon	5
		act_done_in_evening	8
act_involves_a_person	15	act_done_in_night	2
act_involves_two_people	5		
act_involves_several_other_people	5	act_done_in_outside	5
act_involves_lots_of_other_people	5	act_done_in_shopping_area	5
act_involves_one_object	5	act_done_in_residential_area	5
		act_done_in_countryside	5
act_involves_money	6		}

4

Noun Phrase Analysis with Connectionist Networks

Stefan Wermter and Wendy G. Lehnert
Department of Computer and Information Science, University of Massachusetts, U.S.A.

INTRODUCTION

In the past, most systems in knowledge-based natural language processing relied on reverse knowledge engineering (e.g. Cullingford, 1978; Dyer, 1983; Lehnert, 1988; Wilensky, 1978). By carefully examining a domain and a task, knowledge representations and control structures were developed to produce the desired behaviour. In the last decade it has become more obvious that the development of appropriate knowledge structures, their communication, and their control, needs an enormous effort in knowledge engineering (see for example Dyer, 1983). Furthermore, the complexity of the representations and their control makes it difficult to scale up the memory and the language processing capacity of these systems (DeJong, 1979; Dyer, 1983; Lehnert, 1988).

An alternative approach for the acquisition of knowledge for a natural language processing system would be to learn at least part of the necessary knowledge and to use more uniform knowledge structures. A learning system reduces knowledge engineering and more uniform knowledge structures allow us to scale up underlying memory models. Our approach in the NOCON[1] is a step towards this goal. NOCON builds a memory model by learning semantic relationships between nouns in order to disambiguate noun phrases. One key problem for understanding noun phrases is to decide how different constituents within a noun phrase attach to one another. Function words like prepositions

---

[1]NOCON stands for NOun phrase analysis with CONnectionist networks.

generate structural ambiguities, which lead to a combinatorial number of syntactically possible attachments. In general, syntactic, semantic, and contextual knowledge might all be necessary for understanding complex noun phrases with multiple prepositional phrases. In NOCON we focus on syntactic and semantic knowledge for structural noun phrase disambiguation. The noun phrases considered are complex noun phrases of the form $<N><P><N>\ldots$ $<P><N>$ where $<N>$ stands for a noun and $<P>$ for a preposition.

NOCON's architecture is divided into two levels: an integration level at the top and a learning level at the bottom. The *integration level* integrates semantic constraints with syntactic constraints to form a structural interpretation of the complete noun phrase. The integration deals with the structural disambiguation of noun phrases of arbitrary length and consists of a relaxation network. The relaxation network at the integration level is based on plausibility values from the learning level. The *learning level* learns the semantic relationships in a noun–preposition–noun triple and consists of feed forward networks trained with the backpropagation learning rule. Using the NASA thesaurus we identify 16 semantic features to represent nouns in our scientific domain. Based on these features, backpropagation networks are trained to learn the plausibility of noun–preposition–noun triples. After training, the backpropagation networks generalise the learned regularities for new noun–preposition–noun triples and assign plausibility values which are used by the integration level. In this paper[2] we will describe the learning level, outline the integration level, show results from a case study, and discuss alternative approaches.

THE DOMAIN

Noun phrases are extremely frequent in almost all domains, especially in scientific and technical domains (Hirschman, 1986). For instance compare the following sentences:

> The patient showed an unanticipated reaction after the application of Cortison.
> Print the American cruisers' current positions and states of readiness.
> What is the next port of call for the South Carolina?

The first sentence is an example for fact-oriented language and a noun phrase expresses the main content. The second and third sentence are queries from a natural language interface (Hendrix, Sacerdoti, Sagalowicz, & Slocum, 1978). In natural language queries to a database we often find imperative verb forms followed by a noun phrase (second sentence) or interrogative pronouns followed

---

[2]The paper (Wermter & Lehnert, 1989) focused more on details of the learned internal representation and on the combination of symbolic and connectionist techniques.

by a noun phrase (third sentence). Although the imperative verb and interrogative pronoun supply information necessary for answering the query, the essential content of these queries is expressed in the noun phrases.

Because of the importance of noun phrases, natural language processing systems need a powerful and flexible model for understanding them. To investigate such a model we chose noun phrases from the NPL corpus (Sparck-Jones & VanRijsbergen, 1976) as our domain for NOCON. The NPL corpus contains titles of scientific articles and queries from the physical sciences emphasising the fields of meteorology, astronomy, and electrical engineering. For example:

Effects of electromagnetic fields on turbulences in gases.
Note on the cause of ionisation in the f-region.
Radio emission by plasma oscillations in nonuniform plasmas.
Calculation of fields on plasma ions by collective co-ordinates.
An iterative analogue computer for use with resistance network analogues.

For our domain of physical sciences we represented a noun with a binary vector of 16 features (see Table 1). The feature representation was developed by using two abstraction steps. First, we used the NASA thesaurus (1985) for classifying the specific nouns in the noun phrases. Because the NASA thesaurus covers a very similar domain compared with our corpus, it was very useful for a basic classification of the nouns. We classified each noun according to the most

TABLE 4.1
Semantic Features of the Nouns and Examples

Semantic Features	*Examples*
MEASURING-EVENT	Observation, Investigation, Research
CHANGING-EVENT	Amplification, Acceleration, Loss
SCIENTIFIC-FIELD	Mechanics, Ferromagnetics
PROPERTY	Intensity, Viscosity, Temperature
MECHANISM	Experiment, Technique, Theorem
ELECTRIC-OBJECT	Transistor, Resistor, Amplifier
PHYSICAL-OBJECT	Earth, Crystal, Vehicle, Room
RELATION	Cause, Dependence, Interaction
ORGANISATION-FORM	Layer, Level, Stratification, F-Region
GAS	Air, Oxygen, Atmosphere, Nitrogen
SPATIAL-LOCATION	Antarctic, Earth, Range, Region
TIME	June, Day, Time, History
ENERGY	Radiation, Ray, Light, Sound, Current
MATERIAL	Aluminium, Water, Carbon, Vapour
ABSTRACT-REPRESENTATION	Note, Data, Equation, Term, Parameter
EMPTY	Cavity, Vacua

general term in the hierarchy of the thesaurus. This step abstracted from specific nouns like "radio emission" to "emission," from "noise fluctuation" to "variation," from "transistor" to "semiconductor devices."

In the second step we abstracted the found classification of the most general thesaurus terms to features. We identified 16 features for the basic meaning of a noun in our domain. For example, in the first step the term "transistor amplifier" has the most general thesaurus term "amplifier" and "transistor" has the most general thesaurus term "semiconductor device." In the second step we abstracted from "amplifier" and "semiconductor device" to ELECTRIC OBJECT.

Several other feature representations have been developed in the past. For instance, Katz and Fodor (1963) developed a classical structure of a semantic theory, in which the semantics of a word is expressed as a collection of semantic markers and distinguishers. Semantic markers (e.g. "human") reflect the semantic relations between lexical items. Distinguishers reflect more specific unsystematic information (e.g. "first lowest academic degree" as one possible distinguisher for the lexical item "bachelor"). Our semantic features correspond conceptually to the semantic markers but we do not make the distinction between semantic markers and distinguishers. Katz and Fodor use distinguishers to characterise different word senses across different domains (e.g. a bachelor as a young fur seal, as the lowest academic degree, as a young knight). Since different word senses occur less often in a specific domain than in a completely unrestricted domain, we represent words in NOCON exclusively with features. Furthermore, an explicit semantic representation with features is more systematic than a combination of features and unsystematic, informal distinguishers which are still in natural language.

Our set of semantic features differs from several other sets of semantic features (e.g. Dahlgren, 1988; Katz & Fodor, 1963; Wilks, 1975) mainly because of different domains. Some features are not directly applicable, e.g. features like "human," "animal," "male," "female," "living," "non-living," and "emotional." These features would not contribute any distinguishing information in our domain, since all occurring concepts are nonliving. In a similar way, semantic features like "good" are not used since the corpus does not contain evaluating knowledge about morally acceptable things. On the other hand there are features like "physical object" and "abstract representation" which occur in other sets of features as well (e.g. Dahlgren, 1988). In general, there is not a widely accepted theory of how to develop an optimal set of semantic features. However, we believe that examining the regularities of the domain, using a "neutral" thesaurus with a well-known ontology, and comparing the set of semantic features with other feature sets, has led to a set of features in NOCON which serves as a reasonable starting point to express essential properties of the nouns in our domain.

LEARNING LEVEL: LEARNING SEMANTIC PREPOSITIONAL RELATIONSHIPS

In this section we examine how semantic relationships in noun phrases can be learned. Based on our developed feature representation, backpropagation networks learn underlying regularities of semantic relationships from a corpus of training noun phrases. The learned regularities are used for making inferences about the relationships within new test noun phrases.

Backpropagation for Learning Semantic Relationships

Within noun phrases, nouns can be connected with prepositions, for instance: "Diffusion of electrons in gases." The disambiguation of these noun phrases is based on prepositional relationships. A *prepositional relationship* is the semantic relationship between the features of two nouns connected by a preposition. Each prepositional relationship is encoded as the concatenation of the two feature vectors of the two nouns. The set of prepositional relationships for a given preposition describes the multiple word senses of a preposition by determining which noun features can be related. There are two kinds of prepositional relationships: *Plausible prepositional relationships* are possible relationships, for instance, "symposium on hydrodynamics." *Implausible prepositional relationships* are relationships which are not reasonable; for instance "symposium in ionosphere" is implausible because symposiums do not take place in the outer atmosphere.

Knowing about the plausible prepositional relationships "symposium on hydrodynamics" and "hydrodynamics in ionosphere" and knowing about the implausible prepositional relationship "symposium in ionosphere" we must interpret the noun phrase "symposium on hydrodynamics in ionosphere" so that the prepositional phrase "in ionosphere" attaches to "hydrodynamics," but not to "symposium." Since knowledge about the plausibility of the prepositional relationship between two nouns can help to rule out implausible structural interpretations of the whole noun phrase, we train backpropagation networks for learning the plausibility of prepositional relationships.

To learn the plausibility of prepositional relationships within noun phrases, backpropagation networks (Rumelhart, Hinton, & Williams, 1986) are used. For each preposition there is one backpropagation network determining the plausibility of the prepositional relationships (see Fig. 4.1). One network consists of 3 layers of units. The input layer consists of 32 binary units (values 0 and 1) representing 16 features for each of the 2 nouns. The one real-valued output unit determines if the prepositional relationship is plausible (value 1) or implausible (value 0). Twelve real-valued hidden units encode the mapping from the input units to the output units based on the training set.

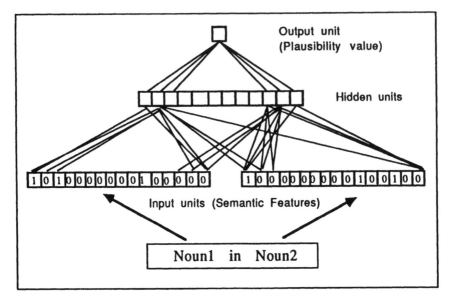

FIG. 4.1.   Backpropagation network for the prepositional relationships of "in."

An alternative network configuration for learning plausibility values of prepositional relationships would be one network for all prepositions instead of one network per preposition (Cosic & Munro, 1988). Then, the input units would represent the semantic features for the two nouns and the features for the particular preposition as well. However, one disadvantage of this approach is the static configuration. If the set of prepositional relationships for *one* preposition is modified, the whole architecture has to be retrained including the prepositional relationships of *all* other prepositions. Furthermore, such an approach cannot be extended to new prepositions without retraining old prepositions. However, in our approach adding a preposition only requires to train one new network with the prepositional relationships for that particular preposition since each preposition has a modular backpropagation network.

Training Results of the Backpropagation Networks

We need one training set of prepositional relationships for each preposition. First we concentrated on the 3 prepositions "in," "of" and "on." We extracted 50 noun phrases from our corpus which contained only these 3 prepositions, for instance:

Note on the cause of ionisation in the f-region.
International symposium on fluid mechanics in the ionosphere.

Based on these 50 noun phrases we built one training set for each preposition focusing on the semantic relationships between nouns and prepositions. Compound nouns (like "fluid mechanics") and simple nouns (like "mechanics") are represented as a 16-bit vector. Other word classes, like adjectives and determiners, are not considered here. Each training example in the training set consists of a prepositional relationship together with its binary plausibility value. The plausibility value is set to 1 if the prepositional relationship in the training set is plausible and is set to 0 otherwise. Each prepositional relationship is encoded with a pair of 16 features for each noun and each noun can have multiple features. For instance, the noun "acceleration" is both a CHANGING-EVENT and a form of ENERGY. Each noun in the 50 noun phrases is stored in a lexicon with its name and the associated 16 features. The following examples show 2 nouns with their features using the same order as in Table 4.1.

F-region	(0 0 0 0 0 0 1 0 1 1 1 0 0 0 0 0)
Ionisation	(0 1 0 1 1 0 0 0 0 0 0 0 0 0 0 0)

Now we will describe the training for the prepositional relationships. Since the training and testing results were very similar for different prepositions, we will just describe the training and test results for the preposition "in" in detail. We selected all 124 prepositional relationships for the preposition "in" from the 50 noun phrases. Since these prepositional relationships are taken from *existing* noun phrases, most are plausible. However, a backpropagation network can only learn to differentiate between plausible and implausible prepositional relationships if it has seen enough plausible and implausible training examples. To get implausible prepositional relationships in the training set, we added the 124 inverse prepositional relationships to the 124 prepositional relationships so that the training sets for "in" consists of 248 prepositional relationships. An inverse prepositional relationship is a prepositional relationship in which the order of the two nouns is changed. Including the inverse prepositional relationships in the training set prevents the networks being overloaded with too many plausible relationships since most of the inverse prepositional relationships are implausible. We illustrate the prepositional relationships and the inverse prepositional relationships for the preposition "in" for our example "Note on cause of ionisation in f-region" together with the plausibility values:

Note in f-region	0
Cause in f-region	1
Ionisation in f-region	1
F-region in note	0
F-region in cause	0
F-region in ionisation	0

Another possible way of generating implausible relationships would be to combine nouns from different noun phrases arbitrarily. Then we could expect that many of the prepositional relationships would be implausible. However, we used the inverse prepositional relationships since most of them were implausible and since they could be generated more systematically than combining nouns from different noun phrases arbitrarily.

Now we describe the results for the training set with the 248 prepositional relationships for "in." We conducted 3 runs training 3 backpropagation networks with the prepositional relationships for "in." The use of 3 different runs prevents the training depending on a randomly good initialisation of the weights in the network. In each run the backpropagation network was trained for 1600 epochs (396,800 prepositional relationships) with the learning rate η 0.01 and the weight change momentum α 0.9. The weights in the backpropagation network were changed after each complete epoch.

Figure 4.2 illustrates the learning for the different runs. Within the training phase the total sum squared error on the training set decreases from 77.8 to 6.6, from 62.5 to 7.1, and from 70.1 to 8.1 for the 3 runs. The learning curves show roughly the same learning behaviour for the 3 runs. Since the learning curves are very similar we show the average learning curve for the total sum squared error over the 3 runs. The similarity of the learning curves indicates that learning prepositional relationships for "in" does not depend significantly on the initial weights in the network. From now on we will refer to the "total sum squared error" as the *total error*.

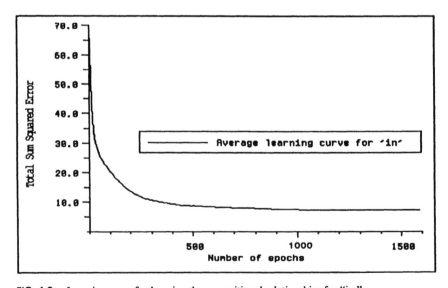

FIG. 4.2.   Learning curve for learning the prepositional relationships for "in."

After the training phase was completed the trained networks were tested with the training set. For the interpretation of the tests we introduce the terms "error tolerance" and "error rate." The *error tolerance* determines how much the actual outcome of the output unit could deviate from the desired outcome 0 for an implausible prepositional relationship and from the desired outcome 1 for a plausible prepositional relationship and still be considered correct. The *error rate* is the percentage of incorrectly classified prepositional relationships on the training set or on the test set.

For the training set the 3 networks of the 3 runs showed an error rate from 6.5% to 6.9% for an error tolerance of 0.49 and from 7.3% to 7.7% for an error tolerance of 0.3 (see Table 4.2). A network which was not trained at all was tested with the training set and showed an error rate of 54.0% for the error tolerance 0.49 and an error rate of 73.4% for the error tolerance 0.3. These tests with the training examples demonstrate that an effective representation for prepositional relationships can be learned.

After the networks had been tested with the 248 training examples, the networks were tested with 30 new test examples which had not been part of the training set. For the test set we chose 15 plausible and 15 implausible prepositional relationships from our corpus, with the only constraint that the prepositional relationships in the test set were not part of the training set. The test results with 30 new prepositional relationships that the networks had not been trained on showed an error rate from 16.7% to 26.7% for the error tolerance 0.49 and from 20% to 30% for the error tolerance 0.3 (see Table 4.3). The performance of the trained network on the test examples, which the network has

TABLE 4.2
Test Results for the Training Set for the Prepositional Relationships of "in"

Run	1	2	3	No learning
Error rate for the training set for error tolerance 0.49	6.9%	6.5%	6.9%	54.0%
Error rate for the training set for error tolerance 0.30	7.7%	7.3%	7.7%	73.4%

TABLE 4.3
Test Results for the Test Set for the Prepositional Relationships of "in"

Run	1	2	3	No learning
Error rate for the test set for error tolerance 0.49	16.7%	26.7%	16.7%	53.3%
Error rate for the test set for error tolerance 0.30	20.0%	30.0%	20.0%	70.0%

never seen before, can be demonstrated by comparing the described error rates with an untrained network.

To sum up the results for training the backpropagation networks with prepositional relationships for "in," we have shown that one trained network currently reaches a performance of providing the plausibility value of a prepositional relationship correctly for about 93% of the prepositional relationships in the training set and for about 83% of the prepositional relationships in the test set. The average performance over the 3 trained networks is 93% on the training set and 80% on the test set.

The results for other prepositional relationships were very similar. For instance, we conducted these same experiments with the prepositional relationships for "on." We trained networks with prepositional relationships for "on" based on our 50 noun phrases using the same network structure and the same parameters. The total error decreased from 69.2 to 3.7, from 61.1 to 4.5, and from 54.0 to 3.4 for 3 runs. That is, the learning curves for the prepositional relationships "on" show almost the same behaviour as the learning curves for the prepositional relationships for "in." The error rates for the training set for the error tolerance 0.49 were between 5.8% and 6.5% for the three runs. The error rates for the test set for the error tolerance 0.49 were between 16.1% and 22.6%. To sum up the results for training the backpropagation networks with prepositional relationships for "on," one trained network reaches a performance of providing the plausibility value of a prepositional relationship correctly for about 94% of the prepositional relationships of the training set and for about 84% of the test set. The average performance over the 3 trained networks is 94% on the training set and 79% on the test set.

We show elsewhere (Wermter, 1989b) that other prepositional relationships also behave similarly. Experiments with semantic relationships for 7 prepositions (by, for, from, if, of, on, with) were conducted, training 3 networks for each of the 7 types of prepositional relationships with 88 prepositional relationships for 1600 epochs. These experiments demonstrated that the plausibility of different prepositional relationships can be learned.

There might still be several possibilities even to increase the performance of the backpropagation networks by "fine-tuning" the representation. The training set could be more comprehensive, the number of features could be increased, the epochs of learning could be prolonged, absolutely known relationships between features could be fixed in the network to speed up learning. However, even now the networks reach an average performance of 93%–94% correct plausibility values on the training set and 79%–80% on the unknown test set.

INTEGRATION LEVEL: INTEGRATION OF SEMANTIC AND SYNTACTIC CONSTRAINTS

Whereas the last section focused on learning semantic prepositional relationships with backpropagation networks at NOCON's learning level, we now turn to a description of NOCON's integration level. First, we will briefly describe some syntactic constraints in noun phrases. Then, we will show how simple syntactic constraints and learned semantic constraints can be integrated in a relaxation network for disambiguating noun phrases.

Syntactic Constraints

The two syntactic constraints considered in NOCON are the locality constraint and the no-crossing constraint. The *locality constraint* says that a prepositional phrase is more likely to attach to a close preceding noun than to a distant preceding noun. For instance, in the noun phrase "influence on intensity on discharges in Van-Allen-belt," the prepositional phrase "in Van-Allen-belt" might attach to "influence," "intensity," and "discharges." The locality constraint suggests that there is a tendency to attach "in Van-Allen-belt" to "discharges" because "discharges" is the closest constituent. We can view the locality constraint as a variation of the principle of Right Association (Frazier & Fodor, 1978). Although Right Association states that words are always attached to the closest preceding constituent (the lowest nonterminal node in a syntax tree), the locality constraint states that there is only a strong tendency for attaching to the closest preceding constituent.

The second syntactic constraint is the no-crossing constraint. The *no-crossing constraint* (Tait, 1983) for noun phrases means that branches for attachment do not cross. The following example in Fig. 4.3 shows a violated no-crossing constraint. Although the attachments "influence on electrons" and "temperature in Fahrenheit" are semantically plausible, the combination of the two attachments in the noun phrase is not acceptable since the attachments cross.

Relaxation for the Integration of Multiple Constraints

Relaxation networks have been used for a number of tasks to integrate multiple constraints in natural language processing, for instance for modelling garden path sentences (Waltz & Pollack, 1985), for word sense disambiguation (Bookman, 1987), for slot filling in conceptual frames (Lehnert, 1991), and for lexical access (Cottrell, 1988). We have demonstrated elsewhere that relaxation networks are useful for integrating semantic and syntactic constraints for noun phrase disambiguation (Wermter, 1989a); in this section we describe the most important properties of a different relaxation network (see Fig. 4.4), which has fewer nodes.

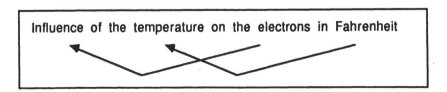

FIG. 4.3.   Noun phrase with a violated no-crossing constraint.

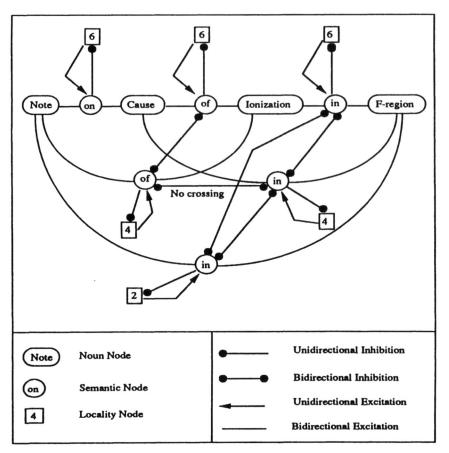

FIG. 4.4.   Relaxation network for the integration of different constraints.

The NOCON relaxation network consists of three types of nodes: *noun nodes* represent the nouns in a noun phrase, *semantic nodes* represent the plausibility of prepositional relationships between nouns, and *locality nodes* represent the distance between two nouns in a noun phrase. Each node has an activation potential between 0 and 10. The activation potential of a semantic node in the relaxation network is initialised with the plausibility value of the output unit of the specific backpropagation network multiplied by a factor of 10 to get values between 0 and 10. The higher the plausibility of a prepositional relationship the higher the initialisation value for the semantic node. The initialisation of the locality nodes is based on the relative distance between the nouns. The closer two nouns are in a noun phrase the higher is the initialisation value for the locality node between these nouns. It is important to point out that the initialisation of the locality nodes does not depend on specific values (6,4, and 2 in Fig. 4.4) but only on the relative distance between nouns (e.g. 3,2,1 would work as well). Noun nodes are initialised with 0 activation since they serve only as the framework to which semantic nodes and locality nodes connect. The semantic constraints are encoded as the semantic nodes, the locality constraints as the locality nodes, and the no-crossing constraints as specific inhibitory connections between semantic nodes in crossing attachment links (see Fig. 4.4).

All nodes are connected via inhibitory and excitatory connections as shown in Fig. 4.4 for a network with three prepositions. Apart from the connections of the locality nodes, all excitatory connections reflect all possible attachment links and all inhibitory connections reflect all mutually competitive attachment links. Networks for noun phrases with a different number of prepositions are built in exactly the same systematic manner. The input nodes are initialised and activation spreads through the network according to the relaxation algorithm (Feldman & Ballard, 1982). After about 20 to 30 update cycles the relaxation network settles into a stable state, and the semantic nodes with the highest activation values determine the preferred structural interpretation. We will see examples for this process in the next section.

A CASE STUDY FOR THE DISAMBIGUATION OF NOUN PHRASES

In this section we describe the results of testing NOCON with 80 noun phrases with up to 3 prepositions. The first 50 noun phrases contained prepositional relationships from the training set of the backpropagation networks; the last 30 noun phrases contained prepositional relationships on which the backpropagation networks had not been trained.

Disambiguation of 50 Noun Phrases with Known Prepositional Relationships

For the first test set 50 noun phrases consisting of nouns and up to 3 prepositions were extracted from the corpus of noun phrases. There were 31 noun phrases with 2 prepositions and 19 noun phrases with 3 prepositions. The input for the test were the 50 noun phrases, the output the structural interpretation of the noun phrase. First, NOCON created all possible prepositional relationships for each noun phrase. The following example shows the prepositional relationships for a noun phrase with 3 prepositions:

> Note on cause of ionisation in f-region
> Note on cause, Note of ionisation, Note in f-region
> Cause of ionisation, Cause in f-region, Ionisation in f-region

The feature representation of each noun in the prepositional relationships is looked up in the lexicon. Then the feature representation is used to initialise the

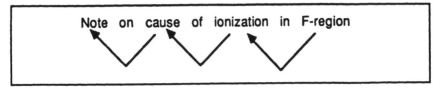

FIG. 4.5.   Structural interpretation of a noun phrase.

backpropagation network for each specific preposition. The output of the backpropagation networks are the plausibility values for the prepositional relationships. Based on these plausibility values NOCON initialises the semantic nodes in the relaxation network. Locality nodes representing constraints for locality and noun nodes are initialised as well. Then the relaxation network starts processing, integrates the syntactic and semantic constraints, and stabilises. The activation of the semantic nodes in the relaxation network determines the structural interpretation of the noun phrase with the preferred interpretation. In our example there are three semantic nodes which have high activation shown in Fig. 4.5.

The following two examples in Fig. 4.6 show two other noun phrases and their structural interpretation. Although these noun phrases consist of the same sequence of four nouns and three prepositions as the noun phrase in Fig. 4.5, they have quite different structural interpretations based on the semantic plausibility of their prepositional relationships and their syntactic constraints. NOCON's overall performance for the 50 noun phrases with known prepositional relationships was 88%; 44 out of 50 noun phrases had all attachments correct after the relaxation and were assigned a correct structural interpretation.

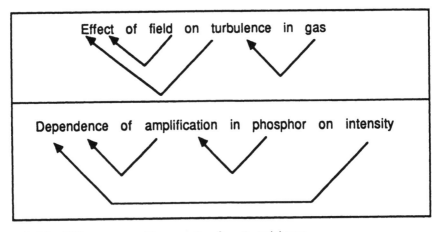

FIG. 4.6.   Different structural interpretations from the training set.

Disambiguation of 30 New Noun Phrases with Unknown Prepositional Relationships

Whereas the prepositional relationships of the first test in the previous section belonged to the training set of the backpropagation networks, the plausibility of the unknown prepositional relationships in the second test had to be generalised from previously learned regularities. The nouns were defined in the lexicon with their feature representation but the backpropagation networks had not been trained with the specific prepositional relationships using these noun phrases.

The set of unknown noun phrases contained 30 noun phrases, 12 noun phrases with 3 prepositions and 18 noun phrases with 2 prepositions. The overall performance for the 30 noun phrases with unknown prepositional relationships was 77%; 23 out of 30 noun phrases had all attachments correct and were assigned a correct structural interpretation. The following 3 examples in Fig. 4.7 show 2 noun phrases with a correct structural interpretation and 1 noun phrase with an incorrect structural interpretation.

The last example also demonstrates that for an incorrect structural interpretation not all prepositional relationships are necessarily incorrect. The first two attachments in the last example are correct but it is more likely for "in layer" to attach to "diffraction" than to "ray." The percentages for the performance of NOCON are based on the conservative evaluation that all attachments have to be correct for a correct structural interpretation of a noun phrase.

In general, prepositional phrases could attach to several nouns if only semantic constraints are considered. For instance, in our example "distortion in

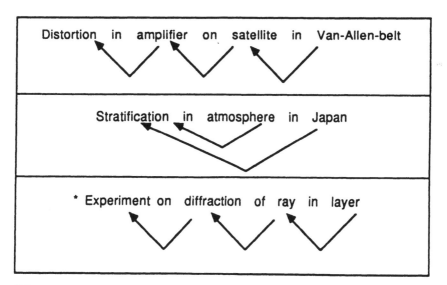

FIG. 4.7.   Different structural interpretation from the test set.

amplifier on satellite in Van-Allen-Belt," the prepositional phrase "in Van-Allen-Belt" could be attached to "distortion," "amplifier," or "satellite," because all the occurring prepositional relationships are plausible. In this case NOCON uses the locality constraints to prefer the closest neighbour ("satellite") as the correct attachment. NOCON's overall strategy is to give semantic constraints preference and to use syntactic constraints (locality and no-crossing of branches) only as a strategy to choose one of several possible structural interpretations.

DISCUSSION

One reason for the development of NOCON was to examine techniques which could reduce the amount of knowledge engineering for the structural interpretation of noun phrases. There have been several general techniques developed to acquire and represent knowledge about the structure of noun phrases. First, some approaches (e.g. Church, 1988; Hindle, 1989) acquire disambiguation rules based on stochastic methods. These stochastic methods are applied to text which is tagged with syntactic information. If the text corpus is appropriate then tagging regularities can be extracted. Although tagging sentences with syntactic categories can be performed with high accuracy, only simple nonrecursive noun phrases are parsed (Church, 1988). In our model recursive noun phrases can be processed. Furthermore, stochastic models developed so far are mainly applied to syntactic processing, whereas prepositional phrase attachment cannot in general be processed without semantic knowledge.

Second, other approaches (e.g. Jensen & Binot, 1988) use standard online dictionaries for deciding about prepositional phrase attachment. Several possible attachments are rated with a "certainty factor." An attachment receives a high certainty factor if there is a "path" in the dictionary which connects the two constituents of an attachment (e.g. fish with bones). Although these approaches of relying on standard dictionaries might seem to be rather promising, the implicit semantic paths in existing online dictionaries are far from being systematic and complete. Making attachment decisions based on a dictionary can only succeed if certainty factors can be computed for all attachments and if the dictionary contains all necessary paths between two constituents.

Third, there are connectionist approaches which deal with a simple form of attachment problems. McClelland and Kawamoto (1986) use a pattern associator to learn a mapping between simple sentences and their categorial representation. The pattern associator is trained with pairs of surface structures and case structures to attach a single prepositional phrase within sentences (e.g. the boy hit the girl with the ball). Since their pattern associator has a fixed length, their approach cannot deal with the attachment of multiple prepositional phrases. Our approach of combining relaxation and backpropagation networks can handle the attachment of multiple prepositional phrases. Of course one could add more units to their pattern associator so that multiple noun phrases could be represented. However, McClelland and Kawamoto state that the pattern associator already uses a "rather excessive number of units." Furthermore, the class of mappings that can be learned in a linear pattern associator without hidden layers using the perception learning rule is small compared with the class of problems that can be learned in an architecture using hidden layers and the backpropagation learning rule.

Fourth, several approaches have been developed, which rely on heuristics to decide whether to attach a prepositional phrase to a noun phrase or a verb phrase. Purely syntactic heuristics are *Right Association* and *Minimal Attachment* (Frazier & Fodor, 1978). Right Association says that terminal symbols should be attached to the lowest nonterminal node in a syntax tree. Minimal Attachment says that constituents should be attached to a higher node in a syntax tree if this produces a tree with less nodes. Frazier and Fodor use these principles in a purely syntactic parsing model. In NOCON we use locality constraints that actually generalise the principle of Right Association by assigning high activation values to noun–preposition–noun triples that are close in the noun phrase. However, our examples in the last section showed that noun phrases with the same length can have totally different structural interpretations and the interpretation depends on semantic relationships between the constituents as well. Since Frazier and Fodor do not integrate semantic constraints in their model, their approach cannot detect different structural interpretations of noun phrases with the same syntactic work classes.

A semantic heuristic approach for prepositional phrase attachment in sentences is described in Wilks, Huang, and Fass (1985). In this approach verbs, nouns, and prepositions are associated with case preferences. These case preferences are the basis for a decision about prepositional phrase attachment. One basic strategy is to move leftwards from the prepositional phrase using noun and verb preferences. A constituent is attached to the first preceding constituent whose preferences are fulfilled. If there is no such constituent then the strategy moves from the main verb rightwards using preposition preferences. If no attachment with fulfilled preferences can be found then the prepositional phrase is attached to the main verb. Our approach and Wilks' approach have in common the dominating influence of semantics over syntax. Only if more than one attachment is possible, or if no attachment is possible, does syntactic knowledge lead to a local attachment. However, representations and processing are quite different in both approaches. Wilks et al. rely on handcoded preferences (case information and rules), but we use backpropagation networks to learn the preferences for noun–preposition–noun triples. Whereas Wilks et al. use a serial "first fit" strategy we use a parallel relaxation strategy, which can avoid too-early commitments for an attachment.

There are several other semantic and contextual heuristic approaches (Ford, Bresnan, & Kaplan, 1982; Crain & Steedman, 1985; Dahlgren & McDowell, 1986; Hirst, 1987). These approaches attack the problem of prepositional phrase attachment in sentences with symbolic predefined knowledge, whereas NOCON was built for learning data-driven preferences for prepositional phrase attachment in noun phrases. However, NOCON can interface with sentence analysers particularly well if the sentence analysers use hybrid symbolic/connectionist techniques (e.g. Lehnert, 1991; Wermter, 1991a). One such hybrid sentence analyser is CIRCUS, which integrates three distinct processing architectures (Lehnert, 1991): (1) a stack; (2) a marker passing algorithm; and (3) numerical relaxation. The stack is used to recognise syntactic constituents and the other two techniques distinguish two types of soft semantic constraints: predictive preferences and data-driven preferences. In particular NOCON could take advantage of the predictive preferences that are associated with semantic case frames. For example, suppose we are analysing:

John gave Mary a hand at the store before work.
The audience gave Mary a hand at the finale before the royal family.

To understand the first sentence we need to understand that "gave a hand" means helped and we need to understand that "at the store" describes a location and "before work" describes a time. Although the second sentence is a bit awkward, we now understand that the audience is applauding Mary, "at the finale" describes a time, and "before the royal family" describes a location. In order to handle these interpretations, we need some case frames associated with the verb "to give" that cover a variety of semantic word senses, and we need a mechanism for triggering and instantiating appropriate word senses when specific types of concepts are encountered as the direct object of "to give."

Two broad types of semantic constraints can co-operate in resolving competition across multiple interpretations. Predictive preferences refer to those semantic constraints which derive from syntactic constituents that are very likely to be present when particular nouns or verbs appear. For example, the verb "to give" will normally appear with a subject, a direct object, and very often an indirect object or prepositional phrase containing the preposition "to." We can therefore predict a set of places in the sentence where useful semantic constraints should appear.

Data-driven preferences as described for NOCON refer to semantic constraints that occur frequently in noun phases. Prepositional phrases describing times and locations are classic examples. If we wanted to predict a prepositional phrase describing a time or place, we would have to associate that prediction with virtually every verb in the lexicon. Although this could be done (indeed, any system that relies on structured inheritance can readily be configured to operate this way), it is simply wrong to set up expectations that are both so broad and so infrequently exercised. If a sentence analyser can only make sense of things that were predicted beforehand, it cannot hope to scale up in the face of a substantial lexicon covering a serious domain. Predictive processing is useful, but only when it is restricted to those constraints that are very likely to appear. Data-driven techniques are needed to handle those cases which are inappropriate for predictive measures, e.g. in relative clauses, participial phrases and prepositional phrases (Wermter, 1991b). Since predictive measures within noun phrases are less applicable than data-driven techniques, data-driven techniques have to be used to understand noun phrases. Using data-driven techniques NOCON was developed to learn structural noun phrase disambiguation based on learned semantic relationships. Learning semantic constraints and integrating them with syntactic constraints gives NOCON the potential to be more independent from specific domains than natural language models, which do not rely on learning.

CONCLUSION

We have described NOCON, a system which learns to disambiguate noun phrases based on connectionist networks. We have demonstrated how learned semantic relationships are integrated with syntactic constraints to provide correct structural interpretations of noun phrases. To our knowledge NOCON is the first noun phrase analyser based on connectionist learning and the parallel integration of semantic and syntactic constraints. We believe that our learning techniques are potentially powerful enough to decrease the knowledge engineering and the domain dependence in natural language processing systems.

ACKNOWLEDGEMENTS

This research is supported by the Advanced Research Projects Agency of the Department of Defense, monitored by the Office of Naval Research under contract #N000-14-87-K-0238, the Office of Naval Research, under a University Research Initiative Grant, Contract #N00014-86-K-0764, NSF Presidential Young Investigators Award NSFIST-8351863 and a grant by the German Academic Exchange Service.

REFERENCES

Bookman, L.A. (1987). A microfeature-based scheme for modelling semantics. *Proceedings of the International Joint Conference on Artificial Intelligence* (pp. 611–614). Milan, Italy. San Mateo, Calif.: Morgan Kaufmann.

Church, K.W. (1988). A stochastic parts program and noun phrase parser for unrestricted text. *Proceedings of the ACL Conference on Applied Natural Language Processing* (pp. 136–143). Austin, Texas. Morristown, N.J.: Association for Computational Linguistics.

Cosic, C. & Munro, P. (1988). Learning to represent and understand locative prepositional phrases. *Proceedings of the Annual Conference of the Cognitive Science Society* (pp. 257–262). Montreal, Canada. Hillsdale, N.J.: Lawrence Erlbaum Associates Inc.

Cottrell, G.W. (1988). A model of lexical access of ambiguous words. In S.I. Small, G.W. Cottrell, & M.K. Tanenhaus, *Lexical ambiguity resolution* (pp. 179–194). San Mateo, Calif.: Morgan Kaufmann Publishers.

Crain, S. & Steedman, M. (1985). On not being led up the garden path: The use of context by the psychological syntax processor. In D.R. Dowty, L. Karttunen, & A.M. Zwicky (Eds.), *Natural language parsing: Psychological, computational, and theoretical perspectives* (pp. 320–358). Cambridge: Cambridge University Press.

Cullingford, R.E. (1978). *Script application: Computer understanding of newspaper stories.* Ph.D. Dissertation, Research Report 116, Computer Science Department, Yale University.

Dahlgren, K. (1988). *Naive semantics for natural language understanding.* Boston, Mass.: Kluwer Academic Publishers.

Dahlgren, K. & McDowell, J. (1986). Using commonsense knowledge to disambiguate prepositional phrase modifers. *Proceedings of the National Conference on Artificial Intelligence* (pp. 589–593). Philadelphia, PA. Menlo Park: American Association for Artificial Intelligence.

DeJong, G.F. (1979). *Skimming stories in real time: An experiment in integrated understanding.* Research Report 158, Department of Computer Science, Yale University.

Dyer, M. (1983). *In-depth understanding.* Cambridge, Mass.: M.I.T. Press.

Feldman, J.A. & Ballard, D.H. (1982). Connectionist models and their properties. *Cognitive Science, 6,* 205–254.

Ford, M., Bresnan, J.W. & Kaplan, R.M. (1982). A competence based theory of syntactic closure. In J.W. Bresnan (Ed.), *The mental representation of grammatical relations* (pp. 727–796). Cambridge, Mass.: M.I.T. Press.

Frazier, L. & Fodor, J.D. (1978). The sausage machine: A new two-stage parsing model. *Cognition, 6,* 291–325.

Hendrix, G., Sacerdoti, D., Sagalowicz, D., & Slocum, J. (1978). Developing a natural language interface to complex data. *ACM Transactions on Database Systems 3* (2), 105–147.

Hindle, D. (1989). Acquiring disambiguation rules from text. *Proceedings of the Annual Meeting of the Association for Computational Linguistics* (pp. 118–125). Chicago, Illinois. Morristown, N.J.: Association of Computational Linguistics.

Hirschman, L. (1986). Discovering sublanguage structures. In R. Grishman & R. Kittredge (Eds.), *Analyzing language in restricted domains: Sublanguage description and processing (pp. 212–234).* Hillsdale, N.J.: Lawrence Erlbaum Associates Inc.

Hirst, G. (1987). *Semantic interpretation and the resolution of ambiguity.* Cambridge: Cambridge University Press.

Jenson, K. & Binot, J.L. (1988). Dictionary text entries as a source of knowledge for syntactic and other disambiguations. *Proceedings of the ACL Conference on Applied Natural Language Processing* (pp. 152–159). Austin, Texas. Morristown, N.J.: Association of Computational Linguistics.

Katz, J.J. & Fodor, J.A. (1963). The structure of a semantic theory. *Language, 39* (2), 170–210.

Lehnert, W.G. (1988). Knowledge-based natural language understanding. In H.E. Shrobe (Ed.), *Exploring artificial intelligence. Survey talks from the national conferences on artificial intelligence* (pp. 83–132). San Mateo, Calif.: Morgan Kaufmann Publishers.

Lehnert, W.G. (1991). Symbolic/subsymbolic sentence analysis: Exploiting the best of two worlds. In J. Barnden & J. Pollack (Eds.), *Advances in connectionist and neural computation theory, Vol. 1.* Norwood, N.J.: Ablex Publishers.

McClelland, J.L. & Kawamoto, A.H. (1986). Mechanisms of sentence processing: Assigning roles to constituents. In J.L. McClelland, D.E. Rumelhart, & the PDP Research Group (Eds.), *Parallel distributed processing, Vol. 2* (pp. 272–326). Cambridge, Mass.: M.I.T. Press.

NASA (1985). *NASA Thesaurus.* National Aeronautics and Space Administration.

Rumelhart, D.E., Hinton, G.E., & Williams, R.J. (1986). Learning internal representations by error propagation. In D.E. Rumelhart, J.L. McClelland, & the PDP Research Group (Eds.), *Parallel distributed Processing, Vol 1.* Cambridge, Mass.: M.I.T. Press.

Schubert, L.K. (1986). Are there preference tradeoffs in attachment decisions? *Proceedings of the National Conference on Artificial Intelligence.*

Sparck-Jones, K. & VanRijsbergen, C.J. (1976). Information retrieval test collections. *Journal of Documentation, 32* (1), 59–75. Philadelphia, PA. Menlo Park: American Association for Artificial Intelligence.

Tait, J.I. (1983). Semantic parsing and syntactic constraints (Mark IV). In K. Sparck-Jones & Y. Wilks (Eds.), *Automated natural language processing* (pp. 169–177). Chichester: Ellis Horwood/John Wiley.

Waltz, D.L. & Pollack, J.B. (1985). Massively parallel parsing: A strongly interactive model of natural language interpretation. *Cognitive Science, 9*, 51–74.

Wermter, S. (1989a). Integration of semantic and syntactic constraints for structural noun phrase disambiguation. *Proceedings of the International Joint Conference on Artificial Intelligence* (pp. 1486–1491). San Mateo, Calif.: Morgan Kaufmann.

Wermter, S. (1989b). Learning semantic relationships in compound nouns with connectionist networks. *Proceedings of the Annual Conference of the Cognitive Science Society* (pp. 964–971). Hillsdale, N.J.: Lawrence Erlbaum Associates Inc.

Wermter, S. (1991a). Learning and representing natural language phrases in a hybrid symbolic/connectionist approach. *Proceedings of the Spring Symposium of the American Association for Artificial Intelligence*. Menlo Park, CA: American Association for Artificial Intelligence.

Wermter, S. (1991b). Learning to classify natural language titles in a recurrent connectionist model. *Proceedings of the International Conference on Artificial Neural Networks* (pp. 1715–1718). Espoo, Finland. Amsterdam: North Holland.

Wermter, S. & Lehnert, W.G. (1989). A hybrid symbolic/connectionist model for noun phrase understanding. *Connection Science, 1* (3), 255–275.

Wilensky, R. (1978). *Understanding goal-based stories.* Ph.D. Dissertation, Research Report 140, Computer Science Department, Yale University.

Wilks, Y. (1975). An intelligent analyzer and understander of English. *Communications of the ACM, 18* (5), 264–274.

Wilks, Y., Huang, X., & Fass, D. (1985). Syntax, preference, and right attachment. *Proceedings of the International Joint Conference on Artificial Intelligence* (pp. 779–784). Los Angeles, California. San Mateo, C.A.: Morgan Kaufmann.

5 Parallel Constraint Satisfaction as a Comprehension Mechanism

Mark F. St. John
Department of Cognitive Science, University of California at San Diego, La Jolla, California, U.S.A.

James L. McClelland
Department of Psychology, Carnegie-Mellon University, Pittsburgh, Pennsylvania, U.S.A.

INTRODUCTION

Parallel distributed processing has facilitated the study of a nontraditional algorithm for comprehension: parallel constraint satisfaction. Traditional algorithms have viewed sentence comprehension as the sequential application of rules which build up an interpretation after some number of intermediate steps (e.g. Marcus, 1980; Woods, 1970). Parallel constraint satisfaction, on the other hand, views sentence comprehension as a parallel computation of an interpretation of the sentence as a whole that best satisfies the constraints derived from the sentence (MacWhinney, 1987; McClelland, & Kawamoto, 1986; Waltz & Pollack, 1985). Similarly, traditional story processing algorithms have viewed comprehension as the sequential building and connecting of text-based propositions (e.g. Charniak, 1983; Schank & Abelson, 1977; van Dijk & Kintsch, 1983; Wilensky, 1983). Parallel constraint satisfaction again views comprehension as a parallel computation of an interpretation of the text that best satisfies the constraints derived from the text. Commensurate with its different view, parallel constraint satisfaction naturally captures a number of important qualities of language comprehension that are difficult for more traditional algorithms:

1. the competition of graded semantic and syntactic constraints;
2. the revision of interpretations based on evidence;
3. the sharing of knowledge between contexts;
4. the inherent drawing of inferences.

This paper discusses a model that applies the approach to the processing of individual simple sentences, and it discusses how this approach can be extended to the processing of simple stories.

First, a simple example of how parallel constraint satisfaction works will be useful. The Schema model described by Rumelhart, Smolensky, McClelland, and Hinton (1986) represents the attributes of rooms in a house or an office. The model is a parallel distributed processing network in which each unit corresponds to a particular feature, such as room size, or an object, such as a typewriter or a sofa. The activity of each unit represents the probability that that attribute is true of a particular room. The connections between units represent constraints among the attributes. A positive connection means that when one attribute is true, the other is typically true as well, and a negative connection means that when one is true, the other is typically false. The strength of the connection represents and imposes the strength of the constraint. The connections, therefore encode a great deal of knowledge about the correlations between room attributes.

When some input activates a unit, or units, the network begins to activate other units that are consistent with this unit, according to the valence and strength of their connections to it. The network gradually settles into a stable state of activations that represents all the attributes of a room that are consistent with the externally activated unit. For example, if the unit for *oven* is externally activated, other units consistent with *oven* will become activated. Gradually, the network will settle into a state that corresponds to a typical kitchen with active units for *oven, toaster, sink*, etc., but not for *sofa, bed*, etc. The externally activated unit represents an external constraint, and the settling process computes an interpretation that best fits that constraint.

The Schema model is actually more powerful than this example would suggest. If both *bed* and *sofa* are externally activated, the model will produce a blend of a bedroom and a living room. Units consistent with either externally activated unit will be activated, and units inconsistent with either will be deactivated. These opposing forces will produce a compromise representation of a room. In this case, the model produces a representation of a large bedroom/ sitting-room that contains a sofa and an easy chair. The Schema model, therefore, has the ability to combine knowledge from different contexts, in this case rooms, to produce novel interpretations of the input.

The Schema model demonstrates parallel constraint satisfaction processing characteristics that are important to language comprehension. First, the Schema model demonstrates the competition among many constraints. Each element of the representation contributes to the global interpretation of a room according to the size of its graded correlations with other elements. The elements all cooperate and compete to find an interpretation that satisfies the strongest, and as many, constraints as possible.

Second, the model can evaluate and revise its interpretation. The model activates units to the degree the evidence supports them. If there is only weak evidence for an interpretation, then the units will be activated only weakly. Additional input will update the interpretation. The evidence from the new input will be added with the previous evidence to support an interpretation. If the new evidence is consistent with the prevailing interpretation, activations will be strengthened. If it is inconsistent, then the network will settle on a new interpretation consistent with all of the evidence. In this sense, the model continually revises its interpretation to reflect the weight of the evidence it receives.

Third, the model demonstrates the sharing of information from different contexts. The bedroom/sitting-room example demonstrates how parallel constraint satisfaction models can easily share information from different contexts. The external constraints from *sofa* and *bed* combine and interact in the network in the same way that constraints from items that are drawn from the same context, such as *sofa* and *floor lamp*, would combine and interact. This ability to combine novel sets of constraints effectively supports generalisation. Novel combinations of external constraints will produce intelligible composite room descriptions.

Fourth, the model can draw inferences. Because of the constraints among elements, the final state into which the network settles will contain information that was not explicit in the input. This extra information constitutes inferences that are drawn automatically as the network settles. In the kitchen example, *oven* was the only explicit room attribute. The rest of the model's interpretation of the kitchen consists of inferences.

SENTENCE COMPREHENSION

A number of difficult processes in sentence comprehension can be viewed as constraint satisfaction problems. Consequently, parallel constraint satisfaction may be applied productively to sentence comprehension. The resolution of ambiguous words, the instantiation of vague words, the inference of missing thematic roles, and the assignment of sentence constituents to their thematic roles all use constraints from themselves and the sentence context to compute an interpretation.

A more sophisticated architecture than that used in the Schema model, however, is required for sentence processing. Sentences contain structure, as well as content, that must be captured by the comprehension process. Additionally, sentence constituents must be processed sequentially because each constituent is read or heard consecutively. Finally, although the constraints among room attributes were relatively easy to specify and assign appropriate strengths, the constraints among sentence constituents are much harder to specify and assign a strength, so a model that learns constraint strengths for itself would be preferred.

We have developed a model that uses parallel constraint satisfaction to process sentences. First we will describe the processing goals for the model more fully, then we will introduce the model and evaluate its performance.

Sentence Comprehension Issues

One problem for sentence comprehension is that the words of a sentence may be ambiguous or vague. In the sentence, "The pitcher threw the ball," each content word is ambiguous. "Pitcher" could either refer to a ball-player or a container, "threw" could either refer to tossed or hosted; and "ball" could refer to a sphere or a dance. How are the appropriate meanings selected so that a single, coherent interpretation of the sentence is produced? Vague words also present difficulties. In the sentences, "The container held the apples" and "The container held the cola," the word "container" refers to two different objects (Anderson & Ortony, 1975). How does the context affect the interpretation of vague words?

A third problem for processing sentences is that a sentence may leave some thematic constituents implicit that are nevertheless present in the event. For example, in the sentence, "Ed ate the spaghetti with clam sauce," the spaghetti was undoubtedly eaten with a fork. Psychological evidence indicates that missing constituents, when strongly related to the action, are inferred and added to the description of the event. McKoon and Ratcliff (1981) found, for example, that "hammer" was inferred after subjects read "Bobby pounded the boards together with nails."

Each of these problems is similar in that a particular constituent is underconstrained: The sentence constituent does not specify the concept to which it refers unambiguously, or, in the case of implicit constituents, the sentence constituent is missing altogether. By viewing the comprehension process as one big constraint satisfaction problem, however, it becomes clear that the context can become a source of additional constraints on the meaning of each particular constituent. Each constituent contributes a few constraints to many aspects of the sentence meaning. Together, they specify a clear meaning for the sentence.

Assigning the correct thematic roles (Fillmore, 1968) to constituents is a similar problem. Consider, "The teacher ate the spaghetti with the bus driver." Semantic knowledge ensures that the bus driver is understood to be another agent, rather than a condiment. Syntactic information can also help. To assign the teacher to a thematic role, syntactic information suggests that the pre-verbal constituent is the agent, and semantic information suggests that the teacher makes a better agent than does spaghetti. These pieces of information combine to constrain the teacher to be the agent. The role assignment process, therefore, can also be viewed as a constraint satisfaction problem. Syntactic constraints, such as word order and verb morphology (for example active and passive voice constructions), and semantic constraints are used together to assign the correct roles.

The processing of sentences, however, is more complicated than the processing that occurred in the Schema model. Whereas the Schema model represents rooms as collections of attributes, sentences have structural properties that cannot be ignored. First, the constituents of a sentence are read sequentially. As each constituent is processed, its constraints are added to the constraints derived from previous constituents. The constraint satisfaction process, therefore, operates as each constituent is processed. As processing continues through the sentence, the interpretation becomes stronger and more accurate. The interpretation of the whole sentence is therefore revised and refined as new constraints from each constituent are added. In the psychological literature this phenomenon is called immediate processing or update (Carpenter & Just, 1977).

A second structural property of sentences is that the order of their constituents matters. Much syntactic information is carried by the order of the constituents. In addition to processing constituents sequentially, then, the model must encode the information that the order of the constituents conveys and use it appropriately to constrain the meaning of the sentence.

Third, the constraints provided by a sentence can be complex and difficult to specify. It is common that more than one constituent is involved in making a constraint. Passive voice sentences are a good example. In "the bus driver was hit by the fireman," the word order and the passive voice markers must be taken together to determine the correct role assignments. Depending on whether the sentence is active or passive, the pre-verbal constituent is either the agent or the patient.

Additionally, constraints are not typically all-or-none. Instead, constraints are typically graded in strength (MacWhinney, 1987): some are strong and others are relatively weak. An example adapted from Marcus (1980) provides an illustration of the competition between constraints.

1. Which dragon did the knight give the boy?
2. Which boy did the knight give the sword?

Apparently, in the first sentence, a syntactic constraint makes us prefer the first noun as the patient and the noun after the verb as the recipient. In the second sentence, however, a stronger semantic constraint over-rides this syntactic constraint: Swords, which are inanimate objects, cannot receive boys. A good method for capturing this competition is to assign real-valued strengths to the constraints, and to allow them to compete or co-operate according to their strength.

Combining evidence from several sources and weighing that evidence on a continuum is easy in parallel constraint satisfaction models, as the schema model demonstrated. Complex and graded constraints, though, are difficult to program by hand. Connectionist learning procedures, however, allow PCS models to learn the appropriate constraints and assign appropriate strengths to them. To take advantage of this feature, learning was added to our list of goals.

The model is given a sentence as input. From the sentence, the model must produce a representation of the event to which the sentence refers. The actual event that corresponds to the sentence is then used as feedback to train the model. But learning is not without its own problems. Several features of the learning task make learning difficult. One problem concerns the difficulty of learning the mapping between the parts of the sentence and the parts of the event (Gleitman & Wanner, 1982). Learning the mapping is sometimes referred to as a boot-strapping problem since the meaning of the content words and significance of the syntax must be acquired from the same set of data. To learn the syntax, it seems necessary to already know the word meanings. Conversely, to learn the word meanings it seems necessary to know how the syntax maps the words onto the event description.

The connectionist learning procedure takes a statistical approach to this problem. Through exposure to large numbers of sentences and the events they describe, the mapping between features of the sentences and characteristics of the events will emerge as statistical regularities. For instance, in the long run, the learning procedure should discover the regularity that sentences beginning with "the boy" and containing a transitive verb in the active voice refer to events in which a young, male human participates as an agent. The discovery of the entire ensemble of such regularities provides a joint solution to the problems of learning the syntax and the meanings of words.

In sum, the model addresses six goals:

1. to disambiguate ambiguous words;
2. to instantiate vague words;
3. to elaborate implied roles;
4. to assign thematic roles;
5. to adjust its interpretation immediately as each constituent is processed;
6. to learn complex and graded constraints.

Description of the Sentence Gestalt Model

Task. The model's task is to process a single clause sentence, without embeddings, into a representation of the event it describes. The sentence is presented to the model as a temporal sequence of constituents. A constituent is either a simple noun phrase, a prepositional phrase, or a verb (including the auxiliary verb, if any). The information each of these sentence constituents yields is immediately used as evidence to update the model's internal representation of the entire event. This representation is called the sentence gestalt because all of the information from the sentence is represented together within a single, distributed representation; the model is called the sentence gestalt, or SG, model because it contains this representation. This general concept of sentence representation comes from Hinton's pioneering work (Hinton, 1981). From the sentence gestalt, the model can produce, as output, a representation of the event. This event representation consists of a set of pairs. Each pair consists of a thematic role and the concept that fills that role. Together, the pairs describe the event.

Architecture and Processing.   The model consists of two parts. One part, the sequential encoder, sequentially processes each constituent to produce the sentence gestalt. The second part is used to produce the output representation from the sentence gestalt.

To process the constituent phrases of a sentence, we adapted an architecture from Jordan (1986) that uses the output of previous processing as input on the next iteration (see Fig. 5.1). Each constituent is processed in turn to update the sentence gestalt. To process a constituent, it is first represented as a pattern of activation over the *current constituent* units. Activation from these units projects to the *intermediate combining* layer and combines with the activation from the *sentence gestalt* created as the result of processing the previous constituent. The actual implementation of this arrangement is to copy the activation from the *sentence gestalt* to the *previous sentence gestalt* units, and allow activation to feed forward from there. Activation in the intermediate layer then creates a new pattern of activation over the *sentence gestalt* units. The sentence gestalt, therefore, is not a superimposition of each constituent. Rather each new pattern in the sentence gestalt is computed through two layers of weights and represents the model's new best guess interpretation of the meaning of the sentence.

Each sentence constituent can be thought of as a surface role/filler pair. It consists of one unit indicating the surface role of the constituent and one unit

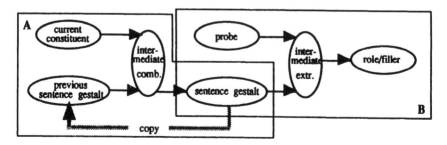

FIG. 5.1.   The architecture of the sentence gestalt network. The boxes highlight the functional parts: area A processes the constituents into the sentence gestalt, and area B processes the sentence gestalt into the output representation. There are 56 input units, 68 output units, 68 probe units, and 100 units in each of the hidden layers. Reproduced from St. John and McClelland (1990) with permission of the publisher, Elsevier Science Publishers BV.

representing each word in the constituent. There are four surface roles: pre-verbal, verbal, first-post-verbal, and other-post-verbal.

For the words in the input, there are units for each of 13 verbs, 31 nouns, 4 prepositions, 3 adverbs, and the auxiliary verb "was." Two of the ambiguous words have two verb meanings, three have two noun meanings, and two have a verb and a noun meaning. Six of the words are vague terms (e.g. someone, something, and food). See Appendix I for details. For prepositional phrases, the preposition and the noun are each represented by a unit in the input. For the verb constituent, the presence of the auxiliary verb "was" is likewise encoded by a separate unit. Articles are not represented, and nouns are assumed to be singular and definite throughout.

Several other models have used a type of sentence gestalt to represent a sentence. McClelland and Kawamoto (1986) used units that represented the conjunction of semantic features of the verb with the semantic features of a concept. To encode a sentence, the patterns of activity produced for each verb/concept conjunction were activated in a single pool of units that contained every possible conjunction. St. John and McClelland (1987) used a similar conjunctive representation to encode a number of sentences at once. These representations suffer from inefficiency and scale badly because so many units are required to represent all of the conjunctions. The current model's representation is far more efficient.

The model's efficiency comes from making the sentence gestalt a trainable, hidden-unit layer. Making the sentence gestalt trainable allows the network to create the primitives it needs to represent the sentence efficiently. Instead of having to represent every possible conjunction, only those conjunctions that are useful will be learned and added to the representation. Further, these primitives do not have to be conjunctions between the verb and a concept. A hidden layer could learn to represent conjunctions between the concepts themselves or other combinations of information if they were useful for solving its task.

Since a layer of hidden units cannot be trained by specifying its activation values explicitly, we invented a way of "decoding" the sentence gestalt into an output layer. Backpropagation (Rumelhart, Hinton, & Williams, 1986) can then be used to train the hidden layers.

The output layer represents the event as a set of thematic role and filler pairs. For example, the event described by "The pitcher threw the ball" would be represented as the set {agent/pitcher(ball-player), action/threw(toss), patient/ball(sphere)}. The words in parentheses designate the concepts to which the ambiguous words correspond.

The output layer can represent one role/filler pair at a time. To decode a particular role/filler pair, the sentence gestalt is probed with half of the pair, either the role or the filler. Activation from the *probe* and the *sentence gestalt* combine in the *intermediate extraction* layer, which in turn activates the entire role/filler pair in the output layer. The entire event can be decoded in this way by successively probing with each half of each pair.

The output has one unit for each of 9 possible thematic roles (e.g. agent, action, patient, instrument) and 1 unit for each of 45 concepts, including 28 noun concepts, 14 actions, and 3 adverbs. Additionally, there is a unit for the passive voice. Finally, there are 13 "feature" units, such as male, female, and adult. These units are included in the output to allow the demonstration of more subtle effects of constraints on interpretation (see Appendix I for the complete set of roles and concepts). This representation is not meant to be comprehensive. Instead, it is meant to provide a convenient way to train and demonstrate the processing abilities of the network. Any one role/filler pattern, then, consists of two parts. For the role, one of the nine role units should be active, and for the filler, a unit representing the concept, action, or adverb should be active. If relevant, some of the feature units or the passive voice unit should be active.

Environment and Training Regime.   Sentence/event pairs are created on-line during training from scaffoldings called sentence-frames. The sentence-frames specify which thematic roles and fillers can be used with a given action. Each of the 14 actions has a separate sentence-frame. Four of the actions, *kissed, shot, hit,* and *gave,* have additional frames to create passive voice sentences.

To create a sentence/event pair, an event description is generated, and then a sentence to describe that event is generated. The generation process creates events with different probabilities so that these events will be trained with different frequencies. For example, the generation process is more likely to generate a sentence/event pair about the bus driver eating steak than eating soup, so the bus driver eating steak will be more frequently trained.

The sentences are limited in complexity because of the limitations of the event representation. Namely, only one filler can be assigned to a thematic role in a particular sentence. Also, all the roles are assumed to belong to the sentence as a whole. Therefore, no embedded clauses or phrases attached to single constituents are allowed.

Although the sentences often include ambiguous or vague words, the events are always specific and complete. Each event consists of a specific action and each thematic role related to this action is filled by some specific concept. Accordingly, each event occurs in a particular location, and actions requiring an instrument always have a specific instrument.

Training consists of trials in which the network is presented with a sentence and the event it describes. The rationale is that the language learner experiences some event and then hears a sentence about it. The learner processes the sentence and compares the conceptual representation its comprehension mechanism produces to the conceptual representation it obtained from experiencing the event.

Discrepancies are used as feedback for the comprehension mechanism. The model's response to a role or filler probe is compared to the correct answer. The error between the two is used to modify the weights of the network using back propagation (Rumelhart et al., 1986). The error measure used is cross–entropy

(Hinton, 1989), where T_j is the target activation, and A_j is the output activation of unit j.

$$C = -\Sigma_j[T_j * \log_2(A_j) + (1-T_j) * \log_2(1-A_j)]$$

Cross-entropy is an appropriate error measure because its minimum is the conditional probability of each unit being fully active given the input constituents. Once the network is trained, the activation of each unit will represent the probability that that unit should be fully active given the sentence input at that point in the sentence.

To promote immediate processing, a special training regime is used. After each constituent has been processed, the network is trained to predict the set of role/filler pairs of the entire event. From the first constituent of the sentence, then, the model is forced to try to predict the entire event. This training regime assumes that the complete event is available to the learning procedure as soon as sentence processing begins, but it does not assume any special knowledge about which aspects of the event correspond to which sentence constituents. Of course, after processing only the first constituent, the model generally cannot guess the entire event correctly. By forcing it to try, this training procedure requires the model to discover the mapping between constituents and aspects of the event, as it forces the model to extract as much information as possible from each constituent. Consequently, as each new constituent is processed, the model's predictions of the event are refined to reflect the additional evidence it supplies.

The model was trained for 330,000 sentence trials until it began processing passive sentences correctly. The learning rate was 0.0005, and the momentum was 0.9. The weights were updated after every 60 sentence trials.

An illustration of processing.   An example of how a trained network processes a sentence will help illustrate how the model works. To process the sentence, "The teacher ate the soup," the constituents of the sentence are processed in turn. As each constituent is processed, the network performs a type of pattern completion. The model tries to predict the entire event by augmenting the information supplied by the constituents processed so far with additional information that correlates with the information supplied by the constituents.

With each additional constituent, the model's predictions improve. Early in the sentence, many possible events are consistent with what little is known about the sentence so far. The completion process activates each of these alternatives slightly, according to their support. As more constituents are processed, the additional evidence supports fewer possible events more strongly.

The pattern of activation over the sentence gestalt can be observed directly, and responses to probes can be examined, to see what it is representing after processing each constituent of the sentence (see Fig. 5.2). After processing the first constituent, "The teacher," of our example sentence, the network assumes the sentence is in the active voice and therefore assigns *teacher* to the agent role.

The teacher ate the soup.

Sentence Gestalt Activations

unit	#1	#2	#3
1			
2			
3			
4			
5			
6			
7			
8			
9			
10			
11			
12			
13			
14			
15			
16			
17			
18			
19			
20			
21			
22			
23			
24			
25			

Role/Filler Activations

	#1	#2	#3
agent			
person			
adult			
male			
female			
bus driver			
teacher			
action			
consumed			
ate			
gave			
threw(host)			
drove(motiv.)			
patient			
person			
adult			
child			
female			
schoolgirl			
thing			
food			
ball(party)			
steak			
soup			
crackers			

FIG. 5.2. The evolution of the sentence gestalt during processing. On the left, the activation of part of the sentence gestalt is shown after each sentence constituent has been processed. On the right, the activation of selected output units is shown when the evolving gestalt is probed with each role. The #s correspond to the number of constituents that have been presented to the network at that point. #1 means the network has seen "The teacher;" #2 means it has seen "The teacher ate;" etc. The activations (ranging between 0 and 1) are depicted as the darkened area of each box. Reproduced from St. John and McClelland (1990) with permission of the publishers, Elsevier Science Publishers BV.

The network also fills in the semantic features of teachers (person, adult, and female) according to its previous experience with teachers. When probed with the action role, the network weakly activates a number of possible actions that the teacher typically performs. The network similarly makes guesses about the other roles for which it is probed.

When the second constituent, "ate," is processed, the sentence gestalt is refined to represent the new information. In addition to representing both that *teacher* is the agent and that *ate* is the action, the network is able to make better guesses about the other roles. For example, it infers that the patient is food. Since, in the network's experience, teachers typically eat soup, the network produces activation corresponding to the inference that the food is *soup*. After the third constituent is processed, the network has settled on an interpretation of the sentence. The thematic roles are represented with their appropriate fillers.

Sentence Gestalt Model Results

Overall Performance.   First, the overall performance of the network will be evaluated. Then, the processing of an example sentence that incorporates most of the characteristics of the model will be presented. Finally, the model's ability to generalise will be examined.

Once the model was able to process correctly both active and passive sentences, the simulation was stopped and evaluated. Correct processing was defined as activating the correct units more strongly than the incorrect units. After 330,000 random sentence trials, the model began processing the passive sentences in the corpus correctly.

One measure of performance is the number of times an output unit that should be on is more active than an output unit that should be off. The idea behind this measure is that as long as the correct unit within any set, such as people or gender, is the most active, it can win a competition with the other units in that set. Checking that all of the correct units are more active than any of the incorrect units is a quick, and conservative, way of calculating this measure. In 55 unambiguous sentences generated randomly from the corpus, an incorrect unit was more active in 14 out of the 1710 possible cases, or on 0.8% of the opportunities. Overall, then, the model processes sentences 99.2% correctly.

The 14 errors were distributed over 8 of the 55 sentences. In 5 of the 8 sentences, the error involved the incorrect instantiation of the specific concept or a feature of that concept referred to by a vague word. Two involved the incorrect activation of the concept representing a non-vague word. In each case, the incorrect concept was similar to the correct concept.

Therefore, errors were not random; they involved the misactivation of a similar concept or the misactivation of a feature of a similar concept. The errors in the remaining sentence involved the incorrect assignment of thematic roles in a passive, reversible sentence: "Someone hit the pitcher."

Performance on Specific Tasks.   Our specific interest was to develop a processor that could perform several important language comprehension tasks correctly. Five typical sentences were drawn from the corpus to test each processing task. The categories and one example sentence for each are presented in Table 5.1. The parentheses denote the implicit, to be inferred, role.

The model performed correctly on each example sentence in each category. To illustrate the model's processing abilities we will first present two examples that demonstrate the model's ability to assign thematic roles correctly. Then, we will present a detailed processing example that demonstrates the model's ability to instantiate vague words, infer additional thematic roles, and change its interpretation as each new constituent is processed.

Role assignment is divided into four sub-categories based on the type of information available to help assign the correct thematic roles to constituents.

TABLE 5.1
Task Categories

Category	Example
Role assignment	
Active semantic	The schoolgirl stirred the kool-aid with a spoon.
Active syntactic	The bus driver gave the rose to the teacher.
Passive semantic	The ball was hit by the pitcher.
Passive syntactic	The bus driver was given the rose by the teacher.
Word ambiguity	The pitcher hit the bat with the bat.
Concept instantiation	The teacher kissed someone.
Role elaboration	The teacher ate the soup (with a spoon).

Sentences in the semantic groups contain semantic information that can help assign roles. In the example from Table 5.1, of the concepts referred to in the sentence, only the schoolgirl can play the role of an agent of stirring. The network can therefore use that semantic information to assign schoolgirl to the agent role. Similarly, kool-aid is something that can be stirred, but cannot stir or be used to stir something else. After an entire sentence was processed, the sentence gestalt was probed with the filler half of each role/filler pair. The network then had to complete the pair by filling in the correct thematic role. For each pair, in each sentence, the unit representing the correct role was the most active. Sentences in the passive semantic category are processed equally well. Of course the semantic knowledge necessary to perform this task is never provided in the input or programmed into the network. Instead, it must be developed internally in the sentence gestalt as the network learns to process sentences.

To process sentences in the active and passive syntactic categories, however, the network cannot rely entirely on semantic constraints to assign thematic roles. Sentences in these categories were created by including in the corpus pairs of reversible events, such as "the bus driver gave a rose to the teachers," and "the teacher gave a rose to the bus driver." Both of these events were trained with equal frequency. Without a difference in frequency, there is no semantic regularity to help predict which of the two events is more likely. The model must rely on syntactic information, such as word order, to assign the thematic roles. Passive sentences further complicate processing by making word order, by itself, unpredictive. The past participle and the "by" preposition provide cues designating the passive, but in themselves do not cue which person plays which role. The word order information must be used in conjunction with the passive cues to determine the correct role assignments.

When sentences in the syntactic categories were tested, for each role/filler pair in each test sentence, the correct role was the most active. Figure 5.3 provides an example of role assignment in the semantic and syntactic categories.

The schoolgirl stirred the kool-aid with a spoon.

agent ■	agent ☐	agent ☐	agent ☐
action ☐	action ■	action ☐	action ☐
patient ☐	patient ☐	patient ■	patient ☐
instrument ☐	instrument ☐	instrument ☐	instrument ■
location ☐	location ☐	location ☐	location ☐
co-agent ☐	co-agent ☐	co-agent ☐	co-agent ☐
co-patient ☐	co-patient ☐	co-patient ☐	co-patient ☐
recipient ☐	recipient ☐	recipient ☐	recipient ☐
schoolgirl	**stirred**	**kool-aid**	**spoon**

The busdriver was given the rose by the teacher.

agent ☐	agent ☐	agent ☐	agent ■
action ☐	action ■	action ☐	action ☐
patient ☐	patient ☐	patient ■	patient ☐
instrument ☐	instrument ☐	instrument ☐	instrument ☐
location ☐	location ☐	location ☐	location ☐
co-agent ☐	co-agent ☐	co-agent ☐	co-agent ☐
co-patient ☐	co-patient ☐	co-patient ☐	co-patient ☐
recipient ■	recipient ☐	recipient ☐	recipient ☐
bus driver	**was given**	**rose(noun)**	**teacher**

FIG. 5.3.   Role assignment. After a sentence is processed, the network is probed with the filler half of each role/filler pair. The activation over a subset of the thematic role units is displayed. The first sentence contains semantic information useful for role assignment, whereas the second sentence contains only syntactic information useful for role assignment. The activations (ranging between 0 and 1) are depicted as the darkened area of each box. Reproduced from St. John and McClelland (1990) with permission of the publishers, Elsevier Science Publishers BV.

A detailed example of processing demonstrates the remaining comprehension phenomena. The model was presented with the sentence "The adult ate the steak with daintiness." Immediate update works by having the model update its interpretation of the whole sentence after each constituent is processed. As each constituent is processed, the information it conveys modifies the sentence gestalt and strengthens the inferences it supports. But the beginning of a sentence may not always accurately predict its eventual full meaning. For example, in "The adult ate the steak with daintiness," the identity of the adult is initially unknown. After "The adult ate" has been processed, *bus driver* and *teacher* are equally active (see Fig. 5.4). After processing "The adult ate the steak," the model guesses that the agent is the *bus driver* since steak is typically eaten by bus drivers. At this point, the model has sufficient information to instantiate "the adult" to be the *bus driver*. Along with this inference, *gusto* is inferred as the manner of eating, since bus drivers eat with gusto. Here the model demonstrates its ability to infer additional thematic roles.

The adult ate the steak with daintiness.

Sentence Gestalt Activations					Role/Filler Activations				
unit	#1	#2	#3	#4		#1	#2	#3	#4
1					**agent**				
2					person				
3					adult				
4					child				
5					male				
6					female				
7					bus driver				
8					teacher				
9					**action**				
10					ate				
11					shot				
12					drove(trans)				
13					drove(motiv)				
14					**patient**				
15					person				
16					adult				
17					child				
18					bus driver				
19					schoolgirl				
20					thing				
21					food				
22					steak				
23					soup				
24					crackers				
25					**adverb**				
26					gusto				
27					pleasure				
28					daintiness				

FIG. 5.4. The sequential processing of a garden-path sentence. After "the steak" has been processed, the network instantiates "the adult" with the concept *bus driver*. When "with daintiness" is processed, network must interpret "the adult" to mean *teacher*. Reproduced from St. John and McClelland (1990) with permission of the publishers, Elsevier Science Publishers BV.

The model has, at this point, been led down the garden path toward an ultimately incorrect interpretation of the sentence. The next constituent processed, "with daintiness," only fits with the teacher and the schoolgirl.

Since the sentence specifies an adult, the agent must be the *teacher*. The model must revise its representation of the event to fit with the new information by de-activating *bus driver* and activating *teacher*.

In general, as each constituent is processed, the information it conveys explicitly is added to the representation of the sentence along with implicit information implied by the constituent in the current situation. When the evidence is ambiguous and supports many conflicting inferences (such as after "The adult ate" has been processed), all the inferences are weakly activated in the sentence gestalt. When new evidence suggests a different interpretation, the sentence gestalt is revised.

Generalisation.   An important remaining question is whether the model is actually learning useful constraints that it can apply to novel sentences or whether it is simply memorising sentence/event pairs.

Generalisation occurs when a regularity is exploited and applied to novel cases. We can test the model's ability to exploit different types of regularities. To this end, separate corpora were developed to test the model's ability to generalise syntactic and semantic regularities. The model was trained and evaluated on each corpus separately.

For syntax, we tested the model's ability to learn and use the syntax of active and passive sentences. Could the model learn to use the active/passive voice markers and the temporal order of the constituents, word order, productively on novel sentences? This is a test of compositionality. The model must learn to compose the familiar constituents of sentences in new combinations. To perform this generalisation task, the model must learn several types of information. First, it must learn the concept referred to by each word in a sentence: "John" refers to *John* and "saw" refers to *saw*. Second, the model must learn that the order of the constituents, which constituent comes before the verb and which after, is important in assigning the agent and patient. Third, the model must learn the relevance of the passive markers: the past participle of the verb and the prepositional phrase beginning with "by." Fourth, the model must learn to integrate the order information and the passive marker information to assign the thematic roles correctly.

The model was trained on a corpus of sentences composed of 10 people and 10 reversible actions, such as "John saw Mary." These sentences could appear either in the active or passive voice. The basic corpus consisted of all 2000 sentences (10 people by 10 actions by 10 people by 2 voices). Before training began, though, 250 of these sentences (12.5%) were set aside for later testing: They were not trained. The model was then trained on the remaining sentences. Once the training corpus was mastered (after 100,000 trials), the 250 test sentences were presented to the model. The model processed 97% of these sentences correctly. In only 11 sentences did the model incorrectly assign a thematic role. In these sentences, when probed with one of the fillers, the model activated an incorrect role more strongly than the correct role.

Semantic regularities may also provide the basis for generalisation. We tested the model's ability to learn some semantic regularities and apply them in novel contexts. There are two basic generalisation effects we would like to see in the model's behaviour. First, as with syntax, the trained model should exhibit compositionality: The model should be able to represent successfully sentences it has never seen before. Secondly, the model should make predictions: It should be able to use information presented early in a sentence to help it process subsequent information.

To test these generalisation effects, we again created a simple corpus for the model to learn. This corpus consisted of 8 adults and 8 children, 5 actions, and

8 objects for each action. The corpus was arranged to make age a semantic regularity. For each action, 3 objects were presented with adults, 3 were presented with children, and 2 were presented with both adults and children. This arrangement created a corpus of 400 sentences (8 adults by 5 actions by 5 objects plus 8 children by 5 actions by 5 objects). For example:

George watched the news.	Bobby watched He-Man.
George watched Johnny Carson.	Bobby watched Smurfs.
George watched David Letterman.	Bobby Watched Mighty Mouse.
George watched Star Trek.	Bobby watched Star Trek.
George watched the Road Runner.	Bobby watched the Road Runner.

The regularity is that the age of the agent, in conjunction with the verb, predicts a set of objects. Age, though, is not explicitly encoded in the input or the output representations. Instead, it is a "hidden" feature. The model must learn which agents are the adults and which are the children based on its experience seeing the objects with which each is paired. The children all watch one set of shows, and the adults all watch another set. Age, therefore, organises the sentences into sets. Since age does not appear in the input, however, it must be induced by the model and accessed as each sentence is processed.

Before the model was trained on the corpus of sentences, 50 of the 400 sentences (12.5%) were randomly picked to be set aside as the generalisation set. The model was then trained on the remaining sentences. When these sentences were processed correctly (after 90,000 trials), the model was tested for compositional and predictive generalisation.

Again, to be compositional, the model should be able to process correctly the sentences on which it has not been trained. The model processed 86% of these sentences correctly. On the remaining 14%, or 7 sentences, the model activated the wrong object more strongly than it activated the correct object. At the point in training when the model was stopped, then, it could compose novel sentences reasonably well.

Semantic organisation should allow the model to predict subsequent information. There are two types of regularities that the model should discover to help make predictions. One is the general regularity that children do children's activities and that adults do adult activities. To test the learning of this regularity we observed which objects the model predicted after the model had processed the agent and action. Given an agent and an action, the model should predict the objects appropriate for that action and an agent of that age. For example, given the partial sentence, "Bobby watched . . . ," the model should predict the object to be either He-Man, Smurfs, Mighty Mouse, the Road Runner, or Star Trek. Specifically, this regularity suggests that the model should activate each of these objects $\frac{1}{5}$ or 0.2.

What makes this a generalisation task is that some of the sentences in the corpus were set aside and not trained: Some agents were never paired with certain objects. For example, the network was never trained on the sentence, "Bobby watched He-Man." To activate each object in the age appropriate set to 0.2, the model must generalise. It must generalise both to discover the complete set of five children's shows, and to associate that set to each of the eight children. This generalisation can be tested by observing whether He-Man is activated as a predicted object for "Bobby watched . . ."

The other type of regularity is specific to each agent. The fact that the training corpus does not contain, "Bobby watched He-Man," is also a regularity that the model can learn. It learns that it should not predict He-Man as an object for "Bobby watched . . ." Since, for Bobby, there are only four shows that he actually watches, each should be given an activation level of $\frac{1}{4}$ or 0.25. The model's tendency to generalise by using the general regularity about children's viewing habits, therefore, is counteracted by the specific regularity about Bobby's personal viewing habits. The activation of the appropriate/untrained (e.g. He-Man for Bobby) objects should be a compromise between the two competing forces. The appropriate/untrained objects, then, should have an activation somewhat less than 0.2. For the appropriate/trained (e.g. Mighty Mouse for Bobby) objects, the activation level should lie between 0.2 and 0.25, and the activation level for the inappropriate/untrained (e.g. the news for Bobby) objects should be close to 0.

The model's predictions on each of the five actions for four of the people in the corpus were tabulated. The activation values for the model's object predictions were categorised into three groups: the appropriate/trained, the appropriate/untrained, and the inappropriate/untrained. The average activation in each group is shown in Table 5.2. The means are significantly different from one another.

Three conclusions can be drawn from these data. One, the appropriate/ trained objects are activated to the appropriate degree. The model correctly predicts the correct set of objects for the action and the age of the agent. Two, the model generalises in that it also activates age-correct objects it has not actually seen in that context before. The substantially weaker activation of these appropriate/untrained objects demonstrates the competition between the

TABLE 5.2
Semantic Prediction

	Trained	Untrained
Appropriate	0.210	0.036
Inappropriate	—	0.006

general and specific regularities. The general regularity activates the objects, but the agent-specific regularities reduce that activation. Three, the set of inappropriate/untrained objects for each action are turned off.

The difference in activation between the appropriate/untrained and inappropriate/untrained objects understates their difference in the network. As the activation of a unit approaches 1 or 0, the nonlinearity of the activation function requires that exponentially more activation be added to move closer to 1 or 0. A large change in the net input, therefore, would be required to reduce the activation level of an appropriate/untrained object to that of an inappropriate/untrained object. Consequently, the two types of objects are substantially different, and the general regularity is having a significant impact on prediction.

Interestingly, there is a trade-off during training between compositional generalisation and predictive generalisation. During training the model improves its ability to compose novel sentences, but loses the ability to make general predictions. The general predictions are lost as the model learns the specific regularities of the training corpus. Compositionality is gained as the input constituents become lexeme-like. As the network trains, it slowly learns which parts of the input are responsible for which parts of the output. The network slowly hones the meanings of the input constituents until they are essentially represented as lexemes.

The model's training procedure encourages predictive generalisation for both types of regularities by requiring the model explicitly to predict the object after processing the agent and action. Recall that the model must answer questions about the entire sentence after processing each constituent. The model learns that all of the untrained objects, both appropriate and inappropriate, should not be predicted because they never occur.

It may seem that the model diverges from human behaviour as it reduces the influence of the general regularity in favour of the person-specific regularities. It must be remembered, though, that the model is trained on a set of only 16 people. If there were many more people, the person-specific regularities would receive less practice and the general regularity would receive more practice. This change would make the age generalisation much stronger.

The model can clearly learn and apply regularities productively from its training corpus to novel sentences. However, the degree to which the model composes novel sentences, 97% in the syntactic corpus, but only 86% in the semantic corpus, is far from the degree we expect from people. Again, this performance may be due to the size and content of the corpus. The effects of these factors on generalisation are not well understood. Our simulation should be taken only as an indication that some degree of compositionality can be acquired.

As demonstrated by learning the rule for the passive voice construction, it can learn syntactic regularities, and as demonstrated by learning the meaning of each word and the hidden-feature age, it can learn semantic regularities.

Generalisation based on these regularities takes two forms. When the regularity consists of input/output pairings, generalisation leads to compositionality. Input/output pairings are like lexemes in that the specific input constrains a specific part of the output. There are few, if any, constraints on other parts of the output. Lexemes will compose in novel combinations easily because each one makes a separate and independent contribution to the interpretation.

When the regularity consists of input/input pairings, generalisation can lead to prediction. For input/input pairings, one part of the input affects multiple parts of the output. Some of the parts may be future constituents, so the input, in effect, predicts future inputs. These input/input pairings may not compose easily. The parts may make mutually contradictory predictions. For example, in "Bobby watched the news," "Bobby" predicts that *the news* will not be watched, and "the news" predicts that *Bobby*, a child, will not be watching. These contradictory predictions will create conflict in the sentence gestalt and make the interpretation hard to represent.

Additionally, a novel pairing may not compose easily because the constraints specific to a pair may not have been learned. In other words, there may be constraints, in the environment, that pertain to a pair of input constituents. If the model has never experienced this pair, it cannot know these constraints, and they will not affect the interpretation.

Discussion of the SG Model

The SG model has been quite successful in meeting the goals that we set out for it, but it is of course far from being the final word on sentence comprehension. Here we briefly review the model's accomplishments. Following this review, we consider some of its limitations and how they might be addressed by further work.

Accomplishments of the Model. One of the principle successes of the SG model is that it correctly assigns constituents to thematic roles, based on syntactic and semantic constraints. Though syntactic constraints can be significantly more subtle than those our model has faced thus far, those it has faced are fairly difficult. To handle active and passive sentences correctly, the model must map surface constituents on to different roles depending on the presence of various surface features elsewhere in the sentence.

The model also exhibits considerable capacity to use context to disambiguate meanings and to instantiate vague terms in contextually appropriate ways.

Indeed, it is probably most appropriate to view the model as treating each constituent in a sentence as a clue or set of clues that constrain the overall event description, rather than as treating each constituent as a lexical item with a particular meaning. Although each clue may provide stronger constraints on some aspects of the event description than on others, it is simply not the case that the meaning associated with the part of the event designated by each constituent is conveyed by only that constituent itself.

The model likewise infers unspecified arguments roughly to the extent that they can be predicted reliably from the context. Here we see very clearly that constituents of an event description can be cued without being specifically designated by any constituent of the sentence. These inferences are graded to reflect the degree to which they are appropriate given the set of clues provided. The drawing of these inferences is also completely intrinsic to the basic comprehension process: No special, separate inference processes must be spawned to make inferences; they simply occur implicitly as the constituents of the sentence are processed.

The model demonstrates the capacity to update its representation as each new constituent is encountered. Our demonstration of this aspect of the model's performance is somewhat informal; nevertheless, its capabilities seem impressive. As each constituent is encountered, the interpretation of all aspects of the event description is subject to change. If we revert to thinking in terms of meanings of particular constituents, both prior and subsequent context can influence the interpretation of each constituent.

Unlike most conventional sentence processing models, the ability to exploit subsequent context is again an intrinsic part of the process of interpreting each new constituent. There is no backtracking; rather, the representation of the sentence is simply updated to reflect the constraints imposed by each constituent as it is encountered.

The gradual, incremental learning capabilities of the network underlie its ability to solve the bootstrapping problem, that is, to learn simultaneously about both the syntax and semantics of constituents. The problem of learning syntax and semantics is central for developmental psycholinguistics. Naigles, Gleitman, and Gleitman (1987, p. 3) state that learning syntax and semantics only from statistical information seems impossible because, "at a minimum, it would require such extensive storage and manipulation of contingently categorised event/conversation pairs as to be unrealistic." Yet it is exactly by using such information that our model solves the problem. The model learns the syntax and semantics of the training corpus simultaneously. Across training trials, the model gradually learns which aspects of the event description each constituent of the input constrains and in what ways it constrains these aspects.

We do not want to overstate the case here, since the child learning a language confronts a considerably more complex version of these problems than our model does. Our sentences are pre-segmented into constituents, are very simple in structure, and are much fewer in number than the sentences a child would hear. However, the results demonstrate that the bootstrapping problem might ultimately be overcome by an extension of the present approach.

Many of the accomplishments of the SG model are shared by predecessors. Cottrell (1985), Cottrell and Small (1983), Waltz and Pollack (1985), and

McClelland and Kawamoto (1986) have all demonstrated the use of syntactic and semantic constraints in role assignment and meaning disambiguation. Of these, the first three embodied the immediate update principle, but did not learn, while the fourth learned in a limited way, and had a fixed set of input slots.

The greater learning capability of our model allows it to find connection strengths that encode the constraints embodied in the corpus, without requiring the modeller to induce these constraints or try to build them in by hand. It also allows the model to construct its own representations in the sentence gestalt, and this ability allows these representations to be considerably more compact than in other cases.

Finally, the model is able to generalise the processing knowledge it has learned to novel sentences. Generalisation can come in two varieties: compositional generalisation and predictive generalisation. Compositional generalisation occurs when the model has learned the constraints on sentence interpretation contributed by each element of the sentence, including both syntax and semantics, and has learned how to combine that information in novel sequences.

The second variety of generalisation is predictive generalisation. This occurs when the model can use a regularity to predict upcoming sentence constituents. In the semantic generalisation experiment, the model learned regularities about the age of agents in the corpus. The model then used these regularities to predict appropriate objects.

Deficiencies and Limitations of the Model.   The model has several limitations. It only addresses a limited number of language phenomena: It does not address quantification, reference and co-reference, co-ordinate constructions, or many other phenomena. Perhaps the most important limitation is the limitation on the complexity of the sentences, and of the events that they describe. The model can only process single-clause sentences. In general, it is necessary to characterise the surface roles and fillers of sentences with respect to their superordinate constituents.

Similarly, in complex events there may be more than one actor, each performing an action in a different sub-event of the overall event or action. Representing these structures requires head/role/filler triples instead of simple role/filler pairs.

One solution is to train the model using triples rather than pairs as the sentence and event constituents. The difficulty lies in specifying the nonsentence members of the triples. These nonsentence members would stand for entire structures. Thus they would be very much like the patterns that we are currently using as sentence gestalts. It would be desirable to have the learning procedure induce these representations, but this is a bootstrapping problem that we have not yet attempted to solve.

Another limitation is the small size of the corpus used in training the model. Given the length of time required for training, one might be somewhat pessimistic about the possibility that a network of this kind could master a substantial corpus. However, it should be noted that the extent to which learning time grows with corpus size is extremely hard to predict for connectionist models, and is highly problem-dependent. For some problems (e.g. parity), learning time per pattern increases more than linearly with the number of training patterns (Tesauro, 1987), whereas for other problems (e.g. negation), learning time per pattern can actually decrease as the number of patterns increases (Rumelhart, 1987).

Where the current problem falls in this continuum is not yet known. A comparison of the learning times between the general corpus and the syntactic corpus used in the generalisation experiments, however, is suggestive. The network required 660,000 trials to learn the 120 events in the general corpus (330,000 trials to learn all but the most irregular events). On the other hand, the network required only 100,000 trials to learn the 2000 events of the syntactic corpus. The syntactic corpus, of course, is extremely regular, and the regularities are compositional. Given the model's good generalisation results on the syntactic corpus, it is possible that the model will scale well to very large corpora if their regularities are composable.

STORY COMPREHENSION

Some aspects of story comprehension can also be viewed as constraint satisfaction problems. The resolution of pronouns and the inference of missing propositions are both problems where constraints from the context are used to compute an interpretation. Parallel constraint satisfaction, therefore, can usefully be applied to story comprehension.

Processing a story is similar to processing a sentence. Each sentence of a story is read sequentially, and it is used immediately to provide additional constraints on the meaning of the story. This similarity to individual sentence comprehension suggests that constraint satisfaction, as embodied in the sentence gestalt model, would be useful for story comprehension.

In fact, Miikkulainen and Dyer (1989) developed a model that learns to process a text into a script-like representation (it can also generate a paraphrase of the text from this representation). The model uses a network similar to the sentence gestalt model to process words sequentially into a propositional representation. Another network with the same architecture then processes the propositions sequentially into a simple script representation. Miikkulainen and Dyer have demonstrated that this architecture can infer missing propositions. These propositions are inferred to the degree that they are supported by the information in the text. Their architecture should also be able to resolve pronouns and revise its interpretation.

One limitation of their model, however, is that it must be provided with a representation for stories, though it learns its own representations for individual concepts. An important ability of the model introduced here is that it learns its story representation for itself.

We now discuss some important aspects of story comprehension in more detail and suggest how the sentence gestalt model can be extended to address them.

Story Comprehension Issues

Pronoun Resolution. Pronouns create substantial ambiguity in text. When referring to people, they provide only gender information, which may or may not be helpful in finding their referents. The pragmatics of discourse, however, dictate that pronouns can only be used when the referent can easily be inferred, so there must be information in the text to help resolve the pronoun. This information constrains the interpretation of the text to the point that only the correct referent assignment is possible. For example in, "Fred picked up the frisbee. He threw it to Betty," the pronoun constrains the agent to be a male individual, and the remainder of the text constrains Betty to be the recipient, thereby ruling her out from being the agent of throwing.

The model should be able to combine the evidence from each of the available constraints to find the best supported interpretation.

Proposition Inference. Inferred propositions can be divided into two categories. Coherence inferences are drawn to explain or justify the text, and prediction inferences are drawn to predict additional information, such as future actions, that fit the story context. Potts, Keenan, and Golding (1988) found that coherence inferences are activated as fully as explicit propositions. Potts et al.'s subjects would read a paragraph of text and then name aloud a target word that described either a coherence inference or an explicit proposition. For both types of targets, naming time was equally well facilitated. Potts et al. concluded that the coherence inferences were fully inferred as the subjects read the paragraphs.

Our explanation for the full activation of coherence inferences is that the text provides substantial evidence for them. Consider the following pair of sentences.

Jolene raced down the track ahead of her rivals.
The judge handed her the trophy.

Having read the second sentence, it is reasonable to infer that Jolene won the race. Causal antecedents are strongly associated to their outcome, so once the outcome is known, the causal antecedents must be true, and so are easily inferred.

Predictive information can also be inferred. Evidence that prediction inferences are drawn during reading has been found by Graesser (1981) and

Millis, Morgan, and Graesser (in press). Graesser had one group of subjects answer *how*, *why*, and *what next* questions as they read through short narrative texts. Graesser then calculated the number of new inferences produced by each sentence and the likelihood that each sentence confirmed a prior expectation.

Different subjects then read the texts, and their sentence reading times were recorded. Graesser found that the more prediction inferences a sentence elicited, the slower it was read, and he found that the more likely it was that a sentence confirmed a prior inference, the faster it was read. Both of these results support the conclusion that readers draw prediction inferences as they read. Millis et al. found similar results for expository texts.

Though predictive inferences seem to be inferred well enough to affect reading times, they do not appear to be inferred as strongly as coherence inferences. Whereas coherence inferences have sufficient evidence supporting them to become fully activated, prediction inferences typically have much less support. This weak support leads to the weak activation of the predicted information. Both McKoon and Ratcliff (1986) and Potts et al. (1988) have investigated how active prediction inferences become. McKoon and Ratcliff found that even well-predicted actions, such as dying after a 14-storey fall, are only weakly inferred. Like Potts et al., they had subjects read paragraphs describing some event, and name a target word after the paragraph. They found that target words describing the predicted actions were only weakly facilitated, and concluded that they were only weakly inferred.

Potts et al. found no facilitation and concluded that there was no evidence that the predicted inferences were inferred. The method these experiments employed may underestimate the degree of activation of these inferences, but it seems clear that they are not activated as strongly as coherence inferences.

Given the available empirical evidence, it seems reasonable to conclude that inferences are drawn roughly to the degree the text supports them. Prediction inferences, which are typically not strongly supported, are drawn only weakly. Coherence inferences, with their much stronger textual support, are drawn fully. Models of text comprehension should incorporate a mechanism that uses the degree of support provided by the text to determine the activation level of inferences.

Two well-known algorithms for text comprehension are good at inferring coherence inferences, but cannot activate prediction inferences partially. Schank and Abelson's (1977) script understander and Wilensky's (1983) plan understander have as one of their central goals the ability to draw coherence inferences. Schank and Abelson's model draws coherence inferences by instantiating a script. As text is matched to actions in a script, the missing actions are filled in from the script. These inferred actions are added to the developing representation in an all-or-none fashion, so inferred actions are as active as explicit actions.

Wilensky's model draws coherence inferences by attempting to explain each new proposition in terms of the previous text. It searches backward in a semantic network for a plan or motive to connect the text. For instance, if the current proposition is an action, the model tries to determine how it helps implement a previously mentioned plan. If this procedure fails, the model will try to infer an appropriate plan that fits with a previously mentioned motive. Once the current proposition is explained, missing actions can be filled in. Again, propositions are added to an all-or-none fashion, so they are all fully activated. In both of these models, inference-making is a process separate from the bottom-up processing of the text. Inference-making occurs after the explicit text has been processed.

Although these procedures work well for coherence inferences, they do not allow prediction inferences to be drawn and activated partially. The representations do not allow levels of activation: Inferences must be drawn fully or not drawn at all. Since it would not be sensible to activate a large number of predictions fully, especially when contradictory predictions can be made, Schank and Abelson's (1977) model and Wilensky's (1983) model make only very conservative prediction inferences, if any.

In parallel constraint satisfaction, inference-making is conceived of differently. As in sentence comprehension, inference-making is inherent to processing the explicit text. The combined set of constraints from the text are used as evidence to support an interpretation that best satisfies the strongest and the most constraints from the text. Each part of the text supports many aspects of the interpretation. A specific proposition, therefore, will constrain the interpretation to represent the information it contains explicitly, and also constrain it, to varying degrees, to represent correlated information. All of this correlated information constitutes inferences.

The reader's hope is that by the end of the story, sufficient constraints have been provided by the text for a complete interpretation to be computed. The interpretation would, at that point, contain fully activated coherence inferences, partially activated prediction inferences, and resolved pronouns.

Interpretation Revision.   Finally, readers revise their interpretations when new information makes their old interpretations unlikely. Rumelhart (1981) asked subjects questions about their interpretation as they read the following story.

> Business had been slow since the oil crisis. Nobody seemed to want anything really elegant anymore. Suddenly the door opened and a well-dressed man entered the showroom floor. John put on his friendliest and most sincere expression and walked toward the man.

Rumelhart found that after reading the first sentence, his subjects held a variety of interpretations. As additional sentences were read, his subjects changed their interpretations, until after reading the final sentence, most subjects agreed that the story was about a car salesman. New information from the text changes the amount of support for the current interpretation of the text. For example, after reading the first sentence, some subjects believed the text was about gas stations. The second sentence, though, does not fit this interpretation: Gas stations have little to do with elegance. For some subjects, the second sentence provided enough evidence to change the interpretation to something other than gas stations. For others, it merely weakened the gas station interpretation. This process of evaluation and revision is a ubiquitous aspect of comprehension.

Neither Schank and Abelson's (1977), nor Wilensky's (1983) model revises its interpretations. Because these models' knowledge bases do not represent the likelihood or frequency of sets of actions, any alternative, if represented, is as good as any other. Consequently, it is difficult to weight alternatives according to their support from the text or their likelihood given background.

One consequence of these models' inability to evaluate their interpretations is that they do not revise their interpretations in light of new evidence. In Wilensky's model, each new proposition must be explained immediately. This model, then, will fall victim to any initially ambiguous text, such as Rumelhart's, as it attempts to explain new propositions in light of an initial faulty interpretation.

Schank and Abelson's model minimises this problem by committing itself to a particular script only after evidence from the text is rather strong. Their model does, then, evaluate its interpretation in this limited sense: It must see two mentions of a script before it commits itself to that script. Once committed, however, it cannot make revisions. New text that is difficult to assimilate into the script is interpreted as the beginning of a new script. Also, by waiting to commit to an interpretation, the model fails to make any initial interpretation.

On the other hand, a parallel constraint satisfaction model can evaluate its interpretation based on the strength with which the constraints support that interpretation. The strength of support can be observed in how strongly elements of the interpretation are activated. Early in a text, there may be little support for any interpretation. This condition will be manifest in the weak activation of possible interpretations. As text-based support for an interpretation grows, that interpretation will become more active. Further evidence may also revise the interpretation to one that is better supported by the combination of new and old evidence.

The constraints in a parallel constraint satisfaction model can represent the likelihood of information. Interpretations can then be activated according to their degree of support from the text and their likelihood to occur. Importantly, a parallel constraint satisfaction model evaluates the whole interpretation: How well the ensemble of propositions fits together. The many interdependencies throughout the representation affect the support for each part interactively. Wilensky's inference-making algorithm, however, requires only that individual propositions from the text be connected, by some cause or motive, to previous text. A problematic text can, therefore, be interpreted as a series of locally coherent, but globally inconsistent, explanations. In a parallel constraint satisfaction model, inconsistent constraints would compete and thereby lower the model's evaluation of its interpretation. By allowing all of the evidence from the text to bear on the whole interpretation as each proposition is processed, a globally consistent interpretation is more likely to be found.

Representation of Multiple Propositions. Stories also have certain structural properties that must be addressed by a model of story comprehension. Stories are composed of a number of propositions, and it is important that the elements of these propositions do not become confused. The bindings between concepts and the thematic roles they play, however, are easily lost. In Charniak's (1983) semantic processor, for example, an interpretation is computed by having each concept in each proposition serve as a source node in a semantic network. Markers are spread through the network, and by tracing back from where they meet, an interpretation can be retrieved. This procedure treats the simple concepts as constraints and searches for an interpretation that satisfies them. But this procedure will create confusion because the concepts are not bound to their thematic roles in their respective propositions. Charniak provides an example. "John wanted to commit suicide. A rope fell down on Fred." One of several paths the marker passer will discover is: John—suicide—rope—hang—John. Rejecting this faulty interpretation requires substantial additional processing.

In parallel constraint satisfaction, there are no such limits on the complexity of the constraints. Constraints, for example, can embody the conjunction of a concept and a thematic role so that who did what does not become confused in the computation of an interpretation. Constraints can also encode conjunctions of a concept and an action so that concepts from different propositions will not be confused. With these more complex constraints, these faulty interpretations will not be computed.

Knowledge sharing. When reading a story, people are often reminded of past events that share some qualities with the current event. When visiting a doctor, people are reminded of previous visits to doctors. More interestingly, people can be reminded of previous visits to their accountants. Aspects of the two situations are the same: Checking in with a receptionist and waiting, for instance. For these reminders to occur, memory must be organised so that the similarities can be noticed and shared between contexts.

Schank (1981) has argued that the ability to share knowledge is crucial. What knowledge sharing buys is better understanding of novel texts. Having never visited an accountant, a reader could still understand the events occurring in an accountant's waiting room because of shared knowledge from other waiting rooms. During reading, if relevant knowledge from another context can be found, it can be used to make predictions about upcoming text.

More importantly, it can help organise and disambiguate text as it is processed, as does any script-like knowledge, by providing the goals and causal structures in the story. The difference is that the shared knowledge is imported from another context.

Appropriate knowledge sharing will depend on the knowledge representation that the model uses. Knowledge about different "sub-schemas" or "scenes" within a story must be represented separately so that they can be noticed and inserted into different contexts. Pieces of text can then activate a particular sub-schema, and this sub-schema will constitute a modular part of the whole interpretation of the story. Knowledge sharing, therefore, is similar to the compositional generalisation demonstrated in the sentence gestalt model. A model learns what constraints arise from each part of the input. These constraints influence separate parts of the entire interpretation. The parts, then, can be combined in novel ways and the model will be able to produce an interpretation by composing the interpretation from each part. For sentences, the parts are words or sentence constituents that are combined to form descriptions of simple events. For stories, the parts are sub-schemas that are combined to form small stories.

On the other hand, the similarities between situations are not complete. Waiting in an accountant's office is not quite the same as waiting in a doctor's office. The art, magazines, and smells are all likely to be different. Consequently, shared knowledge must be massaged to fit the context. The parts of a story, therefore, are not completely modular: There are some interdependencies between the parts that require certain details to be modified to fit the current context.

The interdependence of knowledge between sub-schemas is related to the predictive generalisation in the sentence gestalt model. A particular input constituent provides constraints on several aspects of the interpretation. The constraints betwen sub-schemas simply provide extra information about the sub-schemas, and they are processed like any other constraint. Constraints from each sub-schema, and from their interactions, are used to compute an interpretation.

The representational and processing issues involved here are complex and not completely understood. For instance, it is difficult to know what the interdependencies are among sub-schemas when they are arranged in novel combinations. How to modify the waiting room sub-schema in an unfamiliar context is not clear. It is possible that the context, visiting an accountant or a doctor, provides some general information about the character of events throughout the story. This general information would then have to be applied appropriately to each sub-schema. For example, accountants might be thought to be conservative and business-like. The art, magazines, and the receptionist could reflect these characteristics in specific ways.

Understanding how to share knowledge and how to modify that knowledge to fit the context, then, are important and difficult issues that require further study.

Learning.   In addition to these processing issues, the reader must learn how to encode the schematic knowledge used during reading. The reader must learn what information can be predicted from a text and how reliably it can be predicted.

Further, the reader must learn how to represent this information in such a way that it can be applied usefully in appropriate contexts. It has been argued that the learning of schematic knowledge is difficult, particularly in conventional symbolic frame systems (Rumelhart, Smolensky, et al., 1986; Schank, 1981). The basic problems concern when to begin a new frame, what information to include in a frame, and whether to make that information a constant or a variable.

In his work on scripts, Schank (1981) illustrates the problem of deciding whether to learn a new script using his Legal Seafood example. Legal Seafood is a restaurant in which customers pay a cashier before they receive their food. How should this new sequence of restaurant actions be encoded? It would be wasteful and inefficient to learn a new script for every different sequence. Instead, the Legal Seafood sequence should be organised within the general restaurant script. The question is how to encode this exceptional sequence so that it can be retrieved when it is relevant. Further, if a number of restaurants operate like Legal Seafood, then it ceases to be an exceptional sequence and becomes a common variant. If common variants are encoded differently from exceptions, then how many instances are required to create a variant, and how are the variants encoded?

Deciding what information to include in a frame, or script, is also difficult. If children get ice-cream each time they go to a museum, should they include that event in their script for museums? In general, every experience will contain countless details that make it different from every other instance of a script and that may be only coincidental. Which of these details should be ignored? What should be considered variables within a script? Which details are important enough to motivate considering the experience an exception in which the details would be encoded as constants? Specifying criteria to resolve these questions will be difficult and will most likely fail to transfer to other knowledge domains.

A return to the goal of comprehension will shed some light on these issues. If the interpretation is to be as complete and predictive as possible, every regularity should be learned and applied. If children typically receive ice-cream when they visit museums, receiving ice-cream should be included in their representation of visits to museums.

Among a corpus of instances, there will be many regularities, or correlations, between features and sets of features of the events. Most of the correlations will be small, but each provides some predictive power. Together, they compose a detailed and predictive script. Exceptional events modify some of the correlations, and sets of common exceptional events simply modify them more.

It can be argued that scripts and frames are a rough approximation to the nature of the events they represent. The all-or-none boundaries they impose on the representation of events are artificial (Rumelhart, Smolensky, et al., 1986). The true nature of common events is better described as a set of prototypes that develop from exposure to numbers of instances (McClelland & Rumelhart, 1985; Posner & Keele, 1968). The instances encode all of the salient details. Prototypes emerge seamlessly from the correlations between details. The prototypes most similar to a new instance will make the strongest predictions, and the strength of the correlations between details will determine the strength of the predictions: There is no need to make binary discriminations between script-relevant and script-irrelevant details.

A successful story comprehension mechanism, therefore, should be able to encode instances and extract the correlations among their features. These correlations can then be applied to the comprehension task.

To reiterate, the story comprehension issues are:

1. the resolution of pronouns;
2. the inference of missing information;
3. the revision of interpretations based on evidence;
4. the representation of multiple propositions;
5. the sharing of knowledge across contexts; and
6. the seamless acquisition of knowledge.

Description of the Story Gestalt Model

These comprehension issues can be investigated with a model very similar to the sentence gestalt model. Instead of processing sentence constituents into a sentence gestalt, propositions are processed into a story gestalt. In the following, the story gestalt model is described briefly, and two illustrations of the model's performance are presented.

The model's task is to take a story as input and understand the story so that it can answer questions. The model learns to comprehend stories through experience comprehending example stories. Once trained, the model's performance on the comprehension tasks can be evaluated by using example stories from the corpus or by using novel stories.

Corpus.   The corpus consists of a large number of stories that take place in one of six different contexts: for example, going to the beach or going to a restaurant. Each story consists of a series of propositions that describe actions or attributes of a character or of the situation.

A proposition is represented as a set of thematic roles: agent, predicate, patient or theme, recipient or destination, location, manner, and attribute. For example, the proposition that conveys *the judge gave the trophy to Jolene* would be (agent = judge, predicate = gave, patient = trophy, recipient = Jolene, location = nil, manner = nil, attribute = nil). The "predicate" role is used both for actions and for the predicates of descriptions. For example, the proposition for *it was sunny at the beach* would be (agent = nil, predicate = weather, patient = nil, recipient = nil, location = beach, manner = nil, attribute = sunny).

A proposition is represented in the network as a vector of activation values. The concepts are represented locally, so that each possible concept for each thematic role is represented by a separate single unit. Consequently, there are 19 units to represent each of the 19 agents. There are 34 different units to represent each of the 34 patients, and so on. A *nil* for a role is represented by turning off every unit in that role. Altogether, 136 units are required to represent all of the propositions.

The corpus of stories is generated from a set of six story-frames. Each story-frame contains information about the events that can occur in one of the six contexts. This information is chosen probabilistically to be included in a particular story. The model is trained on the corpus by first generating a story from one of the story-frames and then training the model on that story. Both a story and the event it refers to are generated at the same time. The story may leave out information and contain pronouns, but the event is always complete and specific.

Across the 6 story-frames, the total number of different events is 28,480. For example, in the restaurant story-frame, there are 20 different sequences of events involving 2 of 10 possible characters and one of 4 possible vehicles for a total of 7200 restaurant events (20 * 10 * 9 * 4). The number of possible input stories is much higher because of pronouns and missing propositions.

Architecture and Training Regime.   To comprehend one of these stories, the model processes the propositions one at a time, and evaluates the information in each proposition to build and refine a representation of the whole story iteratively. The network is trained to perform this task by receiving feedback on its comprehension performance. In essence, the model is required to process the propositions so that it can answer questions about them. The questions provide a predicate from a proposition in the event and the network is required to complete the whole proposition from the predicate alone.

The network can be divided into two parts according to their function. Part A of the network (see Fig. 5.5) receives each proposition in turn and processes it to update its representation of the story. Specifically, the proposition is used to activate the units in the *current proposition* layer. The *current proposition* layer sends activation to the *intermediate-combination* layer where it is combined with activation from the *previous story gestalt*. The story gestalt represents what is known about the story at each point during processing. At the beginning of the story, nothing is known, so the units all have 0.0 activation. Activation from the

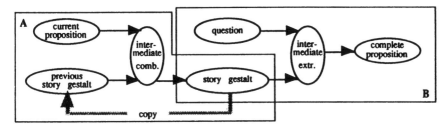

FIG. 5.5.   The architecture of the story gestalt network. The boxes highlight the functional parts: area A processes the propositions into the story gestalt, and area B processes the story gestalt into the output propositions. See the text for details. Reproduced from St. John (1992) with permission of the publishers, Ablex Publishing Corporation.

intermediate-combination layer feeds forward to produce a pattern of activation in the *story gestalt* layer. The new *story gestalt* then represents the whole story as well as it can based on the information provided from the input at that point in the story.

As each new proposition is processed, the new proposition replaces the last one in the *current proposition* layer, and the pattern of activation over the *story gestalt* is copied to the *previous story gestalt* layer. Activation feeds forward again to create a new story gestalt. In this way, information from previous propositions is both maintained and used to compute an updated interpretation of the whole story. It is important to understand that the story gestalt representation need not simply be a weighted sum of the propositions. The two layers of weights between the *previous story gestalt* and the *story gestalt* allow the network to compute more complex and useful representations of the information contained in the propositions.

Part B of the network performs the question-answering computation. A question is created by removing everything except the predicate from a proposition. The question is then used to activate a pattern of activation in the *question* layer. Activation from the layer combines in the *intermediate-extraction* layer with activation from the *story gestalt*. Activation from the *intermediate-extraction* layer then activates the units in the *complete proposition* layer.

There are 136 units in the *current proposition* layer, 100 units in the *story gestalt* and *previous story gestalt* layers, 100 units in the *intermediate combination* and *intermediate-extraction* layers, 34 units in the *question* layer, and 136 units in the *complete proposition* layer.

The propositional representation used in the *complete proposition* layer is identical to the representation used in the *current proposition* layer. The activation pattern over the units in the *complete proposition* layer can be compared to the correct pattern for that question. The error between the two is backpropagated (Rumelhart et al., 1986) to the *current proposition* and *previous story gestalt* layers. As with the sentence gestalt model, the error is calculated using the cross-entropy function (Hinton, 1989).

The model is trained after each proposition on the part of a story that has been presented in the input. After the first proposition, the model is asked only about the first proposition. After the second proposition is presented, the model is asked about both the first and second propositions. Propositions that are missing from the input are only asked about after they have been skipped in the input. For example, if the second proposition were missing, the model would only be asked about it after the third proposition were presented.

Before training on the corpus began, the model was trained on single, random propositions. The propositions are generated by activating one unit in each thematic role randomly, and the model is required to reproduce that proposition in the output. The purpose of this training is to help the model learn to remember the propositions actually presented by learning to map single propositions from the input to the output. Once this mapping has been learned, the model can then be trained on whole stories. Training, then, is composed of two phases: a pretraining phase on single propositions and the normal training phase on whole stories.

Once the model has mastered the pretraining task, training on the full corpus of stories begins. So that the model will not immediately lose the memory mapping it learned in the pretraining, the random, single-proposition training continues on 20% of the training trials. The model was trained for 160,000 story trials with a learning rate of 0.0001 and a momentum of 0.9.

Simulation Results

The model's processing performance will be illustrated with two examples. The first example illustrates the model's ability to resolve a pronoun using the gender of the pronoun. The second example illustrates the model's ability to draw prediction and coherence inferences and bind characters to their roles in a script.

A simple problem in pronoun resolution occurs in the following story.

Sally and Clement decided to go to the restaurant.
She paid the bill.

The pronoun "she" refers to one of the previously introduced characters, and the gender of the pronoun rules out Clement. The gender information, then, can be used as a constraint on the correct referent. The model is presented with this story and then questioned about who paid the bill. The model activates Sally, signifying that it has resolved the pronoun (see Fig. 5.6).

The second example illustrates inference making. The model is given a story about a restaurant; the story is missing a number of propositions. After the third input proposition has been processed, the model is questioned about several propositions from the story, including information that has to be inferred (see Fig. 5.7).

input
(agent=Sally and Clement, predicate=decided to go, destination=restaurant)
(agent=She, predicate=paid, patient=bill, location=restaurant)

question	output		
	agent	**predicate**	**destination**
decided to go	S and C	decided to go	restaurant
	9 9	9	9

	agent	**predicate**	**patient**	**location**
paid	Sally (C)	paid	bill	restaurant
	9 (1)	9	9	9

FIG. 5.6.   Pronoun resolution. The model is shown a story containing a pronoun, then questioned about both propositions. The model resolves the pronoun correctly. The numbers indicate the activation, from 0 to 1.0, of active concepts (decimal points are not shown). The parentheses denote alternative concepts and their activations. When there are two agents, the activation of each is shown.

First the model is questioned with "decided to go." The model must recall the context of this story and it must recall both characters' names. The model strongly activates the correct information.

One inference involves the distance to the restaurant. In the training corpus it was the case that all of the cheap restaurants were near by and all of the expensive restaurants were far away. Since the story says the restaurant was expensive, the model should infer that it was far away. Questioned about distance, the model strongly activates "far."

Within a script, one character may play a particular role in a set of actions. For example, the character who orders (in the simple world of the training corpus) pays the bill and tips the waiter. By knowing which character performed one of these actions, the whole set can be inferred. The input story says that Sally paid the bill. When questioned about any of the actions, the model activates Sally more strongly than Clement.

By definition, inferring that Sally ordered is a coherence inference because ordered comes before the explicitly presented proposition about paying in the story. Inferring that Sally left the tip is a prediction inference because it comes after the last-presented proposition.

The model, however, makes no distinction between these inferences. One process, activating the story based on constraints from the input, is used to produce a complete interpretation. Representing the explicit text, drawing prediction inferences, drawing coherence inferences, and resolving pronouns all result from this same process.

input
(agent=Sally and Clement, predicate=decided to go, destination=restaurant)
(predicate=quality, patient=restaurant, attribute=expensive)
(agent=Sally, predicate=paid, patient=bill, location=restaurant)

question	output				
	agent	**predicate**	**destination**		
decided to go	S and C	decided to go	restaurant		
	9 9	9	9		
	predicate	**patient**	**attribute**		
quality	quality	restaurant	expensive		
	9	9	9		
	predicate	**patient**	**attribute**		
distance	distance	restaurant	far		
	9	9	9		
	agent	**predicate**	**patient**	**recipient**	**location**
ordered	Sally (C)	ordered	cheap wine	waiter	rest.
	8 (5)	9	9	9	9
	agent	**predicate**	**patient**	**location**	**manner**
enjoyed	S and C	enjoyed	cheap wine	restaurant	not
	9 8	9	9	9	9
	agent	**predicate**	**patient**	**location**	
paid	Sally (C)	paid	bill	restaurant	
	9 (1)	9	9	9	
	agent	**predicate**	**patient**	**recipient**	
brought	waiter	brought	credit-card	Sally (C)	
	9	9	9	7 (4)	
	agent	**predicate**	**patient**	**location**	**manner**
tipped	Sally (C)	tipped	waiter	restaurant	small
	9 (3)	9	9	9	8

FIG. 5.7. Conditional inferences. The model is shown three propositions from a restaurant story, then questioned about a number of propositions from the whole event. The numbers indicate the activation, from 0 to 1.0, of active concepts (decimal points are not shown). The parentheses denote alternative concepts and their activations. When there are two agents, the activation of each is shown.

Discussion of the Story Gestalt Model

The resolution of pronouns and the inference of missing information are problems similar to the instantiation of vague words and the inference of missing thematic roles addressed by the sentence gestalt model. The story gestalt model was shown, by example, to perform these two processes. A more thorough analysis of the model's performance on these tasks is in preparation.

The revision of the text's interpretation as comprehension proceeds is also similar to the immediate processing in the sentence gestalt model. Finally, the sharing of knowledge between contexts are, to some degree, similar to the compositional and predictive generalisation shown in the sentence gestalt model. It seems reasonable to believe, therefore, that the story gestalt model will be able to address these issues as well. Evaluation of the story gestalt model's performance on these tasks are also in preparation.

Admittedly, there are many qualities of story comprehension that have not been addressed. Some of the most important are how to check whether the text is coherent, and the problem solving behaviour that occurs when the text is not coherent. It may be best to understand the sentence gestalt model and its story extension as first-pass processors that comprehend texts effortlessly and automatically. When these processors run into significant trouble, other processes are initiated. How these other trouble-shooting processes work, and to what extent they use the knowledge encoded in the sentence gestalt model or the story gestalt model, is not immediately clear.

CONCLUSIONS

Parallel constraint satisfaction provides a different framework for understanding the computations involved in processing sentences and stories. The traditional view is that semantic and syntactic rules construct, through a series of steps, an interpretation of a sentence or story. The parallel constraint satisfaction view, on the other hand, is that the words and propositions of a text are used as evidence for, or constraints on, complete interpretations. This different view makes long-standing problems such as disambiguation, thematic role assignment, and the bootstrapping problem for sentences, and pronoun resolution and inference making for stories, seem feasible and easy. The approach may also lead to important insights into other problems such as sharing information between contexts and modifying that information.

Both the sentence gestalt model and the story gestalt model demonstrate the utility of parallel constraint satisfaction as a language comprehension mechanism. Parallel constraint satisfaction has also been applied successfully to other comprehension tasks. McClelland and Rumelhart (1981) demonstrated how it could be used to process letter features into words, and McClelland and Elman (1986) demonstrated how it could be used to process phonetic features into words. The basic point is that although each of these models may use a different architecture that conforms to the processing demands of each task, the meat of the models lies in their use of parallel constraint satisfaction. Through parallel constraint satisfaction, we can begin to understand much of language comprehension in terms of a single algorithm, whereas before the algorithms for processing words, sentences, and stories were all different.

ACKNOWLEDGEMENTS

The work and ideas described in this chapter have also been described in St. John and McClelland (1990). *Artificial Intelligence*. Correspondence should be addressed to Mark St. John, Department of Cognitive Science, University of California at San Diego, La Jolla, CA 92093-0515. E-mail: stjohn@cogsci.ucsd.edu.

REFERENCES

Anderson, R.C. & Ortony, A. (1975). On putting apples into bottles: A problem of polysemy. *Cognitive Psychology*, *7*, 167–180.

Carpenter, P.A. & Just, M.A. (1977). Reading comprehension as the eyes see it. In M.A. Just & P.A. Carpenter (Eds.), *Cognitive processes in comprehension*. Hillsdale, N.J.: Lawrence Erlbaum Associates Inc.

Charniak, E. (1983). Passing markers: A theory of contextual influence in language comprehension. *Cognitive Science*, *7*, 171–190.

Cottrell, G.W. (1985). *A connectionist approach to word sense disambiguation*. Dissertation, Computer Science Department, University of Rochester, NY.

Cottrell, G.W. & Small, A.L. (1983). A connectionist scheme for modeling word sense disambiguation. *Cognition and Brain Theory*, *6*, 89–120.

Fillmore, C.J. (1968). The case for case. In E. Bach & R.T. Harms (Eds.), *Universals in linguistic theory*. New York: Holt, Rinehart, & Winston.

Gleitman, L.R. & Wanner, E. (1982). Language acquisitions: The state of the state of the art. In E. Wanner & L.R. Gleitman (Eds.), *Language acquisition: The state of the art*. Cambridge: Cambridge University Press.

Graesser, A.C. (1981). *Prose comprehension beyond the word*. New York: Springer-Verlag.

Hinton, G.E. (1981). Implementing semantic networks in parallel hardware. In G.E. Hinton & J.A. Anderson (Eds.), *Parallel models of associative memory*. Hillsdale, N.J.: Lawrence Erlbaum Associates Inc.

Hinton, G.E. (1986). *Learning distributed representations of concepts*. Paper presented to the 8th Annual Conference of the Cognitive Science Society. Amherst, Mass.

Hinton, G.E. (1989). Connectionist learning procedures. *Artificial Intelligence*, *40*, 185–234.

Hinton, G.E., McClelland, J.L., & Rumelhart, D.E. (1986). Distributed representations. In D.E. Rumelhart, J.L. McClelland, & the PDP Research Group (Eds.), *Parallel distributed processing: Explorations in the microstructure of cognition, Volume 1*. Cambridge, Mass: M.I.T. Press.

Jordan, M.I. (1986). *Attractor dynamics and parallelism in a connectionist sequential machine*. Paper presented at the 8th Annual Conference of the Cognitive Science Society. Amherst, Mass.

MacWhinney, B. (1987). Competition. In B. MacWhinney (Ed.), *Mechanisms of language acquisition: The 20th annual Carnegie symposium on cognition*. Hillsdale, N.J.: Lawrence Erlbaum Associates Inc.

Marcus, M.P. (1980). *A theory of syntactic recognition for natural language*. Cambridge, Mass.: M.I.T. Press.

McClelland, J.L. & Elman, J.L. (1986). Interactive processes in speech perception: The TRACE model. In J.L. McClelland, D.E. Rumelhart, & the PDP Research Group (Eds.), *Parallel distributed processing: Explorations in the microstructure of cognition, Volume 2*. Cambridge, Mass.: M.I.T. Press.

McClelland, J.L. & Kawamoto, A.H. (1986). Mechanisms of sentence processing: Assigning roles to constituents. In J.L. McClelland, D.E. Rumelhart, & the PDP Research Group (Eds.), *Parallel distributed processing: Explorations in the microstructure of cognition, Volume 2*. Cambridge, Mass.: M.I.T. Press.

McClelland, J.L. & Rumelhart, D.E. (1981). An interactive activation model of context effects in letter perception: Part 1. An account of basic findings. *Psychological Review*, *88*, 375–407.

McClelland, J.L. & Rumelhart, D.E. (1985). Distributed memory and the representation of general and specific informaton. *Journal of Experimental Psychology: General, 114*, 159–188.

McKoon, G. & Ratcliff, R. (1981). The comprehension processes and memory structures involved in instrumental inference. *Journal of Verbal Learning and Verbal Behaviour, 20*, 671–682.

McKoon, G. & Ratcliff, R. (1986). Inferences about predictable events. *Journal of Experimental Psychology: Learning, Memory, and Cognition, 12*, 82–91.

Miikkulainen, R. & Dyer, M.G. (1989). A modular neural network architecture for sequential paraphrasing of script-based stories. In the *Proceedings of the International Joint Conference on Neural Networks*. Piscataway, N.J.: IEEE.

Millis, K.K., Morgan, D.C., & Graesser, A.C. (in press). The influence of knowledge-based inferences on the reading time of expository text. In A.C. Graesser & G.H. Bower (Eds.), *The psychology of learning and motivation*. New York: Academic Press.

Naigles, L.G., Gleitman, H., & Gleitman, L.R. (1987). *Syntactic bootstrapping in verb acquisition: Evidence from comprehension*. Technical report. Philadelphia, Penn.: Department of Psychology, University of Pennsylvania.

Posner, M.I. & Keele, S.W. (1968). On the genesis of abstract ideas. *Journal of Experimental Psychology, 77*, 353–363.

Potts, G.R., Keenan, J.M., & Golding, J.M. (1988). Assessing the occurrence of elaborative inferencess: Lexical decision versus naming. *Journal of Memory and Language, 27*, 399–415.

Rumelhart, D.E. (1981). Understanding understanding. In H.W. Dechert & M. Raupach (Eds.), *Psycholinguistic models of production*. Norwood, N.J.: Ablex Publishing.

Rumelhart, D.E. (1987). *Colloquium on generalization of semantic information in a PDP network*. Presented to the Department of Computer Science, Carnegie-Mellon.

Rumelhart, D.E., Hinton, G.E., & Williams, R.J. (1986). Learning internal representations by error propagation. In D.E. Rumelhart, J.L. McClelland, & the PDP Research Group (Eds.), *Parallel distributed processing: Explorations in the microstructure of cognition, Volume I*. Cambridge, Mass.: M.I.T. Press.

Rumelhart, D.E., Smolensky, P., McClelland, J.L., & Hinton, G.E. (1986). Schemata and sequential thought processes in PDP models. In D.E. Rumelhart, J.L. McClelland, & the PDP Research Group (Eds.), *Parallel distributed processing: Explorations in the microstructure of cognition, Volume 2*. Cambridge, Mass.: M.I.T. Press.

Schank, R.C. (1981). Language and memory. In D.A. Norman (Ed.) *Perspectives on cognitive science*. Norwood, N.J.: Ablex Publishing.

Schank, R.C. & Abelson, R.P. (1977). *Scripts, plans, goals, and understanding: An inquiry into human knowledge structures*. Hillsdale, N.J.: Lawrence Erlbaum Associates Inc.

St. John, M.F. (1992). The story gestalt: A model of knowledge intensive processes in text comprehension. *Cognitive Science, 16*, 271–306.

St. John, M.F. & McClelland, J.L. (1987). Reconstructive memory for sentences: A PDP approach. Paper presented to the Ohio University Inference Conference, *Proceedings Inference: OUIC 86*. Athens, Ohio: University of Ohio.

St. John, M.F. & McClelland, J.L. (1990). Learning and applying contextual constraints in sentence comprehension. *Artificial Intelligence, 46*, 217–257.

Tesauro, G. (1987). *Scaling relationships in backpropagation learning: Dependence on training set size*. Technical report. Champaign, Illinois: Centre for Complex Systems Research, University of Illinois at Urbana-Champaign.

van Dijk, T.A. & Kintsch, W. (1983). *Strategies of discourse comprehension*. Orlando, Florida: Academic Press.

Waltz, D.L. & Pollack, J.B. (1985). Massively parallel parsing: A strongly interactive model of natural language interpretation. *Cognitive Science, 9*, 51–74.

Wilensky, R. (1983). *Planning and understanding: A computational approach to human reasoning*. Reading, Mass.: Addison Wesley.

Woods, W.A. (1970). Transition network grammars for natural language analysis. *Communications of the Association for Computing Machinery, 13.*

APPENDIX I: INPUT AND OUTPUT REPRESENTATIONS

Input

surface locations (4)

pre-verbal, verbal, post-verbal-1, post-verbal-n

words (52)

consumed, ate drank, stirred, spread, kissed, gave, hit, shot threw
drove, shed, rose
someone, adult, child, dog, busdriver, teacher, schoolgirl, pitcher, spot
something, food, steak, soup, ice cream, crackers, jelly, iced-tea, kool-aid
utensil, spoon, knife, finger, gun
place, kitchen, living-room, park, bat, ball, bus, fur
gusto, pleasure, daintiness
with, in, to, by
was

Output

roles (9)

agent, action, patient, instrument, co-agent, co-patient, location, adverb
recipient

actions and concepts (45)

ate, drank, stirred, spread, kissed, gave, hit, shot, threw (tossed)
threw(hosted), drove(transported), drove(motivated), shed(verb), rose(verb)
busdriver, teacher, schoolgirl, pitcher(person), spot
steak, soup, ice cream, crackers, jelly, iced-tea, kool-aid
spoon, knife, finger, gun
kitchen, living-room, shed(noun), park
rose(noun), bat(animal), bat(baseball), ball(sphere), ball(party), bus
pitcher(container), fur
gusto, pleasure, daintiness

passive marker (1)

passive

features (13)

person, adult, child, dog, male, female, thing, food, utensil, place
indoors, outdoors, consumed

SYNTAX

II

SYNTAX

INTRODUCTION

It has been argued by some (Schank, 1975; Small & Reiger, 1982) that it is possible to reduce the necessity for structural analysis and go directly from individual word meanings to the meaning of the sentence. However, even in these case-based approaches, where the constituents are assigned their respective case roles (e.g. agent, action, patient), word order and function words are important sources of information. Other evidence from neuropsychology (Shallice, 1988), suggests that there are specialised modules in the brain that deal specifically with syntactic aspects of sentence processing. For example, there are patients with lesions that affect their ability to use function words. These same patients show no comprehension deficit. Of course, it depends on one's perspective on natural language processing, whether or not such evidence is considered admissable.

Connectionist approaches to the problem of syntax can be divided into two main categories: those that adopt a localist approach to representation and those that assume a more distributed approach. As already mentioned in the introduction to the semantics section, Hinton (1989) has observed that the terms *localist* and *distributed* are not absolute definitions and should be understood in the context of the relationship between some descriptive language and its connectionist implementation. Therefore, a localist approach is characterised by a preference for using single units to represent specific elements of a representational formalism. For example, one unit might be used to represent a single node in a parse tree. The alternative involves representing the same elements as a pattern of activation over a number of units. The advantage of the localist approach is the ready interpretability of the behaviour of networks comprising localist units. A disadvantage is that localist approaches tend to demand more resources than the distributed alternative and often require unrealistic architectural assumptions to be made. Most distributed approaches, however, tend to involve some localist representation, especially for input and output.

Both papers in this section adopt a localist approach in the tradition of Feldman and Ballard (1982) and Fanty (1985). A common motivation they have for doing so is to facilitate the mapping of pre-existing symbolic techniques into a connectionist framework. In Rager's case (Chapter 6), he takes an approach to grammar definition involving meta-rules called two-level grammars, which he proceeds to implement in a connectionist form. His choice of symbolic formalism is motivated by a need to deal with ungrammaticality in a principled rather than an ad hoc fashion. By implementing it in a connectionist framework he gains the additional advantage of being able to represent competition between multiple parses in a natural way.

Schnelle and Doust (Chapter 7) also favour a localist approach, and this decision is also determined by the need to map a conventional symbolic framework, the Earley parser, onto a connectionist one. Schnelle and Doust argue that we must take Fodor and Pylyshyn's (1988) critique of connectionism seriously and satisfy ourselves, at least initially, with an implementationist approach to modelling cognitive processes. This entails devising connectionist implementations for extant symbolic theories. Fodor and Pylyshyn propose this as the only realistic role for connectionism. They make strong claims for the psychological reality of symbolic processes, but concede that such processes must be *implemented* in some form on neural hardware. Opponents of this view argue that current symbolic theories are abstract and approximate characterisations of what are fundamentally connectionist processes (Smolensky, 1988). Schnelle and Doust dissent from the strong position propounded by Fodor and Pylyshyn (1988). They adopt an implementationist approach for pragmatic reasons, arguing that symbolic theories of language are currently the best theories we have. They do not discount the possibility that at some later date implementational considerations may affect the symbolic level of description, or indeed render it unnecessary.

Whatever the motivation, localist implementations are ultimately unsatisfactory. This is especially true if one is motivated by an interest in models that have some psychological plausibility. Non-localist approaches to syntactic processing are still in their infancy. However, the work of a number of researchers shows considerable promise (Elman, 1989; Pollack, 1990; Servan-Shreiber, Cleeremans, & McClelland, 1989). For example, Elman (1989) has made use of simple recurrent networks (SRNs) in modelling the process of number agreements between nouns and verbs. These networks make use of distributed internal representations that are created by a learning algorithm rather than by hand, as is the case in localist models. A key aspect of Elman's work is the use made of the temporal dimension in encoding the elements in a sentence; something that humans must also do when processing speech. Elman's SRNs only have enough input units to represent one word. Sentence processing is achieved by allowing representational information activated in the hidden units during the processing of one word, to be accessed in the processing of the next word, and so on. Thus a complex internal representation is created in the hidden units that temporally encodes sentential information. A similar network is used by Servan-Shreiber et al. (1989) to study the capacity of networks to act as recognisers for finite state grammars, in particular grammars that allow recursive embeddings. They found that simple recurrent networks could, within certain constraints, act as successful finite state recognisers.

The work of Pollack (1990), although not dealing directly with syntactic issues, provides another important tool for tackling connectionist syntactic processing. He has developed a technique (recursive auto-associative memory, or RAAM) for representing recursive open-ended structures such as lists and trees in distributed fixed-width patterns, of the type one finds in hidden units of feedforward networks, or indeed in the fixed-width neural pathways of the brain. RAAMs can facilitate the encoding, decoding, and manipulation of complex tree-structures, which is a necessary pre-requisite for syntactic processing.

To conclude, the general picture of connectionist syntactic processing is that there are a number of promising techniques becoming available for dealing with some of the limitations of earlier approaches. Although none of these techniques have as yet reached the stage where they can compete with conventional symbolic approaches, the early indications are very positive.

REFERENCES

Elman, J.L. (1989). *Representation and structure in connectionist models*. CRL Technical Report 8903. La Jolla, Calif.: Center for Research in Language, U.C.S.D.

Fanty, M. (1985). *Context-free parsing in connectionist networks*. Technical Report TR-174. Rochester, New York: Dept. of Computer Science, University of Rochester.

Feldman, J.A. & Ballard, D.H. (1982). Connectionist models and their properties. *Cognitive Science, 6*, 205-254.

Fodor, J. & Pylyshyn, Z. (1988). Connectionism and cognitive architecture. *Cognition, 28*, 3-71.

Hinton, G.E. (1989). Connectionist learning procedures. *Artificial Intelligence, 40*, 185-234.

Pollack, J.B. (1990) Recursive distributed representations. *Artificial Intelligence, 46*, 77-105.

Schank, R.C. (1975). *Conceptual information processing*. Amsterdam: North-Holland.

Servan-Schreiber, D., Cleeremans, A., & McClelland, J. (1989). Learning sequential structure in simple recurrent networks. In D. Touretzsky (Ed.), *Advances in neural information processing systems, 2*. San Mateo, Calif.: Morgan-Kaufman.

Shallice, T. (1988). *From neuropsychology to mental structure*. Cambridge: Cambridge University Press.

Small, S. & Rieger, C. (1982). Parsing and comprehending with word experts (a theory and its realisation). In W.G. Lehnert & M.H. Ringle (Eds.), *Strategies for natural language processing*. Hillsdale, N.J.: Lawrence Erlbaum Associates Inc.

Smolensky, P. (1988). *The constituent structure of connectionist mental states*. Technical Report CU-CS-394-88. Boulder, Colorado: Department of Computer Science, University of Colorado.

6 Self-correcting Connectionist Parsing

John E. Rager
Department of Mathematics and Computer Science, Amherst College, Amherst, MA 01002, U.S.A.

INTRODUCTION: CONSTRAINED CHAOS

This paper explores several ways of using connectionist networks to parse sentences which are syntactically "extragrammatical." Extragrammatical is not a well-defined term: A sentence is extragrammatical if it is ungrammatical but would still make sense to many native speakers. Labelling a sentence with any of the terms sensible, ungrammatical, or extragrammatical is a judgment by the person who hears the utterance. It is doubtful that any two people would make the same judgment all the time. In fact, even one person is likely to be inconsistent. Suppose, however, that we look at one user of a language. One of the striking things about human language use is that our speaker will attach an interpretation to almost any utterance she hears. Even a nonsense stream of sounds will be heard as phonemes and words. Sentences with "errors" in them yield enormous amounts of information, e.g. they will be broken into phrases even if they contain mostly (or perhaps all) nonsense words. Contrast this to an interpreter of a formal language. It is relatively easy to build a checker that will decide whether or not a string belongs to the language. If it does, it is also easy to extract a parse of the string; however, it is much harder to derive meaningful information about nonmember strings. This is inadequate for natural language. Even if we had a formal language deriving all of the "correct" sentences of some language, it would be neither an adequate model of the human language faculty nor an adequate basis for a computer natural language processor.

The term "extragrammatical," as introduced here, is not intended to cover the entire range of phenomena attributed to our hearer, but is restricted to sentences which might be judged ungrammatical but meaningful. It is generally accepted that the ability to handle input which is extragrammatical, in this sense, is important for natural language processing systems. Some researchers (e.g. Carbonell & Hayes, 1984) feel that this ability lies inherently outside the realm of syntax; that handling ungrammatical sentences is impossible without semantic and pragmatic input. In contrast, Weischedel and Ramshaw (1986) analyse the knowledge required to handle extragrammatical input and conclude that all phases of processing should be considered seriously, including syntax. We agree. Although it is not possible to detect or repair extragrammaticality using only the syntax of a language, it is useful to study syntax orthogonally to other issues. Some extragrammaticality (e.g. agreement failure or subcategorisation failure) is clearly syntactic and should be handled as such.

Let us review briefly some previous syntactic approaches to handling extragrammatical input. Several systems have worked within the framework of augmented transition networks (ATNs). Kwasny and Sondheimer (1981) allow the relaxation of chosen arc conditions to handle co-occurrence violations and allow the use of "pattern arcs" that encode the possibilities of some patterns explicitly, including extraneous material or missing required material. Weischedel and Black (1980) also allow the relaxation of arc conditions. In addition, they discuss a German tutor which explicitly encodes some incorrect forms (e.g. the frequent verb misplacement error in sentences like * "Ich habe gegessen das Fleisch", as opposed to "Ich habe das Fleisch gegessen").

In a system not based on an ATN, Charniak (1983) describes a parser called Paragram, an extension of Marcus' rule-based, deterministic, wait-and-see parser Parsifal (Marcus, 1980). Parsifal uses rules to build a parse. At any point, only one rule will be applicable. To handle situations where no rule applies, Paragram rates the applicability of rules by giving variable credit for passed tests and deducting credit for failed tests. If no rule fits precisely, the rule with the best "goodness of fit" succeeds and is applied first.

One of the important features of connectionist models of processing is that they can function with "noisy", partly incorrect input or with completely correct input. The functioning in the two cases is much the same: The network "settles" on the "closest" correct answer. In this paper we discuss methods of allowing partly incorrect input in connectionist parsing. That is, we look at connectionist processing of sentences that are not correct in the grammar we use to construct the parser. Two choices were made in the construction of the examples in this paper: first, the choice of connectionist architecture; second, the choice of grammatical representation. It is not our aim to suggest that either of these choices, which will be discussed, were the only possible choices or even the best choices. The intention is to show that a wide range of extragrammatical recovery phenomena can be handled in a connectionist framework. The same ideas will work in other architectures and with some other grammatical representations.

The connectionist architecture we use here is similar to that proposed by Feldman and Ballard (1982) and later used by Fanty (1985) in his parser. Our processing units are complicated, although they can be replaced by larger networks of simpler units. The functioning of various classes of units are described when they are used, but the following is a description of a general unit:

1. Units have a small memory for integer values, which may include thresholds and a small number of state variables.

2. Units produce output according to functions, which will be described in the sections of the chapter in which they are used. The function can depend on the units inputs and stored information.

3. Units have only one output, but they may have multiple input sites. Units are connected by links, which go from the output of one unit to one of the input sites of at least one other unit. All the inputs arriving at one site are combined using some simple function (e.g. sum, maximum, minimum). This means that different units can influence one unit in different ways. We will commonly use this to switch a unit on and off.

Two-level grammars were chosen as the grammatical representation. One of the problems with some previous work on ungrammaticality is the ad hoc nature of the acceptable ungrammaticalities: the relaxation techniques are built in manually; the pattern arcs are an extended part of the parser; the "goodness of fit" parameters are knobs to twiddle. The knowledge that allows the use of extragrammaticality is derived from sources external to the grammar. The ungrammaticality we will accept in two-level grammars is a consequence of the grammar itself.

To illustrate this point with an unnatural example, consider the following context-sensitive grammar.

$S \rightarrow ABSc$ $\quad$ $Aa \rightarrow aa$ $\quad$ $Ab \rightarrow ab$
$S \rightarrow Abc$ $\quad$ $Bb \rightarrow bb$ $\quad$ $BA \rightarrow AB$

This is a grammar for the language $a^n b^n c^n$, although this is probably not obvious at first glance.

Example
$S \rightarrow ABSc \rightarrow ABAbcc \rightarrow AABbcc \rightarrow AAbbcc \rightarrow Aabbcc \rightarrow aabbcc$

Now suppose we have the string aaabbccc. It cannot be generated by this grammar. It is not clear how to derive any relationship between the string and the grammar. This despite the fact that it is obvious (to the superior pattern-matching skills of a human) that the problem is that the number of "a"s and "b"s is different. Consider the string acbbcacb. This is "less close" to being in this grammar than the first string; however, Chomsky grammars are binary devices, and they do not admit degrees of membership. Here follows a two-level grammar for the same language.

Metagrammar
COUNT → {X}+

Grammatical Schema[1]
S →   (A,*,COUNT) (B,*,COUNT) (C,*,COUNT)
(A,*,COUNT X) → (A,*,COUNT) a   (A,*,X) → a
(B,*,COUNT X) → (B,*,COUNT) b   (B,*,X) → b
(C,*,COUNT X) → (C,*,COUNT) c   (C,*,X) → c

Informally, a two-level grammar is a grammar whose rules have variables in them (called grammatical schema). The metagrammar consists of rules, which define legal values for the variables that appear in the schema. The variables are replaced with values obtained from the metagrammar. When a variable appears more than once in a rule scheme, it must be replaced the same way each time that it appears (this is called uniform substitution). In the example just shown, COUNT can be replaced by any string of one or more Xs. If COUNT is replaced by XX, the first rule schema becomes the rule:

S → (A,*,XX) (B,*,XX) (C,*,XX)

The same rule schema can be used multiple times in the same derivation with different metavariable values each time. (This is all the reader needs to know about two-level grammars to understand this paper. For more complete definitions see Greibach [1974]; Krulee [1983]; Pagan [1981]; Rager [1987]; etc.) In this example, a leftmost derivation for aabbcc is given by the following:

S → (A,*,XXX) (B,*,XXX) (C,*,XXX) → (A,*,XX) a (B,*,XXX) (C,*,XXX)
  → (A,*,X) a a (B,*,XXX) (C,*,XXX) → a a a (B,*,XX) b (C,*,XXX)
  → a a a (B,*,X) b b (C,*,XXX)   → a a a b b b (C,*,XXX)
  → a a a b b b (C,*,XX) c   → a a a b b b (C,*,X) c c
  → a a a b b b c c c

Notice that several of the schema are used twice, once with COUNT replaced by XX and once with COUNT replaced by X.

---

[1]The * is a marker used to separate the complex non-terminal into pieces to make the schema easier to read.

This grammar contains an explicit encoding of the equality of the lengths of the three substrings. Consider a bottom-up shift-reduce "parse" of aaabbccc, sketched out in Table 6.1. (In a shift-reduce parse, there are two actions, one of which is taken at any step. First, an input symbol can be moved onto the stack. Or, if the top symbols on the stack match the right-hand side of a rule, then the symbols can be replaced by the left-hand side of the rule. This is the reverse of the application of a rule as in a derivation.)

At step n the parse cannot continue, as there are no applicable rules to reduce and no input to shift. However, if the parser can observe that the first rule would reduce if the COUNT metavariable were ignored (or, more precisely, if the uniform instantiation of the COUNT metavariable were ignored), then an extra-grammatical parse could continue. This metavariable relaxation allows a "parse," with the explanation that the metavariable COUNT had to be ignored. (With this relaxation, the grammar will produce $a^n b^m c^p$.) Notice that this explanation of the extragrammaticality is given in terms of the original grammar.

In the last example, the language is context sensitive. The same phenomena can occur in a context-free language. The language $a^n b^n$ can be represented with a similar two-level grammar (remove the [C,*,COUNT] from the right side of the first rule). This representation is "better" than the usual context-free grammar ($S \to aSb$; $S \to ab$) because it explicitly describes the language as having a length equality constraint. (Better, that is, if this equality is meaningful rather than accidental.)

These examples point out the virtue of two-level grammars in the explanation of extragrammaticality. The grammars come with a specific list of things which

TABLE 6.1
An Error-detecting Shift-reduce Parse

Step	Stack	Input	Action
1		aaabbccc	shift
2	a	aabbccc	reduce
3	(A,#,X)	aabbccc	shift
4	(A,#,X) a	abbccc	reduce
5	(A,#,XX)	abbccc	shift
6	(A,#,XX) a	bbccc	reduce
7	(A,#,XXX) (several more steps)		
n	(A,#,XXX) (B,#,XX) (C,#,XXX)		

can be wrong; the "grammatical" language is defined by requiring the uniform substitution of metavariables to hold; the "extragrammatical" by allowing metavariable mismatches. This gives a formal definition for extragrammaticality, something which is necessary for computer implementation. At the same time, it retains the distinction between grammatical and ungrammatical. Now, one can argue that it is necessary to build in the extragrammaticality by choosing the metagrammar. We claim the argument is at least partly false for natural languages. It is not the case that any two grammars that generate the same string set are equally adequate linguistically. The discussions in Rager (1987) and Krulee (1983) focus on the various kinds of linguistically motivated two-level structures one can build. One of the major sources of data for the existence of linguistic principles and agreement restrictions is the comparison of grammatical and ungrammatical utterances. It is our contention that if the two-level grammar is written with reasons for its metavariables, then it will be these things which, if they fail, will give rise to reasonable extragrammaticality. In other words, if the grammar is explanatory (and not just convenient), it will fail in the ways one would want. The reason for this, of course, is that the grammar writer is encoding his knowledge about what is linguistically related and interesting in the meta-grammar. We will use this explicit encoding as a guide to building connectionist networks. We are not claiming that this will capture all extragrammaticalities, of course. In particular, if a two-level grammar were written specifically for German, it would be unlikely to include the word-order error discussed earlier. Such an error might be covered by a grammar built using universal grammar principles, which could then be allowed to fail.

It would be preferable to allow the extragrammaticality handling to arise naturally from a network built for other reasons, rather than building it in. This may be possible with the right type of network, preferably one which will learn a grammar by itself. There is extensive linguistic evidence that much of the human syntactic language faculty is prewired, not learned (Chomsky, 1985). This may mean that an unstructured network cannot learn language, at least not using the same evidence that humans do. It may be that a learning network would need to have certain abilities or structures built into it. The work in this chapter can be viewed as an examination of one possibility for what such networks might look like.

AGREEMENT

In this section we describe a simple parsing network which handles agreement failure. Agreement failure includes a large class of syntactic failures also called co-occurrence restriction violations. A co-occurrence restriction is a description of two or more grammatical elements which must agree in some property. (The usual examples of agreement are subject-verb agreement in a sentence and adjective-noun agreement in a noun phrase. The simplicity of these is somewhat misleading, as agreement/co-occurrence is a widespread linguistic phenomenon. For a selection of papers dealing with this important topic, see Barlow and Ferguson [1988].)

The two-level grammar following describes a fragment of possible French noun phrases. Only phrases that consist of a determiner, two adjectives, and a noun are included. The adjectives must precede the noun. The metavariables gender1 and gender2 enforce the restriction that all four words in the phrase must have the same gender. The number feature of the words (singular/plural) is ignored.

Metagrammar
gender1, gender2 → masc | fem

Grammatical Schema
(NP,*,gender1) → (preNP,*,gender1) (noun,*,gender1)
(preNP,*,gender2) → (det,*,gender2) (adj1,*,gender2) (adj2,*,gender2)

Sample Derivation
(NP,*,masc) → (preNP,*masc) (noun,*,masc)
       → (det,*,masc) (adj1,*,masc) (adj2,*,masc) (noun,*,masc)

A simple network for building a parse in this grammar is given in Fig. 6.1. In this network, we make the assumption that input activation is applied to at most one of each of the paired nodes (e.g. [det masc] and [det fem]) that represent lexical categories. (For now, ignore the double circles, which indicate active nodes.)

Each of the internal nodes of the network has a threshold which appears below and to the right of the node. The node activates (produces output) if the sum of its inputs is greater than or equal to the threshold. The output of a node is exactly 1, except that the gender nodes output their input if it exceeds the threshold. (This distinction is made for compatibility with later examples.) If a correct input is applied, the nodes will settle into a final state in which the NP is activated and the other internal nodes form a parse tree of the phrase. (This is a distributed representation of the tree.)

Each of the rules has a metavariable associated with it. Each metavariable can have two values. Nodes for these values appear in the network. For example, gender2 appears in the network as two nodes (gender2 masc) and (gender2 fem). Each of these has the same threshold (three) since they must be fed by three identically gendered items (det, adj1 and adj2).

The nodes named something-X are the same as the corresponding nodes without the X, except that they ignore the metavariables. For example, preNP-X will be active if one of each of the input pairs is active, without regard to agreement.

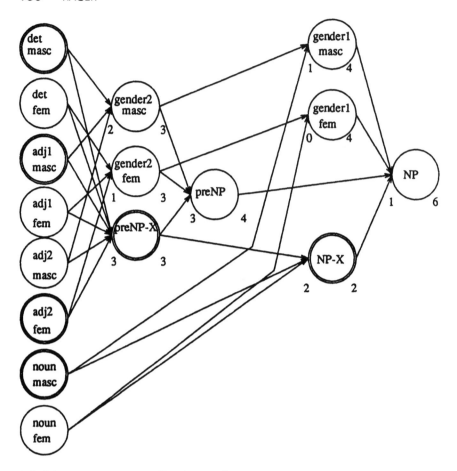

FIG. 6.1.   A network to parse French noun phrases.

In Fig. 6.1 we also show what happens if the input nodes are activated to correspond to the pattern (det masc) (adj1 masc) (adj2 fem) (noun masc), which violates the agreement restriction. Activated nodes are shown as double circles; the total input to each node appears below and to the left of the node. Notice that the nodes (gender2 masc) and (gender2 fem) are not able to fire; this in turn prevents preNP from receiving enough input to fire.

To build a network that will be able to recover gracefully from this type of error, it is necessary to build in an "understanding" that, for example (gender2 masc) and (gender2 fem) are related and that one and only one of them must be active. As the network stands in Fig. 6.1, it has no structure corresponding to the fact that masc and fem are different possible values for the same variable; no explicit evidence of the relationship between the two. We must build in the idea that gender2 is a single-valued variable.

A simple change in the network will do this. In Fig. 6.2, each of the metavariable value groups is connected as a winner-take-all (wta) network (Feldman & Ballard, 1982). A winner-take-all network is a fully connected graph in which each node inhibits all the others. (Inhibitory links are drawn with circles.) The node with the highest external input adds the (lower) competitive inputs to its own outputs, taking the input. Each winner-take-all node has two input sites, one for competitive input from other wta nodes, one for input from outside the wta network. Any node which receives an input from another node which is higher than its external input will remove itself from the competition, setting its output to zero. The result of this is that exactly one of the nodes, the one with the highest initial input, will end up with all the credit and will activate nodes connected to it. (In these agreement nodes the output is the input, regardless of threshold, so that this competition can take place. Notice the nodes

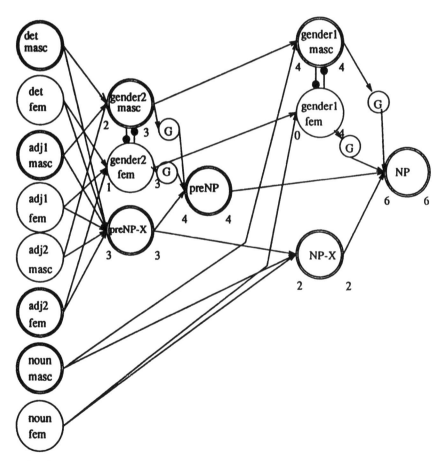

FIG. 6.2.   A network with winner-take-all nodes.

marked "G." These "gate" nodes output their threshold if their threshold is exceeded. Their threshold is the same as the threshold of the preceding agreement node. Without these gates, preNP would receive enough input from the sum of its inputs to fire even before consensus was reached. In future diagrams including wta networks, these gate nodes will be needed, they will not be shown.) If this simple change is made to the network of Fig. 6.1 and the new network is supplied the same input as in the previous example, the network settles into the configuration in Fig. 6.2. This has solved part of the problem. NP will now activate even if an improperly gendered sequence is applied. (It will not activate if a sequence with missing components is used.) Notice that the -X nodes are no longer actually needed, since, e.g., pre-NP will activate eventually if pre-NP-X does.

There are two problems, however, that we would still like to solve. First, this network no longer has the property that the final state of the network looks like a grammatical parse tree. Second, the network neither detects nor signals specific extragrammaticalities.

The network in Fig. 6.3 solves these problems. The nodes marked conflict activate if there is competition, i.e. if more than one input line is active at the same time. Note that all the forward links have been removed, except for the ones which activate the conflict nodes. They are the same as in the previous diagram.

The nodes drawn half hidden by the regular nodes are "shadows," which participate only after a parse is finished. The purpose of this shadow network is to settle into the (corrected) parse tree. Any agreement failure in the forward network will be removed in the shadows. Following Fanty (1985), these nodes are activated starting from the NP (top node) and working back towards the inputs. There is no competition in this shadow network; the winning nodes from the forward parse control (directly or indirectly) the activation. (Only metavariable nodes not connected to higher ones are directly controlled from above. In this example this occurs only at the top of the network.) There are backward links mirroring each forward link and from NP, (gender1 masc), and (gender1 fem) to their own shadows. These last three links are at the "top" of the tree—NP at the very top, gender1 at the top of the network of nodes involving the gender. These links lead the activity to begin its backward journey.

Figure 6.3 shows the final state of the network after the input (det masc) (adj1 fem) (adj2 masc) (noun fem) is applied. Notice the shadows have corrected the sentence to (det masc) (adj1 masc) (adj2 masc) (noun masc). Also note that the conflict nodes are on.

It is worth discussing the timing delays involved in handling the extragrammatical parse. If a grammatical phrase is set up in the input nodes, the winner-take-all networks involve no delay, as a winner is already present. If an extragrammatical phrase is set up, one more cycle must be introduced for each winner-take-all network, so the settling time is potentially doubled. On any particular example, one additional cycle is required for each conflict. Unlike

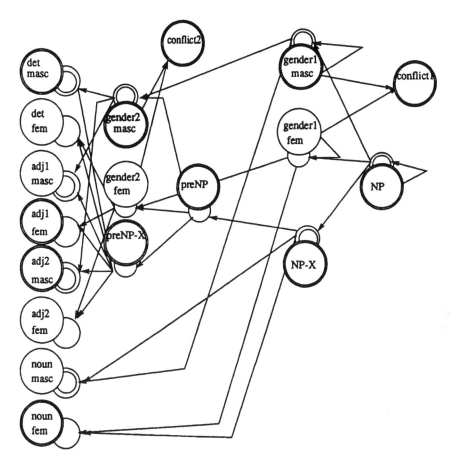

FIG. 6.3.   A shadow network to correct input.

most conventional methods for handling extragrammaticality, this time does not
come from extra processing added after a normal parse fails; the extra processing
happens as the parse progresses. The feedback network adds time proportional
to the depth of the network, but this type of feedback network is needed for other
reasons in more complicated parsing tasks (cf. Fanty, 1985).

Figure 6.3 raises an interesting linguistic question. The network settles into a
masculine configuration, even though the input includes a feminine noun. It is
easy to change the network so that the gender1 winner-take-all network will
always be dominated by input from the noun. This is done by multiplying the
link values from (noun masc) and (noun fem) by, say, four, and changing the
thresholds of gender1 and NP. In this way it is possible to assign more
importance to the head of the phrase. Any competition at gender1 will always be
predestined, but its existence alerts the network to the extragrammaticality.

COUNTING

The mechanism described in the previous section handles simple extragrammaticality by reconciling different nominees for the value of a metavariable. It is only able to handle metavariables with a finite number of possible values, each of which is represented by a node. This will suffice for a wide variety of grammatical constructions, but not all. In this section we discuss a mechanism for handling counting constructions.

The two-level grammar that follows represents the context-sensitive language $\{a^n b^n c^n\}$. It reproduces the grammar from an earlier example. Recall that the metavariables are used to encode the count.

Metagrammar
COUNT → {X}+

Grammatical Schema
S → (A,*,COUNT) (B,*,COUNT) (C,*,COUNT)
(A,*,COUNT X) → (A,*,COUNT) a
(B,*,COUNT X) → (B,*,COUNT) b
(C,*,COUNT X) → (C,*,COUNT) c
(A,*,X) → a
(B,*,X) → b
(C,*,X) → c

There are natural constructions similar to context-sensitive languages that count, e.g. the crossed serial dependencies of Swiss German (Shieber, 1985) and Bambara (Culy, 1985). There are other constructions, e.g. the "respectively" construction of English and the less complex crossed-serial dependency of Dutch, which may naturally follow this pattern, but also have context-free, non-counting grammars (Pullum & Gazdar, 1982). In all these examples, the noncontext-freeness of the grammar arises from the necessity of enforcing a length equality constraint. The metavariables in the grammar do just that.

Because there are arbitrarily deep parse trees for strings in $\{a^n b^n c^n\}$, it is not possible to construct a static (in shape) connectionist network which will settle into a parse of the string $a^n b^n c^n$. Instead, we construct a network in which nodes act as counters and which can reproduce the (corrected) input string.

Consider the network in Fig. 6.4. It functions as follows:

1. The input nodes are turned on to represent an incoming a,b,c, or d. d is used to mark the end of the string. The nodes turn themselves off after two time steps. This allows the counter nodes time to react.

2. A counter node counts the number of times its input line switches from 0 to 1. The output of the counters is just this count. Notice that the b and c counters have inhibitory connections back to a second site on the previous counters. Each

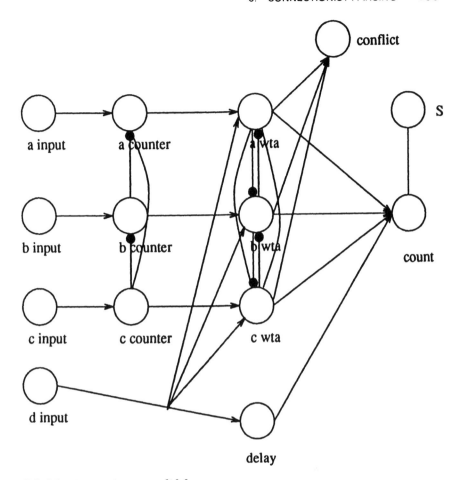

FIG. 6.4.   A network to parse $a^n b^n c^n$.

counter has this second input site for inhibition; if this site is receiving input the node will no longer count. This means that an "a" which appears after a "b" will be ignored. (This may not be desirable; other mechanisms are possible.)

3.   The output of the "d" input unit is connected to the nodes in the winner-take-all network. These nodes do not become receptive (able to act on their input from the counters) until the "d" input node is active. The winner in this case outputs the maximum, rather than the sum of all the inputs, so it's really a winner-pass-input, rather than a winner-take-all network. The final node (count) activates after a delay on the "d" input node and connects to the S node, which marks a completed parse. (The delay allows one time step for the wta conflict to finish before the count can activate.)

This network is designed to settle into the state corresponding to $a^n b^n c^n$ where n is the maximum of $\{r,s,t\}$ if $a^r b^s c^t$ is input. Other functions of r, s, and t are easily possible. For linguistic analysis, there is a weakly appealing reason for choosing the maximum, since in that case $a^n b^n c^n$ at least includes all of the input symbols.

It is also possible to build a mechanism to detect the currently ignored out-of-sequence input (e.g. $a^2 babc^2$ currently parses as correct).

A feedback network of shadow nodes can be constructed to output the corrected string (Fig. 6.5, where only the shadows are shown). The inhibition links make the network finish outputting one letter before continuing with the next one. The output nodes, upon activation, output a 1, then switch to 0 and wait for an input change. The decounter nodes count down, slowly, to zero. (Here slowly means on the same time scale as the receiver of the output.) The node in the wta networks just pass their input to their output.

The network in Fig. 6.6 adds one more wrinkle to the process. It is designed to process $a^n b^m a^n b^m$. Here, only two nodes are used to input a and b. The init node causes acounter1 and bcounter1 to be initially receptive to input. When the first b is counted by bcounter1, its output inhibits the first acounter1 from further change and makes acounter2 receptive. (The "d" input node and its links would play the same role as in the previous example. They have been removed for the sake of clarity.) The sequence of two of each counter allows the input to be directed to the correct counter in each case. Two winner-take-maximum nodes are used to determine count1 (n) and count2 (m).

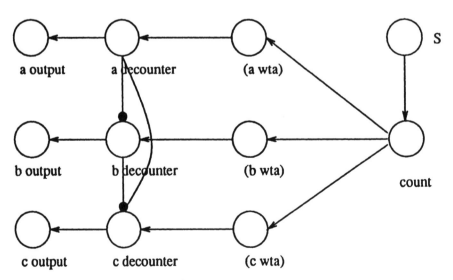

FIG. 6.5.   A network to correct $a^r b^s c^t$.

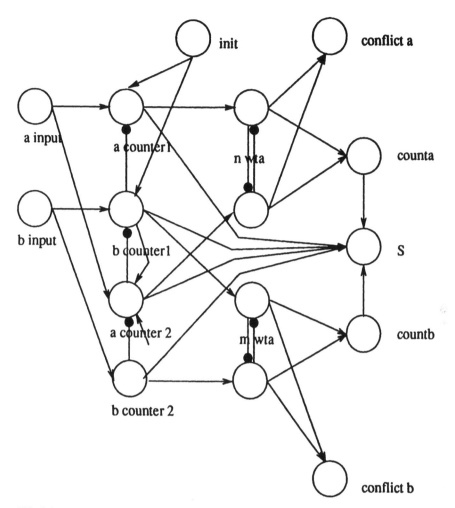

FIG. 6.6.   A network to parse $a^n b^m a^n b^m$.

This method of sequencing activation so that only certain nodes are receptive is quite useful for freeing nodes from absolute position dependence and will be used again in the following sections.

CONSTITUENT MOTION

There are two reasons to consider the question of constituent motion, i.e. the movement of a node from one place in a tree to another. First, there are syntactic errors in which components appear out of order. Correcting them would require movement. Second, in many linguistic theories (e.g. the extended standard theory of transformational grammar or government-binding theory), parsing involves the reversal of transformations, which literally switch the position of components. (E.g. the passive construction of English is explained in both of these theories as arising from a transformation of the structure tree, which, loosely speaking, reverses the object and subject NPs. The advantage of this explanation is that the passive and active versions of a sentence have nearly identical structure before the transformation.)

In the agreement example of Fig. 6.1 each of the input nodes is tied to a particular location in the input string. This requirement is relaxed in the $a^n b^m a^n b^m$ example, where all the "a"s ("b"s) are handled by one input node. To discuss notion of components in this framework, it is necessary to use a similar relaxation in natural language examples.

Consider the network of Fig. 6.7. This network appears more complicated than it really is. The first column (I) is a set of input nodes, one for each syntactic category of input. To signal an input, one is activated, has non-zero input for a while, and then turns itself off. (The assumption here is that input arrives slower than the time required for the network to absorb the input. The node needs to stay active long enough to signal nodes in the next column, but turn itself off before the next input arrives.)

The second column (II) is a temporally organised set of detectors. Each of these has two input sites, one for "normal" input and one for links which make the node receptive or nonreceptive to input. The links that effect the receptivity of the nodes are not shown. (It is possible to combine this into one site, but it is clearer this way. Remember, there is only one output for each node.) Nodes higher in the column, if they have positive output, represent inputs which occur earlier in the sentence. The temporal relation between the nodes is entirely relative. Each node which has non-zero output inhibits itself and the two nodes before it (so they cannot be effected by input) and primes the three nodes after it (so they are receptive). Changing the receptivity of a node has no immediate effect on its output. This sequencing assures that exactly one of each type of receptor node can be effected by input (i.e. is receptive) at any given time. The first three nodes are receptive initially.

To make this clearer, if the first input is a verb, node verb1 will have non-zero output. This will cause det1 and noun1 to be silenced forever. If the first input is a noun and the second a verb, noun1 and verb1 will have non-zero output and det2, noun2, and verb2 will be receptive. Notice that the node verb1 is active in both situations, but in the first corresponds to the first word of the sentence and in the second corresponds to the second word. (Not all the links are shown. I am also assuming that the input should not contain two consecutive words of the same type. If this is not the case counting nodes can be used, as in the last section.)

The third column represents the application of the following productions:

NP → det noun
VP → verb.

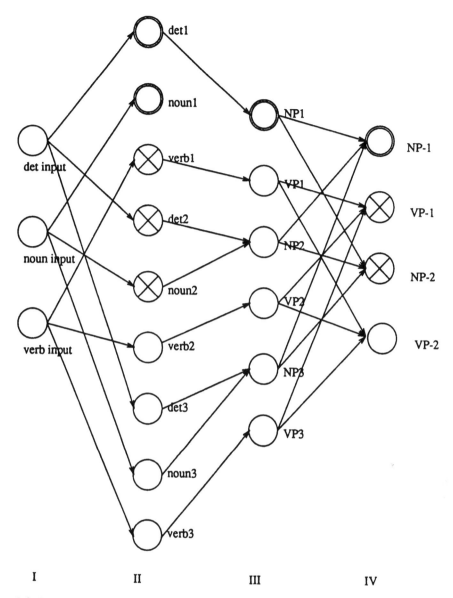

FIG. 6.7.   A network with temporally–varying receptivity.

These productions apply only if the constituents on the right-hand side of the rule are contiguous in the temporally oriented column. (Or if the constituents are separated by other constituents, all of which are off. This cannot happen in this example, but can be handled by inhibitory input links in representing rules where it can.) If one of the productions can be applied, one of the nodes in III will be active, corresponding to application of this production.

Column IV is like column II, with a sequence of NP, VP nodes, two of which are receptive at any given time. (The links that do this have been omitted.) Here, every NP in III is attached to every NP in IV (this can be simplified somewhat). To prevent every NP in IV from responding to the same NP in III, the nodes in IV sample their input when they are first made receptive and set their threshold to their nominal threshold plus the current input level. This means that before an NP in IV can be activated, an NP in III must be activated after the NP in IV becomes receptive.

For example, suppose the first two inputs are a det and a noun. At this point, the network state will be as in Fig. 6.7. Nodes with crossed circles are receptive, nodes with double circles are active and outputting. At this point, the threshold of NP-2 in column IV is two and the input to it is one. This masks the one active NP in column III. If NP-2 in III now becomes active, it can activate NP-2 in column IV.

The reason for introducing this freedom from positional dependence is to allow a representation of constituent motion.

The ability of networks to handle extragrammaticality is tied to another ability: The ability to change the parse by manipulating the nodes that resolve the conflicts. In the simple agreement case shown earlier, if the final winner-take-all network is artificially flooded with activation favouring the feminine value, the feedback will be a feminine phrase even if the input is a syntactically correct masculine phrase. If a similar network were devised for subject/verb agreement, the sentence could be changed from plural to singular by a similar means. (Here we assume the input nodes remain linked to the actual lexical input, which can be switched by the number metavariable from plural to singular.)

Since the syntactic structures of plural and singular sentences (or feminine/masculine noun phrases) are almost identical, it is hardly surprising that such a switch is possible. It is more interesting to contemplate a change where the difference in syntactic structure is larger. We will now consider a change in structure that involves the movement of a constituent.

Consider the following grammar. This is a representation of the idea that a question can be formed by moving the auxiliary verb to the front of the subject noun phrase. It is linguistically inadequate, but does contain the movement idea we want to demonstrate. (This is another example of two externally different sentences with quite similar deep structures.) A network for recognising this grammar is given in Fig. 6.9.

Metagrammar
stype → decl | ques

Grammatical Schema
S → (S,*,stype)
(S,*,decl1) → NP auxverb VP

(S,*,ques) → auxverb NP VP
NP → noun
VP → mainverb

This network is like the one demonstrated earlier, where columns II and IV are temporally oriented (the links which start and stop receptivity are not shown). The winner-take-all network in VI mediates between the value of decl and the value of ques for the metavariable stype.

The figure shows active (double circle) and receptive (crossed circle) nodes after the phrase (noun auxverb mainverb) has been parsed. As in the examples in the previous section, we would like to construct a shadow feedback network that will display the result of the parse. In addition, we would like to be able to force the sentence into the opposite configuration by flooding the ques node of the winner-take-all network with activation. (This is a variation of a "correction.") That is easy, but we would also like to show how to reuse the sections of the input sentence in this new configuration, thereby "moving" the auxverb.

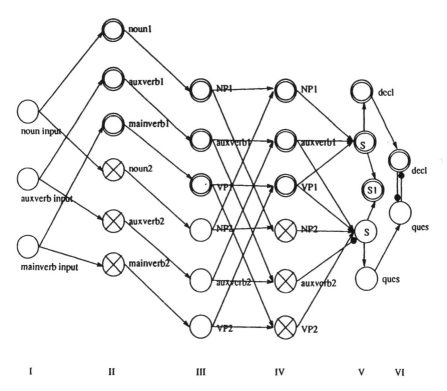

FIG. 6.8.   A network for both declaratives and questions.

Consider the network of Fig. 6.9. In column III, corresponding to the specific NP, auxverb, or VP, the only nodes which are ever receptive are the ones primed from above. That is, there are links from the nonshadow nodes to the shadow nodes. The nodes in the column do not deactivate those above them, but make receptive those below them, which are also receiving from their nonshadow counterparts. (This requires a set of nodes for transmitting receptivity. For clarity, they are not shown in the figure.) In this example, the first three nodes are the only potentially receptive ones.

As the activation flows back from (S-ques) the feedback net settles into configuration in Fig. 6.9. The configuration can be interpreted as a different structure on the same initial node. We allow the temporal interpretation of column IV to over-ride that of II, so that the noun appears after the verb.

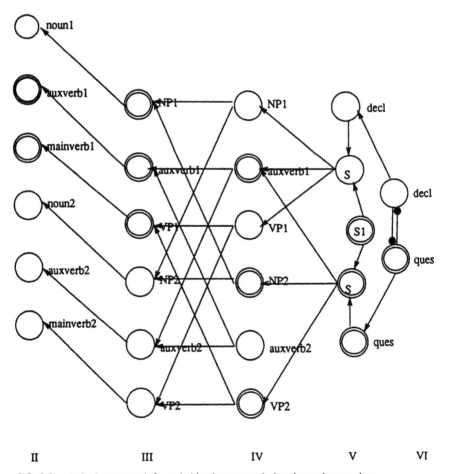

FIG. 6.9.   A shadow network for switching between a declarative and a question.

We have constructed a mechanism for changing the interpreted order of the constituents. It has the drawback that it is a lot harder to examine the network. This difficulty happens because we forced the system to use the same column I nodes, but interpreted in a different, nontemporal order. (Notice that the configuration given is an impossible one, if considered with each temporal column in strict order. If we allow feedback to different column one nodes, the system is easier to understand, but loses the benefit that the actual lexical items, which we imagine as tied to the column I items, can be reshuffled.)

There is an elegant way around this dilemma. Instead of just using spatially represented temporal relations, we can use actual temporal relations as well. Imagine the same feedback network with delays built in so that auxverb becomes active several steps before VP, etc. (in the feedback S → auxverb VP NP). This will cause the column I nodes to activate in the correct time sequence. If they are then connected to the inputs columns of another copy of Fig. 6.8, the feedforward network will settle into the new, changed configuration.

What we have then, is a way (a somewhat crude way) of moving a constituent by trading types of temporal representation. This shows that we can, in fact, rearrange components in a connectionist parsing (or generating) system. This rearrangement corresponds to movement in a transformational grammar. (A full treatment of this connection between connectionism and transformational grammar is beyond the scope of this chapter. It will be explored more fully in Rager & Berg [1990].)

MISSING CONSTITUENTS

One of the most commonly encountered extragrammaticalities is ellipsis, or missing constituents. These are generally hard to explain and process. They may lie outside the realm of syntax, although some theoretical work has been done on the linguistics of syntactic fragments (see, e.g. Barton, 1985).

It is possible to use the ideas we have developed to build parsers which can recover from missing constituents. Suppose we have two rules for NP:

NP → det noun
NP → det adj noun

Consider the network in Fig. 6.10. The numbers on the links are connection strengths. The output of a node (0 or 1) is multiplied by the strength to give the input to the target node. If a grammatical set of input nodes is active, the network activates the node corresponding to the correct rule. If an ungrammatical set is applied, the winner-take-all network mediates in favour of the "closest" rule, where closest is determined by summing the strengths. The values on the nodes were chosen so that each grammatical possibility sums to 6 on its target (the 6 is arbitrary, it's the smallest integer that works here). The choice of -3 for the

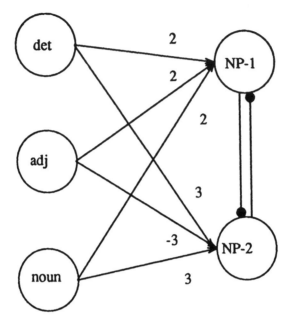

FIG. 6.10.   A network to handle simple ellipsis.

inhibitory link is also somewhat arbitrary, it was simply chosen as the negative of the strength of one of the excitatory links.

Table 6.2 gives the results in all the cases. The results are reasonable, although in some cases there doesn't seem to be a "better" choice.

This method works well for small networks. Since all the completely correct interpretations sum to the same number, grammatical combinations are favoured over extragrammatical ones. In larger networks, with many combining rules, this can be very complicated. More work on ellipsis in connectionism is

TABLE 6.2
Results of Missing Constituent Parses

Output From			Initial Input To			
det	*adj*	*noun*	*NP-1*	*NP-2*	*Winner*	*Judgment*
1	1	1	6	3	NP-1	grammatical, correct winner
1	0	1	4	6	NP-2	grammatical, correct winner
1	1	0	4	0	NP-1	ungrammatical, reasonable winner
1	0	0	2	3	NP-2	ungrammatical, ?
0	1	0	2	0	NP-1	ungrammatical, okay winner
0	0	1	2	3	NP-2	ungrammatical, okay winner
0	1	1	4	0	NP-1	ungrammatical, reasonable winner

definitely needed. This problem will probably not yield to purely syntactic methods.

CONCLUSIONS

To summarise, we have explored mechanisms for detecting and correcting syntactic failures in local connectionist parsing networks. Using the two-level grammar as a representation, we first built networks to handle simple agreement failure and then to handle agreement failure where the agreement is based on a counter. These two together give a powerful representation, able to reach out of the context-free grammars into the indexed grammars to cover a wide range of co-occurrence phenomena, including crossed serial dependencies. These networks are "natural," because they handle the extragrammaticality with minor, real-time modifications of strict syntactic networks. The parallelism available in a network is useful, since following paths on which a mismatch occurs might otherwise waste time. For example, verb subcategorisation for complement type can be represented with a metavariable which links the verb and the rule to expand its complement. There will be mismatches even when there is also a correct match. For example, if the verb requires two NP complements, the rule which requires only one will apply with a mismatch of the subcategorisation variable. The parallelism allows the extragrammatical and grammatical parses to run together.

The ability to run these networks in both directions shows a relationship between recognition and generation. By adding a generating "shadow network" and manipulating the metavariable assignments, we can alter the input into a different, related output. A temporally structured sequence was developed to allow flexible use of the nodes. This sequencing also allowed us to develop a connectionist form of constituent movement. The possibility of constituent movement allows us to also consider transformational analyses.

The sequencing actually can be used for another purpose: Shrinking the network. If we are willing to accept a network that doesn't remember the whole parse, we can attach the bottom of a sequenced column to the top, so that the nodes can be reused. If this is done, then there is always a set of "active" and a set of "receptive" nodes, but once the activation has been used in the next column, the nodes become available for reuse. (This does require some cautious reworking of the way the nodes in this column and the next column handle input.)

It is also worth mentioning that if we accept the assertion of generalised phrase structure grammar (Gazdar, Klein, Pullum, & Sag, 1985) that grammars obey linear precedence (LP) relations then our sequences are simplified if they are ordered according to the LP rules. Linear precedence means that if X . . . Y can appear in the right-hand side of a phrase structure rule, then Y . . . X cannot. This means that a situation where Y is active and X is receptive below it is never required, since this configuration cannot appear in a rule.

Returning to the handling of extragrammaticality, we considered the use of winner-take-all networks to choose among alternate parses when each is missing required constituents. A simple example was given, but this is a complex phenomenon. It if can be handled using syntactic techniques, it will require the use of more information than used here. The same simple winner-take-all technique can be used to ignore excess input in simple cases.

Although we used two-level grammars, a very general representation, in fact any grammatical representation with a strong reliance on feature unification (e.g. definite clause grammars), could be used as a basis for constructing the networks. All that is required is an adequate explicit encoding of linguistic relations in the grammar features, which can be used as the basis for winner-take-all networks, which then allow loose matching of productions.

None of the networks discussed herein have the complexity of a real parser, but the techniques address the same questions that would be found in one. The nodes in the networks here are all simple syntactic markers, which may include metavariables. When a rule is parsed, the constituent nodes activate the dominating node (the nodes representing the right-hand side activate the left-hand side node) and the winner-take-all networks handle possible metavariable conflict among the constituents. In a full parser, for example that of Fanty (1985), the nodes are more complex. In Fanty's case, the node is a (production, length, position) triple. It is still the case that constituent nodes activate their parent, although the children are themselves actually full, finished productions resulting in the required components. If the productions are written with metavariables, as they are here, the matching will include a winner-take-all resolution of the metavariable values. The principle is exactly the same. In fact, it is easy to think about the metavariables with nodes that represent productions, since metavariables are uniformly substituted within production. The handling of extragrammaticality in full parsers based on two-level grammars is discussed in Rager (1987). The techniques used there to extend chart parsing and corner parsing to extragrammaticality give details about how to handle metavariable relaxation with more complex objects.

Much work remains to be done on connectionist parsing of extragrammatical input, including the important subject of its relationship to semantic and pragmatic analysis.

ACKNOWLEDGEMENTS

Experimentation on the networks described was done using the Rochester Connectionist Simulator (Goddard, Lynne, Mintz, & Bukys, 1989), whose contribution I acknowledge. I would also like to thank my colleagues at Northwestern University and at Amherst College for their support and for providing rich, albeit hectic, environments in which to work. Special thanks to my colleague George Berg and to the editors of this volume.

REFERENCES

Barlow, M. & Ferguson, C. (1988). *Agreement in natural language.* Stanford: C.S.L.I.

Barton, E.L. (1985). *A theory of constituent structures and constituent utterances.* Ph.D. dissertation, Northwestern University.

Carbonell, J.G. & Hayes, P.J. (1984). *Recovery strategies for parsing extragrammatical language.* Department of Computer Science Technical Report CMU-CS-84-107. Pittsburgh, Penn.: Carnegie-Mellon University.

Charniak, E. (1983). A parser with something for everyone. In M. King (Ed.) *Parsing Natural Language.* New York: Academic Press, 117–150.

Chomsky, N. (1985). *Knowledge of language.* New York: Praeger.

Culy, C. (1985). The complexity of the vocabulary of Bambara. *Linguistics and Philosophy, 8,* 345–351.

Fanty, M. (1985). *Context-free parsing in connectionist networks.* Department of Computer Science Technical Report TR-174. Rochester, New York: University of Rochester.

Feldman, J. & Ballard, D. (1982). Connectionist models and their properties. *Cognitive Science, 6,* 205–254.

Gazdar, G., Klein, E., Pullum, G., & Sag, I. (1985). *Generalized phrase structure grammar.* Cambridge, Mass.: Harvard University Press.

Goddard, N.H., Lynne, K.L., Mintz, T., & Bukys, L. (1989). *Rochester Connectionist Simulator.* Technical Report 233. Rochester, N.Y.: University of Rochester, Computer Science Department.

Greibach, S. (1974). Some restrictions on W-grammars. *Proceedings of the Annual ACM Symposium on the Theory of Computing,* 256–265.

Krulee, G.K. (1983). *Two-level representations for natural language.* Available from the Indiana University Linguistics Club. Also published as Department of Electrical Engineering and Computer Science Technical Report 83-04-AI-02. Evanston, Il.: Northwestern University.

Kwasny, S.C. & Sondheimer, N.K. (1981). Relaxation techniques for parsing grammatically ill-formed input in natural language understanding systems. *American Journal of Computational Linguistics, 7,* 99–108.

Marcus, M.P. (1980). *A theory of syntactic recognition for natural language.* Cambridge, Mass.: M.I.T. Press.

Pagan, F.G. (1981). *Formal specification of programming languages: A panoramic primer.* Englewood Cliffs, N.J.: Prentice-Hall.

Pullum, G. & Gazdar, G. (1982). Natural languages and context-free languages. *Linguistics and Philosophy, 4,* 471–504.

Rager, J.E. (1987). *Multi-level structures for natural language processing.* Ph.D. dissertation, Northwestern University.

Rager, J.E. (1988). Self-correcting connectionist parsing. *Proceedings of the AAAI spring symposium.* Menlo Park, Calif.: American Association for Artificial Intelligence.

Rager, J.E. & Berg, G. (1990). A connectionist model of motion and government in Chomsky's government and binding theory. *Connection Science, 2,* 35–52.

Shieber, S.M. (1985). Evidence against the context-freeness of natural language. *Linguistics and Philosophy, 8,* 333–343.

Weischedel, R.M. & Black, J.E. (1980). Responding intelligently to unparsable inputs. *American Journal of Computational Linguistics, 6,* 97–109.

Weischedel, R.M. & Ramshaw, L.A. (1986). *Reflections on the knowledge needed to process ill-formed language.* B.B.N. Laboratories Technical Report 6264. Cambridge, Mass.: B.B.N. Laboratories.

Weischedel, R.M. & Sondheimer, N.K. (1983). Meta-rules as a basis for processing ill-formed input. *American Journal of Computational Linguistics, 9,* 161–177.

7   A Net-linguistic "Earley" Parser

H. Schnelle and R. Doust
Ruhr-Universität, Universitätsstr. 150, 4630 Bochum, Germany

INTRODUCTION

This is a chapter about cognitive architecture, i.e. the architecture of the representational states and processes of a cognitive system (Fodor & Pylyshyn, 1988, p. 10). At present, two types of architecture are under discussion: the classical architectures of symbolic rule systems and the connectionist architectures of interactive units. Net-linguistic systems that have been developed in recent years (see Schnelle, 1981; 1988a; 1988b; for an overview) also have a connectionist architecture even though they are intended as definitional variants of symbolic rule systems. It is our belief that notation is secondary for the content of a linguistic system: Linguistic structure should, for instance, be conceived as a fundamentally abstract entity that can, however, be presented notationally in different ways.

However, in the present situation, symbolic rule systems are the standard descriptive means in theoretical linguistics. The challenge is to find out whether combinatorially and compositionally complex linguistic contents, such as those represented in phrase structure rules, can also be defined in connectionist architectures. The challenge has been explicitly put forward by Fodor and Pylyshyn (1988). This chapter tries to justify a positive answer to the challenge. We present a general translation algorithm that defines a net-linguistic or localist connectionist system given an arbitrary context-free constituent structure grammar. Our approach thus seems to belong to a particular variety of connectionism taken as a theory of implementation (Fodor & Pylyshyn, 1988, p.

169

64). This is, indeed, the case for our position as it is put forward here. It is, however, not the case with respect to the principled position we take on this issue.

Before presenting the details of our system in the latter part of this article, the first part will define the parsing problem in connection with the general problems of linguistic theory, then define the form of a connectionist implementation and give a rough outline of its instantiation for an Earley chart-parser.

THE BASIC CHARACTERISTICS OF THE PARSER

The Parsing Task

In our view the core problems of linguistics are defined in terms of what we call grammar systems. A grammar system consists of a set of sub-systems or levels. A level is a system consisting of minimal elements (primes), a mathematical apparatus for defining formal objects from primes and prime structures, the relevant relations that hold for these elements, and a class of designated formal objects (markers) that are assigned to certain simple prime structures, called the expressions for that level. This specification is a slightly generalised formulation of Chomsky's definition (Chomsky 1986, p. 46 and his fn. 28, i.e. 1975, p. 108).

Generative grammar theory started with the assumption that one level of grammar is the phrase structure level and that this level can be defined by a system of context-free constituent structure rules. The present empirical status of Chomsky's theory led to the assumption that this level could be constrained strongly in such a way that its structure could be defined without the help of rule systems merely by specifying the lexical entities together with some general structure principles and a framework of parameters. For the present article, however, we shall still start from a discussion of context-free constituent structure systems, which are well understood and thus very valuable for studies of the architecture of cognitive systems. They are paradigmatic for finitely specifiable systems with unlimited combinatorial power. Showing how such systems could be defined in connectionist architecture would seem to be the best way to answer the challenge.

In a definition of a constituent structure system for a level, the primes of the general definition are rendered by terminal symbols, the operation of forming simple prime structures is concatenation, and the simple prime structures are strings of terminal symbols. Certain strings of prime symbols are representations of the expressions of the language to be described at that level. In some varieties of grammars these expressions are sequences of morphemes (or lexemes and formatives); in others they are the simple syntactic categories corresponding to parts of speech.

The mathematical apparatus of context-free constituent structure systems introduces other symbols (the so-called nonterminal symbols), and from them defines formal objects such as possible phrase markers, phrase marker components, and sets of phrase marker components (phrase marker sets), as well as basic relations (i.e. the possible constituent structure rules). A specific level (for a particular grammar) is characterised by defining the following for each level: the designated formal objects (i.e. the designated phrase markers) and the rules that generate the designated objects and the assignments to representations of expressions in the language.

A phrase structure parser is a mechanism that assigns a representation of the designated object (the phrase marker) automatically to a representation of an expression at the phrase structure level. The ordinary explanations of the use of context-free constituent structure rules as rewrite-rules operating on symbol strings—i.e. strings of terminal and nonterminal symbols—provide the instructions appropriate for a human symbol manipulator. In the case of a computer implementation, strict instructions concerning the sequence and form of rule applications must be added to the rule system. These added specifications transform the rule system into an algorithm.

One of the most efficient parsing algorithms for context-free constituent structure rule systems is the Earley algorithm. This algorithm applies to so-called context-free constituent structure grammars (CFGs).[1]

The parser takes as an input a sequence of symbols—its *input string*—and assigns to it its phrase marker—its *correct parse*. However, during the parsing process, a set of parses of parts of an expression must be considered and stored temporarily, independently of whether they fit together to form a correct parse of the complete expression. These intermediate results are stored in a list which is called a *parse-list set*.

The parsing problem is, then, to find a mechanism which gives the correct parse of an input string—or, if the input string is structurally ambiguous, the correct parses. In some solutions, such as in Earley's, the problem is solved by a tandem of two mechanisms: the first assigns parse-lists to the input string and the second a correct parse (or correct parses) to the final parse-list set (and thus indirectly to the input string).

Features of Connectionist Structure

In the present chapter, we shall describe how the symbolic manipulations used in Earley's algorithm implemented on a universal machine can always be realised by a (special purpose) network of interactive units. Linguistically, our net-linguistic implementation thus applies to the phrase structure level. Technically, it is best understood as the compilation of a connectionist network of interactive units from a grammar together with the rules of the algorithm.

We shall now give a brief definition of our particular understanding of connectionism. There are, of course, broader and narrower conceptions of what

---

[1]Linguistically, these systems are merely parts of the syntactic parts of grammars but for this formally oriented chapter we shall follow the common practice of calling them grammars.

connectionism is. The broadest conception starts from the principle that the behaviour of complicated systems is to be described by the interaction of a large number of simple units. The simple units are in each moment of time in particular activity states and they change their states depending on their own current states and the states of their neighbours, thus realising the interactivity. Mathematically, the interaction is defined by a set of individual state transition functions,

$$S'(i) := F_i \{ S(i) \}, \hspace{4cm} 1$$

one for each unit i. The set $\{ S(i) \}$ is to be understood as the set of states of the *neighbours* of unit i and $S'(i)$ is the activity state of unit i following the state $S(i)$. In our view, any system defined by equations of this type is a connectionist system. In a narrower sense of connectionism, it is required that the degree of interactive dependency of unit i on unit j be given by a parameter w_{ij} and that the functions F_i be expressed in terms of these "connectionist" parameters. In some cases it is even required that the effects of the neighbours on a unit be superposed linearly, i.e. that the function be expressed by a linear equation (perhaps modified by a simple nonlinear output function F'_i)

$$S'(i) := F'_i [\Sigma_{ij} w_{ij} S(j)]. \hspace{3cm} 2$$

As we shall see, our systems are connectionist in the broad sense, with the F_i taken as Boolean functions.

We now consider just what are the connectionist instantiation mappings of algorithms determined from rule systems. Our *mapping criteria* are the following:

1. Each relevant category symbol of a grammar is mapped on a simple unit. Each unit has two activity states: *active* and *inactive*. If the unit is in the state *active*, the behavioural environment—defined by the presence of a particular input string—is such that the category applies to it.

2. Each relevant structural relation between the categories of a grammar, symbolically expressed by the specific ways in which the category terms occur in rules, is expressed either by the functions F_i or by the neighbourhood relations determining the appropriate arguments—i.e. the sets $\{ S(i) \}$—for the functions.

We thus require that the connectionist mapping be behaviourally and structurally equivalent to the definition of a system in terms of rules together with an interpretative algorithm.

The Architecture of our System

Our implementation consists of a system or network of connected interactive units. As we shall see, the units are very compactly arranged in a three-dimensional space. We shall therefore often speak of the system space and the subspaces of subnetworks. Functionally, the complete network is indeed architecturally subdivided into connected subnetworks, such that each subnetwork has a different computational function. Certain subnetworks serve as storage spaces, others as buffers for executing simple computational tasks, and yet others as specialised computational units. The architecture is as presented in Fig. 7.1. There are four storage spaces in all: the input-string space (I), the shifted input-string space (II), the parse-list space (III), and the correct-parse space (IV); four buffers: the input-string buffer (V), the shifted input-string buffer (VI), the parse-list buffer (VII), and the correct-parse buffer (VIII) (together with their corresponding shift control units [VII'] and [VIII']); and, finally, the parse-list processing unit (IX) and the correct-parse processing unit (X).

The essential subnetworks are the processing units (IX) and (X). Their interactivity structure depends on the specific grammar which determines the system. By contrast, the interactivity structure of the other units is completely homogenous and universal; it is the same for all grammars.

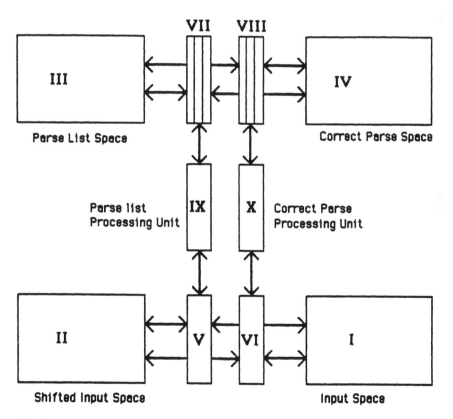

FIG. 7.1.

The role of the units (IX) and (X) is best understood by comparing the architecture of the system with the classical architecture shown in Fig. 7.2. This architecture contains, in addition to the spaces (I) to (IV), storage spaces GR and PR for the storage of the grammar and interpreter rules respectively. These

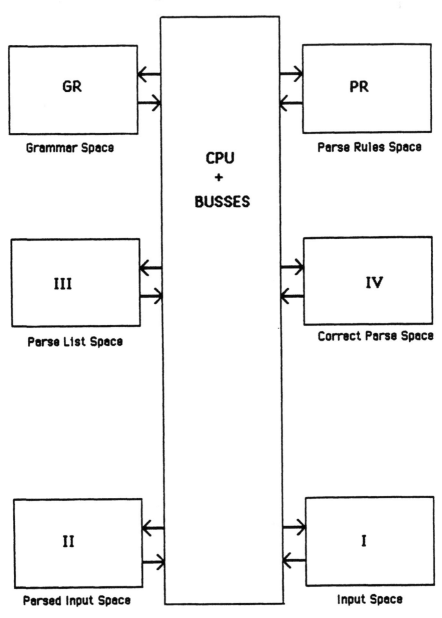

FIG. 7.2.

spaces interpret and control the application of the grammar rules to the input string and the intermediate results of the parse process. As is usual in von Neumann machines, there is a central processing unit together with busses. The changes in the spaces (I) to (IV) are computed by the CPU as the rules of PR and GR flow through this processing unit. Obviously the CPU is the universal processing unit of a von Neumann machine.

The essential properties of the architecture in Fig. 7.2 are the following: the universal processing system CPU (with its storage space) is specialised by the algorithmic rules stored in the PR space to be a machine which is applicable to arbitrary constituent structure grammars. It is further specialised by the grammatical rules stored in the GR space to implement the particular constituent structure grammar determined by GR. We will now discuss how the special purpose architecture given in Fig. 7.1 relates to this architecture of the rule-controlled universal machine. The rules of GR are transformed into a grammar-specific connectivity structure for each of (X) and (IX); the two connectivity structures are similar. The space ER is transformed into a system of functional interdependencies (equivalent to difference equations) describing the dynamic behaviour of the system of elementary units composing (IX) and (X).

As we shall show later, there is a functional reason for specifying the conceptual units of a parser in terms of triples of integers (X, Y, Z). The spaces of our architecture given in Fig. 7.1 can be correspondingly represented in three-dimensional space as in Fig. 7.3. The dimension Y has as many integer positions as there are relevant grammatical concepts, the dimension X all (positive and negative) integers and the dimension Z only 0 and the negative integers. As can be seen from the representation, (IX) and (X) each comprises just one column in the Y dimension; i.e. each comprises just one (processing) position for each relevant grammatical concept. Each integer value of Y defines the plane of all triples with fixed Y; the integers on this surface represent the possible occurrences of the relevant grammatical concepts in the parse-list space and the correct parse space, i.e. the potential occurrences of the concepts in parses.

Each position in the three-dimensional space is in each moment in a particular activity state that will change depending on the current activity states of the neighbours. The neighbours for each unit are specified in advance. All the units in (I) to (IV) have the same neighbourhood relation and so do all those in the buffers (V) to (VIII). Only in (IX) and (X) (and in VII' and VIII') do the neighbourhood relations differ for individual units. This is a consequence of the fact that (IX) and (X) correspond to the structure of the grammar rules. (Similarly, VII' and VIII' correspond to the grammar and the algorithmic iteration conditions.) For each unit there is a function specifying its change of state.

The activity states of a unit will be rendered by mappings S into the set of possible activity values. The changes of state will form a discrete sequence. In this sequential order of states, $S'(X, Y, Z)$ is the state following $S(X, Y, X)$.

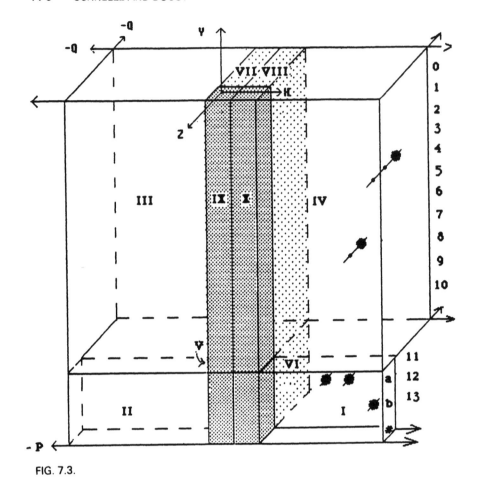

FIG. 7.3.

Furthermore, we take { S (X, Y, Z) } to be the set of states of the neighbours of S (X, Y, Z). The form of the functional dependency of each unit will then be given by equations of the form

$$S'(X, Y, Z) := F_{X, Y, Z} \{ S (X, Y, Z) \} \qquad 3$$

Let us now describe the parsing process in outline. In the starting situation the input string is present in space (I). It is shifted in a stepwise way, symbol for symbol over to space (II). At each symbol shift, it passes through the buffer (V) assigned to the processing unit (IX), and thus causes this unit firstly to compute all the grammatical information relevant for this string position and then to add it to the parse-list information in (III) already computed. The auxiliary buffers at (VIII) help in this process. The process ends after the last symbol of the input string has been transferred to (II) and the last piece of information has been entered to the parse list at (III). After this, the input string now stored at (II) is fed back to (I), in the same stepwise way, passing through unit (VI). But now there is a simultaneous flow of parse-list information passing buffer (VIII). Both buffers activate the processing of (X), which only lets through the parse-list information which fits into a correct parse description, entering it into space (IV). After the last symbol has been passed back from (II) to (I), and the last piece of parse-list information has been checked, the process ends. The correct parse description is now contained in (IV).

The reader should by now have a rough idea of the intended implementation. The details of our system are somewhat involved and understanding them will require a careful reading of this chapter. We believe, however, that this will be rewarding, since the reader should acquire a detailed understanding of how symbolically defined systems can be mapped into systems whose type is similar to systems defined by a set of partial differential/difference equations (i.e. systems of interactive units obeying the rule that the momentary local change of each unit depends on the current states of the neighbours). Formal neural networks are special cases of such systems.

Let us add two general remarks to this introduction. The first remark again concerns the relation of our proposal to connectionist ones. As is easily understood from the outline, our system may be conceived as a version of a localist approach to implementation. We first determine the relevant grammatical concepts and assign interactive units to them and then define the appropriate connectivities and interactivity functions. Since these functions have the form of formula (3) our proposal is connectionist in the broad sense. Our system is, however, not connectionist if one understands by this a subsymbolic, conceptually distributed adaptive and learning system. We nevertheless believe that it contains structural insights which may guide the development of flexible learning systems with appropriately constrained initial structure.

The second remark we wish to make concerns the implementational character of our approach. We believe that in the present state of the art, we must first study the structure and behaviour of systems that are well understood in terms of the classical methods of description in cognitive science. Extended experience may, however, provide techniques which will allow direct design of interactive systems in ways similar to those used in the structural design of computer hardware. It may well be that rule specification of behaviour will then have to be derived from interactive structure, i.e. by a method which would be the inverse of the one specified in this article.

We shall now explain in detail how the connectionist parse list computation is derived from Earley's algorithm. For those who are unfamiliar with it, we shall first give an introduction to some of the details required and shall then proceed by giving the general and specific description of the three-dimensional connectionist parsing system we have constructed as its counterpart.

THE REPRESENTATION OF PARSE-INFORMATION

Motivation and Content

In order to provide a comparison of our work with that of Earley, it will be useful here to first describe the various ways by which the results of the parsing processes can be represented. In Earley's case parse-information is computed symbol configurations stored in lists. In our case, it consists of activity configurations over a space of simple interactive units. Before presenting our representation, we shall give a brief introduction into Earley's representation and its relation to context-free grammars. We shall follow its representation in Aho and Ullman (1972). Readers who are familiar with Earley's methods of representation of parse information can skip these two sections and go to *Our Approach* (p. 187).

For ease of exposition and comparison, we shall refer in this chapter to the following simple example grammar of our choice:

$$G = \{ N, \Sigma, P, S \}$$

where $N = \{ S, A \}$, $\Sigma = \{ a, b \}$, $S = \{ S \}$, and P is the set of the following grammar rules:

$$S -> a A, S -> A b,$$
$$A -> a a, A -> a$$

used to parse the following input string:

a a b

In the parsing of this sentence with this grammar, we can see that right up to the last symbol the possible structure of the sentence remains ambiguous. Were the third symbol to have been an a, the sentence recognised would have had the structure of the first S-rule, i.e. aA. But the third terminal is in fact a b, and so the successful S-rule is the second one. We can thus see clearly the need for an algorithm that retains all possible parse-paths during the processing that are compatible with the terminals so far recognised. The phenomenon shown by this grammar is similar to the switching phenomena observed in the case of the sentences:

The old train the young / The old train broke down

or

The poor shop went bankrupt / The poor shop at the market

We now discuss some different ways of representing the result of parsing the input string according to our example grammar.

The Standard Representation of Parses and Parse-lists for a Given String

A simple way of representing the final result of parsing the sentence, or as we shall say, the *correct parse*, might be as in Fig. 7.4, where the different arcs shown represent the respective categories that have been recognised.

A *correct parse* of a string is thus a description of the constituents of an S-symbol in terms of a tree-like structure, where each node of the tree is governed by a grammar rule, and where the leaves of the tree given by the rules form the *complete* ordered list of terminals making up the string to be parsed.

A *partial parse* of a string is, in contrast, a description of the constituents of an S-symbol as shown, where at the leaves we merely find a *part* of the ordered list of terminals making up the string to be parsed.

If one were to represent these arcs in a parse-tree that shows all the possibilities of partial parses that would have been considered during the left-to-

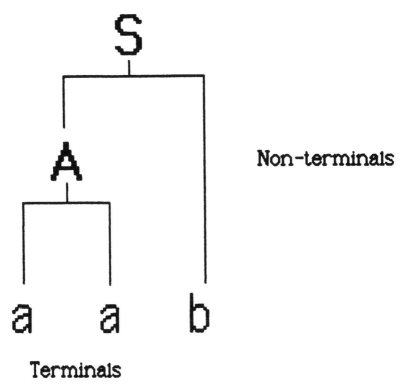

FIG. 7.4.

right parsing process, the definitive or actual correct parse of the sentence would appear along with all the other partial parses that did not, at the end of this particular string, lead to a complete parse (cf. Fig. 7.5).

Tabular Representations

The information represented by a tree-structure can also be represented in a tabular form. We can do this by assigning to each of the possible categories a row, and to each terminal symbol occurrence in a given string a column. An arc (in the sense of Winograd, 1983) is represented by a number indicating its length. We call a *completed category* an arc's category of a particular length in a particular position with respect to a string, of which *all* the necessary elements making it up according to the grammar rules have been found in the input string in the range covered by the length of the category. An *incompleted category* is like a completed category, except that some of the constituents are yet to be found in the range covered by the length of the category.

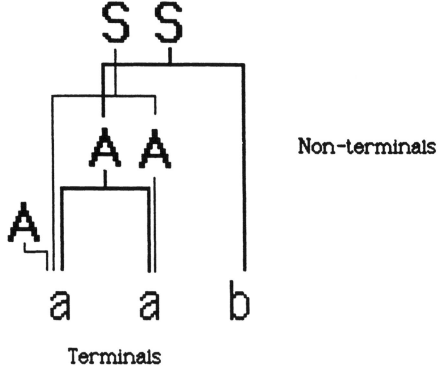

FIG. 7.5.

TABLE 7.1

Lengths of Completed	S:		2	3
Categories	A:	1	1/2	
Occurrence positions	0	1	2	3
Input terminals		a	a	b

1/2 here means that two different occurrences of A end at this position (position 2): one of length 0, the other of length 1.

Representing the information in this way, we could also, for example, choose to show merely the completed categories and their lengths. For our example we would get the representation of Table 7.1.

Alternatively, we could also replace these lengths by pointers to the particular position at which the arc started. The situation would then look as in Table 7.2.

The numbers here refer to the position (shown at the bottom of the table) where the arc started, and thus, in an indirect way, do fix the position and length of the category recognised.

Instead of representing the syntactic categories, we could also represent the rules from which the results were obtained, i.e. we could choose to distinguish the different types of S and A that occur according to the constituents making them up. Combining the rule symbols with the pointer information, we end up with Table 7.3, i.e. an ordered set of lists of objects describing the parsing of a sentence: *parse-lists*. This method of representing parsing is, roughly speaking, also that used by Earley's algorithm, as we shall see. The reader should verify the way in which it corresponds to the earlier representations.

Earley's Representation

In Earley's representation, note is, however, not only taken of completed grammatical categories, but also of the incomplete ones, which mark the intermediate steps leading to recognition of particular grammatical categories. This requires the introduction of symbols for incomplete categories. Earley derives appropriate symbols by the device of "dotting" the rules of a given grammar. The result of dotting a rule we will call a *dotted rule symbol* or an *arc*. It should be noted that a dotted rule symbol does not designate a rule, but a category, in fact usually an incomplete category.

TABLE 7.2

Initial Positions of Completed	S:		0	0
Categories	A:	0	0/1	
Occurrence positions	0	1	2	3
Input terminals		a	a	b

TABLE 7.3

List 0	List 1	List 2	List 3
		$<$S->aA ,0$>$	
		$<$A->aa ,0$>$	
	$<$A->a ,0$>$	$<$A->a ,1$>$	$<$S->Ab ,0$>$
0	1	2	3
	a	a	b

For each CF-rule of the form $X -> Y_1 \ldots Y_n$, n dotted rule symbols of the form $X -> Y_1 \ldots Y_j . Y_{j+1} \ldots Y_n$, for $0 \leqslant j \leqslant n-1$, for incomplete rules, and one dotted rule symbol for the completed category, namely $X -> Y_1 \ldots Y_n$. are constructed.

The set of all dotted rules so constructed from the grammar rules or productions P of a grammar $G = \{N, \Sigma, P, S\}$, we shall call $P.$, and the new "dotted" grammar used by Earley, which results from the dotting process, we shall call $G. = \{\Sigma, P., S\}$.

The dot in a dotted rule symbol separates that part of the right-hand side of the rule which has been recognised at a particular moment in time, from the part which still needs be recognised in order for the rule as a whole to be satisfied. The dotted rule symbols for representing incomplete or complete categories are used in a similar way to that for the nonterminal categories stated earlier: They are placed in the lists of a list-sequence, one for each position of the terminal-string to be parsed.

The following dotted rule symbol, for example, together with its pointer,

$$< S -> a . A , 0 >$$

may be placed in list 1 in Table 7.3. It then indicates that a particular part a of a string S has been found in this list, and that it would require the subsequent finding of an A starting at this list position for recognition of a complete S. The pointer 0 indicates the particular list at which this S-symbol "started" or was predicted. (The pointer cannot, in general, exceed n the length of the given input string.)

This, then, is an important feature of Earley's representation: Instead of representing the ordinary nonterminal symbols occurring in the rules of a given CF-grammar at the nodes in a tree, other symbols are distributed over the lists of a list configuration. An item is a pair of a *dotted rule symbol* (or arc) and a *pointer number*. For each string of length n to be parsed, the list configuration is a sequence of $n+1$ lists: an initial list and a list for each symbol occurrence of the string to be parsed. Each list is a set of items. A pointer in an item is to be taken as the sequence number of the list it refers to. An *item occurrence* is an item occurring as an element of a list. It may be specified by a triple of the form:

< list number, dotted rule symbol, pointer number >

Parses and parse lists for a string of length n may thus also be taken to be sets of item occurrences satisfying the general conditions:

$0 \leqslant$ list number $\leqslant n, 0 \leqslant$ pointer number $\leqslant n$

and certain structure conditions derived from the given grammar in a way still to be dealt with.

THE EARLEY PARSE-LIST ALGORITHM

Motivation

Formally, Earley's algorithm may be taken to contain two kinds of specifications:

1. Structure constraints for the possible distributions of item occurrences over list configurations (given a string and a grammar).
2. A sequential ordering of partial list configurations satisfying the structure constraints together with a functional specification transforming a partial list configuration into the next one in the sequence.

Here, (1) specifies the formal structure of possible parses and (2) the process of algorithmic generation.

More concretely, the algorithm manipulates the items in placing and referring to them in the item-lists I_x, a sequence of lists corresponding to the occurrence positions X of the parsed string of terminals. Importantly, the lists are worked on sequentially, and new lists are thought of as being added to the right of the old ones.

Our aim is to transform Earley's specifications, given in terms of symbol occurrences, into connectionist specifications given in terms of functional dependencies of the current activities of nodes in a space of connected node positions. We apply the localist principle of transformation: One concept—one node. The essential idea of our transformation consists of not taking syntactic categories or dotted rule symbols as the basic concepts but the item occurrences. That is, each possible item occurrence will be rendered by a node. Earley's structure constraint will be transformed into activity dependencies between the nodes and the algorithmic specifications into a structured process of the expansion of activities over the space of nodes whose activity distribution corresponds to distributions of item occurrences (that is, distributions of items over list configurations).

The formal character of our transformation consists of deriving algebraic formulae specifying the interactions of the nodes distributed in space from the symbolic rules given in Earley's algorithm. This derivation is somewhat involved and will require several paragraphs. In the next paragraph we shall give a thorough description of the working of Earley's algorithm for readers who are not familiar with it. Readers conversant with the algorithm may skip this paragraph or merely check the result of the parse at the end of it.

We now give a brief description of how the Earley parse-list algorithm actually works in computing parse-lists given a string. As described earlier, the final parse-list set contains all the possibilities that appeared from consideration of the input string together with its sequential input process. The computation of the correct parse requires an additional algorithm, the correct parse algorithm, which will not be discussed in this chapter.

We shall illustrate here the first algorithm, the parse-list algorithm, with the help of our example grammar. In the following we assume the grammar specification as given earlier. The treatment we will give here will necessarily be somewhat exhaustive, as we wish to make clear the actual nature of what is involved in the working of the algorithm.

The Initialising Part of the Parse-list Algorithm

Firstly, the starting list I_0 is constructed by applying the Earley rules 1, 2, and 3 to the input string "a a b" as follows (we paraphrase here Aho & Ullman, 1972, p. 320):

> 1. For all $S \rightarrow \alpha$ in P, add the item $<S \rightarrow . \alpha, 0>$ to list I_0.
> Now perform (2) and (3) until no new items can be added to list I_0.
> 2. For all $<X \rightarrow \alpha.Y\beta, 0>$ in I_0, if $<Y \rightarrow \tau., 0>$ is in list I_0, add $<X \rightarrow \alpha Y.\beta, 0>$ to list I_0.
> 3. For all $<X \rightarrow \alpha.Y\beta, 0>$ in I_0, and for all $Y \rightarrow \tau$ in P, add $<Y \rightarrow .\tau, 0>$ to I_0.

Thus, for our example determined by the rule system $S \rightarrow aA$, $S \rightarrow Ab$, $A \rightarrow aa$, $A \rightarrow a$, we must first select the dotted rule symbols that apply according to *rule 1*. These are just those arcs corresponding to the first two grammar rules, $S \rightarrow aA$ and $S \rightarrow AB$. We must first, therefore, enter 0 as a pointer in the corresponding items. Thus application of rule 1 yields the adding of $<S \rightarrow .aA,0>$ and $<S \rightarrow .Ab,0>$ to I_0.

According to *rule 2*, we must first of all find a completed dotted rule symbol in I_0. The completed arcs in our grammar are $S \rightarrow aA., S \rightarrow Ab., A \rightarrow aa., A \rightarrow a.$. We must then test to see whether any of these are present in the present list. As we are still dealing with the zeroth list, the length of any arc cannot exceed zero. Clearly all of the possible completed arcs must have at least the length 1. It is therefore clear that there will not be any of the above arcs present[2]. Looking in

---

[2]As a matter of fact, rule 2 will never be applied for grammars that have no null-symbols, since the first application of rule 2 must always be with a rule containing a null-symbol as its first element.

the list we find that this is true, and therefore we cannot apply rule 2 here. Therefore we now have only rule 3 to consider.

From *rule 3* we must first consider all dotted rule symbols with the dot before a non-terminal. In this grammar these are S → a.A and S → .Ab. Since these both have the same non-terminal after the dot (i.e. A), we must consider in relation to these arcs the grammar rules of the form A → τ in the set P. . In this grammar these are the dotted rule symbols A → .aa, and A → .a.

We then test to see which of the dotted rule symbols S → a.A and S → .Ab are present in the list I_0. As the dotted rule symbol $<S → .Ab,0>$ is present, we must enter 0 as pointer into the "A → .τ"—items. Application of rule 3 thus results in the adding of the items $<A → .a,0>$ and $<A → .aa,0>$ to I_0. This ends the process of creating list I_0, since we can now no longer add any new items to it. We thus have an I_0 consisting of four items:

$$I_0: <S → .aA,0>, <S → .Ab,0>, \qquad \text{(from rule 1)}$$
$$<A → .a, 0>, <A → .aa,0>, \qquad \text{(from rule 3)}$$

The Recursive Part of the Algorithm

There now follows a recursive method of constructing the list I_j given the list I_{j-1} and the input string $a_1 a_2 a_3 \ldots a_n$, consisting of the rules 4, 5, and 6:

4. For all items $<X → α.aβ, i>$ in list I_{j-1}, and for all $a = a_j$, add item $<X → αa.β, i>$ to list I_j.

Now perform (5) and (6) until no new items can be added to I_j.

5. For all $<X → α.Yβ, k>$ in list I_i, and for all items $<Y → τ., i>$ in list I_j, add $<X → αY.β, k>$ to list I_j.

6. For all items $<X → α.Yβ, i>$ in list I_j, and for all $Y → τ$ in P, add $<Y → .τ, j>$ to list I_j.

Applying these rules with $j = 1$, in order to create list I_1, we start with *rule 4*. According to rule 4, we must first consider all the arcs with a terminal after the dot. In this grammar these are the arcs: S → .aA, A → .a, A → .aa, S → A.b, with corresponding terminals a and b. The corresponding arcs with the dot after the terminal are: S → a.A, A → a., A → a.a, S → Ab.

We must now test to see which of the first set of arcs is present in the list 0 ($= 1 - 1$), i.e. the previous list, and which of the terminals is present at the current position. The terminal present is *a*, of which the corresponding items $<S → .aA,0>$, $<A → .a,0>$, and $<A → .aa,0>$ are present in list 1_0. We must therefore firstly enter the pointers of these three items into the corresponding three items with the dot after the terminal. We then add these new items to I_1. The items to be added are:

$$<S → a.A, 0>, <A → a., 0>, <A → a.a, 0>$$

According to *rule 5*, we must consider all the arcs with a non-terminal after the dot. In this grammar these are the arcs: $S \to a.A$, $S \to .Ab$, with actually just one common corresponding non-terminal, A. The corresponding arcs with the dot after the non-terminal are: $S \to aA.$, $S \to A.b$. We must also consider in relation to the latter all completed arcs: $S \to aA.$, $S \to Ab.$, $A \to aa.$, and $A \to a.$, of which the complete S—arcs can be ignored; they are not used with any other arcs, since they do not appear on the right-hand side of any grammar rule.

We must now test to see which of the arcs $A \to a.$, $A \to aa.$ are present in the current list, i.e. which, if any, of the non-terminals are present at the current position. The only non-terminal present is given by the item $<A \to a.,0>$, of which there is only one corresponding item with the dot before the A present in list I_0, i.e. $<S \to .Ab,0>$. We must therefore enter the pointer of this latter item into the corresponding item with the dot after the non-terminal, giving the following item:

$$<S \to A.b,0>$$

Applying this rule is then just a matter of adding this new item to I_1.

Now, according to *rule 6*, which is in fact exactly the same as rule 3 for the general case of list I_j, we must first consider all dotted rule symbols with the dot before a non-terminal. In this grammar these are $S \to a.A$ and $S \to .Ab$. Since these both have the same non-terminal after the dot (i.e. A), we must once more consider in relation to these arcs the arcs corresponding to the grammar rules of the form $A \to \tau$ in P with the dot at the beginning. These are of course just as before the arcs $A \to .aa$, and $A \to .a$.

We then test to see which of the arcs $S \to a.A$ and $S \to .Ab$ are present in the list I_1. As the item $<S \to a.A,0>$ is present, we must first enter a 1 in the A-arcs, giving the arcs: $<A \to .a,1>$ and $<A \to .aa,1>$. Applying rule 6 then becomes adding these items to I_1. After this there are no more possible new items to be added to I_1, so we end up with the following:

I_1: $<S \to a.A,0>, <A \to a.,0>, <A \to a.a,0>$,   (from rule 4)
　　$<S \to A.b,0>$,   (from rule 5)
　　$<A \to .a,0>, <A \to .aa,0>$ (from rule 6)

TABLE 7.4

I_0	I_1	I_2	I_3
$<S->.aA,0>$	$<S->a.A,0>$	$<A->aa.,0>$	$<S->Ab.,0>$
$<S->.Ab,0>$	$<A->a.,0>$	$<A->a.,1>$	
$<A->.aa,0>$	$<A->a.a,0>$	$<A->a.a,1>$	
$<A->.a,0>$	$<S->A.b,0>$	$<S->aA.,0>$	
	$<A->.a,1>$	$<S->A.b,0>$	
	$<A->.aa,1>$		

In a similar fashion *we continue applying rules 4, 5 and 6* and obtain Table 7.4. By inspection of the last list produced, which contains an item of the form $<S \to \tau., 0>$, we can see that our input string is in fact a valid sentence according to the grammar.

OUR APPROACH

An Outline

As already indicated, Earley's system is one of constraints on item occurrences, i.e. triples of symbols and a procedure for a step-wise generation of constraints synchronised by the sequence of symbols in an input string. In contrast, our system is a system of nodes, which may be active or inactive, together with a specific neighbourhood relation between nodes; this is the expression of grammatical structure in our system and a system of algebraically formulated equations—one for each node, which is as many arguments as the node has neighbours—each determining the conditions for activity changes of the node given the activities of its neighbours. In the derivation of our system from Earley's specification, we shall make use of two intermediate representations, which conform to the specifications just given, but violate certain basic requirements of connectionism. Only the third representation is our final form.

With a view to the programming of our system on a computer, we present it, moreover, in an abbreviated form appropriate for spread-sheet types of calculation.

The first intermediate form of our system corresponds merely to the *constraints of Earley's system*. That is, it contains exactly one node for each possible item occurrence in Earley's system and their algebraic formulae render the constraints directly between the item occurrences. Since the item occurrences are parse representation symbols, we call the corresponding units in our system *parse representation units*, such that the constraints are interactivity dependencies between these.

Earley's algorithm is transformed into a system in which structurally determined activity changes need only occur in a limited domain of nodes, exactly one for each dotted rule symbol (and not as in the constraints, one for each item occurrence). We shall call these units *grammatical category units*.

The *final version* of our system has to cope with the following problem. In the general case the interactivity changes of the grammatical category units may depend on arbitrarily distant item occurrence nodes. This violates basic principles of connectionism. The problem is solved by the definition (and implementation) of connectionist flow processes, which provide the appropriate information in the immediate neighbourhood of the grammatical category nodes.

The transformation of Earley's constraints and algorithm into a connectionist system will be introduced in four steps:

1. The *definition of the parse representation space* consisting of the interactive representation units, according to the localist representation principle of connectionism.

2. The transformation of Earley's algorithm over the distribution of possible item occurrences into a *structure determined system of algebraic equations specifying the activity changes of all units in the representation space* depending on the activity changes of their neighbours in the parse representation space.

3. The transformation of Earley's algorithm into a system of *algebraic equations solely specifying the activity changes of the units in the grammatical category sub-space*, depending on their neighbours in the parse-list representation space.

4. The transformation of the system in (3) into a *system of algebraic equations* for the grammatical category units *depending merely on their immediate local neighbours* (and no longer on distant neighbours in the parse representation space).

We now present the four definitions of our system in their general compact form in order to give the reader an idea of what they look like. After this, we describe the special case of our system for our example grammar (and given input string) to give the reader a rough idea of our aim. The general definition of our system is somewhat abstract. Readers who want to have a concrete idea should turn to the section titled *The final system illustrated by an example grammar* (p. 196).

The Four Versions of Our System

The Representation Space (0).   We define an *integer representation space* (X, Y, Z) such that:

$$-Q \leqslant X \leqslant Q$$
$$-P \leqslant Y \leqslant 0$$
$$-Q \leqslant Z \leqslant 0$$

where P is a function of the grammar rules $P = P(GR)$, equal to the number of contextualised grammatical categories in the grammar. Every plane specified by a Y co-ordinate *represents* such a category. The variable Q is a function of the length of the input string $Q = Q(INP)$. In order to be able to cope with all grammars and input strings, we assume in general argumentation $p = q = \infty$.)

The particular values at a point (X,Y,Z) are represented by $S(X,Y,Z)$, where S is a mapping of positions (X,Y,Z) onto the binary set of activity values: active (1) and inactive (0). All possibilities for dependencies between the points are allowed here, so we have:

$$S(X_i, Y_i, Z_i) = \pi_j \cap_k S(X_j, Y_j, Z_j) . S(X_k, Y_k, Z_k)$$

Note, however, that the reference to the representation in Fig. 7.3 is only obtained appropriately when the variables in all the following formulae are prefixed by '–', as the numerical constants (i.e. $S(X+1,Y,-Z+1)$ would yield $S(-X-1,-Y,Z-1)$).

General Computational Constraint Generated by a Grammar GR and Earley's Algorithm ER (I).   Earley's algorithm is based on two sets of rules: one for the algorithmic determination of a parse-list assigned to an input string, and one for the corresponding determination of a correct parse. These rules are translated into constraints on the representation space, which allow only a particular set of causal dependencies between the activities 0 or 1 taken on by the points in the space. The list-number in the algorithm is represented by the X co-ordinate, and the pointer-number by the Z co-ordinate.

As described earlier, there are four essential rules for the parse-list algorithm, namely those given by (1), (4), (5) and (6) (see *The Earley Parse-list Algorithm*, earlier). In our system they are transformed into equations of the following form:

$$S(X,Y,Z) = S(X',Y',Z') \cdot S(X'',Y'',Z'')$$

The following relations hold for *all the rules*:

a. $X = X''$
b. $X' = X'' - Z''$
c. $Z = Z' + Z''$

The same relations hold for the lines in which there is no (X',Y',Z') if one takes these to be equal to $(0,0,0)$.

The differences between the rules or their corresponding equations amount merely to differences in the sets of constraints on the variables in this basic form.

For the constraints on the Y-values, we must find for each of rules 1,4,5, and 6 all the dotted rule groups in the grammar that satisfy the relations given in Table 7.5. (Note that c represents a terminal and C a non-terminal.)

TABLE 7.5

Earley Rules	Dotted Rules		
	Y	Y'	Y''
1	$S \rightarrow .\tau$	/	$.S.$
4	$D \rightarrow \alpha c.\beta$	$D \rightarrow \alpha.c\beta$	$.c.$
5	$D \rightarrow \alpha C.\beta$	$D \rightarrow \alpha.C\beta$	$C \rightarrow \tau.$
6	$C \rightarrow .\tau$	/	$D \rightarrow \alpha.C\beta$

These relations are the basic ones to be implemented for each new grammar for which the system is to be implemented. They are used in all the specifications of the connectivities of the system to come.

The additional constraints on the variables for the individual rules 1,4,5 and 6 are as follows:

1. values of X',Y' and Z' are taken as zero for the constraints, and $Y'' = 0$;
4. Z'' is fixed at 1;
5. no additional constraints;
6. values of X',Y', and Z' are taken as zero for the constraints.

We give here the actual form of the equations resulting from the application of these constraints on the basic equation:

1'. $S(X,Y,Z) =$ $\quad\quad\quad\quad\quad$ $S(X,0,Z)$ with $Z = X$
4'. $S(X,Y,Z) = S(X-1, Y',Z-1)$. $S(X,Y'',1)$
5'. $S(X,Y,Z) = S(X-Z'',Y',Z-Z'')$. $S(X,Y'',Z'')$
6'. $S(X,Y,Z) =$ $\quad\quad\quad\quad\quad$ $S(X,Y'',Z)$ with $Z = X$

Let us indicate briefly the meaning of these equations with respect to Fig. 7.3. The equations specify general constraints for simultaneous activities in subspace III (or IV) of this figure, i.e. for possible parse-list representations. No specification of the processes in IX and X by which these constraints are generated is given. The next paragraph will show how we can specify constraints merely on units in IX and X from which the constraints of activities in III and IV just defined follow.

The meaning of (b) earlier is that, if the length of the last computed constituent $C \to \tau$. is subtracted from its position, we *must* get the position of the constituent $D \to \alpha.C\beta$. Correspondingly (c) says that the length of $C \to \tau$. added to the length of $D \to \alpha.C\beta$ *must* provide the length of $D \to \alpha C.\beta$.

We have, in fact, just presented the constraints corresponding to version 2 of the general form. The other two versions 1 and 3 are related in a formally very simple way. Version 1 is obtained by replacing the variables X,X',X'' and Z,Z',Z'' for the numbers in these respective co-ordinate positions, and version 3 is obtained by replacing all of the latter by 0.

The "Algorithmic" Constraint (II). The constraints to be defined presently provide a substantial reduction in the number of the dependencies between the points: the connectivities of only a *finite* number of points will represent the generative conditions of the grammatical structure. That is, together with certain specifications, these points alone generate the constraints under specifications I in the previous section.

This finite space will comprise all the positions $(0,Y,0)$. Their generative capacity lies in the fact of their interdependency and their Boolean dependencies on positions in the representational space as given in the following specification. They are determined from the constraints in (I) plus the following additional constraint:

d. $X = 0$

In order to derive the constraints in I, we apply the following transformation to the above formulae to achieve this finite "grammar space" reduction step.

At the end of each iteration cycle, the activities in each unit with $X <> 0$ are *shifted* one space to the left and the activities of the units with $X = 0$ are set to zero. This is just equivalent to applying a variable transformation of $X := X - 1$ at each iteration cycle, which amounts to having to subtract X from X co-ordinate after X iteration cycles.

The only result of this transformation (apart from being reset to zero) for the grammar space units is the same as that obtained by adding constraint (d). For the other units, however, we must take into account the transformation, and this results in a shifting process being added to our rules, as follows:

The Shift Rule: At the end of each "iteration" X,
for all $X <> 0$
$S(X - 1, Y, Z) := S(X, Y, Z)$

for $X = 0$
$S(X, Y, Z) := 0$

Thus, we can see that the complexity of the connectivities in the grammar representation space units (I and III) has been transferred into a "stepwise shifting in" of the connectivities. We give the new rules here for comparison:

4″. $S(0,Y,Z) = S(-1,Y',Z-1)$. $S(0,Y'',1)$
5″. $S(0,Y,Z) = S(-Z'',Y',Z-Z'')$. $S(0,Y'',Z'')$
6″. $S(0,Y,0) =$ $S(0,Y'',0)$

Let us summarise what this definition amounts to. A step-wise generation of structure in III (Fig. 7.3) by an appropriate interactivity of units in IX. As a consequence, the units in I and III no longer have specific grammatically determined connectivities but merely participate in the shifting process. The problem still left is that the activities of these units in IX may still depend on arbitrarily distant positions in III. This "infinite connectivity" will be eliminated in the next section.

The Localisation Step (III).   As can be seen, the only case where a potentially infinite number of causal dependencies in the X-direction is still necessary in the formulae given is for rule 5″. We now, in turn, eliminate these infinite causal dependencies and also those in the Z-direction, in the same sort of way as before: by introducing shifting processes in these directions. The introduction of these shifting processes has the same effect for the grammar space units as the adding of yet a further general constraint, namely:

  e. $Z'' = 0$ (for elimination of the infinite dependencies in the X-direction)
  f. $Z = 0$ (for elimination of the infinite dependencies in the Z-direction)

We then end up with a completely localist connectionist system, where every point only has causal connections with a finite number of others.

The algorithmic processes from which these connectivities are derived will be described in the Appendix, to enable those readers more used to the normal computational approach to get an idea of the process. Here, we will merely show the functional connectivities necessary to implement this procedure connectionistically.

The shifting processes consist of a series of "fetch-steps," where information is retrieved (shifted), and "return-steps," where this information is shifted back into place. In order to carry out the shifting connectionistically, we create a new set of shift control units for each dotted rule symbol in the system. For each dotted rule we have four units representing respectively the shifting commands for the two dimensions, X and Z, of positive and negative. Each shift control unit sends out a signal to all the units in its row to change their activities according to the direction of the shift. (Strictly speaking, this is not enough for the system to be classed as connectionist, for the shift control unit would have to have infinite connections with its particular units in order to be able to give them all the signal at the same time. However, it has been shown (see Rothacker, 1984) that, in principle, we can nevertheless achieve a connectionist system by letting the shifting take place *asynchronously*. We will carry on under the assumption that this can be performed successfully.)

We place the shift control units for a dotted rule Y in the following positions (the positions specified here for section VII′ co-operate with buffer VII. Correspondingly, other shift control units will have to be defined for VIII):

  $(-2, Y, -1)$ for shifting of the Z-column of the Y-unit in the positive Z-direction, notated Shift $(Y, +Z)$.
  $(-2, Y, -2)$ for shifting of the Z-column of the Y-unit in the negative Z-direction, notated Shift $(Y, -Z)$.
  $(0, Y, -1)$ for Shift $(Y, +X)$.
  $(0, Y, -2)$ for Shift $(Y, -X)$.

We now give the general dependencies of the units in the parse-list space; this expresses their dependence on the shift control units Y. This is also easily derived from the general shift definition given later in the algorithmic definition.

For all $Z > 0$

$S(0,Y,Z) := S(0,Y,Z+1) .S(-2,Y,-1)$ OR $(0,Y,Z-1) .S(-2,Y,-2)$

$S(2,Y,Z) := S(2,Y,Z-1) .S(-2,Y,-1)$ OR $(2,Y,Z+1) .S(-2,Y,-2)$

For all $X < 0, X > 8$

$S(X,Y,Z) := (S(X+1,Y,Z) .S(0,Y,-1)$ OR $(X-1,Y,Z) .S(0,Y,-2)$

In order to secure the termination of the shift search in the Z direction at a position after which there is no further information, we introduce maximum length markers, i.e. other shift registers to be shifted simultaneously with those just described. We also need separate shift control units for these marker buffers as these may need to be shifted independently of the other representation buffer. As they only need to be shifted in the Z-direction, we need only two. We place these units at positions $(-3,Y,-1)$ and $(-3,Y,-2)$ following the same convention as before. The formulae for the marker buffer units dependent on these marker shift control units are the following:

$S(-1,Y,Z) := S(-1,Y,Z+1) .S(-3,Y,-1)$ OR $S(-1,Y,Z-1) .S(-3,Y,-2)$

$S(-3,Y,Z) := S(-3,Y,Z-1) .S(-3,Y,-1)$ OR $S(-3,Y,Z+1) .S(-3,Y,-2)$

In addition we must give a fundamental network starting condition for the marker buffers:

Fundamental Network Starting Condition
For all Y,
    $S(-1, Y, 0) = 1$ (set the limits of the marker to zero)
    $S(-3, Y, 0) = 1$

otherwise, $S(X, Y, Z) = 0$ for all X,Y,Z except for those in the input string.

The shift rule, applied when the calculation of each parse-list position is complete, is implemented by making a unit (at $[1,0,-1]$) dependent on the nonactivity of all the shift units. The unit then sends out a signal to all those units responsible for shifting to the left to become activated. We thus have the following connectivities:

The Shift Rule
For all Y
    $S(0,Y,-2) := S(1,0,-1)$
    $S(1,0,-1) := -\pi_{All\ Y}$ $\quad S(0,Y,-1) . S(0,Y,-2)$
    $\qquad\qquad\qquad\qquad S(-2,Y,-1) . S(-2,Y,-1)$
    $\qquad\qquad\qquad\qquad S(0,Y,-1) . S(0,Y,-1)$
    (i.e. multiplication over all shift units)

We can now give the shifting conditions connectionistically by calculating the Boolean formulae for the shift control units. In order to control the switch-overs from fetch- and return-steps, we need to specify the states of various groups of units in the network. It is fairly easy to derive the appropriate conditions for activation of the shift control units by simple examination of the rules in their *algorithmic form* (see Appendix). Ignoring all commands that are not shifts, the conditions for the groups of shifting commands present in the rule can easily be taken from the state of the units mentioned after the corresponding words "iterate until" in each step of the algorithmic form.

In the following it should be noted that all the possible appropriate Y-values are to be found in Table 7.5, and all are then to be used in the prescriptions we will now give for the connectivities in the X and Z directions for each Earley rule. For positions for which connectivities are defined from different Earley rules, the different positions are to be combined with a Boolean OR-function.

For rule 5, we need to define the following formulae for individual units, as they should only become activated for certain activation patterns of shift control units.

$$S(0,Y,0) := S(0,Y',0) \, .$$
$$S(-2,Y,-2) \, . \, S(-2,Y',-2)$$

$$S(-1,Y,0) := S(0,Y',0) \, .$$
$$S(-2,Y,-2) \, . \, S(-2,Y',-2)$$

The first of these two formulae in fact contains the original rule 5 (with X and Z set equal to zero), together with the conditions as to when this activation can occur. The other formula has the function of activating a marker unit to register the success of rule 5, and thus has exactly the same conditions.

The marker shift control units also have their special formulae for rule 5. Their formulae read:

$$S(-3,Y, 0) := S(-3,Y,1) \, . S(-2,Y,-2) \, U \, S(-3,Y,-1)$$

$$S(-3,Y,-1) = -S(-3,Y',0) \, . \, (S(-1,Y',0) \, U \, S(-2,Y,-1)) \, U$$
$$-S(-3,Y'',0) \, . \, (S(-1,Y'',0) \, U \, S(-2,Y,-1)) \, U$$
$$S(0,Y'',0) \quad . \, S(-2,Y'',-2)$$

$$S(-3,Y,-2) = -S(-1,Y'',0) \, . \, -S(-1,Y',0) \, .$$
$$(start_5 \, U \, S(-3,Y',0) \, U \, S(-2,Y,-2)) \, U$$
$$-S(-3,Y,-2) \, . \, S(-3,Y'',0) \, . \, S(0,Y',-2)$$

Here, we have used the following abbreviation:

$start_5 : S(-3,Y'',0) \, . S(-3,Y,0) \, . S(-3,Y,1).$

It should be noted that the minus sign here signifies the lack of activity at the corresponding position; this is equivalent to the logical NOT. (This could most easily be implemented connectionistically by creating a double for all those units which need this possibility, and placing this unit next to its original in the space. This new unit would then always have to assume the opposing activation value. Another possibility would be to use logical array units for the connections between the units, whereupon this negation could be handled by a normal NOT-gate.)

In addition to the formulae given for each case of the marker shift control units, the units also assume exactly the same conditions as their corresponding standard Z-shift control units, combined with a Boolean OR.

The activation pattern for rule 4 is similar to that for rule 5 except that we can simplify it somewhat as the distance to be shifted back in the X-direction is fixed at one. For instance, we only need to iterate once for many of the shifting types. To do this we only need to change the conditions for changing over to a new shift procedure. We do this by making the end of each type of shifting dependent on its presence, so that it stops as soon as the shifting has been performed once.

The individual conditions for the shift control units for each of the three dotted rules from rules 4 and 5 are in fact determined by the following conditions controlling the switching over of the different shift processes in the algorithm (4/5 signifies that the corresponding condition is to be taken according as the triple Y,Y',Y'' is from rule 4 or 5):

For Rule 4
For rule 4 we use the following abbreviation:

$start_4 : S(0,Y'',1) .S(1,0,-1) . S(-2,Y,0)$

$S(-2,Y ,-1) := -S(-3,Y',-1) .(S(-1,Y',0) \cup S(-2,Y,-1))$

$S(-2,Y',-1) := -S(-3,Y', 0) .(S(-1,Y',0) \cup S(2,Y',-1))$

$S(-2,Y'',-1)$ no determination from rule 4

$S(-2,Y ,-2) := -S(-1,Y',0).(start_4 \cup S(-2,Y,-2))$

$S(-2,Y',-2) := -S(-1,Y',0).(S(0,Y',-2) \cup S(-2,Y',-2))$

$S(-2,Y'',-2)$ no determination from rule 4

$S(0,Y, -1)$ no determination from rule 4

$S(0,Y',-1) := -S(0,Y',-2) . start_4$

$S(0,Y'',-1)$ no determination from rule 4

$S(0,Y ,-2)$ no determination from rule 4

$S(0,Y',-2) := -S(-3,Y',-1) . S(-3,Y',0)$

$S(0,Y'',-2)$ no determination from rule 4

$S(-3,Y,-1) = 0$

$S(-3,Y,-2) = 0$

For Rule 5

$S(-2,Y,-1) := -S(-3,Y',0).(S(-1,Y',0) \cup S(-2,Y,-1))\cup$
$\qquad\qquad -S(-3,Y'',0).(S(-1,Y'',0) \cup S(-2,Y,-1))$

$S(-2,Y',-1) := -S(-3,Y',0) .(S(-1,Y',0) \cup S(2,Y',-1))$

$S(-2,Y'',-1) := -S(-3,Y',-1).(S(-3,Y',0) \text{ U } S(-2,Y'',-1))\text{U}$
$\qquad -S(-3,Y'',0).(S(-1,Y'',0) \text{ U } S(-2,Y,-1))$
$S(-2,Y,-2) := -S(-1,Y'',0).-S(-1,Y',0).$
$\qquad (\text{start}_5 \text{ U } S(-3,Y',0)\text{U } S(-2,Y,-2))$
$S(-2,Y',-2) := -S(-1,Y',0).(S(0,Y'',0) \text{ U } S(-2,Y',-2))$
$S(-2,Y'',-2) := -S(-1,Y'',0).-S(0,Y'',0).$
$\qquad (\text{start}_5 \text{ U } S(-3,Y',0) \text{ U } S(-2,Y'',-2))$
$S(0,Y,-1)$ no determination from rule 5
$S(0,Y',-1) := -S(-1,Y'',0).-S(0,Y'',-1).$
$\qquad (\text{start}_5 \text{ U } S(-3,Y',0) \text{ U } S(0,Y',-1))$
$S(0,Y'',-1)$ no determination from rule 5
$S(0,Y,-2)$ no determination from rule 5
$S(0,Y',-2) := -S(0,Y'',0).S(-3,Y',0) \text{ U }$
$\qquad -S(-3,Y'',0).(S(-1,Y'',0) \text{ U } S(-2,Y,-1))$
$S(0,Y'',-2)$ no determination from rule 5
$S(-3,Y,-1) = -S(-3,Y',0).(S(-1,Y',0) \text{ U } S(-2,Y,-1)) \text{ U }$
$\qquad -S(-3,Y'',0).(S(-1,Y'',0) \text{ U } S(-2,Y,-1)) \text{ U }$
$\qquad S(0,Y'',0).S(-2,Y'',-2)$
$S(-3,Y,-2) = -S(-1,Y'',0).-S(-1,Y',0).$
$\qquad (\text{start}_5 \text{ U } S(-3,Y',0) \text{ U } S(-2,Y,-2)) \text{ U }$
$\qquad -S(-3,Y,-2).S(-3,Y'',0).S(0,Y',-2)$

For rules 1 and 6, we can use very simple conditions which are just that the Y″ in question is in its correct position, and that has at least one length entry, whether this be zero or non-zero. The fact that we do not need to know the exact length of the appropriate dotted rule simplifies things here enormously.

For a particular dotted rule instance Y,Y″ of rule 1 or 6, we have the following conditions:

$S(0,Y,0) := -S(-3,Y'',0).(S(0,Y'',0) \text{ U } -S(-1,Y'',0))$

This completes the specification of the connectivities of our system.

The Final System Illustrated by an Example Grammar

We shall now illustrate the general system of constraints by discussing our implementation for a simple example grammar: S → aA, S → Ab, A → aa, A → a.

In Table 7.6 the dotted rule symbols for this grammar are listed together with labels that will also be taken as the co-ordinate values for the Y co-ordinate. Furthermore a labelling for the terminals of the grammar has been given in order to enable the straightforward description of relations between the two types later on. We have also included the start symbol .S., which punctuates the start of the input string. It is the same for any grammar and is present at the begining of the algorithm.

TABLE 7.6

1	S-> aA.		7	A ->aa.
2	S-> a.A		8	A ->a.a
3	S-> .aA		9	A ->.aa
4	S-> Ab.		10	A ->a.
5	S-> A.b		11	A ->.a
6	S-> .Ab			
0	.S.	12 .a.	13	.b.

We now illustrate the connectivities and functional dependencies. Since the general derivation of these structural determinants from the rules of the Earley algorithm is somewhat involved, it will be useful to have the features of our example in mind. The connectivities for our grammar example (for $X=0$, $Z=0$) can be rendered as in Fig. 7.6.

As can be seen from the figure, there are two types of connectivities: the control connectivities (marked by a bar) and the direct connectivities (left unmarked in the figure).

Figure 7.6 only provides the connectivities inside the set of triples (0,Y,0), i.e. the units in the processor component IX in Fig. 7.3. It does not yet provide the dependencies of parse representation units where X or Z values are defined for 0.

The complete system of dependencies is rendered in Table 7.7. The reader may check that the dependencies between the Y co-ordinates are as given in the general definition.

TABLE 7.7
Parse-list Processor Unit Dependencies

$$S(0, 1, 2) = S(-1, 2, 1) . S(0, 10, 1)$$
$$S(0, 1, 3) = S(-2, 2, 1) . S(0, 7, 2)$$
$$S(0, 2, 1) = S(-1, 3, 0) . S(0, 12, 1)$$
$$S(0, 3, 0) = S(0, 0, 0)$$
$$S(0, 4, 2) = S(-1, 5, 1) . S(0, 13, 1)$$
$$S(0, 4, 3) = S(-1, 5, 2) . S(0, 13, 1)$$
$$S(0, 5, 1) = S(-1, 6, 0) . S(0, 10, 1)$$
$$S(0, 5, 2) = S(-2, 6, 0) . S(0, 7, 2)$$
$$S(0, 6, 0) = S(0, 0, 0)$$
$$S(0, 7, 2) = S(-1, 8, 1) . S(0, 12, 1)$$
$$S(0, 8, 1) = S(-1, 9, 0) . S(0, 12, 1)$$
$$S(0, 9, 0) = S(0, 2, 0)$$
$$S(0, 9, 0) = S(0, 6, 0)$$
$$S(0,10, 1) = S(-1,11, 0) . S(0, 12, 1)$$
$$S(0,11, 0) = S(0, 2, 0)$$
$$S(0,11, 0) = S(0, 6, 0)$$

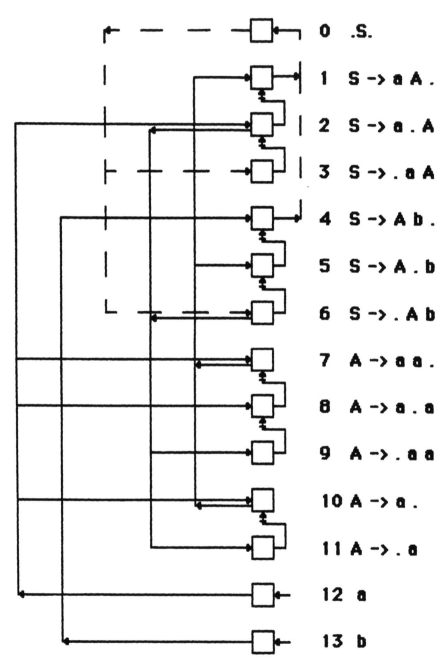

.A   A.

0 .S.

1 S -> a A .

2 S -> a . A

3 S -> . a A

4 S -> A b .

5 S -> A . b

6 S -> . A b

7 A -> a a .

8 A -> a . a

9 A -> . a a

10 A -> a .

11 A -> . a

12 a

13 b

FIG. 7.6.

198

The reader should check in particular that for each line of the form:

$$S(X,Y,Z) = S(X',Y',Z') \cdot S(X'',Y'',Z'')$$

the following relations always hold:

a. $X = X'' = 0$
b. $X' = X'' - Z''$
c. $Z = Z' + Z''$

As before, the same relations hold for the lines in which there is no (X',Y',Z') if one takes these to be equal to $(0,0,0)$.

The meaning of (b) is that, if the length of the last computed constituent $C \to \tau$. is subtracted from its position, we *must* get the position of the constituent $D \to \alpha.C\beta$. Correspondingly (c) says that the length of $C \to \tau$. added to the length of $D \to \alpha.C\beta$ *must* provide the length of $D \to \alpha C.\beta$.

We have, in fact, just presented the constraints corresponding to version 2 of the general form. The other two versions 1 and 3 are related in a formally very simple way. Version 1 is obtained by replacing the variables X,X',X'' and Z,Z',Z'' for the numbers in these respective co-ordinate positions, and version 3 is obtained by replacing all of the latter by 0.

Upon re-examination of the form of our three-dimensional system as implemented for our example grammar, shown in Fig. 7.3, it should be possible to get an overall view of how our system works for a specific example. In the figure we have merely shown the result after the finding of the correct parse of the sentence "a a b" according to our grammar.

The Compilation Procedure Summarised

In conclusion, we define the compilation of one formula for each position in the parse list computation space, expressing the connectivities and interdependencies, from a given CF-grammar. We proceed with the following steps.

I. Set up the Following General Functional Connectivities. (Note that indentification with the positions in Fig. 7.3 requires that *all* variables and constants are multiplied by -1, and that positives become negatives and vice versa.)

1. For units in sections I, II, III, IV, V and VI
For all $X < 0$, $X > 8$
$$S(X,Y,Z) := S(X+1,Y,Z) \cdot S(0,Y,-1) \ U \ S(X-1,Y,Z) \cdot$$
$$S(0,Y,-2)$$
2. For some units in section VII
For all $Z > 0$
$$S(0,Y,Z) := S(0,Y,Z+1) \cdot S(-2,Y,-1) \ U \ S(0,Y,Z-1) \cdot S(-2,Y,-2)$$

$$S(-1,Y,Z) := S(-1,Y,Z+1).S(-2,Y,-1) \cup S(-1,Y,Z-1).S(-2,Y,-2)$$
$$S(-2,Y,Z) := S(-2,Y,Z-1).S(-2,Y,-1) \cup S(-2,Y,Z+1).S(-2,Y,-2)$$
$$S(-3,Y,Z) := S(-3,Y,Z-1).S(-2,Y,-1) \cup S(-3,Y,Z+1).S(-2,Y,-2) \cup$$
$$S(-3,Y,Z-1).S(-3,Y,-1) \cup S(-3,Y,Z+1).S(-3,Y,-2)$$

3. For some units in section VII'

For all Y

$$S(0,Y,-2) := S(1,0,-1)$$
$$S(1,0,-1) := - \pi \qquad S(0,Y,-1).S(0,Y,-2)$$
$$\text{\tiny XII Y} \qquad S(-2,Y,-1).S(-2,Y,-2)$$
$$S(0,Y,-1).S(0,Y,-2)$$

(i.e. multiplication over all shift units)

II. Set up the Grammar-specific Structural Dependencies

1. Create the list of dotted rules from the context-free grammar, together with the dotted rule symbol .S.

2. Calculate the set of appropriate triples Y, Y', Y" or pairs Y, Y" of dotted rules for each individual rule 1, 4, 5 and 6 according to Table 7.7.

III. Set up the Following Grammar-specific Functional Connectivities

1. For the units in IX

For Rules 4 and 5
$$S(0,Y,0) := S(0,Y',0).S(-2,Y,-2).S(-2,Y',-2)$$

For Rules 6 and 1
$$S(0,Y,0) := -S(-3,Y'',0).(S(0,Y'',0) \cup -S(-1,Y'',0))$$

2. For the units in VII

For Rules 4 and 5
$$S(-1,Y,0) := S(0,Y',0).S(-2,Y,-2).S(-2,Y'.-2)$$

TABLE 7.8

Earley Rules	Dotted Rules		
	Y	Y'	Y"
1	$S \rightarrow .\tau$	/	.S.
4	$D \rightarrow \alpha c.b$	$D \rightarrow \alpha.c\beta$	.c.
5	$D \rightarrow \alpha C.\beta$	$D \rightarrow \alpha.C\beta$	$C \rightarrow \tau.$
6	$C \rightarrow .\tau$	/	$D \rightarrow \alpha.C\beta$

NOTE: for grammar rules 1 and 6, only the dotted rule pairs Y and Y" that are different should be taken into account. For example, any pair $Y = A \rightarrow .A$ and $Y'' = A \rightarrow .A$ should not be included in the set of dotted rules.

For Rules 4 and 5

$S(\ 0,Y,0) := S(0,Y,-1).\ \ S(-2,Y,-1)\ U\ S(0,Y,-1).S(-2,Y,-2)$
$S(-1,Y,0) := S(-1,Y,-1).S(-2,Y,-1)\ U\ S(-1,Y,-1).S(-2,Y,-2)$
$S(-2,Y,0) := S(-2,Y,-1).S(-2,Y,-1)\ U\ S(-2,Y,-1).S(-2,Y,-2)$
$S(-3,Y,0) := S(-3,Y,-1).S(-2,Y,-2)\ U\ S(-3,Y,-1)$

3. For the units in VII'

For Rule 4

For rule 4 we will be using the following abbreviation:

$\text{start}_4 : S(\ 0,Y'',1).S(\ 1,0,-1).S(-2,Y,0)$
$S(-2,Y\ ,-1) := -S(-3,Y',-1)\ .\ (\ S(-1,Y',0)\ U\ S(-2,Y,-1)\ )$
$S(-2,Y',-1) := -S(-3,Y',\ 0)\ .\ (\ S(-1,Y',0)\ U\ S(-2,Y',-1)\ )$
$S(-2,Y'',-1)$ no determination from rule 4
$S(-2,Y,\ -2) := -S(-1,Y',0)\ .\ (\text{start}_4\ U\ S(-2,Y,-2))$
$S(-2,Y',-2) := -S(-1,Y',0)\ .\ (S(0,Y',-2)\ U\ S(-2,Y',-2)\ )$
$S(-2,Y'',-2)$ no determination from rule 4
$S(0,Y\ ,-1)$ no determination from rule 4
$S(0,Y',-1) := -S(0,Y',-2)\ .\ \text{start}_4$
$S(0,Y'',-1)$ no determination from rule 4
$S(0,Y\ ,-2)$ no determination from rule 4
$S(0,Y',-2) := -S(-3,Y',-1)\ .\ S(-3,Y',0)$
$S(0,Y'',-2)$ no determination from rule 4
$S(-3,Y,-1) = 0$
$S(-3,Y,-2) = 0$

For Rule 5

For rule 5 we use the following abbreviation:

$\text{start}_5 : S(-3,Y'',0).S(-3,Y,0).S(-3,Y,1)$
$S(-2,Y,-1)\ := (-S(-3,Y',0).(S(-1,Y\ ,0)\ U\ S(-2,Y,-1)\ )\ )\ U$
$\qquad\qquad (-S(-3,Y'',0).(S(-1,Y'',0)\ U\ S(-2,Y,-1)\ )\ )$
$S(-2,Y',-1) := \ -S(-3,Y',0).(S(-1,Y'\ ,0)\ U\ S(2,Y',-1)\ )$
$S(-2,Y'',-1) := (-S(-3,Y',-1).(S(-3,Y',0)\ U\ S(-2,Y'',-1)\ )\ )\ U$
$\qquad\qquad (-S(-3,Y'',0).(S(-1,Y'',0)\ U\ S(-2,Y,-1)\ )\ )$
$S(-2,Y,\ -2) := -S(-1,Y'',0).-S(-1,Y',0).$
$\qquad\qquad (\text{start}_5\ U\ S(-3,Y',0)U\ S(-2,Y,-2)\ )$
$S(-2,Y',-2) := -S(-1,Y',0)\ .\ (S(0,Y'',0)\ U\ S(-2,Y',-2)\ )$
$S(-2,Y'',-2) := -S(-1,Y'',0).-S(0,Y'',0)\ .$
$\qquad\qquad (\text{start}_5\ U\ S(-3,Y',0)\ U\ S(-2,Y'',-2)\ )$
$S(0,Y,\ -1)$ no determination from rule 5
$S(0,Y',-1) := -S(-1,Y'',0)\ .\ -S(0,Y'',-1)\ .$
$\qquad\qquad (\text{start}_5\ U\ S(-3,Y',0)\ U\ S(0,Y',-1)\ )$
$S(0,Y'',-1)$ no determination from rule 5
$S(0,Y,\ -2)$ no determination from rule 5
$S(0,Y',-2) := (-S(0,Y'',0)\ .\ S(-3,Y',0)\ )\ U$
$\qquad\qquad (-S(-3,Y'',0)\ .\ (S(-1,Y'',0)\ U\ S(-2,Y,-1)\ )\ )$

$S(0,Y'',-2)$ no determination from rule 5
$S(-3,Y,-1) = (-S(-3,Y',0).(S(-1,Y',0) \cup S(-2,Y,-1))) \cup$
$\qquad (-S(-3,Y'',0).(S(-1,Y'',0) \cup S(-2,Y,-1))) \cup$
$\qquad S(0,Y'',0) . S(-2,Y'',-2)$
$S(-3,Y,-2) = -S(-1,Y'',0).-S(-1,Y',0).$
$\qquad (start_5 \cup S(-3,Y',0) \cup S(-2,Y,-2)) \cup$
$\qquad -S(-3,Y,-2) . S(-3,Y'',0) . S(0,Y',-2)$

IV. Combine the Connectivities Defined for Each Position in the Space. For positions for which different connectivities have been defined in the previous process, all the different connectivities are to be combined together with a Boolean OR-function.

V. Set the Starting Activation Values of all Units in the Space.
For all Y_i, set
$S(1, Y_i, 0) = 1$
$S(3, Y_i, 0) = 1$

otherwise, set $S(X, Y, Z) = 0$ for all X, Y, Z except for those representing the input string in section I, the input string space, which are set to 1.

VI. Run the System. Let the system run in parallel (and asynchronously), such that each unit executes one operation at each clock pulse of the complete processor (or else asynchronous connectivities can be implemented as indicated in Rothacker, 1984).

Final Note. This article was written in 1988. Another presentation is:
R. Wilkins and H. Schnelle. A connectionist parser for context-free phrase structure grammars. In C. Dorffner (Hrsg.), *Konnektionisms in Artificial Intelligence und Kognitionsforschung.* Berlin et al.: Springer, 1990.

REFERENCES

Aho, A.V. & Ullman, J.D. (1972). *The theory of parsing, translation, and compiling (Vols. 1 & 2).* Englewood Cliffs, N.J.: Prentice Hall.

Chomsky, N. (1975). *The logical structure of linguistic theory.* New York: Plenum Press.

Chomsky, N. (1986). *Knowledge of language—Its nature, origin, and use.* New York: Praeger.

Fodor, J.A. & Pylyshyn, Z.W. (1988). Connectionisms and cognitive architecture: A critical analysis. *Congition, 28,* 3–71.

Rothacker, E. (1984). *Elements of theoretical net-linguistics.* GENET-7 (ms.) Sprachw. Inst., Ruhr-Universität Bochum.

Schnelle, H. (1981). Elements of theoretical net-linguistics, Part 1: Syntactical and morphological nets—Neuro-linguistic interpretations. *Theoretical Linguistics, 8,* 67–100. Berlin: Walter de Gruyter & Co.

Schnelle, H. (1988a). The challenge of concrete linguistic descriptions: Connectionism massively parallel processing, net-linguistics. In H. Schnelle & J. van Bentham (Eds.), *Cognitive science—*

A European perspective, Vol 2: Logic and linguistics. Hillsdale, N.J.: Lawrence Erlbaum Associates Inc.

Schnelle, H. (1988b). Ansätze zur prozessualen Linguistik. In H. Schnelle & G. Rickheit (Eds.). *Sprache in Mensch und Computer.* Opladen: Westdeutscher Verlag.

Winograd, T. (1983). *Language as a cognitive process.* Reading, Mass.: Addison-Wesley.

APPENDIX

We give here the algorithmic versions of the Earley rules; the connectivities for the final version of our system are designed to implement these.

The Shift Rule

If no Shift $(Y, \pm D)$ function is being carried out, (i.e. nothing is being shifted), then

$S(1,0,-1) := 1$

If $S(1,0,-1) = 1$, then for all Y,

$S(-4,Y,0) := 1$

Rule 5′′′

For all triples p,q,r such that $C^N_{p,q} = 1$ and $C_{(\Sigma)}{}^A_{p,r} = 1$

Initial Conditions

If $S(0, Y'', 0) = 1$, and $S(-3, Y'', -2) = 1$ (if a completed category is present and this other process was in the searching shifting state, i.e. if a completed category has been activated), then

$S(-3, Y, Z') := S(-3, Y, Z+1)$
$S(-3, Y, 0) := 1$

(increase by one the number of markers, i.e. the number of times this process needs to be activated).

Recursive Conditions

If (at a later time), $S(-3, Y'', 0) = 1$ and $S(-3, Y, 0) = 1$ and $S(-3, Y, 1) = 1$ (condition start$_5$) (i.e. the activated category has been placed in its correct position, and there is a double marker):

1. iterate until $S(-1, Y'', 0) = 1$ (all the lengths of this completed category have passed)
   a. iterate until $S(0, Y'', 0) = 1$ (the individual lengths)

   Shift$(Y'', -Z)$ (i.e. set $S(0, Y'', -2)$ to be active)
   Shift$(Y, -Z)$ (i.e. set $S(0, Y, -2)$ to be active)
   Shift$(Y', -X)$ (i.e. set $S(0, Y', -2)$ to be active)

   b. iterate until $S(-1, Y', 0) = 1$ (the last of all the incompleted categories at this position that need to be added to)

   Shift$(Y', -Z)$
   Shift$(Y, -Z)$
   $S(0, Y, 0) = S(0, Y', 0) . S(0, Y'', 0)$
   (The transformed rule with X and Z set to zero)
   $S(-1, Y, 0) := S(0, Y', 0) . S(0, Y'', 0)$
   (add new marker if rule 4/5 successful)

c. iterate until $S(-3, Y', 0) = 1$ (shift back the Z shifts made at this X-position)

Shift(Y',+Z)
Shift(Y,+Z)

2. iterate until $S(-3, Y'',0) = 1$ (i.e. until the longest completed category is back in place)

Shift(Y'',+Z)
Shift(Y,+Z)
Shift(Y',+X)
$S(-3, Y, Z') := S(-3, Y, Z-1)$
(get rid of double marker)

Rule 4′′′

For all triples p,q,r such that $C^N_{p,q} = 1$ and $C_{(N)}{}^A_{p,r} = 1$.

Initial Conditions

If $S(0, Y'', 1) = 1$ and $S(1,0,-1) = 1$, and $S(-2,Y,0) = 1$ (condition start$_4$) (i.e. if a terminal has just been shifted into the input string buffer).

Recursive Conditions

1. iterate until $S(0,Y',-2) = 1$ (only once)

Shift(Y,-Z)
Shift(Y',-X) (i.e. set $S(0, Y', -2)$ to be active)

2. iterate until $S(-1, Y', 0) = 1$ (the last of all the incompleted categories at this position that need to be added to)

Shift(Y,-Z)
Shift(Y',-Z)
$S(0, Y, 0) = S(0, Y', 0)$
(The transformed rule 4 with X and Z set to zero)
$S(-1, Y, 0) := S(0, Y', 0)$
(add new marker if rule 4 successful)

3. iterate until $S(-3, Y', 0) = 1$ (shift back the Z shifts made at this X-position)

Shift(Y',+Z)
Shift(Y,+Z)

4. iterate until $S(0,Y',-1) = 1$ (i.e. perform only once)

Shift(Y,+Z)
Shift(Y',+X)

Rule 6/1′′′

For all pairs p,q $(p<>q)$ such that $C^1_{p,q} = 1$.
If $S(-3, Y'', 0) = 1$ and
$S(0, Y'', 0) = 1$ or $S(-1, Y'', 0) = 0$

(if a possible shifting process for Y″ is terminated, and a category Y″, i.e. a predicting category, of length 0 or of any other length is present), then

$S(0,Y,0) := 1$

The definition of these processes contains an abbreviation; we define $Shift(Y, \pm D)$ for $D \, \varepsilon \, \{ X, Z \}$ as follows:

$Shift(Y, \pm Z)$:
$S(0, Y, Z') := S(0, Y, Z \pm 1)$ (for actual representation)
$S(-2, Y, Z') := S(-2, Y, Z \mp 1)$
$S(-1 \mp 1, Y, 0) := S(-1 \pm 1, Y, 0)$
$S(-1, Y, Z') := S(-1, Y, Z \pm 1)$ (for marker part of buffer)
$S(-3, Y, Z') := S(-3, Y, Z \mp 1)$
$S(-2-1, Y, 0) := S(-2+1, Y, 0)$
$S(-2+1, Y, 0) := 0$

(i.e. the marker is set to zero in order to make way for a new maximum length)

$Shift(Y, \pm X)$:
$S(X', Y, Z) := S(X \pm 1, Y, Z)$ (for $1 < X < 8$)
$S(-4 \mp 4, Y, Z) := S(-4 \pm 4, Y, Z)$

III

REPRESENTATIONAL ADEQUACY

REPRESENTATIONAL ADEQUACY

INTRODUCTION

The issue of representational adequacy in connectionist natural language processing has been touched on in other sections of this volume. Indeed, much of the agenda of the connectionist research community interested in language has been dictated by the need to match the representational adequacy of conventional symbolic approaches. The three papers in this section address the topic more directly, or, as with Dorffner, call into question the ground rules of the whole debate.

Given the current debate between the opposing symbolic and connectionist camps, one is put in mind of Thomas Kuhn's (1970) description of the process of transition between scientific paradigms. This is not an original observation with regard to connectionism (cf. Schneider, 1987), but it is a useful vantage point from which to view the debate. According to Kuhn's analysis, a paradigm shift tends to be accompanied by some crisis within the conventional paradigm involving an inability to deal with certain phenomena. Historians of science of this period may see the main source of tension as the inability of symbolic cognitive science models to say anything about how their systems might be implemented in the human brain. The work of Chomsky (1975), Marr (1982), and more recently Fodor (1976) has encouraged a compartmentalised approach to cognitive science, where the messy details of implementation can and should be avoided. The conventional wisdom holds that it is possible to study a cognitive phenomenon using a self-contained calculus, independently of how this calculus might be implemented.

Most cognitive scientists have been happy enough with this state of affairs. What has enthused a small but growing group of researchers is the possibility, still uncertain, that connectionist models will lead to a better fit between cognitive theories and their implementation details. Connectionism bears many of the hallmarks of a paradigm shift, as Kuhn (1970), p. 158 has described it:

> The man who embraces a new paradigm at an early stage must often do so in defiance of the evidence provided by problem-solving. He must, that is, have faith that the new paradigm will succeed with the many large problems that confront it, knowing only that the older paradigm has failed with a few.

Connectionism at this stage is replete with promises, but unable to claim many substantial successes. Nevertheless, those successes there have been (e.g. McClelland & Rumelhart, 1981; Rumelhart, Hinton, & Williams, 1986; Sejnowski & Rosenberg, 1986) have generated sufficient faith to make the paradigm seem worth embracing.

One of the key acts of faith required in adopting a connectionist approach to language centres on the issue of representational adequacy. The papers in this section represent a range of positions with regard to this issue. Bever (Chapter 8) makes a persuasive case for a division of labour between associationistic connectionism and symbolic processes. He defines these as habitual and structural processes, respectively. Bever does not deny that there is a role for habitual processes, but he maintains that connectionist models will never be able to deal with structural processes, and those that do only have the appearance of doing so. In reality, he argues, they have structural properties built into their representations and training schedules. For Bever, the interesting point in this scheme is the way in which the habitual and structural interact. In effect, Bever is proposing a hybrid model which would preserve the acknowledged strengths of the symbolic approach, while at the same time accommodating the advantages of connectionism.

George Berg (Chapter 9), in his contribution to this section, argues explicitly for a hybrid model, on the basis that current connectionist models are representationally inadequate in a number of important ways. One such inadequacy is the inability of connectionist representations to distinguish between concepts and instances of concepts. He terms this *static representational inadequacy*. The other main form is *dynamic representational inadequacy*. This entails an inability on the part of connectionist networks to configure themselves dynamically in response to incoming information, such as a sentence. The ability to create new representations, on demand, and in real time is not found in current connectionist models. To remedy these inadequacies, Berg proposes a hybrid marker-passing network with various extensions for search and expansion.

Dorffner (Chapter 10) adopts a more radical position than the authors of the preceding papers by proposing that an explicit representational level be dispensed with. He proposes that rather than being supplied a priori, symbolic representations evolve as a result of a self-organisation process. The impetus for self-organisation arises from repeated exposure to, and interaction with, the environment. In other words, the symbolic representations are grounded in experience. This view has a number of philosophical and psychological progenitors. Philosophically, the approach suggests the Wittgensteinian injunction to look, not at language in isolation, but at how it is used (Ayer, 1985). In a psychological context, Piaget pioneered the view of a developmental continuum between sensory-motor behaviour and language (Piaget & Inhelder, 1969. He maintained that language has a sensory-motor foundation upon which a symbolic edifice is constructed (see McNeil, 1979 for a more recent version of this view). In general, there is an appreciation among connectionists that if an *explicit* symbolic framework for dealing with language is to be jettisoned, it needs to be replaced with some form of developmental framework, such as that suggested by Piaget. This would then entail the study of language as a tool of communication, evolving within an organism that actively interacts with its environment. The connectionist language-users model of Bob Allen (1990), for example, is one attempt at this approach.

Where does all this leave the debate on representational adequacy? It seems that the dominant view favours some type of interim solution to the perceived inadequacies of current connectionist models (though not everybody sees it as interim). This solution involves either the incorporation of explicit symbolic structures into connectionist models (Berg) or the interfacing of connectionist models with pure symbolic systems (Bever). An alternative view suggests that we must see language as part of a larger developmental picture. From this perspective, the way to representational adequacy is to allow a connectionist system to evolve its own representational framework constrained by sensory and communicative requirements. Though aesthetically appealing, a commitment to the latter approach still requires the type of act of faith that Kuhn describes. One of the main challenges of connectionism is to justify this faith.

REFERENCES

Allen, R.B. (1990). Connectionist language users. *Connection Science, 2,* 279–312.

Ayer, A.J. (1985). *Wittgenstein.* New York: Random House.

Chomsky, N. (1975). *Reflections on language.* Cambridge, Mass.: M.I.T. Press.

Fodor, J.A. (1976). *The language of thought.* Sussex, U.K.: Harvester Press.

Kuhn, T.S. (1970). *The structure of scientific revolutions.* Chicago, Illinois: University of Chicago Press.

Marr, D. (1982). *Vision.* San Francisco, Calif.: Freeman.

McClelland, J.L. & Rumelhart, D.E. (1981). An interactive activation model of context effects in letter perception: Part 1. An account of basic findings. *Psychological Review, 88,* 375–407.

McNeil, D. (1979). *The conceptual basis of language.* Hillsdale, N.J.: Lawrence Erlbaum Associates Inc.

Piaget, J. & Inhelder, B. (1969). *The psychology of the child.* New York: Basic Books.

Rumelhart, D.E., Hinton, G.E., & Williams, R.J. (1986). Learning internal representations by error propagation. In D.E. Rumelhart, J.L. McClelland, & the PDP Research Group (Eds.), *Parallel distributed processing. Explorations in the microstructure of cognition. Volume 1: Foundations.* Cambridge, Mass.: M.I.T. Press, 318–362.

Schneider, W. (1987). Connectionism: Is it a paradigm shift? *Behavior Research Methods, Instruments, & Computers, 19,* 73–83.

Sejnowski, T.J. & Rosenberg, C.R. (1986). *NETtalk: A parallel network that learns to read aloud.* Technical Report JHU/EECS-86/01. Baltimore, Maryland: The Johns Hopkins University Electrical Engineering and Computer Science.

8 The Demons and the Beast— Modular and Nodular Kinds of Knowledge

Thomas G. Bever
The University of Rochester, Wilson Blvd., Rochester, NY 14627, U.S.A.

Chaos often breeds life, when order breeds habit
—Henry Adams

The human brain has to develop analogies to make up for its limitations
—Alan Turing

INTRODUCTION AND SUMMARY

An enduring insight of behavioural science is that most actual behaviour is a function of habit. This was the basis for the enduring popularity of S-R psychology, despite the many empirical inadequacies that ultimately lead to its downfall in the "cognitive revolution." Connectionism appears to be rehabilitating the image of associationistic models of behaviour, by increasing the adequacy of associationistic models to account for structural phenomena invoked by cognitive psychologists as the basis for rejecting S-R psychology.

The negative thesis of this chapter is that connectionist models can capture only habits and are therefore inadequate in principle to capture structural processes. The positive thesis of this chapter is that connectionist models can capture only habits, and therefore are an important new tool in the study of how habitual knowledge interacts with structural processes.

The first part of the chapter reviews evidence that many behaviours are the result of a complex interaction of structural and habitual processes. The second part reviews several recent important connectionist models of a large segment of English knowledge, primarily the verb-learning model of Rumelhart and McClelland, and the word-reading model of Seidenberg and McClelland: In each case, careful examination of the model shows that it has structural properties built into its representation and feeding schemes—thus, the models neither discover nor circumvent knowledge structures; rather, they reflect the relevant probabilities in their input, given their particular representational schemes. The third part presents a framework for modelling language acquisition, in which the child is seen as building up an interaction between structural and associative representations of language. A connectionist model, Baby Clauseau, demonstrates how connectionist models can be utilised to study associatively learnable patterns in the environment. Baby Clauseau recognises only 100 frequent words of motherese and where actual utterances end: It learns, from actual motherese discourses, to segment utterances into distinct phrases which are linguistically appropriate. This exemplifies the positive role of connectionism in the study of how habits and structures may interact.

STRUCTURE AND HABITS—THE KNOWLEDGE AND THE POWER

Small habits well pursued betimes
May reach the dignity of crimes.

—Hannah More

One of the outstanding facts about behaviour is that most of the time we do what we do most of the time. Consequently, much of what psychologists study is based on accumulated habits; patterns of behaviour that are well-oiled. This makes psychology hard to do, if you think that there might be more underlying behaviour than probabilistic habits alone. Reasoning and language are among those skills suggesting that the mind is a non-probabilistic computational machine that carries out discrete operations on symbols. For example, if you see the array on the left in (1) transformed into the one on the right by compression of the upper row, you will reason that the upper row still has more circles than the lower does. Your ability to do this involves manipulation of symbols at an abstract level of representation. It runs something like this: Nothing was added or taken away when the row was compressed, so the number of dots in the two arrays must still be the same. There is nothing concrete or probabilistic about this judgement; it is symbolic and categorical.

1. o o o o o o o o o o o o   oooooooooooo

   0 0 0 0 0 0 0 0 0 0 0   0 0 0 0 0 0 0 0 0 0

     Similarly, if you know English you can decide that (2b) is licensed by (2a) but (2d) is not licensed by (2c). Here, too, your judgement is categorical, following the differentiation of lexical passive adjectives (e.g. "unsuspected") and verbal passives.

2. a. The girl was surprised.
   b. Somebody (or something) surprised the girl.
   c. The girl was unsurprised.
   d. *Somebody (or something) unsurprised the girl.

Even simple observations like these necessitate the development of computational models in which symbols represent categories, and discrete processes state the relations between the symbols. Mental theories of number and grammars of language are typical examples of such models. The independent effect of structural knowledge is hard to bring out in adults because the pathways of ordinary behaviour are so well-practiced: For example, if you simply looked at the array on the right in (1), you might suspend your reasoning capacity and decide that the short line of "o"s is, in fact, less numerous than the line of "0"s, simply because it looks that way—in general it is the case that shorter arrays have fewer components. Similarly, the way one actually understands sentences may draw on probabilistic properties of languages. For example, one may comprehend the relation between the subject and verb in (3a) based on the generalisation that, unless, otherwise marked, as in (3b) and (3c), agents precede their verbs.

3. a. The girl hit the wall.
   b. It's the wall that the girl hit.
   c. The wall was hit by the girl.

These simple observations (confirmed in a variety of experimental settings; see Bever, 1970; 1975b, for reviews) justify the distinction between two kinds of mental entities—a structural demon and an habitual beast. By definition, in everyday behaviour, the habitual beast overwhelms the structural demon. Most number-related behaviour does not involve rendering judgement about unusual configurations, and most language behaviour does not involve rendering grammaticality intuitions about sentences in the abstract: Most of the time, we rely on habitual appearances to make judgement of quantity, and use habitual processes to understand sentences. Accordingly, it is extremely difficult to demonstrate the effect of structural processes in adult behaviour. Indeed, it is a real question whether structural processes play a determining role in everyday behaviour at all, once they are surrounded by a habitual overlay.

A logical solution to this empirical question is also an empirical one—to examine what young children do before they have enough experience to acquire generalisations. Often, a child's behaviour can display the formation of behavioural systems, drawn out in time in such a way that we can disentangle categorical mental structures from habitual overlays on them. On this view, one expects that children will first display categorical and structural processes in relatively pure form, and will subsequently suffuse them with habitual processes based on the statistics of their experience.

However, for a time, various classical demonstrations were taken to show that children actually start out with behavioural strategies and work from them into structural representations and processes. For example, the transformation from the left to the right array in (1) is a variant on a classical Piagetian paradigm, the study of the principle of "conservation". The typical finding is that children do not master the correct answer until they are about six years old—at age four, they seem dependent on the surface appearance only to make their judgement of quantity: They clearly rely on the length strategy to make numerical judgement. Similarly, children at age four systematically misunderstood passive sentences, and object-first sentences like (3b) and (3c). This suggests that they are using the first-noun = agent strategy as the basis for understanding simple sentences. These lines of research supported the view that the child starts out basing its behaviour on statistical generalisations, and subsequently develops structural representations.

The logic of how that might work was never clear: How does one arrive at categorical representations from statistical generalities? One cannot. Equally problematic is the fact that my investigations of two-year-olds (with Jacques Mehler; see Bever, 1982, for a review) suggested that the four-year-olds' reliance on statistical generalisations arises out of more basic structural capacities. For example, two-year-old children characteristically perform conservation tasks like (1) well above chance; similarly, they understand object-first cleft sentences like (3b) quite well. That is, the four-year-old's behaviour represents a change from a dependence on structural representations to a dependence on statistical generalisations. The typical performance curve on the unusual kinds of tasks is U-shaped, which has lead to the view that the child's behaviour shows a "regression".[1]

The observed distinction between children's early categorical capacities and their eventual dependence on generalisations showed that such generalisations could replace structural processing in many instances of comprehension. This was part of the motivation for a strategy-based theory of sentence comprehension in adults (Bever, 1970). On the strategy-based view of comprehension, adults utilise a set of perceptual strategies that represent simultaneous constraints on mapping surface sequences onto underlying semantic representa-

---

[1]There have been two classes of proposals about the function of behavioural regressions: on one view, the statistical generalisations extend the application of initially limited structural capacities (Bever, Mehler, & Epstein, 1968); on the second view, the apparent regressions represent a shift from one kind of representation to another (Bowerman, 1982; Karmiloff-Smith, 1986; Langer, 1982). Either or both of these views might turn out to be right in the end, but they are hopelessly post hoc. For example, there are other ways to correct the limitations on initially limited structural capacities, most notably to develop the adult form of the capacity; similarly, there is no general explanation for the shift from one kind of representation to another.

tions, e.g. (4). Each of these strategies may be statistically supported, though each is subject to contravention in specific cases.

4. a. N – V – N = Agent Action Object.
   b. Animate nouns are agents.
   c. BE Verb + pastparticiple BY . . . indicates an exception to (a).

The perceptual strategies theory of comprehension was also motivated by the apparent failure to show how grammatical knowledge was embedded directly in language behaviour. In the first heyday of transformational psycholinguistics, it was thought that grammatical rules corresponded to mental operations. This underlays the "derivational theory of complexity," the theory that the behavioural complexity of a sentence corresponds to the number of grammatical rules in its derivation. Careful experimental research finally invalidated the derivational theory of sentence complexity, which at least temporarily destroyed the view that the grammar is directly related to the comprehension mechanism (Fodor, Bever, & Garrett, 1974). By the early 70s, the received word was that there is psychological evidence for abstract linguistic representations, but not for the computational rules which map one level of representation onto another. Perceptual strategies were involved as the probalistically valid processes that arrived at linguistic representations without grammatical computation.

The strategies-based theory of sentence comprehension did not spark a great deal of research, for several reasons. First, it is very difficult to ascertain which statistical properties of sentences are reliable cues—an extensive construction count would have been required to assess the frequency with which particular kinds of sequences correspond to particular phrased and semantic relations. In other words, it became necessary to assess the *cue validity* of surface forms for underlying representations, in the Brunswikian (1956) sense. The second difficulty was taken to be more telling: the strategies-based comprehension model is not computational. The strategies apply simultaneously as constraints on the mapping relations between outer form and semantic analysis, but do not specify how the comprehension mapping is carried out. Finally, it did not explain how comprehension works when the strategies fail. For example, most of the strategies are inconsistent with (5a), and most of them are consistent with the initial part of (5b) in a misleading way; yet these sentences can be understood. Hence, the comprehension system had to include either a set of apparently limitless backup strategies or a way of accessing linguistic knowledge as a last resort.

5. a. The girls were unimpressed by midnight
   b. The horse raced past the barn fell

The result of these considerations is that the strategies-based comprehension system was extrapolated only by those who denied the existence of grammatical structures altogether (e.g. Bates & MacWhinney, 1987). Those who accepted the evidence for a categorical representation of language rejected strategies as vague, unformulated, and necessarily incomplete (e.g. Frazier, 1979).

Current connectionist models in artificial intelligence seem to offer a way in which one can meet the difficulties with the original formulation of the perceptual strategies model (for current reviews, see Feldman & Ballard, 1982; Hinton & Sejnowski, 1986; Rumelhart, Hinton, & Williams, 1986). In the connectionist framework, output behaviour is defined in terms of nodes that are active and inactive: Each node itself is activated by a network of connections from a set of input nodes. One result of this kind of modelling is that activation of different input nodes can be applied simultaneously to the same set of output nodes. For (a toy) example, we can envisage a set of input nodes which categorise each phrase in a linguistic sequence on such dimensions as animacy, surface order, and so on. These nodes could be mapped onto an output set, which represents the semantic function with which the phrases are paired. Clearly, the activation strength from an input "animacy" node to an output "agent" node would be high, as would the strength from the input "first nounphrase" node; conversely, the connection from "inanimate" and "second nounphrase" would be stronger to the semantic "patient" node. When given a particular input, all these connections are activated simultaneously, so the output is effectively the average of the connection strengths from the input nodes. In this way, the different constraints can apply simultaneously, as envisaged in the strategies-based model of speech perception.

Such models can also isolate the statistical regularities in the input/output relations. They can be trained by giving them correct input/output sets of nodes, and by adjusting the strength of the connections between nodes on each training trial: Whatever regularities occur in the input/output pairs can gradually exert themselves in the form of differentiated connection strengths. To continue the linguistic example, one could imagine presenting a model with data pairs consisting of a description of the input and an output description of the semantic relations assigned to each phrase in it. On each such presentation, the input/output connections are adjusted in such a way as to increase incrementally the likelihood that the output would occur, given the input. With enough pairings to represent the probabilistic facts that are true of such input/output pairings, the model will reflect them in the accumulated pattern of connection strengths. (For examples of just such toy models, see McClelland and Kawamoto [1986] and St. John and McClelland [1990]).

Connectionist models seem to offer new hope for the strategies-based model of comprehension. Indeed, they might provide a general framework for understanding the relation between the structural demon and the statistical beast in a wide range of behavioural systems. Such a model could offer a third explanation for the formation of statistically based behavioural generalisations: They automatically arise when any structural capacity is embedded in an otherwise uncommitted system. On this view, each innate structural mental mechanism is situated initially in a sea of uncommitted units: As the mechanism performs its computational work, transforming one symbolic representation into another, the uncommitted units inevitably form direct associative connections between the different representations defined by the computational mechanism. For example, a simple grammar may specify for the child that one of the basic options for word order is that subjects precede objects. Once the child has determined that this property is true of English, then it can understand active sentence orders. From this experience, a generalisation is possible: The first phrase in a proposition is always the agent (4a). The computational mechanism for English does not specify this, but it is an inevitable generalisation out of the child's actual capacities, and the statistical properties of the sentences it experiences. Hence, the generalisations are without direct causes, but arise automatically from the interaction of internally specified representations and environmental information.

A major problem with the strategies-based model was that it did not specify the relation between the grammar and the strategies. The combination of a connectionist and structural component might offer an explanation of what has been a riddle: How can there be behavioural evidence for abstract levels of representation in comprehension, but no direct evidence for the computational rules which interrelate and thereby define those levels? On the hybrid model I have in mind, the representations are defined by the child's computational system for language (its grammar); probability-based pairings of representations at different levels automatically emerge, and become the active basis for mapping outer representations into inner ones during comprehension. Hence the representations are real, but the complex computational processes that define them are replaced by efficient probabilistic processes associating the representations.

This seems to be an extremely attractive solution to the problem of accounting for the effect of the frequency beast on the computational demon. There are numerous specific models that we can examine to see if they reveal an interaction of associative and structural knowledge. This discussion is limited to some of those models, which are alleged to learn something about a large subset of natural language. In the best instances, the models suggest that the beast/demon formulation of cognitive modelling may be a viable one—those connectionist models which seem to work by association actually *presuppose* the structural representations defined in grammars. In the specific instances, each connectionist model manages to sneak enough sensitivity to the relevant linguistic structure to guarantee that it will converge on linguistically sensitive behaviour, once it is trained with cases exhibiting the linguistic constraints.

A MODEL THAT LEARNS SOME MORPHOLOGY

> *Our life is like some vast lake that is slowly filling with the stream of our years. As the waters creep surely upward the landmarks of the past are one by one submerged. But there shall always be memory to lift its head above the tide until the lake is overflowing.*
>
> —Bisson

The currently most notorious model is one that purports to learn to produce the past tense of English verbs. Verbs come in two flavours; *regular* (add -ed to form the past) and *irregular* (typically, change vowel colour, in a system partially derived from the Indo-European ablaut).Rumelhart and McClelland (1986; R&M) implemented a connectionist model that learns to associate past tense with the present tense of both the regular and irregular verb types. The first step in setting up this model is to postulate a description of words in terms of individual feature units. Parallel distributed connectionist models are not naturally suited to represent serially ordered representations, since all components are to be represented simultaneously in one matrix. But phonemes, and their corresponding bundles of distinctive features, clearly are ordered. R&M solve this problem by invoking a form of phonemic representation suggested by Wickelgren (1969), which recasts ordered phonemes into "Wickelphones," which can be ordered in a given word in only one way. Wickelphones appear to avoid the problem of representing serial order by differentiating each phoneme as a function of its immediate phonemic neighbourhood. For example, "bet" would be represented as composed of the following Wickelphones:

6. et#, bet, #be

Each Wickelphone is a triple, consisting of the central phoneme and a representation of the preceding and following phonemes as well. As reflected in (6), such entities do not have to be represented in memory as ordered: They can be combined in only one way into an actual sequence, if one follows the rule that the central phone must correspond to the prefix of the following unit and the suffix of the preceding unit. That rule leads to only one output representation for the three Wickelphones in (6), namely "b . . . e . . . t." R&M assign a set of distinctive phonemic features to each phone within a Wickelphone. There are four feature dimensions, two with two values and two with three, yielding ten individual feature values (see Table 8.1). This allows them to represent Wickelphones in feature matrices: For example the central /e/ in "bet" would be represented as shown in (7):

7. Dimension 1   Vowel
   Dimension 2   Low

Dimension 3 Short
Dimension 4 Front

The verb learning model represents each Wickelphone in a set of "Wickelfeatures". These consist of a triple of features, [f1, f2, f3], the first taken from the prefix phone, the second from the central phone, and the third from the suffix phone.

8. f1   f2   f3
  [end,   interrupted, vowel]
  [end,   interrupted, low]
  [stop,   low,   stop]
  [voiced, low,   unvoiced]

There are about 1000 potential Wickelfeatures of this kind (10 prefix values $\times$ 10 central phone values $\times$ 10 suffix values).

Wickelfeature representations of the words occur at the input and the output with a separate node for each of the Wickelfeatures: All of the nodes at each layer are connected to all of the nodes at the other, as depicted in Fig. 8.1. The machine is taught in the following way: The input is provided in the form of a conventional phonemic notation, and transformed into a corresponding set of

TABLE 8.1
Categorisation of Phonemes on Four Simple Dimensions

	Place					
	Front		Middle		Back	
	V/L	*U/S*	*V/L*	*U/S*	*V/L*	*U/S*
Interrupted						
Stop	b	p	d	t	g	k
Nasal	m	–	n	–	N	–
Cont. Consonant						
Fric.	v/D	f/T	z	s	Z/j	S/C
Liq/SV	w/l	–	r	–	y	h
Vowel						
High	E	i	O	ˆ	U	u
Low	A	e	I	a/α	W	*/o

Key: N = ng in *sing*; D = th in *the*; T = th in *with*; Z = z in *azure*; S = sh in *ship*; C = ch in *chip*; E = ee in *beet*; i = i in *bit*; O = oa in *boat*; ˆ = u in *but* or schwa; U = oo in *boot*; u = oo in *book*; A = ai in *bait*; e = e in *bet*; I = i_e in *bite*; a = a in *bat*; α = a in *father*; W = ow in *cow*; * = aw in *saw*; o = o in *hot*.
From Rumelhart & McClelland (1986, p. 235, their Table 2).

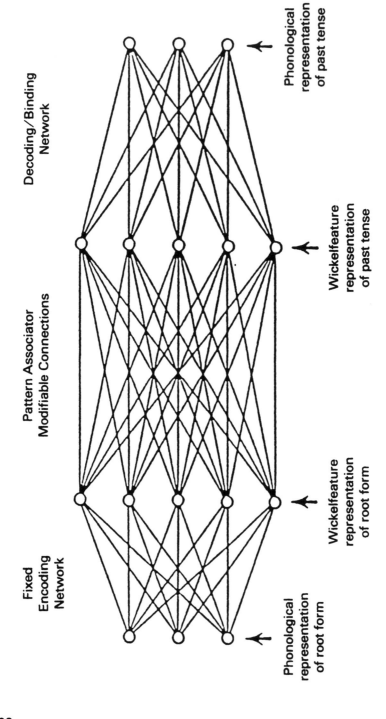

FIG. 8.1. The basic structure at the verb learning model. (From Rumelhart & McClelland (1986b), p. 222, their Figure 1).

222

Wickelfeatures. The input layer of Wickelfeatures is activated by the input. Each input node is connected to each output node with a specific connection weight. On each trial, the weights of these connections determine the influence of the activation of the input node on the activation of the output nodes to which it is connected.

On each training trial, the machine is given the correct output Wickelfeature set as well as the input set. This makes it possible to assess the extent to which each output Wickelfeature node which should be activated, is, and the converse. The model then uses a variant on the standard perceptron learning rule (Rosenblatt, 1962), which changes the weights between the active input nodes and the output nodes that were incorrect on the trial: Lower the weight and raise the threshold for all the output nodes that were incorrectly activated; do the opposite for nodes that were incorrectly inactivated.

The model was given a set of 200 training sessions, with a number of verbs in each session. At the end of this training, the system could take new verbs that it had not processed before, and associate their past tense correctly in most cases. Hence, the model appears to learn, given a finite input, how to generalise to new cases. Furthermore, the model appears to go through several stages of acquisition; these correspond to the stages of learning the past tense of verbs that children go through as well (Brown, 1973; Bybee & Slobin, 1982). During an early phase, the model (and children) produce the correct past tense for a small number of verbs, especially a number of the minority forms (went, ran, etc.). Then the model (and children) "overgeneralise" the attachment of the majority past form, –ed and its variants, so that they make errors on forms on which they had been correct before (goed, wented, runned, etc.). Finally, the model (and children) produce the correct minority and majority forms.

It would seem that the model has learned the rule-governed behaviours involved in forming the past tense of novel verbs. Yet, as R&M point out, the model does not "contain" rules, only matrices of associative strengths between nodes. They argue that the success of the system in learning the rule-governed properties, and in simulating the pattern of acquisition, shows that rules may not be a necessary component of the description of acquisition behaviour. That is, this model is a potential demonstration that rule-governed behaviour is an illusion, and that its real nature is explained by nodes and the associative strengths between networks of nodes. A number of linguistic commentators have drawn this conclusion about connectionist models in general, because of this model in particular (Langackre, 1987; Sampson, 1987).

The model, however, is not without critics. Fodor and Pylyshyn (1988) argued that such models cannot work in principle; Pinker and Prince (1988) argued that this model did not, in fact, work. Lachter and Bever (1988) took a different approach: We stipulated for purposes of argument that the model works, and then investigated *why* it does so. Our forensic method was the following. We examined each arbitrary feature of the model with the rule system in mind, and asked: Would this facilitate or inhibit the behavioural emergence of data which looks like that governed by the past tense rules? Without exception, we found that each "arbitrary" decision would facilitate the emergence of such behaviour. That is, we found that a set of apparently benign simplification devices set the model to be sensitive to the rule-governed properties of the input.

In the formation of the past tense, there are two important features of the present verb form: the final phone (for regular past tenses), and the medial vocalic segment (for irregular past tenses). We described a number of representational devices of the model that insured it would be sensitive to these linguistic properties of past tense formation. (Lachter and Bever acronymically referred to those devices as TRICS—The Representations It Crucially Supposes).

The first simplification of the model involves reducing the number of within-word Wickelfeatures from about 1000 to 260. R&M did this but in an idiosyncratic way: They required that all Wickelfeatures have the same dimension for f1 and f3, whereas f2 can range fully across all feature dimensions and values. Accordingly, the potential Wickelfeatures for the vowel /e/ in "bet" in (9a) are possible; those in (9b) are not.

9. a. [interrupted, vowel, interrupted]
    [voiced, mid, unvoiced]
    [front, short, middle]
  b. [interrupted, vowel, stop]
    [stop, vowel, unvoiced]
    [front, short, unvoiced]

This apparently arbitrary way of cutting down on the number of Wickelfeatures has felicitous consequences for the relative amount of rule-based information contained within each sub-feature. It heightens the relative informativeness f2, since f1 and f3 are mutually predictable, but not with f2. This restriction is entirely arbitrary from the standpoint of the model; but it is an entirely sensible move if the goal were to accommodate to a rule-based account of the phenomena in which the relevant information in a Wickelphoneme is actually in f2. The use of centrally informative Wickelphones automatically emphasises f2.

R&M set up a completely separate set of 200 Wickelfeatures just for phones at word boundaries. Consider word-final phones. R&M allow the available Wickelfeatures to be the cross-product of all possible values of f1 and f2, so long as f3 is the boundary. For example, all the features in (10) are among the possible features for the /et#/ in /bet/.

10. [vowel, interrupted, end]   [low, unvoiced, end]
    [front, stop, end]   [short, middle, end]

We can see that this gives a privileged informational status to phones at the word boundary, compared with any other ordinally defined position within the word: The phones at the boundary are the only ones with their own unique set of Wickelfeatures. This makes the information at the boundary uniquely recognisable. That is, the Wickelfeature representation of the words exhibits the property of "boundary sharpening".

In order to generalise to new cases, these models must have a way of blurring the input so that the model learns on imperfect input. R&M did this by allowing input nodes to be activated if either f1 or f3 were incorrect, so long as f2 is correct. That is, the fidelity of the relationship between an input Wickelphone and the nodes that are actually activated is subject to "peripheral blurring". This effect is not small: The blurring was set to occur with a probability of 0.9 (this value was determined by R&M after some trial and error with other values). That is, a given Wickelnode is activated 90% of the time when either the input does not correspond to its f1 or f3. It can always count on f2, however. This dramatic feature of the model is unmotivated within the connectionist framework, but it has the same felicitous result from the standpoint of the structure of the phenomenon as discussed earlier. It heightens (in this case, drastically) the relative reliability of the information in f2, and tends to destroy the reliability of information in f1 and f3. This further reflects the fact that the structurally relevant information is in f2. It also explains how the model generalises to new cases—by *failing to discriminate them* in the input of old cases. This is a charming resuscitation of the old psychological saw—that generalisation *is* the failure of discrimination—surely, recidivist behaviourism when applied to language.

The period of overgeneralisation of the regular past at the 11th cycle of trials also depends on a real trick. For the first 10 cycles, the machine is presented with only 10 verbs; 8 irregular and 2 regular ones. On the 11th cycle it is presented with an additional 410 verbs of which about 80% are regular. Thus, on the 11th cycle alone, the model is given more instances of regular verbs than in all the training trials it has received before. It is no wonder, therefore, that the regular past ending immediately swamps the previously acquired irregulars. R&M defend this arbitrary move by suggesting that children also experience a sudden surge of regular past tense experience. There are no acquisition data showing anything of the sort (see Pinker & Prince, 1988, who compile evidence to the contrary). Furthermore, if there were to be a sudden increase in the number of verbs a child knows at the time he learns the regular past tense rule, it would be ambiguous evidence between acquiring the rule, and acquiring a lot of verbs. The rule allows the child to memorize half as many lexical-items for each verb, and (with a constant lexical memory) learn twice as many verbs from then on. Therefore, even if it were true that children show a sudden increase in the number of verbs they know at the same time that they start over-generalising, it would be very difficult to decide which was the cause and which the effect.

It is the spirit of connectionist learning models to represent how people learn by inference from masses of individual experiences. Extracting the frequency variation in linguistic experience is what *linguists* do—they are interested in possible patterns, not in the frequency with which individual instances are experienced. Yet R&M presented each verb the same number of times, despite wide variation in actual frequency, thus predigesting the input for their model in much the same way a linguist does—by ignoring real frequency information. This is probably the most important trick of all—and it is absolutely clear why they did it. Irregular past tense verbs are by far and away the most frequently occurring tokens. Hence, if R&M had presented their model with data corresponding to the real frequency of occurrence of the verbs, the model would have learned all the irregulars, and might never receive enough relative data about regulars to learn them. One cannot fault R&M as computer engineers for simplifying the input in this way, but it vitiates any claim that this is a plausible inference-based learning model, and it clarifies further why it is the linguistically relevant patterns that the model tends to extract.

It is clear that a number of arbitrary decisions, made simply to get the model up and working, were made in ways that would facilitate learning the structural regularities inherent to the presented data. It seems obvious what went on: Wickelphones were the representation of choice because they seem to solve the problem of representing serial order (though they do so only for an unnaturally restricted vocabulary, see Pinker & Prince, 1988; Savin & Bever, 1970). But Wickelphones also give equal weight to the preceding and following phone, whereas it is the central phone that is the subject of rule-governed regularities. Accordingly, a number of devices are built into the model to reduce the information and reliability of the preceding and following sub-phones in the Wickelphone. Further devices mark phones at word-boundary as uniquely important elements, as they are in rule-governed accounts of some phonological changes that happen when morphemes are adjoined. Finally, the behavioural learning properties of the model were ensured by making the model learn slowly, levelling all actual frequency information and flooding it with regular verbs at a particular point.

The most important claim for the R&M model is that it conforms to the behavioural regularities described in rule-governed accounts, but without any rules. Pinker and Prince (1988) demonstrate that, in fact, the model is not adequate, even for the basic facts: Hence, the first claim for the model is not correct. Lachter and Bever (1988) showed further, that, even if the model *were* empirically adequate, it would be because the model's architecture and method of data predigestion is designed to extract rule-based regularities in the input data. The impact of the rules for past-tense learning is indirectly embedded in the form of representation and the treatment of the input data: Even Wickelfeatures involve a linguistic theory with acoustic segments and phonological features within them; the work of the special representational devices to render available the segmental phoneme, and emphasise boundary phonemes in terms of segmental features. That is, garbage in/garbage out: Regularities in/regularities out.

One might argue that the special devices are a theory of the child's morphophonological mind—that is, they constitute the theory of what underlies phonological universals. To check for that, one must examine the implications of each of the TRICS for phonological universals. None of the special devices fares well under this kind of scrutiny. For example, "central-informativeness" makes it hard to learn processes in which f1 and f3 are marked for different dimensions. Since such processes are common, the universal predictions this makes are incorrect. Similarly, sharpening information at word boundaries is well-suited to isolate the relevant information in the regular past-tense formation in English, and would seem like a natural way to represent the fact that morphological processes affect segments at the boundaries of morphemes when they are combined. Unfortunately, such processes do not seem to predominate cross-linguistically over within-word processes.

One of the most unrealistic aspects of the Wickelphonological feature system is that a single feature is represented by only one node, regardless of how many times it appears in a given word. But it is often the case that a word can have more than one instance of the same feature: For example, in "deeded", almost all the features with f2 centred on the vowels are identical and thus make the word simpler to represent in Wickelnodes than "seeded", by about 12 Wickelfeatures—this means that learning the past tense of "deed" should be easier than for "seed". The particular configuration of features in R&M makes feature repetitions possible even in monosyllabic words. For example, the number of separate Wickelfeatures for the internal sounds in "fazed" is 55% larger than the corresponding number of separate Wickelfeatures for "dozed". There does not, however, seem to be any evidence that learning the past for one is easier than for the other.

Finally, the child is exposed to tokens, not types: It is difficult to see how the child could learn if it ignored the past-tense experience of a verb until all the other verb past-tense forms have been attended to at least once. One can *imagine* a model which does this—i.e. a model with a "McRumelwell's Demon", which rejects all verbs from the inner sanctum of weight-change until all the other verbs have been admitted once. But this is a demon with considerable analytic powers; knowledge about past forms of verbs that have appeared, and about which ones are being awaited. Furthermore, the demon knows just when to expand the list of to-be-learned past-tense forms (the 11th cycle). All of this without a word-level representation of words in Wickelphones!

So, in the model, the representations it crucially assumes do not define a plausible set of linguistic universals. (As Lachter and Bever [1988, p. 213] put it, "Trics aren't for kids.")[2]

EVIDENCE FOR NODES UNSEEN—SOME MODELS THAT LEARN TO READ ALOUD

English orthography satisfies all the requirements of the canons of reputability under the law of conspicuous waste. It is archaic, cumbrous and ineffective; its acquisition consumes much time and effort; failure to acquire it is easy of detection.

—Veblen

---

[2]Since this writing, there have been several unpublished attempts to meet some of the prevailing criticism. Marchman and Plunkett (1989) argue that regression in performance of single units during training is a natural consequence of connectionist systems with multiple connectivity. A unit may initially be responsive to a particular input, only to lose that unique sensitivity as more trials increase the number of dimensions to be discriminated. Hence, individual units seem to "regress" simply as a function of increased training, without special changes in the model's input. There are several aspects of this work that mitigates its implications for natural developmental regressions. First, the loss of response discrimination found by Marchman and Plunkett is in *single* units, not a whole learning system; second, it is hard to show that the early success and later regressions in single-unit responses is more than statistical noise during early training phases.

MacWhinney and Leinbach (1991) have offered a broad range response to previous critiques of R&M. Their primary method is to construct a new model which acquires past tense morphology allegedly without TRICS. This model is presented somewhat cryptically, so analysing it is difficult. Its salient properties are (1) it is a four-layered model with two cascaded hidden layers; (2) it implements an "onset and rime" representation of sequentially ordered segments with a full complement of features describing each segment; (3) cases for training are presented with their actual relative frequencies; (4) some measure of success is claimed, but the model fails specifically to show a regression on irregular forms. In response, I note (1) two middle layers were used because it did not work with one layer—this is an interesting, possibly important, result bearing on the power of such models to learn sequence transformations. But without some analysis of the hidden units' performance the meaning of any learning is obscure—at best, it is an existence demonstration that some network configuration can learn aspects of orderly data; (2) They admit that the representations are those of standard linguistic analysis, but fail (explicitly) to see that these representations are *not* theory-neutral; rather, they have built into them reflections of how segmental and morphological structure work. Curiously they recognise this, claiming that theirs, and other, models are "implementations" of actual processes, and are therefore immune to independent criticism. This amazing point begs the question: If the models are merely implementations, then they make no claims and hence are of little theoretical interest, specifically connectionist. (3) It is intriguing that presentation of actual relative frequencies worked—indeed, surprising that it was possible in a tractable number of trials given that the frequency ratio between the most and least frequent verb is of the order of 10^4:1. It may turn out that the additional hidden layer is important in filtering out dominant effects of the overwhelmingly frequent irregular verbs. (4) They tout the model as achieving two out of three phases of U-shaped development, namely a phase of poor performance and a subsequent phase of good performance. A regression requires by definition a decrease in performance; accordingly, the most charitable interpretation of the boast that "two out of three isn't bad" is as a joke.

Foreigners always spell better than they pronounce.

—Twain

I want that glib and oily art
to speak and purpose not

—Shakespeare (King Lear)

The R&M model is relatively simple in that it uses a single layer of input nodes and a single layer of output nodes. Obviously, if this is supposed to be like a model of even a minuscule part of the brain, it is much too simple. Also, it is well known that a two-layer activation system cannot learn disjunctive mappings (Minsky & Pappert, 1969). One of the legacies of taxonomic linguistics as one level of representation in language involves disjunctive relations with units at other levels (as in "complementary distribution"). So it is unrealistic to attempt any kind of linguistic modelling with a two-layer system. More recent implementations of connectionist models include an intermediate level of nodes, so-called "hidden units", which do have the power to learn disjunctive mappings. In a scheme of this kind, there are two sets of connection strengths to adjust on each training trial; those between the output nodes and the hidden units, and those between the hidden units and the input nodes. Obviously, little would be gained by setting each layer of connections in the same way. There are a number of schemes for how to apportion the credit and blame to the two levels. A popular technique is so-called "backpropagation". In this scheme, the connections between the output nodes and hidden nodes are adjusted first on each trial, in a manner similar to that of a two-level system. Then the connections between the input nodes and the hidden units are adjusted (the way this is done is not in itself straightforward—it involves integrating the error term over all the connections from an input node to each of the hidden units. But it is a mathematically plausible extrapolation from what happens in two-layer systems. See Rumelhart et al., 1986).

Several models of different kinds of language learning have been developed using models with hidden units. Some of these models appear to learn to read, that is, they learn to pronounce English words, given conventionally spelled input. These models have received a lot of public attention and are worth some consideration as they are applied to linguistic problems.

One would like a spelling system in which letters always correspond to the same sound, but the relation between spelling and pronunciation in English is complex. First, there is a distinction between "regular" and "irregular" spelling correspondences. Even the regular correspondences are not simple, however: Most consonants actually have a small set of phones to which they correspond, and there are also consonantal doublets that map onto single sounds; vowels are pronounced in several ways, with a particular set of changes (from the Old

English vowel shift), being signalled by a final "e" in the next syllable. Part of the reason for this melange is historical—the alphabet was formed before a number of sound changes took place. It is also due to the fact that the spelling corresponds to the underlying morphological structure, which is itself computationally prior to the operation of phonological rules (see Chomsky & Halle, 1968).

Some enthusiastic researchers have referred to the English system as containing spelling-sound "rules" (see, e.g., Venezky, 1970), but nobody has been able to make a rule-based pronunciation program that really works—and the likes of IBM have thrown millions of dollars at the problem. But there are a number of majority regularities, and one can show that children follow them during early stages of reading, pronouncing relatively irregular words as though they were regular. There is also some evidence that brain-damaged adults revert to regular pronunciations of irregular words. A barrage of experimental studies with normal adults has shown that spelling irregularity increases reading time for infrequent words, but not for frequent words. Finally, subjects seem to have access to different strategies for deciding when a letter sequence is a word as a function of the other words in the experiment (see Seidenberg, 1987, for a representative review of these research areas).

All this (and more) has led an army of psychologists to agree that people read words with a "dual route" system (see, e.g., Coltheart, Sartori, & Job, 1986): Frequent words are memorised as a visual whole, whereas infrequent words are sounded out following the regularities (and then corrected if they are actually irregular). With a relatively regular and frequent set of words to decide on, subjects can decide directly on the visual appearance; if the set of words contains rare irregulars, then the subject has to sound out each word to check its legitimacy as a word.

Psychologists persist in believing that the mind is simple: They ponder a two-process model like that just described, and wonder, "why not *one* process?" In this vein, Seidenberg and McClelland (1988; S&M) have constructed a connectionist model which learns to map English monosyllabic uninflected words onto appropriate Wickelphonological feature matrices. The model has three layers of nodes (see Fig. 8.2). The input level is a set of 400 nodes, which represent an encoding of letters. Each input node is connected to 200 hidden units. The output level has two sets of nodes; one is the set of 460 Wickelfeatures as used in the past-tense verb learning model. The other is a set of nodes which encode the letters the same way as in the input nodes. The model was trained for 250 cycles that selected 400–500 words from the 2900 most frequent monosyllabic English words. Words were selected on each cycle in proportion to the log of their real frequency of occurrence (this was accomplished by a random process on each cycle, which is why the number of words on each cycle could differ slightly).

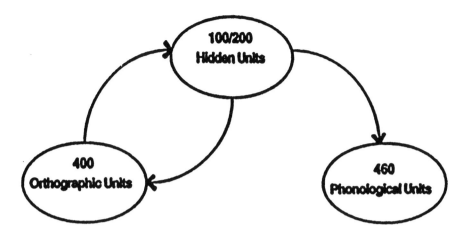

FIG. 8.2. Overall structure of the learning model used by Seidenberg and McClelland (1989).

On each trial, the feedback information was both on the correctness of the Wickelfeatures that were and were not activated, and on the correctness of the encoded letter representations. S&M measure the success of the model in terms of the sum of the squares of the difference between the activation level of each output node and the level it ought to have (0 or 1). The model shows considerable improvement in these terms over the 150,000 individual word trials. Quantitatively, the model learns the frequent regulars and irregulars first, and learns the infrequent regulars last. S&M note that this is similar to the order of learning in children. They also quantify the accuracy of the model after the 150,000 trials and find that the mean squared error is not larger for irregular than regular words unless they are also infrequent: They relate this to the experimental findings on word naming and lexical decision. They show that the model's error score on certain subsets of words corresponds to their relative time to be read aloud in naming experiments. They simulate phonological priming by giving an already trained model *additional* training on a word, and showing that training lowers the error score for other words with similar spelling-sound correspondences. Finally, they train a new model with few hidden units and show that it only learns to pronounce regulars and frequent irregulars, just like developmental dyslexics.

S&M also describe an interpretation of the model that accounts for effects in "lexical decision" studies, a paradigm in which subjects must decide whether a letter sequence is a word or not. S&M suggest that the error term on the reactivation of the input Wickelnodes can serve as a measure of the "wordiness" of the input. They suggest that the word/nonword decision be simulated by whether the letter error term is below or above a particular criterion. First, they demonstrate that in the model, words have lower error terms than nonwords; similarly, nonwords that are pronounceable and legally spelled in English have lower error terms than unpronounceable or illegally spelled nonwords. They apply the model to account for effects on lexical decision time that depend on the experimental set. For example, the effect of word frequency on naming depends on the range of frequencies that is used: the model explains this because when a full range of frequencies is used, it is harder to establish a criterion that separates words from nonwords on the error terms, because they are more continuous. Similarly, if very word-like nonwords are used consistently in an experiment, response latencies are elevated: This corresponds to the fact that word-like nonwords will have small error terms, which will be hard to distinguish from the error terms for real words.

This model is a tour de force. The creators are modest about many aspects of the model, and enjoin us not to take specifics of it too seriously. But they emphasise that the model appears to do away with *two* routes for reading and to replace them with *one*. Seidenberg (1989) also suggests that the model exemplifies how a continuous framework can represent what appears to be categorical knowledge.

But this claim may be premature—just as in R&M, the model works because of the real regularities of the input/output correspondences and because of a set of special devices not dissimilar to those in R&M. First, since it uses the Wickelphonological nodes from R&M, it also buys all the same representational moves (except blurring, which they did not use—there was no need to have a phonology-hearing representation, since they were not attempting to account for phonologically based misreadings). These devices conspire to emphasise the central phone information, which facilitates the learning of individual letter-phone correspondences in regular words. They also emphasise the clarity of initial and final phones, which help differentiate the large number of letters which have a different distribution of pronunciation in word initial and word final position (e.g. y,h,w,c,e,i,q,u,x). Finally, in monosyllabic words, which the model was limited to, consonantal letter combinations almost all occur at word boundaries: Hence giving extra marking to those sounds which break the one-letter/one-sound generalisation.

The use of Wickelphonology also makes predictions about the different ease of learning to pronounce words as a function of the number of distinct Wickelfeatures in their description. For example, since "dozed" has 55% more Wickelfeatures for the medial sounds than "fazed", there should be an enormous difference in the model's accuracy on those words. Given S&M's method of measuring success, "fazed" should be learned sooner and better, but that difference does not correspond to any real effects that have been reported

(actually, S&M do not work with inflected forms, but similar points can be made for uninflected words.)

The second set of representational devices involves the way in which the letters were encoded onto input nodes. Because of the requirement that representations be distributed, they used an encoding of Wickel-letter triples, with L1,L2,L3, as outlined in (6). It might have broken new ground if they had encoded the letters in terms of a set of visual features that differentiate them (they report that Lacouture [1988] has recently done that). But, instead, they created 3-dimensional Wickel-letter-matrices as labels for each input node. A Wickel-letter-matrix has 3 dimensions, each of which has 10 letters chosen randomly from the set of 27 (26 letters and word boundary). Each dimension corresponds to L1 or L2 or L3 in the triple which defines Wickel-letters. Each Wickel-letter-matrix defines 1000 Wickel-letter-matrix points—each point corresponds to a Wickel-letter. Input words are represented in terms of Wickel-letters—a given input node is triggered if any of the 1000 Wickel-letter-matrix-points correspond to any of the Wickel-letters in the input word. Four hundred input Wickel-letter-matrices were created by randomly selecting 10 letters for each of the 3 dimensions 400 times.

This encoding of the letter appears at first to be computationally neutral, except there is a twist: The matrix dimension corresponding to the middle letter of Wickel-letters never has word boundary chosen as one of its ten letters. Prima facie, this is a sensible property, since, by definition, no Wickel-letter of the form X#Y exists in monosyllabic words. But it also has the property that the central letter of Wickel-letters is represented in ˜4% more input node Wickel-letter-matrices than the initial or final letter of Wickel-letters. This is a small difference, but the model does run for 50,000 individual trials, so it is likely that it enhances the relevance of the central member of the Wickel-letters, which is what would be needed to capture those regular letter/sound relations which exist. Also, there is an organisational feature of the feedback that may be critical to its success. Each hidden unit is trained simultaneously with feedback from the letter and phonological nodes. Insofar as there are spelling/sound regularities, this technique allows the hidden units to respond in accord with correlations between letter-sound pairs: Each unit is given feedback on each Wickel-letter-matrix-node Wickelfeature pair, which will tend to isolate the training effect of those pairs which correlate (be it positively or negatively).

As in R&M, the training words are not presented in direct proportion to the actual frequency of word occurrence. In English, about 180 words account for more than half of the word occurrences: The range across all words is at least 70,000 to one. Among monosyllabic words, the 180 most frequent words account for more than 90% of all word occurrences, because most infrequent words are also multisyllabic: More than 97% of the 180 most frequent words are monosyllabic, whereas less than 20% of the least frequent words are monosyllabic (this can be determined from analysis of the Kuçera & Francis [1967] word count). Hence, if words were presented in linear proportion to their real frequency of occurrence, the model might well learn the more frequent irregular words as isolated cases, and never extract regular patterns or differentiate them from the irregulars—a result not consistent with the facts S&M want to simulate. Furthermore, it appears to be the case that irregular spellings are more probable in frequent than infrequent monosyllabic words. Thirty percent of the 90 most frequent monosyllabic words are irregularly spelled, whereas this is true of only 7% of a corresponding sample of the least probable monosyllabic words. Hence, irregular pronunciations would swamp the learning system if words were presented with their actual relative frequencies.

For these reasons, reducing the contrast in exposure to the most and least frequent words was a practical necessity. As I mentioned in the discussion of R&M, this manipulation removes the model from the realm of plausible learning models; at the same time, it converges on what a structural analyst would do when searching for possible spelling/sound patterns. In this case, "McSeidenwell's Demon" collapses the frequency range of tokens via a log transform. Clearly, it had to leave some frequency information intact (unlike McRumelwell's Demon, who manipulated the R&M model by changing its input on cycle 11), because it is frequency-based human behaviour which they are attempting to model. A log transform may have been chosen because it flattens the distribution enough, but also leaves some frequency information available. One might argue that a log transform of actual frequency is justified because the effects of experience often turn out to be a log transform of frequency of training. But, if true, that fact is to be *explained* by the learning model, not artificially built in to the data presentation scheme by a word-knowing demon.

In response to an early version of this paper, Seidenberg and McClelland (1989) tried out a variant of their model in which words are presented more closely in proportion to their real frequencies. Instead of compressing the frequency range with a log transform, they tried a square-root transform. With training, this model displayed the effect of frequency, which S&M note with satisfaction. They also note that the model does *not* display the facilitation of high-frequency regular words, although they do not explain this fact. Furthermore, they do not note that the low-frequency regular words are learned relatively less well. Table 8.2 presents the mean squared error for each of the word categories for about the first 25,000 training trials (the first 40 epochs for the original model, taken from their Fig. 3, and the first 400 epochs for the square-root transform model, taken from their Fig. 27).

The most noticeable fact is that low-frequency regular words are learned relatively less well in the root than the log model. This is *exactly* the kind of difference predicted by the preceding consideration: The high-frequency irregulars occur relatively more often, and drive out the regulars. The root model maintains considerable reduction of the real numerical superiority of the high-frequency irregulars. It remains the case that learning all regulars will be less

TABLE 8.2

Approximate Mean Square Error from Seidenberg and McClelland (1989) Comparing Models in which Words are Presented with a Frequency that is Either the Log or Square Root of their Actual Frequency

	High Frequency		Low Frequency	
	Regular	Irregular	Regular	Irregular
Log Model	7	10	10	15
Root Model	7	8	12	16

effective if real frequencies are used. Of course, with enough training, or enough hidden units, some model will learn all words to some degree. The important fact is that the relative ease of learning will be shifted in favour of irregulars if real frequencies are used. This is disastrous for S&M, because the relative ease of learning different word types is the basis for making predictions about behavioural complexity.

S&M give a scientifically oblique argument for using the log frequency compression: Without it, the model would have to be given 5,000,000 training trials to guarantee training on each word—the relatively frequent words would take up most of the training trials. They estimate that 5,000,000 trials would take about a month with existing equipment. Given the amount of human brain time they and others are spending on their model, the month might have been well spent: Most of the behavioural experiments they model took at least that long to run.

They also offer several potentially empirical justifications for some kind of frequency compression: First, they suggest that infrequent regular words appear more often in inflected variants (less characteristic of some irregularly spelled words such as "have"); hence their true relative frequency is underestimated. Second, they speculate that the frequency range is smaller for children learning to read. The first point could be determined empirically, but since most irregular words are also constant when inflected, it seems unlikely that the frequency levelling effect of inflected forms is very large. The second point is more puzzling. It is true *by definition* that children experience a smaller frequency range: Until the child has read at least 70,001 words, it has no potential to experience the true frequency range of English words. But the child also does not experience most of the individual words at an early stage. So the relevance of the child for the model is obscure. Of course, it would be easy to use a children's text-based frequency count for selecting training trials. I made a small test count of 2,000 sentences of a second-grade text. Irregularly spelled words accounted for more than half of the forms. Furthermore, the mean token frequency of the irregulars was about 30 and of the regulars was 3. This is necessarily a smaller frequency ratio than for adults at least because of the small samples, but it suggests a similar problem.

In brief, S&M's model does just what its designers created and manipulated it to do—it learns spelling/sound regularities, and it learns frequent irregulars more quickly than infrequent irregulars. But, of course, S&M aspire to show that once trained, the model makes distinctions along the frequency and regularity dimensions similar to adult humans: They use the mean squared error between the primed features and the actually correct features as a way of predicting relative reaction times. This presents a problem if one is supposed to take the model as a candidate for reading behaviour: The mean squared error of an output can be calculated only if the correct pronunciation is already known. There is a corresponding circularity in the presumed behavioural model: The reader transforms the letters into the phone-features, and then checks it against his knowledge of the correct pronunciation of the word—the further away the actual word is, the longer the time to pronounce the word. But if the reader "knows" the correct pronunciation of the word, why doesn't he just say it? There might be a way out of this: One might try to assess the distance between the output of the model on a word and the nearest pronounceable sequence (assuming some English phonology filter that defines "pronounceability"—a neat trick in connectionist terms). It *might* turn out to be the case that those words which arrive more closely to a pronounceable sequence are the short and frequent words . . . but that would have to be shown. In any event, S&M make much of the fact there is no word-level set of units, so it is totally mysterious how an error term could be matched against anything at all within the model.

The lack of a transparent relation between the model and a behavioural mechanism further highlights the fact that the learning net is telling us only about redundancies and associative patterns available in the input (once treated to some statistical distortion). That is, it serves as a powerful frequency analyser, operating on a predigested set of actual data. Perhaps this may reveal useful statistical properties of English spelling/sound correspondences; but it is not a model of pronunciation behaviour. Hence, among other things, the claim that it is a "one-process" model of pronunciation is unwarranted.

The "simulation" of lexical decision does not involve a behavioural implementation, because it does not aspire to be a simulation of actual behaviour. Rather, the re-activation letter error term is used as a measure of the definiteness with which a word is recognised. All the predictions are based on the clarity with which different subsets of words and nonwords can be distinguished using the letter error term. Thus, the range of phenomena that the model accounts for are just those which have to do with the statistical properties governing the discriminability of different subsets of English words. I have no quarrel with this application of the model: Indeed, it demonstrates elegantly that subjects use the statistical properties of letter sequences to guide their lexical decisions. It makes no claims about how that process occurs.

The model's statistical success might be taken as a demonstration that lexical decision may not be a very useful task for the study of language behaviour—if the model were a complete account of lexical decision behaviour, using it to study semantic structures or sentence processing would be like studying taste by using the amount of time it takes people to name pictures of vegetables. Also, the flavour of S&M's discussion is redolent of the view that semantic factors are ordinarily unused in lexical decision: Many studies, however, show that associative and other kinds of priming affect lexical decisions (classically, Meyer & Schvaneveldt, 1971, and many others since then). In fact, lexical decision may be sensitive even to structurally mediated semantic information: For example, lexical decisions are faster following a noun-anaphor that refers to the word (Cloitre & Bever, 1986). S&M do not directly deny such possibilities, but the model is irrelevant to them. And, since the model has no word-level representations, it is difficult to see how to integrate it with semantic and syntactic effects in the normal uses of language.

The most striking empirical success of the model is the orderly relation between the phonological error score and actual reaction times in lexical decision tasks: The model predicts with a high correlation the relative decision times for 14 different subsets of words (e.g. "frequent regulars," "infrequent regulars," "infrequent uniquely spelled words"). This correlational success is an initial demonstration that subjects are responsive to statistical regularities that differentiate spelling-sound correspondences in different types of words. But it leaves unspecified how subjects' average performance is accumulated from individual responses. One appeal of the connectionist models is based on the appearance that they reduce apparently complex phenomena to a single process—spreading activation among units. Accordingly, this model's statistical success appears to confirm the hypothesis that subjects also use a single activation process in lexical decision. This conclusion, however, is unwarranted, if for no other reason than that the model is not a behavioural theory.

The ambiguity of the data here parallels that of studies of "one-trial vs. incremental learning" and "probability matching vs. hypothesis formation". In each case, the data overall have an incremental appearance, gradually increasing as a function of number of trials: But closer analysis suggests that the averaging process is obscuring quantal learning acquired by different subjects at different times. There is a directly relevant experimental analogue to consider in the present case—the acquisition of the pronunciation of new written words by young children. Suppose one attempted to teach a young child to read vocabulary in a new language: On each trial, the child is presented with a word, attempts to pronounce it and is given the correct pronunciation as feedback. With a vocabulary of 100 words or so, 75 with a "regular" pronunciation and 25 with a set of irregularities, one would expect to see a gradual improvement across words and children, and such improvement should occur faster with regular pronunciations (assuming equal presentation frequency). But it would not be surprising if individual children learn the pronunciation of individual words quantally, that is, going from not pronouncing a word correctly on trial n to pronouncing it correctly on trial $n+1$, and never misreading it after that. Across children, n should turn out to be greater for irregulars, because on average, their pronunciation is less supported; for any individual word, the acquisition will appear gradual, because the function is averaged across individual children.

In this way, a process that is actually discrete can appear to be continuous: A difference between word classes that is quantal can appear to be gradual. The corresponding possibility exists for tasks such as lexical decision in adults. Each trial may be responded to quantally, with a discrete process: For example, "assume the word is frequent and can be checked automatically; if it isn't, assume that it is spelled regularly. . . ." Across words of different kinds, the average response times will correspond to the extent to which the particular kind of word follows the more favoured strategies. Hence, a multi-strategy model fits the data exactly as well as an alleged "one-process" model. In the absence of a particular behavioural theory, the data and the success of the model do not bear on the behaviour, only on the statistical regularities with which the real behavioural mechanisms are interacting.

There is another, more infamous, model which learns to pronounce English words, also using hidden units. This model, NEttalk, is trained to transform printed words into input phone instructions to a Dectalk machine (Sejnowski & Rosenberg, 1986). The model is trained on each letter, moving from left to right; on each trial, the training occurs on a letter with the 3 preceding and 3 following letters. One can think of this as training on super Wickel-letters, with 3 pre- and 3 post-central phone positions. (In this case each Superwickel-letter is not given its own node, since that would add up to the equivalent of 27 to the 7th power Superwickel-letter nodes. In fact, the relative order of the 6 surrounding letters is not preserved in the input representation.) After 400,000–1,000,000 trials, the model-driven Dectalker sounds very impressive.

How does this work? First, the model is learning the associative information available, which determines the sound of a central phone in a very informative string (7 letters). Second, it dodges the problem of digraphs, by requiring the model to output silent phones for one of the members of the digraph (e.g. "phone" would have at its output level "f-on-".) This solves artificially a big problem in spelling/sound correspondences. Finally, Dectalk itself has a program with a great deal of English phonology built in. For example, it fixes up phonetic transitions, has a lot of stress rules, and includes many phonetic rules of English.

It is striking that both of these models of "reading" miss the real computational problem in reading. Written text provides an input sketch of what to say, but the output is determined not only by the letter sequence but by computational linguistic processes as well. For example, it is well known that the morphological and surface phrase structure of words plays a large role in stress, and therefore in such phonetic features as vowel length, and neutralisation of both vowels and consonants: S&M avoid this problem (a) by not having their model responsible for it and (b) only treating monosyllabic words. Netalk solves it (insofar as it does) by relying on long string of input information and on the rich built-in phonology in Dectalk. But it makes the obvious mistakes which a nonmorphologically aware reader makes, such as not differentiating the pronunciation of "ragged" in the two sequences in (11), or of "delegates" in (12).

11. a. Harry's ragged.
    b. Harry ragged.
12. a. Harry delegates minors in gym.
    b. Harry's delegates minor in gym.

In brief, insofar as these reading models work, they do so because they limit themselves to that information which is indeed associatively determinable, and rely on other devices to pick up some of the pieces.

These models require perfect information and many thousands of trials, even with all the special devices and tricks. Clearly, they are able to extract certain frequency-based information in the input/output relations they are trained on. This may be marvellous engineering; it may lead to conversations with telephone operator modules as intelligent as the current real ones. It may reveal to us frequency properties in the world of which we were unaware. But the value of psychology is limited to knowing that a powerful device shows some adaptation to some frequency information after 100,000 trials involving 400,000 instances of phones and billions of individually computed adjustments in associative strength (e.g. in S&M's model there are 172,000 connections, each of which must be checked and may be changed on each of 10,000 trials. So the training period involves more than 200 billion computations.). Science has given us many analytic tools that tell us about the world, but not directly about ourselves. A spectrometer tells us about the composition of a distant star—but that does not tell us anything about stargazing. Aside from all the limitations and isolated cleverness of current connectionism, maybe what it is showing us is that this cannot be the way that children learn anything, even habits.

One might think that the very large number of trials involved in connectionist models is irrelevant because the human child has so many more units to learn with: Surely, if a model with 200 hidden units requires 100,000 training trials, one with 2,000 will require fewer trials, with 2,000,000 fewer still, and so on. This is undoubtedly true. But the computational load (the number of individual computations and weight changes) on each trial also increases proportionally. Most telling, however, is the fact that as the number of hidden units goes up, the models tend to learn each case as a separate item. Hence, the models converge onto brute-force one-to-one mapping associations that cannot generalise to new cases. So, the prognosis is not a hopeful one: When you make the models powerful enough to deal with more than toys, they memorise everything as a separate instance.

THE STUDY OF STATISTICALLY AVAILABLE INFORMATION

How use doth breed a habit in a man!
—Shakespeare (Two gentlemenof Verona)

Most people don't associate anything—their ideas just roll about like so many dry peas . . . but once you begin lettin' 'em string their peas into a necklace, it's goin' to be strong enough to hang you, what?
Lord Peter Wimsey

Structural Hypotheses and their Statistical Confirmation

I originally observed that connectionist modelling might help us understand the relation between computational and habitual mental structures. This is justified by what I found, but it is difficult to show that from most existing models. This is because these models make a theoretical virtue of obscuring the structural information they contain and presuppose. Indeed, the flavour of the accompanying commercials is that no structural information is required at all. That makes it a chore to show how the models really work, and it reduces the chances that they will tell us anything about the real relations between the structural demon and the statistical beast. This is consistent with the fact that some of the models' creators seem to argue (like Bates & MacWhinney, 1987) that the beast *is* the demon—that is, that the notion of structural rule and category is actually an illusion, and that conceptual nodes and associative strengths between nodes are all there is.

Proponents of this kind of view (e.g. Rumelhart and McClelland) accept the scientific utility of rule-based descriptions of language; but, they argue, rules express vague regularities inherent to the data, whereas connections express what the underlying mechanism actually is. A frequent explanatory allusion is to the relation between Boyle's law (BL) and the internal combustion engine. The idea seems to be that BL is a generalisation about the behaviour of pressure, volume, and temperature, but the engine is a real instance of those generalities. This analogue has been offered to me a number of times, so it may be worth a little direct attention. The analogy is clearly flawed, but perhaps in an instructive way.

The main flaw is that it begs the question about ultimate cause while seeming to answer it. BL states an orderly relation between pressure, volume, and temperature. It exists for a set of reasons—a combination of thermodynamic laws and assumptions about the particulate nature of gases. That is, BL is true in an engine because of a set of laws not contained in the engine. If structural linguistic rules are true of language, then either they are in the language engine or not. If they are not, then they must be true for other reasons, presumably materialistic ones. Hence, just as for BL, there must be other physical principles that explain the existence of the rules, not represented in the connectionist model itself. This would argue that there is some other biological basis for the rules, not included in the connectionist model, but which constrains it to behave as though it included them. So the question is begged.

The currency of connectionist learning is statistical inference. We know, however, that no amount of inference can cause the distinction between something that is always true in the model's experience, and something that is true by categorical designation. Examples of this kind of distinction are not hard to find. National Basketball Association players are tall in *fact*, but they are professional in *principle*. Such categorical distinctions are not mere artefacts of a technological civilisation (assuming professional sport to be civilised): In primitive cultures, it can be a matter of great importance to know who your biological ancestors are and who merely acts like them—it determines everything ranging from politeness forms to marriage. Even in civilised culture, the mere knowledge of such categorical relationships can be a matter of life and death— after all, Oedipus behaved perfectly appropriately with his wife: The basis of the tragedy was that he insisted on *finding out* that she was his mother, very much the wrong category for a wife.

There are varying responses from connectionists concerning the problem of explaining categorical and symbolic knowledge: The most apparently forthcoming is that such knowledge could be built into the models—which is why they are allegedly consistent with nativism. But, insofar as categorical distinctions and symbolic constructs are built in, the connectionist model becomes merely an implementational system of constraints to be explained by some other theory. One such "explanation" for innate categories that the more enlightened connectionists offer is "evolution." This surely must be the true account of whatever is innate. But appeals to "evolution" do not explain the mental nature or role of categorical and symbolic processes, much less why the particular ones have evolved the way they have. It is another example of begging the question. On one view, the constraints leading to the possibility and formation of categories are biological, in which case they are not explained by connectionist models. On the other view, the constraints are metaphysical (e.g. constraints or information processing systems in general). The final possibility is one that I suspect many connectionists will find most satisfactory: There is no explanation for the existence or arrangement of categorical mental structures; there is only biological history.

There is a corresponding problem in accounting for the acquisition of complex systems like language via statistical inference alone: Inference is a mechanism for the confirmation of an hypothesis, but it is a notoriously bad mechanism for *creating* hypotheses about the kinds of structures inherent to human behaviours. Consider a (relatively) simple phenomenon—learning to play tag—in particular, figuring out the concept of "it." (See Bever, Carroll, & Miller, 1984; Lachter & Bever, 1988.) "It" is actually a category defined by one of the recursive rules of the game, not by any particular overt property or necessary behaviour. It seems likely that children can learn this concept without much explicit instruction. But the statistics of the behaviour of the players is not informative enough to account for the creation of the categories: Children have to have a lot of conceptual information, which sets up hypotheses as to what kind of activity they are watching. They have to know about games; they have to know about transitivity of (invisible) properties (like "it"-ness); they have to know about rules and priorities among them. Such prior knowledge allows for the construction of hypotheses about tag. Once the alternative hypotheses are elaborated, the statistical properties exhibited in games of tag provide information that can tend to confirm or disconfirm particular hypotheses.

It would be unreasonable to assume that the child uses none of the statistically available information to confirm its hypotheses. I have argued that some connectionist models of learning work only insofar as their structure (and input data) steer their associative processes towards correct representations. Thus, a successful connectionist model is actually a hybrid between associative and symbolic structures. This dual property may make it possible to investigate the interaction between what is built into a learning model, and the environmental regularities which confirm its hypothesis. In this way, we can separate the symbolic process of forming structural hypotheses from the statistical processes involved in two aspects of language acquisition. First, the statistically supported patterns can confirm specific structural hypotheses. Second, they can become the behavioural bases for extending linguistic performance beyond the current computational capacity. In the next pages, I outline an example of a connectionist model of learning phrase segmentation, and show how the knowledge it isolates might serve each function.

The problem of language acquisition is often framed as the problem of learning the grammatical structures that generate a set of experienced utterances stored with their meaning. On this view, children accumulate a set of sentences they understand, and then apply analytic processes to them which yield a grammatical organisation for them. This view enables theorists to focus on the kind of learning model required for the discovery of a grammar from coded input data, and has been a fruitful strategy. But it also begs an important question: How do children assign both linguistic structure and meaning to sentences for which they have not yet learned a grammar? (See Valian, 1990, for a discussion of this issue and its impact on parameter setting theories of language acquisition). That is, how do children encode sentences they cannot parse? A related question is: How do children make use of partially correct analyses of the utterances they hear?

Consider the role of connectionist modelling in the context of an hypothesis testing model of language acquisition. On this model, children have competing structural hypotheses about their language and use incoming data to choose between the hypotheses. Children could use such data in two ways: Deductively, the possibility of a particular utterance can rule out a structural hypothesis; inductively, accumulation of partial information can confirm one hypothesis statistically over another. Deductive models of hypothesis testing in language acquisition have been the most commonly explored type—children are presented as "little linguists," applying information about which sequences are grammatical to distinguish underlying grammatical hypotheses. A great virtue of such models is that they can be studied in direct relation to a grammar that distinguishes between grammatical and ungrammatical sequences—thus, the learning model is tied directly to the grammar. However, deductive models generally require a body of structurally analysed and comprehended data, and hence beg the question of how sentences that cannot be parsed are understood and recorded as data.

Inductive models have appeared unattractive for three reasons. First, it is axiomatic that pure inductive systems are unable to form hypotheses, so a separate hypothesis-formation process must be postulated anyway. Second, it is not clear how partially coded input could bear on structural hypotheses. Third, it is difficult to assess the availability to children of statistically supported hypotheses. If we interpret connectionist models as inductive analysers, then we can use them to meet the second and third objections to inductive models of hypothesis confirmation. Consider the following general description of connectionist learning and what it can show:

A model has input data, I, under a particular descriptive scheme, R; and output data O, presented in a set of behaviours, B. The model is trained to produce a discriminative response DB that discriminates along some dimension of R, DR. Insofar as the model learns to pair instances of DB and DR correctly on a training set, it can be asserted that R provides the information needed for the discrimination in the training set; insofar as the trained model correctly discriminates new I, it can be asserted that R provides the information needed for the DB/DR discrimination in general.

Or, to put it succinctly, a model can reveal the *cue validity* of information for a discriminative behaviour, under specific descriptions of the environmental input and the behavioural output. On this view, such models are analytic tools for the psychologist, aiding in the discovery of what information lies in the statistical properties of the environment under different descriptions.

The fact that models can operate under different input descriptions allows us to construct an input representation for sentences that is incomplete, and then examine the cue validity of that kind of representation for certain kinds of information children receive. Consider the following model, "Baby Clauseau," which learns to predict when an utterance is going to end (see Juliano & Bever, 1990, for a fuller presentation). It has the following assumptions:

1. Input: examines three words of input at a time. Each word position has:
   a. a separate node for each of the 100 most frequent words in motherese;
   b. a separate node for each of 4 word-length categories;
   c. a node indicating how far to the left the nearest recognised word is.
2. Output: an activation level of one node ranging from 0 to 1, corresponding to the likelihood that the third word ends the utterance.
3. Training feedback: negative feedback when the utterance does not end there; positive feedback when the utterance ends there.

We constructed a three-layer model with these assumptions, using 10 hidden units in the usual arrangement (complete connectivity between layers, a standard backpropagation weight-changing routine, etc.). It was trained on a 21,000 word sample of motherese text (approximately 4000 utterances), and then generalised to a new 800 word text of motherese.[3] The results were quite intriguing. First, the mean output level on the generalisation text for actual utterance boundaries was 0.5, whereas for non-boundary positions it was 0.1. This demonstrates a considerable degree of differentiation of actual boundaries, based on the minimal input assumptions. Second, if we separate the continuous output values into discrete predictions of boundary vs. non-boundary, the results appear as in Table 8.3.

Finally, we assessed the cumulative likelihood at each of 20 output activation values, of an actual utterance boundary (a "hit," a correct prediction by the model that there is an utterance boundary), and the cumulative likelihood at those values of a non-boundary (a "false alarm," or incorrect prediction of a boundary). We used an adaptation of detection theory to scale the discriminability of boundaries from non-boundaries as analysed by the model (Fig. 8.3).

TABLE 8.3
Percentage of Utterance Boundaries in Next Text by Baby Clauseau (BC), Using an Arbitrary Threshold Between .1 and .5 in BC's Output

	Model's Predicted Boundary
Actual Text	
Boundary	76
Non-boundary	18

---

[3]In fact. this model is a variant on one we constructed for a practical reason—to make on-line decisions about formatting text displayed in closed captioning for the deaf.

This technique is useful in assessing discriminability functions of such models, because it utilises information from every level of output. Figure 8.3 shows that there is considerable information at all levels of output that discriminates boundaries from non-boundaries, given the input.

This model demonstrates that a child could learn to predict when an utterance ends, knowing only 100 frequent words, the approximate length of all words and by examining three words at a time. Such knowledge can help the child delimit sentences in multi-sentence utterances without clear acoustic boundaries, clearly an important prerequisite to analysing sentence structure. But such multi-sentence utterances may be relatively rare, and hence the model might be taken a a small tour-de-force but not as an interesting one.

It becomes more interesting if we consider why the child might learn to predict when an utterance ends. The child and adult goal in comprehension includes

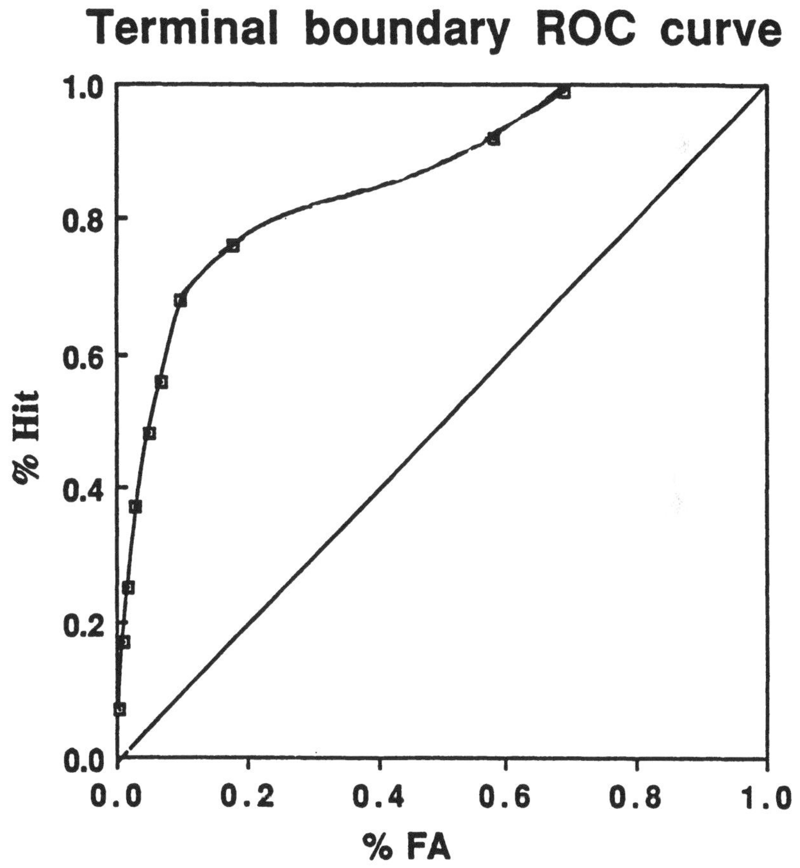

Terminal boundary ROC curve

FIG. 8.3.   Detection-theoretic analysis of the output of Baby Clauseau on new text. Each square represents the number of hits (correct predictions of a boundary) and false alarms (incorrect predictions) at successively higher output values.

segregation of major meaning-bearing phrases. Thus, the learning of utterance-final boundaries may be viewed as a by-product of the attempt to package sentences into meaning units in general. We can assess the significance of this interpretation by generalising the output of the trained model to predict phrase boundaries *within* utterances. We did this on the 800-word generalisation text period. The mean output value was 0.3 for within-utterance phrase boundaries and 0.1 for non-boundaries. Applying the same procedure as earlier to arrive at discrete predictions, we found the results as in Table 8.4.

Finally, the detection-theoretic analysis of the output shows considerable discrimination of phrase boundary from non-phrase boundary positions (Fig. 8.4).

I have argued that a separate function of associative knowledge is to extend the empirical domain of a computationally limited processing system. An adaptation of the output from Baby Clauseau serves as an example of this. We noted that the following "boundary sharpening" procedures lead to a near-perfect phrasing analysis of motherese texts. The input to the boundary sharpening procedures is the sequence of boundary values assigned by BC to an utterance. The rules are:

1. A boundary occurs after a word when the activation level after the next word is lower.

2. Single words surrounded by boundaries and adjoined rightward unless they end the utterance.

Sample phrased output from this procedure is presented in Fig. 8.5. These phrase-segmenting procedures add two assumptions to Baby Clauseau: (a) to assign phrase structure, look ahead one word; (b) a local peak in boundary activation level is a phrase boundary. The first assumption seems typical of boundary-sharpening mechanisms in many other areas of perception. The second constitutes a testable claim—namely that children (and possibly adults) assign segmentation one word after each point.[4]

TABLE 8.4
Same as Table 8.3, but for Phrase Boundaries
Within Utterances in New Texts

	Predicted by Model
In Text	
Boundary	71
Non-boundary	20

[4]Note that this would be easy to implement in a system which assigned a potential phrase boundary whenever the critical BC value is above some criterion (say 0.2 in the current model), and then check that assignment on the next word to make sure that the BC value descended. This system would make empirically testable predictions about local garden paths, predictions which we are now starting to test on adults.

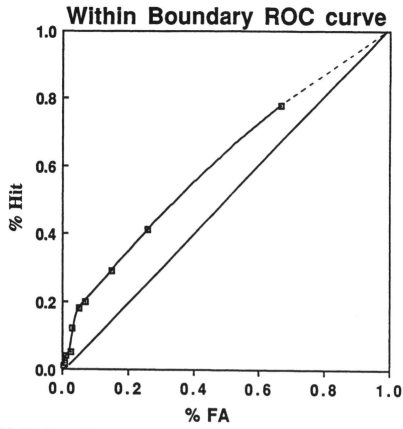

Within Boundary ROC curve

% Hit (y-axis): 0.0, 0.2, 0.4, 0.6, 0.8, 1.0

% FA (x-axis): 0.0, 0.2, 0.4, 0.6, 0.8, 1.0

FIG. 8.4   Same as Fig. 8.3, but for phrase boundaries within utterances in new text.

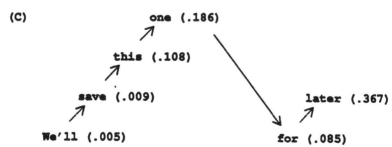

(A)   "We'll save this one for later."

(B)   We'll (.005) save (.009) this (.108) one (.186) for (.085) later (.367).

(C)
                       one (.186)

         this (.108)

  save (.009)   later (.367)

We'll (.005)   for (.085)

(D)   [[We'll save this one] for later.]

FIG. 8.5   Phrase segmentation using output from Baby Clauseau.

247

To summarise the model. It is trained on actual motherese to predict utterance-final boundaries, using a simple set of input, output, and feedback assumptions. It then generalises well, showing a large discriminability function for utterance boundaries in new texts. But it *also* shows good discriminability for phrase boundaries within utterances, *even though it was not trained on sentence-interval phrase boundaries.*

As with the models discussed in the first section of this paper, there is no magic here. The model learns utterance boundaries because of redundancy in the configuration of the three final words, given the descriptive input scheme; the generalisation to phrase boundaries occurs because almost every utterance boundary is *also* a phrase boundary. What the model shows is that the child could use clear information (actual utterance boundaries) to aid it in an early stage of processing phrases when the surface information is unclear. The input representations are schematic and incomplete, but make assumptions that seem reasonable, and do not beg any questions; namely, that the child knows some frequent words and the length of words it does not know, that it is attempting to find natural meaning units, and it recognises actual pauses as boundaries.

Knowing where the major phrases begin and end within utterances is vital information for distinguishing between two kinds of phrase structure organisations, head-first and head-final. In fact, if content and function morphemes are characteristically stressed differently, then a simple strategy of attending within phrases to the stressed word would tend to locate phrase heads in a way that could differentiate between the two types of structure. We are currently constructing a connectionist model of this hypothesis differentiation process.

Such exercises are *not* intended as models of the language-acquiring child: Rather, they are demonstrations that certain kinds of information are statistically available in natural discourses, under particular assumptions of input and output representation. Thus, the models exemplify connectionism as a tool to examine the role that associative-activation knowledge could play in language acquisition.

In any event, this application of BC demonstrates how associative structures, learned from degraded and simple input data, can be used to extend limited computational knowledge and capacity: There are many phrase types which children may not be able to compute structurally as phrases; such phrases would still be assigned a correct segmentation by the associatively based habits, trained on evidentially clear cases of where entire utterances actually end. The point of the exercise, again, is *not* to argue that we have demonstrated a connectionist model of phrase assignment, but rather to show that the specific input representations are adequate to learn, from a natural corpus, a set of associations that combine with a boundary sharpening procedure to segment phrases correctly. How this is actually implemented in the child or adult—if it is—is an entirely different matter, for reasons discussed in the first section of this chapter.

CONCLUSION—BEHAVIOURAL STRATEGIES AND MENTAL STRUCTURES

The overall research programme I have outlined suggests a general rehabilitation of the notion of behavioural "strategy." The theoretical claim is that associative strategies form automatically and are natural bases for extending the range of a limited computational capacity. The perceptual strategy that "bigger = more," discussed at the beginning of this chapter, is probably statistically supported over the range of cases that children can compute (roughly, displays with six items or less): hence, the strategy can be derived from computable cases, and then extended to larger cases. The situation is less clear in the case of a complex linguistic strategy, such as (4a), that an "N-V-N" sequence corresponds to "agent, action, object": how can we be sure that this strategy is justified in the language the child hears? One can envisage a model that would be trained to assign basic grammatical relations to a selected set of short motherese sentences, for example, those which use only the set of 100 most frequent words. How well the trained model generalises to new sentences which have the "n-v-n" pattern would be a measure both of the learnability of the pattern on the short sentences, and how well supported it is as a generalisation applying to longer sentences.

Such an investigation will confirm (or disconfirm) the long-held view that actors precede and agents follow their predicates. Other generalisations (e.g. that agents are animate) can be investigated in similar ways. In the general case, one could assign a surface and semantic analysis to a training text, and train a model to assign the basic semantic relations that link the surface phrases: The success of the model at learning the training text will be a measure of the regularities in that text; its success at generalising to new text will be a measure of the availability of statistical information about the surface input to discriminate underlying thematic relations; finally, and perhaps most important for our general research program, analysis of the trained model may reveal *new* informative properties of the surface input.

Connectionist engines offer empirical answers to the problem of analysing statistically available information. What we called perceptual and production "strategies" in language behaviour are interpretable as implementations of statistically valid relations between structural representations. Connectionist models allow us to explore what kinds of such generalisations exist under different representational and environmental assumptions. That is, in the implied long programme of research, the role of connectionist modelling is to inform us about the kinds of statistical information available to the child, given its structural capacities at each stage. This will define the information which children might use to confirm some structural hypotheses and extend the behavioural application of others. Thus, we can use these frequency engines to the hilt to help us understand what the beast *might* be doing to extend the domains of the demons. But it will be a further empirical matter to see how they co-exist productively in the child.

ACKNOWLEDGEMENTS

A number of the arguments concerning McClelland and Rumelhart were worked out with Joel Lachter. In general, I have learned whatever I know about connectionist modelling from conversations with Lachter, Jerry Feldman, and Gary Dell. Mark Seidenberg and Jay McClelland were generous with their explanations of how their model works, and checked the accuracy of my summary of it. Cornell Juliano is largely responsible for Baby Clauseau.

REFERENCES

Bates, E. & MacWhinney, B. (1987). Competition variation and language learning. In B. MacWhinney (Ed.), *Mechanisms of language acquisition* (pp. 157–197). Hillsdale, N.J.: Lawrence Erlbaum Associates Inc.

Bever, T.G. (1970). The cognitive basis for linguistic universals. In J.R. Hayes (Ed.), *Cognition and the development of language* (pp. 277–360). New York: Wiley & Sons, Inc.

Bever, T.G. (1975a). Functional explanations require independently motivated functional theories. In R. Grossman, J. San, & T. Vance (Eds.), *Papers from the Parasession on Functionalism*, Chicago Linguistic Society. Chicago: University of Chicago, 580–563.

Bever, T.G. (1975b) Psychologically real grammar emerges because of its role in language acquisition. In D.P. Dato (Ed.), *Developmental psycholinguistics: Theory and applications* (pp. 63–75). Washington D.C.: Georgetown University Round Table on Languages and Linguistics.

Bever, T.G. (1982). Regression in the service of development. In T. Bever (Ed.), *Regression in mental development* (pp. 153–188). Hillsdale, N.J.: Lawrence Erlbaum Associates Inc.

Bever, T.G. (1987). The aesthetic constraint on cognitive structures. In W. Brand & R. Harrison (Eds.), *The representation of knowledge and belief* (pp. 314–356). Tucson, Arizona: University of Arizona Press.

Bever, T.G., Carroll, J., & Miller, L.A. (1984). Introduction. In T. Bever, J. Carroll & L.A. Miller (Eds.), *Talking minds: The study of language in the cognitive sciences.* Cambridge, Mass.: M.I.T. Press.

Bever, T.G., Mehler, J., & Epstein, J. (1968). What children do in spite of what they know. *Science, 162,* 921–924.

Bever, T.G. & Hansen, R. (submitted). *The induction of mental structures while learning to use symbolic systems.*

Bowerman, E. (1982). Reorganizational processes in lexical and syntactic development. In E. Wanner & L. Gleitman (Eds.), *Language acquisition: The state of the art* (pp. 319–346). Cambridge, Mass.: Cambridge University Press.

Brown, R. (1973). *A first language: The early stages.* Cambridge, Mass.: Harvard University Press.

Brunswick, E. (1956). *Perception and the representative design of psychological experiments.* Berkeley, C.A.: University of California Press.

Bybee, J. & Slobin, D. (1982). Rules and schemes in the development and use of the English past tense. *Languages, 58,* 265–289.

Chomsky, N. (1981). *Lectures on government and binding.* Dordrecht: Foris.

Chomsky, N. & Halle, M. (1968). *The sound pattern of English.* New York: Harper & Row.

Cloitre, M. & Bever, T.G. (1986). *Linguistic anaphors and levels of representation.* Cognitive Science Technical Report No. 36. Rochester, N.Y.: University of Rochester.

Coltheart, M., Sartori, G., & Job. R. (Eds.) (1986). *Cognitive neuropsychology of language.* London: Lawrence Erlbaum Associates Ltd.

Feldman, J. & Ballard, D. (1982). Connectionist models and their properties. *Cognitive Science,* *6,* 205–254.

Fodor, J.A., Bever, T.G., & Garrett, M. (1974). *Psychology of language.* New York: McGraw Hill.

Fodor, J.A. & Pylyshyn, Z.W. (1988). Connectionism and cognitive architecture: A critical analysis. *Cognition, 28,* 3–71.

Francis, W.N. & Kuçera, H. (1979). *Manual of information to accompany a standard sample of present-day edited American English, for use with digital computers.* Providence, Rhode Island: Department of Linguistics, Brown University.

Frazier, L. (1979). *On comprehending sentences: Syntactic parsing strategies.* Doctoral Thesis, University of Connecticut.

Gerken, L.A. (1987). *Function morphemes in young children's speech perception and production.* Columbia University, Ph.D. Dissertation.

Gerken, L.A., Landau, B., & Remez, R. (in press). Function morphemes in young children's speech perception and production. *Developmental Psychology.*

Hinton, G. & Sejnowski, T. (1986). Learning and relearning in Boltzmann machines. In D. Rumelhart & J. McClelland (Eds.), *Parallel distributed processing: Explorations in the microstructure of cognition: Vol. I.* Cambridge, Mass.: M.I.T. Press.

Jandreau, S.M., Muncer, S.J., & Bever, T.G. (1986). Improving the readability of text with automatic phrase-sensitive formatting. *British Journal of Educational Technology, 17,* May.

Juliano, C. & Bever, T. (1990). *Clever moms: Regularities in motherese that prove useful in parsing.* Presented at the 1990 CUNY Sentence Processing Conference.

Karmiloff-Smith, A. (1986). Cognitive processes and linguistic representations: Evidence from children's metalinguistic and repair data. *Cognition, 23,* 95–147.

Kuçera, H. & Francis, W.N. (1967). *Computational analysis of present-day American English.* Providence, Rhode Island: Brown University Press.

Lachter, J. & Bever, T.G. (1988). The relation between linguistic structure and associative theories of language learning—A constructive critique of some connectionist learning models. *Cognition, 28,* 195–247.

Lacoutre, Y. (1989). From mean square error to reaction time: A connectionist model of word recognition. In D. Touretsky & T. Sejnowski (Eds.), *Proceedings of the 1988 connectionist models summer school.* San Mateo, Calif.: Morgan Kauffman.

Langackre, R. (1987). The cognitive perspective. *Reports of the Centre for Research in Language, San Diego, 1,* (3).

Langer, J. (1982). Mental representations and cognitive development. In T.G. Bever (Ed.), *Regression in mental development.* Hillsdale, N.J.: Lawrence Erlbaum Associates Inc.

Levelt, W. (in press). *Speaking: From intention to articulation.* Cambridge, Mass.: Bradford Books.

MacWhinney, B. & Leinbach, J. (1991). Implementations are not conceptualizations: Revising the verb learning model. *Cognition, 40,* (121–157).

McClelland, J.L. & Kawamoto, A.H. (1986). Mechanisms of sentence processing: Assigning roles to constituents. In J.L. McClelland, D.E. Rumelhart, & The PDP Research Group (Eds.), *Parallel distributed processing. Explorations in the microstructure of cognition, Volume 2: Psychological and biological model* (pp. 272–331). Cambridge, Mass.: M.I.T. Press.

Meyer, D.E. & Schvaneveldt, R.W. (1971). Facilitation in recognizing pairs of words: Evidence of a dependence between retrieval operations. *Journal of Experimental Psychology, 90,* 227–234.

Minsky, M. & Pappert, S. (1969). *Perceptions.* Cambridge, Mass.: M.I.T. Press.

Newport, E.L. (1977). Motherese: The speech of mothers to young children. In N.J. Castellan, D.B. Pisoni, & G.R. Potts (Eds.), *Cognitive theory, Vol. 2.* Hillsdale, N.J.: Lawrence Erlbaum Associates Inc.

Pinker, S. & Prince, A. (1988). On language and connectionism: Analysis of a parallel distributed processing model of language acquisition. *Cognition, 28,* 73–193.

Plunkett, K. & Marchman, V. (1991). U-shaped learning and frequency effects in a multi-layered perception: Implications for child language acquisition. *Cognition, 38*, 43–102.

Rizzi, L. (1982). *Issues in Italian syntax.* Dordrecht: Foris.

Rosenblatt, F. (1962). *Principles of neurodynamics.* New York: Spartan.

Rumelhart, D., Hinton, G.E., & Williams, R. (1986). Learning internal representations by error propagation. In D. Rumelhart, J. McClelland, & the PDP Research Group (Eds.), *Parallel distributed processing: Explorations in the microstructure of cognition: Vol I. Formulations.* Cambridge, Mass.: M.I.T. Press/Bradford Books.

Rumelhart, D. & McClelland, J. (Eds.) (1986). *Parallel distributed processing: Explorations in the microstructure of cognition.* Cambridge, Mass.: M.I.T. Press.

Sampson, G. (1987). A turning point in linguistics: Review of D. Rumelhart, J. McClelland, and the PDP Research Group (Eds.), Parallel distributed processing: Explorations in the microstructure of cognition. *Times Literary Supplement*, June 12, 643.

Savin, H. & Bever, T.G. (1970). The nonperceptual reality of the phoneme. *Journal of Verbal Learning and Verbal Behavior, 9*, 295–302.

Seidenberg, M.S. (1985). Constraining models of word recognition. *Cognition, 20*, 169–190.

Seidenberg, M.S. (1987). Sub-lexical structures in visual word recognition. Access units or orthographic redundancy. In M. Coltheart (Ed.). *Attention and performance XII: Reading* (pp. 245–263). Hillsdale, N.J.: Lawrence Erlbaum Associates Inc.

Seidenberg, M.S. (in press). Cognitive neuropsychology and language. *Cognitive Neuropsychology.*

Seidenberg, M.S. (1989). Visual word recognition and pronunciation: A computational model and its implications. In W.D. Marslen-Wilson (Ed.), *Lexical representation and process* (pp. 25–74). Cambridge, Mass.: M.I.T. Press.

Seidenberg, M.S. & McClelland, J.L. (1989). A distributed, developmental model of word recognition and naming. McGill University Cognitive Science Technical Report. *Psychological Review, 96*, 523–568.

Sejnowski, T.J. & Rosenberg, C. (1986). *NETtalk: A parallel network that learns to read aloud.* (EE and CS Technical Report No. JHU/EECS-86/01). Baltimore, M.D.: Johns Hopkins University.

Slobin, D. (1978). A case study of early language awareness. In A. Sinclair, R. Jarvella, & W. Levelt (Eds.), *The child's conception of language.* New York: Springer-Verlag.

Slobin, D. & Bever, T.B. (1981). Children use canonical sentence schemas in sentence perception. *Cognition, 12*, 229–265.

St John, M. & McClelland, J.L. (1990). Learning and applying contextual constraints in sentence comprehension. *Artificial Intelligence, 46*, 217–257.

Valian, V.V. & Coulson, C. (1990). Anchor points in language learning: The role of marker frequency. *Journal of Memory and Language, 27*, 71–86.

Venezky, R. (1970). *The structure of English orthography.* The Hague: Mouton.

Wickelgren, W. (1969). Context-sensitive coding, associative memory, and serial order in (speech) behavior. *Psychological Review, 76*, 1–15.

9 Representational Adequacy and the Case for a Hybrid Connectionist/Marker-passing Model

George Berg
Department of Computer Science, Department of Linguistics and Cognitive Science, S.U.N.Y. at Albany, LI 67A, Albany, NY 12222, U.S.A.

INTRODUCTION

The heart of any natural language processing (NLP) system is its underlying knowledge representation (KR) model. The limits of its KR become the limits of the entire NLP system. This is well known and accepted by researchers in symbolic systems (cf. Brachman, 1979; Woods, 1975). However, researchers in the various connectionist approaches to NLP are just beginning to come to grips with representing knowledge in artificial neural networks. When compared to their symbolic counterparts, connectionist NLP systems have woefully inadequate KR models. Typical shortcomings include the inability to represent the relationships between concepts in the model ("non-combinational semantics") and the lack of a means of *timely* change in the system's knowledge in response to the natural language input.

To overcome these shortcomings we have developed the autonomous semantic network (ASN) model for representing and processing knowledge (especially for building NLP systems). ASNs are a massively parallel model of both representation and processing. The model has three parts. The first part is a generalised local connectionist network (cf. Feldman & Ballard, 1982). This network serves as the primary knowledge representation. It is also the backbone of the model in that the spreading activation in this part controls the operation of the other two parts. To carry out searches and facilitate relationally-sensitive

The author's émail address is berg@cs.albany.edu

processing, we add a second network, the "WTA-search network." The third part of the ASN model is the "construction network." The construction network adds and deletes links in the model and allocates new nodes.

Both the WTA-search and construction networks are made up of simple, special-purpose processing elements ("nodes"). In each case, a particular node performs a single, fixed task whenever it is activated by the excitation it receives. Because the tasks of the WTA-search and construction network nodes can be implemented using various marker-passing schemes, we refer to the ASN model as a hybrid connectionist/marker-passing model.

Together, the three parts of the ASN constitute a representationally adequate KR model. In addition the WTA-search and construction networks represent a distributed processing ability—one which is free from the bottleneck of a central, serial controller and processor. This represents a major advance in distributed AI systems—a massively parallel model of representation coupled with an equally parallel *general* processing ability.

REPRESENTATIONAL ADEQUACY

In this chapter, we take a view that natural language processing is primarily an application using a knowledge representation system. In one sense, this is a gross oversimplification, but our view is that an adequate model of knowledge representation and processing is a prerequisite to NLP. Without the ability to work from adequate representations, any attempt to understand language will be severely handicapped. This will probably be to the point where it will either not work, or work only in limited circumstances. This is similar to the arguments of Woods (1975) and Brachman (1979) about the representational adequacy of semantic networks. In addition, we consider an *integral part* of a KR model to be its ability to modify its representations in a reasonable amount of time.

What do we mean by representational adequacy? First, we contend that it has two parts—static adequacy and dynamic adequacy. as we show later, they are both fundamental parts of a KR model—parts that are lacking in current connectionist KR models. Later in this chapter we show how our ASN model combines static and dynamic adequacy.

Static Representational Adequacy

Static adequacy is what has traditionally been termed representational adequacy in the KR literature. We choose to rename it in order to underscore the difference between it and dynamic adequacy, discussed later.

There are many separate issues, which together constitute a full notion of the static adequacy of a KR system (cf.; Brachman, 1979; Hayes, 1979; Woods, 1975). The issue of concern here is the ability to represent individual instances of concepts explicitly, as well as their properties and their relationships to other concepts in the system. An adequate knowledge representation system must be able to represent multiple instances of the same concept simultaneously, along with any properties that distinguish these instances (e.g. a small green box and a medium-size blue box).

This is in contrast to the "representation" that we get in many systems based on connectionist models with distributed representations (cf. Hinton, McClelland, & Rumelhart, 1986). In these systems a concept is represented as the co-occurrence of a set of features. These features are represented by connectionist units in the system. The state of the units indicates the presence or absence of features in the concept being represented. In a sense, this represents only types, not intentional concepts. This becomes clear when we try to represent several concepts simultaneously. For distributed representations, two alternative forms have predominated—the undifferentiated, flat representation and role-specific representation.

The flat representation style is clearly inadequate for representing several concepts simultaneously. If we simultaneously activate the feature nodes for several concepts, we do not have a way to decide which features belong to which concepts. For that matter we do not know how many concepts are being represented. This is an instance of the "cross-talk" problem (cf. Feldman & Ballard, 1982).

The alternative is to split the representation into a separate set of features for each concept filling a specific role (cf. Hinton et al., 1986; Hinton, 1988). For example, "Jan phoned Ellen" would have separate sets of features to represent the actor, the action and the object. Although differentiating the features by role allows us to represent more than one concept, it is not a general answer to being able to represent the relationships between concepts. As Fodor and Pylyshyn (1988) point out, the fillers of these roles are often not simple concepts, but complex ones (made up of simple ones in specific relationship to one another). For example, this architecture would be unable to represent "Sue believes Jan phoned Ellen." The concept in the object role is now "Jan phoned Ellen", which cannot be represented without cross-talk confusion. For this reason, current distributed representation connectionist models clearly lack static representational adequacy[1].

In contrast to distributed representation models, local representation connectionist models (cf. Cottrell, 1985; Feldman & Ballard, 1982; Stolcke, 1990) allow an individual connectionist node to represent an entire intensional concept. The properties of a concept are represented by links to other concepts representing the properties. Similarly, links can associate two concepts. Local models use intermediate nodes to represent the relationship between the two concepts. For example "Jean's son is Bill" could be represented by four nodes JEAN, SON, BILL, and a connector node. The connector node is attached to the other three with bidirectional excitation links. It is activated when it receives excitation over

---

[1] We say "current" distributed representation models, because there is some preliminary work that may allow such systems static adequacy (cf. Miikkulainen & Dyer, 1989; Pollack, 1988).

any two of its links and sends its own excitation out to the node connected by the third link. In this way, the relationships between concepts can be represented.

For our purposes, we can conclude that local representation connectionist models may be adequate for static representation (although this is not generally accepted—see Fodor & Pylyshyn, 1988. However, the next section shows that they are dynamically inadequate, and thus unsuitable as a general KR model.

Dynamic Representational Adequacy

Dynamic representational adequacy is the ability of a KR model to change. A defining feature of a NLP system is that it reads in information, usually in the form of text. As the system reads the text, it must be able to represent the concepts introduced in the text, as well as their properties and the relationships that exist between concepts. The KR system must support this. Offhand, this seems very similar to static adequacy—representing concepts, properties, and relationships. Indeed, in a sense dynamic adequacy *is* static adequacy—it is the maintenance of static adequacy *over time*. This last point is where the complications arise. Whereas static adequacy itself is concerned with adequately representing the knowledge of one particular set of concepts, properties, and relationships (the system's "knowledge base"), dynamic adequacy is concerned with turning one static representation into another, different representation as a result of new information. This new information can take several forms. It can be the introduction of a new concept. It can be the addition of a new property to a concept. It can be the addition fo a new relationship between concepts. It could also be the deletion of any of these things from the current knowledge base.[2] Clearly, the nature of a NLP system demands that its KR system be dynamically adequate.

One other aspect of dynamic adequacy is important—the KR model that purports to be dynamically adequate must support *timely* change. Because information is generally given once in a text and is often used subsequently to add further information (e.g. "There once was a boy named Jack. He lived with his mother . . ."), the KR model must allow change which takes place at roughly the same rate as the presentation of the input to the system.

Dynamic adequacy is not achieved by local representation connectionist models. Systems based on such models (cf. Cottrell, 1985; Stolcke, 1990) cannot represent an arbitrary new unit. Their static nature and their fixed interconnections limit them to representing a fixed number of distinct concepts, each represented by a single unit. There have been proposals for learning and change in local representation models (cf. Feldman, 1981). However, no significant systems that can represent new units have come of them.

---

[2]We are not concerned here with representing history or the passage of time (e.g. "Jim had a beard in the seventies"). This issue is problematic for all AI and cognitive science researchers.

The relationship between dynamic adequacy and distributed representation models (cf. Hinton et al., 1986) is more subtle. Since a particular concept in a distributed representation model is not one unit, but rather a pattern of activations over a (potentially large) set of units, one can define a particular unused pattern to correspond to the representation of this new concept. Even in a system where individual units represent low-level features (e.g. "blue", "male", "alive"), and which as a result will map two intentionally unique concepts onto the same representation, there is a solution. Simply augment the model with extra units. Each intentionally unique concept can be given a unique pattern of activation over these units (analogous to an "ID number"—Mikkulainen & Dyer, 1989, use this idea).

Since the units in many connectionist models employ real-number activation levels, we are not restricted to binary encoding of these identifiers. Even with the practical limitations of hardware floating-point precision, and the limits of the discrimination abilities of connectionist learning methods, a reasonable number of units can identify a large enough number of individual concepts uniquely that we concede that encoding a new one is not a problem for distributed representations. This is especially true if we allow concepts, which are otherwise distinguishable based upon their features, to share the same "ID number."

The problem with dynamic adequacy in distributed representation models is *timeliness*. As mentioned earlier, changes in a NLP system's knowledge base must take place at a pace roughly equal to the rate at which the system is reading its input. For a distributed representation system to embody a concept non-trivially, it must not only be able to encode the concept, but it must be able to represent the relationships of the concept. For instance, in the "Jan phoned Ellen" example, the concept for the action must be able not only to identify itself as a distinct "phoning" action, but it must also represent that the actor was Jan and that the object was Ellen. In distributed representation models, this type of relationship is done via one of the connectionist learning methods (cf. Hinton & Sejnowski, 1986; Rumelhart, Smolensky, McClelland, & Hinton, 1986). In general, such learning techniques can establish the necessary associations. Unfortunately, they cannot do it in a *timely* way. The existing techniques will not make the associations quickly. They require many iterations over the concepts to be associated—a process that clearly violates the real-time constraints of NLP. Because they cannot change its representations quickly enough, the current distributed representation connectionist models are inadequate for the KR tasks needed in NLP systems.

AUTONOMOUS SEMANTIC NETWORKS

The autonomous semantic network (ASN) model is designed to provide both a knowledge representation and processing ability for use in massively parallel NLP systems. The model was designed specifically to provide both an adequate representation for the knowledge used in natural language as well as distributed control and processing mechanisms, which change the state of the system's knowledge representation in response to the presentation of the natural language input. There are three parts to the ASN model: (1) the representation/backbone network; (2) the WTA-search network; and (3) the construction network.

The representation/backbone is a generalised spreading-activation, local connectionist network. Input to an ASN is received as excitation of specific units in this network. Output from the system is the activation (or lack thereof) of designated output units, although as a practical matter, the entire network can be designated as output so the state of the entire knowledge base can be examined.

Although the representation/backbone network behaves as if it were a local representation connectionist model, its actual implementation must be more general. In order to support indirection in construction nodes (described shortly) a unit in the representation/backbone network must be able in some fashion to identify the units to which it has links. This makes it much more complex than a purely connectionist model (which needs no such information: A connectionist unit needs only to have the links exist—it does not need information about which other units the links connect to). This added complexity does not hamper our ability actually to implement the ASN model; see the conclusion.

The representation/backbone serves two purposes in the ASN model. First, it is the knowledge representation part of the model. The representational part of this network is similar to a local connectionist model (cf. Cottrell, 1985; Feldman & Ballard, 1982; Shastri, 1988). Units are designated to represent intentional concepts. The relationships between concepts are expressed by excitatory and inhibitory connections between them.

The second purpose of the representation/backbone is to act as the "skeleton" for the entire ASN model. Some of the units in the representation/ backbone network serve to control processing in the ASN model. The activation of a particular unit may stand for a particular word being read and the excitatory and inhibitory links lead out from it to nodes in the WTA-search and construction networks, which together work to change the state of the representation to reflect the effect of "reading" this new word.

The second part of the ASN model is the WTA-search network. This network is composed entirely of special processing elements—the WTA-search nodes. When activated, a WTA-search node examines a fixed set of units from the representation/backbone network. From these it picks a "winner"—the unit with the highest activation value.[3] WTA-search nodes can also be cascaded, so that the "winner" among the units attached to one WTA-search node is then

---

[3]This is similar to the local connectionist "winner-take-all" networks of Feldman and Ballard (1982), and takes its name from them.

examined by another WTA-search node connected to the first. As we show later, cascaded WTA-search nodes can be organised to search the representation/ backbone network's units in the fashion of a taxonomic hierarchy.

The third part of the model is the construction network. The construction network is made up of several different types of nodes. When activated, each node performs a fixed task. These tasks include: add a link between two units in the representation/backbone network; remove a link between two units; and allocate a new unit for use in the representation/backbone network. There are also node types, which perform the corresponding tasks on nodes in the WTA-search network.

Normally a construction node will perform its link-creating or deleting between the same two units. However, the usefulness of these link-changing construction nodes can be greatly increased by allowing a single level of indirection. This is shown in Fig. 9.1. The two parts of this figure are each a

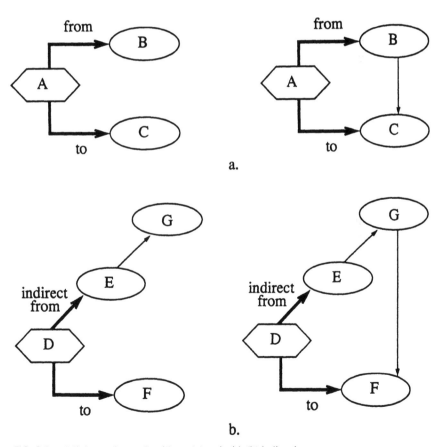

FIG. 9.1.   A link-creating node without (a) and with (b) indirection.

"before and after" illustration of the effect of a different link-creating node. Part (a) of the figure shows a normal link-creating node (A). When it becomes activated the node creates a link from the unit attached at the end of A's "from" link (unit B) to the unit at the end of A's "to" link (unit C). The effect of A is completely fixed. Part (b) shows a similar situation, but one where the from link of the construction node is indirect. In this case the resulting link is created not from the unit at the end of the from link (unit E), but indirectly through it. The link is created from the unit, which is itself linked to unit E (hence the notion of indirection). By connecting different units to E the same construction node can create links to different units. Indirection can also be used for a construction node to gain access to the winner of a WTA-search. As we show later, the use of indirection is a key part of the representational adequacy of the ASN model. The use of indirection is what requires the units in the representation/backbone network to have a pointer to the units to which they are connected. See Berg (1988) or Kulshrestha (1990) for details. As we will see later, the three networks that combine to make up the model give ASNs both static and dynamic representational adequacy.

ASNs AND REPRESENTATIONAL ADEQUACY

In this section we show how the ASN model can perform NLP tasks that require both static and dynamic representational adequacy. The examples are taken from actual ASN-based NLP systems. For the sake of clarity, the examples are highly abstracted from their actual ASN implementations. For an exhaustive treatment, see Berg (1988).

The Style of ASN-based NLP

Before showing how ASNs handle representation-based problems in NLP, it is necessary to discuss some of the underlying assumptions used in the design of our ASN-based systems.

The most fundamental design decision is that ASN-based NLP systems should, as much as possible, exploit the parallelism inherent in the task. Operations should only be serialised or synchronised when absolutely necessary. This follows naturally from the primary thesis underlying ASNs—that high-level NLP can be done in a massively parallel environment.

A second decision is that regularities in language should be mirrored in the structure of the NLP systems. For instance, transitive verbs subcategorise for many of the same structures. This regularity is captured in ASN systems by a single portion of the network, which supports this regularity and which is used by all of the transitive verbs. Specifically, this subnetwork will recognise and build a representation for the verb's actor and object case frames. This is in sharp contrast to a system where these mechanisms are duplicated for each transitive verb. In general, any structure shared by a group of words or concepts will be represented by a single subnetwork, which can be used by any of them.

There is a limit to how much this can be done, however. If a structure is to be used simultaneously in two or more parts of the network, there must be multiple copies of it. An example of this are the subnetworks supporting structural markers (which are described later). Although the subnetworks that operate on them are almost identical, they must be duplicated because they are in use simultaneously. Thus the desire the parallelism takes priority over avoiding duplicate structures.

Another characteristic feature of our ASN-based systems is that they are lexically oriented. Certain units represent the effect of reading a word. These are called *lexical-input* units and are units in the representation/backbone network. To simulate reading, the lexical-input units for the words in the text are activated one after the other. Currently, selecting and activating the lexical-input units is done outside the system. Two simplifying assumptions are made: first, words are presented at a fixed rate, and since all inputs are presented as discrete words, we ignore low-level issues such as morphology.

When a lexical-input unit is activated, it in turn activates a subnetwork of representation/backbone units, construction nodes, and possibly WTA-search nodes. These build the representation of the meaning of the word.

Something to note here is the presence of time. Many of the connectionist NLP systems read all of their words at once, at the beginning of processing (Cottrell, 1985; McClelland and Kawamoto, 1986; Waltz and Pollack, 1985). In contrast, ASN systems read their words serially. One of the consequences of this is that the ASN systems must sequence some of their operations so they are executed in the proper order. Executing operations in the wrong order may lead to an erroneous interpretation of parts of a text. Timing has many implications in such systems. However, other than demonstrating dynamic adequacy, such issues are not the focus of the current work. A good study of some of the consequences of time in a massively parallel NLP system has been done by Gigley (1988a; 1988b).

An important aspect of our NLP systems is their use of distributed search. As the name implies, distributed search is how a controller-less system tries to find a unit in its representation that has certain properties. To do this, an ASN-based system combines two mechanisms, WTA-search and inheritance hierarchies.

In an *inheritance hierarchy*, concepts are organised from most specific at the bottom, to increasingly more general as the hierarchy is traversed upward. The concepts are linked together by what are commonly referred to as IS-A links.[4] To cite a famous example (Fahlman, 1979), suppose there is an elephant, Clyde.

---

[4]We are oversimplifying here. For a more complete account of the semantics of inheritance hierarchies see Touretzky (1986).

Clyde would be represented as a node, CLYDE. The fact that he is an elephant would be represented by an INSTANCE link from the Clyde node to one for elephant. The fact that elephants are mammals would be represented by an IS-A link from ELEPHANT to MAMMAL. The nodes at these higher levels have other links, the semantic interpretation of which indicates the features common at this conceptual level (e.g. "Elephants are grey things", "Mammals have hair"). In this way the relationships between the concepts in the system are represented. This is shown in Fig. 9.2.

By organising the WTA nodes (and the units they search) into a simple inheritance hierarchy, the searches in an ASN system can be done taxonomically. If the structure of the WTA-search network parallels the conceptual inheritance hierarchy, it forms the basis of a search mechanism. For instance, suppose, after talking about Clyde, someone mentions "I'll miss the old grey thing." As the ASN searches for grey things, one of the things it searches will be elephants. As part of our search for elephants, we will search Clyde. Since Clyde was the topic of conversation, the unit which corresponds to him should be highly active. The node CLYDE will be the winner of the WTA-search of grey things. Searches of this type are very important in ASN-based NLP systems. Among other things, they are used to find the referents of pronouns and definite

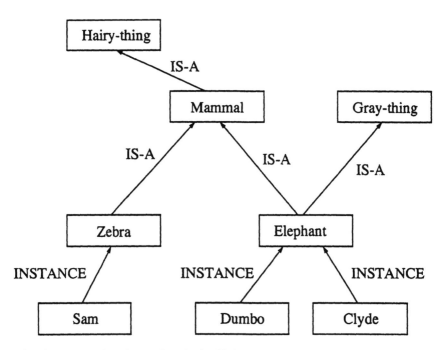

FIG. 9.2.   A simple inheritance hierarchy for Clyde the elephant.

noun phrases. They are also part of the mechanism used for discourse processing (Berg, 1988).

Researchers using connectionist models have touched on ideas similar to this combination of the inheritance hierarchy and WTA nodes. Cottrell (1985, p. 166), in his remarks on aphasia, comments that in an inheritance hierarchy, the subordinates of a common unit will all be linked into a winner-take-all network. Although he is referring to a standard, connectionist winner-take-all network, the idea is nonetheless similar. Shastri and Feldman (1986, p. 194) also have a similar idea. Normally, answers to questions in their system are "multiple-choice" (i.e. one of an enumerated set in a "frame of discernment"). They mention that without a frame of discernment or with a diffuse one they would do an hierarchical search. Shastri (1988) also shows methods for search in a connectionist system using inheritance hierarchies.

Even more important than search in ASN-based NLP systems is the use of indirection in construction nodes. As described in the previous section, any construction node can be either direct or indirect. If it is direct, it performs its operation (e.g. adding a link, deleting a link) directly on the unit to which it is attached. If it is indirect, the directly attached unit is unaffected, but rather determines which unit *is* affected by which it (the directly attached unit) points to (refer to Fig. 9.1). The directly attached node is referred to as a "structural marker," and the use of these units is crucial to the representational adequacy of the ASN model. In Fig. 9.1b, unit E is the structural marker. By attaching and detaching various units to the structural marker, a construction node can operate on different units at different times. In our ASN-based NLP systems, structural markers are similar to variables. More specifically they are used as role specifiers. The units attached to them are the role fillers.

The single most important structural marker in the ASN-based systems is the unit CURRENT-CONCEPT. It represents the head of the noun phrase (NP) currently being processed. By attaching a unit to CURRENT-CONCEPT, the system can add and delete links to change the NP's relationship to the knowledge representation part of the network (and thus its meaning). For instance, this is done when an adjective modifies the noun phrase. Construction nodes acting indirectly through CURRENT-CONCEPT add or delete links to the indirectly attached unit to build a structure reflecting the meaning of the adjective. When processing a verb, CURRENT-CONCEPT also directs subnetworks that determine whether the unit attached to the structural marker (i.e. its filler) is the subject, object, etc. of the sentence.

There are many other structural markers in the ASN systems. For example, to support the case-frame semantics used by the system, there are structural markers such as CURRENT-ACTION, CURRENT-ACTOR, and CURRENT-OBJECT. These are used to identify and process the concepts filling these roles in the current sentence. In addition, most of the processing in ASN systems uses structural markers: distributed search, the transition between sentences, keeping track of prominent concepts in the discourse, etc.

Creating New Representations—The Indefinite NP

There is an important difference between definite and indefinite NPs. As noted in previous work (Cottrell, 1985; Hirst, 1988), a definite NP generally refers to something that is known in the context of the current text. For example, "The black purse was gone when Sam looked" implies that the purse was previously mentioned or otherwise known. In that sense, a definite NP is like a pronoun—it must be matched against some antecedent. The technique used in the ASN-based systems is similar for both define NLPs and pronouns. The general problem that this addresses is known as *anaphora*.

In contrast, an indefinite NP indicates that a new concept should be constructed. When "A gold pen was found at the scene" is read, the NP "a gold pen" is usually meant to be something previously unknown. Whatever the representation that a NLP system uses, somehow a concept representing the previously unknown pen must be established. The pen's attributes must also be represented. The new concept must therefore be a pen, have a gold colour, and have been found "at the scene." The result of processing an indefinite NP must have two properties—it must be distinct from other representations and it must represent the properties of the indefinite NP and its structural relationships to other concepts in the knowledge base.

In our ASN-based systems, an indefinite NP is recognised when an appropriate determiner (e.g. "a," "an") is read. As shown in part (a) of Fig. 9.3, reading the determiner "an" causes excitation from outside the system to activate the input unit AN. This unit then sends activation to construction nodes and units, which build the representation of the indefinite NP.

The result is a new unit which is linked by the structural marker CURRENT-CONCEPT. When adjectives or the head noun for this NP are read, links are created to the units and WTA-search nodes that constitute the appropriate representation for the NP. Part (b) of Fig. 9.3 shows the representation the ASN networks would build for the indefinite NP "a black dog." The unit UNIT_0 represents the NP. The links to BLACK and DOG are normal excitatory links. The links to the WTA-search nodes WTA-BLACK and WTA-DOG indicate that UNIT_0 is included in searches for black things and dogs. The structural marker CURRENT-CONCEPT links UNIT_0 because UNIT_0 is the concept the system is currently processing. This is because the construction nodes, which operate on the concept that is the current focus of the system's attention, have their indirectly acting links running through the structural marker CURRENT-CONCEPT.

Searching—The Definite NP

Just as reading "a" or "an" signals an indefinite NP, reading a definite determiner such as "the" starts the processing of a definite NP. In our current ASN-based NLP systems, the semantics of a definite NP are that a search is made

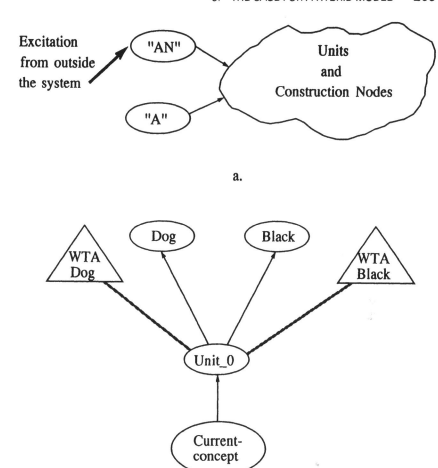

FIG. 9.3.   (a) The effect of reading a determiner. (b) The subnetwork representing the NP "a black dog."

of the knowledge base for an existing concept matching the description given by the NP.

This search is done by the WTA-search hierarchy. If a noun is read after a definite determiner, a WTA-search is started at a point in the search hierarchy (in the WTA-search network). This yields the unit in the domain of this search with the highest activation. This unit is then linked from CURRENT-CONCEPT as the matching concept for the definite NP.

Clearly, this strategy is inadequate for handling anaphora in the general case. One clear extension, which is easily done using ASN networks, is to build a new concept, as in the case of an indefinite NP, if the WTA-search fails to find an active unit. There are more involved methods capturing the discourse constraints on anaphoric reference. An indication of their ASN implementations is given in Berg (1988).

Finding the referent of a pronoun is similar to finding the referent of a definite NP in our systems. In both cases a WTA-search is done of an area of the taxonomic hierarchy in order to find a match. The only major difference is that reading the pronoun itself triggers the processing, whereas the combination of determiner and head noun determine the processing of the definite NP.

Building Structures—Verbs

In the ASN systems verbs are processed using a *case frame* representation (Fahlman, 1979; Fillmore, 1968). A verb in such a representation has several *roles* associated with it. For instance, a transitive verb would have (minimally) "actor," "object," and "instrument" cases. In the sentence "Jane eats her pizza with a fork," Jane is the actor, her pizza is the object, and the fork is the instrument. Case frame semantics can be used in conjunction with inheritance hierarchies and other mechanisms to restrict the concepts that serve as fillers for the roles. For instance "The fire hydrant ate the pizza with a fork" would violate constraints for the actor role. Our ASN systems use an "exploded case representation" (Cottrell, 1985; Fahlman, 1979), where every verb has its own specific case roles (e.g. "eating actor"). These allow further constraints on the role fillers, based on the specific verbs.

The case frame semantics are implemented using both structural markers and the inheritance hierarchy. When the verb is read, it activates subnetworks that will use general case-frame structural markers to identify the parts of the sentence. For a transitive verb such as "eat" these would be CURRENT-ACTOR, CURRENT-ACTION, CURRENT-INSTRUMENT, and CURRENT-OBJECT. The inheritance hierarchy is used to implement the exploded case-frame representation. Just as "a green apple" is linked into the knowledge representation as something that is green and an apple, in the sentence "The boy ate a green apple" it would be linked in as the object in an eating-event. Similarly the boy would be the eating-event's actor and there would be a unit representing the eating-event itself. Constraints allow only semantically plausible fillers for these case roles.

This processing is done when "eats" is read. The lexical entry for the verb starts processing to indicate that it is an active form of a transitive verb. The units and nodes in this subnetwork take the filler of CURRENT-CONCEPT, which at this point is the first noun phrase in the sentence, and make it the filler of the structural marker CURRENT-ACTOR, since this is an active form of the verb.

It is then removed from CURRENT-CONCEPT to free that structural marker for the next noun phrase. When the noun phrase following the verb is read, it will become the filler for CURRENT-OBJECT. Also a new unit will be created to represent the event described by the verb.

In addition to the processing common to all active, transitive verbs, reading "eats" also builds a representation specific to an "eating-event." The general case-frame structural markers are used to link their fillers into the knowledge representation as fillers for verb-specific roles in the sentence (e.g. EAT-ACTOR, EAT-EVENT). Subnetworks activated by the verb do this processing. For example, a subnetwork takes the filler of CURRENT-ACTOR and links it to EAT-ACTOR and to the search node WTA-EAT-ACTOR. The result of all of this processing is a representation of the sentence that is thoroughly integrated into the knowledge base of the system. This is shown in Fig. 9.4 for the sentence "A brown cow ate an apple."

Other Aspects of These Systems

Figure 9.5 shows a portion of the network after the system has read the text "A cow ate an apple. She also ate a brown pear. The apple was green." For clarity the WTA nodes and their connections have been left out of the figure. The shaded units and their connections were added as a result of reading the text. Unit_0 is the representation of the cow. Unit_2 represents the apple. Unit_4 represents the pear. Unit_1 is the concept that represents the eating event in the first sentence. The eating event in the second sentence is Unit_3. As indicated by the new links, the concepts from the text have been properly identified and integrated into the knowledge representation and the WTA-search hierarchy. The pronoun "she" and the definite noun phrase "the apple" were matched to their proper referents. The overall result is that the information in the text has been assimilated into the system's knowledge base. It is now available for use in inference, language generation, question-answering, or as referents for later text. For the sake of clarity this example uses a simplified knowledge base. This is to prevent the example from being unduly cluttered—it reflects no limitation of the system's abilities adequately to process such knowledge bases.

DISCUSSION

In the previous section, we described how ASN-based NLP systems process and represent some simple examples from sentence processing. As a matter of fact, these examples are deceptively simple—by comparison to some of the complex processing, representation, and inference tasks that the best symbolic NLP systems can do (cf. Dyer, 1983), what we have shown here is trivial. They are trivial tasks—but *not* for existing connectionist systems. No extant connectionist system can handle the simple tasks described in the previous section. As stated

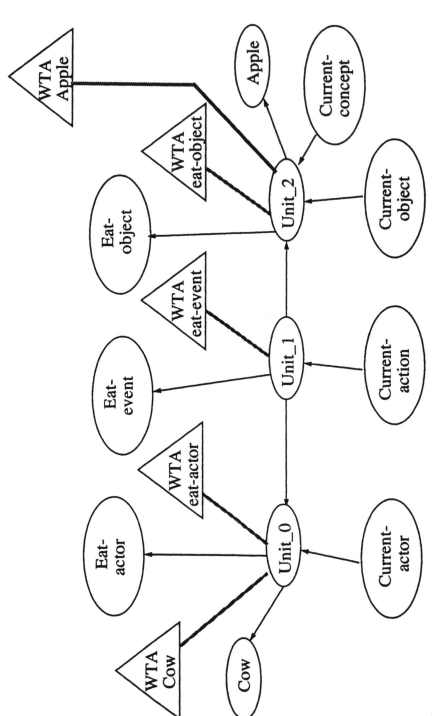

FIG. 9.4. Reading "A brown cow ate an apple."

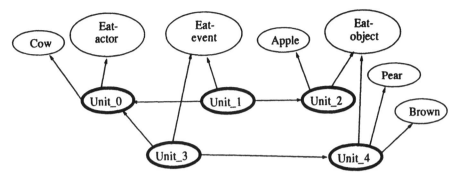

FIG. 9.5.   A portion of the network after the text is read.

earlier, both local and distributed models fall short in some aspect of representational adequacy.

The ASN model succeeds where current connectionist models and architectures fail. It can provide the basis for NLP models with static and dynamic representational adequacy.

But, just like the various connectionist models, the ASM model is massively parallel in both its representation and its processing. It offers the same promise of real-time processing of complex NLP tasks that has eluded the symbolic systems. But, it still remains a "promise"—further research in both conectionism and ASN models is necessary before either can show that the massive parallelism translates into a corresponding performance speed-up on practical problems.

But, what about the properties of ASN-based systems? An important concern in systems such as these is generality. How sensitive are they to slight variations in their environment? How "finely tuned" is each part of a network? This question is partially answered by the use of shared networks in our systems. Throughout ASN-based systems, subnetworks are shared by different lexical-input units as part of their processing (e.g. processing of definite nouns and pronouns, transitive verbs, active verb forms). Another indication is that the same structure for adjectives that works when used in noun phrases also works in sentences such as "The apple is brown." In this type of sentence, forms of "be" cause the noun phrase to remain as the filler of Current-concept and processing the adjective attaches properties of "brown" to the filler. That the same structures are used by different parts of the network indicates that general mechanisms can be constructed. Every individual part of a network need not be individually "hand-tuned" to work properly.

The current ASN systems also use very simple explicit syntax. This is limited to subnetworks which support two structures. The first control the structure of noun phrases. The second control the overall structure of the sentence. The latter use case-frame semantics as constraints to determine allowable noun phrases and their roles in a sentence. The reason for this is that the current research is more concerned with semantics and the representation of knowledge in ASNs. Of special interest at this stage is determining what is necessary for a dynamic system to read and represent extended text. Complicated matters of syntax in these systems will be addressed in future work. However, other, more significant simplifications must be addressed. These have to do with the language the ASN systems currently process. It is readily acknowledged that the English language is much richer and more complex than that used in the examples. In real English not all noun phrases are characterised by determiners; nor is the definite/indefinite distinction a clear-cut one. The allowable sentence structure and the use of forms of the verb "be" are severely restricted in the language currently processed. These omissions and restrictions are deliberate; no claims are implied about the adequacy of the current subnetworks to process these fuller forms of the language. New subnetworks will be necessary. Also, the discourse mechanisms used in these examples are overly simplistic. The existing structural markers, subnetworks, and WTA hierarchies are only the first of the structures necessary to handle discourse issues in multiple-sentence texts (Berg, 1988).

CONCLUSION

In this chapter we discuss how a knowledge representation model is a crucial part of a natural language processing system. In particular we stress the two parts of representational adequacy—static adequacy and dynamic adequacy. Static adequacy to ensure that a NLP system can represent the things it needs to read and infer, and dynamic adequacy to allow this base of represented knowledge to grow and change in response to what the system reads.

Although some research in its early stages promises to give at least some connectionist models representational adequacy, the current ones do not have this property. The ASN model does provide representational adequacy, while retaining connectionism's massive parallelism.

Admittedly, the accomplishments of ASN-based systems have so far been modest compared to their symbolic counterparts. We have two reasons to hope that we can accomplish more in the near future. First, we have just completed a connection machine (Hillis, 1985) implementation of the ASN model (Kulshrestha, 1990). With this we hope to construct larger models than our present simulators have allowed. We also hope to fulfil the promises of actual fast performance, which supporters of massive parallelism have made. Our second reason for hope is that we are making progress on preliminary work in implementing higher-level knowledge structures, such as scripts (cf. Schank, 1982; Schank & Abelson, 1977). With these, we hope to build ASN-based language understanders that are comparable to the best symbolic system in their breadth, but which far exceed them in performance.

ACKNOWLEDGEMENTS

I would like to thank the editors and an anonymous reviewer for suggestions on reorganising the presentation in this chapter. The work described here is supported in part by Faculty Research Awards from the State University of New York in Albany.

REFERENCES

Berg, G. (1988). *A massively parallel natural language processing architecture with distributed control.* Ph.D. thesis, Northwestern University, Department of Electrical Engineering and Computer Science, Evanston, Illinois.

Brachman, R. (1979). On the epistemological status of semantic networks. In N.V. Findler (Ed.), *Associative networks: Representation and use of knowledge by computers.* Orlando, Florida: Academic Press.

Cottrell, G.W. (1985). *A connectionist approach to word sense disambiguation.* Ph.D. thesis, The University of Rochester, Department of Computer Science, Rochester, N.Y.

Dyer, M. (1983). *In-depth understanding.* Cambridge, Mass.: M.I.T. Press.

Fahlman, S. (1979). *NETL: A system for representing and using real-world knowledge.* Cambridge, Mas.: M.I.T. Press.

Feldman, J.A. (1981). Dynamic connections in neural networks. *Biological Cybernetics, 46,* 27–39.

Feldman, J.A. & Ballard, D. (1982). Connectionist models and their properties. *Cognitive Science, 6,* 205–254.

Fillmore, C. (1968). The case for case. In E. Bach & R. Harms (Eds.), *Universals in linguistic theory.* Chicago: Holt, Rinehart, & Winston.

Fodor, J.A. & Pylyshyn, Z.W. (1988). Connectionism and cognitive architecture: A critical analysis. In S. Pinker & J. Mehler (Eds.), *Connections and symbols.* Cambridge, Mass.: MIT Press.

Gigley, H. (1988a). On the role of timing synchronization in parallel models of behavior. In *Proceedings of the 1988 AAAI Spring Symposium Series: Parallel models of intelligence,* Stanford, Calif., 108–124.

Gigley, H. (1988b). Process synchronization, lexical ambiguity resolution, and aphasia. In S.I. Small, G.W. Cottrell & M.K. Tanenhaus (Eds.), *Lexical ambiguity resolution.* San Mateo, Calif.: Morgan Kaufmann.

Hayes, P.J. (1979). The logic of frames. In D. Metzing (Ed.), *Frame conceptions and text understanding.* Berlin: Walter de Gruyter.

Hillis, W.D. (1985). *The connection machine.* Cambridge, Mass.: M.I.T. Press.

Hinton, G.E. (1988). Representing part-whole hierarchies in connectionist networks. In *Proceedings of the Tenth Annual Conference of the Cognitive Science Society,* Montreal, Canada, 48–54.

Hinton, G.E., McClelland, J.L., & Rumelhart, D.E. (1986). Distributed representations. In D.E. Rumelhart, J.L. McClelland, & the PDP Research Group (Eds.), *Parallel distributed processing: Explorations in the microstructure of cognition. Volume 1: Foundations.* Cambridge, Mass.: M.I.T. Press.

Hinton, G.E. & Sejnowski, T.J. (1986). Learning and relearning in Boltzmann machines. In D.E. Rumelhart, J.L. McClelland, & the PDP Research Group (Eds.), *Parallel distributed processing: Explorations in the microstructure of cognition. Volume 1: Foundations.* Cambridge, Mass.: M.I.T. Press.

Hirst, G. (1988). *Semantic interpretation and the resolution of ambiguity.* Cambridge: Cambridge University Press.

Kulshrestha, N.K. (1990). *Implementing autonomous semantic networks on the connection machine.* Technical Report in preparation, Computer Science Department, The State University of New York at Albany, Albany, N.Y.

McClelland, J.L. & Kawamoto, A.H. (1986). Mechanisms of sentence processing: Assigning roles to constituents. In D.E. Rumelhart, J.L. McClelland, & the PDP Research Group (Eds.), *Parallel distributed processing: Explorations in the microstructure of cognition. Volume 2: Psychological and biological models.* Cambridge, Mass.: M.I.T. Press.

Miikkulainen, R. & Dyer, M.G. (1989). A modular neural network architecture for sequential paraphrasing of script-based stories. In *Proceedings of the 1989 International Joint Conference on Neural Networks,* Washington D.C., 49–56.

Pollack, J.B. (1988). Recursive auto-associative memory: Devising compositional distributed representations. In *Proceedings of the Tenth Annual Conference of the Cognitive Science Society,* Montreal, Quebec, 33–39.

Rumelhart, D.E., Smolensky, P., McClelland, J.L., & Hinton, G. (1986). Schemata and sequential thought processes. In J.L. McClelland, D.E. Rumelhart, & the P.D.P. Research Group (Eds.), *Parallel distributed processing: Volume 2: Psychological and biological models.* Cambridge, Mass.: M.I.T. Press.

Schank, R.C. (1982). *Dynamic memory: A theory of reminding and learning in computers and people.* Cambridge: Cambridge University Press.

Schank, R.C. & Abelson, R. (1977). *Scripts, plans, goals, and understanding.* Hillsdale, N.J.: Lawrence Erlbaum Associates Inc.

Shastri, L. (1988). A connectionist approach to knowledge representation and limited inference. *Cognitive Science, 12,* 331–392.

Shastri, L. & Feldman, J. (1986). Neural nets, routines, and semantic networks. In N. Sharkey (Ed.), *Advances in cognitive science 1.* Chichester: Ellis Horwood.

Stolcke, A. (1990). Unification as constraint satisfaction in structured connectionist networks. *Neural Computation, 1,* 559–567.

Touretzky, D.S. (1986). *The mathematics of inheritance systems.* Los Altos, Calif.: Morgan Kaufmann.

Waltz, D. & Pollack, J. (1985). Massively parallel parsing: A strongly interactive model of natural language interpretation. *Cognitive Science, 9,* 51–74.

Woods, W.E. (1975). What's in a link: Foundations for semantic networks. In D.G. Bobrow & A.M. Collins (Eds.), *Representation and understanding: Studies in cognitive science.* New York City: Academic Press.

10 A Step Toward Sub-symbolic Language Models without Linguistic Representations

Georg Dorffner
Austrian Research Institute for Artificial Intelligence, Schottengasse 3, 1010 Vienna, Austria, and Indiana University, Computer Science Dept., Lindley Hall, Bloomington, IN 47405, U.S.A.

INTRODUCTION

The work described in this article is an attempt to view language behaviour in a (almost) completely non-reductionist, non-representationalist, and non-formalist way, and to build a model of basic aspects of language use. The views presented here have several roots: first the dissatisfaction with traditional linguistic theories (e.g. Chomsky, 1965; 1975) and the artificial intelligence (AI) models built around them (e.g. Winograd, 1983) with respect to explanation of important aspects of every-day language processing (cf. Winograd & Flores, 1986). Secondly, the ideas behind the so-called sub-symbolic paradigm, which was initiated, among others, by Smolensky (1988), based on experiences with connectionist networks. And last but not least, there are the ideas of many who advocate the view that cognitive behaviour is not based on representations, i.e. an internal mirror image of the external world, but on self-organisation through motivated interaction with the environment. Among those proposing such a view are Maturana and Varela (1980), Reeke and Edelman (1988), etc.

"Non-representationalist" in this article means that the model should not rely on explicit representations in the strong AI sense, which are brought in by a designer. Instead it should be able to acquire most specific aspects through adaptive self-organisation while interacting with an environment. The basis for such an approach is the sub-symbolic paradigm, which states that symbolic (linguistic) descriptions of mental processes are just an approximation and that many associative and intuitive processes happen on a level underneath. This paradigm puts self-organisation into the centre of attention.

This rather novel approach to language modelling is designed to model many aspects of everyday language use that are left out by more formalist models. An example is the fact that word meaning seems to differ slightly for every individual—especially for more abstract underlying concepts—and that it can gradually vary in changing environments. Context of any kind can play a large role in that process. The assignment of meaning is a largely associative process and therefore belongs to the type of process that the sub-symbolic approach is meant to model. On the other hand, a model has to explain how (linguistic) symbols can evolve as an emergent phenomenon and how they are embedded into the sub-symbolic framework. All this requires a model that can self-adapt and does not start with specific knowledge implanted by a designer.

Trying to build a language model combining many of the ideas just stated requires the refutation of most of the traditional linguistic formalisms. First of all, basing semantics on symbolic descriptions of real-world objects (e.g. *semantic features* or the *language of thought* initiated by Fodor, 1983, and others) will no longer be possible, given the hypothesis that knowledge on a level that is not linguistically describable exists and plays an important role. Second, putting representations such as word categories and syntactic features into the model will also not be considered, given the hypothesis that the system does not mirror the world but self-organises toward adequate behaviour. Under these assumptions the design of a model has to start with very basic functions and has to work itself upward toward more complex versions. Therefore, the focus of this article are processes that are viewed as the core of linguistic behaviour and that are relatively basic compared to the focus of other classical and connectionist approaches, which make more explicit representational assumptions (e.g. Cottrell, 1985; Schnelle & Doust, this volume, etc.). Another model that starts from assumptions similar to those in this chapter is that of Nenov and Dyer (1988).

This chapter is organised into several sections. First, by observing basic language behaviour, a first step is taken toward identifying the fundamental aspects of language. Categorisation and concepts are identified as the fundamentals around which linguistic behaviour can develop. A discussion about symbols (linguistic symbols with intended reference, that is) and how they are motivated by concepts is included. By putting together all the observations of the first section, an implemented model is described. A component for self-organising concept formation is introduced and described in detail. In a next step, symbols—as defined previously—which are the elements of language itself, will be introduced as being embedded into the sub-symbolic formalism, thereby explaining the interaction of symbolic and non-symbolic behaviour. An annotated example and a brief discussion about future extensions concludes this article.

Claimers and Disclaimers

Several claims will be made concerning the language model introduced in this article. But equally many claims can be raised about what this model *cannot* be: First of all, when giving up many of the traditional linguistic formalisms, one also gives up most of the advances on the performance side of language understanding systems. Therefore, one cannot expect such a model to compete directly with systems such as natural language database interfaces (e.g. Trost et al., 1987) or question answering systems (e.g. Berry-Rogghe, Kolvenbach, & Lutz, 1980; Waltz, 1978) that are based on representationalist theories. Instead, one has to start "from scratch," beginning with very fundamental aspects.

Furthermore, the model cannot include conscious phenomena of language—such as learning a foreign language or garden-path sentences—even in an extended version. This is because I concentrate on the associative aspects of language.

Finally, the model will leave out many important aspects, such as the influence that many other cognitive functions have on language understanding. However, the formalism will have easy entry points to include those aspects in the future.

BASIC OBSERVATIONS ABOUT LANGUAGE

In this section I want to collect several observations about human language that will be considered basic to a model of language behaviour. This list is not complete by a long way. Thus, the claim is not that the model introduced later covers all aspects of language; the claim is that it covers many important and basic ones.

From Categories to the Use of Words

Natural human language, to a great extent, consists of linguistic symbols, the *words*. When we use those symbols they are said to *stand for something*. For example, when we use the word "apple," we usually say that it stands for the *concept* of an *apple*, or in other words, it *represents* a set of objects (or, more abstractly, actions, predicates, etc.) in the world, in this case apples. This set of objects is usually called a *category* of objects (or actions, or predicates, etc.).

Thus, in order to deal with language, we first have to deal with categories and concepts and look at them closely. To be able to use words to stand for something, we first have to categorise the elements in the world around us. To be more precise, as we do not have any contact with the world but through our sensory organs, we have to categorise our sensory input before and while we use words. Categorisation, indeed, seems to play a large role in human cognitive behaviour. Lakoff (1987), for example, gives an extensive discussion on "what categories reveal about our mind" (book subtitle). More evidence can be found in Brown (1958), Neisser (1987), and others.

Lakoff (1987) argues (and provides substantive data) that categories are not merely sets of things that have certain features in common. Instead, they depend highly on all kinds of previous knowledge and experience and include radial, metaphorical, and metonymic categories. Therefore, categories are only partially dependent on sensory input (for example, visual patterns), and can also be created internally (and often do not have a direct correspondence to the input). Other authors, like Nelson (1988), have provided more data to support this thesis.

As a result, concepts and categories are *internal* to an individual. Objects in the world are unstructured and dissimilar until some individual *recognises* structure or similarity. Of course, sensory signals are not arbitrary. We are safe to assume that similarities conveyed through the signals correspond to something that "is actually there." However, we have to assume that *not all* relevant aspects for forming concepts are in the sensory signals. For example, to distinguish chairs from tables, more is happening than just discovering similarities through input signals. The surrounding environment, as well as expectations, internal knowledge, and feelings (the context in a general sense), all influence the formation of such a concept. We therefore have to assume that internal influences (the use of language itself being one of them) have a great impact on the recognition of categories and the formation of concepts. This is one of the "constructivist" aspects of the presented view (e.g. Maturana & Varela, 1980): We have made "concepts" largely independent from any objectively existent world.

What, then, is a concept? We could view concepts as mental states that are more or less stable for some time and can become consciously accessible to us (cf. Smolensky, 1988, p. 13). Forming a concept based on external and internal influences can be called *conceptualisation* or *concept formation*. Conceptualisation has much to do with categorisation. Categories are groups of objects that are identified as belonging together and "treated as somewhat equivalent" (Neisser, 1987). Again, we can say that a category does not actually exist in the world, it needs an individual to identify it. Things or situations which are *naturally* categorised together tend to form a concept. For example, the appearance of apples stipulates the forming of a concept *apple*, because they look similar (external aspect) and they can be used for similar purposes like eating (internal aspect). Thus the category of all apples can develop naturally and give rise to a concept. A group of five arbitrary objects (say, an apple, a stone, a book, a cup, and a bug) could—by any outside observer—be viewed as a category, too. But unless some internal motivation exists for viewing them as belonging together, this category does not develop naturally and thus does not help in forming a concept.

Having defined concepts we now recognise one major root to linguistic behaviour. Our initial observation was that humans use words (symbols) to stand for their (internal) concepts. We can therefore say that concepts *motivate* the use of symbols. By forming a *concept* of something, we recognise that there are some instances that are peculiar in that together they stand out from the background. When we want to *communicate* that concept, we generally use a linguistic symbol. This means that we choose an identifiable entity and let it stand for the concept. For this reason, the word "symbol" is used here distinct from "concept," in contrast to many other researchers on the subject (e.g. Hofstadter, 1985; Kaplan, Weaver, & French, 1990).

Such associations between concepts and symbols seem to be the basis of all language functions. However, we do not invent symbols all the time but hear them from others (and have heard them most of our lives). We perceive words, and in order to understand them we want to associate them with one of the concepts we already have. Thus, we use those symbols for a concept that we associated with that concept previously, because we perceived it in a similar context.

As a first result we can state the following assumptions about what basic language processing is:

1. An individual, at all times, categorises sensory input and thus forms concepts about what is perceived. Such categories and concepts are internal entities. No object in the real world must correspond to the concept—albeit, in many cases, there will be some causal dependency between concepts and real world aspects.

2. Attempting to understand a word, in a first step, consists of recognising the word as a symbol and attempting to associate it with currently active concepts. Producing a word, in a first step, consists of finding a word that was associated with the current concept on a previous occasion.

The nature of concepts has thus severe implications as to how individuals assign meaning to a word. We have seen that concepts depend on the history and the experiences of the individual. As no two individuals have the exact same history, it follows that conceptualisation is not absolute but must differ between individuals. When individual A utters a word to stand for a concept that A has in mind, we therefore cannot expect that individual B, who is listening, recalls the exact same concept to which he or she can associate the word. Individual B will only approximately understand what individual A attempted to say. Furthermore, language behaviour is a process of learning and adaptation. When motivated to understand an utterance, we *always* attempt to associate something with the words. When we hear a word and associate a concept that does not match any of the concepts in the current context, we generally try to associate the one closest (Fig. 10.1). Now adaptation comes in. As there is a discrepancy

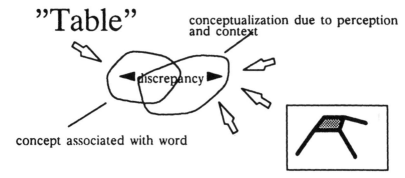

FIG. 10.1.   Learning to match a word with the current context means adaptation toward lesser discrepancies between the two associations.

between the current concepts and the one associated with the word, the asociation tends to be adapted toward lesser discrepancy.

This process of adaptation works in two ways. Not only does the concept associated with the word come closer to the concept of the current context but, vice versa, the latter will tend to be altered as well. This becomes clear when viewing naming by symbols as another contextual influence for conceptualisation. The bidirectionality of influences is also grounded in observations of how language influences perception (Lakoff, 1987; Nelson, 1988; Whorf, 1956) and in theories (e.g. by Edelman, 1978) that advocate symmetry of neural processes.

As a result, we can say that words can influence our concepts, and thus, the way we perceive the world. In many cases—especially in folk psychology—this has lead people to equate words (symbols) with the underlying concepts, in that the only concepts assumed to exist are the ones we have a word for. This is not done here. It is one of the ideas of the sub-symbolic paradigm (Smolensky, 1988) to assume that there are processes besides what is visible through symbolic language. We can summarise the interplay between concepts and symbols thus.

3. Concepts about the world motivate the use of symbols (words). In turn, the use of words by the individual itself and by others tends to influence the concepts (and the natural categories). Within limits, the system is constantly adapting towards lesser discrepancy between associations and expectations.

We see that categorisation and concepts in the context of language consist of at least two aspects: First of all, categorisation means grouping sensory patterns according to their similarities. In our context we could call these *pre-linguistic categories*, as we become aware of them even before communication. Results in literature (such as Roberts & Horowitz, 1986) prove that categorisation happens in humans before language is learned. Then, as we have seen (and is discussed in Lakoff, 1987), categories evolve because there is some kind of *motivation* behind the grouping of stimuli. The motivation I am mainly considering in this chapter is that of trying to communicate and to understand. Thus, a system like this will develop *linguistically influenced* categories or concepts.

Although our main concern in this discussion is linguistic motivation, we have to be aware that the model should be open to a variety of other motivational or contextual influences. This means that a language model has to include at least some of the basic experiences, such as sensory inputs, feelings, motivations, etc., which any human has (see also Dreyfus & Dreyfus, 1985). This has also been called *being grounded to the world* (Maturana & Varela, 1980). Many aspects of language behaviour cannot be accounted for without considering the fact that while interpreting utterances, a cognitive system sees, feels, and has built up internal models based on previous experiences. Again, this does not mean that a model of *only* the language faculty is impossible. It just has to include interface points with additional cognitive functions.

We now have a very simple first understanding of core language behaviour. We have introduced the capability to categorise sensory inputs (*conceptualisation capacity*—Lakoff, 1987), to form concepts, and the capability of associating symbols with concepts, making this association adaptable in both directions. We have also seen that context in all varieties plays an important role in language processing. Among many other questions, we do not yet know the following: What distinguishes symbols from concepts? Where do they come from? How is language behaviour observable and verifiable? I want to discuss those points in the following sub-sections.

Sub-symbolic Knowledge and the Role of Symbols

Although perception and conceptualisation often result in something very concrete (so that we can use a symbol to stand for it), there are many intermediate steps going on before the results are achieved. Sensory input consists of a huge set of stimuli, many of which are discarded on the way to a concept. In order to categorise, the system has to *reduce* information. On the sensory level, probably no two patterns at different times are ever the same, even if they stem from the same object. Perception can thus be seen as an hierarchical process (Fukushima, 1980; Hubel & Wiesel, 1962) of categorising and therefore identifying features on a more and more global level. However, if that process resulted in total reduction of all irrelevant features, we would lose a great deal of capabilities. We could no longer detect similarities and dissimilarities among members of a category, because we would identify them completely (see, for example, Reeke & Edelman, 1988, pp. 158–59).

Total reduction, however, is what happens when we use a symbol for a concept (compare Campbell, 1982). Generally, linguistic symbols are arbitrary in that their shape bears no relation to the underlying concepts. As a result, similar words generally do not stand for similar concepts. When we use a word for a category of things, *all* members of that category are identified; similarities and dissimilarities are erased. To reintroduce them on the symbolic level, one has to identify *sub-concepts* or predicative concepts (usually called *features*), which in turn are replaced by symbols. For example, if we say "apple," all objects we categorise under the concept *apple* could be meant. If we want to be more precise we have to say "Macintosh" or "small green apple," thereby using more symbols for subordinate or orthogonal concepts.

According to the sub-symbolic paradigm, the elements of a cognitive system using language cannot be identical to the elements of language (the symbols). Instead, as it is done in Smolensky (1988), the system is viewed as a dynamic system with a variety of states it can reach (more on tl.at will be seen later). What implications does that have on a language model? When we define understanding of words as trying to associate them with previously learned concepts corresponding to the context, we have to deal with the fact that the basis of conceptualisation is richer than the basis of language (the symbols). Though language itself is largely symbolic, the process of language understanding *cannot be* symbolic. Therefore we need a sub-symbolic process to model conceptualisation and the interaction with symbols. Symbols themselves have to be *embedded* in this process. This is clearly different from the traditional AI view, which suggested that the structures of language and the structures they have to be mapped to have the same overall shape (symbol structures).

This brings us to the major difference between a concept and a symbol. Concepts can evolve slowly within the sub-symbolic state space and do not have to have clear boundaries. Similar concepts (as a result of similar stimuli or of complex internal association and feedback) will have a similar realisation in the system. Symbols, on the other hand, are frequently arbitrary and their similarities do not reflect concept similarities. Thus, they must clearly be separable from each other. When communicating, a *decision* has to be made (influenced, again, by context and previous experience) about which word to use. As a result, symbols will have to possess clear boundaries when it comes to language. In addition, symbols have *referential power* (cf. Hofstadter, 1985); that is, they are used *intentionally* to refer to something by establishing a connection to concepts. A concept by itself does not refer in the same sense, because it develops in a self-organising and uninterpreted process.

A further distinction is in place here. We can see that there is something going on inside an individual, as well as outside. What we usually call a "symbol" in everyday life is an entity that exists in the world, created by one individual and intended to be identified by others. Examples are a string of written letters forming a word, a painted sign, or the acoustic speech signal resulting from pronouncing a word. We could call such entities an *external embodiment of a symbol*. The property that makes something a symbol cannot be found in those entities themselves, but within the individuals using them for communication.

To permit individuals to recognise symbolness, as well as to put symbols to work, there have to be additional mental states in any individual. These mental states can trigger both the production of and the associations with such an external embodiment. We can call such mental states *internal symbols*, or simply *symbols*, because this is the part we have been interested in.

We have thus arrived at a definition of a symbol in a non-representationalist sub-symbolic model. It is a mental state that is activated by conceptual states if the individual intends linguistic reference pointing to the concept. Such a mental state can trigger the production of an external embodiment of the symbol. This embodiment can be recognised as such by other individuals and can subsequently activate another internal symbol. Internal symbols and conceptual states are associatively tied to each other in both directions. Thus not only the production of an external embodiment is possible, but also the association of conceptual states with perceived embodiments. As a result, language processing—even though it deals with symbols—is *not* symbol processing in the sense of merely shuffling symbols around. Instead it is a process of recognising inputs as serving as (external embodiments of) symbols, grounding the corresponding "mental" states in the conceptual framework of the system, and letting them interact with other internal system states. This view also makes clear the major difference between this "sub-symbolic" and "symbolic" AI-approaches. Here a symbol is connected to internal model states and thus gets meaning from inside the model. In classical AI programs—and Turing machines, for that matter—symbols and their referential power usually stem from the model designers and not from any state in the system itself. In a sense, designers communicate their knowledge to the machine by introducing the symbols and writing the program. For the machine these symbols are *not grounded* because they do not map onto a system state that has developed through experience. If they do not even have referential power (i.e. they are just tokens being shuffled around) they should not be called "symbols" in the definition just presented.

It is important to note that the process of identifying external embodiments is not different from "normal" conceptualisation, for they too come into the system as a sensory stimulus (cf. Brown, 1958). We need at least two sensory sources (which could both be of the same nature—say, visual) and two components of concept formation. Internal symbols therefore link conceptual states.

The assumptions about symbols are expressed in Fig. 10.2. *Concepts* (level A) can be overlapping and fuzzy. It many cases these states will be, but never need be, clear and distinguishable. They can also include rich information about individual details and similarities. *Symbols* (level B) can be associated with concepts but have to be clearly separable from each other at the moment when they are used for communication. Those *internal symbols* can trigger the production of *external embodiments* (level C) of the symbol (e.g. a sign, a written

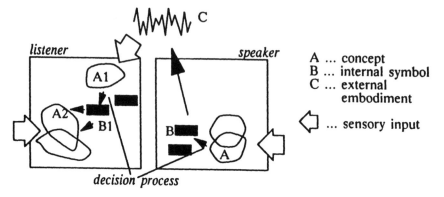

FIG. 10.2.   The function of concepts, internal symbols and external embodiments in both speaker and listener of a language.

word, or an acoustic signal). Those, in turn, are perceived by another individual (a process of concept formation) and mapped onto another internal symbol (B1), which triggers associations (concept A2).

A simple example: If I see a piece of furniture and I cannot decide immediately if it is a chair or a table, the initial concept I am forming will probably be some kind of overlap of the two. However, if I have to refer to that object in a sentence I will have to make a decision about whether to call it "table" (e.g. when I put my cup of coffee on it) or "chair" (e.g. when I plan to sit on it). This decision generally happens unconsciously and is influenced by the context of the situation and my previous experience. Similarly, on the perception side, when taking a word and altering it acoustically, the associations one has will normally not vary to the same degree but stay fixed as long as the word can be recognised. Saying "table" with some quality of "ch" in the beginning does not make the word mean something like "a table that looks a bit like a chair." Therefore, a decision is made again. This does not preclude the possibility that with an input acoustically half-way between "table" and "chair" both words are recognised simultaneously. The decision process rules out *intermediate* forms.

There are, of course, many exceptions to this observation, which will be mentioned later. The assumption is that full abstraction from surface similarities is the *core aspect* of symbolisation.

Testing the Progress of Adaptation

Our last question in this section is about verifiability of the validity of the language model outlined so far. When we have a model that is equipped with the basic architecture to adapt and learn, how can we prove that it is adequate? We cannot look at the internal states and compare it with concepts in the "real world," because there is none. When we permit individual differences within the framework of the basic architecture, we give up the direct verifiability that existed with symbolic linguistic theories. Therefore, we have to resort to external behaviour to test the progress of model adaptation. We have to include at least one output component that produces model behaviour that we can then compare to the behaviour we had expected. For simple concept/word association the most appropriate output component will be the generation of words. For example, when we present sensory stimuli alone to the model (and when we stipulate the motivation for communication), the model should produce a word (or words) that for us describe the stimuli in the current context.

Summary

To summarise, we can now identify the following components of a model that is to simulate simple and basic language behaviour:

1. *A sub-symbolic categoriser of sensory inputs;*
2. *the ability to form internal symbols;*
3. *the interaction between symbols and concepts, going both ways;*
4. *the plasticity of all components toward adaptation;*
5. *an output of testable reactions.*

This simple model covers language tasks such as "naming." Of course, this is not all there is to language behaviour. According to the introductory remarks, however, these aspects are the most basic and important ones, from which more complex ones can be developed. In the last section of this chapter I will give hints as to how to extend the basic model.

Building a Non-representational Connectionist Model

In the beginning, we have asked for a non-representational language model. Considering our observations so far and taking sub-symbolic connectionist networks as implementation, we can see to what degree this goal can be achieved. First of all, we have seen that a model basically has to deal with sensory input, such as visual patterns. By using such input, the problem of how to represent objects of the world does not arise, as unit activations become self-evident (e.g. the luminance of a pixel). Hence we could call them *immediately grounded representations*. Secondly, the fact that connectionist networks can self-organise with the help of learning algorithms frees us from the requirement to formalise a domain into representations, as is necessary in classical AI.

However, we cannot expect such a model to work without presupposing two things:

1. We have to assume certain aspects as given, such as the existence of symbols. In other words, we have to build in "meta-linguistic representations," a formalisation on a more abstract level.

2. We have to assume that the system is motivated to behave adequately. In other words, in the case of language, we have to build in mechanisms that can be interpreted as the motivation to understand and to be understood.

Other than that we do not have to formalise the problem of language understanding. That means that we do not have to identify linguistic concepts such as word category, semantic features, or the like. Instead, the model should acquire such concepts by itself, if they turn out to be relevant. In this sense, the model "constructs" its model of the world, depending on its interactions with the environment (more on this view can be found in Dorffner, 1989).

It should be noted that this is a hypothetical statement about the possibility of a language model. When I say that we do not have to include linguistic representations, then this is based on the general properties of a self-organising connectionist model, and does ot say anything about whether one can succeed in finding the right model.

AN IMPLEMENTATION

In the following sections, I describe an implementation of the model outlined so far. I start with a fundamental architecture for a simple naming task that can gradually be extended to deal with more complex aspects. Architectural details that apply to all model parts are as follows:

1. The definition of units is the one introduced in Rumelhart and McClelland (1986).
2. Unit output values range from 0 to 1 on a continuous scale.
3. The activation function for input units is the sigmoid function; for all others it is the linear threshold function (limited between 0 and 1). The output function for all units is the identity function ($o_i = a_i$).
4. Update is done in a synchronous way, layer by layer.
5. All weights are managed (i.e. stored and altered) by the post-synaptic unit, and not by an independent synapse or connection. Thus, a unit can see an incoming output value of another unit also before weighing it. This is important for several processes, such as detecting if a unit is the winner (the most highly activated unit) of a layer.

Figure 10.3 shows the general architecture of the model, consisting of the components identified previously. The two sensory inputs considered are visual and pseudo-acoustic patterns. The latter consist of an arbitrary n out of m code, which could in theory encode frequency amplitudes or other acoustic parameters.

Due to severe limitations of resources, both inputs have to be extremely simple. So rather than saying "visual" or "acoustic" patterns it would be more

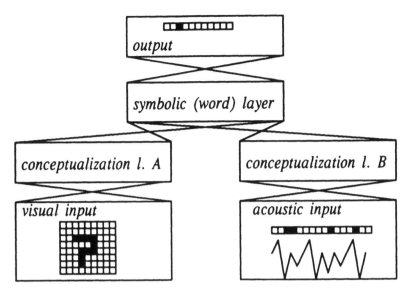

FIG. 10.3. The overall structure of the model.

appropriate to say those patterns "look like primitive visual or acoustic input." I will, however, proceed by calling them visual and (pseudo-) acoustic input, because this is the role they are playing.

Many important aspects of connectionist processing are based on *pattern similarities*. Generalisation in associative networks, for example, works due to the network's ability to cope with novel inputs by exploring the similarities with previous patterns. Similarity of patterns is defined as overlap of active units. A vector of active units can be called a *state* of the model (compare the sub-symbolic hypothesis, Smolensky, 1988), which determines its further behaviour. Thus, overlapping activation patterns can express similar states, to which the model can react in similar ways.

According to the sub-symbolic hypothesis, it is crucial for the model to permit a variety of overlapping states during interaction with the environment. We can call the set of all inputs to a model component, including external sensory input and activations from other components (which do not differ in their nature), a *situation* the component is in. The pattern of activations (the state) that is formed over this component in a certain situation is its *response* to it. If, among the possible states, we can identify a stable one that is distinct from most other states, we could interpret that state as a concept the model has formed. Fuzziness of such concepts is realised through overlaps with other stable states and through continuous transition between states. Context, be it internal (through other model components) or external (through partial patterns) can influence the model states at all times, and thus can alter the concepts gradually.

CATEGORISATION AND CONCEPT FORMATION

According to the previous section, a categorisation layer consisting of a cluster of interconnected units is introduced to realize categorisation and thus concept formation. The ideas behind the functions of that cluster were mainly based on *competitive learning* (Rumelhart & Zipser, 1985), but also bear some relation to the theory of *neuronal group selection* (Edelman, 1978) and to *topographic maps* (Kohonen, 1981).

Figure 10.4 shows the basic categorisation architecture. A layer of *n* units (in this case, four) has inhibitive connections to all units in the same layer (but itself). Furthermore, there are an arbitrary number of connections to external units, whose weights can be positive or negative. In the basic architecture, these units are sensory input units (e.g. visual bitmaps) that form patterns to be categorised. Furthermore, an arbitrary number of additional inputs—external to the layer but internal to the model—are permitted, and will even be required for many basic aspects of the model.

As in competitive learning, one unit in the layer is viewed as standing for a possible "category" of patterns. As no linguistic representation should be brought into the model, none of these categories can be interpreted before running the system. It would be better to say the cluster of units is a set of possible responses to groups of patterns, which after learning might be identified as a

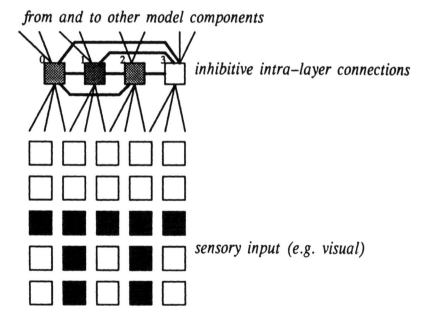

FIG. 10.4.   The connectivity between the visual and a concept (C-) layer.

category. In principle, any unit can respond to any group of patterns. Which patterns are grouped together by one unit depends on pattern similarities and on the (initially random) weight distribution. This response can be influenced to any degree by the other layers connected to the category units. This way there is a *bottom-up*, as well as a *top-down*, component to categorisation. The latter can account for individual differences in the process.

Inhibitive connections between the category units mean that those units *compete* with each other. In general, the layer should tend to have one single unit active for each external pattern. If that is the case, categorisation has reached maximum separation of patterns. In Rumelhart and Zipser (1985), this is forced from the beginning by the mechanism of *winner-take-all*. After an update of the activations of a layer, the winner (i.e. the unit with highest activation) is set to 1 and all others to 0. After that, only the winner is permitted to adapt its weights. This kind of competition, driven to the extreme, makes all responses distinct from each other. The information contained in the activation pattern is fully reduced to category membership.

In the model presented here, the aforementioned aspect is not a desired property. Conceptualisation, as was and will be argued, is information reduction (compare Hubel & Wiesel, 1962) but it is, in general, not *complete* reduction. Put more precisely, information reduction should not set in initially, but evolve *during* conceptualisation to a higher or lesser degree. A distinction has to be made between clear and fuzzy concepts, thus between states with more and ones with less information reduction. Also, according to the sub-symbolic hypothesis, intermediate states with similarities to each other should be permitted at this stage. Complete reduction should not come in until knowledge is expressed symbolically (this will be the content of the next section).

For these reasons, the competitive learning scheme was generalised to categorisation in a wider sense. One unit can still be said to stand for an abstract category, but at any time, especially in the beginning of a training phase, activations over several category units are possible. Only the *general tendency* of the layer (and the weights on each connection) should be toward a single unit responding to each pattern. This has major implications on the learning algorithm.

We now define the state of activations the categorisation layer is in as the concept the model is currently forming, based on patterns external to the layer. If several units have high activations (that is, no clear decision about category membership has yet been made, see Fig. 10.5a), the layer is in an intermediate state. As pattern (and vector) similarity is defined as the overlap of active units, such a state has a potentially large number of similar conditions. We can consider this as a *fuzzy concept*. If, however, one unit is highly activated and all others weakly, then the chance of an overlap with other states is much smaller (Fig. 10.5b). The state is therefore distinct from most other states, and we could consider it as a *clear concept*.

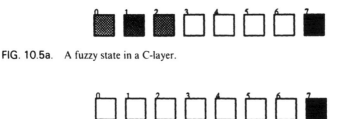

FIG. 10.5a.   A fuzzy state in a C-layer.

FIG. 10.5b.   A clear (identifiable) state in a C-layer.

To distinguish the two types of states, I will henceforth speak of an *identifiable state* if it resembles Fig. 10.5b. Otherwise a state will be considered non-identifiable. As unit activations can vary on a continuous scale, there is no well-defined point that divides identifiable states from others; the shift is always gradual. Only for practical purposes will I later give a mathematical definition of *identifiable state* containing a threshold value. Identifiable states can be compared with stable states that represent schemata in Rumelhart, Smolensky, McClelland, and Hinton (1986).

As one such categorisation layer tends to reach an identifiable state with just one unit highly activated, only one kind of grouping can be discovered. Of course, situations should be classifiable according to more than one aspect. As a simple example, humans can not only classify pictures of objects with relation to their identity (e.g. *table* vs. *chair*), but also with relation to their size, colour, etc. Similarly, categories on different "levels of a hierarchy" are possible (e.g. *table* vs. *furniture*). As a result, for a language model, one categorisation layer as described earlier cannot be enough to account for many cognitive aspects. Thus the layer described should be viewed as one of a large pool of similar layers that work together to yield conceptualisation (cf. the "theory of neuronal group selection," Edelman [1978] and others). Categorisation always depends on random initial conditions and random environmental situations. An expected grouping of patterns is only discovered with a certain probability (usually less than 1) by one given layer. As many such layers exist, the probability that at least one of the layers discovers the expected categories is close to 1. Accordingly, a concept is a state vector over all categorisation layers.

Reaching States

In this section I want to describe in more detail how a categorisation layer reaches identifiable or non-identifiable states and on what conceptualisation depends. As I frequently refer to different layers of units, I shall introduce the following abbreviations. From now on I shall call a categorisation layer, as described earlier, *C-layer* ("C" stands for both *categories* and *conceptualisation*). A layer of units containing sensory patterns, such as the visual layer in Fig. 10.4, is called S-layer. If all units external to a C-layer are relevant, I speak of E-units. In general, E-units contain at least one S-layer.

Through complete connections, patterns over E-units, in a single step, can activate a pattern of activations over the units in the C-layer. This is called the *initial response* of the layer. This is an associative process, just as in a one-layer associative network. The value of the external input to one unit in the C-layer is therefore given as:

$$\text{ext}_i = \Sigma_j \ o_j \ w_{ij} \quad , \qquad j \ldots \text{over all external units} \qquad 1$$

Depending on the weights, the initial response contains some or most of the similarities of the input patterns, or a transformation thereof. Additional update cycles can alter the activation pattern. Assuming that the external input stays constant, the inhibitive connections between all the units in the C-layer come into play. As discussed earlier, units should compete with each other such that strong units should tend to get stronger and weak ones weaker. To achieve this, the *interactive activation* algorithm, first introduced by McClelland and Rumelhart (1981) can be used. According to this algorithm, the activation of a unit can be computed according to the following formula:

$$a_i \ (t+1) := a_i \ (t) + \Delta \, a_i \ (t+1) \qquad 2$$

where:

$$\Delta \, a_i \ (t+1) = (1 - a_i[t]) \ \text{net}_i - \text{decay} \ (a_i \ (t) - \text{rest}) \qquad \text{if net}_i > 0$$
$$= a_i(t) \ \text{net}_i - \text{decay} \ (a_i \ (t) - \text{rest}) \qquad \text{otherwise}$$
$$\text{net}_i = \text{ext}_i + \Sigma_j \ o_j \ w_{ij} \quad j \quad \ldots \text{over all units in the same layer}$$

decay, rest . . . Parameters for decay of activation values

Rumelhart and McClelland (1988) give a detailed description of the behaviour of an interactive activation layer (henceforth called IA-layer). In general, it can be circumscribed as the *rich get richer* effect. This means that a unit which, in the initial response, has higher activations than all the others and increases its activation with each update, while the others decrease (provided *all* weights are negative). In general, after some update cycles, all units converge toward a value that remains virtually unchanged with more cycles.

The strength of this effect depends on the strength of the inhibitive connections. The higher the absolute value of a weight between two units, the more the pre-synaptic unit tends to suppress the post-synaptic one. There are connections in both directions, so in a C-layer it depends on the difference of the two weights between any two units as to which one suppresses the other. The activation value any unit in a C-layer can reach also depends on the value of the external input (for more description of interactive activation see Rumelhart & McClelland, 1988).

In the terms introduced here, the behaviour of a C-layer can be described in the following way. Starting from an initial response, several updating cycles (henceforth, parameter k) drive a C-layer toward a more identifiable state. When all inhibitive weights have the same value, the winner of the initial response is strengthened, and all other units are weakened. Greater absolute weight values increase this effect. In other words, the greater those values are, the more identifiable the resulting state gets. If the weight values differ considerably, a unit other than the initial winner might end up being the winner in the *final response*.

Based on these observations, the learning algorithm for categorisation is designed to strengthen inhibition so as to favour one unit over others under certain circumstances. One such circumstance is the number of times a pattern is present in the input. That means that the layer tends to reach identifiable states for known patterns (as they are recurring). This process can be called *conceptualisation*, or the forming of concepts. What was called *winner take all (WTA)* by Rumelhart and Zipser could, in analogy, now be called *winner take more (WTM)*. While WTA achieved full information reduction in every case, WTM tends to increase reduction gradually.

Incomplete information reduction is very important for this model, even when the inhibitive weights become so strong that a few update cycles virtually amount to WTA. This is because intermediate states only become less likely with increasing inhibitive weights, but are never ruled out completely. If external inputs get high enough, even an otherwise identifiable state can be altered. This is an important aspect for a language model that accounts for the suggestion that meanings of words should be viewed as relative, even when they seem to be fixed and universal. Through large weights, the sought-after state can become very stable, so that it is reached in nearly all similar situations. Almost always, however, there are gateways open for other influences to push the model into another state, or even into virtually every conceivable state.

Another generalisation of the original terminology of competitive learning is this: As more than one unit is permitted to be activated, it is not only useful to speak of *one* winner of an IA-layer, but also of a *degree of winning*. If the winner of a layer could be interpreted as the "best guess" concerning the appropriate category, in analogy the next strongest unit could be seen as the "second-best guess," and so forth. Therefore, it is useful to define a *degree of winning*:

let win_i be the number of units currently weaker than unit i

let $best_i$ be the greatest value of win_i reached until the current moment

let *compet* be the number of competitors for each unit (= no. of units in layer minus 1)

Def:

The *current degree of winning* is equal to *win/compet*

the *degree of winning with respect to previous experience* is equal to

$(compet - (best-win))/compet$

the *current absolute winner* has a current degree of winning equal to *1*

To achieve conceptualisation appropriate for the model behaviour, all units—depending on the degree of winning—should be taken into account during learning. This will be described later.

Context Influences

So far, I have spoken mainly about categorising patterns in *one* S-layer, such as simple visual bitmaps. Input to the units in a C-layer is permitted from an arbitrary number of other units. All such inputs are essentially treated equally. In other words, at least during update, the units in the C-layer cannot distinguish between input coming from an S-layer and input coming from elsewhere. Thus, the activations of some additional external units can change the response to virtually any other conceivable state.

We can see that calling the state of a C-layer a conceptualisation of a pattern in a connected S-layer is only an interpretation I, as the observer, have provided. I could just as well say that the C-layer forms a concept of the activation pattern of *all* external units. In this case, every distinct pattern would have a distinct response (under the assumption that weights are fixed). The aspect of the model permitting it to be interpreted in different ways corresponds to the theory of radical constructivism (Maturana & Varela, 1980): It suggests that a cognitive system has a complex internal architecture that determines its behaviour. External input—as we human observers call it—is not distinct from any activations deriving from inside the model (they are both neural firings). Similarly, language as consisting of symbols that activate associations is also only the interpretation of an observer who has learned to view it that way. Nothing in the functioning of the system, however, depends on such an interpretation.

I prefer the interpretation allowing the C-layer to conceptualise the input from the S-layer. If a cognitive system permits biased interpretation of its behaviour, so can the model. If we view it in this way, responses to the same pattern at different times can be quite different. We can view the factors that influence those changes, namely all the external units other than the S-layer, as the *impact of the context*. Context can be anything; the conceptual activations from other sensory inputs (for example, the recognised words of an utterance, as it will be the case later), the activations from previous experiences, or even simulated moods, drives, and motivations. As every state of the model correlates to a pattern of unit activations, all kinds of context influences can be treated equally. As a result, the model is *always open* to additional components being built in easily. Therefore, if in the following sections I consider only a few model components, it is not a major restriction to the general conception of a complex language model. For practical reasons, I have to start with very simple architectures, which can be extended to more complex versions.

The Learning Rule

Now that I have laid out the basic architecture for categorisation and its fundamental working, I discuss how learning (i.e. weight adaptation) achieves conceptualisations starting from random initial configurations. Here is a summary of the behaviour expected:

a. Repeated presentation of a pattern in the S-layer, or of a pattern sufficiently similar, should tend to strengthen the initial winner and proportionally weaken the others, as well as drive the final response into a more identifiable state.

b. More than one identifiable state for one pattern in the S-layer should be permitted. That means that two or more units can remain highly active in the initial response for a given pattern in the S-layer. With context, that is, when regarding all E-units, there should tend to be only one highly active unit for each pattern.

c. Learning should be bi-directional. This should especially be the case for non-S-layers connected to the C-layer.

Requirement (a) is a generalisation of the basic behaviour of competitive learning, where weights are strengthened such that the winner of the competition (WTA) is more likely to win the next time. Here too, the winner (i.e. the unit that is most highly activated, e.g. unit 7 in Fig. 10.5b) is strengthened, but as other units can also be active, something has to be done with them as well. As the general tendency should be toward more identifiable states, they should be weakened. However, a strongly activated unit that is just barely weaker than the winner might indicate that connections to that unit are important for other conceptualisations (consider also requirement [b]). For this reason, the previously defined *degree of winning* (more precisely, the degree of winning with respect to previous experience) can be introduced and the weights of that unit can be weakened in indirect proportion to that value. As a result, the winner increases and all the others more or less decrease—hence, "winner-take-more."

Weight adaptation on the inhibitive intra-cluster connections is generally different from adaptation on external connections. Those connections are mainly in charge of driving the final response into an identifiable state. To strengthen this effect, all weights are decreased (that means their absolute values are increased) if the pre-synaptic output value is greater than the post-synaptic one. Figure 10.6 shows the current state of a C-layer during adaptation. Lines indicate which connections are made more inhibitive in which direction. The width of the line indicates the strength of weight decrease. Arrows indicate the direction of the connections to be adapted. Note that not only the connections involving the winner are made more inhibitive, but also those involving other active units. In this way, although driving the layer toward more identifiable

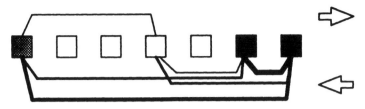

FIG. 10.6.   The adaptation of intra-layer weights.

states, the general structure of the intermediate states (i.e. the hierarchy of stronger and weaker units) is preserved. This is because intermediate states can be essential for many situations (sub-symbolic hypothesis).

In summary, the (verbalised) learning rule looks like this:

For each unit in the C-layer.   3
For each connection to units in the same C-layer, *increase the inhibition to all units that are currently weaker.*
For each connection to units external to the C-layer, *if the unit is the absolute winner, strengthen the weights from all active units; otherwise weaken in indirect proportion to the degree of winning.*

In all cases, both pre- and post-synaptic output values are included directly in the weight increase, just as in the Hebbian learning rule (Hebb, 1949).

The learning algorithm, in general, should favour identifiable states in the C-layer, that is, a state with just one active unit. Requirement (2), to a certain extent, contradicts that general tendency. But remember that it only mentions the S-layer and not any context units. The latter ones should bring a decision. That is, *without any context*, more than one highly active unit should be permitted. In the earlier definition, this amounts to a possible $n : m$ mapping. With the context, the tendency should be toward a unique winner, thus a mapping of $n : 1$. Therefore, weights are decreased when the post-synaptic unit is active and the pre-synaptic unit is inactive (see Mannes, 1989, and Dorffner, 1989, for $n : m$ mappings and the Hebb rule).

To implement that mapping, the learning rule has to be augmented. For that, a definition is necessary:

Def:
A unit is ON if its output value is larger than a threshold; otherwise it is OFF   4

The augmented learning rule can now be stated as follows:

For each connection between unit A and unit B do:
If A and B are both OFF: no change in weights
If both A and B are ON: change weight according to rule (3)

> For internal connections, *if either A or B is ON: change as in (3), while considering only the value of the unit that is ON*
>
> For external connections, *if either A or B is ON: decrease the weight proportionally to the output value of the unit which is ON*

Note that ON and OFF are used only for the conditions of this rule; in all other cases output values are taken as they are (on a continuous scale). This learning rule is applied only if the net activations from the E-units exceed a threshold. Thus some C-layers in the pool do not acquire identifiable states until some particular context is present. Learning is shut off when an identifiable state reaches a distinct quality, thereby preventing over-saturation of acquired states.

To implement the desired behaviour, a unit in such a categorisation layer has to be able to do the following:

a. Compute the number of competitors and the value of *win*;
b. store the best status so far;
c. distinguish between inputs from the same cluster and external ones.

Computing *win* in (a) is done by comparing the output value of the unit with all the other values visible through the incoming connections. An additional storage capacity to memorise the best such value (*best*) implements (b). (c) has already been discussed. All these processes can be done locally, i.e. they do not require a global controller or interpreter, and therefore are within the framework of self-organising networks (Rumelhart & McClelland, 1986; Reeke & Edelman, 1988).

An Experiment on Basic Conceptualisation

The results from a simple experiment illustrates the functions of the described algorithms. For this I consider simple $n \times n$ matrices for visual patterns. Consider the three patterns on a 5×5 bitmap matrix, as shown in Fig. 10.7. For further reference, I call them the "Π"-, the "U"- and the "X"-pattern, respectively, because they roughly resemble these letters. The 3 patterns have some unit

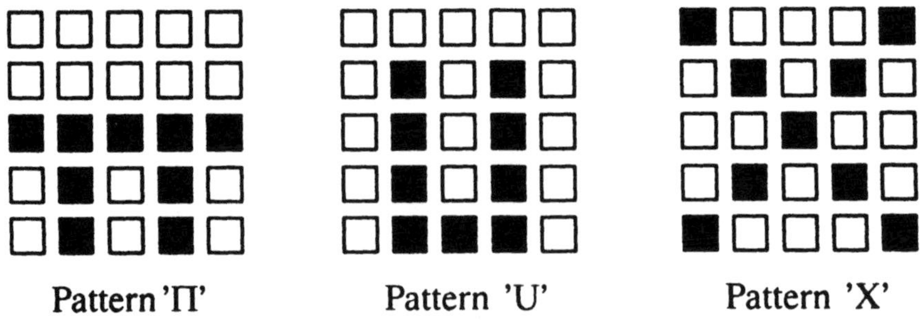

Pattern 'Π'   Pattern 'U'   Pattern 'X'

FIG. 10.7.   Three visual patterns used for training.

overlap, that is, they are similar to each other. "Π" and "U" share 6 active units—thus they have relatively large similarity. "Π" and "X" share 3, "U" and "X" 4 units. In other words, "X" is more dissimilar to both other patterns than those are to each other.

Accordingly, an S-layer with 25 units and a C-layer with 10 units were chosen. The 3 patterns were presented (i.e. the corresponding units in the S-layer were set to 1—for black squares in the pattern—or to 0—for white squares) alternately. Each time, the C-layer was updated 3 times (parameter k) and learning rule (4) was applied. For the next pattern, the activations in the C-layer were erased. Presenting all 3 patterns plus applying all rules is called one *cycle* of learning. For testing, a pattern was presented and the C-layer updated 3 times.

Figure 10.8 shows the responses to the 3 patterns with random initial weight distribution. Note that, in this case, the 3 responses have different winners (units 3 for "Π," unit 8 for "U," and unit 1 for "X"). This is important when patterns are distributed equally during learning. With the lack of any other influence by activations, different concepts can only evolve when the C-layers respond with different winning units. This does not always have to be the case. With a different initial weight distribution, 2 patterns (say, "Π" and "U") might activate the same winner. Despite the different winning units, the responses express the similarities between the patterns. The responses to "Π" and "U," for example, both have units 8 highly active, and units 1 and 3 to a certain degree. This shows that the current weight distribution gives more bias to the "U" pattern (unit 8). In other words, both patterns are close to being thrown in the same abstract category 8. This again, is a random property (nevertheless dependent on pattern similarities) and can be quite different in another setting.

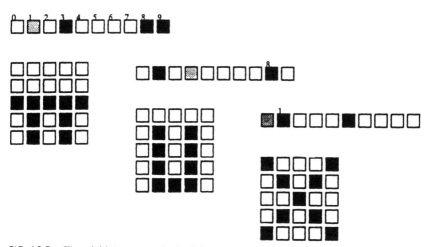

FIG. 10.8.   Three initial responses in the C-layer.

Now learning, shown in the case of pattern "Π," works as follows. Each unit computes its values of *win*: 9 for unit 3 (it is the winner, and there are 9 units activated more weakly), 8 for unit 9, and so on. In the first cycle, *best* is set to the value of *win* for each unit; in all other cycles it reflects the best status the unit ever had. Then all the weights from the active units in the S-layer to unit 3 are increased, and those to the other category units are decreased in proportion to the current degree of winning. Thus, at the next presentation of pattern "Π," unit 3 is stronger and all others weaker, in proportion to their rank in the winning hierarchy. Finally, competition is increased between unit 3 and units 1, 6, 8, and 9 (= all the other units that are ON), between unit 9 and units 1, 6, and 8, and so on. Thus, at the next presentation of "Π," unit 3 suppresses all the other active units more than it does currently. This is expressed in Fig. 10.9, which shows the initial response (upper) and the response after 3 updates (lower, same as in Fig. 10.8) before (left), and after the first learning step (right).

After that, pattern "U" is presented. The values of *win* are computed again. The *best* of unit 8 now becomes 9, whereas that of unit 3 stays at value 9. As earlier, the weights between active units in the S-layer and the winning unit 8 are strengthened. For unit 3, which is below its *best* value (7 compared to 9), the weights are weakened considerably (*degree of winning* < 1), whereas for unit 5, for example, the weights do not change so much (*degree of winning* = 1, because it is at its best). Also, inhibition between unit 8 and 3 (among others) is increased. Both weight adaptations make sure that the responses to the 2 patterns differ further than they did before. A unit which is the winner in one case is weakened more than others in another. Inhibition amplifies this effect.

Figure 10.10a shows the responses to all 3 patterns after 5 cycles. All states have become more identifiable, the initial winner being the most active unit. After 20 cycles (Fig. 10.10b), the response virtually consists of only one unit in

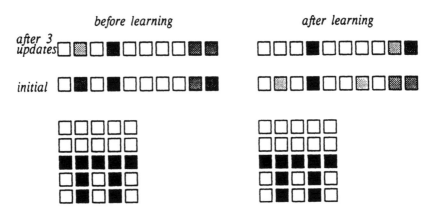

FIG. 10.9. How updates and learning affect the state in a C-layer.

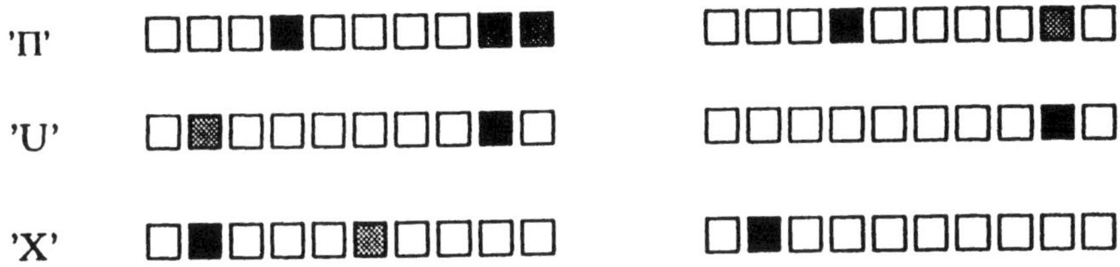

'Π'   □□□■□□□□■■   □□□■□□□□■□

'U'   □■□□□□□□■□   □□□□□□□□■□

'X'   □■□□□■□□□□   □■□□□□□□□□

FIG. 10.10.   The initial responses to the three visual patterns before (fuzzy) and after learning (clear).

each case. That means that, through learning, the responses become increasingly dissimilar.

To make the model adaptable to long-term changes in the environment, the parameter *best*, which is stored with every unit, should decay after some time. In other words, if the unit has not reached its best status of competition for some time, it should lose it. This way, that unit is ready to detect a novel situation again.

Properties of Conceptualisation

C-layers are a simple but powerful approach to letting connectionist models develop concepts about the environment they interact with. With top-down influences, which were not considered in the previous example, such concepts can depend on any kind of internal state in addition to sensory inputs. Simulations have shown that the architecture presented can develop categories that are not solely dependent on surface similarities (Dorffner, 1989). They can show categorisation that resembles radial categories (Lakoff, 1987). They also show the prototypicalisation behaviour underlying many theories about human categories (Rosch, 1978; Lakoff, 1987). It can be shown that categorisation and concept formation of this kind is noise- and error-tolerant, and can even predict many results from psychological literature (see Dorffner, 1989). As suggested earlier, large pools of C-layers will show categorisation behaviour that accounts for individual differences, as well as invariances over individuals.

IMPLEMENTING SYMBOLS

Symbolisation, that is, developing a state with symbolic function as defined earlier, is at the heart of language function. In principle, this is a process that goes a step further than conceptualisation. Remember Fig. 10.2, depicting the role of symbols. There it was crucial to suppose an internal representation of a symbol (level B) with special properties. Accordingly, states in a symbolisation layer have to fulfil the following conditions:

1. They must be clearly identifiable for the model. That means that a stable state distinct from other states has to be reached to permit a clear reaction.

2. Similarities between symbolic patterns should either not exist, or have no consequences on the behaviour of the model (see earlier discussions).

There are exceptions to the second condition, which will be discussed later. All in all, a proper fundamental approach to implement symbolic patterns is to use non-overlapping patterns to realise different internal symbols, and to suppress intermediate states when it comes to linguistic expression. A simple realisation to achieve this is a local implementation of symbols, i.e. let one unit stand for one symbol, just as before, when one unit could stand for a possible category.

Viewed this way, symbolisation and conceptualisation share many properties. Therefore a layer of competitive units can be used again as an implementation, henceforth called an SY-layer. In analogy to the category units in a C-layer, a unit in an SY-layer is called a *symbol unit*. There is one major difference, however: When a symbol is to be used in a language process (such as understanding or production), no other symbol unit can be active at the same time. In other words, full competition (i.e. winner-takes-all strategy) has to set in. For example, *before* transforming the internal symbol into some output (the external embodiment C of a symbol in Fig. 10.2), a *decision has to be made*; in other words, the winner has to suppress all the others totally. This also means *full information reduction*. Intermediate states are possible before and during competition, but cycles have to be continued until the winner is sufficiently distinct from the other symbol units.

Decision, or full competition, is important, because—as discussed earlier—mapping concepts to outputs via symbols is *not* an associative process based on pattern similarities. Similar concepts do not, in general, initiate similar outputs (e.g. similar phonemes). Thus the general working of networks, which is otherwise useful, must be suppressed here. Local realisation and a winner-takes-all strategy do that automatically. As each symbol is realised by only one unit, they are by default maximally dissimilar from each other.

Symbolic Function

Now I have discussed what I consider a symbolic pattern, i.e. the internal realisation of a symbol. But identifying those conditions is not enough for explaining how such a pattern can serve as a symbol in the simple language processes considered here. For that, we have to specify what *symbolic function* is in this view.

As became clear in an earlier section, the central aspect is the identification of at least two concepts and letting one stand for the other. Recognising symbolic function is thus the process of recognising the *co-occurrence* of clear concepts and building a link via an internal symbol between the conceptual states. This was already suggested in Fig. 10.2. Technically this means that the model has to contain at least two C-layers conceptualising two distinct inputs. In this model

I consider simple visual and mock acoustic input. Other aspects will be discussed briefly later.

Therefore we connect the SY-layer so as to form a link between C-layers, as depicted in Fig. 10.11. Bi-directional connections ensure that associations can go two ways. In other words, when strong connections have developed through another learning rule (described later), then one of the two concepts is sufficient to activate a symbol unit and subsequent associations that are similar to the other concept. This is the *recall of concepts* via symbols. In Fig. 10.11 strong connections are drawn by wide lines. Several phases have to be distinguished:

1. *The fuzzy phase (before adaptation):* No symbol unit can be highly activated for a given concept, even if it is clear (identifiable state). Therefore, no strong associations are possible (Fig. 10.12a).

2. *The identification phase (including adaptation):* Two clear concepts co-occur. One symbol unit (the current winner in the SY-layer) is driven towards a maximum value of 1 through competition (WTA). Weights are then adapted, so that associations in both directions are strengthened (Fig. 10.12b).

3. *The recognition phase (after adaptation):* One (clear) concept is activated and a symbol unit is set by WTA in the SY-layer (activated by the trained connections). Through the connections to the other C-layer, another concept is activated associatively (Fig. 10.12c).

Several important aspects can be recognised by observing the described phases. In this basic version, there are no direct connections between concepts and an association can be carried out only via identifying a symbol unit. In this way, similarities between concepts in one C-layer do not have a direct consequence on similarities in the other C-layer. This is essential to a language model. Also, symbols can only evolve after two clear concepts have occurred repeatedly at the same moment. Fuzzy concepts, in this basic version, never develop strong connections with each other. Finally we have to assume that the model is motivated to recognise the symbolic function of the co-occurrence. If it were not, activations in the SY-layer would have to be suppressed.

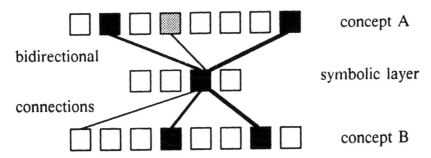

FIG. 10.11.   The connectivity between C-layers and the intermediate symbol (SY-) layer.

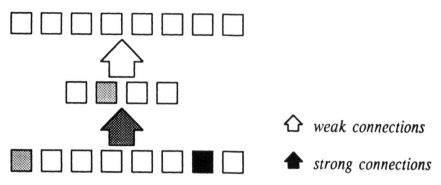

FIG. 10.12a. In the fuzzy phase, a state in the first C-layer hardly activates any state in the SY-layer and the other C-layer.

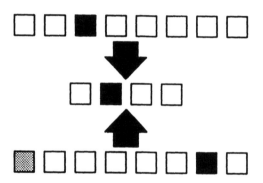

FIG. 10.12b. In the identification phase, identifiable states in both C-layers cause winner-take-all in the SY-layer and adaptation of weights.

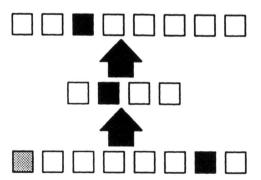

FIG. 10.12c. In the recognition phase, an identifiable state in the first C-layer activates an identifiable state in the other one via the intermediate SY-layer.

Implementing Internal Symbolic Function

To implement the desired behaviour in the three phases just described, a symbol unit has to have the following functions:

1. *it has to recognise if a layer that is connected with it is in an identifiable state;*
2. *it has to have an additional activation value expressing its state in terms of symbolic function;*
3. *it has to be able to initiate or suppress winner-take-all (WTA) of the layer.*

For that, the introduction of several notions is necessary. First, a mathematical definition of "identifiable state" has to be given:

$$\text{id-state:} \quad o_{win} - 1/(n-1) \, \Sigma_{j \neq others} \, o_j > \theta_1 \qquad\qquad 5$$
$$\text{and}$$
$$o_{win} - o_{sec} > \theta_2$$

where:

o_{win} ... output value of winner
others ... set of indices except $_{win}$
o_{sec} ... output value of second-most activated unit
n ... number of units in layer
θ_1, θ_2 ... threshold values

This definition contains two threshold values which clearly divide identifiable states from non-identifiable ones. For several reasons this might not be the most appropriate definition. Here, however, it serves for an easier observation of the model behaviour.

Then, the notion of a *symbol status* is introduced, which can take values between 0 and 1. Value 0 means that the unit has not served as a symbol yet and competition (WTA) cannot be initiated if that unit is the winner, unless two clear concepts co-occur. A value close to 1 means that the unit has often served as a link between two clear concepts, and that one concept can be enough to initiate competition and association.

With these two notions, a rule concerning update and weight adaptation can be formulated:

Given activations in the two C-layers, do the following: 6
Update the SY-layer once and detect the winner.
If the symbol status of the winner is above a threshold,
    then: if at least one C-layer is in an identifiable state
            then: initiate WTA, update the C-layers again, and adapt weights
            else: nothing
        if both C-layers are in an identifiable state, increase symbol status
    else: if both C-layers are in an identifiable state

> then: initiate WTA, increase the symbol status, update and adapt
> weights
> else: nothing

Adapting weights is done in a Hebbian manner, again, similar to rule (4).

Every time two clear concepts occur at the same time, the symbol status of the winner is increased, that is, the winner serves as a symbolic link between the concepts. Also, WTA is applied, so that the winner is now maximally on and all others off. Then weights are adapted, so that the connections between the winners of the C-layers and the winning symbol unit are strengthened by a large amount. When the symbol status exceeds a threshold value (which is true when the same two concepts have co-occurred often enough), one clear concept is sufficient to initiate WTA and thus to recognise the symbol and associate patterns with it. In other words, the symbol status serves to decide whether a symbol unit is the winner only by chance or because it is a unit with symbolic function in the current context.

In terms of the phases discussed here, the rule can be described as follows. In the fuzzy phase no C-layer is in an identifiable state and therefore no symbol unit has a symbol status larger than 0. In the identification phase, two co-occurring identifiable states are detected and the symbol status of the winning units is increased. In the recognition phase one identifiable state is detected and the currently winning symbol unit has a symbol status above threshold.

The Learning Rule in Detail

As was mentioned earlier, weight adaptation in SY-layers is carried out essentially the same way as with C-layers. All connections leading to the winner are strengthened; the others are weakened. However, some important differences remain:

1. adaptation is done in proportion to the current symbol status;
2. adaptation is done according to the 1:1 rule.

The first aspect ensures that links are built only through repeated co-occurrences, which raise the symbol status. Only the weights from and to units with a symbol status greater than zero are adapted. Units that are on by coincidence do not adapt their weights considerably. The second aspect is important, for reasons that will become clearer later. Learning should be towards unique one-to-one links between identifiable states. No two distinct identifiable states (i.e. states with different winners) in one layer should develop strong links to an identifiable state in the other. This means that weights are decreased in both cases where one of the units is *OFF*.

Weakening a connection involves approximately the same increment as in strengthening it. In this way, only consistent pairings of identifiable states form a link. If for example, two distinct identifiable states were paired with the same identifiable state in the other layer equally often, the resulting weights would be around zero.

The following is the verbal description of the learning rule for SY-layers:

For each unit in the SY-layer: 7
If the unit is the winner of WTA:
    then: strengthen the connections to all units in the C-layers that are ON
       and weaken the connections to those that are OFF
       (both in proportion to output value and symbol status)
    else: weaken the connections to all units in the C-layers that are OFF
       (in proportion to the symbol status)
If WTA has not been initiated, do not adapt weights.

The one-to-one learning rule is applied in *both* directions between C- and SY-layers. Symbol units therefore have to be taken into account accordingly in the learning rule (4) for C-layers (1:1 instead of n:1, learning in proportion to symbol status). See the Appendix for a mathematical description of all learning rules.

Directed Identification of a Symbol

No distinction has so far been made as to which of the two inputs represents the (external embodiment of the) symbol and which represents the input referred to by the symbol. In other words, we have identified what *reference* amounts to internally, but we have not talked about the *direction of reference*. Implicitly, we have assumed that the acoustic input is the symbol and the visual input is the reference.

Strictly speaking, it should be a matter of interpretation as to what is viewed as the direction of reference. No essential difference has been and should be made between the (two) kinds of input, because there is none. Another observer of the model (and of humans, for that matter) could say that the visual input represents the symbol that stands for the acoustic input. Indeed, many cases where reference works in this direction occur in real life. For example, written language would be given on the visual side, where a word could stand for acoustic signals. A hypothetical observer (presumably without any knowledge about humans) could assume this direction in every case, if he wanted to.

Nevertheless, in many cases humans are used to preferring one direction over another, because that is what they have learned to see. Thus, under certain circumstances, there has to be an inherent preference for one direction over the other, even in the simple model. One such circumstance is due to the nature of the signals. All speech signals are very similar to each other and are recognised as such. Another one could be motivating influences originating from other aspects of the whole cognitive system. Therefore, a parameter is introduced to the model that indicates if symbolic links are formed, giving preference to a certain direction or not. It is believed that this parameter is dependent on other cognitive functions, such as motivation. Thus it is viewed as an interface to those functions. It can be set by hand for the model described here.

To implement directed identification, strategy (6) has to be modified so as to permit WTA in the symbol layer even when only one identifiable state (on the side that is identified with the external embodiment of the symbol, e.g. the acoustic input) is present.

THE OUTPUT COMPONENT

One of our initial goals was to design a self-organising model with only grounded and meta-linguistic representations. Interpretation, to say it again, could be possible from observing the model, but the system performance should not depend on it. In the context of this implementation, looking at the symbol layer and identifying an activated unit does not do us any good in explaining whether the model works correctly. Therefore, we have to add an output component, at which we train the model to produce some (pseudo-) linguistic behaviour.

A MORE COMPLEX EXAMPLE

An example demonstrating the functions of all model components will show some of the complexities of the first approach.

Introducing multiple layers—as suggested in an earlier section—does not only lend itself to conceptualisation on different dimensions, but also to multiple associations (synonyms and multiple meanings) and for taxonomies of concepts. Many categories that have labels in a language are believed to exist on a hierarchy of subordinate and superordinate categories. Categories on a higher level of this hierarchy (taxonomy) are said to contain all categories on lower levels. Thus, any given object can be named with several labels from different levels of the taxonomy. To introduce such multiple labels, several C- and SY-layers are necessary.

Psychological experiments suggest that there is one particular level of such taxonomies where categories can be learned most naturally (Lakoff, 1987; Nelson, 1988; Rosch, 1>,'3). This is usually attributed to the fact that on that level the objects share most features, but are still distinct enough and thus most easily recognisable. This is called the *basic level* of categorisation. Take, for example, objects like a table or a chair. The taxonomy level with labels like "table" and "chair" would be the basic level. Thus, it is no coincidence that these labels are used most of the time to name any such object. However, there are also categories on a subordinate level (in English, in this case, they are usually labelled with two word phrases such as "kitchen table" or "arm chair") and on a superordinate level, such as the whole of such objects labelled "furniture."

In this model, basic level categories would correspond to concepts that can be most easily learned given only bottom-up activation (cf. Neisser, 1987; Rosch, 1973). All other concepts need more or less context activations, such as linguistic context through naming (Nelson, 1988).

The architecture depicted in Fig. 10.14 was used to learn names for visual inputs on 3 levels of hierarchy. It uses a 5×5 visual bitmap as before, and a layer of 20 units as pseudo-acoustic input. For each distinct input of the latter kind, 4 units were chosen arbitrarily to represent the input. During the process of conceptualisation, these inputs could be distorted by noise of up to 20% false activations. A pool of 4 C-layers with 10 units each was used on the "visual" side, a single C-layer of 15 units on the "acoustic" side. All layers were connected to their respective inputs in both directions with random initial weight configurations. A pool of 4 SY-layers linked the pool of C-layers to the left with the single C-layer to the right. Each SY-layer had connections (initialised randomly) with one of the C-layers to the left and with the single layer to the right, in both directions.

The four patterns in Fig. 10.13 were taken as visual inputs. Seven different pseudo-acoustic inputs were used, which for the sake of explanation we could view as representing the external embodiments of the labels "table," "chair," "baroque (table)," "kitchen (table)," "arm (chair)," "garden (chair)," and "furniture." Alternately, in random order, one visual pattern and one pseudo-acoustic pattern are presented at the input of the model. That is, pattern P1 is presented together with the inputs "baroque," "table," or "furniture;" P2 with "kitchen," "table," or "furniture," and so on.

No output component was used in this example. Output, if using immediately grounded representations again, ideally should be motor output to articulators that form the expected word. In the current implementation this has not yet been done. Instead a simple *labelling technique* was used: Whenever the symbol status of a symbol unit exceeds threshold, the label that was assigned to the most recent pseudo-acoustic input was attached to the symbol unit. This works fine in order to observe the behaviour for simple examples. However, it will not work in any complex case, because such simple interpretation of internal states is not always possible (see earlier discussions about representation-freeness). In future

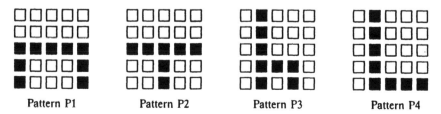

Pattern P1   Pattern P2   Pattern P3   Pattern P4

FIG. 10.13.   Four hierarchically similar visual patterns used for training.

implementations one will not get around including a self-organising output component.

As the model starts in the fuzzy phase (random initial configurations), no symbol links (i.e. connections with large weights via an SY-layer) exist between C-layers on different sides. Therefore, presenting one input alone would not activate any clear state at the other input side. If learning, as described in earlier sections, is turned on, the C-layers will start developing identifiable states for recurring categories of input patterns. It depends on both pattern similarities and initial weights which patterns will be grouped together. According to the similarities of the four patterns, a grouping of P1 + P2 and P3 + P4 will be most likely. Thus there is a high probability that one of the four C-layers in the pool will develop an identifiable state whenever P1 and P2 are present. With equal probability, another identifiable state (in the same or a different layer) will develop for P3 and P4. Any other grouping will be less likely but will still be possible. As long as we do not look at any observable output, however, we cannot care if conceptual states "make sense" to us observers or not.

On the pseudo-acoustic side, similar things will happen. There, no major overlaps occur (only arbitrary but small ones), so there is a high probability that seven different identifiable states develop during concept formation. As soon as there are identifiable states on both sides of a SY-layer, the learning rule (7) comes into play to build up links gradually via a symbol unit, as well as to raise that unit's symbol status. Thus the model is in the identification phase in respect to this pair of concepts. The 1:1-rule ensures that a link with high symbol status develops only when concepts are paired consistently. An identifiable state responding to patterns P1 and P2 will therefore develop a (bi-directional) link to the identifiable state responding to "table," but not to "furniture," or "baroque." The former is also presented with other patterns. The latter is presented only with pattern P1, not with P2. If one of the patterns should be presented more often than the other, some weak links are possible.

Once the symbol status of a symbol unit has reached the threshold, the model has reached the recognition phase with respect to that symbol. Now one of the two inputs can be presented alone, which causes the symbol unit to fire (WTA) and to associate the corresponding identifiable state on the other side via the link that has developed. For example, the input we labelled "table" can fire a symbol unit and activate the identifiable state that used to be the response to patterns P1 and P2. Via connections between the C-layer and the S-layer, even a prototypical pattern (an overlap of P1 and P2) can be activated in the visual input.

As far as the other pairings of inputs are concerned—e.g. P1 with "baroque" or all four patterns with "furniture"—the model cannot enter the identification phase yet, because no identifiable states have developed on the visual side (or only with a slight chance). This is because up till now only bottom-up influences to conceptualisation were considered. To group pattern P1 in one category by itself, or to group all four patterns in one category, a top-down influence is necessary. Theoretically this could be anything, as was argued earlier. Here we are interested in how linguistic naming can influence concept formation. Thus, the top-down component this model can use are the SY-layers connected to the pool of C-layers. With the onset of *directed identification* (see earlier), symbol units can fire even if no identifiable states exist yet on the visual side. These activations can now—provided connections are scaled properly—play a role in concept formation in one of the C-layers of the pool. In other words, the activations in the SY-layer can make the patterns which the C-layers receive seem more similar (in the case of "furniture" for all four patterns) or less similar (in the case of P1 and "baroque"). Thus it increases the probability that identifiable states develop for each of these cases. Such states can then take part in the learning rules and form a pattern that can be activated by either the visual input or by the corresponding symbol unit.

Simulation Results

A simulation was run with the architecture described. As a result, one C-layer in pool 1 (number 1 in Fig. 10.14) acquires conceptualisation on the basic level, grouping together patterns 1 & 2 and 3 & 4, respectively. These are the most natural groupings based on similarities. Experiments with several different initial weight settings revealed that this kind of conceptualisation is the one most likely to be discovered. Three other layers are assumed to have weak initial weight settings, so that they do not start conceptualising without any additional

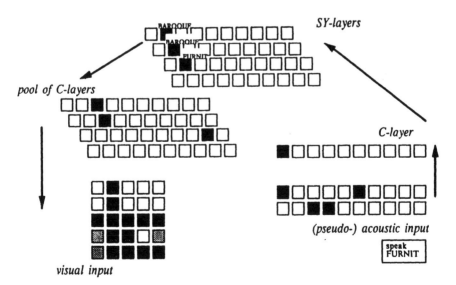

FIG. 10.14. The resulting activations in all layers of the model after training, using the word labelled "furniture" as input at the right (i.e. acoustic) side.

activation (context). These three come into play when the patterns are named on sub- or super-ordinate levels.

After some time, the direction parameter is set to "directed identification." Now, symbol units grow for the other five words in the input. It is left up to chance as to which SY-layer responds to which words. In the simulation, SY-layer 2 developed symbol units for "baroque," "kitchen," "table," "furniture," and "chair;" SY-layer 3 for "baroque," "kitchen," "arm," and "garden;" SY-layer 4 for "baroque," "arm," "garden," and "chair."

The model now started to acquire the following additional symbolic links with more training cycles:

1. *SY-layer 2.* In the given training set, the label "furniture" was used four times in each cycle, whereas "table" was only used twice and "baroque" and "kitchen" only once. As a result, the symbol unit labelled "furniture" started to overwrite all other activations in C-layer 2 of the pool. One identifiable state developed, which is the response of all four visual patterns and is linked to the symbol unit "furniture." The other symbol units did not develop links in either connections. This could be considered unfortunate. Note, however, that other SY-layers are there to acquire links for the other words. Also, the word "furniture" could occur less frequently than the others in a different setting, which would make a big difference.

2. *SY-layer 3.* All four links developed (all labels are on the same taxonomy level and thus occur equally often) in the stipulated direction (from the acoustic side to the visual side). Interestingly, in the other direction, two of the links (for patterns 2 and 3) were not strong enough. This is due to differences in initial weight configurations. More training cycles would probably strengthen them, too.

3. *SY-layer 4.* Again this showed four links developing in the stipulated direction. The activation associated with the symbol unit "chair" was pulled towards that of "garden." As a result, through this layer, "chair" was associated only with pattern 4 but not with pattern 2. As the final results show, such slightly biased links do not have a major impact on overall associations.

In Fig. 10.14, the resulting activations are shown when using the pseudo-acoustic input "furniture" and updating all layers in the order they are connected (see arrows). It can be seen that the imagery pattern gives slight preference to pattern 1, but that it is still the overlap of all four patterns. It can also be seen that the labelling technique fails here. Two units with label "baroque" are active. However, we can judge only observable output—the activations in the visual layer in this case—and cannot say the internal activations are "wrong." Association works similarly in all other six cases.

Through random influences, not all links have been acquired in both directions. Through additional training or with more layers, these random factors would be equalled out. In a few cases ("chair" or "furniture"), a bias has been acquired towards a more specific pattern (pattern 4 in the case of "chair," and pattern 1 in the case of "furniture"). This results in some small random variations in the associated prototypes, but does not completely distort the picture (see Fig. 10.14). This is a desired property. If this experiment is repeated several times with different initial settings, in most cases, prototypical associations will resemble each other. But there are always individual differences depending on chance factors and the history of the model (compare the discussion in the second section).

Note that there are no "false" links (in that a word like "arm" would associate pattern 1, 3, or 4) despite random variations of the said kind. Some links might not get strong enough after a limited number of cycles, but with more layers the chance for every expected link to develop should be equal to one.

FUTURE DIRECTIONS

As was discussed earlier, the model just presented can only include very simple language behaviour, such as the task of naming in connection with sensory input. We must travel a very long way before more complex language processes can be modelled. However, the nature of the given connectionist architecture permits easy integration of other model components. Thus, this model can be viewed as the starting point, which realises the most important aspects of language behaviour according to the view given in the first part of this chapter. From there, the model should be gradually extendable to include more complex cognitive functions that are important to human language. Here is a (not complete) list of future extensions:

1. So far, only pattern similarities based on Hamming distances can play a role in conceptualisation. Therefore, hidden unit layers and more complex sensory inputs (such as one including primitive feature detectors) should be added to the model. The same is true for the output component. Output closer to motor activations and training based on it should lead to a more convincing production side of the model. This is currently under development.

2. Competition should also be introduced *between* layers to permit the model to focus on one aspect (such as one level in the hierarchy).

3. The strict modular structure of the model should not be considered as the ultimate solution. Although many important parts of cognitive processing probably can be modelled in such a modular structure, ways to go around some components should always be permitted. Therefore, in future versions connections other than the ones described should be added to the model. Knowledge on all levels of the abstraction hierarchy (while reducing information, as discussed above) should be able to influence model behaviour. In many cases, for instance, inputs at one end of the model should be permitted to activate patterns on the

other end directly. Phenomena like sound symbolism, or others where similarities among external embodiments do play a role, could partially be explained by that.

Introducing multiple C-layers on the acoustic side (as an example) should permit the model to develop concepts like word categories. Words that are used for concepts on the same dimension will belong to the same category (and have a unit overlap), due to their *use*.

5. As was mentioned initially, language understanding depends on all kinds of context, not just the sensory inputs. This includes experiences (knowledge) through other cognitive functions, drives, motivations, moods, etc. In this model they will be very easy to introduce. The conceptualisation components are open to every input (activation patterns), as was hinted upon in a previous section. This way, conceptualisation can be divorced even more from sensory input and can permit the development of abstract concepts.

6. The next important step will be to go from single words to word sequences, and thus to more complex utterances. Grammar rules to deal with "syntactic structure" of language do not fit into the view of language presented here. They are symbolic and thus brittle, and distinguish between "well-formed" and "malformed" utterances more than seems natural in human language commun-ication. Here, analysing structure of language is considered a problem of how to deal with sequences of patterns (e.g. Jordan, 1986), rather than single patterns presented in parallel. The meaning of word sequences is identified with the associations a listener has, based on the words themselves and the way they are ordered and grouped together. Expectations built up by sequences can also give further evidence for distinguishing word categories (Elman, 1988). As a first step, we at the Research Institute (Mannes & Dorffner, 1990), are developing a simple sequential network that can learn to recognise and react to certain pattern sequences. This network will be inserted into the model between sensory input and the categorisation layers. Sequential processing will also have to be included on the level of phonetics. Phonemes would be viewed as another type of concept. A word then consists of a sequence of external representations of such phonemes, instead of one parallel input.

7. Furthermore, additional input could be made to modify the adaptation during learning, e.g. through so-called *sigma-pi units* (Rumelhart & McClelland, 1986). Thus the model could at times be demotivated to understand and not change conceptualisation.

SUMMARY AND CONCLUSION

In this article, a partial theory has been presented, which views language as an adaptive, self-organising process that does not rely on linguistic representations. It defines semantics and word reference only through adaptive behaviour in an environment. Meanings of utterances are identified with associations a listener has. Those associations do not mirror the world, only reactions by the system have to be interpretable to test the system's performance.

A connectionist implementation of a simple first model within the framework of that theory has been presented. The sub-symbolic paradigm, based on experiences with connectionist networks, has been identified as suitable to the presented view of language. Learning through weight adaptation frees the model of the necessity to possess representations in the strong AI sense. Instead, formalisations have to be brought in only at a meta-linguistic level, as part of pre-wired architecture and built-in mechanisms.

First results with the implemented model verify, on a basic level, the theories and hypotheses underlying this view of language. Future extensions, as they were suggested, should lead to a much more complex self-organising non-representational model of language behaviour.

ACKNOWLEDGEMENTS

I would like to thank Prof. Trappl for his gracious support for this project. I am also very grateful to Stan Kwasny—my dissertation adviser—Robert Port, Michael Gasser, and Paul Smolensky for many helpful discussions, as well as Gerhard Widmer and Christian Mannes for proof-reading and their continuing inspirations to my work. The research for this article has been supported by the Austrian Federal Ministry for Science and Research under grant no. 607.509/4–26/89.

REFERENCES

Berry-Rogghe, G.L., Kolvenbach, M., Lutz, H.D. (1980). Interacting with PLIDIS: A deductive question answering system for German. In L. Bolc (Ed.), *Natural language answering systems.* München: Hanser.

Brown, R. (1958). *Words and things: An introduction to language.* New York: Free Press.

Campbell, J. (1982). *Grammatical man, information, entropy, language, and life.* (Touchstone Book) New York: Simon & Schuster.

Chomsky, N. (1965). *Aspects of the theory of syntax.* Cambridge, Mass.: M.I.T. Press.

Chomsky, N. (1975). *Reflections on language.* Cambridge, Mass.: M.I.T. Press.

Cottrell, G.W. (1985). *A connectionist approach to word sense disambiguation.* Dissertation, TR 154. New York: University of Rochester.

Dorffner, G. (1989). *A sub-symbolic connectionist model of basic language functions.* Dissertation, Indiana University, Computer Science Dept.

Dreyfus, H.L. & Dreyfus, S.E. (1985). *Mind over machine.* New York: The Free Press.

Edelman, G.M. (1978). *Group selection and phasic reentrant signaling: A theory of higher brain function.* New York: Rockefeller University.

Elman, J.L. (1988). *Finding structure in time.* C.R.L. Technical Report 8801. La Jolla: University of California at San Diego.

Fodor, J.A. (1983). *The modularity of mind.* Cambridge, Mass.: M.I.T. Press, Bradford Books.

Fukushima, K. (1980). Neocognitron: A self-organizing neural network model for a mechanism of pattern recognition unaffected by shift in position. *Biological Cybernetics, 36,* 193–202.

Hebb, D.O. (1949). *The organization of behavior.* New York: Wiley.

Hofstadter, D.R. (1985). Waking up from the Boolean dream. In D.R. Hofstadter (Ed.), *Metamagical themas: Questing for the essence of mind and pattern.* New York: Basic Books.

Hubel, D.H. & Wiesel, T.N. (1962). Receptive fields, binocular interaction, and functional architecture in cat's visual cortex. *Journal of Physiology, 160,* 106–154.

Jordan, M.I. (1986). *Serial order: A parallel distributed processing approach* (ICS-UCSD, Report No. 8604). La Jolla: University of California at San Diego.

Kaplan, S., Weaver, M., & French, R. (1990). Active symbols and internal models: Towards a cognitive connectionism, *AI & Society, 1* (4), 51–72.

Kohonen, T. (1981). Self-organized formation of topologically correct featuremaps. In J.A. Anderson (Ed.), *Neurccomputing.* Cambridge, Mass.: A Bradford Book, M.I.T. Press, 511–522.

Lakoff, G. (1987). *Women, fire and dangerous things: What categories reveal about the mind.* Chicago: University of Chicago Press.

Mannes, C. (1989). *Sequentielle konnektionistische Verarbeitung: Detektoren fuer spatiotemporale Muster.* Master's thesis, T.U. Wien.

Mannes, C. & Dorffner, G. (in press). Self-organizing detectors of spatiotemporal patterns. To appear in *Proceedings of the DANIP Workshop.* Oldenbourg: G.M.D.

Maturana, H.R. & Varela, F.J. (1980). *Autopoiesis and cognition.* Dordrecht: Reidel.

McClelland, J.L. & Rumelhart, D.E. (1981). An interactive activation model of context effects in letter perception: Part 1. An account of basic findings. *Psychological Review, 88,* 375–407.

McClelland, J.L. & Rumelhart, D.E. (1986). *Parallel distributed processing: Explorations in the microstructure of cognition. Vol. 2: Psychological and biological models.* Cambridge, Mass.: M.I.T. Press.

Neisser, U. (1987). Introduction: The ecological and intellectual bases of categorization. In U. Neisser (Ed.), *Concepts and conceptual development.* Cambridge: Cambridge University Press, 1–10.

Nelson, K. (1988). Where do taxonomic categories come from? *Human Development, 31,* 3–10.

Nenov, V.I. & Dyer, M.G. (1988). DETE: Connectionist/symbolic model of visual and verbal association. In B. Kosko (Ed.), *IEEE International Conference on Neural Networks, San Diego, Vol. II* (pp. 17–24). San Diego: I.E.E.E.

Reeke, G.N.Jr & Edelman, G.M. (1988). Real brains and artificial intelligence. *Daedalus,* Winter 1988, "Artificial Intelligence."

Roberts, K. & Horowitz, F.D. (1986). Basic level categorization in seven- and nine-month-old infants. *Journal of Child Language, 13,* 191–208.

Rosch, E. (1973). On the internal structure of perceptual and semantic categories. In T. Moore (Ed.), *Cognitive development and the acquisition of language.* New York: Academic Press.

Rosch, E. (1978). Principles of categorization. In E. Rosch & B.B. Lloyd (Eds.), *Cognition and categorization.* Hillsdale, N.J.: Lawrence Erlbaum Associates Inc.

Rumelhart, D.E. & McClelland, J.L. (1986). *Parallel distributed processing: Explorations in the microstructure of cognition, Vol. 1: Foundations.* Cambridge, Mass.: M.I.T. Press.

Rumelhart, D.E. & McClelland, J.L. (1988). *Explorations in parallel distributed processing.* Cambridge, Mass.: M.I.T. Press.

Rumelhart, D.E., Smolensky, P., McClelland, J.L., & Hinton, G. (1986). Schemata and sequential thought processes in PDP models. In J.L. McClelland & D.E. Rumelhart, *Parallel distributed processing: Exploration in the microstructure of cognition, Vol. 2.* Cambridge, Mass.: M.I.T. Press.

Rumelhart, D.E. & Zipser, D. (1985). Feature discovery by competitive learning. *Cognitive Science, 9,* 75–112.

Smolensky, P. (1988). On the proper treatment of connectionism. *The Behavioral and Brain Sciences, 11* (1).

Trost, H., Buchberger, E., Heinz, W., Hoertnagl, C., & Matiasek, J. (1987). "Datenbank-DIALOG"—A German language interface for relational databases. *Applied Artificial Intelligence, 1* (2), 181–203.

Waltz, D.L. (1978). An English language question answering system for a large relational database. *Communications of the ACM, 21* (7), 526–539.

Whorf, B.L. (1956). *Language, thought and reality: Selected writings of Benjamin Lee Whorf* (Edited by John B. Carroll). Cambridge, Mass.: M.I.T. Press.

Winograd, T. (1983). *Language as a cognitive process, 1: Syntax.* Reading: Addison-Wesley.

Winograd, T. & Flores, F. (1986). *Understanding computers and cognition.* Norwood, N.J.: Ablex Publishing Co.

APPENDIX

Formal Description of Learning and Update

Updating C-layers and SY-layers: See page 289.

Updating the symbol status:

$$ss_i(n+1) = \begin{cases} ss_i(n) + \alpha_1(a_i - ss_i(n)) \text{ if } ss_i(n) < a_i \\ ss_i(n) + \alpha_2(ss_i(n) - a_i) \text{ otherwise} \end{cases}$$

Adapting weights:

1. $w_{ij}(n+1) = w_{ij}(n) + \Delta w_{ij}(n)$

2. $w_{ij} := \begin{cases} w_{ij} + 0.5(max - w_{ij}) \text{ if } w_{ij} > max \\ w_{ij} + 0.5(w_{ij} - min) \text{ if } w_{ij} < min \end{cases}$

Adapting weights on internal connections of a C-layer:

$$\Delta w_{ij} = \begin{cases} -\eta o_i o_j - \mu(w_{ij} - w_{rest}) \text{ if } o_i < o_j \wedge win_j \geq best_j \\ -\mu(w_{ij} - w_{rest}) \qquad \text{otherwise} \end{cases}$$

Adapting weights on connections between S-layers and C-layers:

$$\Delta w_{ij} = \begin{cases} \eta o_i o_j & \text{if } ON_i \wedge ON_j \wedge win_i = compet \\ \eta \frac{win_i - best_i}{compet} & \text{if } ON_i \wedge ON_j \wedge win_i \neq compet \\ -\eta ws o_i & \text{if } ON_i \wedge OFF_j \\ -\eta ws o_j & \text{if } OFF_i \wedge ON_j \\ 0 & \text{otherwise} \end{cases}$$

Adapting weights on connections between SY-layers and C-layers:

$$\Delta w_{ij} = \begin{cases} \eta ss_i o_i o_j & \text{if } ON_i \wedge ON_j \wedge win_i = compet \\ \eta \frac{ss_i(win_i - best_i)}{compet} & \text{if } ON_i \wedge ON_j \wedge win_i \neq compet \\ -\eta ss_i ws o_i & \text{if } ON_i \wedge OFF_j \\ -\eta ss_j ws o_j & \text{if } OFF_i \wedge ON_j \\ 0 & \text{otherwise} \end{cases}$$

Adapting weights on connections between C-layers and SY-layers:

$$\Delta w_{ij} = \begin{cases} \eta ss_i o_i o_j & \text{if } ON_i \wedge ON_j \wedge WTA \\ -\eta o_i & \text{if } ON_i \wedge OFF_j \wedge WTA \\ -\eta ss_i o_j & \text{if } OFF_i \wedge ON_j \wedge WTA \\ 0 & \text{otherwise} \end{cases}$$

$$ON_i \equiv o_i > \Theta_{ON}$$
$$OFF_i \equiv o_i \leq \Theta_{ON}$$
$$ws \leq 1$$

IV COMPUTATIONAL PSYCHOLINGUISTICS

IV COMPUTATIONAL PSYCHOLINGUISTICS

INTRODUCTION

The papers in this section cover a range of topics, but they can all be characterised as having a concern with modelling various aspects of human language processing. Although much of the impetus for the development of connectionist models has come from the cognitive modelling domain, the bulk of connectionist research, and this is true of the work described in this volume, is less concerned with psychological plausibility than with building better natural language processing (NLP) systems. The reasons for this are understandable. It can be argued that there are enough attendant difficulties in constructing connectionist models to tackle the hard problems of NLP without the additional constraints of having to provide solutions that are psychologically and/or neurally plausible. A common retort to this complaint, however, is that a good strategy in tackling the hard problems is to pay attention to psychological data.

There are a number of key difficulties in trying to use connectionist models in a cognitive modelling context. The first is the problem of decidability. This is a general problem found in any computational modelling domain, and it arises from the fact that the same set of data can in principle be explained by a range of different models. The second difficulty arises in trying to derive analogues of empirical data from the performance of network models. These two factors are not entirely unrelated, since the decidability issue usually comes down to a competition between models to explain a set of empirical findings. The wider the range of empirical measures one can derive from a set of competing models, the greater the chance of discovering which one gives a better fit to the data.

The decidability issue, although not addressed as such, is the focus of two of the four papers in this section. Massaro (Chapter 11) argues that his fuzzy logic model (FLMP) can explain the same data as that of McClelland and Elman's (1986) TRACE speech perception model. Moreover, he points out a number of inadequacies in TRACE that are not found in FLMP. Norris (Chapter 12) focuses on the issue of interaction between levels of representation. He provides a convincing demonstration of equivalence between the performance of the TRACE model and a recurrent version of a feedforward network in which activation from the hidden units at one time step is fed back to the same units at the next. McClelland and Elman (1986) make a strong case for the kind of interactionism embodied in TRACE, where each level of representation strongly interacts with the ones above and below it in the processing hierarchy. However, Norris demonstrates a range of effects in a model lacking any top-down connections, the type of effects which McClelland and Elman attribute to top-down lexical influences in their model. The key difference between the two models seems to be the ability of Norris's model to learn, and it may be that learning mediates the top-down effects he demonstrates. As a result of his findings, Norris makes the observation that one cannot view feedforward connectionist models as versions of the box models of classical information processing. A more general observation is that two connectionist models with significantly different architectures can account for the same data. This, however, is neither disastrous nor unusual; it merely suggests the need to look for crucial instances in which the models make different predictions.

The kind of data that the various models generate for use in empirical comparisons can vary. However, they usually fall into two main classes: (1) timing data, and (2) response content. The latter class can be sub-divided into two further categories, since the experimenter may be interested in either correct or incorrect responses. The papers by Massaro, Norris, and Mozer and Behrmann (Chapters 11, 12, and 14 respectively) deal with the nature of the response content from connectionist models. Mozer and Behrmann's chapter is unique among the four in that it describes a procedure for deliberately damaging a model with the intention of producing a pattern of errors similar to that found in a class of neuropsychological patients. Both response content and timing data are of interest to O'Seaghdha et al. (Chapter 13). Their paper presents two models; a standard feedforward backpropagation model (Model 1) and an interactive activation model (Model 2), the latter in the tradition of McClelland and Rumelhart (1981). In the interactive activation model, timing is determined as a function of the number of cycles taken by the network to settle. In the backpropagation model, O'Seaghdha et al. use the pattern of error over a number of learning trials to demonstrate response-time priming effects, where error is some function of the difference between the network's output and a desired response. Seidenberg and McClelland (1989) have used error as an analogue of response time, but in their case it was measured after, rather than during, learning. Another way of obtaining a response time measure in feedforward networks is to modify the activation function so that activation builds up, or cascades, over time. The point at which the cascading activation asymptotes is taken to be the time at which a response is triggered. This approach is a modification of a technique first used by McClelland (1979) and adapted for use in a feedforward network by Cohen, Dunbar, and McClelland (1990). Unfortunately, the cascade measure is very time-consuming to obtain, and moreover Seidenberg and McClelland found that the sum of squared error correlated with the number of cycles taken to asymptote. Consequently, one only needs to make a single pass through the network to get a measure that is equivalent to measuring the number of cycles to asymptote. One disadvantage of this error-based measure is that it is only effective if you just have a single module generating the output of interest. However, if the model consists of a number of modules that interact in a time-critical way, then the cascade process needs to be used.

In general, the chapters in this section provide a range of perspectives on connectionist cognitive modelling in the psycholinguistic domain. This is a complex enterprise, since researchers are trying simultaneously to satisfy at least two sets of constraints. On the one hand, there is the struggle to master the new modelling medium of connectionism, and on the other there is the requirement to generate data that is psychologically interpretable and testable. Nonetheless, on the basis of past successes it is likely that the cognitive modelling domain will remain one of the main sources of innovation in connectionism.

REFERENCES

Cohen, J.D., Dunbar, K., & McClelland, J.L. (1990). On the control of automatic processes: A parallel distributed processing model of the Stroop effect. *Psychological Review*, *97*, 332–361.

McClelland, J.L. (1979). On the time relations of mental processes: An examination of systems processing in cascade. *Psychological Review*, *86*, 287–330.

McClelland, J.L. & Elman, J. (1986). The TRACE model of speech perception. *Cognitive Psychology*, *18*, 1–86.

McClelland, J.L. & Rumelhart, D.E. (1981). An interactive activation model of context effects in letter perception: Part 1. An account of basic findings. *Psychological Review*, *88*, 375–407.

Seidenberg, M.S. & McClelland, J.L. (1989). A distributed, developmental model of visual word recognition. *Psychological Review*, *96*, 523–568.

11

Connectionist Models of Speech Perception

Dominic W. Massaro
Program in Experimental Psychology, University of California, Santa Cruz, CA 95064, U.S.A.

INTRODUCTION

Speech offers a viable domain for developing and testing models of perception, pattern recognition, and categorisation. There has been a tradition of fairly elaborate theories of speech perception (for recent reviews, see Jusczyk, 1986; Klatt, 1989; Massaro, 1989). Some of these theories make little direct contact with experimental results, however, and fall outside the mainstream of psychological inquiry. In addition, some theories treat speech as a unique phenomenon and their properties have very little generality beyond speech itself. Different classes of computational models, on the other hand, turn out to have general value and can be formulated to address experimental results directly.

Evaluating different classes of models and testing between them is a highly involved and complex endeavour (Massaro & Friedman 1990). Each class has models that give a reasonable description of the results of interest. Distinguishing between models, therefore, requires a fine-grained analysis of the predictions and observations to determine quantitative differences in their accuracy. Preference for one class of models is also influenced by factors other than just goodness of fit between experiment and theory. Some models are too powerful and thus not falsifiable. With enough hidden units, for example, connectionist models can predict too many different results (Massaro, 1988). Models should also help us understand the phenomena of interest. For example, parameters of a model might provide illuminating dependent measures of the information available in speech perception and the processing of that information. We might

321

not succeed in eliminating all but one class of extant models. Analogous to the wave and particle descriptions of the physics of light, perhaps several classes of models will be valuable rather than just one.

Two classes of connectionist models of speech perception are described, evaluated, and tested. The classes are interactive-activation connectionist models and feedforward connectionist models. Both of these models can account for the influence of multiple information sources in speech perception. Experimental research has documented, for example, that both auditory and visual information influence speech perception in face-to-face communication (Massaro, 1987). These results are described adequately by a process or stage model, the fuzzy logical model of perception (FLMP). It is assumed that auditory and visual sources of information are evaluated independently of one another. Thus, their representation at the evaluation stage maintains modality-specific independence. The two sources are integrated at the next stage, and the representation at this stage reflects the joint contribution of both sources. The final stage makes a decision required by the task. Identification utilises the outcome of integration, whereas discrimination can access the lower-level independent representations resulting from evaluation. The perceiver appears to evaluate and integrate continuous information from the audible and visible sources, and to perceive the pattern that makes the best fit with this information.

The two classes of connectionist models can also account for the results, but in different ways. In interactive activation models, layers of units are connected in hierarchical fashion with two-way connections between units both within and between layers. For example, the TRACE model of speech perception has feature, phoneme, and word layers. There are excitatory two-way connections between pairs of units from different layers and inhibitory two-way connections betwen pairs of units within the same layer. Thus, interactive activation is based on the assumption that the activation of a higher layer eventually modifies the activation and information representation at a lower layer (McClelland & Elman, 1986). In terms of bimodal speech perception, for example, the auditory information can influence the quality of the visual information, and vice versa.

In contrast to interactive activation, feedforward models assume that activation feeds only forward. Two-layer models have an input layer connected to an output layer. Three-layer models assume that the input units activate and inhibit a layer of "hidden" units between input and output layers of units (Minsky & Papert, 1969; Rumelhart, Hinton, & Williams, 1986). In *unconstrained* models, each input unit is connected to each hidden unit and each hidden unit is connected to each output unit. The distinguishing feature of unconstrained models is that separate information sources interact at the hidden layer of processing. In *constrained* models, on the other hand, a given hidden unit is activated only by a single information source. In both constrained and unconstrained models, each hidden unit is connected to all output units.

The goal of the present paper is to describe and test these two classes of models, using the general research strategy proposed by Platt (1964) and developed more fully in the context of speech perception by Massaro (1987). Although the models share certain assumptions and make similar predictions in several experimental paradigms, they differ on one important attribute. The difference has to do with how multiple sources of information interact to influence performance jointly. We begin by describing an experiment on top-down and bottom-up contributions to speech perception and an account of the results in the framework of a fuzzy logical model of perception. The results and model serve as targets for an adequate connectionist model of speech perception.

PHONOLOGICAL CONSTRAINTS IN SPEECH PERCEPTION

To study the joint contribution of stimulus information and phonological constraints in speech perception, subjects were asked to identify a liquid consonant in different phonological contexts (Massaro, 1989). Each speech sound was a consonant cluster syllable beginning with one of the 3 consonants /p/, /t/, or /s/ followed by a liquid consonant ranging (in 5 levels) from /l/ to /r/, followed by the vowel /i/. The 5 different levels along the /l/-/r/ continuum differed in terms of the frequency of the third formant (F_3) at the onset of the liquid—which is higher for /l/ than /r/. (Formants are bands of energy in the syllable that normally result from natural resonances of the vocal tract in real speech.) There were 15 test stimuli created from the factorial combination of 5 stimulus levels combined with 3 initial-consonant contexts. Eight elementary-school children were instructed to listen to each test syllable and to respond whether they heard /li/ or /ri/.

Figure 11.1 gives the average probability of an /r/ response as a function of the two factors. As can be seen in the figure, both factors had a strong effect. The probability of an /r/ response increased systematically with decreases in the F_3 transition. Phonological context also had a significant effect on the judgments. Finally, the significant interaction reflected the fact that the phonological context effect was greatest when the information about the liquid was ambiguous; $F(8, 56) = 8.25, p < 0.001$. Subjects responded /r/ more often given the context /t/ than given the context /p/. Similarly, there were fewer /r/ responses given the context /s/ than given the context /p/. These results will now be described by the FLMP.

Fuzzy Logical Model of Perception (FLMP)

According to the FLMP, speech patterns are recognised in accordance with a general algorithm (Massaro, 1987; Oden & Massaro, 1978). The model assumes three operations in speech recognition: feature evaluation, feature integration,

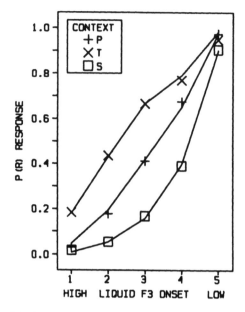

FIG. 11.1. Observed (points) and predicted (lines) probability of an /r/ identification as a function of the F_3 transition onset of the liquid; the initial consonant is the curve parameter (results from Massaro, 1989). The predictions are for the FLMP.

and decision. Continuously valued features are evaluated, integrated, and matched against prototype descriptions in memory, and an identification decision is made on the basis of the relative goodness of match of the stimulus information with the relevant prototype descriptions. The concept of fuzzy logic and how it has influenced the development of the model is discussed more fully in Massaro (1987).

Central to the FLMP are summary descriptions of the perceptual units of the language. These summary descriptions are called prototypes and they contain a conjunction of various properties called features. A prototype is a category and the features of the prototype correspond to the ideal values that an exemplar should have if it is a member of that category. The exact form of the representation of these properties is not known and may never be known. However, the memory representation must be compatible with the sensory representation resulting from the transduction of the speech signals. Compatibility is necessary because the two representations must be related to one another. To recognise the syllable /ba/, the perceiver must be able to relate the information provided by the syllable itself to some memory of the category /ba/.

Prototypes in long-term memory are made active for the task at hand. In speech perception, for example, we might envisage activation of all prototypes corresponding to the perceptual units of the language being spoken. For ease of exposition, consider a speech signal representing a single perceptual unit, such as the syllable /ba/. The sensory systems transduce the physical event and make available various sources of information called features. For each feature and for each prototype, featural evaluation provides information about the degree to which the feature in the speech signal matches the featural value of the prototype.

Given the necessarily large variety of features, it is necessary to determine the degree of match of each feature with its corresponding representation in each prototype. The syllable /ba/, for example, might have visible featural information related to the closing of the lips and audible information corresponding to the second and third formant transitions (Massaro, 1987). These two features must share a common metric if they are eventually going to be related to one another. To serve this purpose, fuzzy truth values (Zadeh, 1965) are used because they provide a natural representation of the degree of match. Fuzzy truth values lie between zero and one, corresponding to a proposition being completely false and completely true. The value 0.5 corresponds to a completely ambiguous situation whereas 0.7 would be more true than false, and so on. Fuzzy truth values, therefore, can represent not only continuous information, but also different kinds of information. Another advantage of fuzzy truth values is that information is couched in a quantitative form and, therefore, allows the natural development of a quantitative description of the phenomenon of interest.

Figure 11.2 gives a schematic diagram of the three operations of the FLMP. Feature evaluation provides the degree to which each feature in the syllable matches the corresponding feature in each prototype in memory. The goal, of course, is to determine the overall goodness of match of each prototype with the syllable. All of the features are capable of contributing to this process and the second operation of the model is called feature integration. That is, the features (actually the degrees of matches) corresponding to each prototype are combined (or conjoined in logical terms). The outcome of feature integration consists of the degree to which each prototype matches the syllable. In the model, all features contribute to the final value, but with the property that the least ambiguous features have the most impact on the outcome.

The third operation, decision, determines the merit of each relevant prototype relative to the sum of the merits of the other relevant prototypes. This relative goodness rule (RGR) gives the proportion of times the syllable is identified as an

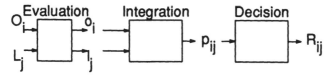

FIG. 11.2. Schematic diagram of the three operations assumed by the FLMP.

instance of the prototype (Massaro & Friedman, 1990). The relative goodness of match could also be determined from a rating judgment indicating the degree to which the syllable matches the category. In pandemonium-like terms (Selfridge, 1959), we might say that it is not how loud some demon is shouting but rather the relative loudness of that demon in the crowd of relevant demons. An important prediction of the model is that one cue has its greatest effect when a second cue is at its most ambiguous level. Thus, the most informative cue has the greatest impact on the judgment.

Test of the FLMP

A critical assumption of the FLMP is that the featural information from the liquid and the phonological context provide *independent* sources of information. It is assumed that subjects adopt the prototypes R and L in the task, and evaluate and integrate the two sources of information with respect to these prototypes. The featural information supporting the R prototype can be represented by the truth value t_i, where the subscript i indicates that t_i changes only with the F_3 transition. For the /l/-/r/ identification, t_i specifies how much the critical F_3 transition feature supports the prototype R. This value is expected to increase as the onset frequency of the F_3 transition is decreased. However, t_i is assumed to be independent of the phonological context. With just two alternatives along the continuum, it can further be assumed that the featural information supporting the L prototype is the complement of t_i. Thus, the support for L is simply one minus the support for R. Therefore, if t_i specifies the support for R given by the F_3 transition, then $(1 - t_i)$ specifies the support for L given by that same transition.

The phonological context also provides independent evidence for R and L. The value c_j represents how much the context supports the prototype R. The subscript j indicates that c_j changes only with changes in phonological context. The value of c_j should be large when /r/ is admissible and small when /r/ is not admissible. Analogous to the treatment of the featural information, the degree to which the phonological context supports the prototype L is indexed by $(1 - c_j)$.

The listener is assumed to have two independent sources of information. The total degree of match with the prototypes R and L is determined by integrating these two sources. Feature integration involves a multiplicative combination of the two truth values. Therefore, the degree of match to R and L for a given syllable can be represented by

$$R = (t_i \times c_j) \qquad\qquad 1$$
$$L = [(1 - t_i) \times (1 - c_j)] \qquad\qquad 2$$

The decision operation maps these outcomes into responses by way of Luce's choice rule. The probability of an /r/ response given test stimulus S_{ij} is predicted to be

$$P(r \mid S_{ij}) = \frac{t_i \, c_j}{t_i \, c_j + (1 - t_i)(1 - c_j)} \qquad 3$$

The FLMP was fit to the proportion of /r/ identifications as a function of the F_3 of the liquid and the initial consonant context. Five levels of the liquid times 3 phonological contexts gives 15 independent data points to be predicted. In order to predict the results quantitatively, the model requires the estimation of 8 free parameters. Five values of t_i are required for the 5 levels of the F_3 transition of the liquid. Unique c_j values are required for each of the 3 different initial consonant contexts. Fitting the model to the observed data, therefore, requires the estimation of $5 + 3 = 8$ parameters.

The model was fit to each of the children's results individually and also to the average results. The quantitative predictions of the model are determined by using the program STEPIT (Chandler, 1969). The model is represented to the program in terms of a set of prediction equations and a set of unknown parameters. By adjusting the parameters of the model iteratively, the program minimises the squared deviations between the observed and predicted points. The outcome of the program STEPIT is a set of parameter values that, when put into the model, come closest to predicting the observed results. Thus, STEPIT maximises the accuracy of the description of each model. The criterion of best fit was based on the root mean square deviation (RMSD) or the square root of the average squared deviation between predicted and observed points. The RMSD values ranged between 0.0157 and 0.0719 and averaged 0.0312. The RMSD for the fit of the average subject was 0.0264. The lines in Fig. 11.1 give the average predictions of the FLMP. The estimated truth values averaged 0.0308, 0.1482, 0.3681, 0.6381, and 0.9752 for the 5 levels going from /l/ to /r/ along the /l/-/r/ continuum. The estimated truth values averaged 0.1780, 0.5672, and 0.7581 for the phonological contexts /s/, /p/, and /t/, respectively. These parameter estimates of the model are meaningful. The t_i values, representing the degree of match with the prototype R, increase systematically with decreases in the starting frequency of F_3. The c_j values change systematically with phonological context; the degree of match with R given by the context is much larger for initial /t/ than for initial /s/.

As noted in the derivation and fit of the FLMP, the model predicts independent effects of stimulus information and context. One way to demonstrate this prediction is to transform the probability of a predicted response, y, by the inverse logistic transform $x = -ln([1 - y]/y)$. Given response probabilities of 0.05 and 0.15, for example, the respective logistic scores would be -2.94 and -1.74. When the predicted responses are transformed in this manner, the predicted functions are now parallel to one another, as illustrated in Fig. 11.3. The logistic transform of the observed results for the middle 3 levels of the liquid continuum are also shown in Fig. 11.3. Only the middle 3 levels are plotted because some of the predicted responses were 0 or 1 at the other levels— precluding a logistic transform. As can be seen in the figure, both the observed

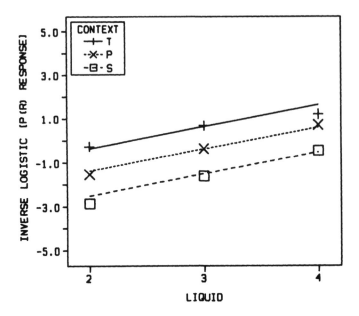

FIG. 11.3. Predicted (lines) and observed (points) inverse logistic transformation of the probability of an /r/ identification for the middle three levels of liquid shown in Fig. 11.1. Context is the curve parameter. The predictions are for the FLMP.

and predicted results are well-described by parallel curves. An analysis of variance on these logistic scores showed no significant interaction between stimulus information and context. We now use these results and predictions to test the assumption of interactive activation.

INTERACTIVE ACTIVATION MODELS

Experimental Test of TRACE

The TRACE model is structured around the process of interactive activation between layers at different levels and also competition within layers. Because of this process, the representation over time of one source of information is modified by another source of information. Contrary to independence predicted by the FLMP, TRACE appears to predict nonindependence of top-down and bottom-up sources of information. Massaro (1989) varied a top-down and a bottom-up source of information in a speech identification task. An important question is whether the top-down context from the lexical level modified the representation at the phoneme level. The TRACE model accounts for the top-down effects of phonological constraints by assuming interactive activation between the word and phoneme levels. Bottom-up activation from the phoneme units activates word units, which in turn activate the phenome units that make them up. Interactive activation appropriately describes this model because it is clearly an interaction between the two levels that is postulated. The amount of bottom-up activation modifies the amount of top-down activation, which then modifies the bottom-up activation, and so on.

In terms of the logistic results in Fig. 11.3, an independent influence of context should simply change the spread among the curves, whereas a nonindependent effect should differentially influence their slopes. Thus, nonindependence effects would be seen in nonparallel functions, contrary to the results that are observed.

I claimed that the concept of interactive activation, as implemented in TRACE, should produce nonindependence effects (Massaro, 1989). Take as an example a liquid phoneme presented after the initial consonant /t/. The liquid would activate both /l/ and /r/ phonemes to some degree; the difference in activation would be a function of the test phoneme. There are many English words that begin with /tr/ but none that begin with /tl/ and, therefore, there would be more top-down activation for /r/ than for /l/. Top-down activation of /r/ would add to the activation of the /r/ phoneme at the phoneme level. What is important for our purposes is that amount of top-down activation is positively related to the amount of bottom-up activation. Now consider the top-down effects for the two adjacent stimuli along the /l/-/r/ continuum. Both test stimuli activate phonemes to some degree, and these phonemes activate words, which then activate these phonemes. Given that two adjacent syllables along the continuum are different, they have different patterns of bottom-up activation, and therefore, the top-down activation must also differ. The difference in the top-down activation will necessarily change the relative activation of the two phonemes. This relationship between top-down and bottom-up activation should be reflected in a nonindependent effect of top-down context.

Because the TRACE model, as originally formulated, cannot be tested directly against the results, a simulation of the experiment with TRACE was compared to the observed results. A simulation allows a test of fundamental properties of TRACE rather than a concern with specific results that are primarily a consequence of the details of the implementation. Differences due to the makeup of the lexicon and specific parameter values are less important than systematic properties of the predictions. Within the current architecture of the TRACE model, the word level appears to play a fundamental role in the discrimination of alternatives at the phoneme level. The most straightforward test of this observation is to simulate results with the standard TRACE model and compare this simulation with the observed results. The simulation used the lexicon, input feature values, and parameter values given in McClelland and Elman (1986, their Tables 1 & 3). Three levels of information about the liquid (l, r, and L) were used as three levels of input information. The phoneme /L/ refers to an intermediate level of a liquid phoneme with neutralised diffuse and acute feature specifications. The other feature specifications for /L/ are the same as those for /l/ and /r/. Thus, the input /L/ activates the two liquids more than the other phonemes, but activates /l/ and /r/ to the same degree. These three liquids were placed after initial /t/, /p/, and /s/ contexts and followed by the vowel /i/. The simulations, therefore, involved a test of these nine stimulus conditions.

A simulation of TRACE involves presentation of a pattern of activation to the units at the feature level. The input is presented sequentially in successive time slices, as would be the case in real speech. The processing of the input goes through a number of cycles in which all of the units update their respective activations at the same time, based on the activations computed in the previous update cycle. The TRACE simulation is completely deterministic; a single run is sufficient for each of the three initial-consonant conditions. The activation of the /l/ and /r/ units at the phoneme level occurred primarily at the 12th time slice of the trace, and these values tended to asymptote around the 54th cycle of the simulation run. Therefore, the activations at the 12th time slice after the 54th cycle were taken as the predictions of the model. The activations of the /r/ and /l/ units as a function of the 3 syllables in the 3 phonological contexts are shown in Table 11.1. These activations cannot be taken as direct measures of the question of the independence of top-down and bottom-up sources of information. In order to assess this question, it is necessary to map these activation levels into predicted responses.

The predicted proportion of /l/ and /r/ responses are not given directly by the activations. McClelland and Elman (1986) assume that the activation a_i of a phoneme unit is transformed by an exponential function into a strength value S_i,

$$S_i = e^{ka_i} \qquad\qquad 4$$

The parameter k is assumed to be 5. The strength value S_i represents the strength of alternative i. The probability of choosing an alternative i, $P(R_i)$, is based on the activations of all relevant alternatives, as described by Luce's (1959) choice rule.

Table 11.1
The TRACE Activations of the /r/ and /l/ Phoneme
Units as a Function of the Bottom-up Information
/l/, /L/, or /r/; and the Top-down Information of
/t/, /p/, or /s/ in Initial Position

| Context | Unit | Test Phoneme | | |
		/l/	/L/	/r/
/t/	/r/	0.46	0.57	0.66
	/l/	0.39	0.12	0.00
/p/	/r/	0.31	0.56	0.65
	/l/	0.52	0.11	0.00
/s/	/r/	0.09	0.23	0.55
	/l/	0.59	0.34	0.17

$$P(R_i) = \frac{S_i}{\Sigma} \qquad\qquad 5$$

where Σ is equal to the sum of the strengths of all relevant phonemes, derived in the manner illustrated for alternative i. The activation values in Table 11.1 were translated into strength values by the exponential function given by Equation 1. The constant k was set equal to 5. The probability of an /r/ judgment was determined from the strength values using Equation 2.

The predicted probability of an /r/ response for three levels of the liquid as a function of whether or not top-down connections are present is shown in Fig. 11.4. To determine if top-down context makes an independent or nonindependent contribution, the response proportions were translated into logistic values. This analysis is analogous to the Braida and Durlach (1972) and Massaro (1979) analyses, except the logistic rather than the Gaussian transform is used. The two transforms are very similar. In addition, the present analysis of independence versus nonindependence parallels the question of sensitivity versus bias in those previous studies and in Massaro (1989). These logistic values are given in Figure 11.5. As can be seen in the figure, the predicted curves are not parallel. In terms of the present analysis, the contribution of top-down context is nonindependent. Thus the simulation is consistent with the intuition that interactive activation between the word and phoneme levels in TRACE produces nonindependent changes at the phoneme level (Massaro, 1988).

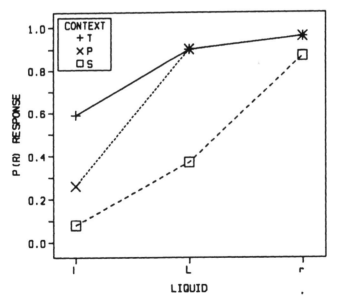

FIG. 11.4.   Probability of an /r/ identification as a function of liquid and context. Predictions of the TRACE model.

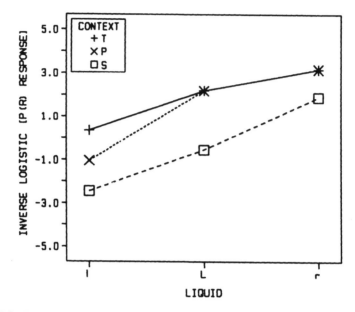

FIG. 11.5 Inverse logistic of the probability of an /r/ identifiction as a function of liquid and context. Predictions of the TRACE model.

At first glance, the effect of the context /p/ seems strange because there is a strong bias for /r/ rather than for /l/. One might have expected very little difference because initial /p/ activates both /pr/ and /pl/ words. However, the makeup of the lexicon used in the simulation favoured /r/ much more than /l/. In this case, the /p/ context functions more like the /t/ context.

The predictions of TRACE were also determined for other values of the constant k, used in Equation 1, that maps activations into strength values. Eight values of k were used, giving a total of eight simulated subjects. The values of k were 0.5, 1, 2, 3.5, 5, 7.5, 10, and 15. For each value of k, there was a nonindependent effect of context. Given that TRACE has been shown to predict nonindependence of stimulus and context, the predictions are falsified by the actual results in Figs. 11.1 and 11.3.

Selective Adaptation with Auditory-Visual Speech

Watching a speaker's face and lips provides important information in speech perception and language understanding (Sumby & Pollack, 1954). This visible speech is particularly effective when the auditory speech is degraded because of noise, bandwidth filtering, or hearing-impairment. The strong influence of visible speech is not limited to situations with degraded auditory input, however. When the visible articulation /pa-pa/ is paired with the sounds /na-na/, subjects often reported hearing /ma-ma/ (McGurk & MacDonald, 1976). A perceiver's recognition of an auditory-visual syllable reflects the contribution of both sound and sight. If a visible /da/ is dubbed with an auditory /ba/, subjects often perceive the speaker to be saying /tha/—a reasonable solution given the psychophysical properties of the two discrepant sources of information (Massaro, 1987).

Roberts and Summerfield (1981) carried out an ingenious study of selective adaptation that provides a critical test of interactive activation (even though the study was carried out independently of the model). In selective adaptation, listeners are exposed to a number of repetitions of an "adapting" syllable and then asked to identify syllables from a speech continuum between two speech categories. Relative to the baseline condition of no adaptation, the identification judgments of syllables along the speech continuum are pushed in the opposite direction of the adapting syllable (a contrast effect). As an example, adaptation with the auditory syllable /be/ (rhymes with *say*) decreases the number of /be/ judgments and increases the number of /de/ judgments along a /be/-/de/ synthetic auditory speech continuum. Roberts and Summerfield (1981) employed different adaptors to evaluate the contribution of auditory and visual information to auditory adaptation along a /be/ to /de/ continuum. After adaptation, subjects identified syllables from an auditory continuum between /be/ and /de/. The adaptors were auditory /be/ and /de/, visual /be/ and /de/, audiovisual (bimodal) /be/ and /de/, and an auditory /be/ paired with a visual /ge/.

How might interactive activation and the TRACE model be formulated to predict the results of selective adaptation? Given auditory and visible speech, separate sets of feature units would be associated with the two different information sources. Figure 11.6 gives a schematic representation of the auditory feature, visual feature, and phoneme layers and the connections between units within and between these layers. The two layers of feature units would both be connected to the phoneme layer. Following the logic of interactive activation, there would be two-way excitatory connections between the feature and phoneme layers, as in the TRACE model. Presentation of auditory speech would activate some units within the auditory feature layer. These activated units would in turn activate certain phoneme units, which would in turn activate units at both feature layers, and so on during the period of interactive activation. Activated units would also inhibit other units within the same layer. If auditory and visual units interact, as assumed by interactive activation, then adaptation to a syllable in one modality should influence later processing of the syllable in the other modality. That is, adaptation with a visual /be/ should activate the phoneme /be/ at the phoneme layer which, in turn, should activate auditory feature units associated with /be/. Thus, a visual /be/ should lead to adaptation along the auditory modality as well as the visual modality. After adaptation with a visual /be/, therefore, the perceiver should be less likely to identify an auditory syllable from a /be/ to /de/ continuum as

PHONEMES

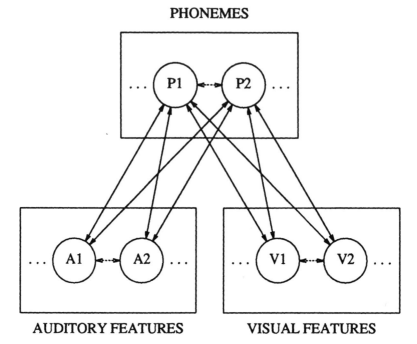

AUDITORY FEATURES   VISUAL FEATURES

FIG. 11.6. Illustration of the TRACE model applied to the recognition of auditory and vidual speech. Two input layers contain auditory and visual feature units, respectively. The third layer contains phoneme units. There are positive connections between two units from different layers and negative connection between two units within the same layer.

/be/. If interactive activation does not occur, on the other hand, auditory adaptation should only be a function of the auditory characteristics of the adaptor and independent of its visual characteristics.

Roberts and Summerfield found no evidence for cross-modal adaptation and thus interactive activation is not supported. The visual adaptors presented alone produced no adaptation along the auditory continuum. Similarly, equivalent levels of adaptation were found for an auditory adaptor and a bimodal adaptor with the same phonetic information. The most impressive result, however, was the adaptation obtained with the conflicting bimodal adaptor. The auditory /be/ paired with visual /ge/ adaptor produced adaptation equivalent to the auditory adaptor /be/. This result occurred even though the subjects usually experienced the bimodal adaptor as /de/ (unfortunately, the authors did not provide an exact measure of the subject's identification of the adaptors). Thus, the adaptation followed the auditory information and was not influenced by the visual information or the phenomenal experience of the bimodal syllable. An interactive activation model would have predicted that the bottom-up activation of the phoneme /d/ would provide top-down activation of the features representing that phoneme. Thus, subjects should not have adapted to the bimodal syllable experienced as /de/ in the same manner as their adaptation to an auditory syllable experienced as /be/. It should be noted that this falsification of interactive-activation models, such as the TRACE model, is solely in the domain of bimodal speech perception and does not address other domains such as the integration of bottom-up and top-down sources of information in speech perception. This latter domain is the topic of the next section.

Phonemic Restoration

Samuel (1981) reports one of the few other existing experiments addressing sensitivity and bias effects in language processing. He employed a signal detection framework in a study of phonemic restoration. In the original type of phonemic-restoration study (Warren, 1970), a phoneme in a word is removed and replaced with some stimulus, such as a tone or white noise. Subjects have difficulty indicating what phoneme is missing. Failure to spot the missing phoneme could be a sensitivity effect or a bias effect. Samuel addressed this issue by creating signal and noise trials. Signal trials contained the original phoneme with superimposed white noise. Noise trials replaced the original phoneme with the same white noise. Subjects were asked to indicate whether or not the original phoneme was present. Sensitivity is reflected in the degree to which the two types of trials can be discriminated, and can be indexed by d' within the context of signal detection theory. Bias would be reflected in the overall likelihood of saying that the original phoneme is present.

To evaluate the top-down effects of lexical constraints, Samuel compared performance on phonemes in test words relative to performance on the phoneme segments presented in isolation. A bias was observed in that subjects were more likely to respond that the phoneme was present in the word than in the isolated segment. In addition, subjects discriminated the signal from the noise trials much better in the segment context than the word context. The d' values averaged about two or three times larger for the segment context than for the word context. In contrast to the results of the study of phonological context discussed in the previous section, there appears to be a large negative effect of top-down context on sensitivity (changes in sensitivity are equivalent to nonindependent effects of stimulus and context). However, the segment versus word comparison in the Samuel study confounds stimulus contributions with top-down contributions. An isolated segment has bottom-up advantages over the same segment presented in a word. Forward and backward masking may degrade the perceptual quality of a segment presented in a word relative to being presented alone. In addition, the word context might provide co-articulatory information about the critical phoneme, which would not be available in the isolated segment.

Samuel carried out a second study that should have overcome the confounding inherent in comparing words and segments. In this study, a word context was compared to a pseudoword context. As an example, the word *living* might be compared to the pseudoword *lathing*, or *modern* might be compared to *madorn*. Samuel also reasoned that pseudowords might show a disadvantage relative to words, simply because subjects would not know what sequence of segments makes up a pseudoword. As an attempt to compensate for this disadvantage for pseudowords, each word or pseudoword was first spoken in intact form (primed) before its presentation as a test item. There was a d' advantage of primed pseudowords over primed words, which Samual interpreted as a sensitivity effect. Analogous to the difference in the segment and word conditions, a stimulus confounding might also be responsible for the difference between pseudowords and words. Natural speech was used and, therefore, an equivalence of stimulus information between the words and pseudowords would not be ensured. In fact, the pseudowords averaged about 10% longer in duration than the words. Longer duration is usually correlated with a higher-quality speech signal, which might explain the advantage of the pseudowords over the words.

In a final experiment, Samuel placed test words in a sentence context. The test word was either predicted or not by the sentence context. The results indicated that the predictability of the test word had a significant influence on bias but not sensitivity. The influence of sentence predictability appears to be a valid comparison because there was no apparent stimulus confounding between the predictable and unpredictable contexts. Given the possibility of stimulus confoundings when sensitivity effects were found and no sensitivity effect with a sentence context, it seems premature to conclude that the phonemic-restoration paradigm produces sensitivity effects. More generally, top-down effects on sensitivity have yet to be demonstrated convincingly, making the concept of top-down activation unnecessary to explain speech perception.

Lexical Context

Elman and McClelland (1988) carried out an ingenious demonstration of context effects in speech perception. Because of coarticulation—the influence of producing one speech segment on the production of another—a given speech segment has different acoustic forms in different contexts. The phonemes /s/ and /ʃ/ are necessarily produced differently, and will differentially influence the production of the following speech segment. Perceivers not only recognise the different speech segments /s/ and /ʃ/, they are apparently able to compensate for the influence of these segments in recognising the following speech segment. During production of speech, coarticulation involves the assimilation of the acoustic characteristics of one sound in the direction of the characteristics of the neighbouring sound. The production of /s/ contains higher-frequency energy than /ʃ/ and coarticulation will result in the sound following /s/ to have higher-frequency energy. The energy in /k/ is somewhat lower in frequency than that in initial /t/—the /t/ has a high burst. Thus, /s/ biases the articulation of a following stop in such a way that the stop segment has somewhat higher-frequency energy. The segment /ʃ/, on the other hand, biases the articulation of a following stop in such a way that the stop segment has somewhat lower-frequency energy. Perceivers apparently take this assimilative coarticulatory influence into account in their perceptual recognition of /t/ and /k/ (and /d/ and /g/), and show a contrast effect. Mann and Repp (1981) showed that recognition of the following segment as /t/ or /k/ is dependent on whether the preceding segment is /s/ or /ʃ/. Given a vowel-fricative syllable followed by a stop-vowel syllable, subjects were more likely to identify the stop as /k/ than /t/ if the preceding fricative was /s/ than if it was /ʃ/ (a contrast effect).

The goal of the Elman and McClelland (1988) study was to induce the same contrast effect, but mediated by the lexical identity of a word rather than the acoustic structure of the preceding syllable. Using synthetic speech, a continuum of speech sounds ranging between *tapes* and *capes* were made by varying the onset properties of the sounds. These sounds were placed after the words *Christmas* and *foolish*. As expected from the Mann and Repp (1981) study, there were more judgments of *capes* following *Christmas* than following *foolish*. However, this dependency could have been triggered directly by the acoustic differences between /s/ and /ʃ/. To eliminate this possibility, Elman and McClelland (1988) created an ambiguous sound half-way between /s/ and /ʃ/ and replaced the original fricatives in *Christmas* and *foolish* with this ambiguous sound. Given a lexical context effect first reported by Ganong (1980) and also replicated by Connine and Clifton (1987), we would expect that the ambiguous segment would tend to be categorized as /s/ when it occurs in *Christmas* and as /ʃ/ when it occurs in *foolish*. The empirical question is whether the same contrast effect would occur given the same ambiguous segment in the two different words? That is, would just the lexical identity of the first word also lead to a contrast effect in the recognition of the following speech segment varying between *tapes* and *capes*? In fact, subjects were more likely to report the test word *capes* following the context word *Christmas* than following the context word *foolish*, and this effect was larger when the segmental information about the /k/–/t/ distinction in the test word was ambiguous.

How does an interactive activation model such as TRACE describe this effect? According to Elman and McClelland (1988), the contrast effect can be induced by assuming connections from the phoneme level in one time slice to the feature level in adjacent time slices (as in TRACE I, Elman & McClelland, 1986). In our example, the units corresponding to /s/ and /ʃ/ would be connected laterally and downward to feature units, which in turn are connected upward to the phoneme units /t/ and /k/. The downward activation from the fricative phoneme to the feature level would modulate the upcoming upward activation from the feature level to the stop phonemes. To describe the lexical effect for the case in which the two words *Christmas* and *foolish* have the same ambiguous final fricative segment, top-down connections from the word level to the phoneme level would activate the appropriate phoneme unit—/s/ and /ʃ/ in *Christmas* and *foolish*, respectively. These units would then activate downward to the feature level, leading to a contrast effect. Because of the assumed top-down activation modulating the bottom-up activation, interactive activation is central to their explanation.

However, an adequate explanation of the Elman and McClelland results does not require interactive activation. Their results simply show that top-down information from the lexical level can influence decisions at the sublexical level. It is the lexical context that disambiguates the final segment of the context word which, in turn, influences identification of the first segment of the following word. That is, we already know that lexical context influences identification of the segments that make up a word (Ganong, 1980). In terms of the FLMP, the lexical context and the segmental information are integrated to achieve perpetual recognition and, therefore, identification of the ambiguous segment. Elman and McClelland (1988) have extended this phenomenon to an indirect measure of identification of the critical segment (/s/ or /ʃ/) by assessing its influence on a following segment (/t/ or /k/). Although this result contributes to the validity of top-down effects on perceptual processing by making the hypothesis of a postperceptual decision less likely, the result appears to be neutral with respect to the existence of interactive activation. In fact, Fig. 11.7 gives the fit of the FLMP to the results (Elman & McClelland, 1988; Experiment 1). Nine free parameters were estimated to predict the 28 data points: 7 for the 7 levels along the tapes-capes continuum, one for the fricative in the intact context word condition, and one for lexical context. The pure lexical context effect is seen in the right panel and the combined effect of lexical context and context segment (/s/ or /ʃ/) is shown in the right panel. It should be emphasised that the FLMP explanation is in terms of perceptual processes, and is not simply a result of a postperceptual decision mechanism. Elman and McClelland (1988) do not justify their argument that process models (such as the FLMP) somehow combine sources of information at a decision level whereas TRACE does so at the level of a perceptual mechanism. Both accounts are computational. Computation is computation—what we attribute it to is more a matter of taste than substance.

AUDITORY/VISUAL SPEECH PERCEPTION

In this section, we describe an experimental study of the perception of auditory and visual speech. The experiment uses an expanded factorial design, illustrated in Fig. 11.8. It provides a powerful method of addressing the issues of the evaluation and integration of audible and visible information in speech perception. Five levels of audible speech varying between /ba/ and /da/ are crossed with five levels of visible speech varying between the same alternatives.

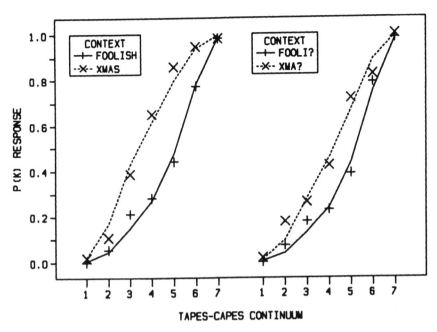

FIG. 11.7.   Observed (points) and predicted (lines) probability of a /k/ identification as a function of stimulus and preceding context for original and ambiguous preceding consonant. The predictions are for the FLMP.

The audible and visible speech are also presented alone, giving a total of $25 + 5 + 5 = 35$ independent stimulus conditions.

Method.   Eleven college students from the University of California, Santa Cruz, participated for one hour in the experiment. Auditory tokens of a male speaker's /ba/ and /da/ were analysed using linear prediction to derive a set of parameters for driving a software formant serial resonator speech synthesiser (Klatt, 1980). By altering the parametric information specifying the first 80msec of the consonant-vowel syllable, a set of 5 400msec syllables covering the range from /ba/ to /da/ was created. During the first 80msec, the first formant (F1) went from 250Hz to 700Hz following a negatively accelerated path. The F2 followed a negatively accelerated path to 1199Hz, beginning with one of 5 values equally spaced between 1125 and 1625Hz from most /ba/-like to most /da/-like, respectively. The F3 followed a linear transition to 2729Hz from one of 5 values equally spaced between 2325 and 2825Hz. All other stimulus characteristics were identical for the 5 auditory syllables. These stimuli were stored in digital form for playback during the experiment.

The visible speech synthesis was based on the work of Parke (1982), who developed an animated face by modelling the facial surface as a polyhedral

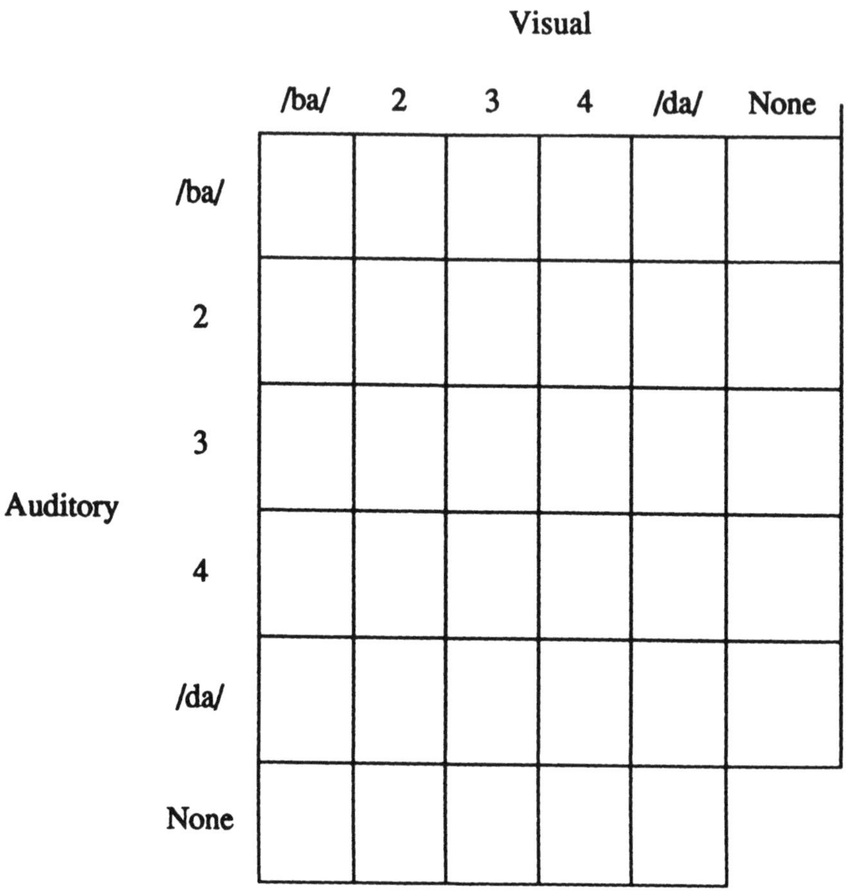

Visual

	/ba/	2	3	4	/da/	None
/ba/						
2						
3						
4						
/da/						
None						

Auditory

FIG. 11.8. Expansion of a typical factorial design to include auditory and visual conditions presented alone. The five levels along the auditory and visible continua represent auditory and visible speech syllables varying in equal steps between /ba/ and /da/.

object composed of about 900 small surfaces arranged in 3 dimensions and joined together at the edges. The surface was shaded to achieve a natural appearance of the skin. The face was animated by altering the location of various points in the face under the control of 50 parameters. The parameters controlling speech animation include the duration of the segment, the manner of articulation, jaw opening angle, mouth width and protrusion values, width of the lip corners, mouth corner, x, y, and z offsets, lower lip /f/ tuck, and degree of upper lip raise. There is no tongue in the current version. Software provided by Pearce, Wyvill, Wyvill, and Hill (1986) was implemented and modified by us on a Silicon Graphics Inc. IRIS 3030 computer to create synthetic visible speech syllables. The control parameters were changed over time to produce a realistic articulation of a consonant-vowel syllable. By modifying the parameters appropriately, a five-step /ba/ to /da/ visible speech continuum was synthesised.

The synthetic visible speech was created frame by frame and recorded on a Betacam video recorder which was later transferred to $\frac{3}{4}''$ U-matic video tape. The 5 levels of visible speech were edited to a second $\frac{3}{4}''$ tape according to a randomised sequence in blocks of 35 trials. There was a 28sec interval between blocks of trials. Six unique test blocks were recorded with the 35 test items presented in each block. The edited tape was copied to $\frac{1}{2}''$ VHS tape for use during the experiment. It was played on a Panasonic NV-9200 and fed to individual NEC C12-202A 12" colour monitors. The auditory speech was presented over the speaker of the NEC monitor. The presentation of the auditory synthetic speech was synchronised with the visible speech for the bimodal stimulus presentations. This synchronisation gave the strong illusion that the synthetic speech was coming from the mouth of the speaker.

Subjects were instructed to listen and to watch the speaker, and to identify the syllable as /ba/ or /da/. Each of the 35 possible stimuli were presented a total of 12 times during 2 sessions of 6 blocks of trials in each session. The subjects identified each stimulus during a 2sec response interval.

Results. The observed proportion of /da/ identifications was computed for each subject for each of the 35 conditions. The mean proportion of /da/ identifications across subjects is shown by the points in Fig. 11.9. As can be seen, the proporation of /da/ responses significantly increased across the visual continuum, both for the unimodal, $F(4,40) = 74.78$, $p < 0.001$, and bimodal, $F(4,40) = 16.50$, $p < 0.001$, conditions. Similarly, the proportion of /da/ responses significantly increased across the auditory continuum, for both the unimodal $F(4,40) = 61.23$, $p < 0.001$, and bimodal, $F(4,40) = 30.82$, $p < 0.001$, conditions. There was also a significant auditory visual interaction, $F(16,160) = 4.61$, $p < 0.001$, in the bimodal condition, because each stimulus dimension had its greatest effect to the extent that the other was most ambiguous.

Test of the FLMP

Applying the model to the task of identifying auditory-visual speech, both sources are assumed to provide continuous and independent evidence for the alternatives /ba/ and /da/. Defining the onsets of the second (F2) and third (F3) formants as the important auditory feature and the degree of initial opening of the Lips as the important visual feature, the prototype for /da/ would be:

/da/ : Slightly Falling F2–F3 & Open Lips.

The prototype for /ba/ would be defined in an analogous fashion,

/ba/ : Rising F2–F3 & Closed Lips,

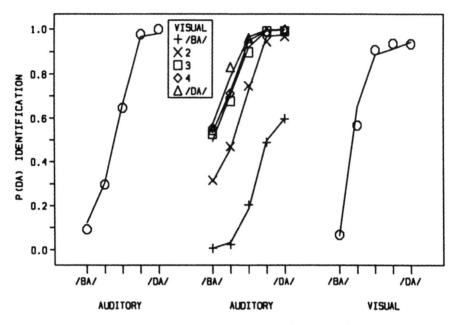

FIG. 11.9. Observed (points) and predicted (lines) proportion of /da/ identifications for the auditory alone (left panel), bimodal (center panel), and visual alone (right panel) conditions as a function of synthetic auditory and visual stimulus conditions. The lines give the predictions for the FLMP.

and so on for the other response alternatives. Given that a prototype has independent specifications for the auditory and visual sources, the value of one source cannot change the value of the other source at the prototype matching stage. The integration of the features defining each prototype is evaluated according to the product of the feature values. If a_i represents the degree to which the auditory stimulus A_i supports the alternative /da/, that is, has Slightly Falling F2–F3; and v_j represents the degree to which the visual stimulus V_j supports the alternative /da/, that is, has Open Lips, then the outcome of prototype matching for /da/ would be;

$$/da/ \quad : \quad a_i \, v_j$$

where the subscripts i and j index the levels of the auditory and visual modalities, respectively. Given the contrasting alternatives /da/ and /ba/, it is reasonable to assume that the feature values for /ba/ are the negation of those for /da/. Following fuzzy logic (Zadeh, 1965), negation is implemented as the additive complement. In this case, the outcome of prototype matching for /ba/ would be:

$$/ba/ \quad : \quad (1 - a_i)(1 - v_j)$$

The decision operation would determine the relative merit of the /ba/ and /da/ alternatives, leading to the prediction that:

$$P(/da/\mid AiVj) = \frac{a_i\,v_j}{\Sigma} \qquad 6$$

where Σ is equal to the sum of the merit of the /ba/ and /da/ alternatives.

The important assumption of the FLMP is that the auditory source supports each alternative to some degree and analogously for the visual source. Each alternative is defined by ideal values of the auditory and visual information. Each level of a source supports each alternative to differing degrees represented by feature values. The feature values representing the degree of support from the auditory and visual information for a given alternative are integrated following the multiplicative rule given by the FLMP. The model requires five parameters for the visual feature values and five parameters for the auditory feature values.

The FLMP was fit to the individual results of each of the 11 subjects. The lines in Fig. 11.9 give the average predictions of FLMP. The model provides a good description of the identifications of both the unimodal and bimodal syllables with an average RMSD of 0.0574 across the individual subject fits.

Table 11.2 gives the average best fitting parameters of the FLMP. As can be seen in the table, the parameter values change in a systematic fashion across the five levels of the audible and visible synthetic speech. The values provide an index of the relative contribution of the two sources of information. They show that the visible speech was as influential as the auditory speech in this situation of face-to-face speech perception. We now use these results to test feedforward models.

FEEDFORWARD CONNECTIONIST MODELS

We now consider several simple feedforward connectionist models in which the connections exist in only one bottom-up direction—from input to output. We formulate and test three classes of models: two-layer, and constrained and unconstrained three-layer models. In all of the models, two of the layers correspond to input and an output, as illustrated in Fig. 11.10. The three-layer models also contain a hidden layer of units between the input and output layers,

Table 11.2

The Average Best Fitting Parameters of the FLMP: The Values Lie Between 0 and 1 and Represent the Degree to which the Alternative /da/ is Supported by Auditory and Visual Sources of Information

Parameter	/ba/	2	3	4	/da/
a_i	0.1206	0.3054	0.6653	0.9667	0.9805
v_j	0.0623	0.6525	0.8880	0.9129	0.9452

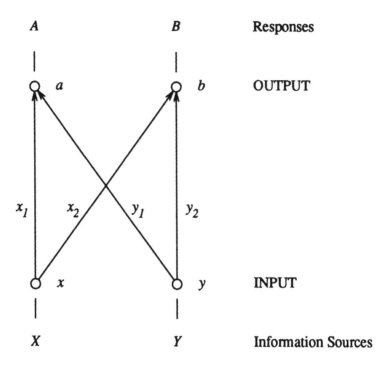

FIG. 11.10. Illustration and connectionist model with inputs X and Y, input units x and y, output units a and b, and responses A and B. The activations entering a from x and y are x_1 and y_1, and analogously for b. In the fit of the model, it is assured that $x_2 = -x_1$ and $y_2 = y_1$.

as illustrated in Fig. 11.11. Unconstrained models with hidden units assume that all input units are connected to all hidden units and all hidden units are connected to all output units (Rumelhart *et al.* 1986). In constrained models, each input unit is connected to only some subset of hidden units. Constrained models allow a reduced reduction of the required number of free parameters (weights). Finally, these models can have a threshold unit associated with each hidden unit and each output unit.

Model Tests

The two-layer model is assumed to have input and output layers of neural units, with all input units connected to all output units. It is assumed that each level of each source of information is represented by a unique unit at the input layer. Each response alternative is represented by a unique unit at the output layer. An input unit has zero activation, unless its corresponding level of the stimulus dimension is presented. This constraint ensures that only one input unit is activated given presentation of a source of information. There are two sources of information in the experiment: auditory place and visual place information—

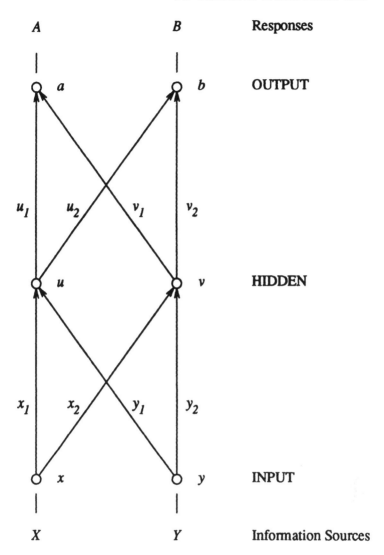

FIG. 11.11.   Illustration of unconstrained connectionist model with inputs X and Y, input units x and y, hidden units u and v, output units a and b, and responses A and B. The activations entering u from x and y are x_1 and y_1, and analogously for v. The activations entering a from u and v are u_1 and v_1, and analogously for b.

abbreviated X and Y, respectively. Given five levels each of X and Y, there are ten input units. Presentation of an input unit's target stimulus gives an input of one. The activation of an output unit by an input unit is given by the multiplicative combination of the input activation and a weight w. This weight can be considered a free parameter, whose value is adjusted to reflect the amount of activation the input unit has on the output unit. Given the design, one or two input units can be activated. With two active inputs X_i and Y_j, the activation entering output unit a is $x_1 + y_1$, where $x_1 = w\, X_i$ and $2y_1 = v\, Y_j$. The weights on the activations entering the other output units are also free parameters. In this case, the activation entering output unit b is $x_2 + y_2$. The total activation leaving an output unit is given by the sum of the input activations, passed through a sigmoid squashing function (Rumelhart, et al., 1986). Therefore, for an $X_i\, Y_j$ stimulus,

$$a = \frac{1}{1 + e^{-[x_1 + y_1]}}$$

7

The "neural processing" of this connectionist model does not specify the stimulus-response function completely. The activations at the output layer have to be mapped into a response, and a relative goodness rule (RGR) is usually assumed to describe this mapping (Massaro & Friedman, 1990). Taking this tack, the activation a transformed into a response probability by the RGR gives

$$P(A \mid X\, Y) = \frac{\dfrac{1}{1 + e^{-[x_1 + y_1]}}}{\dfrac{1}{1 + e^{-[x_1 + y_1]}} + \dfrac{1}{1 + e^{-[x_2 + y_2]}}}$$

8

In summary, evaluation consists of the activation of neural-like units. Integration involves the summation of the separate activations and passing them through the sigmoid squashing function. Decision follows the relative goodness rule. Massaro and Cohen (1987) and Massaro and Friedman (1990) proved that this two-layer model with two response alternatives is mathematically equivalent to the FLMP. Thus, we should not be surprised to find that this model gives an adequate description of the results.

For the 3-layer models, hidden units intervene between the input and output layers. We develop both a constrained and an unconstrained model—each with roughly the same number of free parameters as the 2-layer model. The constrained model has 2 hidden units and the unconstrained model has one hidden unit. In the constrained model, each of the 2 hidden units is connected to only 1 of the two sources of information. In contrast, all inputs are connected to the hidden unit in the unconstrained model. In the fit of the models, it can be assumed that $x_2 = -x_1$ and $y_2 = -y_1$. Thus, the 2-layer model in Fig. 11.10 has 10 and 11 weights for the non-threshold and threshold versions of the 2-layer model. The constrained 3-layer model with 2 hidden units has 15 free weights, and the unconstrained version with 1 hidden unit has 13 free weights. All models provide a reasonable description of the results. The 2-layer models with and without a threshold unit and the 3-layer model gave roughly equivalent descriptions of the results (RMSD of 0.036). The 2-layer model with a threshold unit did not give a better fit than the 2-layer model without a threshold. The unconstrained 3-layer model with one hidden unit did not give a better fit (RMSD of 0.037) than the 2-layer model—even though the 3-layer model has 5 additional free weights. Thus, a third layer is not necessarily beneficial, if roughly the same number of free weights is used. Increasing the number of free weights by assuming 2 hidden units (see Fig. 11.11) allows the 3-layer model to give a better fit (RMSD of 0.016). However, the number of free weights (25) approaches the number of independent observations (35) being predicted.

Superpower of Hidden Unit Models

In a theoretical and analytical analysis, I have shown that models with hidden units are superpowerful—that is, they can predict many types of results and even results that do not occur (Massaro, 1988). Because these models can predict many results—not just those that are empirically observed—superpower might be better described as flabbiness.

Studies using network models with hidden units have been used in a variety of speech recognition tasks. In one study, a network was designed to recognise the 7 syllables, do, re, mi, fa, so, la and ti (Landauer, Kamm, & Singhal, 1987). The input was a continuous utterance of 15 random syllables spoken by a professional media announcer. The input was preprocessed to give a representation assumed to be somewhat analogous to that created by the human ear. This representation consisted of an amplitude measure for each of 15 frequency regions for every 2msec. The unit of analysis was a 150msec "window" of the speech signal. A given 150msec segment had $75 \times 15 = 1125$ continuous measures as input to 1125 input nodes. This 150msec window was moved along the complete utterance in 2msec steps. There were 7 output nodes corresponding to the 7 test syllables and 20 hidden units. This architecture gives a total of $1125 \times 20 + 20 \times 7 + 27 = 22{,}667$ connection weights that are available to describe an input-output mapping.

The system was trained to agree with the performance of a human listener, who judged each 150msec segment of the utterance and rated the degree to which it was a given alternative or gave a rating that indicated that no alternative was viable for that given segment. These ratings were used as target output values for the system. Given these target values, the system learned similar values in about 90 trials—iterations of adjusting the weights. If the complete utterance was 3secs in duration, then there were about 1350 ratings to be predicted, many fewer than the number of connection weights used to make the predictions. Therefore, the model is essentially assuming more than it is predicting and good performance by the model in this situation should not be surprising. For example, a 2-layer model might have done just as well with fewer free parameters. Until more reasonable models are tested, no judgment about the success of network models with hidden units for speech recognition seems possible.

DISCUSSION

Both interactive activation and feedforward connectionist models characterise the transmission and transformation of information between some speech signal and its identification. In the TRACE model, the activation of units in the trace determines which alternative is identified. The input activations generated from bottom-up sources of information are eventually changed by activation at the word level. In contrast, feedforward models are unidirectional and the bottom-up information is not obliterated by the contribution of top down information. As in the FLMP, the feedforward model allows for lower-level information to remain independent of higher-level information, although a *decision* about lower-level information will reflect the contribution of the higher-level information. In interactive-activation models, however, the contribution of higher-level sources of information to lower-level decisions must come at the expense of modifying the representation of the lower-level information. This aspect of the TRACE model has been falsified in several studies (see earlier), and it is noted that there is no unambiguous evidence for interactive activation in the literature.

ACKNOWLEDGEMENTS

The research reported in this paper and the writing of the paper were supported, in part, by grants from the Public Health Service (PHS R01 NS 20314), the National Science Foundation (BNS 8812728), a James McKeen Cattell Fellowship, and the graduate division of the University of California, Santa Cruz. The author would like to thank Jeff Elman for making the simulation program for TRACE available, Alan Kawamoto and Stephen Kitzis for valuable discussions, and Michael Cohen for eclectic assistance.

REFERENCES

Braida, L.D. & Durlach, N.I. (1972). Intensity perception II: Resolution in one-interval paradigms. *Journal of the Acoustical Society of America, 51*, 483–502.

Chandler, J.P. (1969). Subroutine STEPIT—Finds local minima of a smooth function of several parameters. *Behavioral Science, 14*, 81–82.

Cohen, M.M. & Massaro, D.W. (1976). Real-time speech synthesis. *Behavior Research Methods & Instrumentation, 8*, 189–196.

Connine, C.M. & Clifton, C. (1987). Interactive use of lexical information in speech perception. *Journal of Experimental Psychology: Human Perception and Performance, 13*, 291–299.

Elman, J. & McClelland, J. (1986). Exploiting lawful variability in the speech wave. In J.S. Perkell & D.H. Klatt (Eds.), *Invariance and variability in speech processes*. Hillsdale, N.J.: Lawrence Erlbaum Associates Inc.

Elman, J. & McClelland, J. (1988). Cognitive penetration of the mechanisms of perception: Compensation for coarticulation of lexically restored phonemes. *Journal of Memory and Language, 27*, 143–165.

Ganong, W.F. III (1980). Phonetic categorization in auditory word recognition. *Journal of Experimental Psychology: Human Perception and Performance, 6*, 110–125.

Jusczyk, P.W. (1986). Speech perception. In K.R. Boff, L. Kaufman, & J.P. Thomas (Eds.), *Handbook of perception and human performance, Vol.II: Cognitive processes and performance*. New York: John Wiley & Sons.

Klatt, D.H. (1980). Software for a cascade/parallel formant synthesizer. *Journal of the Acoustical Society of America, 67*, 971-995.

Klatt, D.H. (1989). Review of selected models of speech perception. In W. Marslen-Wilson (Ed.), *Lexical representation and process.* Cambridge, Mass.: M.I.T. Press, 169-226.

Landauer, T.K., Kamm, C.A., & Singhal, S. (1987). Network to recognize speech sounds. *Proceedings of the Cognitive Science Society*, 531-536. Hillsdale, N.J.: Lawrence Erlbaum Associates Inc.

Luce, R.D. (1959). *Individual choice behavior.* New York: John Wiley & Sons.

Mann, V.A. & Repp, B.H. (1981). Influence of preceding fricative on stop consonant perception. *Journal of the Acoustical Society of America, 69,* 548-558.

Massaro, D.W. (Ed.) (1975). *Understanding language: An information-processing analysis of speech perception, reading, and psycholinguistics.* New York: Academic Press.

Massaro, D.W. (1979). Letter information and orthographic context in word perception. *Journal of Experimental Psychology: Human Perception and Performance, 5*, 595-609.

Massaro, D.W. (1987). *Speech perception by ear and eye: A paradigm for psychological inquiry.* Hillsdale, N.J.: Lawrence Erlbaum Associates Inc.

Massaro, D.W. (1988). Some criticisms of connectionist models of human performance. *Journal of Memory and Language, 27*, 213-234.

Massaro, D.W. (1989). Testing between the TRACE model and the fuzzy logical model of speech perception. *Cognitive Psychology, 21*, 398-421.

Massaro, D.W. & Cohen, M.M. (1983). Phonological context in speech perception. *Perception and Psychophysics, 34*, 338-348.

Massaro, D.W. & Cohen, M.M. (1987). *Process and connectionist models of pattern recognition.* Proceedings of the Ninth Annual Conference of the Cognitive Science Society. Hillsdale, N.J.: Lawrence Erlbaum Associates Inc.

Massaro, D.W. & Friedman, D. (1990). Models of integration given multiple sources of information. *Psychological Review.*

Massaro, D.W. & Oden, G.C. (1980). Speech perception: A framework for research and theory. In N.J. Lass (Ed.), *Speech and language: Advances in basic research and practice: Vol. 3*, New York: Academic Press, 129-165.

McClelland, J.L. & Elman, J.L. (1986). The TRACE model of speech perception. *Cognitive Psychology, 18*, 1-86.

McGurk, H. & MacDonald. J. (1976). Hearing lips and seeing voices. *Nature, 264*, 746-748.

Minsky, M. & Papert, S. (1969). *Perceptrons.* Cambridge, Mass.: M.I.T. Press.

Oden, G.C. & Massaro, D.W. (1978). Integration of featural information in speech perception. *Psychological Review, 85*, 172-191.

Parke, F.I. (1982). Parametized models for facial animation. *IEEE Computer Graphics, 2*, 61-68.

Pearce, A., Wyvill, B., Wyvill, G., & Hill, D. (1986). Speech and expression: A computer solution to face animation. *Graphics Interface '86*, 136-140. Vancouver, British Columbia: Canadian Information Processing Society.

Platt, J.R. (1964). Strong inference. *Science, 146*, 347-353.

Roberts, M. & Summerfield, Q.U. (1981). Audiovisual presentation demonstrates that selective adaptation in speech perception is purely auditory. *Perception & Psychophysics, 30*, 309-314.

Rumelhart, D.E., Hinton, G.E., & Williams, R.J. (1986). Learning internal representations by error propagation. In D.E. Rumelhart & J.L. McClelland (Eds.), *Parallel distributed processing, Vol. I: Foundations.* Cambridge, Mass.: M.I.T. Press.

Rumelhart, D.E. & McClelland, J.L. (Eds.) (1986a). *Parallel distributed processing: Vol. 1. Foundations.* Cambridge, Mass.: M.I.T. Press.

Rumelhart, D.E. & McClelland, J.L. (1986b). On learning the past tenses of English verbs. In J.L. McClelland & D.E. Rumelhart (Eds.), *Parallel distributed processing, Vol. 2.* Cambridge, Mass.: M.I.T. Press.

Samuel, A.G. (1981). Phonemic restoration: Insights from a new methodology. *Journal of Experimental Psychology: General, 110*, 474–494.

Selfridge, O.G. (1959). Pandemonium: A paradigm for learning. In HMSO, *Mechanization of thought processes* London: Her Majesty's Stationery Office, 511–526.

Sumby, W.H. & Pollack, I. (1954). Visual contribution to speech intelligibility in noise. *Journal of the Acoustical Society of America, 26*, 212–215.

Warren, R.M. (1970). Perceptual restoration of missing speech sounds. *Science, 167*, 392–393.

Zadeh, L.A. (1965). Fuzzy sets. *Information and Control, 8*, 338–353.

12 Connectionism: A New Breed of Bottom-up Model?

Dennis Norris
*Medical Research Council Applied Psychology Unit, 15 Chaucer Road,
Cambridge CB2 2EF, U.K.*

INTRODUCTION

In this chapter I want to consider one aspect of the relation between connectionism and the traditional information processing approach to cognitive psychology. The precise philosophical relationship between connectionism and symbolic approaches to cognitive psychology seems likely to be a subject of fervent debate for many years to come (e.g. Fodor & Pylyshyn, 1988; Pinker & Prince, 1988; Smolensky, 1988). It may seem that the pragmatic psychologist could safely ignore this philosophical debate and concentrate on the more important task of developing and testing new psychological theories. However, like it or not, this debate does have important implications for the way in which psychologists go about their daily activities.

It is often claimed that connectionism gives us a new language for describing psychological theories. The central question, though, is: Does that new language simply give us a way of describing and implementing the processes represented by the boxes of traditional box models, or do connectionist models behave in ways that mean there is no simple mapping between the connectionist models and the box models?

This is an important question for two main reasons. First, most of us are rather more familiar with old-style box models than we are with connectionist models. If we try to understand connectionist models in terms of concepts derived from traditional models, are we likely to be misled? Second, cognitive psychology has developed a number of techniques to simplify the process of mapping between theory and data. For example, additive factors methodology (Sternberg, 1969), cascade systems (McClelland, 1979), double dissociation, and so forth have all been used in an attempt to map out the number and nature of mental processes and the relation between them. But do all of these valued tools apply as well to connectionist models as they do to more familiar forms of psychological theory? If connectionism does turn out to be nothing more than a new technique for implementing old theories, then we can safely continue using our tried and tested procedures—they may not really be very reliable, but at least they won't be any worse because of connectionism. On the other hand, if connectionist models have a new character all of their own, we may have to equip ourselves with an entirely new battery of techniques to help assess them empirically.

In the present chapter I want to examine these issues by concentrating on the problem of deciding whether two processes interact or not. In particular I will be considering the relation between lexical processes and the sublexical processes of letter and phoneme identification. Getting clear-cut evidence that processes interact has always been a difficult problem, although there do seem to be a few cases where we feel we can give a definitive answer. But does connectionism change the way we assess the evidence?

When we describe models as "top down,", "bottom-up,", "interactive," or "autonomous," we think we are doing more than simply attaching a label. The whole purpose of the label is to tell us something about how the system behaves. But in some connectionist systems the behaviour does not seem to fit the label— that is, if we can even get as far as deciding which label is appropriate. Many of these difficulties in characterising connectionist models have their roots in the marriage of connectionism and "interactionism," which took place in the early interactive activation models of visual and spoken word recognition.

INTERACTIVE ACTIVATION MODELS

Despite the tremendous growth in interest in connectionism during recent years, the early interactive activation models remain the most influential connectionist models in cognitive psychology to date. Probably because of their ability to account for a wide range of empirical data, McClelland and Rumelhart's model of visual word recognition (McClelland & Rumelhart, 1981; Rumelhart & McClelland, 1982) and McClelland and Elman's (1986) TRACE model of spoken word recognition continue to have a greater impact than many of the more technologically advanced models of recent years. Part of the appeal of these models is that the interactive activation framework captured what was seen by many as a central characteristic of human language perception; its highly interactive nature and its emphasis on top-down processing.

Although they represent a radical departure from earlier psychological models in having a very novel and highly interactive architecture, they nevertheless have a very conventional hierarchical structure. The internal structure of the models consists of a featural level, a letter or phoneme level, and a word level. Representations are strictly local, and there is a very simple and concrete correspondence between each node and things in the real world. Also, levels in the model echo levels of linguistic description.

It is worth pointing out that subsequent learning models don't represent a simple progression from the interactive activation models. For example, we can't simply present a back-propagation network with suitable training data and expect it to learn to wire itself up like TRACE or the interactive activation model (IAM). There is no problem in getting a simple three-layered net to learn to map between features and words, but with backpropagation there is no control over the kind of representations the network will form at the level of the hidden units. The network will simply construct whatever representations it needs to perform its task. That is, there is no guarantee that the nodes at the middle level will come to represent letters or phonemes. Indeed, it tends to be a characteristic of the standard backpropagation algorithm that it forms distributed rather than local representations. So, even if the hidden units do come to develop phonemic representations, each phoneme will most likely be represented by a pattern of activation distributed across a set of hidden units rather than by a single unit. This means that the individual hidden units themselves cannot serve directly to identify which phonemes are present in the input. If a distributed pattern of activation is to be translated into a single output response, then we would need an additional network to interpret that activation pattern.

It might seem that the difficulty of implementing a learning model with the same hierarchical structure as the interactive activation models is just a temporary problem with the technology. Soon we will be able to do this with unsupervised learning schemes and with backpropagation algorithms designed to develop localised representations. However, it is not clear that this is the right approach to take at all.

Strictly hierarchical models, like TRACE, suffer from a major weakness. Their structure implies that the ability to recognise phonemes is an essential prerequisite to word recognition. Without the phoneme level one could not recognise words. Conversely, the ability to recognise words implies that one can identify phonemes. Words can only be recognised by identifying their constituent phonemes. The problem is that the evidence from human development suggests that the ability to identify phonemes explicitly is only acquired after learning to read (Liberman, Shankweiler, Liberman, Fowler, & Fisher, 1977; Morais, Cary, Algeria, & Bertelson, 1979; Morais, Bertelson, Cary, & Algeria, 1986). Indeed, phoneme identification seems to be contingent on learning to read in an alphabetic orthography (Read, Zhang, Nie, & Ding, 1986). If phoneme identification and word recognition are both dependent on the same set of phoneme nodes, then learning to identify words should immediately confer the listener with the ability to identify phonemes.

Now, strictly speaking, all this implies is that access to the phonemic level is dependent on the skills acquired in learning to read. It certainly does not imply that the development of phonemic representations themselves is contingent on learning to read. Literacy may simply lead to the development of phonemic awareness. In the context of a model like TRACE, this suggests that a learning process is required in order to read out the information available at the phoneme nodes. Activation of a phoneme node does not, of itself, lead to phonemic awareness. Therefore an additional component must be added to the model which is capable of learning how to read out information from the phoneme nodes. However, if phoneme nodes have no direct contact with awareness, one might suggest that it does not really matter too much what sort of sub-lexical representations the net employs. Any kind of representation that will subserve phonemic identification will do perfectly well. No matter what kind of representations develop when learning to recognise words, we could still learn how to map between those representations and phonemes in order to develop phonemic awareness. This suggests that a simple feed-forward backpropagation net with a single layer of hidden units might be a suitable kind of architecture after all. It doesn't really matter if the net doesn't develop hidden units corresponding to individual phonemes. Once the net has been trained to recognise words then it can be taught how to identify phonemes from the patterns of activation at the hidden units. This corresponds to the kind of simple architecture shown in Fig. 12.1. Here phonemes and words are effectively treated as being units at the same level of analysis as far as the network is concerned. As with TRACE and the IAM, there have to be position-specific phoneme (or letter) units in this simple network. Note that there is no direct output from the hidden units. The only way we can examine the representations at this level is by their indirect effects on phoneme or word identification.

The interesting feature of this simple model is that, unlike the interactive activation models, it is entirely bottom-up. In common with most of the new generation of learning models employing backpropagation (e.g. Seidenberg & McClelland 1989), this network has a completely feed-forward architecture. The flow of activation in these networks is entirely bottom-up. No node in the network ever passes activation to a node in an earlier layer in the net. Note that although the figures in Seidenberg and McClelland's papers give the impression that in their model the orthographic output is fed back to the input, a careful reading of the text reveals that this is not the case. The model is strictly feed-forward. As the term "backpropagation" implies, learning in these networks involves passing an error term back down the net even in feed-forward systems. However, the important feature of these networks is that, once the model is trained, it will carry on performing with no top-down flow of information at all. We know that these feed-forward nets are very powerful, but could a bottom-up model of this form account for all of the evidence suggesting that lexical information can influence phoneme and letter identification?

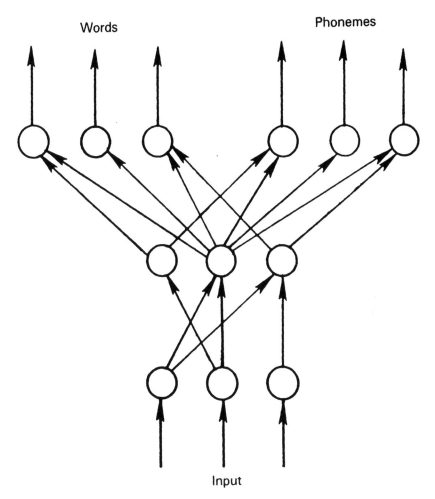

FIG. 12.1. Simple feed-forward network for simulating the word superiority effect (not all connections are shown).

A SIMPLE NETWORK FOR WORD AND LETTER RECOGNITION

As a simple demonstration experiment, a net such as that shown in Figure 12.1 was trained on a set of 50 words and 50 nonwords. In fact all 100 items were real English words, but the net was only trained to classify 50 of these items as "words." Letters were coded in terms of the same feature set used in Rumelhart and McClelland's interactive activation model. The net received two kinds of training, which alternated with each other on successive training cycles. In one kind of training the net was presented with only the words and was trained to activate the corresponding word node in response to each input word. The phoneme/letter nodes were treated as a "don't care" condition. That is, whatever output the net produced at the letter nodes, it was told that it had produced the correct output, or to put it another way, it was never told that it had made an error. This condition was designed to represent teaching a child to recognise words while not giving any feedback about the identities of the letters within those words. In the second kind of training the net was presented with both the word and the nonword inputs. This time the word nodes were treated as a don't care condition while the net was taught to identify the letters in the input. This condition was designed to represent training on identifying letters of the alphabet. Overall, the net was therefore taught how to classify half of the stimuli as words and was given equal training on identifying the letters in both words and nonwords.

At the end of the training procedure the net was found to be able to identify letters in words better than it could identify letters in nonwords. This word-superiority effect still held even when the experiment was repeated with the assignment of stimuli to the word and nonword categories reversed. Whatever the basis of this result, it is clearly not due to the nature of the particular stimuli employed in the word and nonword conditions.

A similar experiment was performed using a set of word and nonword stimuli and a set of "letter" stimuli. In this simulation the net was trained to identify words and letters and was also trained to identify letters appearing "in isolation" (because the net has position-sensitive input slots, the net was trained on position-specific letters, with empty slots set to zero). Subsequent testing revealed that the net was able to identify letters in stimuli it had learned to classify as words better than in nonwords. (In this case the net had never been exposed to nonwords during training.) In this experiment the word superiority effect still held despite the fact that the net had never been taught to identify letters in either the words or the nonwords used in testing.

How can such a simple bottom-up model show what appears to be a strong top-down effect of lexical information? The answer to this question lies with the fact that all backpropagation nets have a top-down flow of information during learning. During the process of recognising a word or phoneme the information flow will be completely bottom-up. In contrast to the IAM models, there is no continuous feedback from higher to lower levels during recognition. However, after each forward pass of information through the net there is a backward pass, in which the error is propagated back down the net in order to update the weights and make the net learn. This means that the success of the net in identifying both phonemes and words will influence the weights in both layers of the net. Errors in identifying words will alter the weights from the hidden units to the word units and also from the input units to the hidden units. The weights from the input units will also be influenced by errors in phoneme identification. The first layer of weights therefore has to subserve both word identification and letter identification. These weights have to be optimised so that they will perform the tasks of word and letter identification simultaneously. This is the source of the "top-down" effect.

If the net had sufficient capacity and learning experience it could potentially learn to perform both tasks independently. For example, it might be possible for the net to allocate one subset of the hidden units (and the weights from the input units to the hidden units) exclusively to word identification and the remainder to letter identification. Letter identiciation would then be totally unaffected by whether the letters appeared in words or nonwords. In fact, increasing the number of hidden units, or making the letters easier to discriminate, does tend to reduce or even eliminate the word-superiority effect. However, with smaller numbers of hidden units, the need to satisfy the constraints imposed by having to identify both words and letters leads the net to develop a set of weights which are better suited to identifying letters in words than letters in nonwords. Even though the net is never trained to identify a word and the letters in a word simultaneously, it still has to develop a set of weights that are suited to both tasks.

Some doubt must remain, though, as to whether this network architecture really should be called "bottom-up." Any network being trained with the backpropagation learning algorithm must be at least partially "top-down." While the net is still learning there must be some top-down flow of information in the form of the error signal being propagated back from the output to alter the weights. However, once learning has been turned off, all information flow is totally bottom-up. So, although learning is top-down processing is entirely bottom-up. Note also that the form of the top-down information is very different from the top-down information in an interactive activation model. In an interactive activation model the processing involved in recognising a word takes place over many cycles through the net. During the recognition of a single word, activation flows in both a bottom-up and a top-down direction. The top-down activation influences the bottom-up activation in the next processing cycle. In this simple backpropagation net there is no top-down flow of information during the recognition of a single word. The word is recognised during a single forward pass through the net. The error signal has no influence on the processing of the current word. However, by determining the weight changes in the net, the error signal can influence how subsequent words are processed.

One might argue that the word superiority effect (WSE) was never a very good example of a top-down effect anyway. Data showing lexicality effects in either written or spoken word recognition can readily be explained by assuming that letter or phoneme identities can be read from a lexical representation rather than from the letter nodes themselves. Cutler, Mehler, Norris, and Segui (1987) have called this kind of model a multiple outlet model. There are two potential sources of letter/phoneme identity information: Letter identities can be established either on the basis of direct perceptual analysis of the stimulus, or by reading the letter information from the lexical representation of the word.

Responses in letter identification tasks can be based on whichever source of information is most readily available. Cutler et al. have argued that this kind of bottom-up model is better able to account for lexicality effects in phoneme monitoring than is TRACE. Lexicality effects in phoneme monitoring come and go according to the composition of the stimulus list. Lexicality effects disappear when the lists change from a mixture of monosyllabic and disyllabic words to a list containing only monosyllabic words. Cutler et al. argue that this should be explained by assuming that subjects shift attention between the lexical outlet and the phonemic outlet. In TRACE, phoneme identification is always based on the activation of phoneme nodes. If lexicality effects vary according to list composition then we have to assume that the structure of the list can alter all the weights between the lexical and the phoneme level. Cutler et al. argue that this is less parsimonious than assuming that subjects are able to shift attention between the lexical and phonemic outlets in a bottom-up level. However, this kind of explanation is unable to handle data from a recent study by Elman and McClelland (1988), which seems to provide categorical evidence that lexical information influence phonetic processing.

ELMAN AND McCLELLAND'S STUDY

Several studies have shown that phoneme identification can be influenced by lexical information. For example, Ganong (1980) has shown that subjects have a lexical bias in phoneme perception. An ambiguous phoneme is more likely to be perceived in such a way as to make it form part of a word rather than a nonword. So, if a subject hears a stimulus midway between "type" and "dype", the initial phoneme is more likely to be perceived as a /t/ forming the word "type" than as a /d/ forming the nonword "dype." On the face of things, this appears to be a top-down effect. It seems that lexical knowledge is having a top-down influence on phoneme identification. However, it is quite possible that this effect simply reflects the combination of two different sources of information about phoneme identity. The initial phoneme can be identified both on the basis of phonemic analysis of the input and by reading out the phonemic representation of the word from the lexicon. Combining these two sources of information leads to a tendency to identify the phoneme as part of a word rather than a nonsense word. According to this view there is a lexical bias, but that bias operates in a totally bottom-up fashion.

In an attempt to overcome the difficulties in interpreting data of this form, Elman and McClelland combined the "top-down" Ganong effect with a second effect that took place entirely within the phonological level. If the Ganong effect really is simply a matter of high-level response bias then, even if a phoneme has its identity influenced by a lexical effect, this should have no impact on the way that phoneme behaves at the phonological level. On the other hand, if the lexical influence in the Ganong effect is really top-down, a phoneme whose identity is determined by lexical information should behave as though its identity had been altered at the phonological level also. The low-level effect that Elman and McClelland used in their experiments was an effect of compensation for coarticulation (Mann & Repp, 1981; Repp & Mann, 1981). The phonemes /s/ and /S/ influence both the production and the perception of following stop consonants. A /t/ produced after an /S/ tends to be rather more like a /k/, and a /d/ is more like a /g/. Conversely, after /s/, a /k/ is more like /t/ and a /g/ is more like /d/. However, listeners compensate for these effects of coarticulation so that phonemes are categorised the same way in different contexts. Because a /t/ will tend to be more like a /k/ after /S/, listeners shift the boundaries between the phonetic categories towards the /k/ end of the continuum. This ensures that the coarticulated /t/ following /S/ will still be categorised correctly as a /t/. The consequence of this boundary shift is that an ambiguous sound half-way between /t/ and /k/ is more likely to be perceived as /t/ after /S/, but as /k/ after /s/.

TRACE accounts for these coarticulatory effects by allowing phoneme nodes to vary the strength of connections between the feature level and the phoneme level in adjacent time slices. Therefore, if the activation of a phoneme node is altered by activation from the lexical level, this will induce the compensation for coarticulation in exactly the same way as if the activation of the phoneme node had been entirely determined by bottom-up perceptual evidence. This predicts that if the identification of a phoneme half-way between /s/ and /S/ could be biased towards /S/ by lexical information, that phoneme should cause compensation for coarticulation just the same as if there were a real /S/ present.

The experiments that Elman and McClelland performed involved presenting subjects with stimuli such as "Christma* ?apes" and "fooli* ?apes," where "*" is a phoneme midway between /s/ and /S/ and "?" is midway between /t/ and /k/. In "Christma* ?apes" the Ganong effect should cause * to be perceived as /s/ since "christmash" is not a word. Compensation for coarticulation should then lead "?" to be perceived as /k/ rather than /t/. With "fooli* ?apes," the effects on phoneme perception should go in the opposite direction and subjects should report hearing "foolish tapes."

Although the effects that Elman and McClelland observed were fairly subtle, and only a small number of stimuli were used, the results were precisely as predicted by TRACE. These findings seem to provide categorical evidence of a top-down influence of lexical-level information on phoneme perception; this cannot be explained simply in terms of the operation of a high-level response bias. The crucial observation in these studies concerns how subjects classify the second word of the pair. Since both "tapes" and "capes" are words there can be no lexical bias favouring either a /t/ or a /k/. Furthermore, the experiment is designed so that the effect following "fooli*" is opposite to the effect following

"Christma*." In addition, there seems to be no reason why the lexical identity of the first word of the pair should exert any bias over the way the second word is perceived.

Taken individually, both the Ganong effect and the coarticulation effect are easily explained by bottom-up models. The Ganong effect can be explained by the simple feed-forward net described earlier. Ambiguous stimuli tend to get identified as the nearest word. Also, the letter nodes tend to identify the ambiguous letters/phonemes as being those in the nearest word. One could also imagine other bottom-up models where phoneme and word information was pooled before coming to a decision about phoneme identity.

The coarticulation effect obviously poses no problem in general for bottom-up models, but it can't be handled by a simple net which deals with only a single word at a time. To explain the coarticulation effect we need a network that is able to take prior context into account as it analyses each phoneme.

A DYNAMIC NET MODEL OF WORD RECOGNITION

The first problem we face in trying to extend a simple model (like that shown in Fig. 12.1) to deal with speech recognition is that the net is unable to cope with time. These nets take an input pattern, presented simultaneously to all input nodes, and map it onto the output pattern. The network has no memory. After processing one input the next input will be processed independently. Therefore such a network will be unable to recognise any pattern that develops over time. The only way that the net can recognise a pattern is if the whole pattern is presented simultaneously. The temporal dimension of a pattern must be recoded as a spatial dimenson. This form of net has to try to recognise speech as if it were a static waveform or spectrograph displayed on an oscilloscope. If it proved successful, recoding the temporal component of speech as a spatial component might form the basis of an acceptable engineering solution to the problem of automatic speech recognition. But a psychologist can't simply pretend that time doesn't exist.

One way to enable a network to deal with patterns with a temporal dimension is to build a memory into the network in such a way that processing of the current input can always take place in the context of the network's memory for its processing of previous inputs. We can achieve this by adding links to the network that have a time delay. Figure. 12.2 shows one example of such a network (Norris, 1988; 1990). The network shown in Fig. 12.2 is in fact a modification of a network architecture first proposed by Jordan (1986) for producing sequences. The steps in the derivation of this architecture from that of Jordan are described more fully in Norris (1990). The same architecture has also been employed by Elman (1988). In this network the input to the next at time t1 causes a pattern of activation at the hidden units. This activation pattern is then copied from the hidden units to the state units. Therefore when a new input

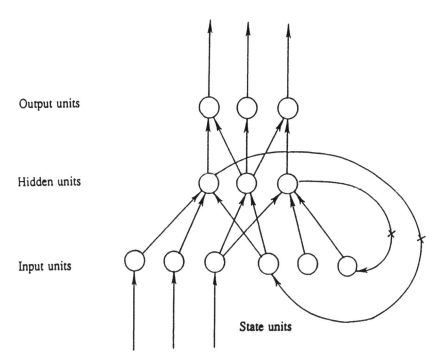

Output units

Hidden units

Input units

State units

FIG. 12.2.   Recurrent net. Not all connections are shown. Links marked "x" have a delay of one time unit.

arrives at time t2, this new input is processed along with the memory for the processing of the previous pattern, which is now stored in the state units. When the next pattern arrives it in turn is processed in the context of the memory for the previous two patterns. Note that the net shown in Fig. 12.2 is equivalent to the net shown in Fig. 12.3. The only difference between the two networks is that the fixed links from the hidden units to the state units have been eliminated and the delay has now been placed in the modifiable weights between the hidden units. The operation of the network is perhaps clearer in the version with state units. However, Fig. 12.3 makes it clear tht this net maintains a bottom-up architecture. There are no feedback links from any layer to earlier layers in the net. The extra interconnectivity required to enable the net to deal with time stems entirely from connections between the hidden units themselves.

This form of network architecture has many interesting properties (Norris, 1990). First, it is very good at coping with temporal variability in its input. It generalises well to patterns with a different rate from the training patterns. Temporal generalisation is something that the simple feedforward nets are very poor at. It is also a major problem for TRACE.

Second, the network automatically displays the "left-to-right" properties of word recognition that Marslen-Wilson and his colleagues (Marslen-Wilson &

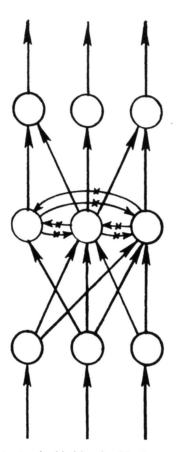

FIG. 12.3.   Simple recurrent network with delayed weights between hidden units.

Welsh, 1979; Marslen-Wilson & Zwitserlood, 1989) have shown to be characteristic of human word recognition. In one simulation the network was trained to
recognise a set of 50 words. The network had 11 input units, 20 hidden units, and
50 output units. Input to the net consisted of phonemes coded as a set of 11
phonetic features. One phoneme was presented to the net at each time slice. The
training words were presented to the net in a continuous sequence, with no gaps
or silences between the words. The net was trained to activate one of the 50
output units for each of the 50 words in its lexicon. The output pattern for a word
was present during the presentation of each phoneme in the word. To simplify
matters, words were actually coded according to their orthographic form rather
than a phonemic transcription. Each letter in the alphabet was coded in terms of
the features of the closest single phoneme.

   The network does a very good job at identifying words from a continuous
input stream. It has some problems learning very short words, but performs very

well with longer words. Note that, unlike TRACE, the network has only a single output node for each word. TRACE has to have a complete lexical network at all positions where a word might start in the input. Because the dynamic net scans through the input in a left-to-right fashion, it only has to have a single output node for each word. That output node indicates which word the net has recognised in the input at that point in time. Output from the net is shown in Table 12.1.

With a model like this we can do exactly the same thing as with the simple feed-forward net we used to simulate the word-superiority effect. We can add phoneme nodes to the output layer and train it to identify both words and phonemes. The structure of such a network is shown in Fig. 12.4. It is very easy to get such a net to show both the Ganong effect and the coarticulation effect. Because it is always identifying each phoneme in the context of the preceding input it can easily learn that in one context a given stimulus should be identified as a /k/, and in another context it should be identified as a /t/. It shows the Ganong effect for precisely the same reason as the simple net shows the WSE.

TABLE 12.1

Activation Levels of the Three Most Highly Activated Items in the Net's Lexicon Following the Presentation of Successive Phonemes/Letters

Input: corner			
c:	calm 0.143	camel 0.142	cold 0.134
o:	cold 0.184	corner 0.175	coroner 0.156
r:	coroner 0.291	corner 0.224	coronet 0.121
n:	corner 0.659	coroner 0.128	coronet 0.066
e:	corner 0.694	coroner 0.108	coronet 0.031
r:	corner 0.942	coroner 0.028	memory 0.007
Input: coroner			
c:	calm 0.143	camel 0.142	cold 0.134
o:	cold 0.184	corner 0.175	coroner 0.156
r:	coroner 0.291	corner 0.224	coronet 0.121
o:	coroner 0.562	coronet 0.319	corner 0.081
n:	coroner 0.627	coronet 0.378	door 0.047
e:	coroner 0.745	coronet 0.460	corner 0.013
r:	coroner 0.862	coronet 0.100	trash 0.017
Input: coronet			
c:	calm 0.143	camel 0.142	cold 0.134
o:	cold 0.184	corner 0.175	coroner 0.156
r:	coroner 0.291	corner 0.224	coronet 0.121
o:	coroner 0.562	coronet 0.319	corner 0.081
n:	coroner 0.627	coronet 0.378	door 0.047
e:	coroner 0.745	coronet 0.460	corner 0.013
t:	coronet 0.788	coroner 0.259	boot 0.002

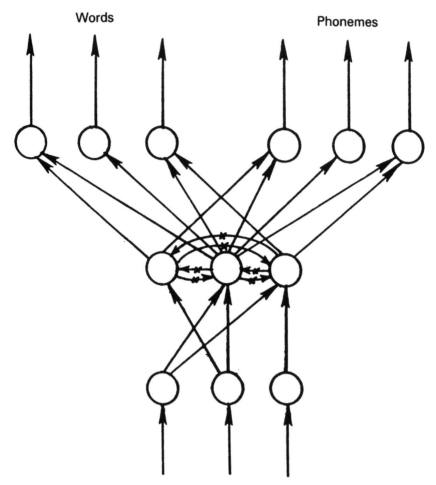

FIG. 12.4.   Recurrent network to identify both words and phonemes.

Note that in TRACE the account of compensation for coarticulation is arbitrary. TRACE is simply wired up to do the job. However, in the dynamic net the process of compensation follows automatically from the structure of the network. It would actually be very difficult to stop the net showing compensation given that it is trained to identify phonemes in different articulatory environments.

So, what happens when we put these two effects together and present the network with Elman and McClelland-style stimuli? Elman and McClelland's experiments were simulated using a lexicon of 12 CVC words constructed from a set of 8 phonemes. The network had 11 input units, 10 hidden units, and 20 output units. There were 12 output units representing the 12 words in the net's vocabulary and 8 output units representing the 8 phonemes. The net was trained on pairs of words and the activation in the hidden units was zeroed after each pair. In the featural coding of the phonemes /t/ and /k/ differed by only the single feature of place of articulation. Normally the place feature for /k/ was coded as 0 and the feature for /t/ was coded as 1. Coarticulation would make the /t/ more like a /k/ after an /S/ and the /k/ more like a /t/ after an /s/. Therefore the input features for /k/ and /t/ following /S/ and /s/ were modified so that after /S/ the place feature for /k/ was set to 0 and the feature for /t/ set to 0.5. After /s/ the place feature for /k/ was set to 0.5 and the feature for /t/ set to 1. In the test phase /t/ and /k/ both had the place feature set to 0.5 in the input after the phonemes /s/ or /s/. During training the net never experienced the test pair in the order they were to appear in the test phase, so there is no possibility that the net could learn any associations between the test words. Also, the probability of the phonemes /t/ or /k/ appearing after any of the words in position 1 of the test pair during training was equated. After training the net was tested by presenting it with the word pairs shown in Table 12.2. The final phoneme in the first word of the pair ws ambiguous between /s/ and /S/ and the initial phoneme in the second pair was ambiguous between /t/ and /k/. Therefore, as in Elman and McClelland's experiments, any bias in the net's response to the initial phoneme of word 2 cannot simply be due to the identity of the preceding phoneme. The results of the stimulation are shown in Fig. 12.5. The top panel shows the identification function for words while the bottom panel shows the identification function for phonemes. Remember that Elman and McClelland's task required subjects to report the identity of the word they heard, not its initial phoneme. Both the word and phoneme identification functions clearly show that the identity of word 1 influences the identification of word 2 in precisely the manner exhibited by the subjects in Elman and McClelland's experiment.

TABLE 12.2
Test Stimuli for Simulating Elman and McClelland's Results

Critical Words in Net's Vocabulary	Nonwords	Test Pairs
Sos	SoS	So? *oS
sos	soS	so? *oS
koS	kos	ko? *oS
toS	tos	to? *oS

? is ambiguous between /S/ and /s/.
* is ambiguous between /t/ and /k/.

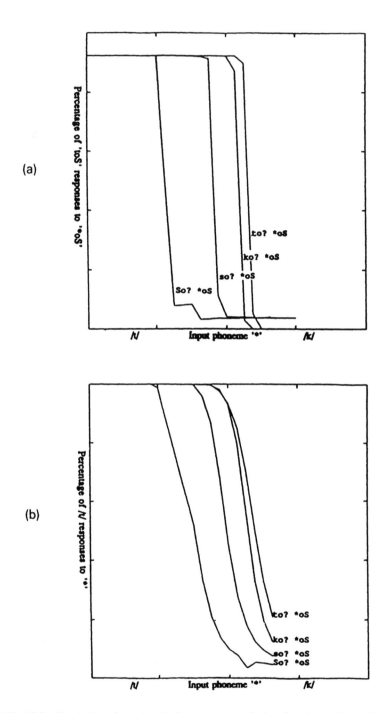

FIG. 12.5 Simulation of word and phoneme categorisation functions. (a) word responses; (b) phoneme responses.

The stimuli "Sos" and "sos" are both words in the network's lexicon but "SoS" and "soS" are not. Therefore, the ambiguous stimuli "So?" and "so?" both have a lexical bias towards /s/. After /s/ an ambiguous phoneme half-way between /t/ and /k/ tends to be perceived more like a /k/ than a /t/. This means that the /t/,/k/ boundary shifts towards the /t/ end of the continuum because more responses are /k/ responses. The converse applies to "to?" and "ko?", which have a lexical bias towards "toS" and "koS." In that case the /t/,/k/ boundary shifts towards the /k/ end of the continuum because more responses are /t/ responses.

CONCLUSIONS

So, contrary to any expectations we might have derived from our experience with conventional bottom-up models, this simple network demonstrates precisely the kind of behaviour we have come to think of as solely the product of highly interactive top-down models. There is no flow of information from lexical nodes to phoneme nodes, yet, nevertheless, lexical constraints influence the way in which the net makes decisions at the phonemic level. Those constraints are pre-compiled into the network weights by the learning process and therefore don't have to be passed around the network during processing.

Although it seems clear how to categorise this network according to the terms bottom-up and top-down, it is rather less obvious whether to describe it as "interactive" or "non-interactive." If we want to classify a model as "top-down" or "bottom-up," all we need to know is the direction of information flow as it passes from input to output. If the information flow is entirely from input to output with no feedback, then the model is clearly bottom-up. However, talk of interaction implies that we have identified two or more processes in the model that might potentially interact. This is the first stumbling block in attempting to characterise parallel distributed processing models. Because we do not always have a series of discrete processing modules connected by clearly identifiable data paths, sometimes it is simply not obvious where to draw the line between one stage and the next. The weights between one layer of nodes and the next in a connectionist network are part of the processing system as well as being a data pathway. If we are unable to establish how many processes the system contains, then we are in no position to ask whether any of the processes interact. Perhaps there are some models where we might want to claim that there is a top-down flow of information, but that this only occurs within processing modules and not between them. The model would then be top-down, but the processes would not interact.

We usually think that top-down models are automatically interactive. Information flows top-down so that a higher-level stage can interact with a stage at a lower level. If information flow is bottom-up then later stages cannot interact with earlier ones. However, if we have a module that can't sensibly be thought of as consisting of a number of smaller modules, we may still want to ask questions about the direction of information flow within that module.

We should remember that the answers to questions of interaction and autonomy depend on the level of granularity of our description of the system. At one level we may wish to describe a system in terms of a small number of autonomous modules. However, to provide a more detailed description we may wish to divide those modules further into a set of more precisely specified modules which interact. Whether the system is interactive or autonomous will depend on which level of description we choose to work at.

The top-down/bottom-up question can therefore be seen as somewhat separate from the question of interaction. When we use terms like "top-down" we need to specify the granularity of our description. The apparent contradictions can arise when we mix talk of interaction between modules with talk of direction of information flow within modules.

In the connectionist models described here there is obviously a problem in determining where the stages are. The weights between the hidden units and the output word units are clearly responsible solely for word recognition. Similarly, the weights between the hidden units and the output phoneme units are responsible solely for phoneme recognition. But everything else in the network is involved in computing some intermediate representation that subserves both word and phoneme recognition. That is, there is some overlap between the parts of the network responsible for word recognition and the parts responsible for phoneme recognition. There is no way to slice the model up into two discrete stages corresponding to word and phoneme recognition.

The conventional box model that comes closest to the architecture of the network is shown in Fig. 12.6. However, for a model of this form to explain Elman and McClelland's results there would have to be some provision for interaction. The lexical processor would either have to interact directly with the phoneme processor, or communicate via the first stage in the model. The behaviour of the network depends on more than simply treating phonemes and words as being at the same level of analysis. A similarly structured non-connectionist model would still have to incorporate some provision for interaction.

Proponents of an interactive view might wish to argue that we should look on these networks as a single highly interactive process that produces two different kinds of output. It might be claimed that the very reason for treating the networks as a single process is that processing is interactive. That is, we really have a single interactive parallel constraint satisfaction network. But this approach would seem to mask crucial aspects of the network's internal structure. Most importantly, it obscures the fact that the phoneme and word nodes don't interact, and that processing is bottom-up.

When I first saw Elman and McClelland's results I thought that this was definitive evidence for interaction between lexical and phonemic processing and

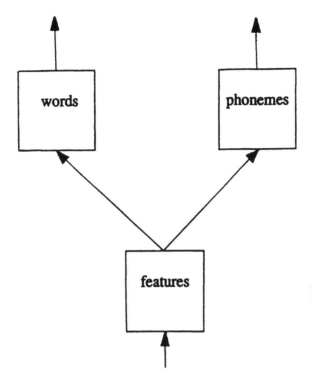

FIG. 12.6. Boxology approximation to the recurrent network shown in Fig. 12.4.

that it was time to throw in the towel and give up on bottom-up models. But, as you can see, this particular bottom-up model gives a very good account of their data, and has a lot of other interesting properties. It explains all of the cohort style data, it's very good at tolerating temporal variability in the input, and it doesn't need to duplicate the network for each time slice the way TRACE does, other than to provide look-ahead.

The fact that proponents of highly interactive models have begun to embrace backpropagation nets which have a simple bottom-up architecture is something of a paradoxical development in connectionist modelling. In itself this is a testimony to the power of these simple models. Of course, as I have already pointed out, backpropagation by its very nature does involve some top-down flow of information. The error terms must be propagated down the network during the learning phase. However, after learning, all information flow in a simple feedforward backpropagation net is bottom-up.

For those of us who thought we understood what it meant to describe a model as "top-down" or "interactive," the behaviour of these rather simple bottom-up models comes as rather a surprise. Contrary to everything we have come to expect from conventional information processing theories, these bottom-up networks can behave in exactly the way we think a highly interactive top-down model should behave. Viewed from the standpoint of traditional box models, Elman and McClelland's results seemed to have provided categorical evidence for an interaction between lexical and phonological processing. If connectionist models were nothing more than implementations of classical models then no connectionist model could change the validity of this conclusion. The fact that we can construct a bottom-up connectionist account of Elman and McClelland's results is a clear, practical demonstration that connectionism is more than just a new way of describing old theories. Even very simple connectionist networks can behave in ways that can't possibly be predicted from a box-model characterisation of the same theory.

REFERENCES

Cutler, A., Mehler, J., Norris, D., & Segui, J. (1987). Phoneme identification and the lexicon. *Cognitive Psychology, 19*, 141–177.

Elman, J. (1988). *Finding structure in time*. Center for Research in Language. Technical Report 8801. San Diego: University of California.

Elman, J. & McClelland, J. (1988). Cognitive penetration of the mechanisms of perception: Compensation for coarticulation of lexically restored phonemes. *Journal of Memory and Language, 27*, 143–165.

Fodor, J.A. & Pylyshyn, Z.W. (1988). Connectionism and cognitive architecture: A critical analysis. *Cognition, 28*, 3–72.

Ganong, W.F. III (1980). Phonetic categorization in auditory word perception. *Journal of Experimental Psychology: Human Perception and Performance, 6*, 110–125.

Jordan, M. (1986). *Serial order: A parallel distributed processing approach*. ICS Report 8604. La Jolla: University of California, San Diego.

Liberman, I.Y., Shankweiler, D., Liberman, A.M., Fowler, C., & Fisher, W.F. (1977). In A.S. Reber & D.L. Scarborough (Eds.), *Towards a psychology of reading*. Hillsdale, N.J.: Lawrence Erlbaum Associates Inc.

McClelland, J.L. (1979). On the time relations of mental processes: An examination of systems in cascade. *Psychological Review, 88*, 375–407.

McClelland, J. & Elman, J. (1986). The TRACE model of speech perception. *Cognitive Psychology, 18*, 1–86.

McClelland, J. & Rumelhart, D. (1981). An interactive activation model of context effects in letter perception: Part 1. An account of the basic findings. *Psychological Review, 88*, 375–407.

Mann, V.A. & Repp, B.H. (1981). Influence of preceding fricative on stop consonant perception. *Journal of the Acoustical Society of America, 69*, 548–558.

Marslen-Wilson, W.D. & Welsh, A. (1978). Processing interactions and lexical access during word-recognition in continuous speech. *Cognitive Psychology, 10*, 29–63.

Marslen-Wilson, W.D. & Zwitserlood, P. (1989). Accessing spoken words: The importance of word onsets. *Journal of Experimental Psychology: Human Perception and Performance, 15*, 576–585.

Morais, J., Bertelson, P., Cary, L., & Algeria, J. (1986). Literacy training and speech segmentation. *Cognition, 24*, 45–64.

Morais, J., Cary, L., Algeria, J., & Bertelson, P. (1979). Does awareness of speech as a sequence of phones arise spontaneously? *Cognition, 7*, 323–331.

Norris, D. (1988). *A dynamic net model of human speech recognition*. Paper presented at the Sperlonga Conference on Cognitive Models of Speech Processing, May.

Norris, D. (1990). A dynamic net model of human speech recognition. In G.T.E. Altman (Ed.), *Cognitive models of speech processing* (pp. 87–104). Cambridge: M.I.T. Press.

Pinker, S. & Prince, A. (1988). On language and connectionism: Analysis of a parallel distributed processing model of language acquisition. *Cognition, 28*, 73–194.

Read, C.A., Zhang, Y., Nie., H., & Ding, B. (1986). The ability to manipulate speech sounds depends on knowing alphabetic reading. *Cognition, 24*, 31–44.

Repp, B.H. & Mann, V.A. (1981). Perceptual assessment of fricative-stop coarticulation. *Journal of the Acoustical Society of America, 69*, 1154–1163.

Rumelhart, D. & McClelland, J. (1982). An interactive activation model of context effects in letter perception: Part 2. The contextual enhancement effect and some tests and extensions of the model. *Psychological Review, 89*, 60–94.

Seidenberg, M. & McClelland, J. (1989). A distributed, developmental model of word recognition and naming. *Psychological Review, 96*, 523–568.

Smolensky, P. (1988). On the proper treatment of connectionism. *Brain and Behavioral Sciences, 11*, 1–74.

Sternberg, S. (1969). The discovery of processing stages: Extensions of Dondors' method. In W.G. Koster (Ed.), *Attention and performance II*. Amsterdam: North Holland, 276–315.

13 Models of Form-related Priming in Comprehension and Production

Padraig G. O'Seaghdha
Lehigh University, Bethlehem, Pennsylvania, U.S.A.

Gary S. Dell
Beckman Institute, University of Illinois, Urbana, Illinois, U.S.A.

Robert R. Peterson
Indiana University, Bloomington, Indiana, U.S.A.

Cornell Juliano
University of Rochester, Rochester, New York, U.S.A.

INTRODUCTION

In comparison to the voluminous semantic priming literature, the dossier on form-related priming effects is rather meagre. For every published experiment that examines how MAT primes CAT, there are many more that look at DOG priming CAT. In a traditional spreading activation framework, form-related priming effects seem both empirically and theoretically straightforward. Similarly spelled and similar-sounding words prime one another by means of activation spreading through common elements, and benefits are accordingly observed in speeded tasks such as naming and lexical decision (e.g. Hillinger, 1980; Meyer, Schvaneveldt, & Ruddy, 1974). Likewise, form priming facilitates perceptual identification (e.g. Evett & Humphreys, 1981; Humphreys, Evett, & Taylor, 1982; Slowiaczek, Nusbaum, & Pisoni, 1987) and retrieval or phonological encoding of words from episodic (e.g. Meyer, 1990) or semantic memory (e.g. Bowles & Poon, 1985). Perhaps because these effects have appeared rather transparent, theoretical and empirical efforts in the areas of lexical perception and production have not made much use of form-related priming as a research tool (e.g. Adams, 1979; Dell, 1986; Glushko, 1979; McClelland & Rumelhart, 1981; Seidenberg, 1985). In this paper, we will demonstrate that form-related priming has an important role to play both in the development of general accounts of lexical processing, and as a tool for the analysis of language comprehension and production.

Although form-relatedness effects are indeed often facilitatory, several instances of either putative or demonstrable inhibition can be cited. One instance is the well-known tip-of-the-tongue (TOT) phenomenon, where a rememberer has the experience of knowing a word but not being able to recover it fully. Persons in TOT states frequently report phonological and prosodic aspects of the target word, and they may also report other words that are similar in form to the target (Brown & McNeill, 1966). Jones and Langford (1987) have recently pointed out that these form-related words, which they call *interlopers*, may be viewed as the cause of a TOT experience if retrieval of an interloper inhibits retrieval of the target (Woodworth, 1938). Bock (1987) reported another form-related inhibitory effect in a production task. Bock found that when subjects produced declarative sentence descriptions of simple pictures, they placed words related to formally similar primes *later* in the sentences. For example, the prime FRIGHTENING increased the likelihood of subjects' describing a picture showing a bolt of lightning striking a church steeple with the sentence "The church was struck by lightning," in which the related word LIGHTNING is late, and reduced the likelihood of using the active sentence "The lightning struck the church," in which LIGHTNING is early. Recently, another challenge has arisen for theories of form-related priming. Several studies have found inhibition from similar primes in a lexical decision task. Specifically, Colombo (1986) reported inhibition of high-frequency targets primed by graphemically and phonologically similar words. Lupker and Williams (1987) replicated this finding, and we report some corroborative studies of our own later.

We will review some of the literature on form-related priming effects in light of this new evidence. We first consider the standard or receptive priming situation, in which the priming process is a perceptual event. Then we will present two different connectionist modelling approaches to form-related priming, the first a backpropagation learning model, and the second an interactive activation model. Along the way, we will present experimental data in support of our arguments. We will also discuss the application of our view of form-related activation to the study of language production. Phonological representations have a clear and necessary role in production, and our models of form-related priming are reciprocally useful in guiding our thinking and research in this domain.

RECEPTIVE PRIMING

The basic procedure in receptive form-related priming experiments involves the presentation of one word or string, the prime, followed by the presentation of a form-related or unrelated target that requires a speeded response. The response might be to identify a masked target, or to name or make a lexical decision to a string of letters presented in clear view.

Several investigators have demonstrated that the processing of a word is influenced by the prior presentation of a phonologically and orthographically related word. Meyer, Schvaneveldt, and Ruddy (1974) found shorter lexical decision latencies to words following phonologically and orthographically similar primes (e.g. BRIBE-TRIBE) than to targets following unrelated primes (e.g. FENCE-TRIBE). Meyer et al. did not interpret this result in terms of phonological activation per se. Rather, they proposed a phonological recoding hypothesis (see Coltheart, 1978), whereby processing of the prime activates grapheme-to-phoneme recoding rules, which are then available to expedite recoding of a related target word. In cases of grapheme-phoneme mismatch (e.g. COUCH-TOUCH), the rules misapply, and inhibition results. Subsequent research, however, has not supported the phonological recoding hypothesis. Hillinger (1980) reported form-related facilitation for visual probes when primes were presented visually or auditorily. Because grapheme-to-phoneme conversion is not required in the auditory case, Hillinger favoured an automatic phonological activation interpretion of the effect.

A similar stance was taken by Tanenhaus, Flanigan, and Seidenberg (1980), who found evidence of phonological activation in a cross-modal Stroop paradigm, and by Humphreys et al. (1982), who found facilitation from masked, nonhomographic homophone primes (e.g. STAIR-STARE) in a perceptual identification procedure. Humphreys et al. argued that the facilitation effect was genuinely phonological because the same effect was found with orthographically dissimilar homophones (e.g. SHOOT-CHUTE), but only a weak effect was observed for matched orthographic controls (e.g. STARK-STARE). Humphreys et al. also did not find an effect with nonword pseudohomophone primes (e.g. TODE-TOAD), and therefore argued that the phonological facilitation effect with word primes was lexically mediated.

So far, the studies reviewed suggest that phonological representations are automatically accessed, and that they result in facilitation of responses to similar words. Two problems for this view have recently appeared. In a series of lexical decision experiments, Martin and Jensen (1988) failed to replicate the Hillinger (1980) experiments and found little evidence of any kind of robust effect of form-related primes. They concluded that automatic phonological activation does not play a significant role in lexical decision. In this connection, it is also worth pointing out that the often cited Meyer et al. (1974) rhyme-priming effect was in fact not statistically significant. However, as Martin and Jensen acknowledge, their experiments do not warrant stronger conclusions concerning the status of automatic phonological activation. Although the failure to replicate Hillinger's experiments is disquieting, there appears to be good evidence of phonological activation across the range of experiments and tasks we review in this paper.

The second challenge to the emerging consensus may help account for the weak or inconsistent results in the literature. In conrast to all the preceding research, Colombo (1986) observed form-related inhibition of high-frequency targets in lexical decision. This was the case whether the targets and primes were rhymes or shared initial letters. However, when the targets were low-frequency words, Colombo found facilitation in the case of rhyme primes, and substantially reduced inhibition for primes and targets sharing initial letters. The fact that Colombo found the standard facilitation effect for low-frequency rhymes, but inhibition for high-frequency targets, suggests that the weak facilitatory effects reported by Martin and Jensen and Meyer et al. could be a consequence of averaging over higher and lower frequency items in their experiments. We will refer to the pattern of low-frequency facilitation and high-frequency inhibition as the Colombo Effect.

Colombo's finding of form-related inhibition of high-frequency words appears to be empirically well founded. It has been replicated by Lupker and Williams (1987), as well as in an experiment of our own in which the task was naming rather than lexical decision. In our experiment, primes and targets were multisyllabic words which, in the related condition, shared two or more initial phonological segments (e.g. CHILDREN-CHIMNEY), and often the entire first syllable (e.g., CAMEL-CAMPUS). The primes were presented for 500msec, and were followed by high- or low-frequency, related or unrelated, targets which subjects named as quickly as possible. The naming latencies, shown in Table 13.1, show a highly significant interaction of priming with target frequency. Our replication indicates that the Colombo Effect is not particular to the lexical decision task.

Colombo proposed an explanation of high-frequency target inhibition in terms of lexical suppression. In this account, based on the McClelland and Rumelhart (1981) model of letter perception, words sharing letters with a presented word (orthographic neighbours) receive partial activation. They also receive inhibition as target recognition proceeds because of competition among activated words. An additional scaling factor or mechanism was required to account for differential inhibition of high-frequency words. For this purpose, Colombo proposed an inhibition threshold, whereby inhibition affects only nodes exceeding a certain level of activation. Because high-frequency words have

TABLE 13.1

Mean Naming Latencies and Error Percentages in Form-related Receptive Priming Experiments

(a) *Frequency Manipulation*	*High Frequency*		*Low Frequency*	
	Related	*Unrelated*	*Related*	*Unrelated*
	507	495	528	552
	(3.3)	(3.0)	(5.3)	(5.8)
(b) *Homophony Manipulation*	*Homophones*		*Nonhomophones*	
	Related	*Unrelated*	*Related*	*Unrelated*
	480	495	502	488
	(1.3)	(0.9)	(3.1)	(2.7)

higher resting levels of activation, they are more likely to exceed the threshold and incur inhibition.

We will discuss this proposal in more detail later. For now, we note that Colombo's account of form-related effects differs from the previous literature by disregarding phonological effects. It will become clear that we regard this omission as mistaken. However, we agree that the Colombo Effect presents a challenge to theories of form activation, and the ability to meet this challenge will be an important criterion in evaluating our models.

THE MODELS

We now examine the ability of two rather different models to simulate the empirical effects of form-related priming, and in particular, their ability to account for inhibitory effects. First, we will consider how form-related priming is handled in a parallel distributed processing (PDP) backpropagation model of word production (see Dell & Juliano, 1990). We will examine the assumption that priming in backpropagation models is related to learning (see Seidenberg & McClelland, 1989, pp. 540–541). On this assumption, prime processing is conceived as a pattern of connection weight changes that reflect the network's disposition to reduce the error in the output for the prime. The PDP model contains very few explicit information processing assumptions. Rather, it learns to map between input letter representations and output phonological feature representations, and produces effects based on the nature of this mapping.

In contrast, our second model (Peterson, Dell, & O'Seaghdha, 1989), an interactive activation model of the type pioneered by McClelland and Rumelhart 1981; Rumelhart & McClelland, 1982), is structurally very explicit. This model was purpose-built to produce the Colombo Effect. The interest, therefore, is less in whether it produces the effect than in how it does so. The interactive activation model produces facilitation via bidirectional letter-to-word and word-to-phonological segment[1] excitatory connections, and inhibition as a result of competition at the phonological level. After presenting this model, we will compare it to the lexical-level explanation of form-related effects proposed by Colombo (1986), and present some experimental results related to it. Finally, we will draw some conclusions concerning the value of both models.

Model 1: A Sequential Backpropagation Model of Word Production

In this section we describe a sequential backpropagation model that learns to produce phonological segments in order. Specifically, we examine how the model, considered as a representative of a broader class of PDP models, simulates priming data. The model has affinities with and is indebted to

---

[1]We use the term *segment* throughout this chapter in place of the traditional phoneme, except in established expressions such as grapheme-to-phoneme correspondence.

Sejnowski and Rosenberg's (1986) NETtalk, which was the first application of the backpropagation algorithm (Rumelhart, Hinton, & Williams, 1986) to graphemic-phonological transcoding. From the point of view of modelling form-related activation, it is also comparable to the recent nonsequential word naming model of Seidenberg and McClelland (1989). It owest more specific debts concerning its sequential architecture to Jordan (1986) and Elman (1988). Jordan outlined a general scheme for modelling action sequences in a parallel distributed framework. The essence of his proposal is that the input layer should contain both an invariant plan, and a *state* representation derived from the model's output during the sequential execution of the plan. The corresponding entities in our model (see Fig. 13.1) are the input letter representations and the *last output*, which is simply a copy of the output on the previous pass. Elman (1988) has recently explored a related architecture where, instead of feeding the output back to the input layer, the state representation consists of a replica of the last state of the hidden units. Elman called these state representations *context* units. Our model incorporates such a state representation, labelled *last hidden* in Fig. 13.1. Thus, both the output and the hidden unit activations are fed back to the input layer in our model.[2]

In its current implementation, the model is designed to pronounce the three-letter words of English. It consists of an input layer, a layer of hidden units, and an output layer (see Fig. 13.1). The input layer contains both orthographic word representations and the copies of the previous hidden and output states described earlier. The orthographic units are fixed representations, five nodes per letter, for three-letter words. Each letter was assigned a binary code over these nodes, and in principle could appear in any position in a word. As we shall see, the replication of previous hidden and output representations is what enables the model to reproduce an output sequence in time. They also enable a valuable simplification of the input representation. Because the model can keep track of sequence, it can dispense with context-sensitive encoding at output. That is, it is not necessary to resort to such cumbersome and often criticised devices as wickelunits (Rumelhart & McClelland, 1986; Seidenberg & McClelland, 1989) to represent output position. Finally, the output layer contained nodes for 18 phonological features, taken from Chomsky and Halle (1968).

The model's task is to produce the phonological features of the segments of words with which it is presented. It learns to produce the next segment, given a

---

[2]Note that with both output and hidden unit feedback, one aspect of Jordan's (1986) architecture may be dispensed with. In Jordan's scheme, there are recurrent connections on the state units, such that these units carry an exponentially weighted average of their previous activations. In our model, the replication of previous hidden unit values serves a similar purpose. The *last hidden* units reflect the combined effect of the current word and *last output* units, together with their own previous values. Because the *last hidden* units carry an activation history, the *last output* units need not do so and are simple copies.

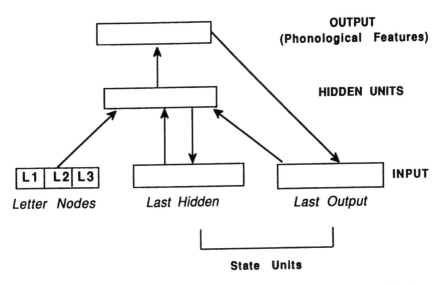

FIG. 13.1.   Structure of the distributed sequential backpropagation model. The ascending lines are trainable connections. The descending lines indicate copying of activation values to state units.

current word and a replica of its last output and hidden layer activations. That is, it produces words, segment by segment, in sequence. The model can, in principle, pronounce all the three-letter words of English. When it errs, it does so in conformity with some well-established constraints observed in the speech-error literature. In particular, it behaves very much like speakers with respect to what are called noncontextual errors—errors that do not involve movement of elements to new positions within an utterance. For example, the errors tended to obey syllabic constituency and to follow phonetic well-formedness constraints (see Dell & Juliano, 1991, for details of these aspects of the model's performance).

For the simulations described here, there were 20 hidden nodes, fully connected to the input and output layers. In addition, each node of the hidden and output layers were given a *bias*. Each bias is an additional weight from a node that is always on, and is learned in the same way as other weights. The logistic activation function was employed, and both the learning rate and the momentum term were set at 0.5.[3]

The interest here is specifically in the model's ability to simulate priming data. For this purpose we trained the model on a purpose-built lexicon of 50 words, all of which were CVCs (CVC = consonant-vowel-consonant). Thus, in the

---

[3]See Rumelhart et al. (1986) and McClelland & Rumelhart (1988) for background on backpropagation.

terminology of current phonological theory (e.g. Selkirk, 1984), each word consisted of an onset (first consonant), nucleus (vowel), and coda (final consonant), and we will use these terms for ease of reference in what follows. The use of such a structurally regular set of words ensured that the model would learn easily and reliably. Because we had already evaluted the model's performance on more diverse sets of words, we were not concerned with the loss of generality entailed by this decision. This simplication is also justified because the interest of the simulations is not in how well the model learns, but in how it simulates priming phenomena *given* that it has learned. Most importantly, it enabled us to test form-related priming effects in a systematic manner.

In effect, the model was presented with a designed experiment. Table 13.2 shows the critical materials used in this experiment, defined by their roles in the experimental design. There were 10 target words, 10 initial condition primes (CV overlap with a CVC target), and 10 rhyme condition primes (VC overlap with a CVC target). The remaining 20 words were fillers, included to add some generality to the model. The critical items and fillers were selected from a listing of all the 3-letter words in the Kučera and Francis (1967) norms. They were chosen to be informally representative of the range of letters in the language. For example, the input letter representations for the initial-rhyme-target triplets included 2 instances each of the letters, a, e, i, o, u, in the nucleus or vowel position. Likewise, a wide range of consonantal letters was sampled, subject to the constraints of the design. No words except for the designated primes and targets shared bigrams.

Training the Model

Training of each word, which we will call a *cycle*, involved four complete passes, one for each segment, through the following regimen. An *epoch* of

TABLE 13.2
Materials Used in the Simulated Experiment

Primes		Related Target	Unrelated Targets	
Initial	Rhyme		Initial	Rhyme
bad	rag	bag	hut	lid
fan	sat	fat	peg	rug
lip	bid	lid	rug	peg
fig	kit	fit	sop	bag
hub	cut	hut	bag	sop
lob	pot	lot	wed	wed
pet	leg	peg	lid	fat
rum	tug	rug	fit	fit
sod	top	sop	fat	hut
web	red	wed	lot	lot

training involved presentation of the complete 50-word vocabulary in a random order. Before training, the weights on the connections were initialised to small random values in the range +/–100. After several epochs, the output representations began to approximate the phonological features of the segments of the current word. There were 4 main steps in each pass of training.

Feedforward Activation. Activation was passed from the input to the hidden, and from the hidden to the output layer. On the first pass, the *last hidden* units were initialised to zero, and the *last output* nodes to 500, the target value for the features of a null segment.[4] For segments other than the first, the previous hidden and output values were determined by the model, as described later.

Error Evaluation. The value of each output feature was compared to the target value of that feature in the relevant phonological segment of the word. Deviations from the target values were used in the next step, backpropagation.

Backpropagation. The model was trained by adjusting the weights on the connections, following the standard backpropagation algorithm. In essence, the algorithm adjusts the weights in such a way that, over the course of training, the difference between the target values and the model's output is minimised.

Input Update. The activation values of the nodes of the output and hidden layers, calculated in the first step, were copied to the last output and last hidden sections of the input layer in preparation for the next pass.

Now consider the complete cycle of training for a word, for instance the word PEG. On the first pass, the input layer contained the fixed letter representations of the current word, as well as initialised state values. The model first produced an approximation to the phonological features of the segment /p/. Error comparison and backpropagation were applied, and the hidden and output values were copied to the input layer, as described earlier. On the second pass, the input layer contained the same letter representations as before, but new values of the *last hidden* and *last output* units. The model then produced its approximation to the features of /e/. Likewise, on the third pass, the model yielded an approximation to /g/. Finally, the model was trained to produce a null value for the offset of the word, using a "featureless" null segment having a value of 500 on all of its features as the training pattern. This completed the cycle of training.

The model's performance was evaluated at two levels. Categorically, the features of the model's output were compared to those of the 40 possible phonological segments (39 phonemes listed by Chomsky and Halle, 1968, plus

---

[4]Activation values ranged from 0 to 1000 (see Goddard, Lynne, Mintz, & Bukys, 1989).

the null segment) and the closest match was selected. The output was correct when the target segment was a better match than any other.[5] At a continuous level, the output features were compared to those of the target segment and an error score was calculated. The target value for each phonological feature was either 0 or 1000. In the *error evaluation* step, each output value was compared to its target activation, and the sum of the squared deviations was calculated over the 18 features. The error scores we report are the square roots of the sums of squares, which return the scores to the original units of measurement. As a rule of thumb, the error score will be off by approximately 1000 for each unwanted or absent feature. However, because the trained model is usually approximately correct on all of the features, the mean error scores are never higher than 400 in the data we report. After 100 epochs, the model was correct on all but 3 segments (all onsets), and none of these involved a target word. The model's performance was also evaluated after 200 and 300 epochs. As we shall see, error scores continued to decline as training proceeded. For the purposes of the priming tests we conducted, epochs of training may be thought of as equivalent to word frequency.

Rationale of Priming Tests

In models of graphemic-phonological transcoding, it is possible, as Seidenberg and McClelland (1989) have demonstrated, to simulate a wide range of empirical results without making many of the structural and processing assumptions of traditional information processing theories. Rather, these models rely on the learning procedure itself. In our tests, priming was simulated by means of the backpropagation algorithm. In effect, as explained later, the short-term activations that presumably determine priming effects were emulated by means of exaggerated weight changes in the model. In practice, these weight changes were effected by consecutive repeated presentations of the prime. Priming is thus conceived of as a strong learning trial. Therefore, with respect to its treatment of priming effects, there is a wide separation between the model's implementation and the generally agreed account of the process as reflecting activation levels irrespective of learning (e.g. Collins & Loftus, 1975). The interest, therefore, is largely in whether the model can simulate the effects in spite of this discrepancy.

Seidenberg and McClelland (1989, pp. 540–541) conducted form-related priming tests in their model, and reported a facilitatory effect in keeping with the results of Meyer et al. (1974) and Hillinger (1980). However, they did not address the inhibitory effect for high-frequency targets reported by Colombo (1986). Our model resembles the Seidenberg-McClelland model in many respects, but it differs in being sequential rather than simultaneous. In examining form-related

---

[5]Note that correctness in this sense did not enter into the training process.

priming in the model, we will consider whether its segmental output might not provide a means by which inhibition could be realised. Consider the rhyme condition pair LEG-PEG in Table 13.2. Presentation of the prime LEG is simulated by repeated presentation, allowing it a disproportionate influence on the configuration of weights in the model. This means that the model may develop a tendency to produce the first segment of this word, /l/. When the related target PEG is presented, this tendency may come into play. Relative to a control target such as CUT, which shares no segments with LEG, the model may be more likely to produce /l/ or at least some of its phonological features when the target is PEG. Conversely, in the initial condition, for the pair PET-PEG, the model may be more likely to produce some of the features of /t/ as the third segment of the target PEG.

Such an outcome would provide the model with a means of simulating inhibition, given the additional assumption that all the segments of a word, or of a sublexical entity such as a syllable (see Dell, 1986), must be specified prior to articulation. On this assumption, output would be paced by the specification time of the slowest segment, and if this time were longer in the context of a related than of an unrelated prime, inhibition would result.[6] Further, for such an outcome to conform to the Colombo Effect, relative inhibition should be greater in more highly trained networks.

We examined rhyme and initial conditions separately. Rhymes are more commonly employed in the receptive and retrieval literatures (but see Colombo, 1986, and our experiments). On the other hand, there is evidence that onsets have a special status in production (e.g. Shattuck-Hufnagel, 1987). There is also motivation in the model for comparing effects of initial and rhyme primes. For the onset, the model is given no *last hidden* context, and only a generic, null *last output* context. Production of this segment, as reflected in the error score (see Fig. 13.2) is therefore the least constrained and the most difficult, and it should accordingly yield the greatest influence of priming.

Priming Tests

The priming trials were conducted following the logic of a counterbalanced experiment. To control for item effects, the model was presented with an initial or rhyme condition prime (see Table 13.2), and then tested on a target and a control word. In this way, each target word was tested in the context of a related and an unrelated prime, just as would be done across subjects in an experiment. The "dependent variable" was the error score on the test trials, as defined earlier.[7] The same words were tested in all conditions, but the balancing of

---

[6]See Model 2, where a process of this kind plays an important role.

[7]No response mechanism is implemented. We are simply assuming a direct relation between error score and latency.

unrelated controls was slightly different for the initial and rhyme conditions to ensure that no letters or segments were shared between primes and unrelated targets (see Table 13.2).

Two measures were recorded for each prime and five measures for each target. For the primes, we measured the error score before presentation and after presentation. For the targets, we measured

1. *the prior score*, the score for each word before the prime was presented;
2. *the initial score*, the score for each word after presentation of the initial prime;
3. *the rhyme score*, the score after presentation of a rhyme prime;
4. *the initial control score*, the score for a target after presentation of an initial prime sharing no segments; and
5. *the rhyme control score*, the score for a target after presentation of a rhyme prime sharing no segments.

In keeping with the experimental literature, a reduced error score in the related condition relative to an unrelated control would indicate facilitation, and a larger error score would indicate inhibition. A more subtle evaluation of the effects within the model is possible by comparing the target error scores to the error scores of the same words in the prior condition, which provides a ready-made neutral baseline, but our concern with the Colombo Effect directs our attention primarily to the related–unrelated contrasts.

As described here, priming in this kind of model may be thought of as a strong learning trial. To generate a strong priming effect, the primes were presented to the network repeatedly. First, we examined the effect of increasing numbers of prime presentations on the "strength" of the prime. Figure 13.2 shows error scores as a function of number of prime presentations (0, 10, 20, and 60) for the relatively poorly trained 100 epoch network. Clearly, much of the effect of priming occurs within the first 10 trials. This shows that we would obtain similar results if we conducted the target tests after 10, 20, or 60 prime cycles. However, we decided to use 60 prime cycles in the actual tests in order to assess the effects of maximal priming. Note also that error scores are much larger for the onset, and that prime presentation has most effect on this segment, much less on the nucleus, and virtually none on the final consonant or coda.

Results

The data we present are the error scores for the 3 segments of the primes and targets at 3 levels of network training. The left-hand panels of Fig. 13.3 show the effect of prime presentation on the primes' error scores. As described earlier, the perception of a prime was simulated by presenting the prime 60 times in succession. The figure shows the error score for each of the prime's segments

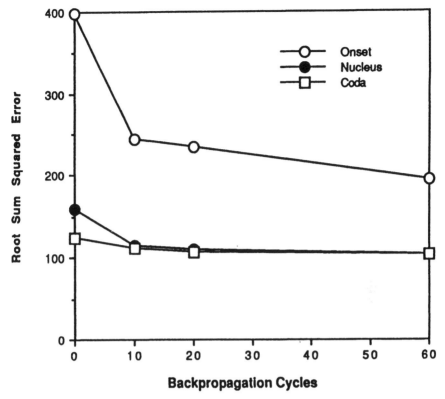

FIG. 13.2.   The effect of prime presentation on the error score for the primes as a function of number of presentations when the network had been trained for 100 epochs.

before and after prime presentation. The priming effects on the targets are shown in the right-hand panels of Fig. 13.3, and the results, averaged over segments, are summarised in Table 13.3. Unless otherwise stated, priming effects in what follows refer to differences between the error scores of initial or rhyme condition targets and their unrelated controls, but we will sometimes point to the relative standing of the prior state in interpreting effects.

The summary data in Table 13.3 indicate facilitatory priming in the initial condition at 100 epochs. There is also some evidence of facilitatory priming at 100 epochs in the rhyme condition, relative to its own control, though not relative to the prior states of the targets. At 200 and 300 epochs, there is little evidence of overall facilitation and no evidence of inhibition. However, our hypothesis is that inhibition might occur at the level of individual segments. The following observations describe additional details of priming effects for each segment, as depicted in the right-hand panels of Fig. 13.3.

TABLE 13.3

Root Sum Squared Error as a Function of Priming Condition and Epochs of Pretest Training
Averaged Over the Three Segments of Target Words

Condition	Epochs of Training		
	100	200	300
Initial	148	111	98
Rhyme	176	116	99
Prior	172	113	98
Initial Control	180	113	99
Rhyme Control	187	116	106

Segment 1 (Onset).   Here, we observe the clearest effect on the first segment
of the initial condition at 100 epochs. Facilitation was present both relative to the
prior state of the target and to the unrelated initial condition. Note, however,
that the other conditions, including the rhyme condition, all showed inhibition
relative to the prior state. This would indicate that the model developed a
preference for the onset of the prime when prime activation was simulated. The
facilitation in the related initial condition persisted at 200 and 300 epochs, but the
effect was very much attenuated.

We suggested earlier that the model's preference for the onset of the prime
might provide a way of simulating inhibition. The similarity of the prime and
target might dispose the model to produce the prime's onset in the rhyme
condition more than in the other conditions. If this were so, the error score
should be greater in the rhyme condition than in the unrelated rhyme control
condition. However, there is no evidence for this at 100 and 300 epochs, and only
a hint of what could be such a tendency at 200 epochs. Thus it appears that
preference for the prime's onset is quite specific, and does not depend on
subsequent segments. The model therefore does not have a means of emulating
inhibitory outcomes in a rhyme priming condition.

Segment 2 (Nucleus).   The first thing to notice here is that the level of the
error scores is much less than that of the onsets. In keeping with this, priming
effects are reduced at the nucleus. We find facilitation in the rhyme condition,
and also in the initial condition at 100 epochs. Note also that there is no
inhibition in the control conditions relative to the prior. However, the benefits of
priming disappear in the initial condition by 200 epochs, and they are largely lost
in the rhyme condition also. Likewise, the effect of prime presentation on prime
error scores is very slight at 200 and 300 epochs (see Fig. 13.3, left panels).

Segment 3 (Coda).   This segment shows little effect of priming. There is no
rhyme priming even at 100 epochs, whereas the initial condition, in which prime

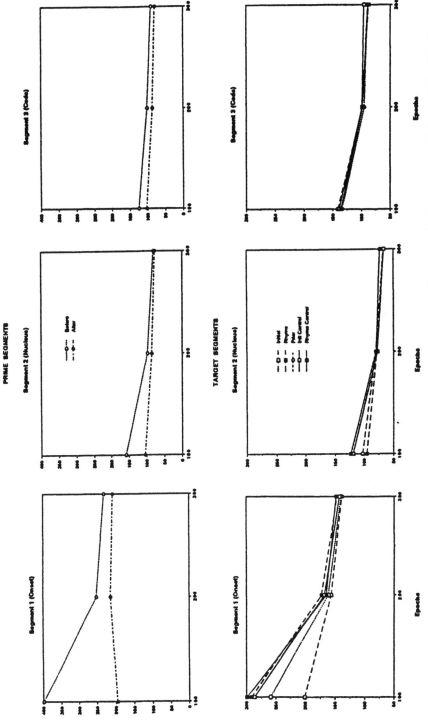

FIG. 13.3. Error scores for prime and target segments as a function of epochs of pretest training. The top panels show error scores before and after 60 cycles of prime presentation. The bottom panels show the effect of prime presentation as reflected in the various target conditions.

387

and target codas differ, shows a slight tendency to inhibition relative to its control. Again, such a tendency could provide a means of simulating inhibition in the model. However, the tendency to inhibition in the initial condition was not observed at 200 and 300 epochs. Therefore, it does not bear the empirically observed relation to target frequency whereby, viewing epochs of training as analogous to increasing word frequency, inhibition should be observed in the 200 and 300 epoch conditions. We conclude that the model is not equipped to reproduce the Colombo Effect in the initial condition.

Overall, we observed some facilitatory priming in both the initial and rhyme conditions when the network was less trained, but a rapidly diminishing effect as training proceeded. The model did not produce the inhibitory effect observed in recent experiments with high-frequency targets. These conclusions hold both across segments and at the level of individual segments.

Although the model was correct in finding facilitation for "low-frequency" words (100 epochs), further consideration shows that the basis of this effect is unsatisfactory. This can be seen most clearly by considering the effect of prime presentation in the model. Just as the priming effect measured on the targets falls off with training, so does the effect of prime presentation (Fig. 13.3, left-hand panels). As one would expect, repeated presentation of primes to an under-trained network has a large effect, but prime presentation has much less effect on the more fully-trained 200 and 300 epoch networks. Unfortunately, this means that, within the model, high-frequency primes have less effect than low-frequency primes. Because a prime's activation is represented only by its influence on the weights in the network, there is less room for this influence to be expressed as training proceeds. For example, the onset, which shows a 51% reduction in error at 100 epochs, shows only a 9.8% reduction at 300 epochs. These effects of prime presentation translated into a 30% priming effect in the test phase at 100 epochs, but only a negligible 2.8% at 300 epochs. Extrapolating from this pattern, the best learned words, at the limit, can have no priming effect, an eventuality that makes little sense.

Clearly, Model 1 does not provide a plausible implementation of priming. First, it does not provide a satisfactory way to represent the activation of high-frequency words. The activation of a prime must be implemented in some way that is independent of its distance from a learning asymptote. Second, this architecture does not reproduce the empirically observed inhibition effect on high-frequency targets. Following presentation of our second model of form-related effects, we will return to the evaluation of the PDP model.

Model 2: Interactive Activation Model of Form-Related Priming

Our second model is designed specifically to produce the empirically observed pattern of form-related facilitation and inhibition that we call the Colombo Effect. It does not involve any learning process. Rather it is driven by activation levels in the style of many pre-PDP connectionist models. In particular, it draws on aspects of Dell's (1986) language production model and McClelland & Rumelhart's (1981) model of letter and word perception.

The essence of the model is the proposal that form-related inhibition arises as a result of competition among phonological segments of activated words. The model incorporates the distinction between nonphonological word nodes or *lemmas* (Kempen & Huijbers, 1983; see further discussion later in the section on *Phonological Competition and Language Production*) and phonologically specified words that is intrinsic to most models of language production (e.g. Dell, 1986; Garrett, 1975; 1980). Our model contrasts with Colombo's (1986) proposal that inhibition is determined at the lexical level.

In the framework of our model, we propose two qualitatively different effects of a prime. The first effect is facilitation of the lemmas of words sharing letters with the prime. The second is competition in the process of phonological specification among segments of currently activated words. In a priming paradigm, these words are the prime and the target. In the model, the competition arises only if an attempt is made to select the target's phonological segments while the prime's segments are highly activated. A form-related prime therefore augments lemma-level activation, but it may interfere with the specification of a word's phonological form. As we shall see, these assumptions are sufficient to enable the model to simulate the range of facilitation and inhibition effects observed in the empirical literature.

Components of the Model

The model has three distinct levels: letters, lemmas, and segments (see Fig. 13.4). As in the PDP simulations, it processes CVCs, though in principle it is general. Nodes at the letter and segment levels represent both letter identities and word positions. That is, each letter and segment is replicated at each of three possible word positions; initial, medial, and final. In the instantiation of the model described here, six words are represented at the lemma level. These words are: CAT, CAP, CAD, PEG, PEN, and PEZ. As in the PDP model, these words may be thought of as realising the conditions of an experiment. Thus, the words CAT and PEG serve as related, and unrelated primes, and CAP and CAD serve as target items. CAP is a high-frequency target and CAD a low-frequency target. The words PEN and PEZ were included so that related and unrelated primes would have equivalent lexical neighbourhoods. PEN represented a high-frequency neighbour of PEG, and PEZ a low-frequency neighbour. Word frequency was represented as a lemma's resting level of activation. High-frequency words were assigned a resting level of 0, low-frequency words were assigned a resting level of –50, and primes were given an intermediate resting level of –25. This assignment of frequencies and resting levels does not, of course, correspond to the actualities of the language. The particular words that we used can best be thought of as convenient labels for the lemmas to which they are attached.

Connections. There are both excitatory and inhibitory connections in the model. All connections are between nodes at adjacent levels. Specifically, lemmas have excitatory connections (weight = 0.03) to their constituent letter and segment nodes; letter nodes have excitatory connections (weight = 0.03) to the lemmas of words that contain them and inhibitory connections (weight = 0.04) to other lemmas; and segment nodes have excitatory connections to lemmas to which they subscribe (weight = 0.03), but no inhibitory connections. Note that there are no intralevel inhibitory connections, and in particular no inhibitory connections between lemmas. We do not intend this omission as a proscription against intralevel inhibition, but this aspect of the model does, underline our contention that intralevel inhibition is not responsible for the Colombo Effect.

The activation of a node was determined by three factors: the node's activation at the beginning of the timestep, $a_i(t)$; activation received from other nodes during the current timestep, $n_i(t)$; and decay of activation during the current timestep, $d_i(t)$. Specifically, the activation of a node at time $t + \Delta t$ was:

$$a_i(t + \Delta t) = a_i(t) + n_i(t) - d_i(t) \qquad 1$$

On each timestep, the amount of activation sent by each node was equal to its current potential, provided the potential was positive. If the node's potential was

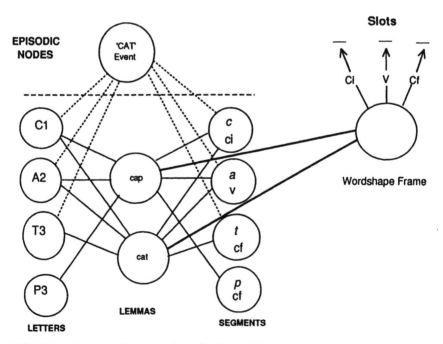

FIG. 13.4.   Structure of the interactive activation model.

zero or less, it sent no output. Activation *received* by a particular node, the net input to the node, was defined as:

$$n_i(t) = \sum_j a_{ij} e_j(t) - \sum_k \gamma_{ik} i_k(t) \qquad\qquad 2$$

where $e_j(t)$ is the activation of an excitatory neighbour of the node, and $i_k(t)$ is the activation of an inhibitory neighbour of the node. a_{ij} and γ_{ik} are weight constants for excitatory and inhibitory links.

Decay of activation, $d_i(t)$, is defined as:

$$d_i(t) = \Theta_i(a_i(t) - r_i) \qquad\qquad 3$$

where Θ_i is a constant decay rate (set to 0.09), $a_i(t)$ is the node's current level of activation, and r_i is the node's resting level of activation. Thus, decay is proportional to a node's distance from its resting level. Finally, activation was bounded by a minimum, which was the resting level of each node, and a maximum, which was set at 300 for all nodes.

Episodic Node.   Figure 13.4 also shows an episodic node. This node resides at the lemma level, has a resting level of 0, and has a decay rate of 1.0. This means that its activation at each timestep is solely a function of new input. On a priming trial, the episodic node establishes connections with the letter and segment nodes of the prime, and serves as an episodic memory of the prime when the target is presented. Thus, the episodic node is a short-term memory representation that stores the mapping between the letters and phonological segments of the prime. We assume that a new episodic memory is established during target processing, but this is irrelevant to the priming process and therefore is not realised in the model.

Simulation of the Priming Process

The model is intended to simulate a priming paradigm, in which a prime is presented long enough to allow strong activation, and in which a target word is presented immediately after the prime. Figure 13.4 depicts the network when the prime is CAT and the target is the high-frequency target CAP.

Prime Presentation.   Prime presentation was simulated by clamping the activation of each of the prime's letter nodes to the maximum level of 300. The model was then run for 20 timesteps. During this time, activation spread throughout the model, from letters to lemmas, from lemmas to segments and letters, and from segments to lemmas. The prime's lemma was highly activated, primarily due to inputs from its 3 letter nodes. Orthographically similar words were also activated, although to a much lesser extent. These nodes received excitatory input from the 2 consistent letter nodes, and inhibitory input from the inconsistent third letter. Thus, in the case where CAT is the prime, CAT would be highly activated, and CAP would be slightly activated.

After the 20 timesteps, links were created from the prime's letter nodes to the episodic node (weight = 0.10), and from the episodic node to the prime's segments (weight = 0.015). In this way, the episodic node was recruited as a temporary memory of the prime. In Fig. 13.4, CAT occupies the episodic node.

Target Presentation.   As in the case of the prime, presentation of the target was simulated by clamping its letter nodes to the maximum level of 300. The model was then run until the target's lemma reached its asymptote. Activation spread through the model in the same manner as for the prime, except that the episodic links were also present. If the target shared letters with the prime, as it did on related trials, it activated the episodic node. Thus, the presentation of a related target reinstated the prime, and thus indirectly reactivated the prime's segments.

Response.   We simulated response latency in terms of the probability of mis-selecting the critical third segment at the point when the target's lemma had reached full activation. The third segment is critical because it distinguishes the primes and targets in the related conditions. By focusing on this segment, we imply that its selection controls most of the variance in responding. Notice that this is just the kind of mechanism that we proposed might regulate facilitation and inhibition in the PDP model.

As shown in Fig. 13.4, we assume that the activation and retrieval of a lexical item makes available an abstract wordshape frame that guides the selection of the target's segments (see Dell, 1986; Stemberger, 1990; for discussion of wordshape frames). The model does not contain explicit wordshape frames, but we capture the functional effect of such frames by making the selection of phonological segments contingent on the activation of lemmas. Specifically, the critical third segment was selected when the target's lemma reached its maximum activation level. Although only selection of the critical segment was implemented, the model carries the implication that all segments must be selected prior to a response.

The model's response time involves three components, and was computed as follows:

$$RT = \beta l_i + \psi(1 - p(R_i, t)) + \kappa \qquad 4$$

Here, the term βl_i is a measure of lexical access time, l_i is the number of timesteps required for the target's lemma to reach asymptote, and β is a constant specifying the duration of one timestep (set to 5msec). The component $\psi(1 - p(R_i, t))$ is an estimate of the processing time incurred when the target's critical segment is incorrectly selected. The probability of correctly selecting the critical segment, $p(R_i, t)$, depends on its activation relative to other competing segments at the same word position. This probability was determined using the same Luce choice rule as in McClelland and Rumelhart (1981), except that it was based on the activation at the timestep when the target's lemma reached asymptote rather than being based on a running average of activation over time. The probability that a segment other than the correct segment is selected is given by $(1 - p(R_i, t))$, and ψ is a constant specifying the time associated with an incorrect selection (set to 150msec in the model). Finally, κ is a constant (set to 450msec) that reflects the time required for all of the processing not explicitly represented in the model, including encoding of letters and response execution.

Simulating the Colombo Effect

As described earlier, Colombo (1986) reported slower lexical decision latencies to high-frequency targets in the context of form-related primes. For low-frequency targets, on the other hand, the priming effect was facilitatory. We successfully simulated the Colombo results with our model.

In the simulation, the model was presented with either a high- or low-frequency target word (CAP or CAD) preceded by either a related or an unrelated prime (CAT or PEG). Figure 13.5 shows the results of the simulation. The probability of selecting the critical segment correctly is plotted as a function of the number of timesteps following the presentation of the target. In this figure, each of the four frequency X relatedness conditions is plotted separately. The endpoint of each line reflects the timestep at which the target reached asymptote and at which segment selection occurred.

Notice that, across timesteps, the probability of selecting the correct segment is higher for unrelated than for related targets. This is because, on related trials, the target tends to reactivate the prime's phonological segments, thus increasing the likelihood of selecting a segment from the prime rather than the target. On an unrelated trial, there is no overlap in letters between the prime and target, so the prime's lemma is inhibited by each of the target's letter nodes. With no lemma-level support, the activation of the prime's segments quickly decays, thereby increasing the probability of correctly selecting the target's critical segment.

A second effect shown in Fig. 13.5 is that, at a given timestep, the probability of correct selection is greater for high-frequency targets than for low-frequency targets. This can be seen most clearly by comparing high- and low-frequency unrelated targets. This frequency effect occurs because high-frequency words have higher resting levels of activation than do low-frequency words and therefore activate their segments more quickly.

Of primary interest, however, is the probability of correct segment selection when the lemmas reach asymptote—that is, at the endpoints of the lines. At these points, the probability of selecting the critical segment correctly is less for high-frequency than for low-frequency words, and this frequency effect interacts with relatedness. For unrelated targets, there is no difference in the probability of

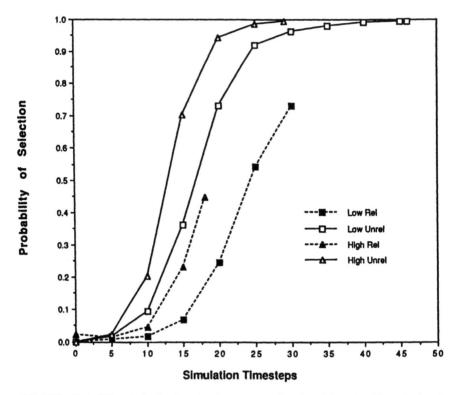

FIG. 13.5   Probability of selecting the critical segment as a function of timesteps. The endpoint of each line indicates the timestep where the lemma reached asymptote and selection actually occurred.

correct selection for high- and low-frequency targets. Both have reached a ceiling probability when selection occurs. For a related target, on the other hand, there is a large advantage for low-frequency words (a 76% chance for a low-frequency target, and 45% for a high-frequency target). This difference is due to the fact that the high-frequency lemma reaches its maximum activation before its critical segment has had enough time to become sufficiently activated. The early initiation of the selection process occurs both because the target is a high-frequency word and because it has been primed. Thus, for high-frequency words, facilitation at the lemma level actually exacerbates the problem of segment selection.

The response time for each of the four conditions was calculated using Equation 4. The results are presented in Fig. 13.6, along with data from the Colombo (1986) study. Clearly, the model's fit to the Colombo data is quite good. In both the simulation and Colombo's data there is a large facilitation effect for low-frequency targets, and an inhibition effect for high-frequency targets.

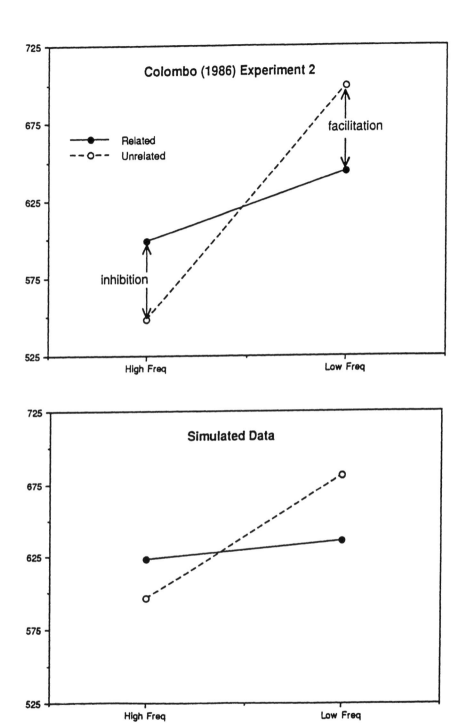

FIG. 13.6. Simulation of the relatedness x frequency interaction.

Phonological Competition or Lexical Suppression?

Our model successfully simulated the Colombo Effect. However, the view of form-related priming that our model implements differs substantially from the account proposed by Colombo (1986). Colombo proposed that words are inhibited in the process of recognition when they pass an activation threshold, and elaborated this proposal in terms of the McClelland and Rumelhart (1981) model of letter perception. As in our model, there are excitatory connections between affiliated letters and words, and inhibitory connections between nonaffiliates in the McClelland-Rumelhart model. In addition, unlike our model, there are intralevel inhibitory connections among letters and words. The model contains orthographic, lexical, and phonological representations, but only the orthographic and lexical representations are considered in their simulations. McClelland and Rumelhart found they could simulate most of the letter perception phenomena they were concerned with without considering phonology. However, though the model deals mainly with letter perception, it readily lends itself to recasting in word recognition terms. Likewise, although the model does not address form-related priming, the existence of intra-level inhibition means that it is a trivial matter to set the model in such a way that it produces form-related inhibition (see McClelland & Rumelhart, 1981, p. 384, where activation of the word WORK falls below its resting level when the related word WORD is presented). The problem Colombo faced was that a uniformly applied inhibition process would produce across-the-board inhibition rather than the observed interaction of priming with target frequency. Her solution was to suggest the inhibition threshold mentioned earlier, whereby only words exceeding a certain level of activation would be inhibited. Because high-frequency words have higher resting levels, they would be more likely to reach the threshold. As Colombo (1986, p. 232) admits, however, this is very much an ad hoc proposal, and we know of no independent motivation for the notion of an inhibition threshold. It would also appear that selectively inhibiting more active lexical nodes would lead to lower overall levels of target activation. In contrast to the use of inhibition in the McClelland and Rumelhart model to promote perceptual sharpening by suppressing weakly activated nodes, Colombo's proposal would leave such nodes immune to inhibition, but damp the activation of more active nodes, including targets.

Apart from the implausibility of the notion of an inhibition threshold, we believe the lexical suppression view to be mistaken. We have proposed an alternative phonological competition model that reproduces the empirical patterns, and which depends on a phonological level of representation that is not addressed at all in Colombo (1986). Note that our emphasis on the phonological level is consistent with most of the literature cited earlier (e.g. Hillinger, 1980; Humphreys et al., 1982; Tanenhaus et al., 1980). However, like Colombo, we found that the explanation of form-related inhibition required an additional mechanism. Whereas the previous studies could account for facilitation in terms of simple phonological activation, our model imports additional structure in the form of wordshape frames, and an additional process of selecting phonological segments to fill them.

The inclusion of wordshape frames entails another important difference between our view and Colombo's. In our model, the constituents of related targets are preactivated due to residual activation left by processing of the prime, but in Colombo's view the lexical nodes of related high-frequency targets are suppressed below their resting levels. In Colombo's conception, facilitation and inhibition are determined by the effects of prime processing on lexical activation levels. That is, these effects are entirely determined during prime processing. In our scheme, there is some effect of prime presentation, but the emphasis is on events occurring during target processing, in particular, selection of the phonological segments of the target and episodic reactivation of the prime. We now consider these two important aspects of the model in some detail.

Selection of Phonological Segments

Although we argue that our account is more plausible than Colombo's, and more consonant with the consensus in the literature on the existence of phonological effects, we have not presented any definitive evidence that would arbitrate between the two accounts. An experiment we have recently conducted, however, suggests that we are correct in giving priority to processes at the phonological level. What we wanted was a condition involving form-related words in which phonological competition did not arise. This condition is provided by nonhomographic homophones. We conducted a naming experiment comparing priming effects among the nonhomographic homophones (e.g. MUSSEL-MUSCLE) and form-related nonhomophones. The nonhomophones (e.g. MUSKET-MUSCLE) were related but orthographically divergent in just the same way as in the experiment we described earlier (see *Receptive Priming*). We followed exactly the same procedure as in the previously described experiment. Since the targets are the same and the primes are lexical competitors, Colombo would predict the same result in both conditions. Our model, however, predicts the results we actually obtained: Facilitation in the homophonous condition where there is no phonological competition, but inhibition in the nonhomophone condition (see Table 13.1).[8]

In a study cited earlier, Humphreys et al. (1982) used nonhomographic homophones in a similar way to evaluate effects of phonological activation. Humphreys et al., however, used a perceptual identification task in which both primes and targets were exposed for very brief durations. With this procedure,

---

[8]Note that the strength of the inhibition effect in this experiment is less critical than the interaction of priming with homophony. The strength of the inhibition effect depends on target frequency and possibly other factors.

facilitation, measured in terms of probability of correct identification, is obtained whether there is phonological competition or not. Indeed, facilitation is even obtained in cases of spelling-to-sound mismatch (e.g. COUCH-TOUCH; see Evett & Humphreys, 1981). Our finding of an interaction between relatedness and homophony in a speeded naming task provides strong support for Humphreys et al.'s conclusions concerning automatic phonological activation, but it also points to the need for an additional mechanism to account for inhibition in the nonhomophone case. Our candidate for this mechanism, described earlier, is competition in the process of segment selection when the sounds of words are being specified.

Although our conclusions are compatible with those of Humphreys et al., our procedures and response measures differ. One reason we obtain inhibition to high-frequency form-related targets is that we use a speeded response task in which transitory difficulty in assigning phonological segments is likely to be disruptive. In addition, the nature of prime processing, as represented by the episodic node, has an important role in our model.

Episodic Memory of the Prime

Inhibition occurs in our model as a result of difficulty in forming a phonological representation of the target word. This difficulty arises because the target tends to activate the prime's lemma and its accompanying episodic representation, as well as the target's own lemma (see Fig. 13.4). By incorporating the episodic node, we are proposing that the inhibition effect depends on the formation of an episodic trace of the prime. We would predict, therefore, that the strength of this representation should influence the size of the inhibition effect. For example, if the primes were masked, as they were in the Humphreys et al. studies, no episodic representation would be developed, and therefore inhibition of high-frequency targets would be eliminated or at least substantially reduced.

To quantify the relationship between the strength of the episodic representation and form-related priming, we ran a series of simulations in which the strength of the letter-to-episode connections in the model was varied. Whereas the weights were 0.10 in the previously described simulations, we varied them from 0 to 0.15 in these tests. By this manipulation, we changed the impact of the episodic memory of the prime. A zero weight on the letter-to-episode links means that the prime's effect is limited to its influence on the activation levels of letters and lemmas. A large weight means that the prime episode is reactivated during the processing of the related target.

Except for varying the letter-to-episodic node weights, the model was run as before. Figure 13.7 shows the results of these simulations. As the weights were increased, there was a general reduction in the priming effect for both low- and high-frequency targets. With very weak or non-existent episodic traces there was

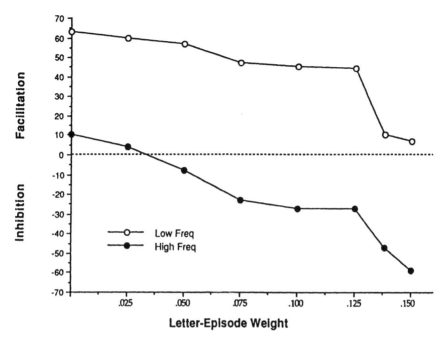

FIG. 13.7.   Priming effects for high- and low-frequency words as a function of the strength of the episodic memory of the prime.

actually a small facilitation effect for the high-frequency target, accompanied by a large facilitation effect for the low-frequency target. With increases in episodic strength, the high-frequency target began to show inhibition, and the low-frequency target showed decreasing facilitation. With the maximum weight of 0.15 there was little facilitation for the low-frequency target, and a large inhibitory effect for the high-frequency target.

Lexical decision data reported by Forster, Davis, Schoknecht, & Carter (1987), showing facilitation of high-frequency targets following masked primes, indicate that our predictions for masked priming are correct. However, the strongest confirmation of our position would be a demonstrastion of inhibition under normal priming conditions and facilitation in masked prime conditions with the same materials. Initial results indicate that this pattern obtains for both the high-frequency and nonhomophone conditions shown in Table 13.1 (Peterson, O'Seaghdha, & Dell, 1989).

Phonological Competition and Language Production

Although the interactive activation model is cast in terms of receptive priming, several aspects of the model have a more direct bearing on language production than comprehension. These include the distinction between nonphonological lemmas and phonologically specified words; the use of wordshape frames, which derives directly from the study of production (Dell, 1986; 1988; Stemberger, 1990); and the last-discussed episodic representations. In production, both syntactic and phonological representations must be constructed prior to articulation, and we suggest that episodic representations are required to maintain these constructions in a state of preparation until they are used. Thus, many of the critical aspects of our model are informed by ideas that derive from the study of production. In this section, we elaborate on the nature of language production with a view to highlighting the indebtedness of our thinking on form activation to language production theory. Then we will describe briefly some recent research in which this debt is repaid by applying our perspective on form-related priming to the study of production.

Production models, beginning with Garrett (1975), share the noncontroversial assumption that production involves successive stages of nonphonological and phonological representation (see Bock, 1982; Dell, 1986; Levelt, 1989; Stemberger, 1985). This conclusion follows from the evident sequence, from intention or message to phonetically explicit speech, in the formulation of utterances. We do not concern ourselves here with details of production models but with a broad characterisation of the consensus view of stages in production.

Figure 13.8 shows some of the main stages of preparation for production in Garrett's (1975) model: a message or conceptual level, a syntactic level, and a phonological level. A speaker begins with an idea or intention, which passes through stages of syntactic formulation and phonological specification. The level of syntactic encoding captures the structural relations between lemmas, which, as described earlier, are nonphonological representations carrying semantic and syntactic aspects of lexical information (Kempen & Huijbers, 1983;

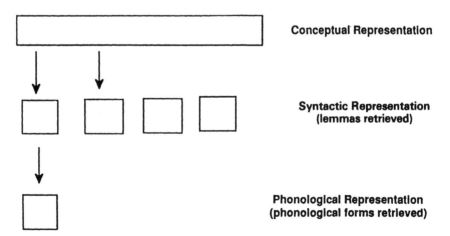

FIG. 13.8.   Some components of planning in speech production.

see Levelt, 1989). A lemma may therefore be thought of as the subset of information in a word's lexical entry that is relevant at the syntactic level of speech planning. At the phonological level, the words are phonologically specified and inserted in a prosodic structure preparatory to articulation. In short, there are distinct stages at which words are first selected and later specified in terms of their sounds. Error corpora, which provide the primary data base for theories of production, support this distinction. To take just one example, lexical exchanges span longer distances than sound errors (Garrett, 1975), and are relatively indifferent to phonological similarity (but see Dell & Reich, 1981).

The empirical work on production, that we now describe, primarily concerns effects at the syntactic and phonological levels. The lemmas of words are activated at the syntactic level, but their forms are fully specified only at the phonological level. In terms of our model, we would expect the phonological segments of a word fully prepared for production to be highly activated. This would likely lead to phonological competition in specifying the sounds of a related probe word. If a longer utterance such as a sentence were prepared, we might expect the initial content words of the utterance to be specified phonologically. Again, responses to probes related to these words should be inhibited. However, in production theory, there is a point in sentence preparation where the lemmas of words are selected for production, but where their sounds are not specified. Our model predicts that inhibition should not affect probes related to elements of this nonphonological portion of a planned utterance.

Production Priming. The difference between production priming and receptive priming for present purposes is that in the receptive case the prime is a recently presented word, whereas in the simplest production case the prime is a subject's intention to say a particular word. In the first production experiment we describe here, subjects prepared to say prime words, and were required to produce them on presentation of a cue on most experimental trials. But on critical trials a form-related or unrelated target was presented, and subjects were required to name this word instead.

Figure 13.9 summarises the procedure in this experiment. A display containing two words at upper and lower screen locations was presented for 1500msec. Then the screen was blanked for 1sec, and an arrow appeared, pointing to the former location of one of the two words. This was the subject's cue to prepare the designated word. Let us say the display contained the words CAT and PEG, and the arrow pointed to the location of CAT. The subject then prepared to say "*cat*." After a preparation interval of 1000msec, one of two things happened. On two-thirds of the trials, a cue appeared signalling the subject to say the prepared word as quickly as possible. On the remaining, critical trials, a probe word appeared. In this case, the subject said the presented word as quickly as possible instead of the prepared word. The probe word could be

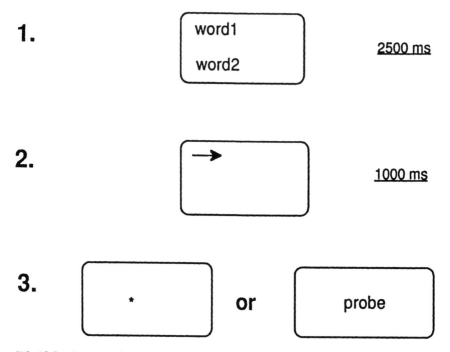

FIG. 13.9.   Procedure in the single-word production priming experiment.

related to the prepared word, related to the alternate (unprepared) word, or it could be unrelated to either word. For example, the related targets could be CAP (prepared) and PEN (alternate).[9] The alternate condition was included to distinguish effects of preparation from effects of merely displaying a word.

We found an inhibitory effect of form-related primes in the prepared condition, relative to the unrelated condition. In addition, we found no effect of form-relatedness in the unprepared alternate condition (see Table 13.4). We suggest that the form of the word was fully specified in the Prepared condition. In terms of the model, a strong episodic representation was established (see Fig. 13.4), and this interfered with the specification of the sounds of the contiguously presented target.

In another study, we had subjects prepare entire sentences rather than single words. Subjects were given 2500msec to read and prepare the sentences. Then, as in the single-word preparation study, subjects either reiterated the sentence on the appearance of a cue, or, on critical trials, they named a probe word. The

---

[9]The examples are merely illustrative, and are chosen because they are the words used in the model. Note that frequency was not manipulated in this experiment. We are currently exploring the effects of target frequency in production priming.

TABLE 13.4

Naming Latencies and Error Percentages in Form-related Production Priming Experiments

(a) *Single-word Production*		
Prepared	*Alternate*	*Unrelated*
601	582	583
(3.9)	(3.4)	(2.8)

(b) *Sentence Production*			
Actives (Critical Word Late)		*Passives* (Critical World Early)	
Related	*Unrelated*	*Related*	*Unrelated*
613	633	634	621
(9.8)	(10.2)	(7.5)	(7.7)

probes were related or unrelated in form to a critical word in the subject or object position of the sentences. For example, a subject might read the sentence "*The hiker lifted the log*," prepare to say it, and then be presented with the form-related probe LOCK. To manipulate the position of the critical word, we used active and passive versions of the same sentences. Thus, in the passive condition, a subject might prepare the sentence, "*The log was lifted by the hiker*," in which the critical word LOG is in subject position. One might expect that the critical word would be prepared for articulation in the passive sentence in much the same way as it would be in a single-word preparation experiment, and in fact the outcome supported this expectation. Related probes were inhibited relative to unrelated controls in the passive condition, where the critical word was in subject position (see Table 13.4). In contrast, when the critical word was in sentence-final object position, we observed facilitation of the form-related probes. We take this to mean that the object nouns were not phonologically specified when the targets were presented. Our model suggests that if a lemma is selected, but the sounds of the word are not specified, related lemmas should be facilitated.

We suggested earlier that production has the advantage of unambiguously requiring full phonological preparation of primes prior to their articulation. In the production priming experiments summarised here, we found inhibition of probes related in form to single prepared words or to the initial nouns of prepared sentences. We suggest that this is because the phonological form of these words was fully specified. We believe that this result provides clear evidence of an effect of phonological preparation, and therefore provides important corroboration of the phonological competition view of form-related inhibition that we advocate.

CONCLUSIONS

We have presented two different models, one a backpropagation model that produces the sounds of orthographic words sequentially, and the other a model specifically designed to simulate form-related priming effects, and in particular what we have called the Colombo Effect. Not surprisingly, the latter model did better at reproducing form-related priming effects. In concluding this paper, we will consider some differences between the models with a view to identifying what it would take for the learning model to simulate the range of empirical results.

Much of the appeal of PDP learning models lies in their seeming ability to reproduce many empirical phenomena without making many structural assumptions. Our backpropagation model too has this quality, but in this paper we have focused on some of its limitations. The performance of our model can be summarised as follows. Similarity between primes and targets engendered facilitation. Facilitation was inversely related to degree of learning of primes and targets. But the model had no means of producing the empirically observed inhibition effects on high-frequency targets (Colombo, 1986; Lupker & Williams, 1987; and see Table 13.1).

Because the backpropagation model's only way of representing the prime is in terms of the learning process for the prime, the model failed to reproduce the data. It might be possible to rectify this limitation of the model by incorporating a short-term weight-change mechanism that is distinct from long-term learning. This would at least remove the anomaly whereby a perfectly learned prime, in principle, has no effect on the model's subsequent processing. Whether such a mechanism would produce form-related inhibition, though, remains to be seen.

The success of our second model, the interactive activation model, leads us to speculate that priming phenomena require articulated representations of the prime and target. The model actually provides two mechanisms for representing the prime. First, the lemma, letter, and segment nodes of the prime retain some activation when the target is presented. Second, an episodic memory for the prime is added to the network. Both kinds of articulation are required to produce the variety of phenomena, at least in our implementation. Thus, we are led to conclude that a model of the type represented by our backpropagation model, to be successful, must separate the *training* of a word, in the sense of learning to say it, from the memory of that word. In other words, one must separate procedural from propositional/episodic memory.

We noted a related point in our attempts to get a variation of Model 1 to produce speech error phenomena (see Dell & Juliano, 1991). The model produced procedural noncontextual errors adequately, but failed to produce segmental movement errors (e.g. CAT PEG → /paet kɛg/). We suggest that, just as the absence of an explicit representation of the prime's occurrence limits its ability to simulate priming data, the lack of articulated representations of multiple words precludes the occurrence of movement errors.

Although we do not claim that it is necessarily correct in all its details, our second, interactive activation model does demonstrate what we believe is a plausible account of form-related priming. Model 2 assumes automatic activation of both orthographic and phonological representations, and identifies the process of phonological specification as the locus of inhibitory effects of form-related primes. The model also stresses events occurring during processing of the target, rather than concentrating only on prime processing. Therefore, our emphasis on phonology does not carry with it the implication that phonological preactivation has a significant impact on early word recognition or on-line reading (see Coltheart, 1978; Seidenberg, 1985; Van Orden, Johnston & Hale, 1988). However, we do contend that models of lexical processing cannot ignore the phonological level or leave it unimplemented (Colombo, 1986; McClelland & Rumelhart, 1981).

Despite the relative success of Model 2, we do not want to make excessive claims for it. For one thing, it is too powerful, building in many assumptions, and including many parameters. For another, it has no learning capability. A more complete model of form-related priming might combine learning with articu-lated representation of competing entities in an integrated architecture. Cohen, Dunbar, and McClelland (1990), for example, have recently developed such a model of Stroop phenomena, suggesting that the goal of an integrated model may be attainable for at least some problems. However, the Stroop model produces interference by means of output competition among colours and words trained in separate networks, whereas the form-related inhibition with which we are concerned arises within a single system.

At present we do not have a solution to the problem of generating form-related inhibition in a unified learning-activation model, and therefore we leave this problem as a challenge to ourselves and others. In the meantime, we hope to have demonstrated at least two things. One is that form-related priming presents a nontrivial theoretical and modelling problem. The other is that the improved understanding of form-related priming that is emerging from current empirical and theoretical work equips us with a valuable tool for use in the study of language comprehension and, perhaps even more so, language production.

ACKNOWLEDGEMENTS

The simulations described in this paper were conducted on the Rochester Connectionist Simulator (Goddard, Lynne, Mintz, & Bukys, 1989). The research was supported by NIH Grant NS 25502. We thank Antje Meyer for comments on the manuscript. Address correspondence to Pat O'Seaghdha, Department of Psychology, Lehigh University, Bethlehem, PA 18015, U.S.A.

REFERENCES

Adams, M.J. (1979). Models of word recognition. *Cognitive Psychology*, *11*, 133–176.

Bock, K. (1982). Toward a cognitive psychology of syntax: Information processing contributions to sentence formulation. *Psychological Review*, *89*, 1–47.

Bock, K. (1987). An effect of the accessibility of word forms on sentence structures. *Journal of Memory and Language*, *26*, 119–137.

Bowles, N.L. & Poon, L.W. (1985). Effects of priming in word retrieval. *Journal of Experimental Psychology: Learning, Memory, and Cognition*, *11*, 272–283.

Brown, R. & McNeill, D. (1966). The "tip of the tongue" phenomenon. *Journal of Verbal Learning and Verbal Behavior*, *5*, 325–337.

Chomsky, N. & Halle, M. (1968). *The sound pattern of English.* New York: Harper & Row.

Cohen, J.D., Dunbar, K., & McClelland, J.L. (1990). On the control of automatic processes: A parallel distributed processing model of the Stroop effect. *Psychological Review*, *97*, 332–361.

Collins, A.M. & Loftus, E.F. (1975). A spreading-activation theory of semantic processing. *Psychological Review*, *82*, 407–428.

Colombo, L. (1986). Activation and inhibition with orthographically similar words. *Journal of Experimental Psychology: Human Perception and Performance*, *12*, 226–234.

Coltheart, M. (1978). Lexical access in simple reading tasks. In G. Underwood (Ed.), *Strategies of information processing.* London: Academic Press, 151–216.

Dell, G.S. (1986). A spreading activation theory of retrieval in sentence production. *Psychological Review*, *93*, 283–321.

Dell, G.S. (1988). The retrieval of phonological forms in production: Tests of predictions from a connectionist model. *Journal of Memory and Language*, *27*, 124–142.

Dell, G.S. & Juliano, C. (1991). *Connectionist approaches to the production of words* (Cognitive Science Technical Report CS-91-5). Urbana, Illinois: University of Illinois, Beckman Institute.

Dell, G.S. & Reich, P.A. (1981). Stages in sentence production: An analysis of speech error data. *Journal of Verbal Learning and Verbal Behavior*, *20*, 611–629.

Elman, J. (1988). *Finding structure in time.* Technical Report 8801. San Diego: University of California, San Diego, Center for Research in Language.

Evett, L.J. & Humphreys, G.W. (1981). The use of abstract grapheme information in lexical access. *Quarterly Journal of Experimental Psychology*, *33A*, 325–350.

Forster, K.I., Davis, C., Schoknecht, C., & Carter, R. (1987). Masked priming with graphemically related forms: Repetition or partial activation. *Quarterly Journal of Experimental Psychology*, *39A*, 211–251.

Garrett, M.F. (1975). The analysis of sentence production. In G.H. Bower (Ed.), *The psychology of learning and motivation.* New York: Academic Press, 133–177.

Garrett, M.F. (1980). Levels of processing in sentence production. In B. Butterworth (Ed.), *Language production, Vol. 1: Speech and talk.* New York: Academic Press, 177–220.

Glushko, R. (1979). The organization and activation of orthographic information in reading aloud. *Journal of Experimental Psychology: Human Perception and Performance*, *5*, 674–691.

Goddard, N.H., Lynne, K.L., Mintz, T., & Bukys, L. (1989). *Rochester Connectionist Simulator.* Technical Report 233. Rochester, N.Y.: University of Rochester, Computer Science Department.

Hillinger, M.L. (1980). Priming effects with phonemically similar words: The encoding bias hypothesis reconsidered. *Memory and Cognition*, *8*, 115–123.

Humphreys, G.W., Evett, L.J., & Taylor, D.E. (1982). Automatic phonological priming in visual word recognition. *Memory and Cognition*, *10*, 576–590.

Jones, G.V. & Langford, A.S. (1987). Phonological blocking in the tip of the tongue state. *Cognition*, *26*, 115–122.

Jordan, M.I. (1986). *Serial order: A parallel distributed processing approach.* Technical Report 8604. San Diego: University of California, San Diego, Institute for Cognitive Science.

Kempen, G. & Huijbers, P. (1983). The lexicalization process in sentence production and naming: Indirect election of words. *Cognition, 14,* 185–209.

Kuçera, H. & Francis, W.N. (1967). *Computational analysis of present-day American English.* Providence: Brown University Press.

Levelt, W.J.M. (1989). *Speaking: From intention to articulation.* Cambridge, Mass.: M.I.T. Press.

Lupker, S.J. & Williams, B.A. (1987). *When do rhyming primes inhibit target processing?* Paper presented at the 28th annual meeting of the Psychonomic Society, Seattle, Washington.

McClelland, J.L. & Rumelhart, D.E. (1981). An interactive activation model of context effects in letter perception: Part 1. An account of basic findings. *Psychological Review, 88,* 375–407.

McClelland, J.L. & Rumelhart, D.E. (1988). *Explorations in parallel distributed processing: A handbook of models, programs, and exercises.* Cambridge, Mass.: M.I.T. Press.

Martin, R.C. & Jensen, C.R. (1988). Phonological priming in the lexical decision task: A failure to replicate. *Memory and Cognition, 16,* 505–521.

Meyer, A.S. (1990). The time course of phonological encoding in language production: Phonological encoding inside the syllable. *Journal of Memory and Language, 29,* 524–545.

Meyer, D.E., Schvaneveldt, R.W., & Ruddy, M.G. (1974). Functions of graphemic and phonemic codes in visual word-recognition. *Memory & Cognition, 2,* 309–321.

O'Seaghdha, P.G., Dell, G.S., & Peterson, R.R. (1988). *Indexing representations in language production.* Paper presented at the 29th annual meeting of the Psychonomic Society, Chicago, Illinois.

Peterson, R.R., Dell, G.S., & O'Seaghda, P.G. (1989). *A connectionist model of form-related priming effects.* Proceedings of the 11th Annual Conference of the Cognitive Science Society, Hillsdale, N.J.: Lawrence Erlbaum Associates Inc.

Peterson, R.R., O'Seaghdha, P.G., & Dell, G.S. (1989). *Phonological competition in form-related priming.* Paper presented at the 30th Annual Meeting of the Psychonomic Society, Atlanta, Georgia.

Rumelhart, D.E., Hinton, G.E., & Williams, R.G. (1986). Learning internal representations by error propagation. In D.E. Rumelhart & J.L. McClelland (Eds.), *Parallel distributed processing: Explorations in the microstructure of cognition, Vol. 1.* Cambridge, Mass.: M.I.T. Press, 318–364.

Rumelhart, D.E. & McClelland, J.L. (1982). An interactive activation model of context effects in letter perception: Part 2. The contextual enhancement effect and some tests and extensions of the model. *Psychological Review, 89,* 60–94.

Rumelhart, D.E. & McClelland, J.L. (1986). On learning the past tenses of English verbs. In J.L. McClelland & D.E. Rumelhart (Eds.), *Parallel distributed processing: Explorations in the microstructure of cognition, Vol. 2.* Cambridge, Mass.: M.I.T. Press.

Seidenberg, M.S. (1985). The time course of information activation and utilization in visual word recognition. In D. Besner, T. Waller, & G.E. McKinnon (Eds.), *Reading research: Advances in theory and practice, Vol. 5.* New York: Academic Press.

Seidenberg, M.S. & McClelland, J.L. (1989). A distributed developmental model of visual word recognition. *Psychological Review, 96,* 523–568.

Sejnowski, T. & Rosenberg, C. (1986). *NETtalk: A parallel network that learns to read aloud* (Technical Report EECS-86/01). Baltimore, Maryland: Johns Hopkins University.

Selkirk, E. (1984). *Phonology and syntax: The relation between sound and structure.* Cambridge, Mass.: M.I.T. Press.

Shattuck-Hufnagel, S. (1987). The role of word onset consonants in speech production planning. In E. Keller & M. Gopnik (Eds.), *Motor and sensory processes in language.* Hillsdale, N.J.: Lawrence Erlbaum Associates Inc.

Slowiaczek, L.M., Nusbaum, H.C., & Pisoni, D.B. (1987). Phonological priming in auditory word recognition. *Journal of Experimental Psychology: Learning, Memory, and Cognition, 13,* 64–75.

Stemberger, J.P. (1985). An interactive activation model of language production. In A. Ellis (Ed.), *Progress in the psychology of language, Vol. 1.* Hillsdale, N.J.: Lawrence Erlbaum Associates Inc.

Stemberger, J.P. (1990). Wordshape errors in language production. *Cognition, 35,* 123–158.

Tanenhaus, M.K., Flanigan, H.P., & Seidenberg, M.S. (1980). Orthographic and phonological activation in auditory and visual word recognition. *Memory and Cognition, 8*, 513–520.

VanOrden, G.C., Johnston, J.C., & Hale, B.L. (1988). Word identification in reading proceeds from spelling to sound to meaning. *Journal of Experimental Psychology: Learning, Memory, and Cognition, 14*, 371–386.

Woodworth, R.S. (1938). *Experimental psychology.* New York: Holt.

14

Reading with Attentional Impairments: A Brain-damaged Model of Neglect and Attentional Dyslexias

Michael C. Mozer
Department of Computer Science and Institute of Cognitive Science, University of Colorado, Boulder, CO 80309-0430, U.S.A.

Marlene Behrmann
Department of Psychology and Rotman Research Institute, University of Toronto, Toronto, Ontario M5S 1A1, Canada

INTRODUCTION

Qualitatively different forms of acquired dyslexia have been identified and described in recent years (Coltheart, 1981; Ellis & Young, 1987; Shallice, 1988). These reading disorders arise as a consequence of brain damage—stroke, trauma, or diffuse degenerative conditions—in adults who were competent readers premorbidly, thus differentiating them from the developmental dyslexias observed in children who have difficulty acquiring reading skills in the first place. Although the acquired dyslexias have been characterised extensively in the neuropsychological literature, attempts are only now being made to relate the disorders to explicit computational accounts of reading (Hinton & Shallice, 1989; Patterson, in press; Patterson, Seidenberg, & McClelland, 1989).

A broad distinction that has arisen from the behavioural research in acquired dyslexia is the separation between impairments at peripheral and central stages of the reading process (Shallic & Warrington, 1980). Before a written word can be pronounced or understood, it must be classified as a single orthographic entity. This classification or attainment of a *visual word-form* (Shallice, 1988) occurs following the encoding of the visual percept. Once the stimulus features are registered and analysed, the integrated orthographic word-form serves as the

The authors' e-mail addresses are mozer@cs.colorado.edu and marlene@psych.toronto.edu respectively.

key to later, cognitive stages of processing (e.g. semantic access). Selective disturbances of reading that prevent the attainment of the visual word-form are classified as peripheral deficits, whereas those that affect processing beyond the word-form system or visual lexicon are classified as central dyslexias.

One of the most thoroughly studied forms of peripheral impairment, currently enjoying a considerable degree of interest (see, for example, the special edition of *Cognitive Neuropsychology, 7* (5/6)), is neglect dyslexia. The hallmark of neglect dyslexia is the failure to report information appearing on the left. Neglect dyslexia patients may ignore the left side of an open book, the beginning words of a line of text, or the beginning letters of a single word.[1] Neglect dyslexia is traditionally interpreted as a disturbance of selective attention (for detailed discussion, see Caramazza & Hillis, in press; Riddoch, Humphreys, Cleton, & Fery, in press). In neglect dyslexia, attention is unevenly distributed across the visual field, with maximal attention deployed to the right hemispace and considerably less to the left (Kinsbourne & Warrington, 1962). The consequence of such a deficit is that perceptual information on the left is not adequately processed and is thus often ignored.

A central question surrounding neglect dyslexia is exactly how much processing the neglected information receives, that is, at what stage of processing does the attentional deficit take its toll. One line of evidence indicates the neglect dyslexia occurs with respect to a retinal co-ordinate frame, as opposed to an intrinsic object-centred frame.[2] For example, 180° rotation of words leads to neglect with respect to the left of the retinal frame, not the object-centred frame,[3] and the retinal location of a word affects performance, even in the right visual field—the further to the right a word is presented relative to fixation, the better it is reported (Behrmann, Moscovitch, Black & Mozer, 1990; Ellis, Flude & Young, 1987; Young, Newcombe, & Ellis, in press). These findings suggest an attentional disruption occurring at an early stage of analysis for the following reason. The initial encoding of the visual world is certainly retinotopic, and one can argue on computational grounds that object recognition requires as a precondition a recoding of the perceptual data into an object-centred representation (Hinton, 1981; Marr, 1982). Thus, if the attentional disruption affects a retinotopic encoding, it must occur prior to recognition.

---

[1] Because neglect dyslexia occurs more frequently following lesions to the right hemisphere than to the left, all descriptions in this chapter refer to left-sided neglect.

[2] We use the term *retinal co-ordinate frame* loosely to describe a reference frame that depends on head and/or body position of the observer, not just eye position. See Ladavas (1987) and Farah, Brunn, Wong, Wallace, and Carpenter (1990) for further discussion of possible reference frames used in spatial attention.

[3] However, see Barbut and Gazzaniga (1987) and Hillis and Caramazza (1989) for an alternative conceptualisation.

However, puzzling evidence to the contrary indicates that the neglected items *are* recognised. For instance, neglect is less severe for words than nonwords (Behrmann et al., 1990; Brunn & Farah, in press; Sieroff, Pollatsek, & Posner, 1988). Why should there be a difference in performance between words and nonwords unless the items are analysed to the point where the lexical status of the item can be determined? As a further example, when patients are shown pairs of words presented simultaneously, say SUN and FLY, they often fail to read the left word. Surprisingly, though, neglect of the left word is less likely if the two words can be combined to form a compound, say COW and BOY (Behrmann et al., 1990). Surely, if the relation between the left and right words influences performance, then the left word must be read even if the patient fails to report it.

In this chapter, we propose an account of these and other phenomena associated with neglect dyslexia within the framework of an existing connectionist model. We show that the effects of damage to the model resemble the reading impairments observed in neglect dyslexia. We then sketch an account of another peripheral disorder, attentional dyslexia, in the same framework. We begin by describing the model, called MORSEL, originally developed by Mozer (1987; 1988; 1991).

MORSEL

MORSEL is a connectionist model of two-dimensional object recognition and spatial attention. MORSEL was originally developed with two goals in mind: (1) to build a computational mechanism that could analyse several visual objects simultaneously, and (2) to account for a broad spectrum of psychological data, including perceptual errors that occur when several objects appear simultaneously in the visual field, facilitatory effects of context and redundant information and attentional phenomena. The architecture and details of MORSEL arose from constraints imposed by these two goals. In this section, we summarise the aspects of MORSEL that are relevant to the task of word identification, but we refer the interested reader to Mozer (1991) for a more complete description and justification of the model.

MORSEL has three essential components (Fig. 14.1). The central component is a connectionist network called BLIRNET, which builds location invariant representations of visually-presented letters and words. BLIRNET has the capacity to analyse multiple strings in parallel, but perceptual interactions arise as the amount of information to be processed increases. Consequently, two additional components are required: a "clean up" mechanism that constructs a consistent interpretation of the somewhat noisy perceptual data provided by BLIRNET, called the *pull-out net*; and an *attentional mechanism* (AM for short) that guides the efforts of BLIRNET and prevents BLIRNET from attempting to process too much information at once.

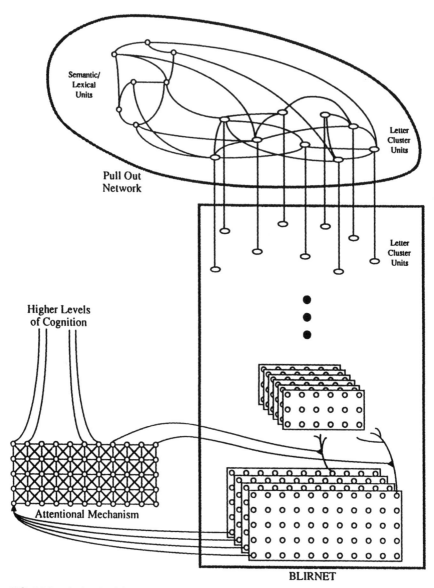

FIG. 14.1.   A sketch of the essential components of MORSEL.

To illustrate the typical operation of the system, consider a simple example in which MORSEL is shown a display containing two words, PEA and BOY. These words cause a pattern of activity on MORSEL's "retina," which serves as input to BLIRNET as well as to the AM. The AM then focuses on one retinal region, say the location of PEA. Information from that region is processed by

BLIRNET, which activates an orthographic representation suggesting that the item is PEA or possibly TEA, PFA, or RER. The pull-out net then selects the most plausible interpretation of BLIRNET's output, based partly on lexical and semantic knowledge, in this case hopefully PEA. The representation at this level of the system encodes the identity of the word but not its retinal location. Location information is recovered from the AM, which indicates the current location of focus. Shape and location information can then be bound together and stored in a visual short-term memory or used however desired by higher-level systems. Next, attention shifts to BOY and this process is repeated.

Input to MORSEL

Presentation of a visual display causes a pattern of activity on MORSEL's "retina." In the current implementation, the retina is a feature map arranged in a 36 × 6 spatial array, with detectors for 5 feature types at each point in the array (line segments at 4 orientations and line-segment terminator detectors). Letters of the alphabet are encoded as an activity pattern over a 3 × 3 retinal region. For instance, Fig. 14.2 depicts the retinal representation of PEA BOY.

The Letter and Word Recognition System (BLIRNET)

BLIRNET was designed on computational grounds to achieve the greatest amount of processing power given a limited amount of hardware. BLIRNET's architecture consists of a hierarchy of processing levels, starting at the lowest level with location-specific detectors for primitive visual features—the retinal representation—and progressing to a level composed of location-independent detectors for abstract letter identities. Units at intervening levels register successively higher order features over increasingly larger regions of retinotopic space. The effect of this architecture is that both location invariance and featural complexity increase at higher levels of the system.

Units in the output layer of BLIRNET have been trained to detect the presence of particular sequences of letters. These *letter-cluster units* respond to local arrangements of letters but are not sensitive to the larger context or the absolute retinal location of the letters. For example, there may be a unit that detects the sequence MON; it would become activated by words like MONEY or DIAMOND.

The letter-cluster units respond to triples of letters in four consecutive slots, either a sequence of three adjacent letters, such as MON, or two adjacent letters and one nearby letter, such as MO_E or M_NE, where the underbar indicates that any single letter may appear in the corresponding position. An asterisk is used to signify a blank space; for example, **M is an M with two spaces to its left. Presentation of MONEY should result in the activation of the following letter-cluster units: **M, **_O, *MO, *_ON, *M_N, MON, M_NE, MO_E, ONE, O_EY, ON_Y, NEY, NE_*, N_Y*, EY*, E_**, and Y**.The representation of words in the output

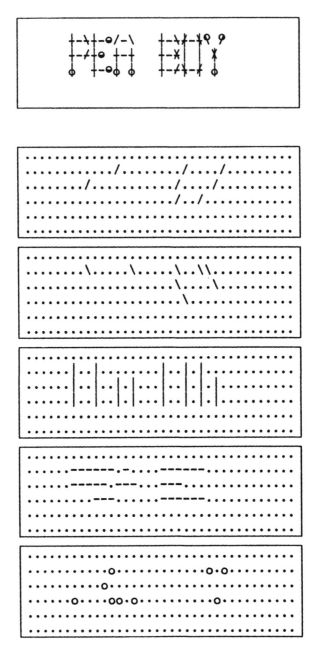

FIG. 14.2.   The top array shows the superimposed feature activations for a sample input PEA BOY, positioned on MORSEL's retina. The remaining arrays represent the individual feature maps. Each character in an array represents the activity of a single unit. A "." indicates that the unit is off. A "-", "/" "|", or "\" indicates activity of the corresponding unit in the 0°, 45°, 90°, 135° line segment map, respectively, and "o" indicates activity in the line segment terminator map.

414

layer of BLIRNET is thus distributed: a word corresponds to a pattern of activity across the letter-cluster units.

In most cases, the letter-cluster scheme is *faithful* (Smolensky, 1990), meaning that the set of units associated with a word is unique to that word (but see Pinker & Prince, 1988, and Prince & Pinker, 1988, for limitations to this type of scheme). The letter-cluster coding scheme also allows for the faithful representation of multiple words in parallel, provided that the words are not too similar (Mozer, 1991).

The details of BLIRNET's architecture are not particularly important; there are many possible implementations of the same basic idea (e.g. Uhr, 1987; Zemel, Mozer, & Hinton, 1989). The key aspect of BLIRNET is that although it can process multiple letters and words simultaneously in principle, it has resource limitations that cause a degradation in the quality of analysis as the amount of information to be processed increases. Consequently, when one or more words are presented to BLIRNET, appropriate clusters are not always fully activated and some "spurious" clusters achieve partial activation. These spurious clusters are related to the presented stimuli; they tend to be clusters that would be appropriate if a letter of the stimulus were substituted for a visually-similar letter (e.g. MOV instead of MON), if a letter or two were deleted from or inserted into the stimulus (e.g. ONY or MO_N), or if adjacent letters in the stimulus were transposed (e.g. ENY).

The Pull-out Network

The noisy pattern of letter-cluster activity produced by BLIRNET is not always easy to interpret. Interpretation is further complicated when several words are processed simultaneously because clusters of one word are entangled with clusters of another. The pull-out network (henceforth, *PO net*) has the task of selecting a set of clusters that represent a single item: it must "clean up" the noise and "disentangle" the hodgepodge of activations from multiple words (Fig. 14.3).

The PO net contains a set of units in one-to-one correspondence with the letter-cluster units of BLIRNET. Each letter-cluster unit excites its corresponding unit in the PO net; thus, the pattern of letter-cluster activity is copied to the PO net. Co-operative and competitive interactions then take place with the PO net to activate a set of letter clusters that exactly correspond to a single letter string. The resulting activity pattern is taken as MORSEL's response.

The basic idea behind the PO net interactions is that *compatible* clusters—ones likely to appear together in a letter string, e.g. MON and ONE—should excite one another and *incompatible* clusters—ones unlikely to appear together, e.g. MON and MOV—should inhibit one another. Thus, the connection strengths are related to how strongly one can predict the presence or absence of one cluster given another cluster. These predictions serve as weak constraints on how the

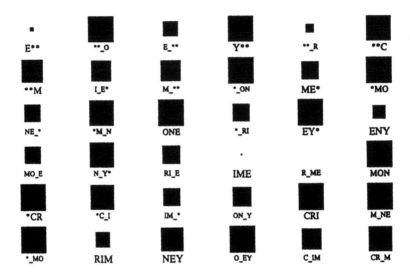

BLIRNET Activations

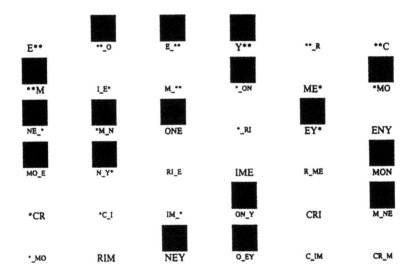

PO Net Activations

FIG. 14.3. Desired behaviour of the PO net. Suppose that two words, CRIME and MONEY, are processed by BLIRNET, and the resulting activations include those shown in the upper half of the figure. In this contrived example, clusters of MONEY are, on average, more active than clusters of CRIME. (The area of the black square above a cluster name is proportional to the cluster's activity level.) The lower half of the figure depicts the final activations of letter cluster units in the PO net: Clusters of MONEY have been enhanced (e.g. MO_E) and clusters of CRIME suppressed.

416

letter clusters might be assembled to form valid strings. The PO net attempts to satisfy as many of these weak constraints as possible while maintaining consistency with the perceptual data. Details of the dynamics are described in Appendix 1. Similar clean-up mechanisms have proven useful for recovering information from noisy signals in other connectionist models (Hinton & Shallice, 1989; Touretzky & Hinton, 1988).

The connections among letter cluster units embody syntactic knowledge about which pairs of clusters can appear together with a letter string. An additional source of information can assist the PO net selection process: Higher-order knowledge about valid English words. Some form of lexical or semantic knowledge certainly plays a role in reading, as abundant evidence suggests that lexical status has a significant effect on performance (e.g., Carr, Davidson, & Hawkins, 1978; McClelland & Johnston, 1977).

The utility of units representing semantic features (hereafter, *semantic units*) is easiest to envisage if word meanings are represented locally, that is, if there is one semantic unit per word meaning. For instance, suppose there was a semantic unit representing the "wealth" sense of MONEY. It would be connected to all clusters of MONEY. Activation of some clusters of MONEY would result in activation of the "wealth" semantic unit, which in turn would reinforce these clusters and help activate the remaining ones. Inhibitory interactions among the semantic units are also necessary to prevent multiple meanings from remaining simultaneously active. The end result of the pull-out process is then selection of one internally-consistent spelling pattern in the letter-cluster units and one word meaning in the semantic units.

The semantic units serve two critical computational roles. First, because all interactions between letter-cluster units are pairwise, the semantic units are necessary to provide a higher-order linking of the letter clusters. This linking helps clusters of a word to cohere. Indeed, without the semantic units, the pull-out net has the strong tendency to combine bits of information from different stimuli. Second, the semantic units allow semantic access to perform within the PO net. Semantic representations are clearly needed by higher-order processes.

These two computational benefits of semantic units hold even with distributed semantic representations. In the current implementation, the semantic unit representation is semi-distributed: There are many semantic units corresponding to each word meaning, but each semantic unit is associated with only one word meaning. Thus, the "semantic" units are actually a lexical representation, albeit a distributed representation, so to be honest we call them *semlex units*. However, the only reason for not constructing a fully-distributed semantic representation is the difficulty of devising a complete set of semantic features.[4]

---

[4]It might seem implausible that a distributed orthographic representation could have any systematic relationship to a distributed semantic representation, but Hinton and Shallice (1989) have demonstrated otherwise in a model that learns orthographic-semantic associations.

On grounds of parsimony, we would like to believe that an explicit lexical representation is not necessary; the semantic representation can serve the same function in the pull-out process and is necessary in any case to represent word meanings. Further, the architecture we propose—direct association between orthographic and semantic knowledge without mediation by a lexicon—is entirely consistent with Hinton and Shallice's (1989) model of acquired dyslexia.

The Attentional Mechanism (AM)

MORSEL has an attentional mechanism, the AM, that controls the amount and temporal order of information flowing through BLIRNET. The AM receives input about where to focus from various sources, resolves conflicting suggestions, and then constructs a "spotlight" centred on the selected region of the retina. The attentional spotlight serves to enhance the activation of input features (such as those depicted in Figure 14.2) within its bounds relative to those outside. As activity is propagated through BLIRNET, the highlighted region maintains its enhanced status, so that at the output of BLIRNET, letter-cluster units appropriate for the attended item tend to become most active as well. Consequently, the PO net will choose the attended item. Note that attention causes the preferential processing of certain items, but it does not act as an all-or-none filter. Information from the unattended regions of the retina undergoes some degree of analysis by BLIRNET. This partial processing of unattended information distinguishes the AM from other early-selection filtering mechanisms that have been proposed (e.g. Koch & Ullman, 1985; LaBerge & Brown, 1989).

The attentional system receives input about where to focus from two sources. First, attention can be guided in a *bottom-up* manner by stimulus information so as to bias selection towards locations where stimuli are actually present. Second, higher-levels of cognition can supply top-down control on the basis of task demands. For instance, if the task instructions are to report the left item in a multi-item display first, selection can be biased towards the left portion of the display initially; if the instructions are to read a page of text, a scanning mechanism can bias selection towards the top-left corner initially, and then advance left to right, top to bottom. (Butter, 1987, argues for a similar distinction between "reflex" and "voluntary" control of attention in humans.)

As shown in Fig. 14.1, the AM is a set of units in one-to-one correspondence with the retinotopic feature maps serving as input to BLIRNET. Activity in an AM unit indicates that attention is focused on the corresponding retinal location and serves to *gate the flow of activity* from the input layer to the next layer of BLIRNET. Specifically, the activity level of an input unit in a given location is transmitted to the next layer with a probability that is monotonically related to the activity of the AM unit in the corresponding location. However, the AM serves only to bias processing: it does not absolutely inhibit activations from unattended regions, but these activations are transmitted with a lower probability.

Each unit in the AM gets bottom-up input from the corresponding location in all of the retinotopic feature maps, as well as an unspecified top-down input. The dynamics of the AM generate a single, continuous region of activity over the retinotopic space, with a bias towards locations indicated by bottom-up and top-down inputs. Details of the AM selection process are a provided in Appendix 2.

Key Properties of MORSEL

Many details of MORSEL (e.g. the letter-cluster representation, the operation of BLIRNET) are not critical in the present work. Consequently, we have no strong commitment to the nuts and bolts of MORSEL, only to the framework that it provides. In fact, if we have any commitment at all, it is to the belief that the nuts and bolts are *wrong*. The input representation is not rich enough; the AM dynamics are too brittle; the PO net is not based on a rigorous computational foundation (cf. Hopfield, 1982). Nonetheless, we experimented with a wide variety of alternatives to the mechanisms and parameters reports in this chapter, and were pleased to discover that the qualitative behaviour of the model was remarkably insensitive to these details.

Four properties of MORSEL, however, are essential in accounting for the behaviour of neglect dyslexia patients.

1. Attentional selection by location occurs early in the course of processing. With all other things being equal, there is a preference for locations where stimuli appear.

2. Attention attempts to select a single item. In this regard, an item is defined as a relatively dense bundle of features separated from other bundles by a relatively sparse region. This crude definition does not always suffice, but it allows for early segmentation of the image without higher-order knowledge.

3. Attention gates the flow of activity through the object recognition system. The activities of features outside the attended region are relatively attenuated but not completely suppressed. Consequently, unattended information receives some degree of analysis.

4. After the recognition system has processed the perceptual data in a bottom-up fashion, a clean-up mechanism acts on the resulting representation to recover information that is orthographically and semantically meaningful. This clean-up mechanism can compensate for noise and inaccuracy in the recognition system and in the perceptual data itself.

Any model with these four properties should suffice for the present purpose. There is surely a large class of models with these properties; MORSEL is not unique. The interesting thing about MORSEL is that it was developed to account for a variety of perceptual and additional data in normal subjects, but, as we will show, it is entirely consistent with a neglect dyslexia data as well. It would be difficult to justify the development of a simulation model as large as MORSEL for the present purpose alone. However, the details of MORSEL had been worked out previously, except for a few tweaks and extensions to specify aspects of the model that were not previously required (e.g. the semlex unit representation). In this sense, the simulations we report are natural predictions of the model.

Damaging MORSEL to Produce Neglect Dyslexia

We propose that neglect dyslexia results when the bottom-up connections to the AM from the input feature maps are damaged. The damage is graded monotonically, most severe at the left extreme of the retina and least severe at the right (assuming a right-hemisphere lesion, as we have throughout the chapter). This account may be contrasted with one claiming that the damage to connections in the left field is absolute and connections in the right field are entirely intact.

The consequence of the damage is to affect the probability that features present on the retinotopic input maps are detected by the AM. To the extent that features in a given location are not detected, the AM will fail to focus attention at that location. Note that this is not a "perceptual" deficit, in the sense that if somehow attention can be mustered, features will be analysed normally by BLIRNET.

To give the gist of our account, MORSEL and the hypothesised deficit are compatible with the early, peripheral effects observed in neglect dyslexia because the disruption directly affects a low-level representation. MORSEL is also compatible with the late, higher-order effects in neglect dyslexia: The PO net is able to reconstruct the elements of a string that are attenuated by the attentional system via lexical and semantic knowledge.

Three Caveats Regarding MORSEL

We feel it somewhat premature to map the model, and hence the locus of damage, to particular anatomical sites in the brain. Roughly speaking, the AM might be associated with the dorsal visual system and BLIRNET with the ventral (Ungerleider & Mishkin, 1982), or in another framework, the AM might be associated with the posterior attention system and BLIRNET with the ventral-occipital word-form system (Posner & Peterson, 1989; Posner, Peterson, Fox, & Raichle, 1988). In either framework, the lesion to the AM that we propose would correspond to parietal damage.

We have also deliberately avoided the issue of where eye fixation rests with respect to MORSEL's retinotopic map, and hence, which input information is processed by which cerebral hemisphere. The only strong claim we wish to make is that, regardless of hemifield, the left-right gradient of damage is present. However, the absolute severity of damage may show a sharp discontinuity when crossing from one hemifield to the other (Mesulam, 1985), and the quantitative nature of the gradient and discontinuity may differ from one patient to another.

Finally, we do not regard the AM as a complete model of human spatial attention, for the following reason. A fundamental question in studies of neglect has been the frame of reference with respect to which neglect occurs: viewer centred (including eyes, head, body), object centred, or environment centred. That is, do patients neglect objects on the left side of their visual field, objects on the left side of a room? Evidence suggests that a viewer-centred representation is primary, but that other frames of reference are involved (Calvanio, Patrone, & Levine, 1987; Farah et al., 1990; Gazzaniga & Ladavas, 1987). Although the AM is capable of explaining effects that occur in a viewer-centred frame, other mechanisms need be postulated to account for effects that appear to be object- or environmentally-based. A more abstract scene-based encoding of object locations seems necessary (e.g. Hinton, 1981; LaBerge & Brown, 1989), and might well correspond to the anterior attention system discussed by Posner and Peterson (1989). Fortunately, the data we consider next can be explained purely in terms of a viewer-centred frame.

SIMULATIONS OF NEGLECT DYSLEXIA

We now turn to a detailed description of the performance of patients with neglect dyslexia and demonstrate through simulation experiments how the lesioned version of MORSEL can account for these behaviours. The patient descriptions and simulation results are grouped according to six basic phenomena. The first three—extinction, modulation of attention by task demands, and the effect of retinal presentation position on accuracy—appear compatible with a deficit localised at an early stage of processing, whereas the last three—relative sparing of words versus nonwords, distinctions in performance within the class of words, and the influence of lexical status on extinction—appear to arise at later stages of processing. MORSEL provides a unifying framework to account for these disparate behaviours.

An important finding in neglect dyslexia, and in neuropsychology in general, is that there is great variability in performance across patients. Thus, we have not attempted to model every individual case of neglect dyslexia. We have chosen a set of phenomena to model that seem relatively common and for which some agreement is found in the literature. Nonetheless, we believe that much of the observed heterogeneity across patients can be explained by parametric variation of the model's lesion—i.e. adjusting the gradient and severity of damage. Although it is sensible to begin by modelling phenomena that have been reliably observed, we fully believe that understanding individual differences is likely to be of as much interest as similarities in behaviour.

The Extinction Effect

A well-documented finding in the literature on neglect is that a patient who can detect a single contralesional stimulus may fail to report that stimulus when a second stimulus appears simultaneously in the ipsilesional space. This phenomenon, termed *extinction*, has been reported to occur with visual, tactile, and auditory stimuli and has a direct analogue in reading. When two words are presented simultaneously in the two visual fields, patients tend to neglect the contralesional stimulus. Sieroff and Michel (1987) demonstrated further that with a single word, centred across the fovea and subtending the same visual angle as the two non-contiguous words, extinction of information in the contralesional hemifield is less severe. In a similar experiment, Behrmann et al. (1990) showed that a compound word (such as PEANUT) is read better when the two component morphemes (PEA and NUT) are physically contiguous than when they are separated by a single blank space. Further, when the two words are separated by a pound sign (PEA#NUT), performance is still better than in the spaced condition, despite possible perceptual complications introduced by the pound sign, lending additional support to the conclusion that extinction is strongly dependent on the physical separation between items in the display.

The phenomenon of extinction is consistent with the view that the visual attentional system attempts to select one of multiple items in the visual field; in neglect patients, the selection is heavily biased towards the rightmost item. An "item" here can simply be defined by the physical adjacency of its components and physical distinctiveness from its neighbours. (We conjecture that the distinctiveness need not be one of physical separation; any simple property such as colour or texture boundaries could suffice.)

MORSEL's AM operates in this manner. In the unlesioned model, when two 3-letter words are presented to the AM, attention selects the left word on 41.3% of trials and the right on 40.8%; some combination of the two words is selected on the remaining 17.9% of trials. (See Appendix 3 for details of this and other simulations involving the AM.) In the lesioned model, the right word is nearly always selected because the bottom-up input to the AM from the retinotopic feature maps is degraded for the left word, thereby weakening its support. Figure 14.4 illustrates the bottom-up input detected by the lesioned AM upon presentation of two 3-letter words. Two blobs of activity are apparent, corresponding to the two words, but the left blob is weaker. The consequence of this left-sided degradation can be seen in Fig. 14.5, which shows activities of the AM units over time arising from this input. The AM settles on the right word.

Table 14.1 shows the distribution of attention in the lesioned model for displays containing two three-letter words. Each row indicates the percent of presentations in which a given combination of letters is selected; "1," "2," and "3" are letters of the left word, "4," "5," and "6" letters of the right word. The right word is selected over 75% of the time, with the remainder of the

FIG. 14.4.   The bottom-up input detected by the lesioned AM upon presentation of two three-letter words. The area of a white square at a given location indicates the relative strength of the input at that location in the retinotopic map. The black dots indicate the locations in the map for which there is no input.

presentations involving selection of the right word along with the rightmost portions of the left, or selections of only the rightmost portions of the right word. The AM clearly demonstrates extinction of the left item when 2 words are presented. However, extinction does not occur when the left item is present alone: The entire item is attended 86% of the time, and its rightmost portion is attended the remaining 14% of the time.

In the normal model, when two items are presented, one will be selected arbitrarily. If the AM is allowed to refocus on the same stimulus display, it will select the other item about half the time. Thus, simply by resetting the AM and allowing it to settle again, possibly with a slight inhibitory bias on the location just selected, both display items can be sampled. In the lesioned model, however, refocusing attention is unlikely to alter the selection. As long as the right item is present the left item is prevented from attracting attention; this masking does not occur in the normal model.

Because the AM serves only to bias processing in BLIRNET toward the attended region, as opposed to completely filtering out the unattended

TABLE 14.1
Distribution of Attention in the Lesioned
AM for Displays Containing Two Three-
Letter Words

Letters Attended	Relative Likelihood of Attentional State
1 2 3 4 5 6	6.6%
2 3 4 5 6	9.7%
3 4 5 6	0.1%
4 5 6	76.2%
5 6	7.2%
6	0.2%

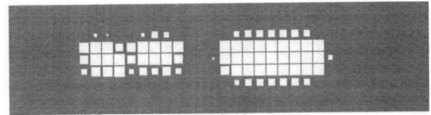

Iteration 3

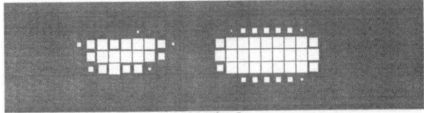

Iteration 9

Iteration 15

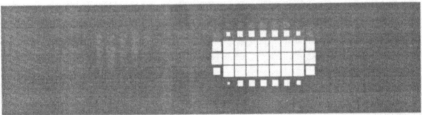

Iteration 20

FIG. 14.5. Activities of the AM units at several points in time as the right word is selected. By iteration 20, activities within the AM have reached equilibrium.

information, MORSEL will not necessarily fail to detect the unattended information. This depends on the operation of the PO net, which attempts to combine the outputs of BLIRNET into a meaningful whole. Thus, one cannot directly translate the distribution of attention into a distribution of responses. Nonetheless, the strong right-sided bias will surely affect responses, particularly for simple stimuli that cannot benefit from the PO net's application of higher-order knowledge. For instance, in the task of detecting a single or a pair of simultaneously-presented flashes of light, commonly used to test extinction, responses can only be based on the stimulus strength following attenuation by the AM.

Modulation of Attention by Task Demands

The strong predominance of right-biased responses in neglect patients can be modulated under certain conditions. Butter (1987) has suggested that the rightward orientation of these patients is a reflexive or involuntary response but that attention can wilfully be deployed to the left. Karnath (1988) showed that patients always reported the right-sided stimulus first when given the free choice of order of naming two bilaterally presented stimuli. The left-sided stimulus was often neglected in these cases. When patients were instructed to report the left-sided stimulus first, they were able to report both stimuli. A similar result in the domain of reading was found by Behrmann et al. (1990). One of their patients with neglect dyslexia (AH) reported the left-sided word on only 4% of trials when two words were presented simultaneously. When instructed to report the left-hand word first, AH reported both words correctly on 56% of trials.

An overt attentional shift provided by cueing patients to a stimulus on the left has been shown to overcome the neglect deficit in other tasks too. For example, Riddoch and Humphreys (1983) placed a single letter at each end of a line and instructed their patients to report the identity of the letter prior to bisecting the line. The degree of neglect on the line bisection task was significantly reduced with the additional letter reporting task. These findings suggest that the distribution of attention can be influenced by task instructions.

In MORSEL, two sources of information can guide attention: bottom up and top down. These two sources simply add together to bias the selection of a location. In a lesioned model, the bottom-up inputs for the left portion of the retina are weakened, but the top-down inputs are undamaged; hence, sufficiently strong top-down "task driven" guidance can compensate for the deficit in bottom-up control of attention. Figure 14.6 illustrates the effect on the AM when a top-down input to the left field is superimposed on the degraded bottom-up input shown in Fig. 14.4. Without the top-down input, the right word would have been selected (Fig. 14.5). This bias, however, compensates for the bottom-up degradation and the left word is selected.

This example makes the point that the deficit in MORSEL is attentional and not perceptual. A true perceptual deficit would occur if, say, the connections within BLIRNET were lesioned. Our account of neglect dyslexia places the locus of damage outside the recognition system; further, the effect of the damage on perception can be overcome via alternative routes—the top-down inputs. That neglect is primarily an attentional deficit is widely held in the neuropsychological

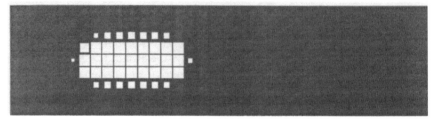

FIG. 14.6. The upper diagram depicts the top-down input to the AM superimposed on the degraded bottom-up input of Fig. 14.4. The lower diagram depicts the resulting equilibrium state of the AM. The left word is selected here, but without the top-down input, the right word would have been selected (Fig. 14.5).

literature (Heilman, Watson, & Valenstein, 1985; Kinsbourne, 1987; Mesulam, 1981; Posner & Petersen, 1989).

The Effect of Retinal Presentation Position on Accuracy

One finding in the literature compatible with a deficit at an early stage of processing is that performance changes as a function of stimulus location. Behrmann et al. (1990) presented words to a neglect dyslexia patient with their left edge immediately next to a central fixation point (the *near position*), or in the fourth character position to the right of fixation (the *far position*). Words appearing in the far position were still in the region of high acuity in the patient's intact visual field. The words were 3 to 5 letters in length. The patient reported only 28% of the words correctly in the near position, but 44% in the far position. This finding was confirmed with a second set of 6- and 7-letter words in which 39% and 77% of the words were reported correctly from the near and far positions, respectively. Thus, performance improved as the stimuli were displaced farther into ipsilesional space. This result is also obtained using a line bisection task in which the severity of neglect decreased for lines appearing further to the right (Butter, Mark, & Heilman, 1989).

The effect of presentation position argues that attention must be operating at least partially in a retinotopic reference frame, as opposed to an object-centred frame. If neglect occurred with respect to an object-centred frame, the left side of an item might be neglected relative to the right, but the stimulus position in the visual field would not matter.[5]

That attention operates on a retinotopic frame is clearly consistent with the architecture of MORSEL. Nonetheless, it requires a bit of explanation to see how MORSEL accounts for the effect of presentation position on accuracy. We begin with an overview of the account. Consider first the normal model being shown a single word. Independent of word length, if the letters are arranged sufficiently close to each other, the AM will always select the region of retinotopic space corresponding to the entire word. In the lesioned model, however, the input strength of the left side of the word is less than the right side, often causing the left side to be suppressed in the AM selection process. Consequently, BLIRNET analyses the word with a relative degradation of the left side. This degradation propagates through BLIRNET, and to the extent that it prevents the PO net from reconstructing the word's identity, accuracy will be higher in the normal model than in the lesioned model. The same reasoning applies with the lesioned model alone when considering presentation of a word on the relative right versus the left. The farther to the right the word appears, the stronger and more homogeneous its bottom-up input to the AM, and the less likely the AM will be to neglect the leftmost letters. Consequently, accuracy will be higher.

Figure 14.7 illustrates three examples of the AM suppressing the left side of a six-letter word: in the top row, the rightmost five letter positions are attended; in the middle row, four letters are attended; and in the bottom row, three letters are attended. Table 14.2 summarises the distribution of attention for a six-letter word presented to the AM in each of three retinal positions. The "standard" position refers to the presentation position used in Fig. 14.7; the shifted positions refer to moving the word one or two letter positions (three or six pixels) to the right of the standard position. As expected, when the word is moved farther to the right, the AM is more likely to focus on its initial letters.

The attentional focus produced by the AM affects BLIRNET's processing of a word and, ultimately, the accuracy of report. Although we are interested in the accuracy of the report, we have chosen not to simulate the detailed operation of BLIRNET for two reasons. First, the version of BLIRNET implemented by Mozer (1991) was trained to recognize a relatively small set of letter clusters—

---

[5] Although eye movements have not been carefully controlled for in these studies, the possibility of eye movements cannot fundamentally alter our conclusion concerning the role of the retinotopic frame, for the following reason. If patients were able to foveate on the stimuli then, independent of presentation position, all items would be analysed in approximately the same retinal position. To explain the effect of presentation position on performance, one would need to postulate that it is easier to move the eyes to a given location than to a location on its relative left. Because eye movements and attention shifts are intertwined, this is tantamount to claiming that attention operates in a retinotopic frame as well.

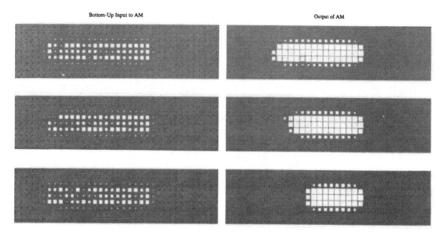

FIG. 14.7.   The bottom-up input to the lesioneu AM and the resulting AM equilibrium state for three different presentations of a six-letter word. In the top row, the rightmost five letter positions are attended; in the middle row, four letters are attended; and in the bottom row, three letters are attended.

about 600 of the approximately 6500 needed to represent most English words. The present simulations require a much larger set of letter clusters, and the training procedure is quite computation-intensive. Second, the exact activity levels produced by BLIRNET are not critical for the present modelling effort, and in fact, simulation of a large network like BLIRNET obscures the essential properties that are responsible for interesting behaviours. Consequently, rather than simulating BLIRNET, we have incorporated its essential properties into a simple algorithm that determines letter cluster activations for a particular input stimulus and attentional state (see Appendix 4 for further details).

In Fig. 14.8, one can see the simulated activations of various letter units in response to the stimulus PARISH on a trial where the AM has successfully focused

TABLE 14.2
Distribution of Attention in the Lesioned AM for Displays Containing One Six-Letter Word

Letters Attended	Relative Likelihood of Attentional State		
	Standard Position %	Shifted Right One Position %	Shifted Right Two Positions %
1 2 3 4 5 6	8.1	18.2	37.2
2 3 4 5 6	14.6	24.5	31.9
3 4 5 6	30.1	33.7	25.8
4 5 6	33.0	20.0	5.0
5 6	13.9	3.6	0.1
6	0.3	0.0	0.0

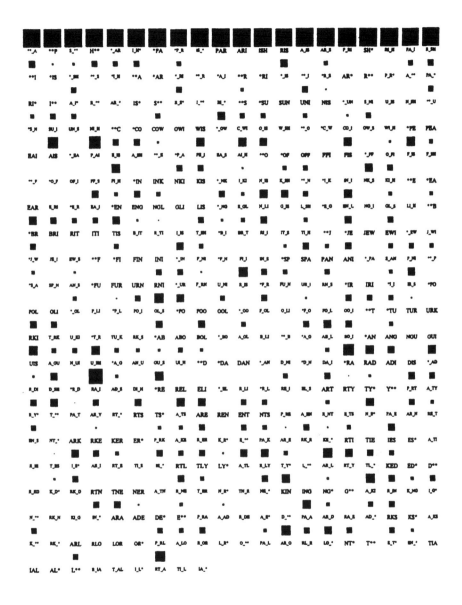

FIG. 14.8.   Activations of various letter cluster units in response to the stimulus PARISH on a trial where the AM has selected all six letters of the word.

429

on all six letters of the word. Activity levels range from zero to one. The activity of a cluster is indicated by the area of the black square above it. The letter clusters of PARISH (first row of figure) are highly active. In addition, clusters with letters visually similar to the stimulus word are partially activated, for example, RTS, PA_T, RA_I, and DIS, as are clusters that would be appropriate were letters of the stimulus slightly rearranged, for example, AR_I and I_S*. Finally, a bit of noise is thrown into the activation process, which creates random fluctuations in the activity pattern.

If only the last three letters of PARISH are attended, the resulting pattern of letter cluster activity looks quite different (Fig. 14.9). Clusters representing the initial segment of the word are less active than in Fig. 14.8. Further, because the initial segment is suppressed, clusters such as **I and **_S will become more active, as if ISH was presented instead of PARISH.

The next stage in processing the stimulus is to feed the output of BLIRNET to the PO net, allow the PO net to settle, and then determine which of a set of alternative responses best matches the final PO net activity pattern. (The procedure for selecting alternative responses—and which letter clusters to include in the PO net simulation—is explained in Appendix 4.) In the case of the fully attended PARISH (Fig. 14.8), the PO net almost always reads out the correct response. In the case of the partially attended PARISH (Fig. 14.9), the PO net often is able to reconstruct the original word; other times it fabricates a left side, reading out instead RADISH or POLISH or RELISH; and occasionally it just reads out the attended portion, ISH, although the influence of the semlex units acts against the read out of nonwords.

To test the effect of stimulus presentation position in MORSEL, we conducted a simulation using six six-letter words: PARISH, BEGGAR, FOSTER, SILVER, MORSEL, and SHADOW. Although the obvious way to test MORSEL is to present a stimulus on the retina, allow the AM to settle, determine the resulting BLIRNET activations, feed these to the PO net, and read out a response, we have decoupled the AM and PO net simulations to reduce the computational burden. Running a simulation of the AM alone on a six-letter stimulus, we can determine the probability of the AM selecting a particular combination of letters (the *attentional state*, see Table 14.2). Independently, the PO net simulation can be run in its entirety for each possible attentional state. The probability of being in attentional state i, p (*state i*), can then be combined with the probability of the PO net responding correctly given a particular attentional state, p (*correct | state i*), to yield an overall probability of correct response:

$$p \text{ (correct)} = \sum_i p \text{ (state i) } p \text{ (correct | state i)}.$$

Table 14.3 presents the results of the PO net simulation on our collection of 6 words, each line showing the accuracy in a particular attention state. These

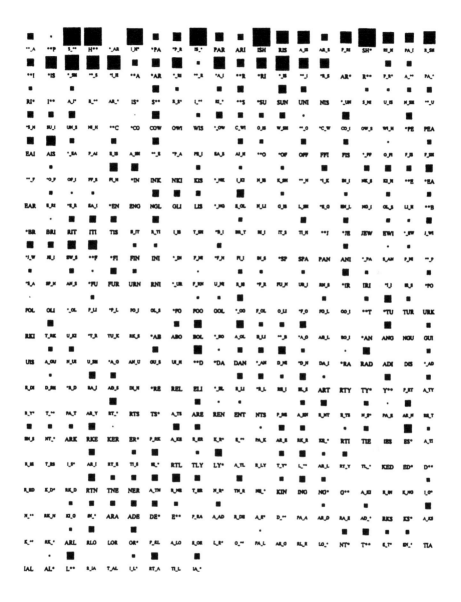

FIG. 14.9. Activations of various letter cluster units in response to the stimulus PARISH on a trial where the AM has selected the last three letters of the word.

431

TABLE 14.3
Performance of Lesioned MORSEL on
Displays Containing One Six-Letter
Word

Letters Attended	Correct Responses Given Attentional State
1 2 3 4 5 6	100%
2 3 4 5 6	85%
3 4 5 6	51%
4 5 6	33%
5 6	17%
6	18%

figures are averaged across the 6 words and 100 replications of each word. The replications are necessary to obtain a reliable measure of accuracy because noise introduced by BLIRNET can cause different responses on each trial. (See Appendix 4 for further details of the simulation methodology.) The table indicates that performance drops as fewer letters of the word are attended. Even with only one letter attended, the residual accuracy is quite high, no doubt due to the partial activation of unattended information. Combining the conditional probabilities of Table 14.3 with the marginal probabilities of being in a given attentional state of Table 14.2, one obtains an overall probability of correct response: 49% for words presented in the standard position, 63% for words one position to the right, and 79% for words 2 positions to the right.

Thus, the peripheral lesion in MORSEL does result in a retinotopic deficit as measured by reading performance. Performance is better than would be expected by examining the distribution of attention alone, thanks to the reconstruction ability of the PO net: Although the entire word is attended on only 8% of trials (for the standard position), the word is correctly reported far more frequently—49% of trials. Nonetheless, the retinal position of the stimulus does come into play; the PO net is not so effective that accuracy is absolute.

Not surprisingly, when MORSEL does produce an error, the error generally occurs on the left side of a word. For example, with PARISH, the alternative responses include left-sided completions such as POLISH or IRISH and right-sided completions such as PARKER or PARTS, yet the PO net always prefers the left-sided completions. Figure 14.10 shows a graph of activity over time for the stimulus PARISH on a trial where the AM has selected just the right side—ISH. On this trial, the PO net eventually reads out POLISH.

The account provided by MORSEL suggests that neglect—the difficulty in reading single words—goes hand in hand with extinction—the difficulty in selecting one of two items. Both behaviours are caused by the same underlying deficit. This does not imply, however, that the two behaviours must necessarily co-occur. With a milder gradient of damage than the one we have simulated,

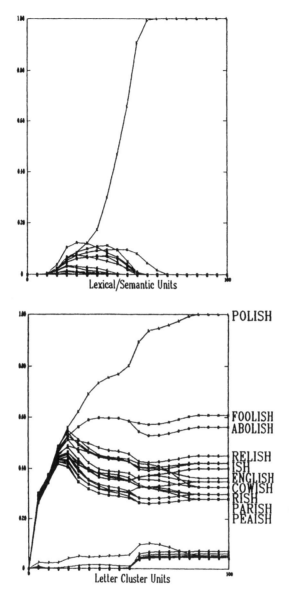

FIG. 14.10.   Activity in the PO net as a function of time for the stimulus PARISH on a trial where the AM has selected the last three letters of the word. The PO net eventually reads out POLISH. The top graph summarises activations of the semlex units over time, and the bottom graph activations of the letter cluster units. Each trace represents aggregate activity of a particular response and is labelled with a single digit or letter symbol. Traces corresponding to the same word in the two graphs use the same symbol. The ten most active responses in the letter cluster graph are shown on the far right, roughly next to the corresponding trace. The aggregate semlex activity of a response is simply the average activity of its semlex units. The aggregate letter cluster activity of a response is a measure of the activity of the target clusters relative to nontarget clusters (see Appendix 4). Note that due to the distributed word representations, there will always be partial activity of response alternatives similar to the chosen one.

433

MORSEL shows minimal neglect in reading words due to the compensation action of the PO net, yet even a slight right-sided bias leads to extinction. This is consistent with reports in the literature: Neglect and extinction generally co-occur, and on the path to recovery, neglect diminishes in severity, leaving extinction as the only manifestation of the brain damage (Kolb & Whishaw, 1985). At present, there are no data in the domain of reading that challenge MORSEL's claim that both neglect and extinction of words are caused by the same deficit; however, several studies from the general hemispatial neglect literature find a double dissociation (Bisiach, Perani, Vallar, & Berto, 1986; Ogden, 1985).

The deficit in MORSEL occurs with respect to a retinotopic reference frame, but irrespective of the retinal position of a word, the left part of the word tends to be reported more poorly than the right due to the attentional gradient. Consequently, one could easily interpret the deficit as occurring with respect to an object-based frame. Indeed, Baxter and Warrington (1983), in finding neglect errors for short as well as long words, suggest that the phenomenon is due to the "faulty distribution of attention to the central representation of a word." MORSEL allows the data to be interpreted from a different perspective, one in which a deficit that produces a retinotopic gradient can lead to a relative difference between the left and right components of an object, independent of the object's size and position.

Relative Sparing of Words Versus Nonwords

A general finding in the neglect dyslexia literature is that the reading of words is less affected by neglect than the reading of nonwords. For example, Sieroff et al. (1988) demonstrated that their patients with right parietal lesions showed superior overall performance on words compared to nonpronounceable nonwords. The relative superiority of words is observed both under brief tachistoscopic presentation of the stimuli and under unlimited exposure duration, and has been replicated in several other studies using pronounceable nonwords (or *pseudowords*) as well as nonpronounceable nonwords (Behrmann et al., 1990; Brunn & Farah, in press; Sieroff, 1989).

Sieroff and Posner (1988) reproduced this effect in normal subjects by modulating attention to foveally presented words. They instructed their subject to report the identity of a cue prior to reading the target; the cue was a single digit appearing to the immediate left or right of the target. As in the case of neglect dyslexia, performance on words is significantly better than on nonwords. The locus of this word superiority effect is controversial. One popular explanation is that word reading is attention free because the orthographic string makes direct contact with its existing lexical entry (LaBerge & Samuels, 1974; Sieroff et al., 1988). Such a view affords privileged processing status to words. Nonwords, on the other hand, do not benefit from this mode of lexical access and are subject to attentional control. The implication of such a view is that two distinct modes or processing exist. It is not clear, however, where the two paths diverge—at an early level prior to the encoding of the integrated "word form" (Warrington & Shallice, 1980) or as a means for sequential readout of information into phonological or semantic codes (Mewhort, Marchetti, Gurnsey, & Campbell, 1984).

An alternative interpretation, which has been used to account for the perceptual advantage of letters in words over letters in nonwords, is that letters in words are supported by an existing lexical representation (McClelland & Rumelhart, 1981; Rumelhart & McClelland, 1982). Such support does not benefit nonprounceable nonwords. On this account, letter strings are processed through the same channel independent of lexical status. This account can explain the word advantage in neglect dyslexia: The superiority of words is obtained from the fact that partially encoded contralesional information may be enhanced by lexical support in the case of words but not in the case of nonwords (Brunn & Farah, in press; Sieroff et al., 1988).

This latter account is embodied in MORSEL. Specifically, the PO net acts to recover the portion of a letter string suppressed by the AM using both orthographic knowledge (the connections among letter cluster units) and semantic/lexical knowledge (the connections between letter cluster and semlex units). This gives words an advantage over pseudowords, which lack the support of semantic/lexical knowledge, and a double advantage over nonprounceable nonwords, which lack the support of orthographic, lexical, and semantic knowledge.

We conducted a simulation study using the lesioned version of MORSEL to compare performance on 5-letter words and pseudowords (Table 14.4). The 2 conditions differ in that the words have an associated representation in the semlex units whereas the pseudowords do not. In the first stage of the simulation, we measured the likelihood of the AM attending to a given portion of a 5-letter stimulus string (second column in Table 14.5). Then, the PO net simulation was run for 100 replications of each stimulus in each attentional state to obtain the probability of a correct response for a given stimulus type in a given attentional state (third and fourth columns of Table 14.5). Combining the AM and PO net

TABLE 14.4
Stimuli for Word/Pseudoword Simulation

Words			Pseudowords		
CATCH	PRESS	WATER	FATCH	FRESS	SATER
TRUCK	CRIME	MONEY	DRUCK	TRIME	SONEY
FLESH	STICK	FRONT	BLESH	PLICK	DRONT
FRAME	SOUTH	GROUP	TRAME	POUTH	BROUP

TABLE 14.5
Performance of Lesioned MORSEL Word/Pseudoword Experiment

Letters Attended	Relative Likelihood of Attentional State (%)	Correct Responses Given Attentional State (%)	
		Words	Pseudowords
1 2 3 4 5	8	100	81
2 3 4 5	21	79	0
3 4 5	35	19	0
4 5	32	19	0
5	3	21	0

simulation results as described for the previous simulation, we obtain an overall probability of correct response: The lesioned MORSEL correctly reported 39% of words but only 7% of pseudowords. In comparison, the neglect dyslexia patient HR studies by Behrmann et al. (1990) correctly reported 66% of words and 5% of pseudowords for stimuli of 4 to 6 letters.[6]

To summarise the implications of the current simulation, MORSEL provides a mechanism by which lexical or semantic knowledge can help compensate for noisy sensory data. This results in differential performance for words versus pseudowords because pseudowords do not benefit from such knowledge. MORSEL's account does not require the assumption that words and nonwords are processed along separate channels, or that the processing of words somehow bypasses the attentional system. In MORSEL, the attentional system and the recognition system operate identically for words and nonwords. Ultimately, however, words are less affected by the distribution of attention because of the compensating action of the PO net.

---

[6]HR's data is used for comparison to MORSEL in all simulations. We took little effort to obtain quantitative fits to HR's data for three reasons. First, the data we report is self-contradictory: HR performs quite well in one experiment but then poorly with similar stimulus materials in another. This is because the experiments were conducted sometimes weeks apart, and therefore reflect different stages of recovery of the patient and different overall levels of arousal and motivation. Second, the parameter values used to fit the data of one patient at a particular stage of recovery can hardly be expected to apply to other patients with somewhat different brain lesions. Third, given the number of free parameters of the model—that is, parameters not required in earlier work on MORSEL (e.g. connections involving semlex units, the nature of the attentional deficit)—relative to the small number of data points in this and subsequent simulations, a precise fit should not be considered terribly impressive. The important fact about parameter settings is that the qualitative behaviour of the model is remarkably insensitive to the specific parameter values.

Distinctions in Performance within the Class of Words

Studies examining the lexical status of a letter string have shown a difference in accuracy between words and nonwords, but recent work has found a more subtle influence of psycholinguistic variables on performance. Behrmann et al. (1990) compared performance on words that have a morpheme embedded on the right side—for example, PEANUT, which contains the morpheme NUT, and TRIANGLE, which contains ANGLE—and words having no right-embedded morphemes—for example, PARISH and TRIBUNAL. Although the patient studied by Behrmann et al. showed no difference in accuracy for the two stimulus types, a distinction was found in the nature of the errors produced. The upper portion of Table 14.6 summarises the responses of the patient for words that contain right-embedded morphemes (hereafter, *REM words*) and words that do not (*control words*). Words were presented in two positions, either immediately to the right of fixation (the *near condition*) or several letter spaces further to the right (the *far condition*). Responses were classified into three categories: *correct responses*, *neglect errors* (in which the right morpheme or its syllable control is reported— NUT for PEANUT or ISH for PARISH), and all *other errors*. The other errors consist mainly of responses in which the rightmost letters have been reported correctly but alternative letters have been substituted on the left to form an English word—for example, IRISH or POLISH for PARISH (these errors have been termed *backward completions*). In both near and far conditions, overall accuracy is comparable for REM and control words, but neglect errors are the predominant error response for REM words and backward completions for control words. Sieroff et al. (1988) have also studied compound words and found no significant difference in overall accuracy between compound and noncompound words. However, they provide no information about the distribution of error responses.

Our simulation study used 12 compound words—half 6 letters long and half 7—from the stimulus set of Behrmann et al. (Table 14.7). As in our earlier simulations, the PO net simulation was conducted for each attentional state to obtain the probability of correct and neglect responses for REM and control words conditional upon the attentional state. These conditional probabilities were then combined with the probability of being in each attentional state (measured separately for 6- and 7-letter words) to generate the distribution of responses shown in the lower portion of Table 14.6. Comparing the upper and lower portions of the table, it is evident that the model produces the same pattern of results as the patient. The difference in accuracy between near and far conditions confirms that the previous finding concerning of the effect of retinal presentation position. Overall accuracy is about the same for REM and control words. Neglect errors are frequent for REM words, whereas backward completion errors (the primary error type in the "other error" category for the simulation as well as the patient) are most common for control words.

TABLE 14.6
Distribution of Responses on Word Reading Task (in %)

	Near Condition		Far Condition	
Response Type	REM Words (e.g. PEANUT)	Control Words (e.g. PARISH)	REM Words (e.g. PEANUT)	Control Words (e.g. PARISH)
(a) Neglect Dyslexia Patient (from Behrmann et al., 1990)				
Correct Response	43	40	79	76
Neglect Error	39	4	13	4
Other Error	18	56	9	20
(b) Simulation of Lesioned MORSEL				
Correct Response	39	44	75	76
Neglect Error	32	0	9	0
Other Error	29	56	16	24

The difference in performance for the two word classes is explained by the action of the semlex units. These units support neglect responses for REM words but not control words. The same effect was responsible for the basic word advantage in the word/pseudoword simulations. However, in the present simulation, the influence of semlex units acts not to increase the accuracy of report for one stimulus type but to bias the model towards one type of error response over another when the perceptual data is not strong enough to allow the PO net to reconstruct the target.

The only discrepancies between the patient and simulation data in Table 14.6 are that the model produces about a 5% lower neglect error rate uniformly across all conditions and a slight accuracy advantage for control words. The accuracy advantage for control words can be eliminated by adjusting parameters of

TABLE 14.7
Stimuli for Embedded-morpheme Experiment

REM Words		Control Words	
Six-letter	*Seven-letter*	*Six-letter*	*Seven-letter*
PEANUT	INKWELL	PARISH	DARLING
SUNSET	SKILIFT	BEGGAR	PROMISE
COWBOY	NEWBORN	FOSTER	CUSTARD
SUNTAN	EARRING	SILVER	TORMENT
OFFSET	NETWORK	MORSEL	GESTURE
SUNDAY	BEDROOM	SHADOW	COMPLEX

model, but in truth, the advantage is present for most parameter settings. It is not difficult to see why this is so. Consider the behaviour of the PO net when the AM has selected the last three letters of either PEANUT or PARISH. With PEANUT, the predominant response of the PO net is NUT because the clusters of NUT receive strong support from the semlex units. With PARISH, however, the semlex units do not support ISH but instead favour PARISH or one of the alternative backward completions. If the number of backward completions is relatively small, PARISH is more likely to be read correctly than PEANUT. Such behaviour is at variance with the patient data.

We have an escape from this dilemma. Our implementation of the PO net utilises only a limited number of alternative responses for a given stimulus. This was necessary to make simulations computationally feasible, yet by cutting down on the number of alternative responses, it raises the likelihood of the PO net producing the correct response simply by guessing. Such guessing behaviour occurs when the combination of perceptual data and semlex biases do not strongly agree on a candidate response—the case of PARISH when only ISH is attended. In support of this argument, our pilot simulations used even fewer alternative responses, and the advantage of control words over REM words was even further exaggerated.

The Influence of Lexical Status on Extinction

The last two sections presented experimental results that were explained by MORSEL in terms of an interaction between attentional selection and higher-order stimulus properties. However, the tie to attentional selection is somewhat indirect because the stimuli were single words or pseudowords, and attention is generally thought of as selecting between two competing items, not selecting between portions of a single item.

Using the extinction paradigm, Behrmann et al. (1990) have been able to show that the ability of a neglect dyslexia patient to select the leftmost of 2 words is indeed influenced by the relation between the words. When the patient was shown pairs of semantically unrelated 3-letter words separated by a space, e.g. SUN and FLY, and was asked to read both words, the left word was reported on only 12% of trials; when the 2 words could be joined to form a compound word, e.g. COW and BOY, the left word was read on 28% of trials. (On all trials where the left word was reported, the right word was also reported.) Thus, it would seem that the operation of attention to select among stimuli interacts with higher-order stimulus properties.

One natural interpretation of this interaction is that the attentional system is directly influenced by semantic or lexical knowledge, as proposed by late-selection theories of attention (e.g., Deutsch & Deutsch, 1963; Norman, 1968; Shiffrin & Schneider, 1977). MORSEL provides an alternative account in which attention operates at an early stage, but because unattended information is partially processed, later stages can alter the material selected. Thus, one need not posit a direct influence of higher-order knowledge on attentional selection to obtain behaviour in which the two interact.

To describe how MORSEL can account for the interaction, we begin with a description of the lesioned model's behaviour and then turn to simulation results. When two items are presented to the lesioned AM, usually the right word is selected (Table 14.1). Consequently, BLIRNET strongly activates the clusters of BOY when COW BOY is presented, partially activates the clusters of COW and, because BLIRNET has some difficulty keeping track of the precise ordering of letters, weakly activates clusters representing a slight rearrangement of the stimulus letters, OWB and WB_Y. These latter clusters support the word COWBOY. The overall pattern of letter cluster activity is thus consistent with COWBOY as well as BOY. Because both words receive support from the semlex units, the PO net can potentially read out either; thus, in the case of COWBOY, the left morpheme is read out along with the right. When the two morphemes cannot be combined to form a word, however, the semlex units do not support the joined-morpheme response, and the PO net is unlikely to read the two morphemes out together.

There is another avenue by which the left morpheme may be read out: the patient may be able to shift attention to the left and reprocess the display. In the experiment of Behrmann et al., this seems a likely possibility because all trials contained two words and the patient's task was to report the entire display contents. Although the patient was not explicitly told that two words were present, the observation of both words on even a few trials may have provided sufficient incentive to try reporting more than one word per trial. The patient may therefore have had a top-down control strategy to shift attention leftward. MORSEL is likewise able to refocus attention to the left on some trials using top-down control of the sort illustrated in Fig. 14.6. This will cause an increase in reports of the left morpheme both for related and unrelated stimulus pairs.

Table 14.8 lists the 12 word pairs used in the stimulation. *Related morphemes* can be joined to form a compound word; *unrelated morphemes* do not combine in this manner. As with previous simulations, each stimulus was presented 100 times in each additional state to obtain a probability of reporting the joined morpheme (e.g. COWBOY or SUNFLY) conditional upon the additional state (Table 14.1) to obtain overall response rates. The left morpheme was reported on

TABLE 14.8
Stimuli for Extinction Simulation

Unrelated Morphemes		Related Morphemes	
COW NUT	PEA SET	COW BOY	PEA NUT
OFF TAN	SUN FLY	OFF SET	SUN TAN
BAR DAY	SUN BOY	BAR FLY	SUN DAY

14.1% of trials for related morphemes but only 2.8% for unrelated morphemes. Thus, the strength of lexical/semantic knowledge is sufficient to recover the extinguished information on the left for 2 morphemes that can be combined to form a word. Fig. 14.11 shows a graph of activity over time for COW BOY on a trial where the AM has focused attention only on BOY. Nonetheless, the semlex units of COWBOY and the partial activations from the left morpheme converge to eventually cause the PO net to read out COWBOY.

Assuming that top-down control of the AM allows MORSEL to shift attention to the left and reprocess the display on some proportion of the trials, δ, we can obtain a good quantitative fit to the data. We arbitrarily pick δ to be 10%, which makes the total per cent of trials in which the left morpheme is reported 24.1% for related morphemes and 12.8% for unrelated morphemes. These results are in line with the patient data obtained by Behrmann et al.—28% and 12%.

Interestingly, on trials in which just the right morpheme is reported, MORSEL occasionally produces left neglect errors, for example, reporting ROY for BOY. Behrmann et al.'s patient produced similar errors. Thus, both left-item extinction and left-sided neglect can be observed on a single trial.

MORSEL makes further predictions concerning the factors that influence extinction for morpheme pairs. We mention here three such factors that have yet to receive thorough testing on neglect patients. First, the physical separation between the two morphemes is important: The further apart the morphemes are, the less activation BLIRNET will produce for the internal clusters of the joined morpheme—e.g. OWB and W_OY of COWBOY. This will reduce the likelihood of the PO net reading out COWBOY. Patients have been shown to perform better when there is no space between two morphemes than when there is a fixed space (Behrmann et al., 1990; Sieroff & Michel, 1987), but these studies have not manipulated spacing as a continuous variable. Inter-item spacing could explain the result of Sieroff et al. (1988) that performance on COW BOY (with *two* spaces between the words) is not better than on BOY COW, in apparent contradiction to the effect of related morphemes obtained by Behrmann et al. The second factor that may influence extinction is semantic relatedness of the two morphemes. The particular effect we have simulated depends not on the two morphemes being semantically related, but on the fact that they can be joined to form a lexical item. Semantic relatedness alone may allow for a reduction in extinction, but it would not be by exactly the same mechanism.[7] Third, task instructions should alter behaviour because top-down guidance to the AM can affect the distribution of

---

[7]If the two morphemes are semantically related but do not combine to form a compound word, e.g. BOY and MAN, one mechanism whereby one morpheme could affect the read-out of the other morpheme involves priming of the semantic units. That is, activation of the semantic units of MAN will support the related word BOY to some extent. This account requires an elaboration of temporal processing in MORSEL which has not been necessary in the present work.

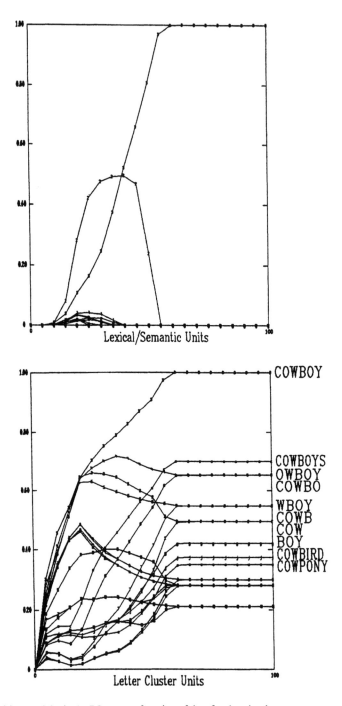

FIG. 14.11. Activity in the PO net as a function of time for the stimulus COW BOY on a trial where the AM has focused attention only on BOY. The PO net eventually reads out COWBOY.

442

attention. Thus, in the case where two related morphemes appear with a space between them, MORSEL predicts that performance will differ depending on whether patients are instructed that the display contains two unrelated morphemes or a single word with a space in the middle. In the latter case, patients should attempt to spread attention broadly, and thereby obtain stronger activations for the left morpheme. Experimental work is currently underway using the Sieroff and Posner (1988) cueing paradigm to simulate neglect in normals and examine these three predictions of MORSEL.

ATTENTIONAL DYSLEXIA

Having provided a detailed account of phenomena surrounding neglect dyslexia, we turn to another acquired reading disorder, attentional dyslexia, and sketch an account in the framework of MORSEL.

As documented by Shallice and Warrington (1977) and Shallice (1988), attentional dyslexia patients correctly read single words presented in isolation, as well as single letters, but performance falters when multiple items are present. For instance, when several words appear simultaneously, letters from one word often migrate to the homologous position of another word. For example, WIN FED might be read as FIN FED. These *letter migration errors* have also been observed with normal subjects under conditions of brief masked exposure of multiple words (Mozer, 1983; Shallice & McGill, 1978). Although patients have no difficulty processing multiple letters as part of a word, as evidenced by normal performance on reading single words, when the task focuses on the letters instead of the word, a deficit is observed. Patients are, for example, unable to name the constituent letters of a visually presented word. The difficulty is clearly in processing a letter when surrounded by other letters, because naming performance is near perfect on individually presented letters. Even when a target letter is flanked by digits that are of a different colour and do not have to be reported (e.g. the target V in 1 3 V 4 7), patients still make some errors. A striking feature of the disorder is that the category of irrelevant flankers affects performance: If the flanking characters are letters—members of the same category (e.g. H L V R C), performance is much poorer. This category effect cannot be due to interference occurring at the response production stage: When the target is a digit and is surrounded by other digits, interference is marked, but when the target digit is replaced by dots that the patient is to count, performance is significantly better. Thus, when the output demands are equated, there is still a significant effect of the category of the flankers in relation to the targets.

Acquired attentional dyslexia has only been reported in the two patients described by Shallice and Warrington (1977). However, Geiger and Lettvin (1987) have described a group of developmental dyslexic readers who show many of the same characteristics as the acquired attentional dylexics. When letters are presented foveally and in isolation, their subjects are able to identify the letters with no difficulty. If, however, the foveal letters are presented simultaneously with letters in the parafovea, the dyslexic subjects are significantly worse than control subjects at reporting letters closest to fixation. Geiger and Lettvin suggest that, whereas normal readers learn a strategy for suppressing information that is not fixated, the dyslexic subjects do not. Shaywitz and Waxman (1987) propose a related explanation in terms of an impairment in covert attentional shifts (in the absence of explicit eye movements).

Rayner, Murphy, Henderson, and Pollatsek (1989) report a similar phenomenon in their subject, SJ, an adult with developmental dyslexia. Although SJ could read whole words and could report the constituent letters (unlike the subjects of Shallice & Warrington, 1977), letters in parafoveal vision interfered with his processing of the currently fixated word. The deficit could not be attributed to an impairment in overt eye movements: Although SJ's average eye fixations were longer than normal and he made more fixations than normal, he did not show an abnormal pattern of eye movements. Interestingly, SJ's reading performance improved when information outside the fixated window region was replaced with Xs or with random letters.

The common finding of all these studies is that the presence of extraneous information in the visual field interferes with processing of the relevant information. As with neglect dyslexia, we propose a straightforward explanation in terms of damage to the attentional system: The damage in attentional dyslexia results in difficulty focusing on a single item in a multi-item display. Consequently, information that ought to be filtered out still gains access to higher levels of processing, thereby overloading the system and interfering with the processing of the relevant information.

In MORSEL, two different types of damage to the AM could yield this deficit. First, there are many ways that internal parameters of the AM could be garbled, which would result in attention capturing everything present in the visual field (Fig. 14.12). Second, if the AM is prevented from reaching equilibrium, attention will be distributed over multiple items. This is because the AM initially activates all locations where items appear and then narrows its focus over time (see, for example, Fig. 14.5). In the case of developmental dyslexia, a plausible reason why the AM cannot reach equilibrium is that the time course of attentional settling is slowed. This behaviour is readily modelled in the AM by scaling down all connection strengths proportionately. Consequently, under conditions of brief exposure or speeded response, the AM will not have sufficient time to focus on a single item.

When multiple items are attended in MORSEL, they are simultaneously processed by BLIRNET and interference among the items can occur. One manifestation of this interference in attentional dyslexia patients is the letter migration phenomenon described earlier. Mozer (1991) has simulated letter migration errors in MORSEL by presenting two words simultaneously and limiting processing time so as to prevent the AM from selecting a single word. As

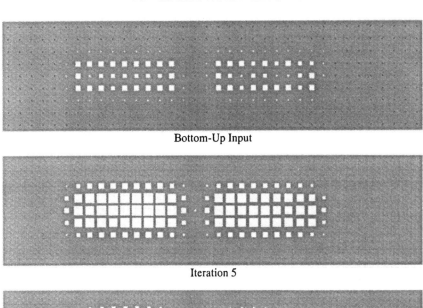

Bottom-Up Input

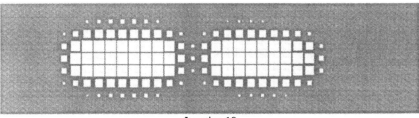

Iteration 5

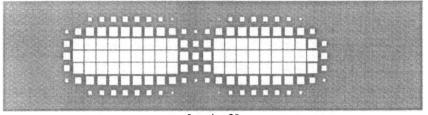

Iteration 10

Iteration 20

FIG. 14.12.   Behaviour of the AM on two three-letter words with 0 set to 25. Rather than selecting one word or another, as would the model with 0 set to .5, the AM settles on both simultaneously.

a result, BLIRNET activates letter clusters of both words simultaneously, and the PO net occasionally recombines clusters of the two words into a single migration response. Note that if one of the words is replaced by a string of Xs or random letters, there should be less interference because there is less ambiguity in the resulting pattern of letter-cluster activity. Thus, MORSEL can account for the improved reading performance of Rayner et al.'s (1989) subject SJ.

Letter migration errors are just one illustration of interference caused by the presence of multiple items. Another is observed when individual letters are processed simultaneously, for example H L V R C. Although BLIRNET may be capable of identifying multiple letters in parallel, performance degrades with multiple letters because of interactions within BLIRNET that produce unpredictable spurious activations (see introductory section on MORSEL here, or Mozer, 1991). For instance, V and L might result in some activation of the letter N. Consequently, it becomes more difficult to discern what is actually present from the pattern of activity produced by BLIRNET. This explains why performance on a target letter is better when the letter is presented in isolation than when embedded in other letters or digits.

What remains is for us to explain the category effect—why performance is so much worse for a letter flanked by irrelevant letters than digits. Our account is based on the fact that the output of BLIRNET specifies letter and word identities, but no location information (see introductory section on MORSEL). Localisation is achieved when the AM focuses on single objects. When the AM is unable to do so, location information cannot be recovered. Consequently, when the target and flankers are all of the same category, for example, H L V R C, MORSEL will generally be able to detect the individual items but will be unable to determine which is the target. Localisation is irrelevant when the target and flankers are members of different categories, for example, 1 3 V 4 7. In this example, it is trivial to determine which item to report on the basis of identity alone because there is only one letter present.

The final phenomenon regarding attentional dyslexia that we need to explain is why patients are unable to name the constituent letters of a visually presented word. This requires a bit of elaboration as to how MORSEL would read letter-by-letter. The pattern of activity produced by BLIRNET in response to an isolated letter is quite different than for the same letter in the context of a word. For example, an isolated E yields activity in the letter clusters **E, *E*, and E**, whereas the E in, say, FED yields activity in **_E, FE_*, E_** *_ED, *FE, FED, and ED*. Although the former pattern of activity is tied to the verbal response "E," the latter is not. Thus, to report letters of a word individually, it is necessary to process them individually. This involves focusing attention on single letters in sequence, thereby suppressing activation from the neighbours and obtaining a pattern of activity identical to that which would be obtained by a single letter presented in isolation. Of course, because the damaged attentional system is unable to focus on individual letters, letter-by-letter reading is impossible.

DISCUSSION

MORSEL was originally developed to explain word recognition and early stages of reading in normal subjects. In this chapter, we have demonstrated that damaging the model leads to behaviours observed in patients with acquired reading impairments. Two distinct forms of peripheral dyslexia—neglect and attentional dyslexia—have been conceptualised as arising from deficits in the distribution of attention that impact the processing of visual stimuli. In neglect dyslexia, damage results in an inability to draw attention to information on the left side of the visual field or the left side of the stimulus. In attentional dyslexia, damage results in difficulty focusing on a single item in a multi-item display. The fact that MORSEL can be lesioned to perform in a manner comparable to both neglect and attentional dyslexia patients is a further, compelling validation of the model.

The co-existence of a word recognition system and an attentional mechanism in MORSEL has provided the means for exploring a range of seemingly disparate behaviours in neglect dyslexia. Previous neuropsychological studies of neglect dyslexia have identified phenomena that appear to be mutually exclusive. For example, the fact that stimulus position, orientation, and physical features are important determinants of performance has been taken as support for the fact that the attentional deficit arises at an early stage of processing (Behrmann et al., 1990; Ellis et al., 1987; Young et al., in press). This interpretation will not suffice, however, since it cannot explain why lexical and morphemic factors— usually associated with deficits at a later stage—play an important role. Although researchers have recognised the need for a unified explanation that can take into account both early and later stages of processing, MORSEL provides the first explicit, computational proposal. According to MORSEL, it is critical to consider interactions between attention and higher-order knowledge: The primary deficit indeed arises at an early stage of processing, but higher-order knowledge at later stages may compensate for the peripheral dysfunction. This explanation allows interpretations that previously appeared contradictory to be brought into alignment.

Adopting the same computational framework, we have also been able to account for a range of behaviours associated with attentional dyslexia. The primary one is that patients with attentional dyslexia are unable to process multiple items appearing simultaneously in the field. Moreover, there is an interaction with identity of the items: When the items are all members of a category, performance is more adversely affected than when the items are drawn from different categories. As with neglect dyslexia, we have shown that damage to the attentional system that occurs at a fairly early stage of processing can nonetheless have consequences that trickle up to higher stages.

Simulations of neuropsychological phenomena, especially acquired dyslexia, have become increasingly popular of late and, as demonstrated earlier, have been successful in modelling pathological performance (see also Hinton & Shallice, 1989; Patterson et al., 1989). Although computational modelling could feasibly be applied to many domains of human performance, it is particularly suitable for the study of acquired dyslexia because research in the cognitive neuropsychology of reading has been prolific in recent years and has provided a solid empirical database from which to venture. Further, certain aspects of connectionist networks are well suited for modelling patient performance: As a network is incrementally damaged, performance is gradually, rather than abruptly, degraded (Hinton & Shallice, 1989; Patterson, in press). Further, because representations in these networks are distributed, no single element is critical to success on any one item and the resulting behaviour is variable and inconsistent. Such is the case with patients; on one occasion performance might be reasonably well preserved, whereas on other occasions, the impairment is significant.

In addition to capturing the quantitative aspects of pathological behaviour, cognitive modelling of the sort described here has also provided considerable explanatory power for interpreting and explaining complex neuropsychological phenomena. Until recently, the predominant theoretical paradigm in cognitive neuropsychology has been to utilise models of normal cognitive processing for analysing the locus of the functional lesion in subjects with impaired performance. These models typically consist of box-and-arrow flow diagrams, with the underlying assumption that discrete and selective damage may affect a single subsystem without influencing the functioning of other components. Information derived from experiments with brain-damaged subjects is then used to guide and constrain the development of models of normal cognition. According to Seidenberg (1988), models of this sort are limited because they do not incorporate specific proposals about knowledge representation or processing mechanisms. These types of models represent a descriptive, first-order decomposition of tasks such as reading and spelling and thus tend to serve as recharacterisations of empirical data. Computational models, in which explicit assumptions about processing are made, provide an alternative, more constructive paradigm for examining normal cognition and its breakdown, and have yielded interesting, counterintuitive results that challenge the more traditional box-and-arrow models.

In our study, as well as those of Hinton and Shallice (1989) and Patterson et al. (1989), complex interactions between the processing components have been studied. These nontransparent interactions are often difficult to account for in the context of box-and-arrow flow diagrams but are more easily explicable in the dynamic framework provided by a working computational model. Although MORSEL is made up of a set of discrete and relatively simple components (not too dissimilar from the box-and-arrow, Fodorian modules), damage at one point may have ramifications for the rest of the system. Thus, analysing each component in isolation provides a restricted view of the overall system. Analysing the operation of the system in its entirety is far more informative, since the net effect of a lesion on behaviour is complicated by interactions among the components.

ACKNOWLEDGEMENTS

Our thanks to Paul Smolensky, Geoffrey Hinton, Sandra Black, and Morris Moscovitch for insightful comments regarding this work. This work was supported by NSF PYI award IRI-9058450 and grant 90-21 from the James S. McDonnell Foundation to the first author, a Postgraduate Scholarship from the Natural Sciences and Engineering Research Council of Canada to the second author, grant 87-2-36 from the Sloan Foundation to Geoffrey Hinton, and NSERC grant A8347.

REFERENCES

Barbut, D. & Gazzaniga, M. (1987). Disturbances in conceptual space involving language and speech. *Brain, 110*, 1487–1496.

Baxter, D. & Warrington, E.K. (1983). Neglect dysgraphia. *Journal of Neurology, Neurosurgery, and Psychiatry, 46*, 1073–1078.

Behrmann, M., Moscovitch, M., Black, S.E., & Mozer, M.C. (1990). Perceptual and conceptual mechanisms in neglect dyslexia: Two contrasting case studies. *Brain, 113*, 1163–1183.

Bisiach, E., Perani, D., Vallar, G., & Berti, A. (1986). Unilateral neglect: Personal and extra-personal. *Neuropsychologia, 24*, 759–767.

Brunn, J.L. & Farah, M.J. (in press). The relation between spatial attention and reading: Evidence from the neglect syndrome. *Cognitive Neuropsychology*.

Butter, C.M. (1987). Varieties of attention and disturbances of attention: A neuropsychological analysis. In M. Jeannerod (Ed.), *Neurophysiological and neuropsychological aspects of spatial neglect*. Amsterdam: North Holland, 1–24.

Butter, C.M., Mark, V., & Heilman, K.M. (1989). An experimental analysis of factors underlying neglect in line bisection. *Journal of Neurology, Neurosurgery, and Psychiatry, 51*, 1581–1583.

Calvanio, R., Patrone, P.N., & Levine, D.N. (1987). Left visual spatial neglect is both environment-centred and body-centred. *Neurology, 37*, 1179–1183.

Caramazza, A. & Hillis, A.E. (in press). Levels of representation, co-ordinate frames, and unilateral neglect. *Cognitive Neuropsychology*.

Carr, T.H., Davidson, B.J., & Hawkins, H.L. (1978). Perceptual flexibility in word recognition: Strategies affect orthographic computation but not lexical access. *Journal of Experimental Psychology: Human Perception and Performance, 4*, 674–690.

Coltheart, M. (1981). Disorders of reading and their implications for models of normal processing. *Visible Language, 15*, 245–286.

Coltheart, M. (1985). Cognitive neuropsychology and the study of reading. In M.I. Posner & O.S.M. Marin (Eds.), *Attention and performance XI*. Hillsdale, N.J.: Lawrence Erlbaum Associates Inc., 3–37.

Deutsch, J.A. & Deutsch, D. (1963). Attention: Some theoretical considerations. *Psychological Review, 70*, 80–90.

Ellis, A.W., Flude, B., & Young, A.W. (1987). Neglect dyslexia and the early visual processing of letters in words and nonwords. *Cognitive Neuropsychology, 4*, 439–464.

Ellis, A.W. & Young, A. (1987). *Human cognitive neuropsychology*. London: Lawrence Erlbaum Associates Ltd.

Farah, M.J., Brunn, J.L., Wong, A.B., Wallace, M.A., & Carpenter, P.A. (1990). Frames of reference for allocating attention to space: Evidence from the neglect syndrome. *Neuropsychologia, 28*, 335–347.

Gazzaniga, M. & Ladavas, E. (1987). Disturbances in spatial attention following lesion or disconnection of the right parietal lobe. In M. Jeannerod (Ed.), *Neurophysiological and neuropsychological aspects of spatial neglect*. Amsterdam: North Holland, 203–214.

Geiger, G. & Lettvin, J.Y. (1987). Peripheral vision in persons with dyslexia. *New England Journal of Medicine, 316*, 1238–1243.

Grossberg, S. & Mingolla, E. (1985). Neural dynamics of perceptual grouping: Textures, boundaries, and emergent segmentations. *Perception and Psychophysics, 38*, 141–171.

Heilman, K.M., Watson, R.T., & Valenstein, E. (1985). Neglect and related disorders. In K.M. Heilman & E. Valenstein (Eds.), *Clinical neuropsychology* (2nd edn.). New York: Oxford University Press.

Hillis, A.E. & Caramazza, A. (1989). *The effects of attentional deficits on reading and spelling*. Technical Report 44. Baltimore, Maryland: Cognitive Neuropsychology Laboratory, Johns Hopkins University.

Hinton, G. & Shallice, T. (1989). *Lesioning a connectionist network: Investigations of acquired dyslexia*. Technical Report CRG-TR-89-3. Toronto: University of Toronto, Department of Computer Science, Connectionist Research Group.

Hinton, G.E. (1981). A parallel computation that assigns canonical object-based frames of reference. In *Proceedings of the Seventh International Joint Conference on Artificial Intelligence*. Los Altos, Calif.: Morgan Kaufmann, 683–685.

Hopfield, J.J. (1982). Neural network and physical systems with emergent collective computational abilities. *Proceedings of the National Academy of Sciences, 79*, 2554–2558.

Karnath, H.O. (1988). Deficits of attention in acute and recovered hemi-neglect. *Neuropsychologia, 26*, 27–43.

Kinsbourne, M. (1987). Mechanisms of unilateral neglect. In M. Jeannerod (Ed.), *Neurophysiological and neuropsychological aspects of spatial neglect*. Amsterdam: North Holland, 69–86.

Kinsbourne, M. & Warrington, E.K. (1962). A variety of reading disability associated with right-hemisphere lesions. *Journal of Neurology, Neurosurgery, and Psychiatry, 25*, 339–344.

Koch, C. & Ullman, S. (1985). Shifts in selective visual attention: Towards the underlying neural circuitry. *Human Neurobiology, 4*, 219–227.

Kolb, B. & Whishaw, I.Q. (1985). *Fundamentals of human neuropsychology*. New York: W.H. Freeman.

Kuçera, H. & Francis, W.N. (1967). *Computational analysis of present-day American English*. Providence, R.I.: Brown University Press.

LaBerge, D. & Brown, V. (1989). Theory of attentional operations in shape identification. *Psychological Review, 96*, 101–124.

LaBerge, D. & Samuels, S.J. (1974). Toward a theory of automatic processing in reading. *Cognitive Psychology, 6*, 293–323.

Ladavas, E. (1987). Is the hemispatial deficit produced by right parietal lobe damage associated with retinal or gravitational coordinates? *Brain, 110*, 167–180.

McClelland, J.L. & Johnston, J.C. (1977). The role of familiar units in perception of words and nonwords. *Perception and Psychophysics, 22*, 249–261.

McClelland, J.L. & Rumelhart, D.E. (1981). An interactive activation model of context effects in letter perception: Part I. An account of basic findings. *Psychological Review, 88*, 375–407.

Marr, D. (1982). *Vision*. San Francisco: Freeman.

Mesulam, M.-M. (1981). A cortical network for directed attention and unilateral neglect. *Annals of Neurology, 10*, 309–325.

Mesulam, M.-M. (1985). *Principles of behavioral neurology*. Philadelphia, Penn.: F.A. Davis Company.

Mewhort, D.J., Marchetti, F.M., Gurnsey, R., & Campbell, A.J. (1984). Information persistence: A dual-buffer model for initial visual processing. In H. Bouma & D.G. Bouwhuis (Eds.), *Attention and performance X*. Hillsdale, N.J.: Lawrence Erlbaum Associates Inc., 287–498.

Mozer, M.C. (1983). Letter migration in word perception. *Journal of Experimental Psychology: Human Perception and Performance, 9,* 531–546.

Mozer, M.C. (1987). Early parallel processing in reading: A connectionist approach. In M. Coltheart (Ed.), *Attention and performance XII: The psychology of reading.* Hillsdale, N.J.: Lawrence Erlbaum Associates Inc., 83–104.

Mozer, M.C. (1988). A connectionist model of selective attention in visual perception. In *Proceedings of the Tenth Annual Conference of the Cognitive Science Society.* Hillsdale, N.J.: Lawrence Erlbaum Associates Inc., 195–201.

Mozer, M.C. (1991). *The perception of multiple objects: A connectionist approach.* Cambridge, Mass.: M.I.T. Press/Bradford Books.

Norman, D.A. (1968). Toward a theory of memory and attention. *Psychological review, 75,* 522–536.

Ogden, J.A. (1985). Anterior-posterior interhemispheric differences in the loci of lesions producing visual hemineglect. *Brain and Cognition, 4,* 59–75.

Patterson, K.E. (1990). Alexia and neural nets. *Japanese Journal of Neuropsychology, 6,* 90–99.

Patterson, K.E., Seidenberg, M.S., & McClelland, J.L. (1989). Connections and disconnections: Acquired dyslexia in a computational model of the reading process. In R.G.M. Morris (Ed.), *Parallel distributed processing: Implications for psychology and neurobiology.* Oxford: Oxford University Press.

Pinker, S. & Prince, A. (1988). On language and connectionism. *Cognition, 28,* 73–193.

Posner, M. & Petersen, S.E. (1989). *The attention system of the human brain.* Technical Report 89-3. Eugene, Oregon: Institute of Cognitive and Decision Sciences, University of Oregon.

Posner, M.I., Petersen, S.E., Fox, P.T., & Raichle, M.E. (1988). Localization of cognitive operations in the human brain. *Science, 240,* 1627–1631.

Prince, A. & Pinker, S. (1988). Wickelphone ambiguity. *Cognition, 30,* 189–190.

Rayner, K., Murphy, L.A., Henderson, J.M., & Pollatsek, A. (1989). Selective attentional dyslexia. *Cognitive Neuropsychology, 6,* 357–378.

Riddoch, M.J. & Humphreys, G.W. (1983). The effect of cueing on unilateral neglect. *Neuropsychologia, 21,* 589–599.

Riddoch, J., Humphreys, G., Cleton, P., & Fery, P. (in press). Levels of coding in neglect dyslexia. *Cognitive Neuropsychology.*

Rumelhart, D.E. & McClelland J.L. (1982). An interactive activation model of context effects in letter perception: Part II. The contextual enhancement effect and some tests and extensions of the model. *Psychological Review, 89,* 60–84.

Seidenberg, M.S. (1988). Cognitive neuropsychology and language: The state of the art. *Cognitive Neuropsychology, 5,* 403–426.

Shallice, T. (1988). *From neuropsychology to mental structure.* Cambridge: Cambridge University Press.

Shallice, T. & McGill, J. (1978). The origins of mixed errors. In J. Requin (Ed.), *Attention and performance VII.* Hillsdale, N.J.: Lawrence Erlbaum Associates Inc., 193–208.

Shallice, T. & Warrington, E.K. (1977). The possible role of selective attention in acquired dyslexia. *Neuropsychologia, 15,* 31–41.

Shallice, T. & Warrington, E.K. (1980). Single and multiple component central dyslexic syndromes. In M. Coltheart, K.E. Patterson, & J.C. Marshall (Eds.), *Deep dyslexia.* London: Routledge & Kegan Paul.

Shaywitz, B.A. & Waxman, S.G. (1987). Dyslexia. *New England Journal of Medicine, 316,* 1268–1270.

Shiffrin, R.M. & Schneider, W. (1977). Controlled and automatic human information processing: II. Perceptual learning, automatic attending, and a general theory. *Psychological Review, 84,* 127–190.

Sieroff, E. (1991). *Perception of visual letter strings in a case of left neglect: Manipulation of the word form.* Brain and Language, 41, 565–589.

Sieroff, E. & Michel, F. (1987). Verbal visual extinction in right/left hemisphere lesion patients and the problem of lexical access. *Neuropsychologia, 25,* 907–918.

Sieroff, E., Pollatsek, A., & Posner, M.I. (1988). Recognition of visual letter strings following injury to the posterior visual spatial attention system. *Cognitive Neuropsychology, 5,* 451–472.

Sieroff, E. & Posner, M.I. (1988). Cueing spatial attention during processing of words and letter strings in normals. *Cognitive Neuropsychology, 5,* 451–472.

Smolensky, P. (1986). Information processing in dynamical systems: Foundations of harmony theory. In D.E. Rumelhart & J.L. McClelland (Eds.), *Parallel distributed processing: Explorations in the microstructure of cognition. Volume I: Foundations.* Cambridge, Mass.: M.I.T. Press/ Bradford Books, 194–281.

Smolensky, P. (in press). Tensor product variable binding and the representation of symbolic structures in connectionist networks. *Artificial Intelligence.*

Touretzky, D.S. & Hinton, G.E. (1988). A distributed connectionist production system. *Cognitive Science, 12,* 423–466.

Uhr, L. (1987) *Highly parallel, hierarchical, recognition cone perceptual structure.* Technical Report 688. Madison, Wisconsin: Computer Sciences Department, University of Wisconsin.

Ungerleider, L.G. & Mishkin, M. (1982). Two cortical visual systems. In D.J. Ingle, M.A. Goodale, & R.J.W. Mansfield (Eds.), *Analysis of visual behavior.* Cambridge, Mass.: M.I.T. Press.

Warrington, E.K. & Shallice, T. (1980). Word-form dyslexia. *Brain, 103,* 99–112.

Young, A.W., Newcombe, F., & Ellis, A.W. (in press). Different impairments contribute to neglect dyslexia. *Cognitive Neuropsychology.*

Zemel, R.S., Mozer, M.C., & Hinton, G.E. (1989). TRAFFIC: A model of object recognition based on transformations of feature instances. In D.S. Touretzky, G.E. Hinton, & R.J. Sejnowski (Eds.), *Proceedings of the 1988 Connectionist Models Summer School.* San Mateo, Calif.: Morgan Kaufmann, 452–461.

APPENDIX 1: PO NET DYNAMICS

The task of the PO net is to select a set of letter cluster units that can be assembled to form a unique letter string and that is consistent with the activations produced by BLIRNET. If the letter string read out by the PO net is an English word the PO net must also select a set of semlex units that represent the semantic/lexical entry.

Letter-cluster Unit Connections

Two letter clusters are said to be *neighbours* if they can be aligned so as to overlap on two letters or delimiters ("*"). Some examples of neighbours are: MON and ONE (overlap on O and N), **M and •MO (• and M), M_NE and V_NE (N and E), and E_•• and F_•• (• and •). Two neighbours are said to be *compatible* if, when aligned, they do not conflict in any letter position. The first two examples above are compatible, the second two incompatible.

Based on this classification of compatible and incompatible neighbours, four types of connections between letter-cluster units are warranted: (1) *excitatory*—between compatible neighbours; (2) *inhibitory*—between incompatible neighbours; (3) •_ *excitatory*—a special case of an excitatory connection where both letter clusters contain delimiters and the presence of one cluster necessitates the presence of another (e.g. •MO implies **M and ••_O). Note that these connections are not symmetric (neither **M nor ••_O alone implies •MO). (4) *-inhibitory*—a special case of an inhibitory connection where both letter clusters contain delimiters. For these pairs, the presence of one cluster precludes the presence of the other (e.g. •MO and ••_A, Y** and E**). These connections are symmetric.

Each connection type has associated with it a different weight. The excitatory connections have positive weights, inhibitory negative. The *-connections have weights of a greater magnitude. The values used in our simulations, as well as other parameters of the PO net described later, are listed in Table 14.9.

Semlex Unit Connections

As stated in the text, the semlex representation is intended to be a distributed encoding of word meanings. Because of the difficulty in devising a complete distributed semantic representation, the PO, net instead uses a semi-distributed representation in which each word meaning is associated with a distinct pool of units. These units are not shared by different words. In our simulations, this is effectively equivalent to a *lexical* representation because simulations involved few if any synonyms.

The number of semlex units associated with each word in MORSEL's lexicon was twice the number of letters in the word. Each of these units was connected to five randomly selected letter clusters of the word, with the restriction that all letter clusters had approximately the same number of semlex connections. Because the number of letter clusters in an l-letter word is $3l+2$ and the total number of semlex-letter cluster connections is $10l$, each letter cluster unit of a word is on average connected to slightly over three of the word's semlex units. This particular scheme was selected because, unlike other schemes we considered, it made the PO net fairly neutral with regard to word length; there was no bias towards either shorter or longer words.

The connections between letter cluster and semlex units are symmetric and excitatory. In addition, each semlex unit slightly inhibits all letter cluster units to which it is not connected. Semlex units also inhibit all semlex units that are associated with different words. It is this inhibition that forces the PO net to select a pattern of activity in the semlex units corresponding to a single word. (See Table 14.9 for values of these parameters.)

PO Net Activation Function

Initially, the PO net receives feedforward excitation from the letter cluster units of BLIRNET. Interactions then take place within the PO net and it gradually iterates towards a stable state. PO units were given the same dynamical properties as units in McClelland and Rumelhart's (1981) interactive-activation model. Units are continuous-valued in the range [–0.2,1.0]. Information

TABLE 14.9
PO Net Connection Strengths

Connection Type	Value
excitatory	0.06
inhibitory	–0.18
*-excitatory	0.24
*-inhibitory	–0.24
letter cluster to semlex	0.10
semlex to letter cluster excitatory	0.10
semlex to letter cluster inhibitory	–0.001
semlex to semlex inhibitory	–0.05
feedforward (ω_F)	0.0005
global suppression (ω_G)	–0.14

coming in to each unit is summed algebraically, weighted by the connection strengths, to yield a "net input":

$$net_i = \sum_{\substack{j \in \\ ACTIVE}} w_{ij} p_j \, \omega_F b_i + \omega_G \bar{p},$$

where *ACTIVE* is the set of all PO units with positive activity at the current time, w_{ij} is the strength of connection to PO unit i from PO unit j, p_j is the activity of PO unit j, b_i is the activity of letter-cluster i of BLIRNET (if i is a semlex unit, then b_i is zero), and ω_F is the strength of feedforward connections from BLIRNET to the PO net. The final term, $\omega_G \bar{p}$, applies only to the letter-cluster units and is explained later.

The activation value of each PO unit is updated by the net input according to the rule:

$$\Delta p_i = \begin{cases} net_i[1.0 - p_i] & \text{if } net_i > 0 \\ net_i[p_i - (-0.2)] & \text{otherwise.} \end{cases}$$

If the net input is positive, activation is pushed towards the maximum value of 1.0; if negative, activation is pushed towards the minimum value of –0.2. The effect of the net input is scaled down as the unit approaches its maximum or minimum activation level.

The network as described thus far is inadequate. The problem is as follows. Many letter clusters compete and co-operate directly with one another, in particular, the clusters representing ends of words and the clusters sharing letters. Often, however, these interactions are not enough. For instance, suppose two words are presented, LINE and FACT, and that clusters of LINE are more active initially. Clusters like ••F and CT• of FACT experience direct competition from the corresponding clusters of LINE, and are therefore suppressed, but the inner clusters of FACT such as FAC and F_CT do not. The pull-out process thus yields LINE along with the inner clusters of FACT. To get around this problem, some type of "global inhibition" is useful.

The mechanism we opted for inhibits each letter-cluster unit in proportion to the average activity of all clusters above threshold, which can be computed as follows:

$$\bar{p} = \frac{1}{|ACTIVE_L|} \sum_{\substack{i \in \\ ACTIVE_L}} p_i,$$

where $ACTIVE_L$ is the set of all letter cluster units with positive activity at the current time. The equation for net_i incorporates this term, weighted by the parameter ω_G. This scheme allows the set of letter cluster units whose activity grows the fastest to shut off the other units. Activity grows fastest for units that have many active compatible neighbours.

APPENDIX 2: AM DYNAMICS

The goal of the AM is to construct a "spotlight" of activity that highlights a single item appearing on MORSEL's retina. Defining an item to be a set of features in close proximity, the spotlight should form a *contiguous* region on the retina consistent with the bottom-up and top-down inputs to the AM.

In connectionism, the standard method of transforming this description of the target behaviour of the AM into a network architecture is to view the AM's task as an *optimisation* problem: To what activity value should each unit in the AM be set in order to best satisfy a number of possibly conflicting constraints? The two primary constraints here are that the AM should focus on locations suggested by the bottom-up and top-down inputs, and the AM should focus on a single item.

The first step in tackling such an optimisation problem is to define a *harmony* function (Smolensky, 1986) that computes the goodness of a given pattern of activity over the entire AM (the

AM *state*). This goodness is a scalar quantity indicating how well the AM state satisfies the optimisation problem. The maxima of the harmony function correspond to desired states of the AM.

Given a harmony function, H, one can ask how the activity of the AM unit at a retinal location (x, y), denoted a_{xy}, should be updated over time to increase harmony and eventually reach states of maximal harmony. The simplest rule, called *steepest ascent*, is to update a_{xy} in proportion to the derivative $\partial H/\partial a_{xy}$. If $\partial H/\partial a_{xy}$ is positive, then increasing a_{xy} will increase H; thus a_{xy} should be increased. If $\partial H/\partial a_{xy}$ is negative, then decreasing a_{xy} will increase H; thus a_{xy} should be decreased.

Returning to the problem faced by the AM, devising a harmony function that computes whether the pattern of activity is contiguous is quite difficult. Instead of constructing a function that rewards contiguity explicitly, we have combined several heuristics that together generally achieve convex, contiguous patterns of activity.[8] The harmony function we use is:

$$H = \sum_{\substack{(x,y) \\ \in ALL}} ext_{xy}\, a_{xy} - \frac{\mu}{4} \sum_{\substack{(x,y) \\ \in ALL}} \sum_{\substack{(i,j) \in \\ NEIGH_{xy}}} (a_{ij} - a_{xy})^2 + \frac{\theta}{2} \sum_{\substack{(x,y) \in \\ ACTIVE}} (\gamma\bar{a} - a_{xy})^2 ,$$

where ALL is the set of all retinal locations, ext_{xy} is the net external (bottom-up and top-down) activity to the AM at location (x, y), $NEIGH_{xy}$ is the set of eight locations immediately adjacent to (x,y)—the *neighbours*, $ACTIVE$ is the set of locations of all units with positive activity, $\bar{a}$ is the mean activity of all units with positive activity—

$$\bar{a} = \frac{1}{|ACTIVE|} \sum_{\substack{(x,y) \in \\ ACTIVE}} a_{xy} ,$$

and μ, θ, and γ are weighting parameters.

The first term encourages each unit to be consistent with the external bias. The second term encourages each unit to be as close as possible to its neighbours (so that if a unit is off and the neighbours are on, the unit will tend to turn on, and vice versa). The third term encourages units below the mean activity in the network to shut off, and units above the mean activity to turn on. The constant γ serves as a discounting factor: with γ less than 1, units need not be quite as active as the mean in order to be supported. Instead of using the average activity over *all* units, it is necessary to compute the average over the *active* units. Otherwise, the effect of the third term is to limit the total activity in the network, i.e. the number of units that can turn on at once. This is not suitable because we wish to allow large or small spotlights depending on the external input. (The same type of scheme was used to limit activity in the PO net, as described in Appendix 1.)

The update rule for a_{xy} is:

$$\Delta a_{xy} = \frac{\partial H}{\partial a_{xy}} = ext_{xy} + \mu \sum_{\substack{(i,j) \in \\ NEIGH_{xy}}} (a_{ij} - a_{xy}) - \theta\, (\gamma\bar{a} - a_{xy}).$$

Further, a_{xy} is prevented from going outside the range [0,1] by capping activity at these limits.[9]

To explain the activation function intuitively, consider the time course of activation. Initially, the activity of all AM units is reset to zero. Activation then feeds into each unit in proportion to its external bias (first term in the activation function). Units with active neighbours will grow the fastest

---

[8]We should note that many other harmony functions would suffice equally well if not better than the one we devised. In fact, we experimented with several different functions, and the qualitative system behaviour was unaffected by the details of the harmony function.

[9]To follow the objective function exactly, the third term should actually be zero if a_{xy} is currently inactive. However, including this term at all times prevents oscillation in the network and does not otherwise appear to affect the quality of the solution.

because of neighbourhood support (second term). As activity progresses, high-support neighbourhoods will have activity above the mean; they will therefore be pushed even higher, whereas low-support neighbourhoods will experience the opposite tendency (third term).

In all simulations, μ was fixed at $1/8$, θ at $1/2$, and γ at 0.11 times the total external input.

APPENDIX 3: DETAILS OF AM SIMULATIONS

In this Appendix, we describe the stimuli used as input to the AM and the simulation methodology.

Input Assumptions

In the font we have designed, letters presented on MORSEL's retina each occupy a 3×3 region of the input map. Letters within a word are presented in horizontally adjacent positions. Thus, a 3-letter word subtends a 3×9 retinal region. Two 3-letter words, with a single space between them (a 3×3 gap), subtend a 3×21 region.

The featural activations arising on MORSEL's retina at a given location serve as a bottom-up input to the corresponding location of the AM. The input is thus nonzero only at locations where letters are present. To simplify our simulations, rather than presenting real words on MORSEL's retina and using the resulting featural activations as input to the AM, we assumed, for a stimulus string occupying a given retinal region, a uniform distribution of input within that region—an external input of 0.01 at each location. We assumed an additional input of 0.01 along the outer border of the region, representing an input from a boundary contour system (e.g. Grossberg & Mingolla, 1985).[10] Finally, we assumed a bit of blurring: Each retinal activation provided not only bottom-up input to the corresponding location in the AM but also to the horizontally, vertically, and diagonally neighbouring locations. This activation strength was only 0.0002, much smaller than the direct input.

With the input as described, 2 3-letter words presented simultaneously produce exactly the same pattern of bottom-up input. Without some degree of randomness, the AM has no means of breaking symmetry and selecting one word or the other. Thus, for simulations of the normal model, we assumed that each bottom-up input is transmitted to the AM with only 90% probability. This causes the strength of a word to vary from one trial to the next.

The basic claim of MORSEL is that neglect dyslexia results from graded damage to the bottom-up AM inputs, most severe on the left and least on the right. One way of expressing this damage is in terms of the probability of transmitting an input to the AM. Rather than a uniform probability close to 1, we assumed in the damaged model that the probability varies with lateral retinal position: At the left edge of the retina, the probability was 48% and increased by 2% for each successive location to the right, with a maximum of 90%. Thus, words presented in the "standard" position (starting 6 pixels from the left end of the retina; this was the position used in most simulations) had a transmission probability of 60% for their left edge, and the probability reached the 90% ceiling by the sixth letter position (21 pixels from the left of the retina).

Simulation Methodology

Simulation experiments were conducted for 2 simultaneous 3-letter words and single 5–7 letter words, presented in the standard position or shifted one or 2 letter positions to the right. For each simulation, 1000 replications were run. On each replication, every source of bottom-up input was

---

[10]Such an input seems of critical importance in determining the focus of attention. Attention should turn to changes in the visual environment, not homogeneous regions.

considered independently and was fed to the AM in accordance with the probabilistic transmission function. Thus, on each replication the AM detected a slightly different subset of the inputs.

The AM was then allowed to run until equilibrium was reached, that is, until all units settled on stable activation values. The total attention to each letter position was then measured by averaging the activities of the 9 AM units in the region corresponding to a given letter. If this average activity was greater than 0.5, the letter was considered to have been attended. The attentional state for the stimulus was then determined by combining the individual letter results. By the 0.5 activity criterion, there were occasional responses that didn't fit into one of the expected attentional states, for example, attending to positions 2 and 4–6 of a 6-letter word but not position 3. We placed such responses into the closest reasonable category; here, the state of attending to positions 2–6.

APPENDIX 4: DETAILS OF BLIRNET AND PO NET SIMULATIONS

About 6000 letter clusters are required to represent the most common words of English. However, running a simulation with this number of clusters is computationally infeasible. If each cluster is connected to, say, 200 other clusters, the total number of connections will exceed 1.2 million, and this estimate completely ignores the cost of the semlex units, which is a major factor if the simulation includes many lexical items. Constructing a full-scale PO net is wasteful, too: For a given stimulus, most of the units will not come into play in determining the PO net's response. Thus, rather than constructing one gigantic PO net to handle all simulations, we constructed a specialised PO net for each stimulus item. This smaller net contained only the letter-cluster and semlex units that seemed relevant for the particular stimulus.

In this Appendix, we describe the procedure used to select letter-cluster and semlex units for inclusion in the PO net simulation, the rules used for determining the BLIRNET activation levels of these units, and finally, the PO net simulation methodology.

Selection of Alternative Responses

For each stimulus, we generated a set of *alternative responses*—strings that had enough in common with the stimulus to be plausible responses. For the single word stimuli, the alternative responses included:

1. The stimulus word itself (e.g., PARISH).
2. All right segments and left segments of the stimulus with three or more letters (e.g., ARISH, PARIS, RISH, PARI, ISH, PAR).
3. All words in the Kuçera and Francis (1967) corpus ending with the last 3 letters of the stimulus and having the same length as the stimulus, plus or minus one letter (e.g. ENGLISH, BRITISH, JEWISH, FINISH, SPANISH, FURNISH, IRISH, POLISH, FOOLISH, TURKISH, ABOLISH, ANGUISH, DANISH, RADISH, RELISH). If more than 15 such words existed, the 15 with the highest word frequency counts were selected.[11]

---

[11]Note that by including only alternative responses that had approximately the same length as the stimulus, we artificially limited the model to responses that preserve stimulus word length. Neglect dyslexia patients do in fact show a preservation of word length (Behrman et al. 1990; Ellis et al., 1987), but clearly not because all the words they know are of the same length as the stimulus. We believe that a fuller implementation of MORSEL should include a processing module similar to BLIRNET that computes word shape information instead of word identity information. The word shape and identity information could then be integrated by the PO net to select responses that were consistent with both, thereby allowing a preservation of word length even in neglect dyslexia patients.

4. All words in the Kuçera and Francis corpus beginning with the first 3 letters of the stimulus and having the same length as the stimulus, plus or minus one letter (e.g. PARTY, PARTS, PARENTS, PARKER, PARTIES, PARTLY, PARKED, PARTNER, PARKING, PARADE, PARKS, PARLOUR, PARENT, PARTIAL). If more than 15 such words existed, the 15 with the highest word frequency counts were selected.

5. Six pseudowords having the same final three letters and overall length as the stimulus (e.g. SUNISH, COWISH, PEAISH, OFFISH, INKISH, EARISH).

For the two-word stimuli used in the extinction experiment, the alternative responses were determined by combining the two words into a single string (e.g. SUN and FLY to SUNFLY) and using the criteria just given in addition to:

1. The individual three-letter stimuli (e.g., SUN, FLY).

2. All three-letter words in the Kuçera and Francis corpus ending with the last two letters of either stimulus (e.g. RUN, GUN, FUN, HUN, NUN, BUN, PUN, SLY, PLY).

3. All three-letter words beginning with the first two letters of either stimulus (e.g. SUM, SUE, SUB, FLA, FLU).

The net constructed for a given stimulus included all letter-cluster units composing each of the alternative responses as well as a set of semlex units for each alternative response that was an English word. This allowed the PO net potentially to read out any of the alternative responses. Table 14.10 presents the average number of alternative responses generated for stimuli in each of the four simulation experiments we conducted, as well as the average number of units and connections contained in the PO net.

Rules for Determining BLIRNET Activations

Once the set of letter cluster units has been selected for a given stimulus, the BLIRNET activation of each unit must be determined. As we explained in the main text, we did not actually simulate BLIRNET. Instead, we used a simple algorithm to obtain activations similar to what BLIRNET would have produced had a full-scale simulation been conducted. Given an input stimulus and a focus of attention produced by the AM, this algorithm worked as follows for a particular letter cluster.

The letter cluster is compared to every subsequence of the stimulus by aligning the cluster in every possible way with the stimulus. For a given alignment, each of the three characters of the cluster (i.e. letters or delimiters—the "don't care" underscores were ignored) is matched against the corresponding character of the stimulus. If the cluster character is a letter, the match score is $\alpha\rho$; if the character is a delimiter, the match score is $1-\alpha(1-\rho)$. α is the level of attention to the corresponding character of the stimulus; α is 1 if the character is attended or 0.368 if unattended.

TABLE 14.10
PO Net Statistics

| Experiment | Number of Alternative Responses | | | Avg. Number of Units | | Avg. Number of Connections |
	Average	Minimum	Maximum	Letter Cluster	Semlex	
Retinal position	35	29	42	324	281	15090
Word/pseudoword	28	20	35	216	245	9916
Right-embedded morpheme (REM)	32	22	42	303	254	13558
Related/unrelated morpheme	50	38	62	393	412	27274

ρ lies in the range [0,1] and is a measure of the featural similarity of the stimulus and cluster characters. If the characters are identical—a perfect match, ρ is 1; to the extent that the characters are physically similar (as measured by the dot product of their feature vectors), ρ is greater than zero. Thus, the physical appearance of the letters comes into play in determining BLIRNET activations.

To summarise, the match will be close to 1 for a letter of a cluster if the corresponding stimulus letter is attended and is physically similar to the cluster's letter. For delimiters of the cluster, however, the match will be close to 1 *either* if the corresponding stimulus position contains a blank space (ρ is 1) or if the corresponding stimulus position is unattended (α is small). The reason for the second condition is that if the position is unattended, few features are transmitted through BLIRNET; consequently, it will appear as if the position is blank.

A cluster character is not only matched against the corresponding stimulus character but also against the left and right neighbours of the stimulus character. The scores obtained for the neighbour matches are multiplied by 0.5, and the largest of these two scores and the original match score is selected as the overall character match. The reason for matching neighbours is that BLIRNET confuses exact letter positions and often produces partial activations of clusters with letters in a slightly incorrect order.

The geometric mean of the overall character matches is computed to obtain an *overall cluster match*; i.e. $(m_1 m_2 m_3)^{1/3}$, where m_i is the match for character i. Character matches involving a delimiter in the cluster and a blank space in the stimulus are ignored in computing overall cluster match. This overall cluster match is computed for each possible alignment of the cluster and the stimulus, and the activation level of the cluster is simply the sum of the overall cluster matches over all alignments.

What this procedure boils down to is simply that a cluster is assigned an activity level of 1.0 if the cluster is contained in the attended portion of the word; the cluster is assigned an activity level of 0.05 ($=0.368^3$) if it is contained in the unattended portion; the cluster is assigned an activity level intermediate between 0.05 and 1.0 if it crosses the boundary between the unattended and attended portions. If a cluster does not match the stimulus exactly because some letters are different or the letters are in a slightly different order, the cluster still attains some degree of activation.

To obtain different responses on each run, gaussian noise with mean zero and standard deviation 0.10 was added to the activity level of each cluster, and the activities were thresholded to lie in the range [0,1].

PO Net Simulation Methodology

To obtain reliable simulation results, each stimulus was tested with alternative sets of semlex unit connections and random fluctuations in the BLIRNET activities. To elaborate, for each stimulus we reconstructed the PO net 10 times, each time with the semlex units connected to a different random subset of their associated letter clusters. For each version of the network thus constructed, we allowed the net to settle 10 times, each time starting with a different pattern of noise added to the BLIRNET activations. In total, then, every stimulus item was presented 100 times.

A measure of the strength of a particular response was computed according to the formula:

$$strength = \frac{1}{2} \left[\frac{t}{n} + \frac{t}{T} \right],$$

where t is the summed activity of target clusters—those composing the response, n is the number of target clusters, and T is the summed activity of all clusters. Cluster activities were thresholded to lie in the range [0,1]. The first term in the formula represents the average activity of the target clusters and approaches 1 as the clusters of the response increase in activity. The second term represents the activity of the target clusters relative to nontarget clusters. The strength ranges from 0 to 1 and reaches 1 only if all target clusters are fully active and no nontarget cluster is active.

On each run, the PO net was allowed to run until it reached equilibrium (usually within 50 processing iterations) and the response with the greatest strength was taken as MORSEL's selection. Generally, this response had strength 1. It was necessary to use only the letter-cluster activity in determining MORSEL's selection; use of the semlex units would have precluded nonword responses.

This simulation procedure was carried out for each stimulus and each attentional state. The individual stimulus results were then averaged to produce a distribution of responses conditional upon a particular attentional state. These conditional probabilities could then be combined with the relative probabilities of different attentional states to obtain an overall distribution of responses.

Author Index

Subject Index

469

Printed and bound by CPI Group (UK) Ltd, Croydon, CR0 4YY

22/10/2024

01777625-0019